Course   Biology of Childhood
BIO 318
Shelly Kirn
CALIFORNIA STATE UNIVERSITY CHICO
BIOLOGICAL SCIENCE

http://create.mheducation.com

ISBN-10: 1308196725   ISBN-13: 9781308196725

Contents

Credits

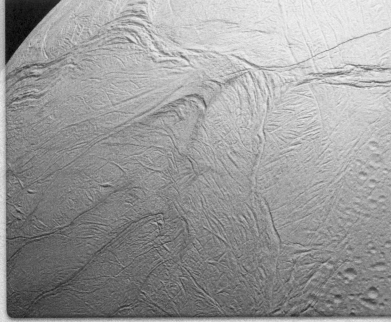

Source: NASA/JPL/Space Science Institute

CHAPTER

1

Exploring Life and Science

CASE STUDY: THE SEARCH FOR LIFE

What do Enceladus, Europa, Titan, Mars, and Earth all have in common? Besides being part of our solar system, they are all at the front line of our species' effort to understand the nature of life.

You may never have heard of Enceladus (shown above) or Europa, but they are both now prime candidates to harbor life outside of Earth. Enceladus is one of Saturn's moons, and Europa orbits Jupiter. Why are these moons so special? Because scientists believe that both of these moons contain water, and plenty of it. Even though Enceladus and Europa are far from the sun, the gravitational pull of their parent planets means that each of these moons may have an ocean of liquid water beneath its frozen surface. And as we will see, water has an important relationship to life.

Titan is the second-largest satellite in the solar system, larger than even our moon. Although it is in orbit around Saturn, and thus located some distance from the influence of the sun, Titan has become a focal point for the study of extraterrestrial life since the NASA space probe *Cassini-Huygens* first arrived at Saturn in 2004. *Cassini* has detected on Titan the presence of the building blocks of life, including lakes of methane and ammonia, and vast deposits of hydrogen and carbon compounds called hydrocarbons.

On Earth, scientists are exploring the extreme environments near volcanoes and deep-sea thermal vents to get a better picture of what life may have looked like under the inhospitable conditions that dominated at the time when, we now know, life first began on our planet. There is evidence that water is still present on Mars, raising the hopes that we may still find evidence of early life there.

In this chapter we will explore what it means to be alive. By looking to other areas of our solar system, we may develop a better understanding of how life first developed and our place in the universe.

As you read through the chapter, think about the following questions:

1. What are the basic characteristics that define life?
2. What evidence would you look for on one of these moons that would tell you that life may have existed on it in the past?
3. What does it tell us if we discover life on one of these moons and it has characteristics similar to those of life on Earth? What if it is very different?

CHAPTER CONCEPTS

1.1 The Characteristics of Life
The process of evolution accounts for the diversity of living organisms and explains why all life shares the same basic characteristics.

1.2 Humans Are Related to Other Animals
Humans are eukaryotes and are further classified as vertebrate mammals in the animal kingdom.

1.3 Science as a Process
Biologists use a scientific process when they make observations and study the natural world. Data is collected, analyzed, and sent to be reviewed by the scientific community.

1.4 Challenges Facing Science
Technology is the application of scientific information. Many challenges, including climate change, the loss of biodiversity, and emerging diseases, are actively being studied by scientists.

2   **Chapter 1**   Exploring Life and Science

1.1 The Characteristics of Life

The science of **biology** is the study of living organisms and their environments. All living organisms (Fig. 1.1) share several basic characteristics. They (1) are organized, (2) acquire materials and energy, (3) are homeostatic, (4) respond to stimuli, (5) reproduce and grow, and (6) have an evolutionary history.

Life Is Organized

Figure 1.2 illustrates the levels of biological organization. Note that, at the bottom of the figure, **atoms** join together to form the **molecules** that make up a cell. A **cell** is the smallest structural and functional unit of an organism. Some organisms, such as bacteria, are single-celled organisms. Humans are *multicellular,* because they are composed of many different types of cells. A nerve cell is one of the types of cells in the human body. It has a structure suitable to conducting a nerve impulse.

A **tissue** is a group of similar cells that perform a particular function. Nervous tissue is composed of millions of nerve cells that transmit signals to all parts of the body. An **organ** is made up of several types of tissues, and each organ belongs to an **organ system.** The organs of an organ system work together to accomplish a common purpose. The brain works with the spinal cord to send commands to body parts by way of nerves. **Organisms,** such as trees and humans, are a collection of organ systems.

The levels of biological organization extend beyond the individual. All the members of one **species** (a group of interbreeding organisms) in a particular area belong to a **population.** A tropical grassland may have a population of zebras, acacia trees, and humans, for example. The interacting populations of the grasslands make up a **community.** The community of populations interacts with the physical environment to form an **ecosystem.** Finally, all the Earth's ecosystems collectively make up the **biosphere** (Fig. 1.2, *top*).

Figure 1.1 **All life shares common characteristics.**
From the simplest one-celled organisms to complex plants and animals, all life shares several basic characteristics.
(leech): © St. Bartholomews Hospital/Science Source; (mushrooms): © IT Stock/age fotostock RF; (bacteria): © Science Source; (meerkats): © Jami Tarris/Getty Images; (sunflower): © Dave Thompson/Life File/Getty RF; (*Giardia*): Source: Dr. Stan Erlandsen/CDC

Figure 1.2 **Levels of biological organization.**
Life is connected from the atomic level to the biosphere. The cell is the basic unit of life, and it comprises molecules and atoms. The sum of all life on the planet is called the biosphere.

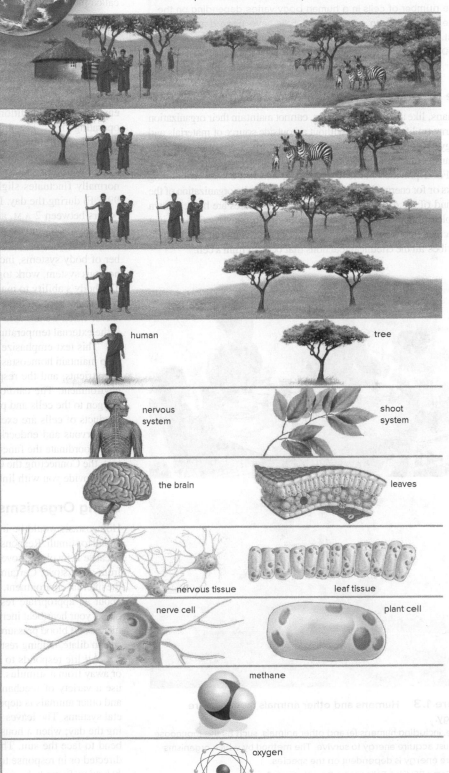

Biosphere
Regions of the Earth's crust, waters, and atmosphere inhabited by living organisms

Ecosystem
A community plus the physical environment

Community
Interacting populations in a particular area

Population
Organisms of the same species in a particular area

Species
A group of similar, interbreeding organisms

Organism
An individual; complex individuals contain organ systems

Organ System
Composed of several organs working together

Organ
Composed of tissues functioning together for a specific task

Tissue
A group of cells with a common structure and function

Cell
The structural and functional unit of all living organisms

Molecule
Union of two or more atoms of the same or different elements

Atom
Smallest unit of an element; composed of electrons, protons, and neutrons

human   tree

nervous system   shoot system

the brain   leaves

nervous tissue   leaf tissue

nerve cell   plant cell

methane

oxygen

4   Chapter 1 Exploring Life and Science

Life Requires Materials and Energy

Humans, like all living organisms, cannot maintain their organization or carry on life's activities without an outside source of materials and energy. **Energy** is the capacity to do work. Like other animals, humans acquire materials and energy by eating food (Fig. 1.3).

Food provides nutrient molecules, which are used as building blocks or for energy. It takes energy to maintain the organization of the cell and of the organism. Some nutrient molecules are broken down completely to provide the energy necessary to convert other nutrient molecules into the parts and products of cells. The term **metabolism** describes all the chemical reactions that occur within a cell.

Figure 1.3 Humans and other animals must acquire energy.

All life, including humans (**a**) and other animals, such as this mongoose (**b**), must acquire energy to survive. The method by which organisms acquire energy is dependent on the species.

(a): © Corbis RF; (b): © Gallo Images-Dave Hamman/Getty RF

The ultimate source of energy for the majority of life on Earth is the sun. Plants, algae, and some bacteria are able to harvest the energy of the sun and convert it to chemical energy by a process called **photosynthesis.** Photosynthesis produces organic molecules, such as sugars, that serve as the basis of the food chain for many other organisms, including humans and all other animals.

Living Organisms Maintain an Internal Environment

For the metabolic pathways within a cell to function correctly, the environmental conditions of the cell must be kept within strict operating limits. The ability of a cell or an organism to maintain an internal environment that operates under specific conditions is called **homeostasis.** In humans, many of our organ systems work to maintain homeostasis. For example, human body temperature normally fluctuates slightly between 36.5 and 37.5°C (97.7 and 99.5°F) during the day. In general, the lowest temperature usually occurs between 2 A.M. and 4 A.M., and the highest usually occurs between 6 P.M. and 10 P.M. However, activity can cause the body temperature to rise, and inactivity can cause it to decline. A number of body systems, including the cardiovascular system and the nervous system, work together to maintain a constant temperature. The body's ability to maintain a normal temperature is also somewhat dependent on the external temperature. Even though we can shiver when we are cold and perspire when we are hot, we will die if the external temperature becomes overly cold or hot.

This text emphasizes how all the systems of the human body help maintain homeostasis. For example, the digestive system takes in nutrients, and the respiratory system exchanges gases with the environment. The cardiovascular system distributes nutrients and oxygen to the cells and picks up their wastes. The metabolic waste products of cells are excreted by the urinary system. The work of the nervous and endocrine systems is critical, because these systems coordinate the functions of the other systems. Throughout the text, the Connecting the Concepts feature at the end of each section will provide you with links to more information on homeostasis.

Living Organisms Respond

Homeostasis would be impossible without the body's ability to respond to stimuli. Response to external stimuli is more apparent to us, because it involves movement, as when we quickly remove a hand from a hot stove. Certain sensory receptors also detect a change in the internal environment, and then the central nervous system brings about an appropriate response. When you are startled by a loud noise, your heartbeat increases, which causes your blood pressure to increase. If blood pressure rises too high, the brain directs blood vessels to dilate, helping restore normal blood pressure.

All life responds to external stimuli, often by moving toward or away from a stimulus, such as the sight of food. Organisms may use a variety of mechanisms to move, but movement in humans and other animals is dependent on their nervous and musculoskeletal systems. The leaves of plants track the passage of the sun during the day; when a houseplant is placed near a window, its stems bend to face the sun. The movement of an animal, whether self-directed or in response to a stimulus, constitutes a large part of its *behavior.* Some behaviors help us acquire food and reproduce.

Figure 1.4   **Growth and development define life.**
(a) A small acorn becomes a tree, and (b) following fertilization an embryo becomes a fetus by the process of growth and development.
(seedling): © Herman Eisenbeiss/Science Source; (tree): © Photographer's Choice/Getty RF; (egg): © David M.Phillips/Science Source; (fetus): © Brand X Pictures/Punchstock RF

Living Organisms Reproduce and Develop

Reproduction is a fundamental characteristic of life. Cells come into being only from preexisting cells, and all living organisms have parents. When organisms **reproduce,** they pass on their genetic information to the next generation. Following the fertilization of an egg by a sperm cell, the resulting zygote undergoes a rapid period of growth and development. This is common in most forms of life. Figure 1.4*a* illustrates that an acorn progresses to a seedling before it becomes an adult oak tree. In humans, growth occurs as the fertilized egg develops into a fetus (Fig. 1.4*b*). **Growth,** recognized by an increase in size and often in the number of cells, is a part of development. In multicellular organisms, such as humans, the term **development** is used to indicate all the changes that occur from the time the egg is fertilized until death. Therefore, it includes all the changes that occur during childhood, adolescence, and adulthood. Development also includes the repair that takes place following an injury.

The genetic information of all life is **DNA (deoxyribonucleic acid).** DNA contains the hereditary information that directs not only the structure of each cell but also its function. The information in DNA is contained within **genes,** short sequences of hereditary material that specify the instructions for a specific trait. Before reproduction occurs, DNA is replicated, so that an exact copy of each gene may be passed on to the offspring. When humans reproduce, a sperm carries genes contributed by a male into the egg, which contains genes contributed by a female. The genes direct both growth and development, so that the organism will eventually resemble the parents. Sometimes **mutations,** minor variations in these genes, can cause an organism to be better suited for its environment. These mutations are the basis of evolutionary change.

Organisms Have an Evolutionary History

Evolution is the process by which a population changes over time. The mechanism by which evolution occurs is **natural selection** (see Section 23.2). When a new variation arises that allows certain members of a population to capture more resources, these members tend to survive and have more offspring than the other, unchanged members. Therefore, each successive generation will include more members with the new variation, which represents an **adaptation** to the environment. Consider, for example, populations of humans who live at high altitudes, such as the cultures living at elevations of over 4,000 meters (m) (14,000 ft) in the Tibetan Plateau. This environment is very low in oxygen. As the Science feature "Adapting to Life at High Elevations" investigates, these populations have evolved an adaptation that reduces the amount of hemoglobin, the oxygen-carrying pigment in the blood. As the feature explains, this adaptation makes life at these altitudes possible.

Evolution, which has been going on since the origin of life and will continue as long as life exists, explains both the unity and the diversity of life. All organisms share the same characteristics of life because their ancestry can be traced to the first cell or cells. Organisms are diverse because they are adapted to different ways of life.

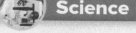

BIOLOGY TODAY   Science

Adapting to Life at High Elevations

Humans, like all other organisms, have an evolutionary history. This means not only that we share common ancestors with other animals but also that over time we demonstrate adaptations to changing environmental conditions. One study of populations living in the high-elevation mountains of Tibet (Fig. 1A) demonstrates how the processes of evolution and adaptation influence humans.

Figure 1A
Individuals living at high elevations, such as these Tibetans, have become adapted to their environment.
© Michael Freeman/Corbis RF

Normally when a person moves to a higher altitude, his or her body responds by making more hemoglobin, the component of blood that carries oxygen, which thickens the blood. For minor elevation changes, this does not present much of a problem. But for people who live at extreme elevations (some people in the Himalayas can live at elevations of over 13,000 ft, or close to 4,000 m), excess hemoglobin can present a number of health problems, including chronic mountain sickness, a disease that affects people who live at high altitudes for extended periods of time. The problem is that, as the amount of hemoglobin increases, the blood thickens and becomes more viscous. This can cause elevated blood pressure, or hypertension, and an increase in the formation of blood clots, both of which have negative physiological effects.

Because high hemoglobin levels would be a detriment to people at high elevations, it makes sense that natural selection would favor individuals who produce less hemoglobin at high elevations. Such is the case with the Tibetans in this study. Researchers have identified an allele of a gene that reduces hemoglobin production at high elevations. Comparisons between Tibetans at both high and low elevations strongly suggest that selection has played a role in the prevalence of the high-elevation allele.

The gene is *EPSA1*, located on chromosome 2 of humans. *EPSA1* produces a transcription factor, which basically regulates which genes are turned on and off in the body, a process called gene expression. The transcription factor produced by *EPSA1* has a number of functions in the body. For example, in addition to controlling the amount of hemoglobin in the blood, this transcription factor also regulates other genes that direct how the body uses oxygen.

When the researchers examined the variations in *EPSA1* in the Tibetan population, they discovered that the Tibetan version greatly reduces the production of hemoglobin. Therefore, the Tibetan population has lower hemoglobin levels than people living at lower altitudes, allowing these individuals to escape the consequences of thick blood.

How long did it take for the original population to adapt to living at higher elevations? Initially the comparison of variations in these genes between high-elevation and low-elevation Tibetan populations suggested that the event may have occurred over a 3,000-year period. But researchers were skeptical of that data because it suggested a relatively rapid rate of evolutionary change. Additional studies of genetic databases yielded an interesting finding—the *EPSA1* gene in Tibetans was identical to a similar gene found in an ancient group of humans called the Denisovans (see Section 23.5). Scientists now believe that the *EPSA1* gene entered the Tibetan population around 40,000 years ago, either through interbreeding between early Tibetans and Denisovans, or from one of the immediate ancestors of this now-lost group of early humans.

Questions to Consider

1. What other environments do you think could be studied to look for examples of human adaptation?
2. In addition to hemoglobin levels, do you think that people at high elevations may exhibit other adaptations?

CONNECTING THE CONCEPTS

Both homeostasis and evolution are central themes in the study of biology. For more examples of homeostasis and evolution, refer to the following discussions:

Section 4.8 explains how body temperature is regulated.

Section 11.4 explores the role of the kidneys in fluid and salt homeostasis.

Section 23.3 examines the evolutionary history of humans.

CHECK YOUR PROGRESS 1.1

1. List the basic characteristics of life.
2. Summarize the levels of biological organization.
3. Explain the relationship between adaptations and evolutionary change.

1.2 Humans Are Related to Other Animals

LEARNING OUTCOMES

Upon completion of this section, you should be able to

1. Summarize the place of humans in the overall classification of living organisms.
2. Understand that humans have a cultural heritage.
3. Describe the relationship between humans and the biosphere.

Biologists classify all life as belonging to one of three **domains.** The evolutionary relationships of these domains are presented in Figure 1.5. Two of these, domain Bacteria and domain Archaea, contain prokaryotes, single-celled organisms that lack a nucleus. Organisms in the third domain, Eukarya, all contain cells that possess a nucleus. Some of these organisms are single-celled; others are multicellular. Humans are multicelled Eukarya.

Domain Eukarya is divided into one of four **kingdoms** (Fig. 1.6)—plants (Plantae), fungi (Fungi), animals (Animalia), and protists (Protista). Most organisms in kingdom Animalia are *invertebrates,* such as earthworms, insects, and mollusks. *Vertebrates* are animals that have a nerve cord protected by a vertebral column, which gives them their name. Fish, reptiles, amphibians, and birds are all vertebrates. Vertebrates with hair or fur and mammary glands are classified as *mammals.* Humans, raccoons, seals, and meerkats are examples of mammals.

Humans are most closely related to apes. We are distinguished from apes by our (1) highly developed brains, (2) completely upright stance, (3) creative language, and (4) ability to use a wide variety of tools. Humans did not evolve from apes; apes and humans share a common, apelike ancestor. Today's apes are our evolutionary cousins. Our relationship to apes is analogous to you and your first cousin being descended from your grandparents. We could not have evolved directly from our cousins, because we are contemporaries—living on Earth at the same time.

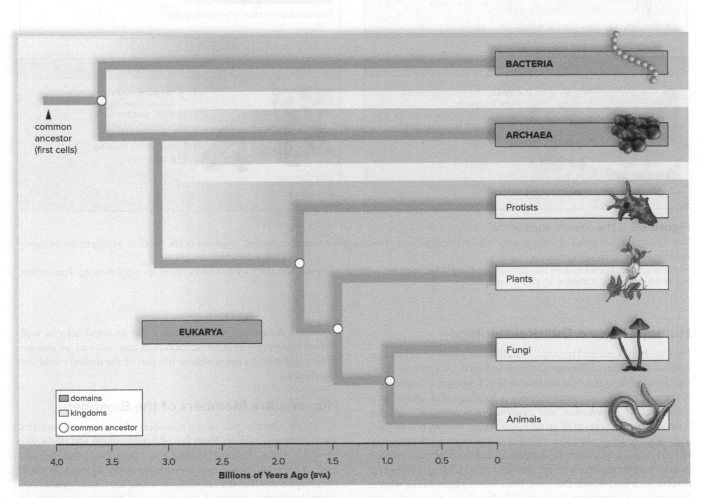

Figure 1.5   The evolutionary relationships of the three domains of life.
Living organisms are classified into three domains: Bacteria, Archaea, and Eukarya. The Eukarya are further divided into kingdoms (see Fig. 1.6).

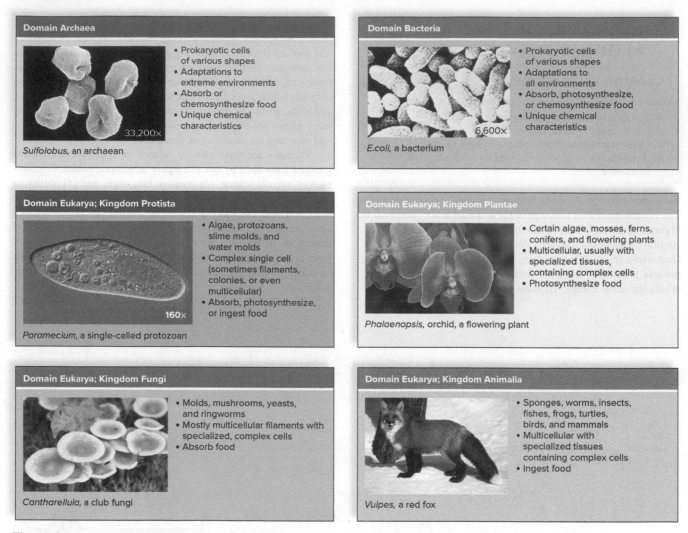

Figure 1.6   The classification of life.

This figure provides some of the characteristics of the organisms of each of the major domains and kingdoms of life. Humans belong to the domain Eukarya and kingdom Animalia.

(archaea): © Eye of Science/Science Source; (bacteria): © A. B. Dowsett/SPL/Science Source; (paramecium): © M. I. Walker/Science Source; (orchid): © Pixtal/Age Fotostock RF; (mushrooms): © Ingram Publishing RF; (fox): © Corbis RF

Humans Have a Cultural Heritage

Humans have a cultural heritage in addition to a biological heritage. *Culture* encompasses human activities and products passed on from one generation to the next outside of direct biological inheritance. Among animals, only humans have a language that allows us to communicate information and experiences symbolically. We are born without knowledge of an accepted way to behave, but we gradually acquire this knowledge by adult instruction and the imitation of role models. Members of the previous generation pass on their beliefs, values, and skills to the next generation. Many of the skills involve tool use, which can vary from how to hunt in the wild to how to use a computer. Human skills have also produced a rich heritage in the arts and sciences. However, a society highly dependent on science and technology has its drawbacks as well. Unfortunately, this cultural development may mislead us into believing that humans are somehow not part of the natural world surrounding us.

Humans Are Members of the Biosphere

All life on Earth is part of the biosphere, the living network that spans the surface of the Earth into the atmosphere and down into the soil and seas. Although humans can raise animals and crops for food, we depend on the environment for many services. Without microorganisms that decompose, the waste we create would soon cover the Earth's surface. Some species of bacteria can clean up pollutants like heavy metals and pesticides.

Freshwater ecosystems, such as rivers and lakes, provide fish to eat, drinking water, and water to irrigate crops. Many of our crops and prescription drugs were originally derived from plants that grew naturally in an ecosystem. Some human populations around the globe still depend on wild animals as a food source. The water-holding capacity of forests prevents flooding, and the ability of forests and other ecosystems to retain soil prevents soil erosion. For many people, these forests provide a place for recreational activities like hiking and camping.

SCIENCE IN YOUR LIFE

How many humans are there?

As of 2016, it was estimated that there were over 7.4 billion humans on the planet. Each of those humans needs food, shelter, clean water and air, and materials to maintain a healthy lifestyle. We add an additional 80 million people per year—that is like adding ten New York Cities per year! This makes human population growth one of the greatest threats to the biosphere.

CHECK YOUR PROGRESS 1.2

1. Define the term *biosphere*.
2. Define *culture*.
3. Explain why humans belong to the domain Eukarya and kingdom Animalia.

CONNECTING THE CONCEPTS

To learn more about the preceding material, refer to the following discussions:

Chapter 23 examines recent developments in the study of human evolution.

Chapter 24 provides a more detailed look at ecosystems.

Chapter 25 explores how humans interact with the biosphere.

1.3 Science as a Process

LEARNING OUTCOMES

Upon completion of this section, you should be able to

1. Describe the general process of the scientific method.
2. Distinguish between a control group and an experimental group in a scientific test.
3. Recognize the importance of scientific journals in the reporting of scientific information.
4. Interpret information that is presented in a scientific graph.
5. Recognize the importance of statistical analysis to the study of science.

Science is a way of knowing about the natural world. When scientists study the natural world, they aim to be objective, rather than subjective. Objective observations are supported by factual information, whereas subjective observations involve personal judgment. For example, the fat content of a particular food would be an objective observation of a nutritional study. Reporting about the good or bad taste of the food would be a subjective observation. It is difficult to make objective observations and conclusions, because we are often influenced by our prejudices. Scientists must keep in mind that scientific conclusions can change because of new findings. New findings are often made because of recent advances in techniques or equipment.

Religion, aesthetics, ethics, and science are all ways in which humans seek order in the natural world. The nature of scientific inquiry differs from these other ways of knowing and learning, because the scientific process uses the **scientific method,** a standard series of steps used in gaining new knowledge that is widely accepted among scientists. The scientific method (Fig. 1.7) acts as a guideline for scientific studies.

The approach of individual scientists to their work is as varied as the scientists. However, much of the scientific process is descriptive. For example, an observation of a new disease may lead a scientist to describe all the aspects of the disease, such as the environment, the age of onset, and the characteristics of the disease. Some areas of biology, such as the study of biodiversity in the ecological sciences (see Section 1.4), lend themselves more to this descriptive approach. Regardless of their area of study, most scientists spend a considerable amount of time performing a descriptive analysis of their observation before proceeding into the steps of the scientific method. Scientists often modify or adapt the process to suit their particular field of study, but for the sake of discussion it is useful to think of the scientific method as consisting of certain steps.

Start with an Observation

Scientists believe that nature is orderly and measurable—that natural laws, such as the law of gravity, do not change with time—and that a natural event, or *phenomenon,* can be understood more fully through **observation**—a formal way of watching the natural world.

Observations may be made with the senses, such as sight and smell, or with instruments; for example, a microscope enables us to see objects that could never be seen by the naked eye. Scientists may expand their understanding even further by taking advantage of the knowledge and experiences of other scientists. For instance, they may look up past studies on the Internet or at the library, or they may write or speak to others who are researching similar topics.

Develop a Hypothesis

After making observations and gathering knowledge about a phenomenon, a scientist uses inductive reasoning. **Inductive reasoning** occurs whenever a person uses creative thinking to combine isolated facts into a cohesive whole. Chance alone can help a scientist arrive at an idea. The most famous case pertains to the antibiotic penicillin, which was discovered in 1928. While examining a petri dish of bacteria that had accidentally become contaminated with the mold *Penicillium*, Alexander Fleming observed an area around the mold that was free of bacteria. Fleming had

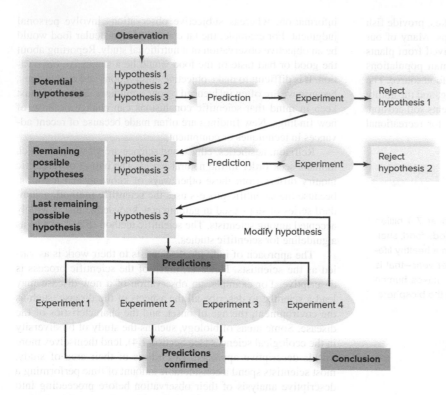

Figure 1.7   The scientific method.
On the basis of new and/or previous observations, a scientist formulates a hypothesis. The hypothesis is tested by further observations and/or experiments, and new data either support or do not support the hypothesis. The return arrow from experiment 4 indicates that a scientist often chooses to retest the same hypothesis or to test a related hypothesis. Conclusions from many different but related experiments may lead to the development of a scientific theory. For example, studies pertaining to development, anatomy, and fossil remains all support the theory of evolution.

long been interested in finding cures for human diseases caused by bacteria, and he was very knowledgeable about antibacterial substances. So when Fleming saw the dramatic effect of *Penicillium* mold on bacteria, he reasoned that the mold might be producing an antibacterial substance.

We call such a possible explanation for a natural event a **hypothesis.** A hypothesis is based on existing knowledge, so it is much more informed than a mere guess. Fleming's hypothesis was supported by further study, but sometimes a hypothesis is not supported and must be either modified and subjected to additional study or rejected.

All of a scientist's past experiences, no matter what they might be, may influence the formation of a hypothesis. But a scientist considers only hypotheses that can be tested by experiments or further observations. Moral and religious beliefs, although very important to our lives, differ among cultures and through time and are not always testable.

Make a Prediction and Perform Experiments

Scientists often perform an **experiment,** which is a series of procedures, to test a hypothesis. To determine how to test a hypothesis, a scientist uses deductive reasoning. **Deductive reasoning** involves "if, then" logic. In designing the experiment, the scientist may make a **prediction,** or an expected outcome, based on knowledge of the factors in the experiment.

The manner in which a scientist intends to conduct an experiment is called the **experimental design.** A good experimental design ensures that scientists are examining the contribution of a specific variable, called the **experimental variable,** to the

observation. The result is termed the **responding variable,** or dependent variable, because it is due to the experimental variable.

To ensure that the results will be meaningful, an experiment contains both test groups and a **control group.** A test group is exposed to the experimental variable, but the control group is not. If the control group and test groups show the same results, the experimenter knows that the hypothesis predicting a difference between them is not supported.

Scientists often use **model** organisms and model systems to test a hypothesis. Some common model organisms are shown in Figure 1.8. Model organisms are chosen because they allow the researcher to control aspects of the experiment, such as age and genetic background. Cell biologists may use mice for modeling the effects of a new drug. Like model organisms, model systems allow the scientist to control specific variables and environmental conditions in a way that may not be possible in the natural environment. For example, ecologists may use computer programs to model how human activities will affect the climate of a specific ecosystem. While models provide useful information, they do not always answer the original question completely. For example, medicine that is effective in mice should ideally be tested in humans, and ecological experiments that are conducted using computer simulations need to be verified by actual field experiments. Biologists, and all other scientists, continuously design and revise their experiments to better understand how different factors may influence their original observation.

Collecting and Analyzing the Data

The **data,** or results, from scientific experiments may be presented in a variety of formats, including tables and graphs. A graph shows

Drosophila melanogaster

Caenorhabditis elegans   64×

Arabidopsis thaliana

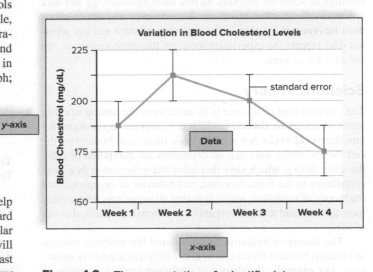

Mus musculus

Figure 1.8   Model organisms used in scientific studies.
Drosophila melanogaster is used as a model organism in the study of genetics. *Mus musculus* is used in the study of medicine. *Caenorhabditis elegans* is used by developmental biologists, and *Arabidopsis thaliana* is used by botanists to understand plant genetics.
(D. melanogaster) © Graphic Science/Alamy; *(C. elegans)* © Sinclair Stammers/Science Source; *(A. thaliana)* © Wildlife GmbH/Alamy; *(M. musculus)* © Steve Gorton/Getty Images

the relationship between two quantities. In many graphs, the experimental variable is plotted on the *x*-axis (horizontal), and the result is plotted along the *y*-axis (vertical). Graphs are useful tools to summarize data in a clear and simplified manner. For example, the line graph in Figure 1.9 shows the variation in the concentration of blood cholesterol over a 4-week study. The bar above and below each data point represents the variation, or standard error, in the results. The title and labels can assist you in reading a graph; therefore, when looking at a graph, first check the two axes to determine what the graph pertains to. By looking at this graph, we know that the blood cholesterol levels were highest during week 2, and we can see to what degree the values varied over the course of the study.

Statistical Data

Most scientists who publish research articles use statistics to help them evaluate their experimental data. In statistics, the standard error, or standard deviation, tells us how uncertain a particular value is. Suppose you predict how many hurricanes Florida will have next year by calculating the average number during the past 10 years. If the number of hurricanes per year varies widely, your standard error will be larger than if the number per year is usually about the same. In other words, the standard error tells you how far off the average could be. If the average number of hurricanes is

four and the standard error is ± 2, then your prediction of four hurricanes is between two and six hurricanes. In Figure 1.9, the standard error is represented by the bars above and below each data point. This provides a visual indication of the statistical analysis of the data.

Statistical Significance

When scientists conduct an experiment, there is always the possibility that the results are due to chance or to some factor other than the experimental variable. Investigators take into account several factors when they calculate the probability value (p) that their results were due to chance alone. If the probability value is low, researchers describe the results as statistically significant. A probability value of less than 5% (usually written as $p < 0.05$) is acceptable; even so, keep in mind that the lower the p value, the less likely it is that the results are due to chance. Therefore, the lower the p value, the greater the confidence the investigators and you can have in the results. Depending on the type of study, most scientists like to have a p value of < 0.05, but p values of < 0.001 are common in many studies.

Scientific Publications

Scientific studies are customarily published in scientific journals, such as *Science* or *Nature,* so that all aspects of a study are available to the scientific community. Before information is published in scientific journals, it is typically reviewed by experts, who ensure that the research is credible, accurate, unbiased, and well executed. Another scientist should be able to read

Variation in Blood Cholesterol Levels

y-axis

x-axis

Figure 1.9   The presentation of scientific data.
This line graph shows the variation in the concentration of blood cholesterol over a 4-week study. The bars above and below the data points represent the variation, or standard error, in the results.

about an experiment in a scientific journal, repeat the experiment in a different location, and get the same (or very similar) results. Some articles are rejected for publication by reviewers when they believe there is something questionable about the design of an experiment or the manner in which it was conducted. This process of rejection is important in science because it causes researchers to critically review their hypotheses, predictions, and experimental designs, so that their next attempt will more adequately address their hypothesis. Often it takes several rounds of revision before research is accepted for publication in a scientific journal.

People should be especially careful about scientific information available on the Internet, which is not well regulated. Reliable, credible scientific information can often be found at websites with URLs containing .edu (for educational institution), .gov (for government sites such as the National Institutes of Health or the Centers for Disease Control and Prevention), and .org (for nonprofit organizations, such as the American Lung Association or the National Multiple Sclerosis Society). Unfortunately, quite a bit of scientific information on the Internet is intended to entice people into purchasing some sort of product for weight loss, prevention of hair loss, or similar maladies. These websites usually have URLs ending with .com or .net. It pays to question and verify the information from these websites with another source (a primary source, if possible).

Develop a Conclusion

Scientists must analyze the data in order to reach a **conclusion** about whether a hypothesis is supported or not. Because science progresses, the conclusion of one experiment can lead to the hypothesis for another experiment (see Fig. 1.9). In other words, results that do not support one hypothesis can often help a scientist formulate another hypothesis to be tested. Scientists report their findings in scientific journals, so that their methodology and data are available to other scientists. Experiments and observations must be *repeatable*—that is, the reporting scientist and any scientist who repeats the experiment must get the same results, or else the data are suspect.

Scientific Theory

The ultimate goal of science is to understand the natural world in terms of **scientific theories,** which are accepted explanations for how the world works. Some of the basic theories of biology are the cell theory, which says that all organisms are composed of cells; the gene theory, which says that inherited information in a gene contributes to the form, function, and behavior of organisms; and the theory of evolution, which says that all organisms have a common ancestor and that each organism is adapted to a particular way of life.

The theory of evolution is considered the unifying concept of biology, because it pertains to many different aspects of organisms. For example, the theory of evolution enables scientists to understand the history of life, the variety of organisms, and the anatomy, physiology, and development of organisms. The theory of evolution has been a very fruitful scientific theory, meaning

that it has helped scientists generate new testable hypotheses. Because this theory has been supported by so many observations and experiments for over 100 years, some biologists refer to the theory of evolution as the **principle** of evolution, a term sometimes used for theories that are generally accepted by an overwhelming number of scientists. Others prefer the term **law** instead of *principle*.

An Example of a Controlled Study

We now know that most stomach and intestinal ulcers (open sores) are caused by the bacterium *Helicobacter pylori* (see the Science feature "Discovering the Cause of Ulcers").

Experimental Design

Let's say investigators want to determine which of two antibiotics is best for the treatment of an ulcer. When clinicians do an experiment, they try to vary just the experimental variables—in this case, the medications being tested. Each antibiotic is administered to an independent test group. The control group is not given an antibiotic. If by chance the control group shows the same results as one of the test groups, the investigators may conclude that the antibiotic in that test group is ineffective, because it does not show a result that is significantly different from that of the control group. The study depicted in Figure 1.10 shows how investigators may study this hypothesis:

Hypothesis: Newly discovered antibiotic B is a better treatment for ulcers than antibiotic A, which is in current use.

In any experiment, it is important to reduce the number of possible variables (differences). In this experiment, those variables may include factors such differences in the subjects' sex, weight, and previous illnesses. Therefore, the investigators *randomly* divide a large group of volunteers equally into experimental groups. The hope is that any differences will be distributed evenly among the three groups. The larger the number of volunteers (the sample size), the greater the chance of reducing the influence of external variables. This is why many medical studies involve thousands of individuals.

In this experiment, the researchers divide the individuals into three groups:

Control group: Subjects with ulcers are not treated with either antibiotic.
Test group 1: Subjects with ulcers are treated with antibiotic A.
Test group 2: Subjects with ulcers are treated with antibiotic B.

After the investigators have determined that all volunteers do have ulcers, they will want the subjects to think they are all receiving the *same* treatment. This is an additional way to protect the results from any influence other than the medication. To achieve this end, the subjects in the control group can receive a **placebo,** a treatment that appears to be the same as that administered to the other two groups but that actually contains no medication. In this study, the use of a placebo would help ensure that all subjects are equally dedicated to the study.

The Results and Conclusion

After 2 weeks of administering the same amount of medication (or placebo) in the same way, researchers examine the stomach and intestinal linings of each subject to determine if ulcers are still present. Endoscopy is one way to examine a patient for the presence of ulcers. This procedure, which is performed under sedation, involves inserting an endoscope—a small, flexible tube with a tiny camera on the end—down the throat and into the stomach and the upper part of the intestine. Then, the doctor can see the lining of these organs and can check for ulcers. Tests performed during an endoscopy can also determine if *Helicobacter pylori* is present.

Because endoscopy is somewhat subjective, it is probably best if the examiner is not aware of which group the subject is in; otherwise examiner prejudice may influence the examination. When neither the patient nor the technician is aware of the specific treatment, it is called a *double-blind* study.

In this study, the investigators may decide to determine the effectiveness of the medication by the percentage of people who no longer have ulcers. So, if 20 people out of 100 still have ulcers, the medication is 80% effective. The difference in effectiveness is easily read in the graph portion of Figure 1.10.

Conclusion: On the basis of their data, the investigators conclude that their hypothesis has been supported.

State Hypothesis:
Antibiotic B is a better treatment for ulcers than antibiotic A.

Perform Experiment:
Groups were treated the same except as noted.

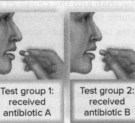

| Control group: received placebo | Test group 1: received antibiotic A | Test group 2: received antibiotic B |

Collect Data:
Each subject was examined for the presence of ulcers.

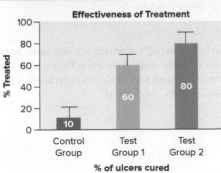

Effectiveness of Treatment

% of ulcers cured

Control Group: 10
Test Group 1: 60
Test Group 2: 80

(% Treated)

CHECK YOUR PROGRESS 1.3

1. Describe each step of the scientific method.
2. Explain why a controlled study is an important part of the experimental design.
3. List a few pros and cons of using a scientific journal versus other sources of information.
4. Summarize how the use of graphs and statistics aids in data analysis.

CONNECTING THE CONCEPTS

For more information on the topics presented in this section, refer to the following discussions:

Section 8.4 discusses how resistance to antibiotics occurs.

Section 9.3 provides more information on ulcers.

Figure 14.3 shows the relationship between an action potential and voltage across a plasma membrane.

Figure 1.10 A controlled laboratory experiment to test the effectiveness of a medication in humans.
In this study, a large number of people were divided into three groups. The control group received a placebo and no medication. One of the test groups received antibiotic A, and the other test group received antibiotic B. The results are depicted in a graph, and it shows that antibiotic B was more effective than antibiotic A for the treatment of ulcers.

BIOLOGY TODAY   Science

Discovering the Cause of Ulcers

In 1974, Barry James Marshall (Fig. 1B) was a young resident physician at Queen Elizabeth II Medical Center in Perth, Australia. There he saw many patients who had bleeding stomach ulcers. A pathologist at the hospital, Dr. J. Robin Warren, told him about finding a particular bacterium, now called *Helicobacter pylori*, near the site of peptic ulcers. Marshall compiled data showing a possible correlation between the presence of *H. pylori* and the occurrence of both gastritis (inflammation of the stomach) and stomach ulcers. On the basis of these data, Marshall formulated a hypothesis: *H. pylori* is the cause of gastritis and ulcers.

Marshall decided to make use of Koch's postulates, the standard criteria that must be fulfilled to show that a pathogen (bacterium or virus) causes a disease:

- The suspected pathogen (virus or bacterium) must be present in every case of the disease.
- The pathogen must be isolated from the host and grown in a lab dish.
- The disease must be reproduced when a pure culture of the pathogen is inoculated into a healthy susceptible host.
- The same pathogen must be recovered again from the experimentally infected host.

By 1983 Marshall had fulfilled the first and second of Koch's criteria. He was able to isolate *H. pylori* from ulcer patients and grow it in the laboratory. Despite Marshall's presentation of these findings to the scientific community, most physicians continued to believe that stomach acidity and stress were the causes of stomach ulcers. In those days, patients were usually advised to make drastic changes in their lifestyle to cure their ulcers. Many scientists believed that no bacterium would be able to survive the normal acidity of the stomach.

Marshall had a problem in fulfilling the third and fourth of Koch's criteria. He had been unable to infect guinea pigs and rats with the bacteria, because the bacteria did not flourish in the intestinal tracts of those animals. Marshall was not able to use human subjects because of ethical reasons. Marshall was so determined to support his hypothesis that in 1985 he decided to perform the experiment on himself! To the disbelief of those in the lab that day, he and another volunteer swallowed a foul-smelling, foul-tasting solution of *H. pylori*. Within the week, they felt lousy and were vomiting up their stomach contents. Examination by endoscopy showed that their stomachs were now inflamed, and biopsies of the stomach lining contained the suspected bacterium (Fig. 1B). Their

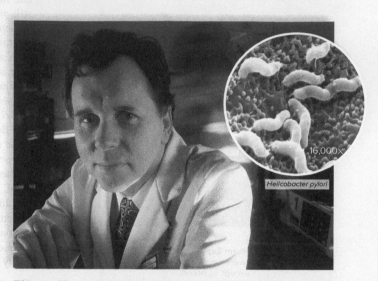

Figure 1B   Dr. Marshall and the cause of stomach ulcers.
Dr. Barry Marshall, pictured here, fulfilled Koch's postulates to show that *Helicobacter pylori* is the cause of peptic ulcers. The inset shows the presence of the bacterium in the stomach.
(Dr. Marshall): © Tony McDonough/epa/Corbis; (bacteria): © Eye of Science/Science Source

symptoms abated without need for medication, and they never developed an ulcer. Marshall challenged the scientific community to refute his hypothesis. Many tried, but ultimately the investigators supported his findings.

In science, many experiments, often involving a considerable number of subjects, are required before a conclusion can be reached. By the early 1990s at least three independent studies involving hundreds of patients had been published showing that antibiotic therapy can eliminate *H. pylori* from the intestinal tract and cure patients of ulcers wherever they occurred in the tract.

Dr. Marshall and Dr. Warren received a Nobel Prize in Physiology or Medicine in 2005. The Nobel committee reportedly thanked Marshall and Warren for their "pioneering discovery," stating that peptic ulcer disease now could be cured with antibiotics and acid-secretion inhibitors rather than becoming a "chronic, frequently disabling condition."

Questions to Consider

1. Explain how Marshall's approach was similar to, and different from, the scientific method shown in Figure 1.7.
2. How could Marshall have done this experiment if he had had an animal model to work with?

1.4 Challenges Facing Science

As we have learned in this chapter, science is a systematic way of acquiring knowledge about the natural world. Science is a slightly different endeavor than technology. **Technology** is the application of scientific knowledge to the interests of humans. Scientific investigations are the basis for the majority of our technological advances. As is often the case, a new technology, such as your cell phone or a new drug, is based on years of scientific investigations. In this section, we are going to explore some of the challenges facing science, technology, and society.

Biodiversity and Habitat Loss

Biodiversity is the total number and relative abundance of species, the variability of their genes, and the different ecosystems in which they live. The biodiversity of our planet has been estimated to be around 8.7 million species (not counting bacteria), and so far, around 2.3 million have been identified and named. *Extinction* is the death of a species or larger classification category. It is estimated that presently we are losing hundreds of species every year due to human activities and that as much as 38% of all species, including most primates, birds, and amphibians, may be in danger of extinction before the end of the century. Many biologists are alarmed about the present rate of extinction and hypothesize it may eventually rival the rates of the five mass extinctions that occurred during our planet's history. The last mass extinction, about 65 million years ago, caused many plant and animal species, including the dinosaurs, to become extinct.

The two most biologically diverse ecosystems—tropical rain forests and coral reefs—are home to many organisms. These ecosystems are also threatened by human activities. The canopy of the tropical rain forest alone supports a variety of organisms, including orchids, insects, and monkeys. Coral reefs, which are found just offshore of the continents and of islands near the equator, are built up from calcium carbonate skeletons of sea animals called corals. Reefs provide a habitat for many animals, including jellyfish, sponges, snails, crabs, lobsters, sea turtles, moray eels, and some of the world's most colorful fishes. Like tropical rain forests, coral reefs are severely threatened as the human population increases in size. Some reefs are 50 million years old, yet in just a few decades human activities have destroyed an estimated 25% of all coral reefs and seriously degraded another 30%. At this rate, nearly three-quarters could be destroyed within 40 years. Similar statistics are available for tropical rain forests.

The destruction of healthy ecosystems has many unintended effects. For example, we depend on healthy ecosystems for food,

Figure 1.11 Preserving biodiversity.
Snails of the genus *Conus* are known to produce powerful painkillers. Unfortunately, their habitat on coral reefs is threatened by human activity.
© Franco Banfi/Waterframe/Age fotostock

medicines (Fig 1.11), and various raw materials. Draining of the natural wetlands of the Mississippi and Ohio Rivers and the construction of levees have worsened flooding problems, reducing the amount of fertile farmland that is available for agriculture. The destruction of South American rain forests has killed many species that might have yielded the next miracle drug and has decreased the availability of many types of lumber. We are only now beginning to realize that we depend on ecosystems even more for the services they provide. Just as chemical cycling occurs within a single ecosystem, so all ecosystems keep chemicals cycling throughout the biosphere. The workings of ecosystems ensure that the environmental conditions of the biosphere are suitable for the continued existence of humans. And several studies show that ecosystems cannot function properly unless they remain biologically diverse. We will explore the concept of biodiversity in greater detail in Chapters 23 and 24.

Emerging and Reemerging Diseases

Over the past decade, avian influenza (H5N1 and H7N9), swine flu (H1N1), severe acute respiratory syndrome (SARS), and Middle East respiratory syndrome (MERS) have been in the news. These are called **emerging diseases,** meaning that they are relatively new to humans. Where do emerging diseases come from? Some of them may result from new or increased exposure to animals or insect populations that act as vectors for disease. Changes in human behavior and use of technology can also result in new diseases. SARS is thought to have arisen in Guandong, China, due to the consumption of civets, a type of exotic cat considered a delicacy. The civets were possibly infected by exposure to horseshoe bats sold in open markets. Legionnaires' disease emerged in 1976 due to bacterial contamination of a large air-conditioning system in a hotel. The bacteria thrived in the cooling tower used as the water source for the air-conditioning system. In addition, with increasing globalization, diseases that were previously restricted to isolated communities are now transported all over the world. The first SARS cases were reported in southern China in November 2002. By the end of February 2003, SARS had reached nine countries/provinces, mostly through airline travel.

Some pathogens mutate and change hosts—jumping from birds to humans, for example. Before 1997, avian flu was thought to affect only birds. A mutated strain jumped to humans in the 1997 outbreak. To control that epidemic, officials killed 1.5 million chickens to remove the source of the virus. New forms of avian influenza (bird flu) are being discovered every few years.

Reemerging diseases are also a concern. Unlike an emerging disease, a reemerging disease has been known to cause disease in humans for some time, but generally has not been considered a health risk due to a relatively low level of incidence in human populations. However, reemerging diseases can cause problems. An excellent example is the Ebola outbreak in West Africa of 2014–2015. Ebola outbreaks have been known since 1976, but generally have affected only small groups of humans. The 2014–2015 outbreak was a regional event, but it affected the lives of millions of people before it was finally brought under control.

Both emerging and reemerging diseases have the potential to cause health problems for humans across the globe. Scientists investigate not only the causes of these diseases (for example, the viruses) but also their effects on our bodies and the mechanisms by which they are transmitted. We will take a closer look at viruses and emerging diseases in Section 8.3.

Climate Change

The term **climate change** refers to changes in the normal cycles of the Earth's climate that may be attributed to human activity. Climate change is primarily due to an imbalance in the chemical cycling of the element carbon. Normally carbon is cycled within an ecosystem. However, due to human activities, more carbon dioxide is being released into the atmosphere than is being removed. In 1850 atmospheric CO_2 was at about 280 parts per million (ppm); today, it is over 400 ppm. This increase is largely due to the burning of fossil fuels and the destruction of forests to make way for farmland and pasture. Today, the amount of carbon dioxide released into the atmosphere is about twice the amount that remains in the atmosphere. It's believed that most of this dissolves in the ocean. The increased amount of carbon dioxide (and other gases) in the atmosphere is causing a rise in temperature called **global warming.** These gases allow the sun's rays to pass through, but they absorb and radiate heat back to Earth, a phenomenon called the greenhouse effect.

There is a consensus among scientists around the globe that climate change and global warming are causing significant changes in many of the Earth's ecosystems and are one of the greatest challenges of our time. We will take a closer look at climate change and the concept of sustainability in Chapters 24 and 25.

CHECK YOUR PROGRESS 1.4

1. Explain how a new technology differs from a scientific discovery.
2. Explain why the conservation of biodiversity is important to human society.
3. Summarize how emerging diseases and climate change have the potential to influence the entire human population.

CONNECTING THE CONCEPTS

Section 8.3 provides additional information on emerging and reemerging diseases.

Section 24.3 examines the impact of climate change and global warming on ecosystems.

Section 25.3 explores the importance of preserving biodiversity.

CASE STUDY: CONCLUSION

In this chapter you have explored some of the basic characteristics of life as we know it. One question we might ask is, How can we apply our knowledge of life on Earth to detect life on other planets? Most likely, the life on moons such as Europa and Titan is not highly organized. Most scientists believe that simple multicellular organisms may be the only life-forms that can survive at such a great distance from the sun. Thus, future missions to planets and moons in our solar system will likely look for evidence of life. When you eat food, you produce carbon dioxide and other waste products. Living organisms on other planets should do the same. By studying the extreme environments of the moons of Saturn and Jupiter, and our own planet, we may be better able to define the basic properties of life and what it really means for something to "be alive."

SUMMARIZE

1.1 The Characteristics of Life

Biology is the study of life. All living organisms share common characteristics:

- They have levels of organization—**atoms, molecules, cells, tissues, organs, organ systems, organisms, species, populations, community, ecosystem,** and **biosphere.**
- They acquire materials and **energy** from the environment. **Metabolism** is the sum of the reactions involved in these processes. **Photosynthesis,** which occurs in organisms such as plants, is responsible for producing the organic molecules that serve as food for most organisms.
- They **reproduce** and experience **growth,** and in many cases **development.** The instructions for these processes are contained within the **deoxyribonucleic acid (DNA)** and organized as **genes.** **Mutations** cause variation of those instructions.
- They maintain **homeostasis** to maintain the conditions of an internal environment.
- They respond to stimuli.
- As species, they are influenced by **natural selection** as the process that results in **evolution** and **adaptation** to their environment over time.

1.2 Humans Are Related to Other Animals

The classification of living organisms mirrors their evolutionary relationships. Humans are mammals, a type of vertebrate in the animal **kingdom** of the **domain** Eukarya.

In addition to their evolutionary history, humans have a cultural heritage in which language, tool use, values, and information are passed on from one generation to the next.

Like all life, humans are members of the biosphere. Humans depend on the biosphere for its many services, such as absorption of pollutants, sources of water and food, prevention of soil erosion, and natural beauty.

1.3 Science as a Process

When studying the natural world, scientists use a process called the **scientific method.**

- **Observations,** along with previous data, are used to formulate a hypothesis. **Inductive reasoning** allows a scientist to combine facts into a **hypothesis.**
- New observations and/or experiments are carried out in order to test the hypothesis. Through **deductive reasoning** scientists can develop a **prediction** of what may occur as a result of the experiment. A good **experimental design** includes an **experimental variable** and a **control group.** Scientists may use **models** and model organisms in their experimental design.
- The **data** from the experimental and observational results are analyzed, often using statistical methods. The results are often presented in tables or graphs for ease of interpretation.
- A conclusion is made as to whether the results support the hypothesis or do not support the hypothesis.
- The results may be submitted to a scientific publication for review by the scientific community.
- Over time multiple conclusions in a particular area may allow scientists to arrive at a **theory** (or **principle** or **law**), such as the cell theory or the theory of evolution. The theory of evolution is a unifying concept of biology.

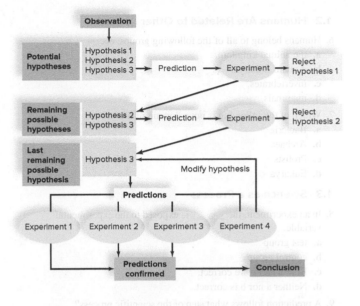

1.4 Challenges Facing Science

While science investigates the principles of the natural world, **technology** applies this knowledge to the needs of society. Some challenges that scientists are investigating include:

- The loss of **biodiversity** and habitats such as coral reefs and rain forests. This often results in the **extinction** of species.
- **Emerging diseases,** such as avian influenza and SARS, and reemerging diseases, such as Ebola.
- The impact of **climate change** and **global warming.**

ASSESS

TESTING YOURSELF

Choose the best answer for each question.

1.1 The Characteristics of Life

In questions 1–4, match each description with the correct characteristic of life from the key.

Key:

- a. Life is organized.
- b. Living organisms reproduce and grow.
- c. Living organisms respond to stimuli.
- d. Living organisms have an evolutionary history.
- e. Living organisms acquire materials and energy.

1. The human heart rate increases when the person is scared.
2. Humans produce only humans.
3. Humans need to eat to get building blocks and energy.
4. Similar cells form tissues in the human body.
5. Which of the following represents the process by which organisms become adapted to changes in their environment over time?
   - a. homeostasis
   - b. development
   - c. evolution
   - d. technology

1.2 Humans Are Related to Other Animals

6. Humans belong to all of the following groups, except
   a. the animal kingdom.
   b. domain Eukarya.
   c. invertebrates.
   d. mammals.

7. Which of the following is not a domain of life?
   a. Bacteria
   b. Archaea
   c. Protists
   d. Eukarya

1.3 Science as a Process

8. In an experiment, the _____ is exposed to the experimental variable.
   a. test group
   b. control group
   c. Both a and b are correct.
   d. Neither a nor b is correct.

9. A prediction follows what step of the scientific process?
   a. formation of a hypothesis
   b. development of a conclusion
   c. analysis of the data
   d. design of an experiment

10. Which comes first in the scientific process?
    a. a hypothesis
    b. a theory
    c. design of an experiment
    d. an observation

11. Information collected from a scientific experiment is known as
    a. a scientific theory.
    b. data.
    c. a hypothesis.
    d. a conclusion.

1.4 Challenges Facing Science

12. _____ is the application of scientific investigations for the benefit of humans.
    a. Bioethics
    b. Adaptation
    c. Evolution
    d. Technology

13. Human influence can be associated with which of the following challenges facing science?
    a. loss of biodiversity
    b. emerging diseases
    c. climate change
    d. All of these are correct.

ENGAGE

BioNOW

Want to know how this science is relevant to your life? Check out the BioNow video below:

• Characteristics of Life

At the end of the day, you head over to the gym for a game of basketball with your friends. Afterward, you go out to eat at a local restaurant. Explain how the characteristics of life apply to you during these activities.

THINKING CRITICALLY

1. Explain how climate change and loss of biodiversity may produce health threats for humans. Give an example of how scientists have already documented instances where this is occurring.

2. You are a scientist working at a pharmaceutical company and have developed a new cancer medication that has the potential for use in humans. Outline a series of experiments, including the use of a model, to test whether the cancer medication works.

3. In the cases of Europa and Titan, if life is found to exist there, will that change our definition of the basic characteristics of life? Will it change our definition of a biosphere?

© nyul/123RF

CHAPTER

3

Cell Structure and Function

CASE STUDY: WHEN CELLS MALFUNCTION

Mary and Kevin first noticed that something was wrong with their newborn about 4 months after birth. Whereas most newborns rapidly strengthen and are developing the ability to hold their head up and are demonstrating hand-eye coordination, their baby seemed to be weakening. In addition, Mary began to sense that something was wrong when their baby started having trouble swallowing his formula. After consulting with their pediatrician, Mary and Kevin decided to take their child to a local pediatric research hospital to talk with physicians trained in newborn developmental disorders.

After a series of tests that included blood work and a complete physical examination, the specialists at the research center informed Kevin and Mary that the symptoms their newborn was exhibiting are characteristic of a condition called Tay-Sachs disease. This condition is a rare metabolic disorder that causes one of the internal components of the cell, the lysosome, to malfunction. Because of this malfunction, fatty acids were accumulating in the cells of their child. These accumulations were causing the neurons to degrade, producing the symptoms noted by the parents.

What puzzled the research team was the fact that neither Kevin nor Mary were of Eastern European descent. Populations from this area are known to have a higher rate of the mutation that causes Tay-Sachs disease. However, genetic testing of both Kevin and Mary indicated that they were carriers for the trait, meaning that although they each had one normal copy of the gene associated with Tay-Sachs disease, each carried a defective copy as well. Only one good copy of the gene is needed for the lysosome to function correctly. Unfortunately, each had passed on a copy of the defective gene to their child.

Despite the poor prognosis for their child, both Kevin and Mary were determined to learn more about how this defect caused the lysosome to malfunction and about what treatments were being developed to prolong the life span of a child with Tay-Sachs disease.

As you read through the chapter, think about the following questions:

1. What organelle produces the lysosomes?
2. What is the role of the lysosome in a normally functioning cell?
3. Why would a malfunction in the lysosome cause an accumulation of fatty acids in the cell?

CHAPTER CONCEPTS

3.1 What Is a Cell?
Cells are the basic units of life. Cell size is limited by the surface-area-to-volume ratio.

3.2 How Cells Are Organized
Human cells are eukaryotic cells, with a plasma membrane, cytoplasm, and a nucleus.

3.3 The Plasma Membrane and How Substances Cross It
The structure of the plasma membrane influences its permeability. Substances cross the membrane using passive and active transport mechanisms, protein carriers, and vesicles.

3.4 The Nucleus and Endomembrane System
The nucleus and ribosomes are involved in the processing of information within the cell. The endomembrane system is a series of interchangeable organelles.

3.5 The Cytoskeleton, Cell Movement, and Cell Junctions
The cytoskeleton is composed of fibers that maintain the shape of the cell and assist in the movement of organelles.

3.6 Metabolism and the Energy Reactions
Mitochondria are the sites of cellular respiration, an aerobic process that produces the majority of ATP for a cell. Fermentation, an aerobic process, produces smaller amounts of ATP.

BEFORE YOU BEGIN

Before beginning this chapter, take a few moments to review the following discussions:

Section 2.2 What properties of water make it a crucial molecule for life as we know it?

Sections 2.3 to 2.7 What are the basic roles of carbohydrates, fats, proteins, and nucleic acids in the cell?

Section 2.7 What is the role of ATP in a cell?

3.1 What Is a Cell?

LEARNING OUTCOMES

Upon completion of this section, you should be able to

1. State the basic principles of the cell theory.
2. Explain how the surface-area-to-volume ratio limits cell size.
3. Summarize the role of microscopy in the study of cells.

All organisms, including humans, are composed of cells. From the single-celled bacteria to plants and complex animals such as ourselves, the cell is the fundamental unit of life. Despite their importance, most cells are small and can be seen only under a microscope. The small size of cells means that they are measured using the smaller units of the metric system, such as the *micrometer* (μm). A micrometer is 1/1,000 millimeter (mm). The micrometer is the common unit of measurement for people who use microscopes professionally (see Appendix A for a complete list of metric units).

Most human cells are about 100 μm in diameter, about the width of a human hair. The internal contents of a cell are even smaller and, in most cases, may only be viewed using powerful microscopes. Because of this small size, the **cell theory,** one of the fundamental principles of modern biology, was not formulated until after the invention of the microscope in the seventeenth century.

The Cell Theory

A cell is the basic unit of life. According to the cell theory, nothing smaller than a cell is considered to be alive. A single-celled organism exhibits the basic characteristics of life that were presented in Section 1.1. There is no smaller unit of life that is able to reproduce and grow, respond to stimuli, remain homeostatic, take in and use materials from the environment, and become adapted to the environment. In short, life has a cellular nature.

All living organisms are made up of cells. While many organisms, such as the bacteria, are single-celled, other organisms, including humans and plants, are multicellular. In multicellular organisms, cells are often organized as tissues, such as nervous tissue and connective tissue. Even bone consists of cells (called osteocytes) surrounded by the material that they have deposited. Cells may differ in their appearance, as shown in the comparison of several cell types in Figure 3.1. However, despite these differences, they all have certain structures in common. In general, it is important to recognize that the structure of a cell is directly related to its function.

New cells arise only from preexisting cells. Until the nineteenth century, most people believed in spontaneous generation, that nonliving objects could give rise to living organisms. For example, maggots were thought to arise from meat hung in the butcher shop. Maggots often appeared in meat to which flies had access. However, people did not realize that the living maggots did not spontaneously generate from the nonliving meat. A series of

Figure 3.1   Cells vary in structure and function.
A cell's structure is related to its function. Despite differences in appearance, all cells exchange substances with their environment.
(blood cells) © Prof. P. Motta, Dept. of Anatomy, Univ. LaSapienza Rome/SPL/Science Source; (nerve cells) © SPL/Science Source; (bone) © McGraw-Hill Education

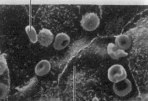

red blood cell

blood vessel cell

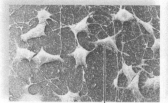

nerve cell

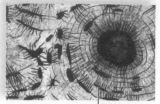

osteocyte

experiments by Francesco Redi in the seventeenth century demonstrated that meat that was placed within sealed containers did not generate maggots. In other words, life did not generate spontaneously. In 1864 the French scientist Louis Pasteur conducted a now-classic set of experiments using bacterial cells. His experiments proved conclusively that spontaneous generation of life from nonlife is not possible.

When mice or humans reproduce, a sperm cell joins with an egg cell to form a zygote. By reproducing, parents pass a copy of their genetic information to their offspring. The zygote is the first cell of a new multicellular organism. Through the process of cell division, every cell in the new organism will contain a copy of the parents' genes.

Cell Size

A few cells, such as the egg of a chicken or frog, are large enough to be seen by the naked eye. In comparison, a human egg cell is around 100 μm in size, placing it right at the limit of what can be viewed by our eyes. However, most cells are much smaller. The small size of cells is explained by considering the *surface-area-to-volume ratio* of cells. Nutrients enter a cell—and waste exits a cell—at its surface. Therefore, the greater the amount of surface, the greater the ability to get material into and out of the cell. A large cell requires more nutrients and produces more waste than a small cell. However, as cells become smaller in volume, the proportionate amount of surface area actually increases. You can see this by comparing the cubes in Figure 3.2.

We would expect, then, that there would be a limit to how large an actively metabolizing cell can become. An example is a chicken's egg. Once a chicken's egg is fertilized and starts metabolizing, it divides repeatedly without increasing in size. This increases the amount of surface area needed for adequate exchange of materials in these rapidly dividing cells.

	One 4-cm cube	Eight 2-cm cubes	Sixty-four 1-cm cubes
Total surface area (height × width × number of sides × number of cubes)	96 cm²	192 cm²	384 cm²
Total volume (height × width × length × number of cubes)	64 cm³	64 cm³	64 cm³
Surface area: **Volume per cube** (surface area÷volume)	1.5:1	3:1	6:1

Figure 3.2   Surface-area-to-volume ratio limits cell size.
As cell size decreases, the ratio of the surface area to volume increases.

Microscopy

Microscopes provide scientists with a deeper look into how cells function. There are many types of microscopes, from compound light microscopes to powerful electron microscopes. The *magnification,* or the ratio between the observed size of an image and its actual size, varies with the type of microscope. In addition, the resolution of the image varies between microscopes (Table 3.1). *Resolution* is the ability to distinguish between two adjacent points, and it represents the minimum distance between two objects that allows them to be seen as two different objects. Usually, the more powerful the microscope, the greater the resolution. Figure 3.3 illustrates images of a red blood cell taken by three different types of microscopes.

Table 3.1	Resolving Power of the Eye and Common Microscopes	
	Magnification	**Resolving Power**
Eye	N/A	0.1 mm (100 µm)
Light microscope	1,000×	0.0001 mm (0.1 µm)
Transmission electron microscope	100,000× (or greater)	0.000001 mm (0.01 µm)

A *compound light microscope* (Fig. 3.3*a*) uses a set of glass lenses and light rays passing through the object to magnify objects. The image can be viewed directly by the human eye.

The *transmission electron microscope* makes use of a stream of electrons to produce magnified images (Fig. 3.3*b*). The human eye cannot see the image. Therefore, it is projected onto a fluorescent screen or photographic film to produce an image (called a *micrograph*) that can be viewed. The magnification and resolution produced by a transmission electron microscope is much higher than that of a light microscope. Therefore, this microscope has the ability to produce enlarged images with greater detail.

A *scanning electron microscope* provides a three-dimensional view of the surface of an object (Fig. 3.3*c*). A narrow beam of electrons is scanned over the surface of the specimen, which is coated with a thin layer of metal. The metal gives off secondary electrons, which are collected to produce a television-type picture of the specimen's surface on a screen.

In the laboratory, the light microscope is often used to view live specimens. However, this is not the case for the electron microscopes. Because electrons cannot travel very far in air, a strong vacuum must be maintained along the entire path of the electron beam. Often cells are treated before being viewed under a microscope. Because most cells are transparent, they are often stained with colored dyes before being viewed under a light microscope. Certain cellular components take up the dye more than other

Figure 3.3   Micrographs of human red blood cells.
a. Light micrograph (LM) of many cells in a large vessel (stained).
b. Transmission electron micrograph (TEM) of just three cells in a small vessel (colored).
c. Scanning electron micrograph (SEM) gives a three-dimensional view of cells and vessels (colored).
(a): © Ed Reschke/Getty Images;
(b): © Alfred Pasieka/Science Source;
(c): © Science Photo Library RF/Getty RF

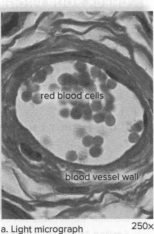

a. Light micrograph   250×

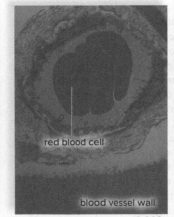

b. Transmission electron micrograph   10,000×

c. Scanning electron micrograph

BIOLOGY TODAY   **Science**

Coloring Organisms Green: Green Fluorescent Proteins and Cells

Most cells lack any significant pigmentation. Thus, cell biologists frequently rely on dyes to produce enough contrast to resolve organelles and other cellular structures. The first of these dyes were developed in the nineteenth century from chemicals used to stain clothes in the textile industry. Since then, significant advances have occurred in the development of cellular stains.

In 2008 three scientists—Martin Chalfie, Roger Y. Tsien, and Osamu Shimomura—earned the Nobel Prize in Chemistry or Medicine for their work with a protein called *green fluorescent protein,* or GFP. GFP is a bioluminescent protein found in the jellyfish *Aequorea victoria,* commonly called the crystal jelly (Fig. 3A*a*). The crystal jelly is a native of the West Coast of the United States. Normally this jellyfish is transparent. When it is disturbed, though, special cells in the jellyfish release a fluorescent protein called aequorin. Aequorin fluoresces with a green color. The research teams of Chalfie, Tsien, and Shimomura were able to isolate the fluorescent protein from the jellyfish and develop it as a molecular tag. These tags can be generated for almost any protein within the cell, revealing not only its cellular location but also how its distribution within the cell may change as a result of a response to its environment. Figure 3A*b* shows how a GFP-labeled antibody can be used to identify the cellular location of the actin proteins in a human cell. Actin is one of the prime components of the cell's microfilaments, which in turn are part of the cytoskeleton of the cell. This image shows the distribution of actin in a human cell.

Questions to Consider

1. Discuss how a researcher might use a GFP-labeled protein in a study of a disease, such as cancer.
2. How do studies such as these support the idea that preserving the diversity of life on the planet is important?

a. Jellyfish

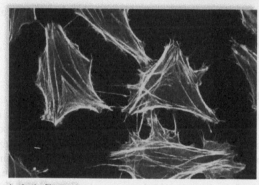

b. Actin filaments

Figure 3A   GFP shows details of the interior of cells.
a. The jellyfish *Aequorea victoria* and (**b**) the GFP stain of a human cell. This illustration shows a human cell tagged with a GFP-labeled antibody to the actin protein.

(a): © Alexander Semenov/Getty RF; (b): © Dr. Gopal Murti/Science Source

components, which enhances contrast. A similar approach is used in electron microscopy, except the sample is treated with electron-dense metals (such as gold) to provide contrast. The metals do not provide color, so electron micrographs may be colored after the micrograph is obtained. The expression "falsely colored" means that the original micrograph was colored after it was produced. In addition, during electron microscopy, cells are treated so that they do not decompose in the vacuum. Frequently they are also embedded into a matrix, which allows a researcher to slice the cell into very thin pieces, providing cross sections of the cell's interior.

These are just a few of the types of microscopes and techniques available to scientists and researchers who study cells (see the Science feature "Coloring Organisms Green: Green Fluorescent Proteins and Cells"). Although microscope technology is evolving rapidly, it still is dependent on the principles of resolution and magnification.

CHECK YOUR PROGRESS 3.1

1. Summarize the cell theory, and state its importance to the study of biology.
2. Explain how a cell's size relates to its function.
3. Compare and contrast the information that may be obtained from a light microscope and an electron microscope.

CONNECTING THE CONCEPTS

For more on the cells mentioned in this section, refer to the following discussions:

Section 6.2 discusses how red blood cells transport gases within the circulatory system.

Section 6.6 provides an overview of how red blood cells help maintain homeostasis in the body.

Section 18.1 examines the complex structure of a human egg cell.

3.2 How Cells Are Organized

Biologists classify cells into two broad categories—the prokaryotes and eukaryotes. The primary difference between a prokaryotic cell and a eukaryotic cell is the presence or absence of a nucleus, a membrane-bound structure that houses the DNA. **Prokaryotic cells** lack a nucleus, whereas **eukaryotic cells** (Fig. 3.4) possess a nucleus. The prokaryotic group includes two groups of bacteria,

Figure 3.4   The structure of a typical eukaryotic cell.
a. A transmission electron micrograph of the interior structures of a cell. **b.** The structure and function of the components of a eukaryotic cell.

(a): © Alfred Pasieka/Science Source

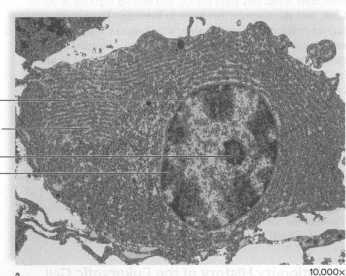

nuclear envelope
endoplasmic reticulum
nucleolus
chromatin

a.   10,000×

Plasma membrane: outer surface that regulates entrance and exit of molecules

protein
phospholipid

CYTOSKELETON: maintains cell shape and assists movement of cell parts:

Microtubules: cylinders of protein molecules present in cytoplasm, centrioles, cilia, and flagella

Intermediate filaments: protein fibers that provide support and strength

Actin filaments: protein fibers that play a role in movement of cell and organelles

Centrioles: short, cylinders of microtubules

Centrosome: microtubule organizing center that contains a pair of centrioles

Lysosome: vesicle that digests macromolecules and even cell parts

Vesicle: membrane-bounded sac that stores and transports substances

Cytoplasm: semifluid matrix outside nucleus that contains organelles

b.

NUCLEUS:

Nuclear envelope: double membrane with nuclear pores that encloses nucleus

Chromatin: diffuse threads containing DNA and protein

Nucleolus: region that produces subunits of ribosomes

ENDOPLASMIC RETICULUM:

Rough ER: studded with ribosomes, processes proteins

Smooth ER: lacks ribosomes, synthesizes lipid molecules

Ribosomes: particles that carry out protein synthesis

Mitochondrion: organelle that carries out cellular respiration, producing ATP molecules

Polyribosome: string of ribosomes simultaneously synthesizing same protein

Golgi apparatus: processes, packages, and secretes modified cell products

the eubacteria and the archaebacteria. We will take a look at their structure in more detail in Section 8.1. Within the eukaryotic group are the animals, plants, and fungi, as well as some single-celled organisms called protists.

Despite their differences, both types of cells have a **plasma membrane,** an outer membrane that regulates what enters and exits a cell. The plasma membrane is a phospholipid bilayer—a "sandwich" made of two layers of phospholipids. Their polar phosphate molecules form the top and bottom surfaces of the bilayer, and the nonpolar lipid lies in between. The phospholipid bilayer is **selectively permeable,** which means it allows certain molecules—but not others—to enter the cell. Proteins scattered throughout the plasma membrane play important roles in allowing substances to enter the cell. All types of cells also contain **cytoplasm,** which is a semifluid medium that contains water and various types of molecules suspended or dissolved in the medium. The presence of proteins accounts for the semifluid nature of the cytoplasm.

The cytoplasm of a eukaryotic cell contains **organelles,** internal compartments that have specialized functions. Originally the term *organelle* referred to only membranous structures, but we will use it to include any well-defined subcellular structure. Eukaryotic cells have many types of organelles (Fig. 3.4). Organelles allow for the compartmentalization of the cell. This keeps the various cellular activities separated from one another.

Evolutionary History of the Eukaryotic Cell

The first cells on Earth were prokaryotic cells. Today these cells are represented by the bacteria and archaea, which differ mainly by their chemistry.

Early prokaryotic organisms, such as the archaeans, were well adapted to life on the early Earth. The environment that they evolved in contained conditions that would be instantly lethal to life today: The atmosphere contained no oxygen; instead it was filled with carbon monoxide and other poisonous gases; the temperature of the planet was above 200°F, and there was no ozone layer to protect organisms from damaging radiation from the sun.

Despite these conditions, prokaryotic life survived and in doing so gradually adapted to Earth's environment. In the process, most of the archaebacteria went extinct. However, we now know that some are still around and can be found in some of the most inhospitable places on the planet, such as thermal vents and salty seas. The study of these ancient bacteria is still shedding light on the early origins of life.

Evidence widely supports the hypothesis that eukaryotic cells evolved from the archaea. The internal structure of eukaryotic cells is believed to have evolved as the series of events shown in Figure 3.5. The nucleus could have formed by *invagination* of the plasma membrane, a process whereby a pocket is formed in the plasma membrane. The pocket would have enclosed the DNA of the cell, thus forming its nucleus. Surprisingly, some of the organelles in eukaryotic cells may have arisen by engulfing prokaryotic cells. The engulfed prokaryotic cells were not digested; rather, they then evolved into different organelles. One of these events would have given the eukaryotic cell a mitochondrion. Mitochondria are organelles that

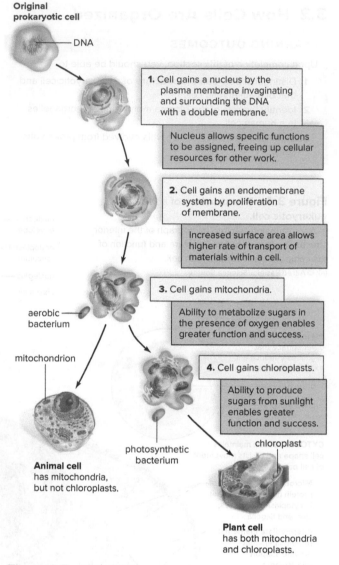

Original prokaryotic cell

DNA

1. Cell gains a nucleus by the plasma membrane invaginating and surrounding the DNA with a double membrane.

Nucleus allows specific functions to be assigned, freeing up cellular resources for other work.

2. Cell gains an endomembrane system by proliferation of membrane.

Increased surface area allows higher rate of transport of materials within a cell.

3. Cell gains mitochondria.

aerobic bacterium

Ability to metabolize sugars in the presence of oxygen enables greater function and success.

mitochondrion

4. Cell gains chloroplasts.

Ability to produce sugars from sunlight enables greater function and success.

Animal cell has mitochondria, but not chloroplasts.

photosynthetic bacterium

chloroplast

Plant cell has both mitochondria and chloroplasts.

Figure 3.5   The evolution of eukaryotic cells.
Invagination of the plasma membrane of a prokaryotic cell could have created the nucleus. Later the cell gained organelles, some of which may have been independent prokaryotes.

carry on cellular respiration. Another such event may have produced the chloroplast. Chloroplasts are found in cells that carry out photosynthesis. This process is often called *endosymbiosis.*

CHECK YOUR PROGRESS 3.2

1. Summarize the role of the plasma membrane in a cell.
2. Describe the main differences between a eukaryotic and a prokaryotic cell.
3. Describe the possible evolution of the nucleus, mitochondria, and chloroplast.

The material in this section summarizes some previous concepts of eukaryotic and prokaryotic cells and the role of phospholipids in the plasma membrane. For more information, refer to the following discussions:

Section 1.2 examines the difference in the classification of eukaryotic and prokaryotic organisms.

Section 8.1 provides more information on the structure of bacterial cells.

3.3 The Plasma Membrane and How Substances Cross It

LEARNING OUTCOMES

Upon completion of this section, you should be able to

1. Describe the structure of the plasma membrane and list the type of molecules found in the membrane.
2. Distinguish among diffusion, osmosis, and facilitated transport, and state the role of each in the cell.
3. Explain how tonicity relates to the direction of water movement across a membrane.
4. Compare passive-transport and active-transport mechanisms.
5. Summarize how eukaryotic cells move large molecules across membranes.

Like all cells, a human cell is surrounded by an outer plasma membrane (Fig. 3.6). The plasma membrane marks the boundary between the outside and the inside of the cell. The integrity and function of the plasma membrane are necessary to the life of the cell.

The plasma membrane is a phospholipid bilayer with attached or embedded proteins. A phospholipid molecule has a polar head and nonpolar tails (see Fig. 2.19). When phospholipids are placed in water, they naturally form a spherical bilayer. The polar heads, being charged, are *hydrophilic* (attracted to water). They position themselves to face toward the watery environment outside and inside the cell. The nonpolar tails are *hydrophobic* (not attracted to water). They turn inward toward one another, where there is no water.

At body temperature, the phospholipid bilayer is a liquid. It has the consistency of olive oil. The proteins are able to change their position by moving laterally. The **fluid-mosaic model** is a working description of membrane structure. It states that the protein molecules form a shifting pattern within the fluid phospholipid bilayer. Cholesterol lends support to the membrane.

Short chains of sugars are attached to the outer surface of some protein and lipid molecules. These are called *glycoproteins* and *glycolipids,* respectively. These carbohydrate chains, specific to each cell, help mark the cell as belonging to a particular individual. They account for why people have different blood types, for example. Other glycoproteins have a special configuration that

allows them to act as a receptor for a chemical messenger, such as a hormone. Some plasma membrane proteins form channels through which certain substances can enter cells. Others are either enzymes that catalyze reactions or carriers involved in the passage of molecules through the membrane.

Plasma Membrane Functions

The plasma membrane isolates the interior of the cell from the external environment. In doing so, it allows only certain molecules and ions to enter and exit the cytoplasm freely. Therefore, the plasma membrane is said to be selectively permeable (Fig. 3.7). Small, lipid-soluble molecules, such as oxygen and carbon dioxide, can pass through the membrane easily. The small size of water molecules allows them to freely cross the membrane by using protein channels called *aquaporins*. Ions and large molecules cannot cross the membrane without more direct assistance, which will be discussed later.

Diffusion

Diffusion is the random movement of molecules from an area of higher concentration to an area of lower concentration, until they are equally distributed. Diffusion is a passive way for molecules to enter or exit a cell. No cellular energy is needed to bring it about.

Certain molecules can freely cross the plasma membrane by diffusion. When molecules can cross a plasma membrane, which way will they go? The molecules will move in both directions. But the *net movement* will be from the region of higher concentration to the region of lower concentration, until equilibrium is achieved. At equilibrium, as many molecules of the substance will be entering as leaving the cell (Fig. 3.8). Oxygen diffuses across the plasma membrane, and the net movement is toward the inside of the cell. This is because a cell uses oxygen when it produces ATP molecules for energy purposes.

Osmosis

Osmosis is the net movement of water across a selectively permeable membrane. The direction by which water will diffuse is determined by the tonicity of the solutions inside and outside the cell. Tonicity is based on dissolved particles, called solutes, within a solution. The higher the concentration of solutes in a solution, the lower the concentration of water, and vice versa. Typically water will diffuse from the area that has less solute (low tonicity, and therefore more water) to the area with more solute (high tonicity, and therefore less water).

Normally body fluids are *isotonic* to cells (Fig. 3.9a). There is the same concentration of nondiffusible solutes and water on both sides of the plasma membrane. Therefore, cells maintain their normal size and shape. Intravenous solutions given in medical situations are usually isotonic.

Solutions that cause cells to swell or even to burst due to an intake of water are said to be *hypotonic*. A hypotonic solution has a lower concentration of solute and a higher concentration of water than the cells. If red blood cells are placed in a hypotonic solution,

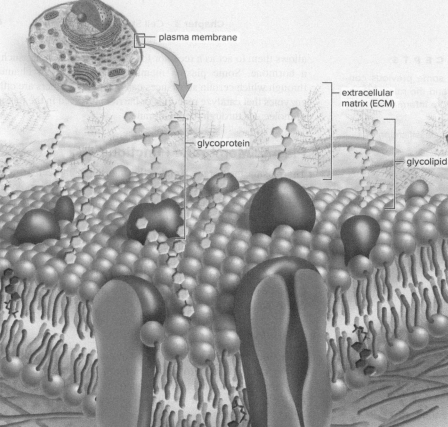

plasma membrane

carbohydrate chain

Outside

extracellular matrix (ECM)

hydrophobic tails

hydrophilic heads

phospholipid bilayer

glycoprotein

glycolipid

filaments of cytoskeleton

Inside

peripheral protein

integral protein

cholesterol

Figure 3.6   Organization of the plasma membrane.
A plasma membrane is composed of a phospholipid bilayer in which proteins are embedded. The hydrophilic heads of phospholipids are a part of the outside surface and the inside surface of the membrane. The hydrophobic tails make up the interior of the membrane. Note the plasma membrane's asymmetry—carbohydrate chains are attached to the outside surface, and cytoskeleton filaments are attached to the inside surface. Cholesterol lends support to the membrane.

water enters the cells. They swell to bursting (Fig. 3.9b). *Lysis* is used to refer to the process of bursting cells. Bursting of red blood cells is termed *hemolysis.*

Solutions that cause cells to shrink or shrivel due to loss of water are said to be *hypertonic.* A hypertonic solution has a higher concentration of solute and a lower concentration of water than do the cells. If red blood cells are placed in a hypertonic solution, water leaves the cells; they shrink (Fig. 3.9c). The term *crenation* refers to red blood cells in this condition. These changes have occurred due to osmotic pressure. **Osmotic pressure** controls water movement in our bodies. For example, in the small

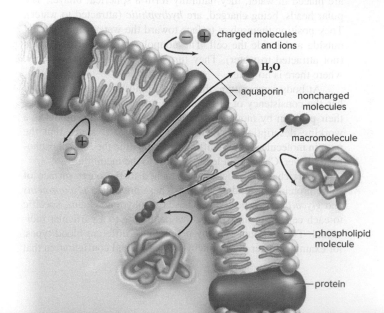

charged molecules and ions

H_2O

aquaporin

noncharged molecules

macromolecule

phospholipid molecule

protein

Figure 3.7   Selective permeability of the plasma membrane.
Small, uncharged molecules are able to cross the membrane, whereas large or charged molecules cannot. Water travels freely across membranes through aquaporins.

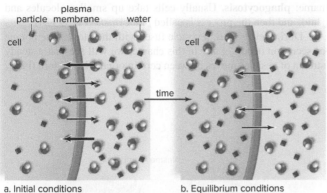

a. Initial conditions   b. Equilibrium conditions

Figure 3.8 **Diffusion across the plasma membrane.**
a. When a substance can diffuse across the plasma membrane, it will move back and forth across the membrane, but the net movement will be toward the region of lower concentration. **b.** At equilibrium, equal numbers of particles and water have crossed in both directions, and there is no net movement.

9,030×   9,030×   11,500×

a. Isotonic solution (same solute concentration as in cell)   b. Hypotonic solution (lower solute concentration than in cell)   c. Hypertonic solution (higher solute concentration than in cell)

Figure 3.9 **Effects of changes in tonicity on red blood cells.**
a. In an isotonic solution, cells remain the same. **b.** In a hypotonic solution, cells gain water and may burst (lysis). **c.** In a hypertonic solution, cells lose water and shrink (crenation).
(all) © Dennis Kunkel/Phototake

and large intestines, osmotic pressure allows us to absorb the water in food and drink. In the kidneys, osmotic pressure controls water absorption as well.

Facilitated Transport

Many solutes do not simply diffuse across a plasma membrane. They are transported by means of protein carriers within the

membrane. During **facilitated transport,** a molecule is transported across the plasma membrane from the side of higher concentration to the side of lower concentration (Fig. 3.10). This is a passive means of transport, because the cell does not need to expend energy to move a substance down its concentration gradient. Each protein carrier, sometimes called a *transporter,* binds only to a particular molecule, such as glucose. Type 2 diabetes results when cells lack a sufficient number of glucose transporters.

Figure 3.10 **Facilitated transport across a plasma membrane.**
This is a passive form of transport in which substances move down their concentration gradient through a protein carrier. In this example, glucose (green) moves into the cell by facilitated transport. The end result will be an equal distribution of glucose on both sides of the membrane.

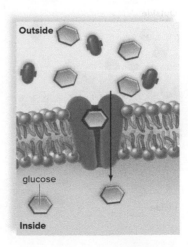

Outside

glucose

Inside

Active Transport

During **active transport,** a molecule is moving from an area of *lower* to an area of *higher* concentration. One example is the concentration of iodine ions in the cells of the thyroid gland. In the digestive tract, sugar is completely absorbed from the gut by cells that line the intestines. In another example, water homeostasis is maintained by the kidneys by the active transport of sodium ions (Na^+) by cells lining kidney tubules.

Active transport requires a protein carrier and the use of cellular energy obtained from the breakdown of ATP. When ATP is broken down, energy is released. In this case, the energy is used to carry out active transport. Proteins involved in active transport often are called *pumps*. Just as a water pump uses energy to move water against the force of gravity, energy is used to move substances against their concentration gradients. One type of pump active in all cells moves sodium ions (Na^+) to the outside and potassium ions (K^+) to the inside of the cell (Fig. 3.11). This type of pump is associated especially with nerve and muscle cells.

The passage of salt (NaCl) across a plasma membrane is of primary importance in cells. First sodium ions are pumped across a membrane. Then chloride ions diffuse through channels that allow their passage. In cystic fibrosis, a mutation in these chloride ion channels causes them to malfunction. This leads to the symptoms of this inherited (genetic) disorder.

Bulk Transport

Cells use bulk transport to move large molecules, such as polysaccharides or polypeptides, across the membrane. These processes use vesicles rather than channel or transport proteins. During *endocytosis,* a portion of the plasma membrane invaginates, or forms a pouch, to envelop a substance and fluid. Then the membrane pinches off to form an endocytic vesicle inside the cell (Fig. 3.12a). Some white blood cells are able to take up pathogens (disease-causing agents) by endocytosis. This process is given a special name: **phagocytosis.** Usually cells take up small molecules and fluid, and then the process is called *pinocytosis* (Fig. 3.12b).

During *exocytosis,* a vesicle fuses with the plasma membrane as secretion occurs. Later in this chapter we will see that a steady stream of vesicles moves between certain organelles, before finally

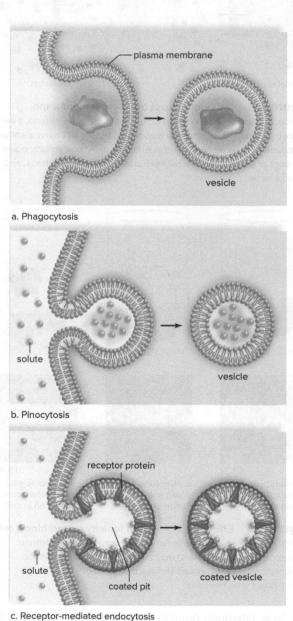

a. Phagocytosis

b. Pinocytosis

c. Receptor-mediated endocytosis

Figure 3.12   Examples of bulk transport.
a. Large substances enter a cell by phagocytosis. **b.** Small molecules and fluids enter a cell by pinocytosis. **c.** In receptor-mediated endocytosis, molecules first bind to specific receptors and are then brought into the cell by endocytosis.

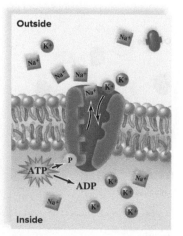

Figure 3.11   Active transport and the sodium-potassium pump.
This is a form of transport in which a molecule moves from low concentration to high concentration. It requires a protein carrier and energy. Na^+ exits and K^+ enters the cell by active transport, so Na^+ will be concentrated outside and K^+ will be concentrated inside the cell.

fusing with the plasma membrane. This is the way that signaling molecules, called *neurotransmitters,* leave one nerve cell to excite the next nerve cell or a muscle cell.

One form of endocytosis uses a receptor, a form of membrane protein, on the surface of the cell to concentrate specific molecules of interest for endocytosis. This process is called *receptor-mediated endocytosis* (Fig. 3.12c). An inherited form of cardiovascular disease occurs when cells fail to take up a combined lipoprotein and cholesterol molecule from the blood by receptor-mediated endocytosis.

CHECK YOUR PROGRESS 3.3

1. Summarize how the fluid-mosaic model describes the structure of the plasma membrane.
2. Compare and contrast diffusion, osmosis, facilitated transport, and active transport.
3. Discuss the various ways cells can move materials in bulk into and out of the cell.

CONNECTING THE CONCEPTS

The movement of materials across a plasma membrane is crucial to the maintenance of homeostasis for many organ systems in humans. For some examples, refer to the following discussions:

Section 9.3 examines how nutrients, including glucose, are moved into the cells of the digestive system.

Section 11.4 investigates how the movement of salts by the urinary system maintains blood homeostasis.

Section 21.2 explains the patterns of inheritance associated with cystic fibrosis.

3.4 The Nucleus and Endomembrane System

LEARNING OUTCOMES

Upon completion of this section, you should be able to

1. Describe the structure of the nucleus and explain its role as the storage place of genetic information.
2. Summarize the function of the organelles of the endomembrane system.
3. Explain the role and location of the ribosomes.

The nucleus contains the genetic instructions that are necessary for the manufacture of the proteins that are involved in most cellular functions. The endomembrane system is a series of membrane organelles that function in the processing of materials for the cell.

The Nucleus

The nucleus, a prominent structure in eukaryotic cells, stores the genetic information (Fig. 3.13) as DNA organized into linear structures called **chromosomes.** Located on the chromosome are collections of genes. **Genes** are segments of DNA that contain information for the production of specific proteins. These proteins have many functions in cells, and they help determine a cell's specificity. While every cell in the body contains the same genes, cells vary in which genes are turned on and off, and this enables them to perform their function in the tissue or organism.

Chromatin is the combination of DNA molecules and proteins that make up the chromosomes. The chromosomes are responsible for transmitting genetic information from one generation to the next. Chromatin can coil tightly to form visible chromosomes during cell division. Most of the time, however, the chromatin is uncoiled. While uncoiled, the individual chromosomes cannot be distinguished and the chromatin appears grainy in electron micrographs of the nucleus. Chromatin is surrounded by a semifluid medium called the *nucleoplasm.* A difference in pH suggests that nucleoplasm has a different composition than cytoplasm.

Micrographs of a nucleus often show a dark region (or sometimes more than one) of chromatin. This is the **nucleolus,** where ribosomal RNA (rRNA) is produced. This is also where rRNA joins with proteins to form the subunits of ribosomes.

The nucleus is separated from the cytoplasm by a double membrane known as the **nuclear envelope.** This is continuous with the endoplasmic reticulum (ER), a membranous system of saccules and channels, discussed in the next section. The nuclear envelope has **nuclear pores** of sufficient size to permit the passage of ribosomal subunits out of the nucleus and proteins into the nucleus.

Ribosomes

Ribosomes are organelles composed of proteins and rRNA. Protein synthesis occurs at the ribosomes. Ribosomes are often attached to the endoplasmic reticulum, but they also may occur free within the cytoplasm, either singly or in groups called *polyribosomes.* Proteins synthesized at ribosomes attached to the endoplasmic reticulum have a different destination from that of proteins manufactured at ribosomes free in the cytoplasm.

The Endomembrane System

The **endomembrane system** consists of the nuclear envelope, the endoplasmic reticulum, the Golgi apparatus, lysosomes, and **vesicles** (tiny, membranous sacs) (Fig. 3.14). This system compartmentalizes the cell, so that chemical reactions are restricted to specific regions. The vesicles transport molecules from one part of the system to another.

The Endoplasmic Reticulum

The **endoplasmic reticulum (ER)** has two portions. *Rough ER* is studded with ribosomes on the side of the membrane that

Figure 3.13 **The nucleus and endoplasmic reticulum.**
a. The nucleus contains chromatin. Chromatin has a region called the nucleolus, where rRNA is produced and ribosome subunits are assembled. **b.** The nuclear envelope contains pores that allow substances to enter and exit the nucleus to and from the cytoplasm. **c.** The nuclear envelope is attached to the endoplasmic reticulum, which often has attached ribosomes, where protein synthesis occurs.
(b): © Don W. Fawcett/ Science Source; (c): © Martin M. Rotker/Science Source

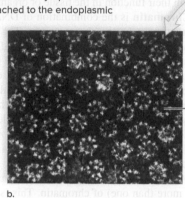

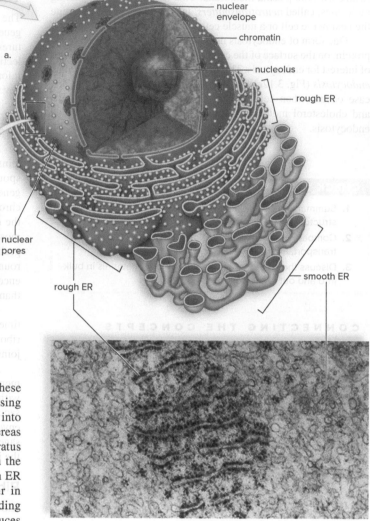

nuclear envelope
chromatin
nucleolus
rough ER
smooth ER
nuclear pores
rough ER

a.

b.

c.   52,500×

faces the cytoplasm. The proteins that are synthesized at these ribosomes enter the interior of the ER for additional processing and modification. Some of these proteins are incorporated into the plasma membrane (for example, channel proteins), whereas others are packed into vesicles and sent to the Golgi apparatus (see below) for export. The *smooth ER* is continuous with the rough ER, but it does not have attached ribosomes. Smooth ER synthesizes the phospholipids and other lipids that occur in membranes. It also has various other functions, depending on the particular cell. For example, in the testes it produces testosterone, and it helps detoxify compounds (such as drugs) in the liver.

The ER forms transport vesicles in which large molecules are transported to other parts of the cell. Often these vesicles are on their way to the plasma membrane or the Golgi apparatus.

The Golgi Apparatus

The **Golgi apparatus** is named for Camillo Golgi, who discovered its presence in cells in 1898. The Golgi apparatus consists of a stack of slightly curved saccules, whose appearance can be compared to a stack of pancakes. Here proteins and lipids received from the ER are modified. For example, a chain of sugars may be added to them. This makes them glycoproteins and glycolipids, molecules often found in the plasma membrane.

The vesicles that leave the Golgi apparatus move to other parts of the cell. Some vesicles proceed to the plasma membrane, where they discharge their contents. In all, the Golgi apparatus is involved in processing, packaging, and secretion.

Lysosomes

Lysosomes, membranous sacs produced by the Golgi apparatus, contain *hydrolytic enzymes.* Lysosomes are found in all cells of the body but are particularly numerous in white blood cells that engulf disease-causing microbes. When a lysosome fuses with such an endocytic vesicle, its contents are digested by lysosomal enzymes into simpler subunits, which then enter the cytoplasm. In a process called autodigestion, parts of a cell may be broken down by the lysosomes. Some human diseases are caused by the lack of a particular lysosome enzyme. Tay-Sachs disease, as discussed in the chapter opener, occurs when an undigested substance collects in nerve cells, leading to developmental problems and death in early childhood.

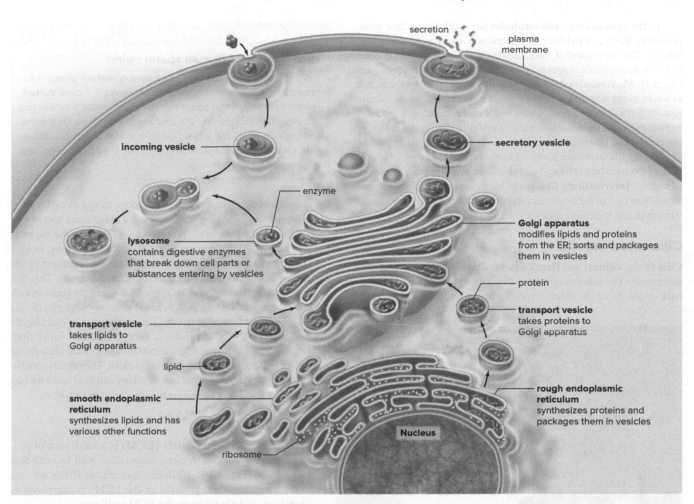

Figure 3.14   The endomembrane system.
The organelles in the endomembrane system work together to produce, modify, and secrete products for the cell. Some of these may be loaded into vesicles to produce lysosomes to digest incoming materials.

CHECK YOUR PROGRESS 3.4

1. Describe the functions of the following organelles: endoplasmic reticulum, Golgi apparatus, and lysosomes.

2. Explain how the nucleus, ribosomes, and rough endoplasmic reticulum contribute to protein synthesis.

3. Describe the organelles of the endomembrane system involved in the export of a protein from the cell.

CONNECTING THE CONCEPTS

For a more detailed look at how the organelles of the endomembrane system function, refer to the following discussions:

Section 18.5 contains information on how aging is related to the breakdown of cellular organelles.

Section 21.2 explores the patterns of inheritance associated with Tay-Sachs disease.

Section 22.2 provides a more detailed look at how ribosomes produce proteins.

3.5 The Cytoskeleton, Cell Movement, and Cell Junctions

LEARNING OUTCOMES

Upon completion of this section, you should be able to

1. Explain the role of the cytoskeleton in the cell.
2. Summarize the major protein fibers in the cytoskeleton.
3. Describe the role of flagella and cilia in human cells.
4. Compare the functions of adhesion junctions, gap junctions, and tight junctions in human cells.

It took a high-powered electron microscope to discover that the cytoplasm of the cell is crisscrossed by several types of protein fibers, collectively called the **cytoskeleton** (see Fig. 3.4). The cytoskeleton helps maintain a cell's shape and either anchors the organelles or assists in their movement, as appropriate.

56   Unit 1 Human Organization

In the cytoskeleton, **microtubules** are much larger than actin filaments. Each is a cylinder that contains rows of a protein called tubulin. The regulation of microtubule assembly is under the control of a microtubule organizing center called the **centrosome** (see Fig. 3.4). Microtubules help maintain the shape of the cell and act as tracks along which organelles move. During cell division, microtubules form spindle fibers, which assist in the movement of chromosomes. **Actin filaments,** made of a protein called *actin,* are long, extremely thin fibers that usually occur in bundles or other groupings. Actin filaments are involved in movement. Microvilli, which project from certain cells and can shorten and extend, contain actin filaments. **Intermediate filaments,** as their name implies, are intermediate in size between microtubules and actin filaments. Their structures and functions differ according to the type of cell.

Cilia and Flagella

Cilia (sing., **cilium**) and **flagella** (sing., **flagellum**) are involved in movement. The ciliated cells that line our respiratory tract sweep back up the throat the debris trapped within mucus. This helps keep

the lungs clean. Similarly, ciliated cells move an egg along the uterine tube, where it may be fertilized by a flagellated sperm cell (Fig. 3.15). Motor molecules, powered by ATP, allow the microtubules in cilia and flagella to interact and bend and, thereby, move.

The importance of normal cilia and flagella is illustrated by the occurrence of a genetic disorder called ciliary dyskinesia. This is a recessive disorder (see Section 21.3) in which one of the genes associated with the production of a protein found in the microtubules of cilia and flagella is not formed correctly. The result are cilia and flagella that will not bend. Not surprisingly, these individuals suffer from recurrent and severe respiratory infections. The ciliated cells lining respiratory passages fail to keep their lungs clean. They are also unable to reproduce naturally due to the lack of ciliary action to move the egg in a female or the lack of flagella action by sperm in a male.

Extracellular Matrix

A protective **extracellular matrix (ECM)** is a meshwork of proteins and polysaccharides in close association with the cell that produced them (Fig. 3.16). Collagen and elastin fibers are two well-known structural proteins in the ECM; collagen resists stretching, and elastin gives the ECM resilience.

Fibronectin is an adhesive protein (colored green in Fig. 3.16) that binds to a protein in the plasma membrane called integrin. Integrins are integral membrane proteins that connect to fibronectin externally and to the actin cytoskeleton internally. Through its connections with both the ECM and the cytoskeleton, integrin plays a role in cell signaling, permitting the ECM to influence the activities of the cytoskeleton and, therefore, the shape and activities of the cell. Amino sugars in the ECM

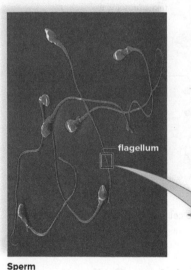

Sperm

Cilia

The shaft of the flagellum has a ring of nine microtubule doublets anchored to a central pair of microtubules.

flagellum

Flagellum

shaft

plasma membrane

Figure 3.15 Structure and function of the flagella and cilia.
The shaft of a flagellum (or cilium) contains microtubule doublets, whose side arms are motor molecules that cause the projection to move. Sperm have flagella. Without the ability of sperm to move to the egg, human reproduction would not be possible. Cilia cover the surface of the cells of the respiratory system, where they beat upward to remove foreign matter.
(sperm): © David M. Phillips/Science Source; (cilia): © Dr. G. Moscoso/Science Source, Inc.

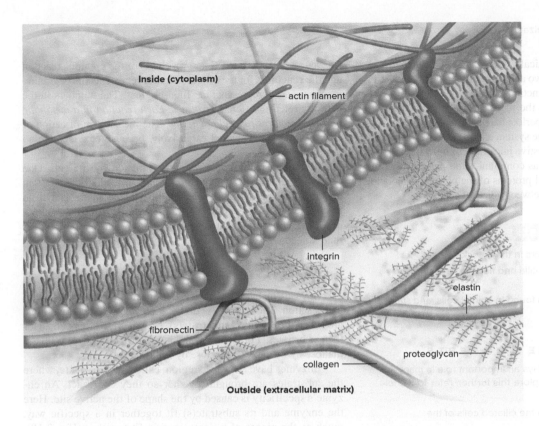

Figure 3.16 **Extracellular matrix.** In the extracellular matrix (ECM), collagen and elastin have a support function, whereas fibronectins bind to integrin, thus assisting communication between the ECM and the cytoskeleton.

form multiple polysaccharides, which attach to a protein and are therefore called proteoglycans. Proteoglycans, in turn, attach to a very long, centrally placed polysaccharide. The entire structure resists compression of the extracellular matrix. Proteoglycans also influence the process of cell signaling by regulating the passage of molecules through the ECM to the plasma membrane, where receptors are located.

In Section 4.2, during the discussion of connective tissue, we will explore how the extracellular matrix varies in quantity and consistency: being quite flexible, as in loose connective tissue; semiflexible, as in cartilage; and rock solid, as in bone. The

extracellular matrix of bone is hard because, in addition to the components mentioned, mineral salts, notably calcium salts, are deposited outside the cell.

Junctions Between Cells

As we will see in Chapter 4, human tissues are known to have junctions between their cells that allow them to function in a coordinated manner. Figure 3.17 illustrates the three main types of cell junctions in human cells.

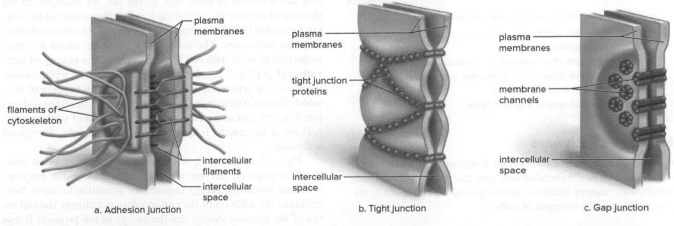

Figure 3.17 **Junctions between cells.**
a. Adhesion junctions mechanically connect cells. **b.** Tight junctions form barriers with the external environment. **c.** Gap junctions allow for communication between cells.

Adhesion junctions mechanically attach adjacent cells. In these junctions, the cytoskeletons of two adjacent cells are interconnected. They are a common type of junction between skin cells. In *tight junctions,* connections between the plasma membrane proteins of neighboring cells produce a zipperlike barrier. These types of junctions are common in the digestive system and the kidney, where it is necessary to contain fluids (digestive juices and urine) within a specific area. *Gap junctions* serve as communication portals between cells. In these junctions, channel proteins of the plasma membrane fuse, allowing easy movement between adjacent cells.

CHECK YOUR PROGRESS 3.5

1. List the three types of fibers in the cytoskeleton.
2. Describe the structure of cilia and flagella, and state the function of each.
3. List the types of junctions found in animal cells, and state a function for each.

CONNECTING THE CONCEPTS

The cytoskeleton of the cell plays an important role in many aspects of our physiology. To explore this further, refer to the following discussions:

Section 10.1 investigates how the ciliated cells of the respiratory system function.

Section 17.2 explains the role of the flagellated sperm cell in reproduction.

Section 19.3 explores how the cytoskeleton is involved in cell division.

3.6 Metabolism and the Energy Reactions

LEARNING OUTCOMES

Upon completion of this section, you should be able to

1. Understand the relationship of products and reactants in a metabolic reaction.
2. Identify the role of an enzyme in a metabolic reaction.
3. Summarize the roles of the anaerobic and aerobic pathways in energy generation.
4. Illustrate the stages of the ATP cycle.

Metabolic Pathways

Cellular respiration is an important component of **metabolism,** which includes all the chemical reactions that occur in a cell. Often metabolism requires metabolic pathways and is carried out by enzymes sequentially arranged in cells:

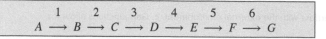

$$A \xrightarrow{\ 1\ } B \xrightarrow{\ 2\ } C \xrightarrow{\ 3\ } D \xrightarrow{\ 4\ } E \xrightarrow{\ 5\ } F \xrightarrow{\ 6\ } G$$

The letters, except *A* and *G,* are **products** of the previous reaction and the **reactants** for the next reaction. *A* represents the beginning reactant, and *G* represents the final product. The numbers in the pathway refer to different enzymes. *Each reaction in a metabolic pathway requires a specific enzyme.* The mechanism of action of enzymes has been studied extensively, because enzymes are so necessary in cells.

Metabolic pathways are highly regulated by the cell. One type of regulation is *feedback inhibition.* In feedback inhibition, one of the end products of the metabolic pathway interacts with an enzyme early in the pathway. In most cases this feedback slows down the pathway, so that the cell does not produce more product than it needs.

Enzymes

Enzymes are metabolic assistants that speed up the rate of a chemical reaction. The reactant(s) that participate(s) in the reaction is/are called the enzyme's **substrate(s).** Enzymes are often named for their substrates. For example, lipids are broken down by lipase, maltose by maltase, and lactose by lactase.

Enzymes have a specific region, called an **active site,** where the substrates are brought together so they can react. An enzyme's specificity is caused by the shape of the active site. Here the enzyme and its substrate(s) fit together in a specific way, much as the pieces of a jigsaw puzzle fit together (Fig. 3.18). After one reaction is complete, the product or products are released. The enzyme is ready to be used again. Therefore, a cell requires only a small amount of a particular enzyme to carry out a reaction. A chemical reaction can be summarized in the following manner:

$$E + S \longrightarrow ES \longrightarrow E + P$$

where E = enzyme, S = substrate, ES = enzyme-substrate complex, and P = product. An enzyme can be used over and over again.

Molecules frequently do not react with one another unless they are activated in some way. In the lab, for example, in the absence of an enzyme, activation is very often achieved by heating a reaction flask to increase the number of effective collisions between molecules. The energy that must be added to cause molecules to react with one another is called the **energy of activation (E_a)** (Fig. 3.19). Even though the reaction will proceed, the energy of activation must be overcome. The burning of firewood releases a tremendous amount of energy, but firewood in a pile does not spontaneously combust. The input of some energy, perhaps a lit match, is required to overcome the energy of activation.

Figure 3.19 shows E_a when an enzyme is not present compared to when an enzyme is present, illustrating that enzymes lower the amount of energy required for activation to occur. Nevertheless, the addition of the enzyme does not change the end result of the reaction. Notice that the energy of the products is less than the energy of the reactants. This indicates that the reaction will occur, but not until the energy of activation is overcome. Without the enzyme, the reaction rate will be very slow. By

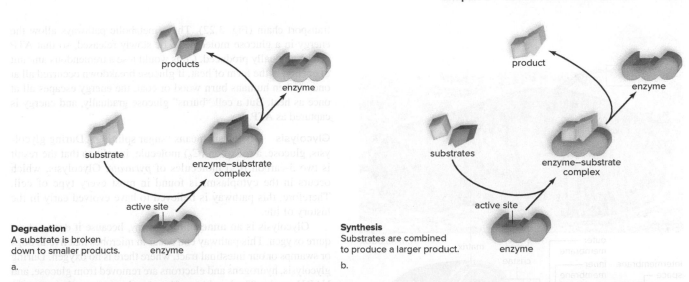

products

enzyme

substrate

enzyme–substrate
complex

active site

Degradation
A substrate is broken
down to smaller products.   enzyme

a.

product

enzyme

substrates

enzyme–substrate
complex

active site

Synthesis
Substrates are combined
to produce a larger product.   enzyme

b.

Figure 3.18   **Action of an enzyme.**
An enzyme has an active site, where the substrates and enzyme fit together in such a way that the substrates are oriented to react. Following the reaction, the products are released and the enzyme is free to act again. **a.** Some enzymes carry out degradation, in which the substrate is broken down to smaller products. **b.** Other enzymes carry out synthesis, in which the substrates are combined to produce a larger product.

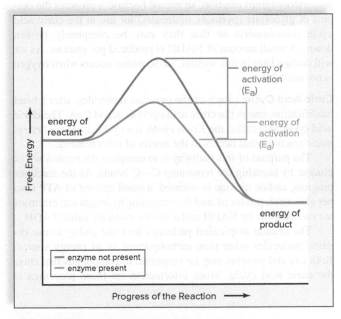

Progress of the Reaction ⟶

energy of
activation
(E_a)

energy of
reactant

energy of
activation
(E_a)

energy of
product

— enzyme not present
— enzyme present

Free Energy ⟶

Figure 3.19   **Energy of activation.**
Enzymes accelerate the rate of a metabolic reaction by lowering the amount of energy of activation needed to start the reaction.

lowering the energy of activation, the enzyme increases the rate of the reaction.

Coenzymes are nonprotein molecules that assist the activity of an enzyme and may even accept or contribute atoms to the reaction. It is interesting that vitamins are often components of coenzymes. The vitamin niacin is a part of the coenzyme **NAD$^+$** (**nicotinamide adenine dinucleotide**), which carries hydrogen (H) and electrons.

Mitochondria and Cellular Respiration

Mitochondria (sing., mitochondrion) are often called the powerhouses of the cell. Just as a powerhouse burns fuel to produce electricity, the mitochondria convert the chemical energy of glucose products into the chemical energy of ATP molecules. In the process, mitochondria use up oxygen and give off carbon dioxide. Therefore, the process of producing ATP is called **cellular respiration.** The structure of mitochondria is appropriate to the task. The inner membrane is folded to form little shelves called *cristae*. These project into the matrix, an inner space filled with a gel-like fluid (Fig. 3.20). The matrix of a mitochondrion contains enzymes for breaking down glucose products. ATP production then occurs at the cristae. Protein complexes that aid in the conversion of energy are located in an assembly-line fashion on these membranous shelves.

The structure of a mitochondrion supports the hypothesis that mitochondria were originally prokaryotes that became engulfed by a cell. Mitochondria are bound by a double membrane, as a prokaryote would be if it were taken into a cell by endocytosis. Even more interesting is the observation that mitochondria have their own genes—and they reproduce themselves!

ATP-ADP Cycle   ATP is the energy currency of the cell, it is involved in a variety of cellular processes. The ATP (Fig. 3.21) resembles that of a rechargeable battery. The breakdown of glucose during cellular respiration is used to produce ATP from ADP and inorganic phosphate ℗. This ATP is then used for the metabolic work of the cell. Muscle cells use ATP for contraction, and nerve cells use it for conduction of nerve impulses. ATP breakdown releases heat, ADP, and phosphate ℗.

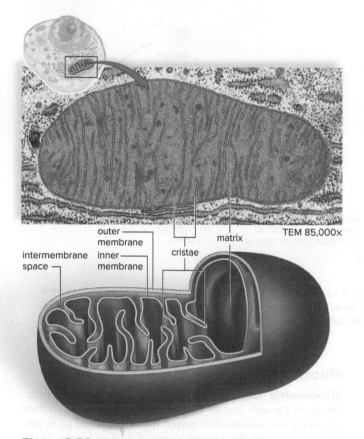

Figure 3.20   The structure of a mitochondrion.
A mitochondrion is bound by a double membrane, and the inner membrane folds into projections called cristae. The cristae project into a semifluid matrix that contains many enzymes.
photo: © Keith R. Porter/Science Source

Cellular Respiration

After blood transports glucose and oxygen to cells, cellular respiration begins. Cellular respiration breaks down glucose to carbon dioxide and water. Three pathways are involved in the breakdown of glucose—glycolysis, the citric acid cycle, and the electron

transport chain (Fig. 3.22). These metabolic pathways allow the energy in a glucose molecule to be slowly released, so that ATP can be gradually produced. Cells would lose a tremendous amount of energy, in the form of heat, if glucose breakdown occurred all at once. When humans burn wood or coal, the energy escapes all at once as heat. But a cell "burns" glucose gradually, and energy is captured as ATP.

Glycolysis   Glycolysis means "sugar splitting." During glycolysis, glucose, a 6-carbon (C_6) molecule, is split so that the result is two 3-carbon (C_3) molecules of *pyruvate*. Glycolysis, which occurs in the cytoplasm, is found in most every type of cell. Therefore, this pathway is believed to have evolved early in the history of life.

Glycolysis is an **anaerobic** pathway, because it does not require oxygen. This pathway can occur in microbes that live in bogs or swamps or our intestinal tract, where there is no oxygen. During glycolysis, hydrogens and electrons are removed from glucose, and NADH results. The breaking of bonds releases enough energy for a net yield of two ATP molecules.

Preparatory Reaction   Pyruvate is a pivotal molecule in cellular respiration. When oxygen is available, the molecule enters the preparatory (prep) reaction, so named because it prepares the outputs of glycolysis (pyruvate molecules) for use in the citric acid cycle mitochondria so that they may be completely broken down. A small amount of NADH is produced per glucose. As we will discuss later in this section, fermentation occurs when oxygen is not available.

Citric Acid Cycle   Each of the pyruvate molecules, after a brief modification, enters the citric acid cycle as acetyl CoA. The **citric acid cycle,** also called the *Krebs cycle,* is a cyclical series of enzymatic reactions that occurs in the matrix of mitochondria.

The purpose of this pathway is to complete the breakdown of glucose by breaking the remaining C—C bonds. As the reactions progress, carbon dioxide is released, a small amount of ATP (two per glucose) is produced, and the remaining hydrogen and electrons are carried away by NADH and a similar molecule called $FADH_2$.

The cellular respiration pathways have the ability to use organic molecules other than carbohydrates as an energy source. Both fats and proteins may be converted to compounds that enter the citric acid cycle. More information on these processes is

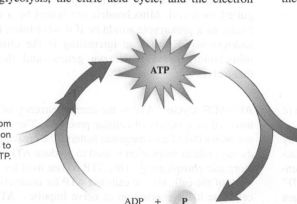

Energy from cellular respiration is used to produce ATP.

Energy from ATP breakdown is used for metabolic work.

ADP + P

Figure 3.21   The ATP cycle.
The breakdown of organic nutrients, such as glucose, by cellular respiration transfers energy to form ATP. ATP is used for energy-requiring reactions, such as muscle contraction. ATP breakdown also gives off heat. Additional food energy rejoins ADP and P to form ATP again.

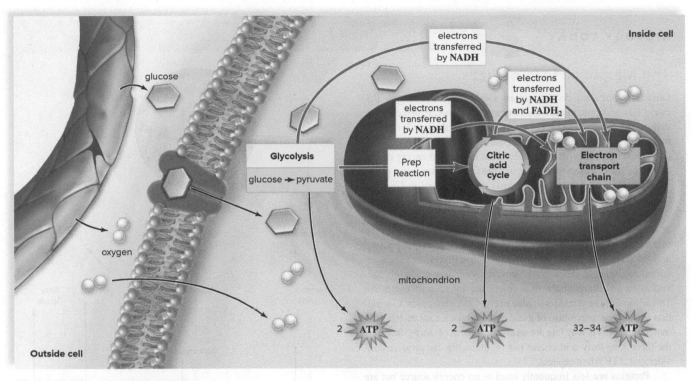

Figure 3.22 Production of ATP.
Glucose enters a cell from the bloodstream by facilitated transport. The three main pathways of cellular respiration (glycolysis, citric acid cycle, and electron transport chain) all produce ATP, but most is produced by the electron transport chain. NADH carries electrons to the electron transport chain from glycolysis and the citric acid cycle. ATP exits a mitochondrion by facilitated transport.

provided in the Health feature "The Metabolic Fate of Pizza," located later in this section.

Electron Transport Chain   NADH molecules from glycolysis and the citric acid cycle deliver electrons to the **electron transport chain.** The members of the electron transport chain are carrier proteins grouped into complexes. These complexes are embedded in the cristae of a mitochondrion. Each carrier of the electron transport chain accepts two electrons and passes them on to the next carrier. The hydrogens carried by NADH molecules will be used later.

High-energy electrons enter the chain, and as they are passed from carrier to carrier, the electrons lose energy. Low-energy electrons emerge from the chain. Oxygen serves as the final acceptor of the electrons at the end of the chain. After oxygen receives the electrons, it combines with hydrogens and becomes water.

The presence of oxygen makes the electron transport chain **aerobic.** Oxygen does not combine with any substrates during cellular respiration. Breathing is necessary to our existence, and the sole purpose of oxygen is to receive electrons at the end of the electron transport chain.

The energy, released as electrons pass from carrier to carrier, is used for ATP production. It took many years for investigators to determine exactly how this occurs, and the details are beyond the scope of this text. Suffice it to say that the inner mitochondrial membrane contains an ATP–synthase complex that combines ADP + Ⓟ to produce ATP. The ATP–synthase complex produces about 32 ATP per glucose molecule. Overall, the reactions of cellular respiration produce 36 to 38 ATP molecules.

Fermentation

Fermentation is an anaerobic process, meaning that it does not require oxygen. When oxygen is not available to cells, the electron transport chain soon becomes inoperative. This is because oxygen is not present to accept electrons. In this case most cells have a safety valve, so that some ATP can still be produced. Glycolysis operates as long as it is supplied with "free" NAD^+ that is available to pick up hydrogens and electrons. Normally, NADH takes electrons to the electron transport chain and, thereby, is recycled to become NAD^+. However, if the system is not working due to a lack of oxygen, NADH passes its hydrogens and electrons to pyruvate molecules, as shown in the following reaction:

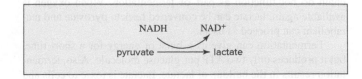

BIOLOGY TODAY  **Health**

The Metabolic Fate of Pizza

Obviously our diets do not consist solely of carbohydrates. Because fats and proteins are also organic nutrients, it makes sense that our bodies can utilize the energy found in the bonds of these molecules. In fact, the metabolic pathways we have discussed in this chapter are more than capable of accessing the energy of fats and proteins. For example, let's trace the fate of a pepperoni pizza, which contains carbohydrates (crust), fats (cheese), and protein (pepperoni).

We already know that the glucose in the carbohydrate crust is broken down during cellular respiration. When the cheese in the pizza (a fat) is used as an energy source, it breaks down to glycerol and three fatty acids. As Figure 3B indicates, glycerol can be converted to pyruvate and enter glycolysis. The fatty acids are converted to an intermediate that enters the citric acid cycle. An 18-carbon fatty acid results in nine acetyl CoA molecules. Calculation shows that respiration of these can produce a total of 108 ATP molecules. This is why fats are an efficient form of stored energy—the three long fatty acid chains per fat molecule can produce considerable ATP when needed.

Proteins are less frequently used as an energy source but are available if necessary. The carbon skeleton of amino acids can enter glycolysis, be converted to acetyl groups, or enter the citric acid cycle at another point. The carbon skeleton is produced in the liver when an amino acid undergoes deamination, or the removal of the amino group. The amino group becomes ammonia (NH_3), which enters the urea cycle and becomes part of urea, the primary excretory product of humans.

In Chapter 9, "Digestive System and Nutrition," we will take a more detailed look at the nutritional needs of humans, including discussions on how vitamins and minerals interact with metabolic pathways and the dietary guidelines for proteins, fats, and carbohydrates.

Questions to Consider

1. How might a meal of a cheeseburger and fries be processed by the cellular respiration pathways?
2. Even though Figure 3B does not indicate the need for water, it is an important component of our diet. Where would water interact with these pathways?

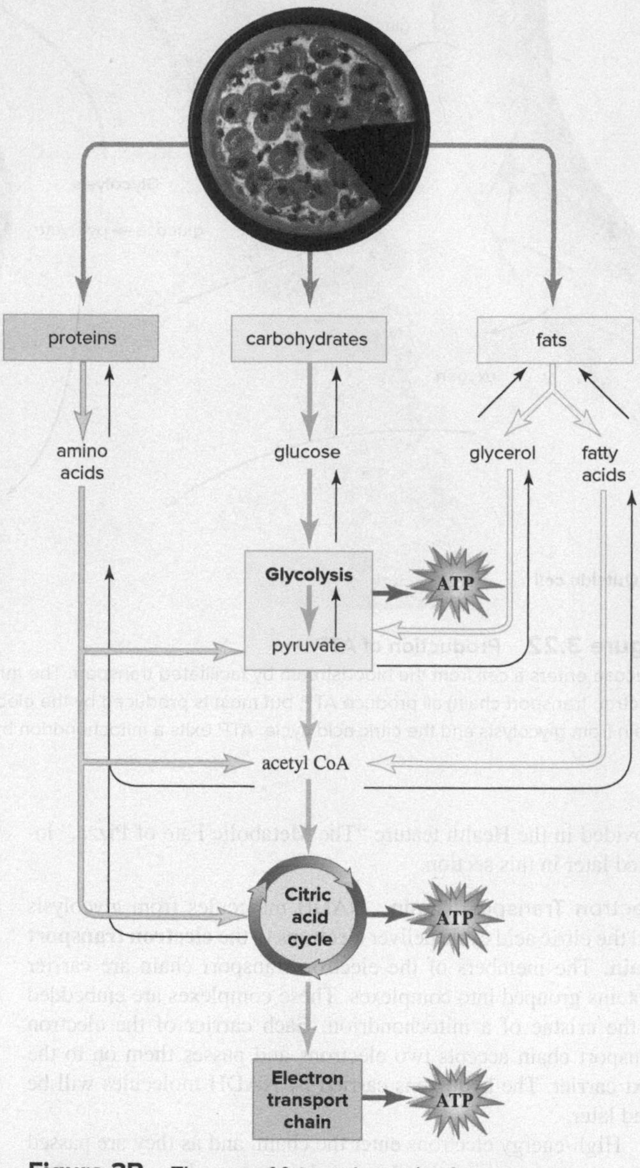

Figure 3B   The use of fats and proteins for energy.
Carbohydrates, fats, and proteins can be used as energy sources, and their monomers (carbohydrates and proteins) or subunits (fats) enter degradative pathways at specific points.
© C Squared Studios/Getty RF

This means that the citric acid cycle and the electron transport chain do not function as part of fermentation. When oxygen is available again, lactate can be converted back to pyruvate and metabolism can proceed as usual.

Fermentation can give us a burst of energy for a short time, but it produces only two ATP per glucose molecule. Also, fermentation results in the buildup of lactate. Lactate is toxic to cells and causes muscles to cramp and fatigue. If fermentation continues for any length of time, death follows.

Fermentation takes its name from yeast fermentation. Yeast fermentation produces alcohol and carbon dioxide (instead of lactate). When yeast is used to leaven bread, carbon dioxide production makes the bread rise. When yeast is used to produce alcoholic beverages, it is the alcohol that humans make use of.

CHECK YOUR PROGRESS 3.6

1. Summarize the roles of enzymes in chemical reactions.
2. Describe the basic steps of required to break down glucose by cellular respiration.
3. Explain why the ATP cycle resembles that of a rechargeable battery.
4. Explain the differences between cellular respiration and fermentation.

CONNECTING THE CONCEPTS

For additional information on the processing of nutrients for energy, refer to the following discussions:

Sections 2.3 to **2.5** provide a more detailed look at carbohydrates and other energy nutrients.

Section 9.3 explores how the small intestine processes nutrients for absorption.

Section 9.6 describes the importance of carbohydrates, fats, and proteins in the diet.

CASE STUDY: CONCLUSION

Over the next few months, both Kevin and Mary dedicated hours to understanding the causes of and treatments for Tay-Sachs disease. They learned that the disease is caused by a recessive mutation that limits the production of an enzyme called beta-hexosaminidase A. This enzyme is loaded into a newly formed lysosome by the Golgi apparatus. The enzyme's function is to break down a specific type of fatty acid chain called *gangliosides*. Gangliosides play an important role in the early formation of the neurons in the brain. Tay-Sachs disease occurs when the gangliosides over-accumulate in the neurons.

Though the prognosis for their child was initially poor—very few children with Tay-Sachs live beyond the age of 4—the parents were encouraged to explore how recent advances in a form of medicine called gene therapy might be able to prolong the life of their child. In gene therapy, a correct version of the gene is introduced into specific cells in an attempt to regain lost function. Some initial studies using mice as a model had demonstrated an ability to reduce ganglioside concentrations by providing a working version of the gene that produced beta-hexosaminidase A to the neurons of the brain. Though research was still ongoing, it was a promising piece of information for both Kevin and Mary.

STUDY TOOLS http://connect.mheducation.com

SMARTBOOK® Maximize your study time with McGraw-Hill SmartBook®, the first adaptive textbook.

SUMMARIZE

3.1 What Is a Cell?

The **cell theory** states that cells are the basic units of life and that all life comes from preexisting cells. Microscopes are used to view cells, which must remain small to have a favorable surface-area-to-volume ratio.

3.2 How Cells Are Organized

The human cell is a **eukaryotic cell** with a **nucleus** that contains the genetic material. **Prokaryotic cells,** such as the bacteria, are smaller than eukaryotic cells and lack a nucleus.

The cell is surrounded by a **plasma membrane,** a **selectively permeable** barrier that limits the movement of materials into and out of the cell. Between the plasma membrane and the nucleus is the **cytoplasm.** In eukaryotic cells, the cytoplasm contains various **organelles,** each with specific functions.

3.3 The Plasma Membrane and How Substances Cross It

The **fluid-mosaic model** describes the structure of the plasma membrane. The plasma membrane contains

- A phospholipid bilayer that selectively regulates the passage of molecules and ions into and out of the cell.
- Embedded proteins, which allow certain substances to cross the plasma membrane.

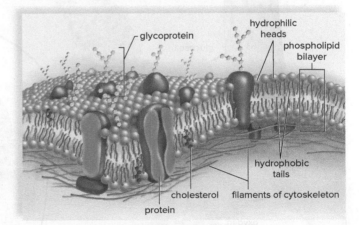

Passage of molecules into or out of cells can be passive or active.

- Passive mechanisms do not require energy. Examples are **diffusion, osmosis,** and **facilitated transport. Tonicity** and **osmotic pressure** control the process of osmosis.
- Active mechanisms require an input of energy. Examples are **active transport** (sodium-potassium pump), endocytosis (**phagocytosis** and pinocytosis), receptor-mediated endocytosis, and exocytosis.

64 Unit 1 Human Organization

3.4 The Nucleus and the Endomembrane System

- The nucleus houses DNA, which contains **genes** that specify the order of amino acids in proteins. **Chromatin** is a combination of DNA molecules and proteins that make up **chromosomes.**
- The nucleus is surrounded by a **nuclear envelope** that contains **nuclear pores** for communication and the movement of materials.
- The **nucleolus** produces ribosomal RNA (rRNA).
- Protein synthesis occurs in **ribosomes,** small organelles composed of proteins and rRNA.

The Endomembrane System

The **endomembrane system** consists of the nuclear envelope, **endoplasmic reticulum (ER)**, Golgi apparatus, lysosomes, and **vesicles.**

- The rough ER has ribosomes, where protein synthesis occurs.
- Smooth ER has no ribosomes and has various functions, including lipid synthesis.
- The **Golgi apparatus** processes and packages proteins and lipids into vesicles for secretion or movement into other parts of the cell.
- **Lysosomes** are specialized vesicles produced by the Golgi apparatus. They fuse with incoming vesicles to digest enclosed material, and they autodigest old cell parts.

3.5 The Cytoskeleton, Cell Movement, and Cell Junctions

- The **cytoskeleton** consists of **microtubules, actin filaments,** and **intermediate filaments** that give cells their shape; and it allows organelles to move about the cell. Microtubules are organized by **centrosomes. Cilia** and **flagella,** which contain microtubules, allow a cell to move.

- Cell junctions connect cells to form tissues and to facilitate communication between cells.
- The **extracellular matrix (ECM)** is located outside the plasma membrane. It may provide structure and regulate the movement of materials into the cell.

3.6 Metabolism and the Energy Reactions

Metabolic Pathways

- **Metabolism** represents all the chemical reactions that occur in a cell. A metabolic pathway is a series of reactions, each of which has its own enzyme. The materials entering these reactions are called **reactants,** and the materials leaving the pathway are called **products.**

Enzymes

- **Enzymes** bind their **substrates** in the **active site.**
- Enzymes accelerate chemical reactions by lowering the **energy of activation (E_a)** needed to start the reaction.
- **Coenzymes,** such as NAD^+ (**nicotinamide adenine dinucleotide**), are nonprotein molecules that assist enzymes.

Mitochondria and Cellular Respiration

- **Mitochondria** are involved in **cellular respiration,** which uses oxygen and releases carbon dioxide.
- During cellular respiration, mitochondria convert the energy of glucose into the energy of ATP molecules.

Cellular Respiration and Metabolism

- Cellular respiration includes three pathways: glycolysis, the citric acid cycle, and the electron transport chain.

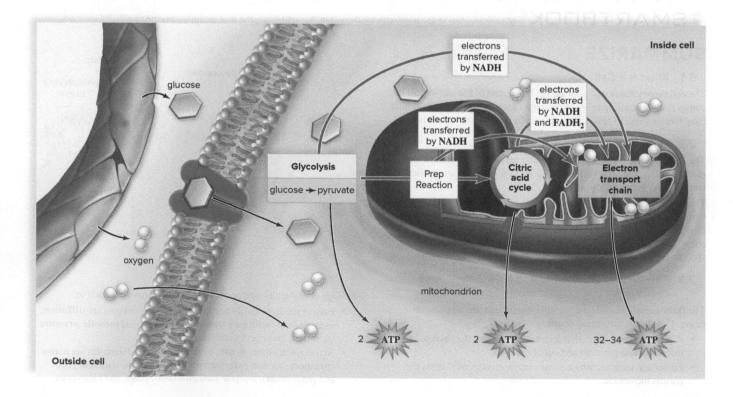

- **Glycolysis** occurs in the cytoplasm and is **anaerobic.** It produces two pyruvate molecules and small amounts of ATP and NADH.
- The pyruvate molecules are modified by the preparatory reactions in the mitochondria before entering the citric acid cycle.
- The **citric acid cycle** occurs in the matrix of the mitochondria. Its role is to break C—C bonds and generate ATP, NADH, and $FADH_2$.
- The **electron transport chain** is located along the cristae of the mitochondria. It is an **aerobic** pathway that uses the electrons in the NADH and $FADH_2$ molecules to generate the majority of the ATP in the cell.
- If oxygen is not available in cells, the electron transport chain is inoperative, and **fermentation** (which does not require oxygen) occurs. Fermentation recycles NAD^+ molecules so that the cell can produce a small amount of ATP by glycolysis.

ASSESS

TESTING YOURSELF

Choose the best answer for each question.

3.1 What Is a Cell?

1. As the size of a cell decreases, the ratio of its surface area to volume
   a. increases.
   b. decreases.
   c. stays the same.

2. The cell theory states that
   a. all life comes from preexisting cells.
   b. all life is composed of cells.
   c. the cell is the basic unit of life.
   d. All of these are correct.

3.2 How Cells Are Organized

3. Prokaryotic cells contain all of the following, except
   a. cytoplasm.
   b. plasma membrane.
   c. DNA.
   d. a nucleus.

4. The endosymbiotic theory explains which of the following?
   a. the origins of the first prokaryotic cell
   b. the formation of the plasma membrane
   c. why DNA is the genetic material in all cells
   d. how eukaryotic cells evolved from prokaryotic cells

3.3 The Plasma Membrane and How Substances Cross It

5. Which of the following is not part of the fluid-mosaic model?
   a. phospholipids
   b. proteins
   c. cholesterol
   d. chromatin

6. Facilitated transport differs from diffusion in that facilitated diffusion
   a. involves the passive use of a carrier protein.
   b. involves the active use of a carrier protein.
   c. moves a molecule from a low to a high concentration.
   d. involves the use of ATP molecules.

7. When a cell is placed in a hypotonic solution,
   a. solute exits the cell to equalize the concentration on both sides of the membrane.
   b. water exits the cell toward the area of lower solute concentration.
   c. water enters the cell toward the area of higher solute concentration.
   d. solute exits and water enters the cell.

3.4 The Nucleus and Endomembrane System

For questions 8–11, match the description to the correct answer in the following key. Answers may be used more than once.

Key:
   a. Golgi apparatus
   b. nucleus
   c. ribosome
   d. lysosome

8. location of the chromatin and nucleolus
9. organelle where proteins and lipids from the ER are modified
10. contains digestive enzymes
11. the site of protein synthesis

12. The ribosomes on the rough endoplasmic reticulum assemble _____, while _____ are assembled in the smooth endoplasmic reticulum.
   a. proteins; phospholipids
   b. cholesterol; proteins
   c. DNA; proteins
   d. cholesterol; phospholipids

3.5 The Cytoskeleton, Cell Movement, and Cell Junctions

13. The cytoskeleton of a cell consists of all of the following, except
   a. microtubules.
   b. actin filaments.
   c. extracellular matrix.
   d. intermediate filaments.

14. Cilia and flagella are involved in
   a. forming junctions between cells.
   b. establishing the extracellular matrix.
   c. cell-to-cell communication.
   d. cell movement.

3.6 Metabolism and the Energy Reactions

15. The active site of an enzyme
   a. is identical to that of any other enzyme.
   b. is the part of the enzyme where the substrate can fit.
   c. is destroyed during a chemical reaction.
   d. is where the coenzyme binds.

16. Enzymes accelerate a chemical reaction by
   a. reducing the amount of substrate produced.
   b. lowering the energy of activation of the reaction.
   c. increasing the energy of activation of the reaction.
   d. reducing the amount of reactant needed.

17. Which of the following pathways produces the greatest amount of ATP?
   a. citric acid cycle
   b. glycolosis
   c. electron transport chain
   d. fermentation

18. Which of the following reactions is aerobic and recycles NAD⁺ molecules?
    a. glycolosis
    b. citric acid cycle
    c. electron transport chain
    d. fermentation

ENGAGE

BioNOW

Want to know how this science is relevant to your life? Check out the BioNow videos below:

- Cell Size
- Saltwater Filter
- Energy Part I: EnergyTransfers
- Energy Part III: Cellular Respiration

1. **Cell Size:** Why would a larger surface-area-to-volume ratio increase metabolic efficiency?

2. **Saltwater Filter:** Explain how the potato uses the principles of diffusion to measure the salt concentration in the branch samples.

3. **Energy Transfers:** Explain how both laws of thermodynamics apply to the experiments in this video.

4. **Cellular Respiration:** What cellular processes are producing the CO_2 being measured in this experiment?

THINKING CRITICALLY

In the case study at the beginning of the chapter, the child had malfunctioning lysosomes, which caused an accumulation of fatty acid in the system. Each part of a cell plays an important role in the homeostasis of the entire body.

1. What might occur if the cells of the body contain malfunctioning mitochondria?

2. What would happen to homeostasis if enzymes were no longer produced in the body?

3. Knowing what you know about the function of a lysosome, what might occur if the cells' lysosomes are overproductive instead of malfunctioning?

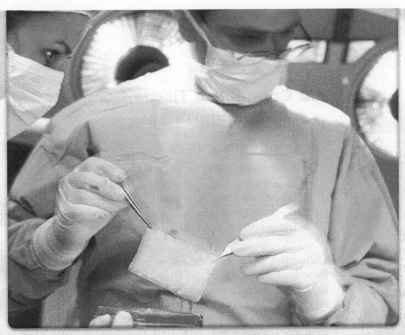

© PHANIE/Science Source

Organization and Regulation of Body Systems

CASE STUDY: ARTIFICIAL SKIN

When Kristen awoke in the hospital, she discovered that a fire in her home had produced third-degree burns over a large portion of her legs. The doctors informed Kristen that the burns on her legs covered too large an area for autografting, the traditional grafting technique that would remove skin from other parts of her body to cover the burn areas. Another available option was allografting, in which skin is removed from another person, or a cadaver, and used to cover the burn areas. However, Kristen's specialists were not eager to take that route because complications often develop due to rejection of the foreign tissue or infections.

Instead, the doctors recommended a relatively new technique—artificial skin. Just a decade ago, the concept of artificial skin may have been found only in a science-fiction movie, but advances in medical technology have made the use of artificial skin a reality. The purpose of using artificial skin is not to permanently replace the damaged tissue; rather, the procedure is designed to protect the damaged tissue and allow time for the patient's skin to heal itself.

The first step of the procedure, after the removal of the burned tissue, is to cover the wound with the artificial skin. This skin contains collagen, a connective tissue, and an adhesive-like carbohydrate that allows the artificial skin to bind to the underlying tissue. Initially the artificial skin contains a plastic wrapping that simulates the epidermis and protects the tissue from water loss and infection. The next step is to remove a small sample of epidermal cells from an unburned area of skin on the patient's body. These are taken to a laboratory and placed in incubators to grow sheets of skin. Once ready, the plastic covering on the patient is replaced by the sheets of epidermal cells. Over time, the laboratory-grown artificial skin is integrated into the newly growing skin.

As you read through the chapter, think about the following questions:

1. What types of tissue are normally found in skin?
2. Why would burn damage to the skin be such a serious challenge to Kristen's health?
3. Why would it be more difficult to produce new dermis in the laboratory than new epidermis?

CHAPTER CONCEPTS

4.1 Types of Tissues
The body contains four types of tissues: connective, muscular, nervous, and epithelial.

4.2 Connective Tissue Connects and Supports
Connective tissues bind and support body parts.

4.3 Muscular Tissue Moves the Body
Muscular tissue moves the body and its parts.

4.4 Nervous Tissue Communicates
Nervous tissue transmits information throughout the body.

4.5 Epithelial Tissue Protects
Epithelial tissues line cavities and cover surfaces.

4.6 Integumentary System
The skin is the largest organ and plays an important role in maintaining homeostasis.

4.7 Organ Systems, Body Cavities, and Body Membranes
Organ systems contain multiple organs that interact to carry out a process.

4.8 Homeostasis
Homeostasis maintains the internal environment and is made possible by feedback mechanisms.

BEFORE YOU BEGIN

Before beginning this chapter, take a few moments to review the following discussions:

Section 1.1 How do tissues and organs fit into the levels of biological organization?

Section 3.2 How are eukaryotic cells structured?

Section 3.5 How are cells linked together to form tissues?

4.1 Types of Tissues

LEARNING OUTCOME

Upon completion of this section, you should be able to

1. Understand where tissues relate in the biological levels of organization.
2. Describe the four types of tissues and provide a general function for each.

Recall from the material on the levels of biological organization (see Fig. 1.2) that cells are composed of molecules; a tissue is a group of similar cells; an organ contains several types of tissues; and several organs are found in an organ system. In this chapter we will further explore the tissue, organ, and organ system levels of organization.

A **tissue** is composed of specialized cells of the same type that perform a common function in the body. The tissues of the human body can be categorized into four major types:

Connective tissue binds and supports body parts.
Muscular tissue moves the body and its parts.
Nervous tissue receives sensory information and conducts nerve impulses.
Epithelial tissue covers body surfaces and lines body cavities.

SCIENCE IN YOUR LIFE

How are cancers named?

Cancers are classified according to the type of tissue from which they arise. Sarcomas are cancers arising in muscular or connective tissue (especially bone or cartilage). Leukemias are cancers of the blood. Lymphomas are cancers of lymphoid tissue. Carcinomas, the most common type, are cancers of epithelial tissue. The chance of developing cancer in a particular tissue is related to the rate of cell division. Both epithelial cells and blood cells reproduce at a high rate. Thus, carcinomas and leukemias are common types of cancer.

CHECK YOUR PROGRESS 4.1

1. Explain how tissues relate to cells and organs in the biological levels of organization.
2. Distinguish between muscular tissue and nervous tissue.
3. Distinguish between connective tissue and epithelial tissue.

CONNECTING THE CONCEPTS

For more information on the roles of each of these tissues in the body, refer to the following discussions:

Section 6.1 explores how blood functions as a connective tissue.

Section 9.3 examines how the epithelial tissues of the digestive system absorb nutrients.

Section 13.2 examines how muscular tissue provides for movement.

4.2 Connective Tissue Connects and Supports

LEARNING OUTCOMES

Upon completion of this section, you should be able to

1. Describe the primary types of connective tissue and provide a function for each.
2. Compare the structure and function of bone and cartilage.
3. Differentiate between blood and lymph.

Connective tissue is diverse in structure and function. Despite these apparent differences, all types of connective tissue have three similar components: specialized cells, ground substance, and protein fibers. These components are shown in Figure 4.1, a diagrammatic representation of loose fibrous connective tissue. The ground substance is a noncellular material that separates the cells. It varies in consistency from solid (bone) to semifluid (cartilage) to fluid (blood).

The fibers are of three possible types. White **collagen fibers** contain collagen, a protein that gives them flexibility and strength. **Reticular fibers** are very thin collagen fibers, highly branched proteins that form delicate supporting networks. Yellow **elastic fibers** contain elastin, a protein that is not as strong as collagen but is more elastic. Elastic fibers return to their original shape and may stretch to over 100 times their relaxed size without damage. Inherited connective tissue disorders arise when people inherit genes that lead to malformed fibers. For example, in Marfan syndrome, there are mutations in the fibrillin gene (*FBN1*). Fibrillin is a component of elastic fibers, and these mutations cause a decrease in the elasticity of the connective tissues that are normally rich in elastic fibers, such as the aorta. Individuals with this disease often die from aortic rupture, which occurs when the aorta cannot expand in response to increased blood pressure.

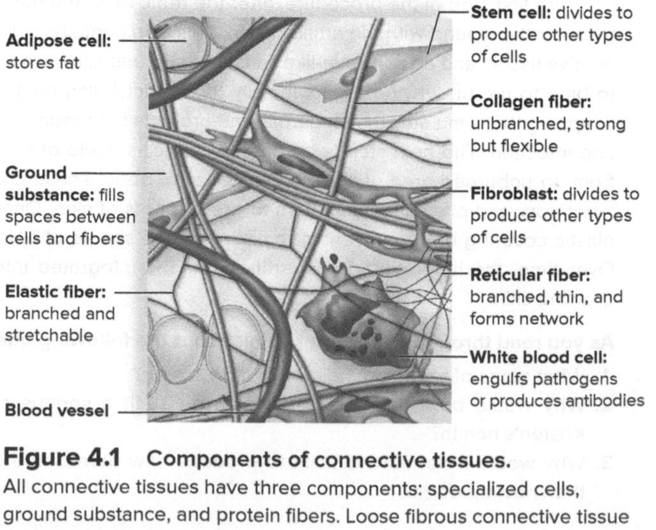

Adipose cell: stores fat

Ground substance: fills spaces between cells and fibers

Elastic fiber: branched and stretchable

Blood vessel

Stem cell: divides to produce other types of cells

Collagen fiber: unbranched, strong but flexible

Fibroblast: divides to produce other types of cells

Reticular fiber: branched, thin, and forms network

White blood cell: engulfs pathogens or produces antibodies

Figure 4.1   Components of connective tissues.
All connective tissues have three components: specialized cells, ground substance, and protein fibers. Loose fibrous connective tissue is shown here.

Fibrous Connective Tissue

Fibrous tissue exists in two forms: loose fibrous tissue and dense fibrous tissue. Both loose fibrous and dense fibrous connective tissues have cells called **fibroblasts** located some distance from one another and separated by a jellylike ground substance containing white collagen fibers and yellow elastic fibers (Fig. 4.2). **Matrix** includes ground substance and fibers.

Loose fibrous connective tissue, which includes areolar and reticular connective tissue, supports epithelium and many internal organs. Its presence in lungs, arteries, and the urinary bladder allows these organs to expand. It forms a protective covering enclosing many internal organs, such as muscles, blood vessels, and nerves.

Adipose tissue is a special type of loose connective tissue in which the cells enlarge and store fat. Adipose tissue has little extracellular matrix. Its cells, which are called **adipocytes,** are crowded, and each is filled with liquid fat. The body uses this stored fat for energy, insulation, and organ protection. Adipose tissue also releases a hormone called *leptin,* which regulates appetite-control centers in the brain. Adipose tissue is primarily found beneath the skin, around the kidneys, and on the surface of the heart.

Dense fibrous connective tissue contains many collagen fibers packed together. This type of tissue has more specific functions than does loose connective tissue. For example, dense fibrous connective tissue is found in **tendons,** which connect muscles to bones, and in **ligaments,** which connect bones to other bones at joints.

Supportive Connective Tissue

Cartilage and bone are the two main supportive connective tissues. Each provides structure, shape, protection, and leverage for movement. Generally cartilage is more flexible than bone, because it lacks mineralization of the matrix. The supportive connective tissues are covered in more detail in Section 12.1.

Cartilage

In **cartilage,** the cells lie in small chambers called *lacunae* (sing., lacuna), separated by a solid, yet flexible, matrix. This matrix is formed by cells called *chondroblasts* and *chondrocytes.* Because this tissue lacks a direct blood supply, it often heals slowly. The three types of cartilage are distinguished by the type of fiber found in the matrix.

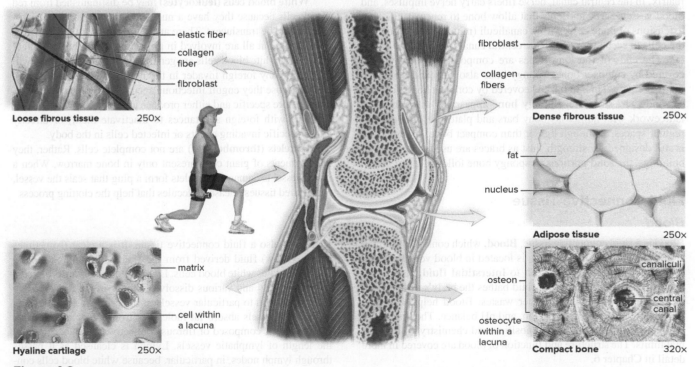

Loose fibrous tissue   250×

— elastic fiber
— collagen fiber
— fibroblast

Hyaline cartilage   250×

— matrix
— cell within a lacuna

fibroblast —
collagen fibers —

Dense fibrous tissue   250×

fat —
nucleus —

Adipose tissue   250×

osteon —
osteocyte within a lacuna —

— canaliculi
— central canal

Compact bone   320×

Figure 4.2   Connective tissues in the knee.
Most types of connective tissue may be found in the knee.
(all photos): © Ed Reschke

70 Unit 1 Human Organization

Hyaline cartilage (Fig. 4.2), the most common type of cartilage, contains only fine collagen fibers. The matrix has a glassy, translucent appearance. Hyaline cartilage is found in the nose and at the ends of the long bones and the ribs, and it forms rings in the walls of respiratory passages. The fetal skeleton also is made of this type of cartilage. Later, the cartilaginous fetal skeleton is replaced by bone.

Elastic cartilage has more elastic fibers than hyaline cartilage does. For this reason, it is more flexible and is found, for example, in the framework of the outer ear.

Fibrocartilage has a matrix containing strong collagen fibers. Fibrocartilage is found in structures that withstand tension and pressure, such as the disks between the vertebrae in the backbone and the cushions in the knee joint.

Bone

Bone is the most rigid connective tissue. It consists of an extremely hard matrix of inorganic salts, notably calcium salts. These salts are deposited around protein fibers, especially collagen fibers. The inorganic salts give bone rigidity. The protein fibers provide elasticity and strength, much as steel rods do in reinforced concrete. Cells called *osteoblasts* and *osteoclasts* are responsible for forming the matrix in bone tissue.

Compact bone makes up the shaft of a long bone (Fig. 4.2). It consists of cylindrical structural units called *osteons* (see Section 12.1). The central canal of each osteon is surrounded by rings of hard matrix. Bone cells are located in lacunae between the rings of matrix. In the central canal, nerve fibers carry nerve impulses, and blood vessels carry nutrients that allow bone to renew itself. Thin extensions of bone cells within canaliculi (minute canals) connect the cells to each other and to the central canal.

The ends of the long bones are composed of spongy bone covered by compact bone. Spongy bone also surrounds the bone marrow cavity. This, in turn, is covered by compact bone, forming a "sandwich" structure. **Spongy bone** appears as an open, bony latticework with numerous bony bars and plates, separated by irregular spaces. Although lighter than compact bone, spongy bone is still designed for strength. Just as braces are used for support in buildings, the solid portions of spongy bone follow lines of stress.

Fluid Connective Tissue

Blood

Blood is a fluid connective tissue. **Blood,** which consists of formed elements (Fig. 4.3) and plasma, is located in blood vessels. Blood transports nutrients and oxygen to **interstitial fluid,** also called extracellular fluid. Interstitial fluid bathes the body's cells and removes carbon dioxide and other wastes. Blood helps distribute heat and plays a role in fluid, ion, and pH balance. The systems of the body help keep blood composition and chemistry within normal limits. The structure and function of blood are covered in more detail in Chapter 6.

Each formed element of blood has a specific function. The **red blood cells (erythrocytes)** are small, biconcave, disk-shaped cells without nuclei. The presence of the red pigment hemoglobin

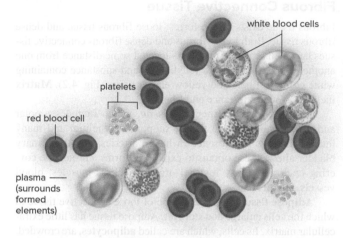

Figure 4.3 **The formed elements of blood.**
Red blood cells, which lack a nucleus, transport oxygen. Each type of white blood cell has a particular way to fight infections. Platelets, fragments of a particular cell, help seal injured blood vessels.

makes the cells red, which in turn makes the blood red. Hemoglobin is composed of four units. Each unit is composed of the protein globin and a complex, iron-containing structure called *heme*. The iron forms a loose association with oxygen; therefore, red blood cells transport oxygen.

White blood cells (leukocytes) may be distinguished from red blood cells because they have a nucleus. Without staining, leukocytes would be translucent. There are many different types of white blood cells, but all are involved in protecting the body from infection. Some white blood cells are generalists, meaning that they will respond to any foreign invader in the body. These are phagocytic cells, because they engulf infectious agents, such as bacteria. Others are more specific and either produce antibodies (molecules that combine with foreign substances to inactivate them) or directly attack specific invading agents or infected cells in the body.

Platelets (thrombocytes) are not complete cells. Rather, they are fragments of giant cells present only in bone marrow. When a blood vessel is damaged, platelets form a plug that seals the vessel, and injured tissues release molecules that help the clotting process.

Lymph

Lymph is also a fluid connective tissue. It is a clear (sometimes faintly yellow) fluid derived from the fluids surrounding the tissues. It contains white blood cells. Lymphatic vessels absorb excess interstitial fluid and various dissolved solutes in the tissues. They transport lymph to particular vessels of the cardiovascular system. Lymphatic vessels absorb fat molecules from the small intestine. Lymph nodes, composed of fibrous connective tissue, occur along the length of lymphatic vessels. Lymph is cleansed as it passes through lymph nodes, in particular, because white blood cells congregate there. Lymph nodes enlarge when you have an infection.

Figure 4.4 summarizes the classification of each of the major types of connective tissue.

Types of Connective Tissue

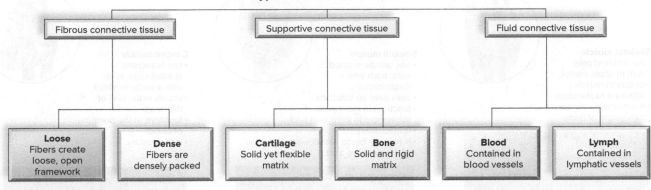

Figure 4.4 **Types of connective tissue.**
Connective tissue is divided into three general categories—fibrous, supportive, and fluid.

CHECK YOUR PROGRESS 4.2

1. Describe the three general categories of connective tissue, and provide some examples of each type.
2. Explain the difference in the composition of the matrix in each of the three classes of connective tissue.
3. Describe how each of the two fluid connective tissues is important to homeostasis.

CONNECTING THE CONCEPTS

The tissue types discussed in this section are examined in greater detail later in the book. For more information, refer to the following discussions:

Section 6.1 details the types of formed elements found in blood.

Section 7.2 explains the role of the lymphatic system in moving lymph through the body.

Section 12.1 provides a more detailed examination of cartilage and bone.

4.3 Muscular Tissue Moves the Body

LEARNING OUTCOME

Upon completion of this section, you should be able to

1. Distinguish among the three types of muscles with regard to location and function in the body.

Muscular tissue is specialized to contract. It is composed of cells called *muscle fibers,* which contain actin and myosin filaments. The interaction of these filaments accounts for movement. These interactions, and the structure of the muscles of the body, are covered in greater detail in Chapter 13. The three types of vertebrate muscular tissue are skeletal, smooth, and cardiac.

Skeletal muscle is also called *voluntary muscle* (Fig. 4.5a). It is attached by tendons to the bones of the skeleton. When it

contracts, body parts move. Contraction of skeletal muscle is under voluntary control and occurs faster than in the other muscle types. Skeletal muscle fibers are cylindrical and long—some run the length of the muscle. They arise during development when several cells fuse, resulting in one fiber with multiple nuclei. The nuclei are located at the periphery of the cell, just inside the plasma membrane. The fibers have alternating light and dark bands that give them a **striated,** or striped, appearance. These bands are due to the placement of actin filaments and myosin filaments in the cell.

Smooth muscle is so named because the cells lack striations (Fig. 4.5b). Each spindle-shaped cell has a single nucleus. These cells form layers in which the thick middle portion of one cell is opposite the thin ends of adjacent cells. Consequently, the nuclei form an irregular pattern in the tissue. Smooth muscle is involuntary, meaning that it is not under conscious control. Smooth muscle is found in the walls of viscera (intestine, bladder, and other internal organs) and blood vessels. For this reason, it is sometimes referred to as *visceral muscle.* Smooth muscle contracts more slowly than skeletal muscle but can remain contracted for a longer time. When the smooth muscle of the bladder contracts, urine is sent into a tube called the urethra, which takes it to the outside. When the smooth muscle of the blood vessels contracts, the blood vessels constrict, helping raise blood pressure.

Cardiac muscle (Fig. 4.5c) is found only in the walls of the heart. Its contraction pumps blood and accounts for the heartbeat. Cardiac muscle combines features of both smooth and skeletal muscle. Like skeletal muscle, it has striations, but the contraction of the heart is involuntary for the most part. Cardiac muscle cells also differ from skeletal muscle cells in that they usually have a single, centrally placed nucleus. The cells are branched and seemingly fused together. The heart appears to be composed of one large, interconnecting mass of muscle cells. Cardiac muscle cells are separate, but they are bound end to end at *intercalated disks.* These are areas where folded plasma membranes between two cells contain adhesion junctions and gap junctions (see Section 3.5).

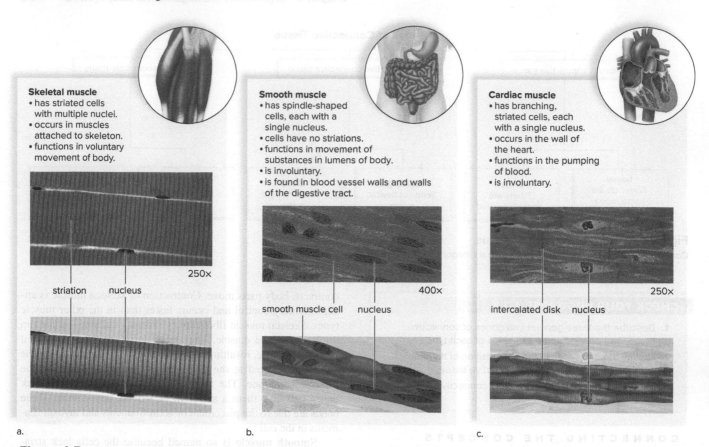

Skeletal muscle
• has striated cells with multiple nuclei.
• occurs in muscles attached to skeleton.
• functions in voluntary movement of body.

striation   nucleus   250×

Smooth muscle
• has spindle-shaped cells, each with a single nucleus.
• cells have no striations.
• functions in movement of substances in lumens of body.
• is involuntary.
• is found in blood vessel walls and walls of the digestive tract.

smooth muscle cell   nucleus   400×

Cardiac muscle
• has branching, striated cells, each with a single nucleus.
• occurs in the wall of the heart.
• functions in the pumping of blood.
• is involuntary.

intercalated disk   nucleus   250×

a.   b.   c.

Figure 4.5 The three types of muscular tissue.
a. Skeletal muscle is voluntary and striated. **b.** Smooth muscle is involuntary and nonstriated. **c.** Cardiac muscle is involuntary and striated.

photos: (a): © Ed Reschke; (b): © McGraw-Hill Education/Dennis Strete; (c): © Ed Reschke

---

CHECK YOUR PROGRESS 4.3

1. Explain the difference in the structure and function of skeletal, smooth, and cardiac muscle.

2. Describe where each type of muscle fiber is found in the body.

3. Explain why smooth muscle and cardiac muscle are involuntary, and summarize what advantage this provides homeostasis.

CONNECTING THE CONCEPTS

Muscular tissue plays an important role in our physiology. For more information on each of the three types of muscles, refer to the following discussions:

Section 5.3 provides a more detailed look at how the heartbeat is generated.

Figure 9.2 illustrates how smooth muscle lines the digestive tract.

Section 13.2 examines the structure and function of skeletal muscle.

4.4 Nervous Tissue Communicates

LEARNING OUTCOMES

Upon completion of this section, you should be able to

1. Distinguish between neurons and neuroglia.
2. Describe the structure of a neuron.

Nervous tissue consists of nerve cells, called neurons, and neuroglia, the cells that support and nourish the neurons. Nervous tissue is the central component of the nervous system (see Section 14.1), which serves three primary functions in the body: sensory input, integration of data, and motor output.

Neurons

A **neuron** is a specialized cell that has three parts: dendrites, a cell body, and an axon (Fig. 4.6). A *dendrite* is an extension that receives signals from sensory receptors or other neurons. The *cell body* contains most of the cell's cytoplasm and the nucleus. An *axon* is an extension that conducts nerve impulses. Long axons are

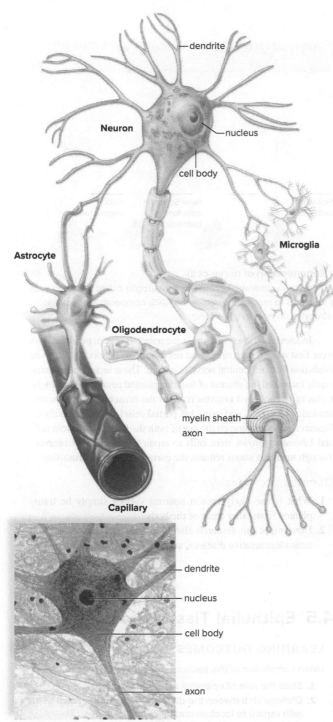

dendrite

Neuron

nucleus

cell body

Microglia

Astrocyte

Oligodendrocyte

myelin sheath
axon

Capillary

dendrite

nucleus

cell body

axon

Micrograph of neuron   200x

Figure 4.6   A neuron and examples of supporting neuroglia.
Neurons conduct nerve impulses. Neuroglia support and service
neurons. Microglia are a type of neuroglia that become mobile in
response to inflammation and phagocytize debris. Astrocytes lie between
neurons and a capillary. Therefore, substances entering neurons from the
blood must first pass through astrocytes. Oligodendrocytes form the
myelin sheaths around fibers in the brain and spinal cord.
photo: © Ed Reschke

covered by myelin, a white, fatty substance. The term *fiber*[1] is used
several different ways when discussing human anatomy, here it
refers to an axon along with its myelin sheath, if it has one. Outside
the brain and spinal cord, fibers bound by connective tissue form
nerves. **Nerves** conduct signals from sensory receptors to the spinal cord and the brain, where integration, or processing, occurs.
However, the phenomenon called sensation occurs only in the
brain. Nerves also conduct signals from the spinal cord and brain
to muscles, glands, and other organs. This triggers a characteristic
response from each tissue. For example, muscles contract, and
glands secrete. In this way, a coordinated response to the original
sensory input is achieved.

Neuroglia

In addition to neurons, nervous tissue contains neuroglia. **Neuroglia**
are cells that outnumber neurons nine to one and take up more
than half the volume of the brain. Although the primary function
of neuroglia is to support and nourish neurons, research is being
conducted to determine how much they directly contribute to
brain function. Neuroglia do not have long extensions (axons or
dendrites). However, researchers are gathering evidence that
neuroglia communicate among themselves and with neurons,
even without these extensions. Examples of neuroglia in the
brain are microglia, astrocytes, and oligodendrocytes (Fig. 4.6).
Microglia, in addition to supporting neurons, engulf bacterial
and cellular debris. *Astrocytes* provide nutrients to neurons and
produce a hormone known as glial-derived neurotrophic factor
(GDNF). This growth factor is currently undergoing clinical trials as a therapy for Parkinson disease and other diseases caused
by neuron degeneration. *Oligodendrocytes* form the myelin
sheaths around fibers in the brain and spinal cord. Outside the
brain, *Schwann cells* are the type of neuroglia that encircle long
nerve fibers and form a myelin sheath. The Science feature
"Nerve Regeneration and Stem Cells" examines how these cells
are being used to generate new nerve cells.

SCIENCE IN YOUR LIFE

What causes MS?

The disease multiple sclerosis, or MS, is a disease that occurs
when the immune system of the body mistakenly targets the
myelin sheath of neurons. This causes the signals traveling
along the neurons to become scrambled, which may lead to a
wide variety of symptoms. Anyone may develop MS, but scientists believe that those highest at risk have a combination of
genetic susceptibility and exposure to yet-unidentified environmental factors.

---

[1]In connective tissue, a fiber is a component of the matrix; in muscular tissue, a fiber is
a muscle cell; in nervous tissue, a fiber is an axon.

BIOLOGY TODAY   Science

Nerve Regeneration and Stem Cells

In humans, axons outside the brain and spinal cord can regenerate—but axons inside these organs cannot (Fig. 4A). After injury, axons in the human central nervous system (CNS) degenerate, resulting in permanent loss of nervous function. Interestingly, about 90% of the cells in the brain and the spinal cord are not even neurons. They are neuroglia cells. In nerves outside the brain and spinal cord, the neuroglia cells are Schwann cells that help axons regenerate. The neuroglia cells in the CNS include microglial cells, oligodendrocytes, and astrocytes, and they inhibit axon regeneration.

The spinal cord contains its own stem cells. When the spinal cord is injured in experimental animals, these stem cells proliferate. But instead of becoming functional neurons, they become neuroglia cells. Researchers are trying to understand the process that triggers the stem cells to become neuroglia cells. In the future, this understanding would allow manipulation of stem cells into neurons.

In early experiments with neural stem cells in the laboratory, scientists at Johns Hopkins University caused embryonic stem (ES) cells to differentiate into spinal cord motor neurons, the type of nerve cell that causes muscles to contract. The motor neurons then produced axons. When grown in the same dish with muscle cells, the motor neurons formed neuromuscular junctions and even caused muscle contractions. The cells were then transplanted into the spinal cords of rats with spinal cord injuries. Some of the transplanted cells survived for longer than a month within the spinal cord. However, no improvement in symptoms was seen and no functional neuron connections were made.

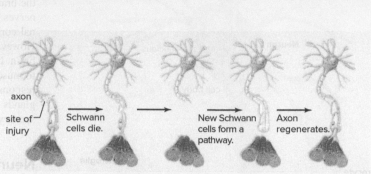

Figure 4A   **Regeneration of nerve cells.**
Outside the CNS, nerves regenerate, because new neuroglia called Schwann cells form a pathway for axons to reach a muscle. In the CNS, comparable neuroglia called oligodendrocytes do not have this function.

In later experiments by the same research group, paralyzed rats were first treated with drugs and nerve growth factors to overcome inhibition from the central nervous system. These techniques significantly increased the success of the transplanted neurons. Amazingly, axons of transplanted neurons reached the muscles, formed neuromuscular junctions, and provided partial relief from the paralysis. Research is being done on the use of both the body's own stem cells and laboratory-grown stem cells to repair damaged CNS neurons. Though many questions remain, the current results are promising.

Questions to Consider

1. What is the likely reason neurons cannot simply be transplanted from other areas of the body?
2. How might this research also help patients who suffer from neurodegenerative diseases, such as Parkinson disease?

CHECK YOUR PROGRESS 4.4

1. Describe the structure and function of a neuron.
2. Discuss the different types of neuroglia and the function of each.
3. Explain how the neurons and neuroglia work together to make nervous tissue function.

CONNECTING THE CONCEPTS

Nervous tissue plays an important role in transmitting the signals needed to maintain homeostasis. For more information on how neurons work, refer to the following discussions:

Section 14.1 provides a more detailed examination of how neurons function.

Section 15.1 discusses how neurons are involved in sensation.

4.5 Epithelial Tissue Protects

LEARNING OUTCOMES

Upon completion of this section, you should be able to

1. State the role of epithelial cells in the body.
2. Distinguish between the different forms of epithelial tissue with regard to location and function.

Epithelial tissue, also called *epithelium* (pl., epithelia), consists of tightly packed cells that form a continuous layer. Epithelial tissue covers surfaces and lines body cavities. Usually it has a protective function. It can also be modified to carry out secretion, absorption, excretion, and filtration.

Epithelial cells are named based on their appearance (Fig. 4.7). All epithelial cells are exposed to the environment on one side. On the other side, they are bounded by a **basement membrane.** The

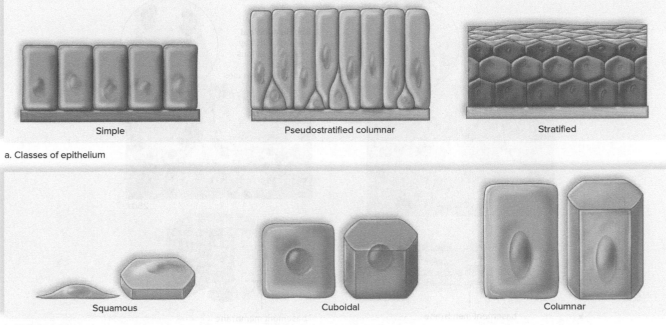

a. Classes of epithelium

b. Cell shapes

Figure 4.7   **Shapes of epithelial cells.**
Epithelial cells have a variety of shapes and configurations in tissues.

basement membrane should not be confused with the plasma membrane (in the cell) or the body membranes that line the cavities of the body. Instead, the basement membrane is a thin layer of various types of carbohydrates and proteins that anchors the epithelium to underlying connective tissue.

Simple Epithelia

Epithelial tissue is either simple or stratified. Simple epithelia have only a single layer of cells (Fig. 4.8) and are classified according to cell type. **Squamous epithelium,** composed of flattened cells, is found lining the air sacs of lungs and walls of blood vessels. Its shape and arrangement permit exchanges of substances in these locations. Oxygen–carbon-dioxide exchange occurs in the lungs, and nutrient-waste exchange occurs across blood vessels in the tissues.

Cuboidal epithelium consists of a single layer of cube-shaped cells. This type of epithelium is frequently found in glands, such as the salivary glands, the thyroid, and the pancreas. Simple cuboidal epithelium also covers the ovaries and lines kidney tubules, the portions of the kidney in which urine is formed. When cuboidal cells are involved in absorption, they have *microvilli* (minute cellular extensions of the plasma membrane). These increase the surface area of the cells. When cuboidal cells function in active transport, they contain many mitochondria.

Columnar epithelium has cells resembling rectangular pillars or columns, with nuclei usually located near the bottom of each cell. This epithelium lines the digestive tract, where microvilli expand the surface area and aid in absorbing the products of

digestion. Ciliated columnar epithelium is found lining the uterine tubes, where it propels the egg toward the uterus.

Pseudostratified columnar epithelium (Fig. 4.8) is so named because it appears to be layered (*pseudo,* "false"; *stratified,* "layers"). However, it does not have true layers, because each cell touches the basement membrane. Its appearance of having several layers is largely due to the irregular placement of the nuclei. The lining of the windpipe, or trachea, is pseudostratified ciliated columnar epithelium. A secreted covering of mucus traps foreign particles. The upward motion of the cilia carries the mucus to the back of the throat, where it may either be swallowed or expectorated (spit out). Smoking can cause a change in the secretion of mucus and can inhibit ciliary action, resulting in a chronic inflammatory condition called *bronchitis.*

In some cases, columnar and pseudostratified columnar epithelium secrete a product. In this case, it is said to be glandular. A **gland** can be a single epithelial cell, as in the case of a mucus-secreting goblet cell, or a gland can contain many cells. Glands with ducts that secrete their product onto the outer surface (e.g., sweat glands and mammary glands) or into a cavity (e.g., salivary glands) are called **exocrine glands.** Ducts can be simple or compound:

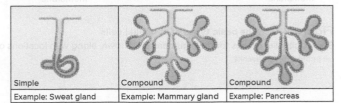

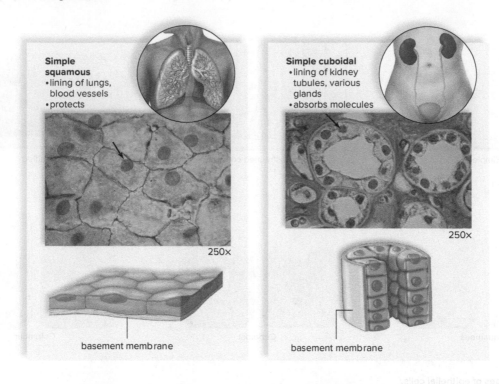

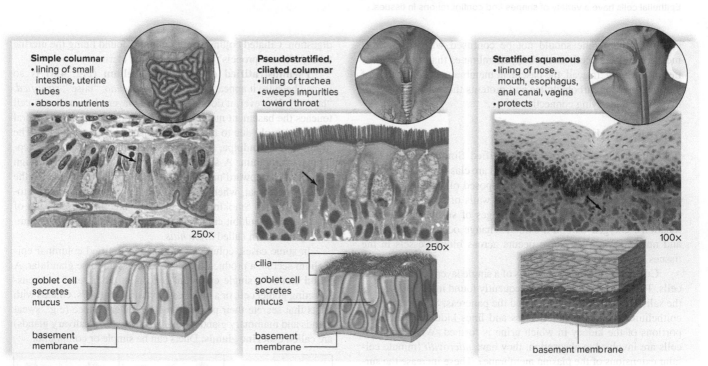

Figure 4.8 **The basic types of epithelial cells.**

Basic epithelial tissues found in humans are shown, along with locations of the tissue and the primary function of the tissue at these locations.

(all photos): © Ed Reschke

Glands that have no ducts are appropriately known as the ductless glands, or endocrine glands. We will explore the function of endocrine glands (e.g., pituitary and thyroid), which secrete hormones directly into the bloodstream, in Section 16.1.

Stratified Epithelia

Stratified epithelia have layers of cells piled one on top of the other (Fig. 4.8). Only the bottom layer touches the basement membrane. The nose, mouth, esophagus, anal canal, outer portion of the cervix (adjacent to the vagina), and vagina are lined with stratified squamous epithelium. During a *Pap smear* these cells are examined to detect any abnormalities, which may indicate the onset of cervical cancer.

As we will see, the outer layer of skin is also stratified squamous epithelium, but the cells are reinforced by keratin, a protein that provides strength. Stratified cuboidal and stratified columnar epithelia also are found in the body.

Transitional epithelium was originally so named because it was thought to be an intermediate form of epithelial cell. Now the term is used to imply changeability, because the tissue changes in response to tension. It forms the lining of the urinary bladder, the ureters (the tubes that carry urine from the kidneys to the bladder), and part of the urethra (the single tube that carries urine to the outside). All are organs that may need to stretch. When the bladder is distended, this epithelium stretches and the outer cells take on a squamous appearance.

CHECK YOUR PROGRESS 4.5

1. List the functions of epithelial tissue.
2. Describe the structure of each major type of epithelial tissue.
3. Summarize how the structure of some epithelial tissue relates to its function. Give some specific examples.

CONNECTING THE CONCEPTS

Epithelial tissue is involved in the operation of most organs of the body. For more information, refer to the following discussions:

Section 9.3 describes how specialized epithelial cells in the stomach secrete hydrochloric acid.

Section 10.6 examines how gas exchange occurs across the epithelial cells of the lungs.

Section 16.1 provides more information on the endocrine and exocrine glands of the body.

4.6 Integumentary System

LEARNING OUTCOMES

Upon completion of this section, you should be able to

1. Explain the function of human skin.
2. Describe the structure of the epidermis and dermis.
3. Identify the function of the accessory organs associated with the skin.

In Section 1.1 we saw that an **organ** is composed of two or more types of tissues working together to perform particular functions, while an **organ system** contains many different organs that cooperate to carry out a process, such as the digestion of food. The **skin** is an organ comprising all four tissue types: epithelial, connective, muscular, and nervous tissue. Because the skin has several accessory organs (hair, nails, sweat glands, and sebaceous glands), it is also sometimes referred to as the **integumentary system.**

Because it covers our bodies, and is largely associated with our physical appearance, the skin is the most conspicuous organ system in the body. In an adult, the skin has a surface area of about 1.8 square meters (m^2) (over 19.5 square feet [ft^2]). It accounts for nearly 15% of the weight of an average human.

The skin has numerous functions. It protects underlying tissues from physical trauma, pathogen invasion, and water loss. It also helps regulate body temperature. Therefore, skin plays a significant role in homeostasis, the relative constancy of the internal environment. The skin even synthesizes certain chemicals that affect the rest of the body. Skin contains sensory receptors, such as touch and temperature receptors. Thus, it helps us to be aware of our surroundings and to communicate with others.

Regions of the Skin

The skin has two regions: epidermis and dermis (Fig. 4.9). A **subcutaneous layer,** sometimes called the *hypodermis,* is found between the skin and any underlying structures, such as muscle or bone.

The Epidermis

The **epidermis** is made up of stratified squamous epithelium. New epidermal cells for the renewal of skin are derived from stem (basal) cells. The importance of these stem cells is observed when there is an injury to the skin. If an injury, such as a burn, is deep enough to destroy stem cells, then the skin can no longer replace itself. As soon as possible, the damaged tissue is removed and skin grafting begins. The skin needed for grafting is usually taken from other parts of the patient's body. This is called *autografting,* as opposed to allografting. In *allografting,* the graft is received from another person and is sometimes obtained from cadavers. Autografting is preferred, because rejection rates are low. If the damaged area is extensive, it may be difficult to acquire enough skin for autografting. In that case, small amounts of epidermis are removed and cultured in the laboratory. This produces thin sheets of skin that can be transplanted back to the patient (see the chapter opener).

Newly generated skin cells become flattened and hardened as they push to the surface (Fig. 4.10). Hardening takes place because the cells produce *keratin,* a waterproof protein. These cells are also called *keratinocytes*. Outer skin cells are dead and keratinized, so the skin is waterproof. This prevents water loss and helps maintain water homeostasis. The skin's waterproofing also prevents water from entering the body when the skin is immersed. Dandruff occurs when the rate of keratinization in the skin of the scalp is two or three times the normal rate. Genetically unique fingerprints and footprints are formed by a thick layer of dead, keratinized cells arranged in spiral and concentric patterns.

Figure 4.9   Anatomy of human skin.

Skin consists of two regions: epidermis and dermis. A subcutaneous layer (the hypodermis) lies below the dermis.

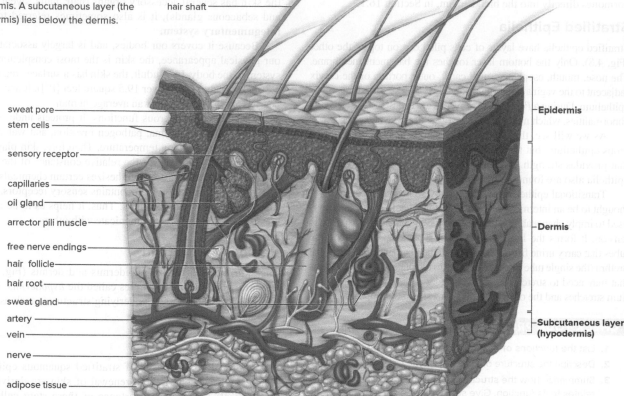

hair shaft

- Epidermis

- Dermis

- Subcutaneous layer (hypodermis)

sweat pore
stem cells
sensory receptor
capillaries
oil gland
arrector pili muscle
free nerve endings
hair follicle
hair root
sweat gland
artery
vein
nerve
adipose tissue

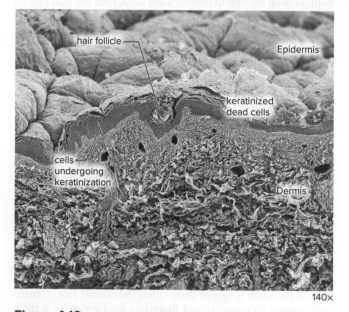

hair follicle

Epidermis

keratinized dead cells

cells undergoing keratinization

Dermis

140×

Figure 4.10   A light micrograph of human skin.

The keratinization of cells is shown in this image.
© Eye of Science/Science Source

Two types of specialized cells are located deep in the epidermis. **Langerhans cells** are macrophages, white blood cells that phagocytize infectious agents and then travel to lymphatic organs. There they stimulate the immune system to react to the pathogen. **Melanocytes,** lying deep in the epidermis, produce melanin, the main pigment responsible for skin color. The number of melanocytes is about the same in all individuals, so variation in skin color is due to the amount of melanin produced and its distribution. When skin is exposed to the sun, melanocytes produce more melanin. This protects the skin from the damaging effects of the ultraviolet (UV) radiation in sunlight. The melanin is passed to other epidermal cells, and the result is tanning. In some people, this results in the formation of patches of melanin called freckles. Another pigment, called carotene, is present in epidermal cells and in the dermis. It gives the skin of some Asian populations its yellowish hue. The pinkish color of fair-skinned people is due to the pigment hemoglobin in the red blood cells in the blood vessels of the dermis.

Some ultraviolet radiation does serve a purpose, however. Certain cells in the epidermis convert a steroid related to cholesterol into vitamin D with the aid of UV radiation (see Section 9.6). However, only a small amount of UV radiation is needed. Vitamin D leaves the skin and helps regulate both calcium and phosphorus metabolism in the body. Calcium and phosphorus have a variety of roles and are important in the proper development and mineralization of the bones.

Skin Cancer   Whereas we tend to associate a tan with good health, it signifies that the body is trying to protect itself from the dangerous rays of the sun. Too much ultraviolet radiation is dangerous and can lead to skin cancer. Basal cell carcinoma (Fig. 4.11a), derived from stem cells gone awry, is the most common type of skin cancer and is the most curable. Melanoma (Fig. 4.11b), skin cancer derived from melanocytes, is extremely serious.

To prevent skin cancer, you should stay out of the sun between the hours of 10 A.M. and 3 P.M. When you are in the sun, follow these guidelines:

- Use a broad-spectrum sunscreen that protects from both UVA (long-wave) and UVB (short-wave) radiation and has a sun protection factor (SPF) of at least 15. This means that if you usually burn, for example, after a 20-minute exposure, it will take 15 times longer, or 5 hours, before you will burn. For extended outdoor activity, use a sunscreen with an SPF of 30 or greater.
- Wear protective clothing. Choose fabrics with a tight weave, and wear a wide-brimmed hat.
- Wear sunglasses that have been treated to absorb UVA and UVB radiation.

Also, avoid tanning machines; even if they use only high levels of UVA radiation, the deep layers of the skin will become more vulnerable to UVB radiation.

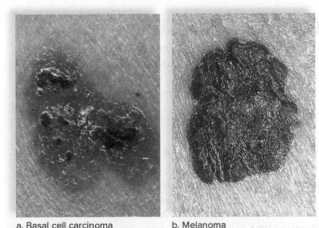

a. Basal cell carcinoma   b. Melanoma

Figure 4.11   Cancers of the skin.
a. Basal cell carcinoma derived from stem cells and (**b**) melanoma derived from melanocytes are types of skin cancer.
(a): © PhotoMix/Alamy; (b): © James Stevenson/SPL/Science Source

The Dermis

The **dermis** is a region of dense fibrous connective tissue beneath the epidermis. *Dermatology* is a branch of medicine that specializes in diagnosing and treating skin disorders. The dermis contains collagen and elastic fibers. The collagen fibers are flexible but offer great resistance to overstretching. They prevent the skin from being torn. The elastic fibers maintain normal skin tension but also stretch to allow movement of underlying muscles and joints. The number of collagen and elastic fibers decreases with age and with exposure to the sun, causing the skin to become less supple and more prone to wrinkling. The dermis also contains blood vessels that nourish the skin. When blood rushes into these vessels, a person blushes. When blood is minimal in them, a person turns "blue." Blood vessels in the dermis play a role in temperature regulation. If body temperature starts to rise, the blood vessels in the skin dilate. As a result, more blood is brought to the surface of the skin for cooling. If the outer temperature cools, the blood vessels constrict, so less blood is brought to the skin's surface.

The sensory receptors—primarily in the dermis—are specialized for touch, pressure, pain, hot, and cold. These receptors supply the central nervous system with information about the external environment. The sensory receptors also account for the use of the skin as a means of communication between people. For example, the touch receptors play a major role in sexual arousal.

The Subcutaneous Layer

Technically speaking, the subcutaneous layer beneath the dermis is not a part of skin. It is a common site for injections, which is why the instrument is called a hypodermic needle. This layer is composed of loose connective tissue and adipose tissue, which stores fat. Fat is a stored source of energy in the body. Adipose tissue helps thermally insulate the body from either gaining heat from the outside or losing heat from the inside. A

Are there side effects of Botox treatments?

Botox is a drug used to reduce the appearance of facial wrinkles and lines. Botox is the registered trade name for a derivative of botulinum toxin A, a protein toxin produced by the bacterium *Clostridium botulinum*. Botox stops communication between motor nerves and muscles, causing muscle paralysis. Treatments are direct injections under the skin, where the toxin causes facial muscle paralysis. The injections reduce the appearance of wrinkles and lines that appear as a result of normal facial muscle movement. However, Botox treatment is not without side effects. Excessive drooling and a slight rash around the injection site are among the milder side effects. Spreading of Botox from the injection site may also paralyze facial muscles unintended for treatment. In a few cases, muscle pain and weakness have resulted. Though rare, more serious side effects, including allergic reactions, may also occur. When performed in a medical facility by a licensed physician, Botox treatment is generally considered safe and effective.

well-developed subcutaneous layer gives the body a rounded appearance and provides protective padding against external assaults. Excessive development of the subcutaneous layer accompanies obesity.

Accessory Organs of the Skin

Nails, hair, and glands are structures of epidermal origin, even though some parts of hair and glands are largely found in the dermis. **Nails** are a protective covering of the distal part of fingers and toes, collectively called *digits* (Fig. 4.12). Nails grow from

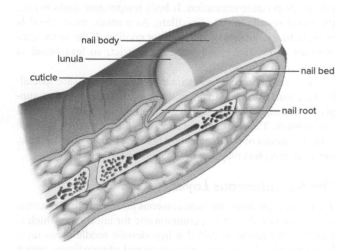

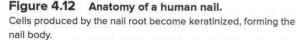

Figure 4.12   Anatomy of a human nail.
Cells produced by the nail root become keratinized, forming the nail body.

epithelial cells at the base of the nail in the portion called the *nail root*. The *cuticle* is a fold of skin that hides the nail root. The whitish color of the half-moon-shaped base, or *lunula,* results from the thick layer of cells in this area. The cells of a nail become keratinized as they grow out over the nail bed.

Hair follicles begin at a bulb in the dermis and continue through the epidermis, where the hair shaft extends beyond the skin (see Fig. 4.9). A dark hair color is largely due to the production of true melanin by melanocytes present in the bulb. If the melanin contains iron and sulfur, hair is blond or red. Graying occurs when melanin cannot be produced, but white hair is due to air trapped in the hair shaft.

Contraction of the *arrector pili muscles* attached to hair follicles causes the hairs to "stand on end" and goosebumps to develop. Epidermal cells form the root of a hair, and their division causes a hair to grow. The cells become keratinized and die as they are pushed farther from the root.

Each hair follicle has one or more **oil glands** (see Fig. 4.9), also called *sebaceous glands,* which secrete sebum. *Sebum* is an oily substance that lubricates the hair in the follicle and the skin. The oil secretions from sebaceous glands are acidic and retard the growth of bacteria. If the sebaceous glands fail to discharge (usually because they are blocked with keratinocytes), the secretions collect and form "whiteheads." Over time, the sebum in a whitehead oxidizes to form a "blackhead." Acne is an inflammation of the sebaceous glands, which most often occurs during adolescence due to hormonal changes.

Sweat glands (see Fig. 4.9), also called *sudoriferous glands,* are numerous and present in all regions of skin. A sweat gland is a tubule that begins in the dermis and either opens into a hair follicle or, more often, opens onto the surface of the skin. Sweat glands play a role in modifying body temperature. When body temperature starts to rise, sweat glands become active. Sweat absorbs body heat as it evaporates. Once the body temperature lowers, sweat glands are no longer active.

CHECK YOUR PROGRESS 4.6

1. Briefly list the functions of the skin.
2. Compare structures and functions of the epidermis and dermis.
3. Explain how each accessory organ of the skin aids in homeostasis.

CONNECTING THE CONCEPTS

For more information on the role of the skin in human physiology, refer to the following discussions:

Section 9.6 provides more information on the relationship between vitamin D and bone calcium homeostasis.

Sections 20.1 and **20.2** explain how cells develop into cancer cells and present some of the different forms of cancer.

Section 23.5 explores the evolutionary reasons for variations in skin color.

BIOLOGY TODAY   **Science**

Face Transplantation

In 2005 a French surgical team led by Professors Bernard Devauchelle and Jean Michel Dubernard was able to perform the world's first partial face transplant. The recipient was a woman, Isabelle Dinoire, severely disfigured by a dog mauling. Muscles, veins, arteries, nerves, and skin were transplanted onto the lower half of Isabelle's face (Fig. 4B, *top left*). The donor's lips, chin, and nose were transplanted. The donor was a brain-dead patient whose family had agreed to donate all their loved one's organs and tissues. The donor shared Isabelle's blood type and was a good tissue match. Eighteen months after the surgery (Fig. 4B, *top right*), Isabelle was able to eat, drink, and smile.

In 2008 a surgical team at Henri-Mondor Hospital in France was able to perform the first full face transplant. The patient, Pascal Coler, suffered from a condition called neurofibromatosis, which caused tumors to grow on his face, producing severe disfiguration.

Patrick Hardison (Fig. 4B, *bottom left* and *right*) was a Mississippi fireman whose injuries occurred when a house fire he was fighting collapsed around him. In 2015, doctors were able to successfully transplant the face of a recently deceased bicycling enthusiast.

Although the ability to do these types of transplant has existed for some time, doctors remain concerned about the ethical aspects of the procedure. Organ transplantation has always involved some moral concerns, because the donor must still be alive when the organs are harvested. Historically, face transplants have been a "quality-of-life" issue and not a "life-or-death" surgery. However, this attitude changed as injured soldiers returning from wars in Afghanistan and Iraq underwent face transplants to treat injuries sustained in combat. Recipients of face transplants must undergo extensive counseling to prepare themselves emotionally for the "new face" and must spend the remainder of their lives on immunosuppressive drugs.

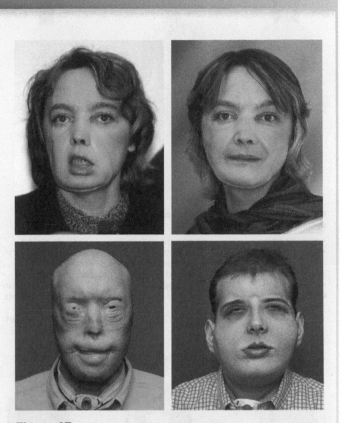

Figure 4B   Face transplant recipients.
Isabelle Dinoire (*top, left* and *right*) and Patrick Hardison (*bottom, left* and *right*) are examples of successful face transplants.
(Isabelle Dinoire): © AFP/Getty Images; (Patrick Hardison): © Cortesia/Notimex/Newscom

Questions to Consider

1. What area of the skin would likely be the hardest for a surgeon to reattach? Why?

2. What functions of the skin might be impaired in the recipient of a face transplant?

4.7 Organ Systems, Body Cavities, and Body Membranes

LEARNING OUTCOMES

Upon completion of this section, you should be able to

1. Summarize the function of each organ system in the human body.
2. Identify the major cavities of the human body.
3. Name the body membranes and provide a function for each.

Recall from our discussion of the skin in Section 4.6 that a group of tissues performing a common function is called an *organ*. Organs with a similar function, in turn, form *organ systems*.

Some of these organ systems, such as the respiratory system, occupy specific cavities of the body, and others, such as the muscular and circulatory systems, are found throughout the body. The organs and cavities of the body are lined with membranes, many of which secrete fluid to aid in the physiology of the organ or organ system.

Organ Systems

Figure 4.13 illustrates the organ systems of the human body. Just as organs work together in an organ system, so do organ systems work together in the body. In some cases it is arbitrary to assign a particular organ to one system when it also assists the functioning of many other systems. In addition, the organs listed in Figure 4.13 represent the major structures in the body. Often, other structures and glands contribute to the operation of the organ system.

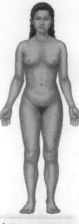
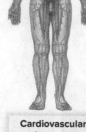
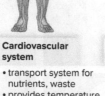

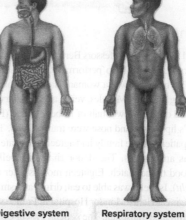
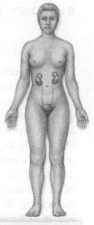

Integumentary system

- protects body
- provides temperature homeostasis
- synthesizes vitamin D
- receives sensory input
Organ: Skin

Cardiovascular system

- transport system for nutrients, waste
- provides temperature, pH, and fluid homeostasis
Organ: Heart

Lymphatic and immune systems

- defends against infectious diseases
- provides fluid homeostasis
- assists in absorption and transport of fats
Organs: Lymphatic vessels, lymph nodes, spleen

Digestive system

- ingests, digests, and processes food
- absorbs nutrients and eliminates waste
- involved in fluid homeostasis
Organs: Oral cavity, esophagus, stomach, small intestine, large intestine, salivary glands, liver, gallbladder, pancreas

Respiratory system

- exchanges gases at both lungs and tissues
- assists in pH homeostasis
Organs: Lungs

Urinary system

- excretes metabolic wastes
- provides pH and fluids homeostasis
Organs: Kidneys, urinary bladder

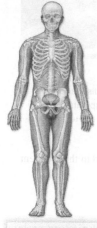

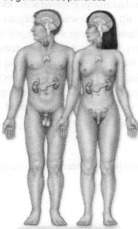

Skeletal system

- provides support and protection
- assists in movement
- stores minerals
- produces blood cells
Organ: Bones

Muscular system

- assists in movement and posture
- produces heat
Organ: Muscles

Nervous system

- receives, processes, and stores sensory input
- provides motor output
- coordinates organ systems
Organs: Brain, spinal cord

Endocrine system

- produces hormones
- coordinates organ systems
- regulates metabolism and stress responses
- involved in fluid and pH homeostasis
Organs: Testes, ovaries, adrenal glands, pancreas, thymus, thyroid, pineal gland

Reproductive system

- produces and transports gametes
- nurtures and gives birth to offspring in females
Organs: Testes, penis, ovaries, uterus, vagina

Figure 4.13   Organ systems of the body.

Body Cavities

The human body is divided into two main cavities: the ventral cavity and the dorsal cavity (Fig. 4.14a). Called the *coelom* in early development, the *ventral cavity* later becomes the thoracic, abdominal, and pelvic cavities. The thoracic cavity contains the lungs and the heart. The thoracic cavity is separated from the abdominal cavity by a horizontal muscle called the *diaphragm*. The stomach, liver, spleen, pancreas, and gallbladder and most of the small and large intestines are in the abdominal cavity. The pelvic cavity contains the rectum, the urinary bladder, the internal reproductive

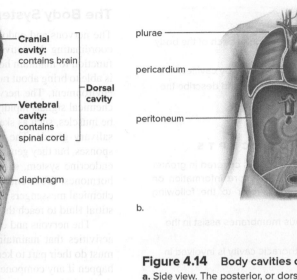

Figure 4.14   Body cavities of humans.
a. Side view. The posterior, or dorsal (toward the back), cavity contains the cranial cavity and the vertebral canal. The brain is in the cranial cavity, and the spinal cord is in the vertebral canal. In the anterior, or ventral (toward the front), cavity, the diaphragm separates the thoracic cavity from the abdominal cavity. The heart and lungs are in the thoracic cavity; the other internal organs are in either the abdominal cavity or the pelvic cavity. **b.** Frontal view of the thoracic cavity, showing serous membranes.

organs, and the rest of the small and large intestines. Males have an external extension of the abdominal wall called the *scrotum,* which contains the testes.

The *dorsal cavity* has two parts: (1) the cranial cavity within the skull contains the brain; (2) the vertebral canal, formed by the vertebrae, contains the spinal cord.

Body Membranes

Body membranes line cavities and the internal spaces of organs and tubes that open to the outside. The body membranes are of four types: mucous, serous, and synovial membranes and the meninges.

Mucous membranes line the tubes of the digestive, respiratory, urinary, and reproductive systems. They are composed of an epithelium overlying a loose fibrous connective tissue layer. The epithelium contains specialized cells that secrete mucus. This mucus ordinarily protects the body from invasion by bacteria and viruses. Hence, more mucus is secreted and expelled when a person has a cold and has to blow his or her nose. In addition, mucus usually protects the walls of the stomach and small intestine from digestive juices. This protection breaks down when a person develops an ulcer.

Serous membranes line and support the lungs, the heart, and the abdominal cavity and its internal organs (Fig. 4.14*b*). They secrete a watery fluid that keeps the membranes lubricated. Serous membranes support the internal organs and compartmentalize the large thoracic and abdominal cavities.

Serous membranes have specific names according to their location. The pleurae (sing., **pleura**) line the thoracic cavity and cover the lungs. The pericardium forms the pericardial sac and

covers the heart. The peritoneum lines the abdominal cavity and covers its organs. A double layer of peritoneum, called mesentery, supports the abdominal organs and attaches them to the abdominal wall. Peritonitis is a life-threatening infection of the peritoneum.

Synovial membranes composed only of loose connective tissue line the cavities of freely movable joints. They secrete synovial fluid into the joint cavity. This fluid lubricates the ends of the bones, so that they can move freely. In rheumatoid arthritis, the synovial membrane becomes inflamed and grows thicker, restricting movement.

The **meninges** (sing., meninx) are membranes within the dorsal cavity. They are composed only of connective tissue and serve as a protective covering for the brain and spinal cord. Meningitis is a life-threatening infection of the meninges.

SCIENCE IN YOUR LIFE

What causes meningitis?

Meningitis is caused by an infection of the meninges by either a virus or a bacterium. Viral meningitis is less severe than bacterial meningitis, which can result in brain damage and death. Bacterial meningitis is usually caused by one of three species of bacteria: *Haemophilus influenzae* type b (Hib), *Streptococcus pneumoniae,* and *Neisseria meningitidis.* Vaccines are available for Hib bacteria and some forms of *S. pneumoniae* and *N. meningitidis.* The Centers for Disease Control and Prevention (CDC) recommends that individuals between the ages of 11 and 18 be vaccinated against bacterial meningitis.

CHECK YOUR PROGRESS 4.7

1. Briefly summarize the overall function of each of the body systems.
2. Describe the location of the two major body cavities.
3. List the four types of body membranes, and describe the structure and function of each.

CONNECTING THE CONCEPTS

Each of the organ systems in this section is covered in greater detail in later chapters of the text. For more information on body cavities and body membranes, refer to the following discussions:

Section 7.3 describes how mucous membranes assist in the immune response of the body.

Section 10.4 illustrates how the thoracic cavity is involved in breathing.

Section 12.4 explains how synovial joints (and their associated membranes) allow movement.

4.8 Homeostasis

LEARNING OUTCOMES

Upon completion of this section, you should be able to

1. Define *homeostasis* and provide an example.
2. Distinguish between positive and negative feedback mechanisms.

Homeostasis is the body's ability to maintain a relative constancy of its internal environment by adjusting its physiological processes. Even though external conditions may change dramatically, we have physiological mechanisms that respond to disturbances and limit the amount of internal change. Conditions usually stay within a narrow range of normalcy. For example, blood glucose, pH levels, and body temperature typically fluctuate during the day, but not greatly. If internal conditions change to any great degree, illness results.

The Internal Environment

The internal environment has two parts: blood and interstitial fluid. Blood delivers oxygen and nutrients to the tissues and carries away carbon dioxide and wastes. Interstitial fluid, not blood, bathes the body's cells. Therefore, interstitial fluid is the medium through which substances are exchanged between cells and blood. Oxygen and nutrients pass through interstitial fluid on their way to tissue cells from the blood. Then carbon dioxide and wastes are carried away from the tissue cells by the interstitial fluid and are brought back into the blood. The cooperation of body systems is required to keep these substances within the range of normalcy in blood and interstitial fluid.

The Body Systems and Homeostasis

The nervous and endocrine systems are particularly important in coordinating the activities of all the other organ systems as they function to maintain homeostasis (Fig. 4.15). The nervous system is able to bring about rapid responses to any changes in the internal environment. The nervous system issues commands by electro-chemical signals rapidly transmitted to effector organs, which can be muscles, such as skeletal muscles, or glands, such as sweat and salivary glands. The endocrine system brings about slower responses, but they generally have more lasting effects. Glands of the endocrine system, such as the pancreas and the thyroid, release hormones. *Hormones,* such as insulin from the pancreas, are chemical messengers that must travel through the blood and interstitial fluid to reach their targets.

The nervous and endocrine systems together direct numerous activities that maintain homeostasis, but all the organ systems must do their part to keep us alive and healthy. Picture what would happen if any component of the cardiovascular, respiratory, digestive, or urinary system failed (Fig. 4.15). If someone is having a heart attack, the heart is unable to pump the blood to supply cells with oxygen. Or think of a person who is choking. The trachea (windpipe) is blocked, so no air can reach the lungs for uptake by the blood; unless the obstruction is removed quickly, cells will begin to die as the blood's supply of oxygen is depleted. When the lining of the digestive tract is damaged, as in a severe bacterial infection, nutrient absorption is impaired and cells face an energy crisis. It is important not only to maintain adequate nutrient levels in the blood but also to eliminate wastes and toxins. The liver makes urea, a nitrogenous end product of protein metabolism. Urea and other metabolic wastes are excreted by the kidneys, the urine-producing organs of the body. The kidneys rid the body of nitrogenous wastes and help adjust the blood's water-salt and acid-base balances.

A closer examination of how the blood glucose level is maintained helps us understand homeostatic mechanisms. When a healthy person consumes a meal and glucose enters the blood, the pancreas secretes the hormone insulin. Then glucose is removed from the blood as cells take it up. In the liver, glucose is stored in the form of glycogen. This storage is beneficial, because later, if blood glucose levels drop, glycogen can be broken down to ensure that the blood level remains constant. Homeostatic mechanisms can fail, however. In diabetes mellitus, the pancreas cannot produce enough insulin or the body cells cannot respond appropriately to it. Therefore, glucose does not enter the cells and they must turn to other molecules, such as fats and proteins, to survive. This, along with too much glucose in the blood, leads to the numerous complications of diabetes mellitus.

Another example of homeostasis is the body's ability to regulate the acid-base balance. When carbon dioxide enters the blood, it combines with water to form carbonic acid. However, the blood is buffered, and pH stays within normal range as long as the lungs are busy excreting carbon dioxide. These two mechanisms are backed up by the kidneys, which can rid the body of a wide range of acidic and basic substances and, therefore, adjust the pH.

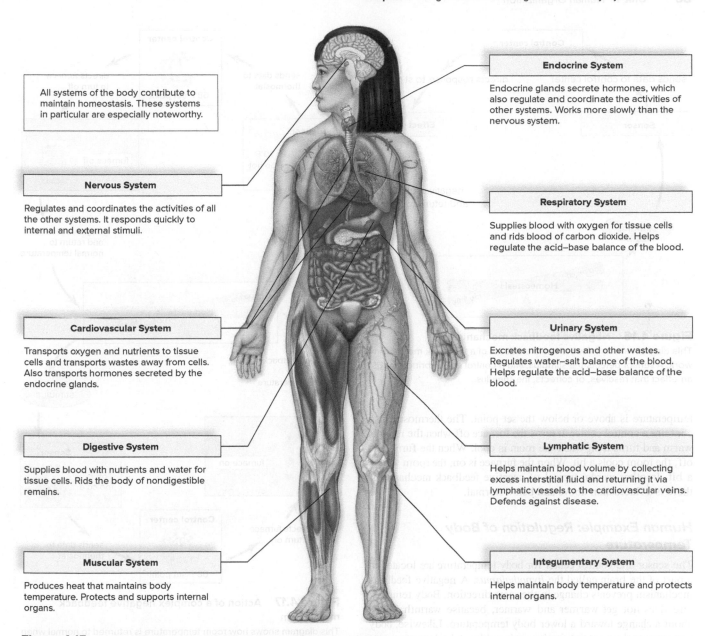

All systems of the body contribute to maintain homeostasis. These systems in particular are especially noteworthy.

Endocrine System

Endocrine glands secrete hormones, which also regulate and coordinate the activities of other systems. Works more slowly than the nervous system.

Nervous System

Regulates and coordinates the activities of all the other systems. It responds quickly to internal and external stimuli.

Respiratory System

Supplies blood with oxygen for tissue cells and rids blood of carbon dioxide. Helps regulate the acid–base balance of the blood.

Cardiovascular System

Transports oxygen and nutrients to tissue cells and transports wastes away from cells. Also transports hormones secreted by the endocrine glands.

Urinary System

Excretes nitrogenous and other wastes. Regulates water–salt balance of the blood. Helps regulate the acid–base balance of the blood.

Digestive System

Supplies blood with nutrients and water for tissue cells. Rids the body of nondigestible remains.

Lymphatic System

Helps maintain blood volume by collecting excess interstitial fluid and returning it via lymphatic vessels to the cardiovascular veins. Defends against disease.

Muscular System

Produces heat that maintains body temperature. Protects and supports internal organs.

Integumentary System

Helps maintain body temperature and protects internal organs.

Figure 4.15   Homeostasis by the organ systems of the human body.
All the organ systems contribute to homeostasis in many ways. Some of the main contributions of each system are given in this illustration.

Negative Feedback

Negative feedback is the primary homeostatic mechanism that keeps a variable, such as blood glucose level, close to a particular value, or set point. A homeostatic mechanism has at least two components: a sensor and a control center (Fig. 4.16). The sensor detects a change in the internal environment. The control center then brings about an effect to bring conditions back to normal. Then the sensor is no longer activated. In other words, a negative feedback mechanism is present when the output of the system resolves or corrects the original stimulus. For example, when blood pressure

rises, sensory receptors signal a control center in the brain. The center stops sending nerve signals to muscle in the arterial walls. The arteries can then relax. Once the blood pressure drops, signals no longer go to the control center.

Mechanical Example

A home heating system is often used to illustrate how a more complicated negative feedback mechanism works (Fig. 4.17). You set the thermostat at 68°F. This is the *set point*. The thermostat contains a thermometer, a sensor that detects when the room

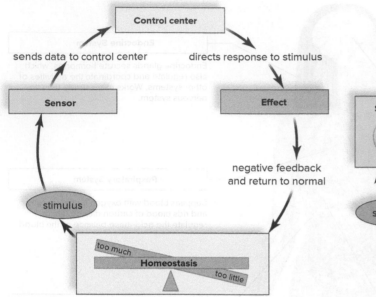

Figure 4.16   Negative feedback mechanisms.
This diagram shows how the basic elements of a feedback mechanism work. A sensor detects the stimulus, and a control center brings about an effect that resolves, or corrects, the stimulus.

temperature is above or below the set point. The thermostat also contains a control center. It turns the furnace off when the room is warm and turns it on when the room is cool. When the furnace is off, the room cools a bit. When the furnace is on, the room warms a bit. In other words, typical of negative feedback mechanisms, there is a fluctuation above and below normal.

Human Example: Regulation of Body Temperature

The sensor and control center for body temperature are located in a part of the brain called the *hypothalamus*. A negative feedback mechanism prevents change in the same direction. Body temperature does not get warmer and warmer, because warmth brings about a change toward a lower body temperature. Likewise, body temperature does not get continuously colder. A body temperature below normal brings about a change toward a warmer body temperature.

Above-Normal Temperature   When the body temperature is above normal, the control center directs the blood vessels of the skin to dilate (Fig. 4.18, *top*). This allows more blood to flow near the surface of the body, where heat can be lost to the environment. In addition, the nervous system activates the sweat glands, and the evaporation of sweat helps lower body temperature. Gradually body temperature decreases to 98.6°F.

Below-Normal Temperature   When the body temperature falls below normal, the control center directs (via nerve impulses) the blood vessels of the skin to constrict (Fig. 4.18, *bottom*). This

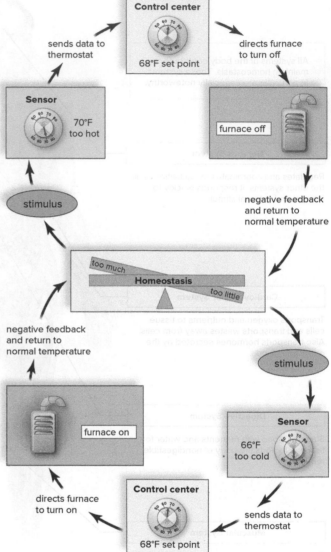

Figure 4.17   Action of a complex negative feedback mechanism.
This diagram shows how room temperature is returned to normal when the room becomes too hot *(top)* or too cold *(bottom)*. The thermostat contains both the sensor and the control center. *Top:* The sensor detects that the room is too hot, and the control center turns the furnace off. The stimulus is resolved, or corrected, when the temperature returns to normal. *Bottom:* The sensor detects that the room is too cold, and the control center turns the furnace on. Once again, the stimulus is resolved, or corrected, when the temperature returns to normal.

conserves heat. If body temperature falls even lower, the control center sends nerve impulses to the skeletal muscles and shivering occurs. Shivering generates heat, and gradually body temperature rises to 98.6°F. When the temperature rises to normal, the control center is inactivated.

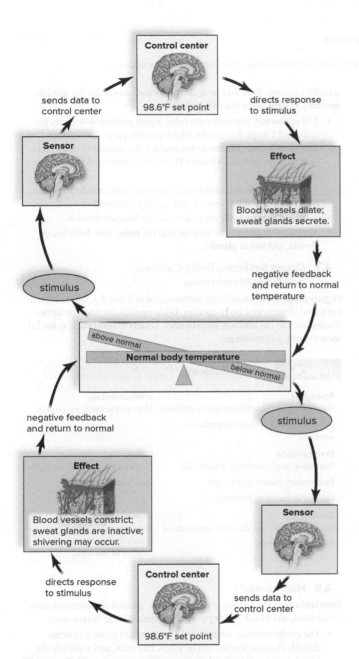

Figure 4.18 Body temperature homeostasis.
Top: When body temperature rises above normal, the hypothalamus senses the change and causes blood vessels to dilate and sweat glands to secrete, so that temperature returns to normal. *Bottom:* When body temperature falls below normal, the hypothalamus senses the change and causes blood vessels to constrict. In addition, shivering may occur to bring temperature back to normal. In this way, the original stimulus is resolved, or corrected.

Positive Feedback

Positive feedback is a mechanism that brings about an increasing change in the same direction. When a woman is giving birth, the head of the baby begins to press against the cervix (entrance to the womb), stimulating sensory receptors there. When nerve signals reach the brain, the brain causes the pituitary gland to secrete the hormone oxytocin. Oxytocin travels in the blood and causes the uterus to contract. As labor continues, the cervix is increasingly stimulated, and uterine contractions become stronger until birth occurs.

A positive feedback mechanism can be harmful, as when a fever causes metabolic changes that push the fever higher. Death occurs at a body temperature of 113°F, because cellular proteins denature at this temperature and metabolism stops. However, positive feedback loops, such as those involved in childbirth, blood clotting, and the stomach's digestion of protein, assist the body in completing a process that has a definite cutoff point.

CHECK YOUR PROGRESS 4.8

1. Define *homeostasis,* and explain why it is important to body function.
2. Summarize how the body systems contribute to homeostasis.

CONNECTING THE CONCEPTS

The maintenance of homeostasis is an important function of all organ systems. For more information on the organ systems, refer to the following discussions:

Section 6.6 describes how the cardiovascular system helps maintain homeostasis.

Section 11.4 explores the role of the urinary system in maintaining homeostasis.

Section 14.2 describes the role of the hypothalamus as part of the central nervous system.

CASE STUDY: CONCLUSION

Skin is a very complex organ, consisting of all four types of tissues. By developing an understanding of how tissues interact to form organs, it is now possible to develop synthetic tissues, such as artificial skin. Though scientists are now expanding these techniques to include the development of artificial dermal tissue, the complexity of the interactions of the various tissues (nervous, muscular, connective) in this layer has presented some obstacles. However, there have been some important advances. Recently, scientists have developed newer forms of artificial skin that release antibiotics directly onto the healing tissue, further protecting the patient against life-threatening infections. Research on artificial tissues is not confined to epithelial tissue. Scientists are exploring the development of artificial cardiac tissue and artificial replacement organs, such as the kidneys, liver, and lungs. Like Kristen's artificial skin, these will not be plastic substitutes but, rather, organic material that integrates with the patient's living cells to replace damaged tissue.

STUDY TOOLS http://connect.mheducation.com

SMARTBOOK® Maximize your study time with McGraw-Hill SmartBook®, the first adaptive textbook.

SUMMARIZE

4.1 Types of Tissues

Tissues are made of specialized cells of the same type that perform a common function. Human tissues are categorized into four groups: connective, muscular, nervous, and epithelial.

4.2 Connective Tissue Connects and Supports

Connective tissues have cells separated by a **matrix** that contains ground substance and fibers. Examples of fibers include **collagen fibers, reticular fibers,** and **elastic fibers.** There are three general classes of connective tissue:

- Fibrous connective tissue contains cells called **fibroblasts.** An example of **loose connective tissue** is **adipose tissue,** which contains cells called **adipocytes. Dense fibrous connective tissue** is found in **tendons** and **ligaments.**
- Supportive connective tissue consists of **cartilage** and bone. The matrix for cartilage is solid yet flexible. The cells are found in chambers called lacunae. Examples are **hyaline cartilage, elastic cartilage,** and **fibrocartilage.** The matrix for bone is solid and rigid. Examples are **compact bone** and **spongy bone.**
- Fluid connective tissue is found in the **blood** and **lymph.** The cells of blood include **red blood cells (erythrocytes), white blood cells (leukocytes),** and **platelets (thrombocytes)** in an **interstitial fluid** called plasma.

4.3 Muscular Tissue Moves the Body

Muscular tissue is of three types: skeletal, smooth, and cardiac.

- **Skeletal muscle** and **cardiac muscle** are **striated.**
- Cardiac and smooth muscle are involuntary.
- Skeletal muscle is found in muscles attached to bones.
- **Smooth muscle** is found in internal organs.
- Cardiac muscle makes up the heart.

4.4 Nervous Tissue Communicates

- **Nervous tissue** is composed of **neurons** and several types of **neuroglia.**
- Each neuron has dendrites, a cell body, and an axon. Axons conduct nerve impulses.
- Neurons may be organized into **nerves,** which are surrounded by connective tissue.

4.5 Epithelial Tissue Protects

Epithelial tissue covers the body and lines its cavities.

- Types of simple epithelia are **squamous, cuboidal, columnar,** and **pseudostratified columnar.**
- Certain epithelial tissues may have cilia or microvilli.
- Stratified epithelia have many layers of cells, with only the bottom layer touching the **basement membrane.**
- Epithelia may be structured as a **gland,** which secretes a product either into ducts (exocrine glands) or into the blood (endocrine glands).

4.6 Integumentary System

Organs comprise two or more tissues working together for a common function. An **organ system** involves multiple organs cooperating for a specific function. **Skin** and its accessory organs constitute the **integumentary system.** Skin has two regions:

- The **epidermis** contains stem cells, which produce new epithelial cells, and **Langerhans cells,** which provide protection against infectious agents. **Melanocytes** produce the coloration of the skin. Within the epidermis, **vitamin D** may be synthesized from cholesterol.
- The **dermis** contains epidermally derived glands and hair follicles, nerve endings, blood vessels, and sensory receptors.
- A **subcutaneous layer** (hypodermis) lies beneath the skin.
- Accessory organs of the skin include the **nails, hair follicles, oil glands,** and **sweat glands.**

4.7 Organ Systems, Body Cavities, and Body Membranes

Organs make up organ systems, summarized in Table 4.1. Some organs are found in particular body cavities. Body cavities are lined by membranes, such as the **mucous membranes, serous membranes, synovial membranes,** and **meninges.**

Table 4.1	Organ Systems
Transport	**Integumentary**
Cardiovascular (heart and blood vessels)	Skin and accessory organs
Lymphatic and immune (lymphatic vessels)	
Maintenance	**Motor**
Digestive (e.g., stomach, intestines)	Skeletal (bones and cartilage)
Respiratory (tubes and lungs)	Muscular (muscles)
Urinary (tubes and kidneys)	
Control	**Reproduction**
Nervous (brain, spinal cord, and nerves)	Reproductive (tubes and testes in males; tubes and ovaries in females)
Endocrine (glands)	

4.8 Homeostasis

Homeostasis is the relative constancy of the internal environment, interstitial fluid, and blood. All organ systems contribute to homeostasis.

- The cardiovascular, respiratory, digestive, and urinary systems directly regulate the amount of gases, nutrients, and wastes in the blood, keeping interstitial fluid constant.
- The lymphatic system absorbs excess interstitial fluid and functions in immunity.
- The nervous system and endocrine system regulate the other systems.

Negative Feedback

Negative feedback mechanisms keep the environment relatively stable. When a sensor detects a change above or below a set point, a control center brings about an effect that reverses the change and returns conditions to normal. Examples include the following:

- Regulation of blood glucose level by insulin
- Regulation of room temperature by a thermostat and furnace
- Regulation of body temperature by the brain and sweat glands

Positive Feedback

In contrast to negative feedback, a **positive feedback** mechanism brings about rapid change in the same direction as the stimulus and does not achieve relative stability. These mechanisms are useful under certain conditions, such as during birth.

ASSESS

TESTING YOURSELF

Choose the best answer for each question.

4.1 Types of Tissues

1. Tissues are formed from _____ and are arranged together to form _____.
   a. organs; organ systems
   b. cells; organs
   c. cells; molecules
   d. molecules; cells

2. This type of tissue is associated with communication.
   a. epithelial tissue
   b. connective tissue
   c. nervous tissue
   d. muscular tissue

4.2 Connective Tissue Connects and Supports

3. Which of the following is found in a connective tissue?
   a. ground substance
   b. protein fibers
   c. specialized cells
   d. All of these are correct.

4. This type of connective tissue contains collagen fibers and is used in areas of the body that undergo compression or need flexibility.
   a. bone
   b. blood
   c. cartilage
   d. adipose tissue

4.3 Muscular Tissue Moves the Body

5. This type of muscle lacks striations.
   a. smooth muscle
   b. skeletal muscle
   c. cardiac muscle
   d. All of these have striations.

6. This form of muscle tissue is under voluntary control in the body.
   a. cardiac muscle
   b. skeletal muscle
   c. smooth muscle
   d. None of these are correct.

4.4 Nervous Tissue Communicates

7. Which of the following form the myelin sheath around nerve fibers outside the brain and spinal cord?
   a. microglia
   b. Schwann cells
   c. neurons
   d. astrocytes

8. These cells support neurons by providing nutrients and growth factors.
   a. oligodendrocytes
   b. Schwann cells
   c. microglia
   d. astrocytes

4.5 Epithelial Tissue Protects

9. Which of these is not a type of epithelial tissue?
   a. simple cuboidal and stratified columnar
   b. bone and cartilage
   c. stratified squamous and simple squamous
   d. pseudostratified and transitional
   e. All of these are epithelial tissues.

10. What type of epithelial tissue is found in the digestive tract to increase the surface area?
   a. cuboidal epithelium
   b. transitional epithelium
   c. columnar epithelium
   d. squamous epithelium

4.6 Integumentary System

11. Which of the following is a function of skin?
   a. temperature regulation
   b. manufacture of vitamin D
   c. protection from invading pathogens
   d. All of these are correct.

12. Keratinization of epithelial cells occurs in which layer of the skin?
   a. subcutaneous layer
   b. dermis
   c. epidermis
   d. All of these are correct.

4.7 Organ Systems, Body Cavities, and Body Membranes

13. Which system helps control pH balance?
   a. digestive
   b. respiratory
   c. urinary
   d. Both b and c are correct.

14. Which type of membrane lines systems that are open to the outside environment, such as the respiratory system?
   a. serous
   b. synoval
   c. mucous
   d. meningeal

4.8 Homeostasis

15. Which of the following allows rapid change in one direction but does not achieve stability?
   a. homeostasis
   b. positive feedback
   c. negative feedback
   d. All of these are correct.

16. Which of the following is an example of negative feedback?
   a. Uterine contractions increase as labor progresses.
   b. Insulin decreases blood sugar levels after a meal is eaten.
   c. Sweating increases as body temperature drops.
   d. Platelets continue to plug an opening in a blood vessel until blood flow stops.

ENGAGE

THINKING CRITICALLY

In the hierarchy of biological organization, you have learned that groups of cells make tissues and two or more tissue types compose an organ. In this chapter, the four types of tissues (connective, muscular, nervous, and epithelial) have been discussed in detail. The skin is an organ system referred to as the integumentary system, containing all four tissue types. In addition to the epidermis and dermis, the integumentary system also includes accessory structures, such as nails, sweat glands, sebaceous glands, and hair follicles. Each of these components of the skin aids in the various functions of the integumentary system. In the case study, Kristen has burns severe enough to need artificial skin treatment. This treatment will help Kristen's skin repair itself while mimicking some of the functions the integumentary system does for homeostasis.

1. The doctor diagnosed Kristen's burns as severe. Which of the following best describes a severe burn versus a superficial burn?
   a. Superficial burns include the epidermis, dermis, and hypodermis layers.
   b. Severe burns include only the layers of the epidermis.
   c. Severe burns include the dermis and anything below it.
   d. Superficial burns occur on the limbs only.

2. What accessory structures and tissues are damaged in a severe burn? Why?

3. What types of functions will the artificial skin perform while Kristen's own skin is repairing itself?

4. What effects can a severe burn have on overall homeostasis of the body? Give a few examples.

5. Which structures in the dermis will have the slowest repair time compared to others? Which might never repair themselves fully? Why?

6. Without the integumentary system, what might happen to the functions of the cardiovascular system? the nervous system?

CHAPTER

17

Reproductive System

CHAPTER CONCEPTS

17.1 Human Life Cycle
The reproductive system produces gametes, each of which has only 23 chromosomes due to meiosis.

17.2 Male Reproductive System
The male reproductive system produces sperm and the male sex hormones.

17.3 Female Reproductive System
In the female, the ovaries produce eggs and the female sex hormones.

17.4 The Ovarian Cycle
The female sex hormones fluctuate in monthly cycles, resulting in ovulation once a month, followed by menstruation if pregnancy does not occur.

17.5 Control of Reproduction
Numerous birth control methods are available for those who wish to prevent pregnancy. Infertile couples may use assisted reproductive technologies to have a child.

17.6 Sexually Transmitted Diseases
Medications have been developed to control AIDS and genital herpes, but these STDs are not curable. STDs caused by bacteria are curable with antibiotic therapy, but resistance is making this increasingly difficult.

BEFORE YOU BEGIN

Before beginning this chapter, take a few moments to review the following discussions.

Section 8.1 What factors contribute to an increased risk of an HIV infection?

Section 16.6 Where is testosterone produced, and what is its function in the male body?

Section 16.6 Where are estrogen and progesterone produced, and what are their functions in the female body?

CASE STUDY: CERVICAL CANCER

Ann had always dreaded her visits to the gynecologist. At each visit her doctor had warned her to quit smoking. However, for the past 20 years she had been a regular smoker, and even though she had cut back considerably in the past few years, she was still smoking around a pack of cigarettes a day. Ann's annual Pap tests had always been normal, so Ann was beginning to view her annual trip to the gynecologist as just a formality. After she turned 40, her visits had become more sporadic, and over the past few years, she had stopped the visits completely.

Until recently, Ann had felt fine. However, a few months ago she had started to experience some abnormal vaginal bleeding, usually shortly after sexual intercourse with her partner. This was often accompanied by small amounts of pain. Concerned about these recent changes, Ann scheduled an appointment with her doctor.

At the appointment, the doctor performed a complete physical exam, which included a Pap test. As the doctor expected, the results of her test were abnormal. Her doctor sent the results to an oncologist, a cancer specialist, who confirmed that Ann's symptoms were being caused by an early stage of cervical cancer. To check the extent of the cancer and to see if it had spread to any additional organs, the oncologist ordered a computed axial tomography (CT) scan of Ann's pelvis and abdomen, as well as a series of blood tests to look for evidence of cancer. Both the CT scan and the blood tests indicated that Ann was lucky—they had caught the cancer at an early stage of development. Her oncologist was convinced that a hysterectomy could be avoided, but Ann would have to immediately begin both chemotherapy and radiation treatment to stop the spread of the cancer.

As you read through the chapter, think about the following questions:

1. What is the role of the cervix in the female reproductive system?
2. What is a Pap test used to detect?
3. What is a hysterectomy?

Unit 5 Reproduction in Humans

C H A P T E R

17

Reproductive System

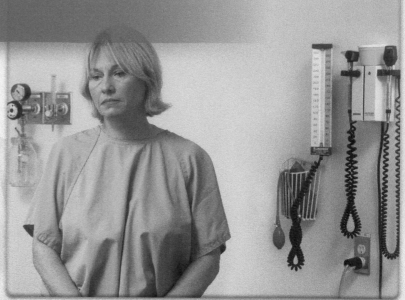

© UpperCut Images/Getty RF

CHAPTER CONCEPTS

17.1 Human Life Cycle
The reproductive system produces gametes, each of which has only 23 chromosomes due to meiosis.

17.2 Male Reproductive System
The male reproductive system produces sperm and the male sex hormones.

17.3 Female Reproductive System
In the female, the ovaries produce eggs and the female sex hormones.

17.4 The Ovarian Cycle
The female sex hormones fluctuate in monthly cycles, resulting in ovulation once a month followed by menstruation if pregnancy does not occur.

17.5 Control of Reproduction
Numerous birth control methods are available for those who wish to prevent pregnancy. Infertile couples may use assisted reproductive technologies to have a child.

17.6 Sexually Transmitted Diseases
Medications have been developed to control AIDS and genital herpes, but these STDs are not curable. STDs caused by bacteria are curable with antibiotic therapy, but resistance is making this increasingly difficult.

BEFORE YOU BEGIN

Before beginning this chapter, take a few moments to review the following discussions:

Section 8.1 What factors contribute to an increased risk of an HIV infection?

Section 16.6 Where is testosterone produced, and what is its function in the male body?

Section 16.6 Where are estrogen and progesterone produced, and what are their functions in the female body?

CASE STUDY: CERVICAL CANCER

Ann had always dreaded her visits to the gynecologist. At each visit her doctor had warned her to quit smoking. However, for the past 20 years she had been a regular smoker, and even though she had cut back considerably in the past few years, she was still smoking around a pack of cigarettes a day. Ann's annual Pap tests had always been normal, so Ann was beginning to view her annual trip to the gynecologist as just a formality. After she turned 40, her visits had become more sporadic; and over the past few years, she had stopped the visits completely.

Until recently, Ann had felt fine. However, a few months ago she had started to experience some abnormal vaginal bleeding, usually shortly after sexual intercourse with her partner. This was often accompanied by small amounts of pain. Concerned about these recent changes, Ann scheduled an appointment with her doctor.

At the appointment the doctor performed a complete physical exam, which included a Pap test. As the doctor expected, the results of her test were abnormal. Her doctor sent the results to an oncologist, a cancer specialist, who confirmed that Ann's symptoms were being caused by an early stage of cervical cancer. To check the extent of the cancer and to see if it had spread to any additional organs, the oncologist ordered a computed axial tomography (CT) scan of Ann's pelvis and abdomen, as well as a series of blood tests to look for evidence of cancer. Both the CT scan and the blood tests indicated that Ann was lucky—they had caught the cancer at an early stage of development. Her oncologist was convinced that a hysterectomy could be avoided, but Ann would have to immediately begin both chemotherapy and radiation treatment to stop the spread of the cancer.

As you read through the chapter, think about the following questions:

1. What is the role of the cervix in the female reproductive system?
2. What is a Pap test used to detect?
3. What is a hysterectomy?

17.1 Human Life Cycle

LEARNING OUTCOMES

Upon completion of this section, you should be able to

1. List the functions of the reproductive system in humans.
2. Describe the human life cycle and explain the role of mitosis and meiosis in this cycle.

Unlike the other systems of the body, the **reproductive system** is quite different in males and females. In both males and females, the reproductive system is responsible for the production of gametes, the cells that combine to form a new individual of the species. In females, the reproductive system has the added function of protecting and nourishing the developing fetus until birth. The reproductive organs, or genitals, have the following functions:

1. Males produce sperm within testes, and females produce eggs within ovaries.
2. Males nurture and transport the sperm in ducts until they exit the penis. Females transport the eggs in uterine tubes to the uterus.
3. The male penis functions to deliver sperm to the female vagina, which receives the sperm. The vagina also transports menstrual fluid to the exterior and acts as the birth canal.
4. The uterus of the female allows the fertilized egg to develop within her body. After birth, the female breast provides nourishment in the form of milk.
5. The testes and ovaries produce the sex hormones. The sex hormones have a profound effect on the body, because they bring about masculinization or feminization of various features. In females, the sex hormones also allow a pregnancy to continue.

Unlike many other animals, humans are not reproductively capable at birth. Instead, they undergo a sequence of events called *puberty,* during which a child becomes a sexually competent young adult. The reproductive system does not begin to fully function until puberty is complete. Sexual maturity typically occurs between the ages of 10 and 14 in girls and 12 and 16 in boys. At the completion of puberty, the individual is capable of producing children.

Mitosis and Meiosis

Before examining the two different forms of cell division that occur during the human life cycle, it is important to recognize that our genetic instructions, or DNA, are distributed among 46 chromosomes within the nucleus. These 46 chromosomes exist in 23 pairs, with each pair containing a contribution from both the male and female parent. Most of the cell types in the body have 46 chromosomes. During the majority of our life cycle, our cells divide by a process called **mitosis** (see Section 19.3). Mitosis is *duplication division,* meaning that each of the cells that exit mitosis has the same complement of 46 chromosomes. In other words, when a cell divides, it produces exact copies of itself by mitosis, much as a copier machine does with a page of notes. In the life cycle of a

human, mitosis is the type of cell division that plays an important role during growth and repair of tissues (Fig. 17.1).

For the purposes of reproduction, special cells in the body undergo a type of cell division called **meiosis.** Meiosis takes place only in the testes of males during the production of sperm and in the ovaries of females during the production of eggs. Meiosis has two functions (see Section 19.4), the first of which is called *reduction division.* During meiosis, the chromosome number is reduced from the normal 46 chromosomes, called the diploid or 2n number, down to 23 chromosomes, called the haploid or n number of chromosomes. This process requires two successive divisions, called meiosis I and meiosis II, and is involved in the formation of **gametes,** or sex cells. As explained in Section 19.4, meiosis also introduces genetic variation, thus ensuring that the new individual is not an exact copy of either parent.

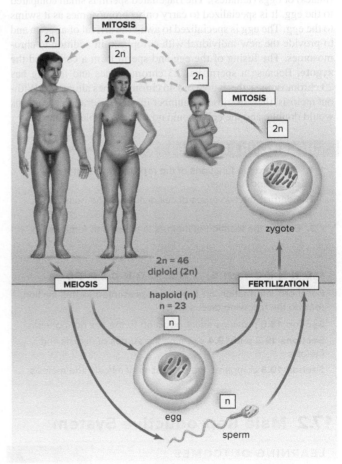

Figure 17.1 The human life cycle.
The human life cycle has two types of cell division: mitosis, in which the chromosome number stays constant, and meiosis, in which the chromosome number is reduced. During growth or cell repair, mitosis ensures that each new cell has 46 chromosomes. During production of sex cells, the chromosome number is reduced from 46 to 23. Therefore, an egg and a sperm each have 23 chromosomes, so that when the sperm fertilizes the egg, the new cell, called a zygote, has 46 chromosomes.

SCIENCE IN YOUR LIFE

What types of cells do not have 46 chromosomes?

In humans, the cell types that do not have the standard 23 pairs of chromosomes are the red blood cells and the cells of the liver. Recall from Section 6.2 that red blood cells lack a nucleus; therefore, they do not have any chromosomes. Cells in the liver, called hepatocytes, typically have more than three copies of each chromosome (giving them 69 or more chromosomes). This condition is called polyploidy, and it is believed to provide the liver with its ability to degrade toxic compounds.

Table 17.1	Male Reproductive Organs
Organ	**Function**
Testes	Produce sperm and sex hormones
Epididymides	Ducts where sperm mature and some sperm are stored
Vasa deferentia	Conduct and store sperm
Seminal vesicles	Contribute nutrients and fluid to semen
Prostate gland	Contributes fluid to semen
Urethra	Conducts sperm
Bulbourethral glands	Contribute mucus-containing fluid to semen
Penis	Organ of sexual intercourse

Following meiosis, the haploid cells develop into either sperm (males) or eggs (females). The flagellated sperm is small compared to the egg. It is specialized to carry only chromosomes as it swims to the egg. The egg is specialized to await the arrival of a sperm and to provide the new individual with cytoplasm in addition to chromosomes. The fusing of the egg and sperm form a cell called the **zygote.** Because a sperm has 23 chromosomes and the egg has 23 chromosomes, the zygote has 46 chromosomes altogether. Without meiosis, the chromosome number in each generation of humans would double, and the cells would no longer be able to function.

CHECK YOUR PROGRESS 17.1

1. Compare the functions of the reproductive system in males and females.
2. Contrast the two types of cell division in the human life cycle.
3. Explain the location of meiosis in males and females.

CONNECTING THE CONCEPTS

For more information on the topics presented in this section, refer to the following discussions:

Section 16.6 provides an introduction to the sex hormones.

Sections 19.3 and **19.4** examine the stages of mitosis and meiosis.

Section 19.5 compares the processes of mitosis and meiosis.

17.2 Male Reproductive System

LEARNING OUTCOMES

Upon completion of this section, you should be able to

1. Identify the structures of the male reproductive system and provide a function for each.
2. Describe the location and stages of spermatogenesis.
3. Summarize how hormones regulate the male reproductive system.

The male reproductive system includes the organs listed in Table 17.1 and shown in Figure 17.2. The male gonads, or primary sex organs, are paired **testes** (sing., testis), suspended within the sacs of the **scrotum.**

Sperm produced by the testes mature within the **epididymis** (pl., epididymides), a tightly coiled duct lying just outside each testis. Maturation seems to be required for sperm to swim to the egg. When sperm leave an epididymis, they enter a **vas deferens** (pl., vasa deferentia), also called the ductus deferens. The sperm may be stored for a time in the vas deferens. Each vas deferens passes into the abdominal cavity, where it curves around the bladder and empties into an ejaculatory duct. The ejaculatory ducts enter the **urethra.**

At the time of ejaculation, sperm leave the penis in a fluid called **semen.** The seminal vesicles, the prostate gland, and the bulbourethral glands add secretions to seminal fluid. A pair of **seminal vesicles** lie at the base of the bladder, and each has a duct that joins with a vas deferens. The **prostate gland** is a single, doughnut-shaped gland that surrounds the upper portion of the urethra just below the bladder. In older men, the prostate can enlarge and squeeze off the urethra, making urination painful and difficult. This condition is discussed in more detail in the Health feature "Urinary Difficulties Due to an Enlarged Prostate" in Section 11.5. **Bulbourethral glands** (also called Cowper's glands) are pea-sized organs that lie posterior to the prostate on either side of the urethra. Their secretion makes the seminal fluid gelatinous.

Each component of seminal fluid has a particular function. Sperm are more viable in a basic solution; seminal fluid, milky in appearance, has a slightly basic pH (about 7.5). Swimming sperm require energy; seminal fluid contains the sugar fructose, which serves as an energy source. Semen also contains prostaglandins, chemicals that cause the uterus to contract. These contractions help propel the sperm toward the egg.

The Penis and Male Orgasm

The **penis** (Fig. 17.3) is the male organ of sexual intercourse. It also contains the urethra of the urinary system. The penis has a long shaft and an enlarged tip called the glans penis. The layer of skin covering the glans penis, called the foreskin, may be removed surgically by **circumcision** shortly after birth (see the Health feature "Male and Female Circumcision" in Section 17.3).

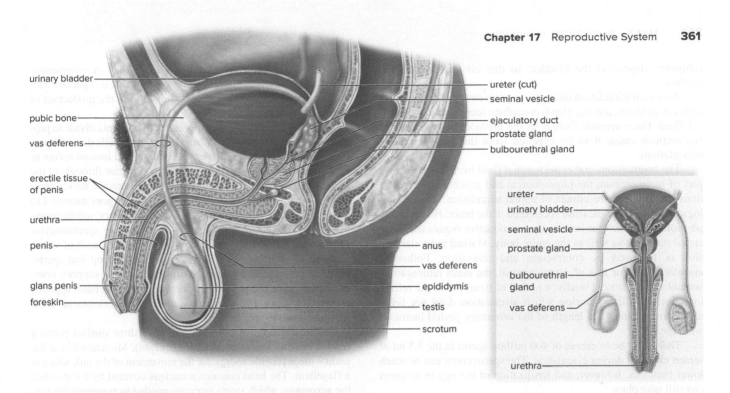

urinary bladder

pubic bone

vas deferens

erectile tissue
of penis

urethra

penis

glans penis

foreskin

ureter (cut)

seminal vesicle

ejaculatory duct

prostate gland

bulbourethral gland

anus

vas deferens

epididymis

testis

scrotum

ureter

urinary bladder

seminal vesicle

prostate gland

bulbourethral
gland

vas deferens

urethra

Figure 17.2   The male reproductive system.
The testes produce sperm. The seminal vesicles, the prostate gland, and the bulbourethral glands provide a fluid medium for the sperm, which move from the vas deferens through the ejaculatory duct to the urethra in the penis. The foreskin (prepuce) is removed when a penis is circumcised.

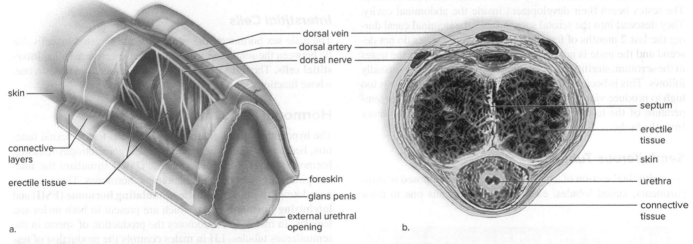

dorsal vein

dorsal artery

dorsal nerve

skin

connective
layers

erectile tissue

foreskin

glans penis

external urethral
opening

a.

septum

erectile
tissue

skin

urethra

connective
tissue

b.

Figure 17.3   The structure of the penis.
a. The shaft of the penis ends in an enlarged tip called the glans penis. In uncircumcised males, this is partially covered by a foreskin (prepuce).
b. Micrograph of shaft in cross section showing location of erectile tissue.
(b) © Anatomical Travelogue/Science Source

Spongy, erectile tissue containing distensible blood spaces extends through the shaft of the penis. During sexual arousal, autonomic nerves release nitric oxide (NO). This stimulus leads to the production of cGMP (cyclic guanosine monophosphate), a high-energy compound similar to ATP. The cGMP causes the smooth muscle of incoming arterial walls to relax and the erectile tissue to fill with blood. The veins that take blood away from the penis are compressed, and the penis becomes erect. **Erectile**

dysfunction (ED) (formerly called *impotency*) is the inability to achieve or maintain an erection suitable for sexual intercourse. ED may be caused by a number of factors, including poor blood flow, certain medications, and many illnesses. Medications for the treatment of erectile dysfunction inhibit the enzyme that breaks down cGMP, ensuring that a full erection will take place. Some of these medications can cause vision problems, because the same enzyme occurs in the retina. During an erection, a sphincter closes off the bladder, so that no urine enters the urethra.

As sexual stimulation intensifies, sperm enter the urethra from each vas deferens, and the glands contribute secretions to the seminal fluid. Once seminal fluid is in the urethra, rhythmic muscle contractions cause it to be expelled from the penis in spurts (ejaculation).

The contractions that expel seminal fluid from the penis are a part of male orgasm, the physiological and psychological sensations that occur at the climax of sexual stimulation. The psychological sensation of pleasure is centered in the brain. However, the physiological reactions involve the reproductive organs and associated muscles, as well as the entire body. Marked muscular tension is followed by contraction and relaxation. Following ejaculation and/or loss of sexual arousal, the penis returns to its normal flaccid state. Usually, a period of time, called the refractory period, follows during which stimulation does not bring about an erection. The length of the refractory period increases with age.

There may be in excess of 400 million sperm in the 3.5 ml of semen expelled during ejaculation. The sperm count can be much lower than this, however, and fertilization of the egg by a sperm can still take place.

Male Gonads: The Testes

The testes, which produce sperm as well as the male sex hormones, lie outside the abdominal cavity of the male, within the scrotum. The testes begin their development inside the abdominal cavity. They descend into the scrotal sacs through the inguinal canal during the last 2 months of fetal development. If the testes do not descend and the male is not treated or operated on to place the testes in the scrotum, sterility (the inability to produce offspring), usually follows. This is because the internal temperature of the body is too high to produce viable sperm. The scrotum helps regulate the temperature of the testes by holding them closer to or farther away from the body.

Seminiferous Tubules

A longitudinal section of a testis shows that it is composed of compartments, called lobules, each of which contains one to three

Boxers or briefs?

The scrotum's role in male physiology is to keep the temperature of the testes lower than body temperature. The lower temperature is necessary for normal sperm production. It might follow that the man's type of underwear can change that temperature, affecting sperm production. However, research has not supported this assumption. The style of underwear worn by a man, loose or close fitting, has not been shown to affect sperm count or fertility significantly.

tightly coiled **seminiferous tubules** (Fig. 17.4a). A microscopic cross section of a seminiferous tubule reveals that it is packed with cells undergoing **spermatogenesis** (Fig. 17.4b), the production of sperm.

During the production of sperm, spermatogonia divide to produce primary spermatocytes (2n). One of these cells does not proceed with the remainder of spermatogenesis and instead serves as a stem cell, allowing spermatogenesis to continue throughout the lifetime of the male. The other primary spermatocyte moves away from the outer wall, increases in size, and undergoes meiosis I to produce secondary spermatocytes. Each secondary spermatocyte has only 23 chromosomes (Fig. 17.4c). Secondary spermatocytes (n) undergo meiosis II to produce four spermatids, each of which also has 23 chromosomes. Spermatids then develop into sperm. Note the presence of **Sertoli cells** (purple), which support, nourish, and regulate the process of spermatogenesis. It takes approximately 74 days for sperm to undergo development from spermatogonia to sperm.

Mature **sperm,** or spermatozoa, have three distinct parts: a head, a middle piece, and a tail (Fig. 17.4d). Mitochondria in the middle piece provide energy for the movement of the tail, which is a flagellum. The head contains a nucleus covered by a cap called the **acrosome,** which stores enzymes needed to penetrate the egg. The ejaculated semen of a normal human male contains several hundred million sperm, but only one sperm normally enters an egg. Sperm usually do not live more than 48 hours in the female genital tract.

Interstitial Cells

The male sex hormones, the androgens, are secreted by cells that lie between the seminiferous tubules. These cells are called **interstitial cells.** The most important of the androgens is testosterone, whose functions are discussed next.

Hormonal Regulation in Males

The hypothalamus has ultimate control of the testes' sexual function, because it secretes a hormone called gonadotropin-releasing hormone (GnRH) (see Section 16.2). GnRH stimulates the anterior pituitary to secrete the gonadotropic hormones. There are two gonadotropic hormones, **follicle-stimulating hormone (FSH)** and **luteinizing hormone (LH),** which are present in both males and females. In males, FSH promotes the production of sperm in the seminiferous tubules. LH in males controls the production of testosterone by the interstitial cells.

All these hormones are involved in a negative feedback relationship that maintains the fairly constant production of sperm and testosterone (Fig. 17.5). When the amount of testosterone in the blood rises to a certain level, it causes the hypothalamus and anterior pituitary to decrease their respective secretion of GnRH and LH. As the level of testosterone begins to fall, the hypothalamus increases its secretion of GnRH and the anterior pituitary increases its secretion of LH. These stimulate the interstitial cells to produce testosterone. A similar feedback mechanism maintains the continuous production of sperm. The Sertoli cells in the wall

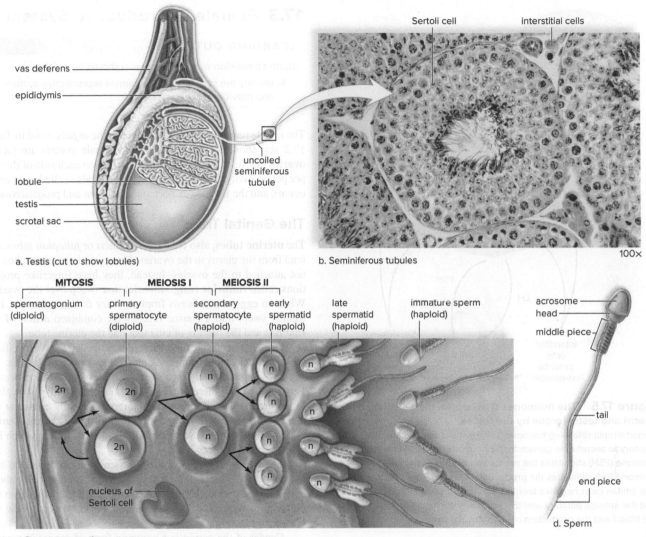

Figure 17.4   Spermatogenesis produces sperm cells.
a. The lobules of a testis contain seminiferous tubules. **b.** Electron micrograph of a cross section of the seminiferous tubules, where spermatogenesis occurs. Note the location of interstitial cells in clumps among the seminiferous tubules. **c.** Diagrammatic representation of spermatogenesis, which occurs in wall of tubules. **d.** A sperm has a head, a middle piece, and a tail. The nucleus is in the head, capped by the enzyme-containing acrosome.
(b) © Ed Reschke

of the seminiferous tubules produce a hormone called *inhibin* that blocks GnRH and FSH secretion when appropriate (Fig. 17.5).

Testosterone, the main sex hormone in males, is essential for the normal development and functioning of the organs listed in Table 17.1. Testosterone also brings about and maintains the male secondary sex characteristics that develop at the time of puberty. Males are generally taller than females and have broader shoulders and longer legs relative to trunk length. The deeper voices of males compared with those of females are due to a larger larynx with longer vocal cords. The Adam's apple, part of the larynx, is usually more prominent in males

than in females. Testosterone causes males to develop noticeable hair on the face, the chest, and occasionally other regions of the body, such as the back. A related chemical also leads to the receding hairline and male-pattern baldness that occur in males.

Testosterone is responsible for the greater muscular development in males. Knowing this, both males and females sometimes take anabolic steroids, either testosterone or related steroid hormones resembling testosterone. Health problems involving the kidneys, the cardiovascular system, and hormonal imbalances can arise from such use.

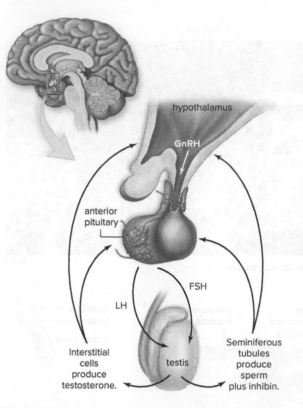

Figure 17.5   **The hormones that control the production of sperm and testosterone by the testes.**
Gonadotropin-releasing hormone (GnRH) stimulates the anterior pituitary to secrete the gonadotropic hormones: Follicle-stimulating hormone (FSH) stimulates the production of sperm, and luteinizing hormone (LH) stimulates the production of testosterone. Testosterone and inhibin exert negative feedback control over the hypothalamus and the anterior pituitary, and this regulates the level of testosterone in the blood and the production of sperm by the testes.

CHECK YOUR PROGRESS 17.2

1. List the structures of the male reproductive system, and then trace the movement of sperm through the system.
2. Describe the process of spermatogenesis.
3. Explain the importance of testosterone to the male reproductive system.

CONNECTING THE CONCEPTS

For more information on the topics presented in this section, refer to the following discussions:

Figure 2.20 provides the chemical structure of testosterone.

Section 16.6 provides additional information on the male sex hormones.

Section 19.4 examines how meiosis reduces the chromosome number during spermatogenesis.

17.3 Female Reproductive System

LEARNING OUTCOME

Upon completion of this section, you should be able to

1. Identify the structures of the female reproductive system and provide a function for each.

The female reproductive system includes the organs listed in Table 17.2 and shown in Figure 17.6. The female gonads are paired **ovaries** that lie in shallow depressions, one on each side of the upper pelvic cavity. The ovaries produce **eggs**, also called *ova* (sing., ovum), and the female sex hormones estrogen and progesterone.

The Genital Tract

The **uterine tubes,** also called the *oviducts* or *fallopian tubes,* extend from the uterus to the ovaries. However, the uterine tubes are not attached to the ovaries. Instead, they have fingerlike projections called **fimbriae** (sing., fimbria) that sweep over the ovaries. When an egg (ovum) bursts from an ovary during ovulation, it is usually swept into a uterine tube by the combined action of the fimbriae and the beating of cilia that line the uterine tube.

Once in the uterine tube, the egg is propelled slowly by ciliary movement and tubular muscle contraction toward the uterus. An egg lives approximately 6 to 24 hours, unless fertilization occurs. Fertilization, and therefore zygote formation, usually takes place in the uterine tube. A developing embryo normally arrives at the uterus after several days, and then **implantation** occurs. During implantation, the embryo embeds in the uterine lining, which has been prepared to receive it.

The **uterus** is a thick-walled, muscular organ about the size and shape of an inverted pear (Fig. 17.6). Normally, it lies above and is tipped over the urinary bladder. The uterine tubes join the uterus at its upper end; at its lower end, the **cervix** enters the vagina nearly at a right angle.

Cancer of the cervix is a common form of cancer in women (see the chapter opener). Early detection is possible by means of a **Pap test,** which requires the removal of a few cells from the region of the cervix for microscopic examination. If the cells are cancerous, a physician may recommend a *hysterectomy*. A hysterectomy is the removal of the uterus, including the cervix. Removal of the ovaries in addition to the uterus is termed an *ovariohysterectomy*

Table 17.2	Female Reproductive Organs
Organ	**Function**
Ovaries	Produce eggs and sex hormones
Uterine tubes	Conduct eggs; location of fertilization
Uterus	Houses developing fetus
Cervix	Contains opening to uterus
Vagina	Receives penis during sexual intercourse; serves as birth canal and as an exit for menstrual flow

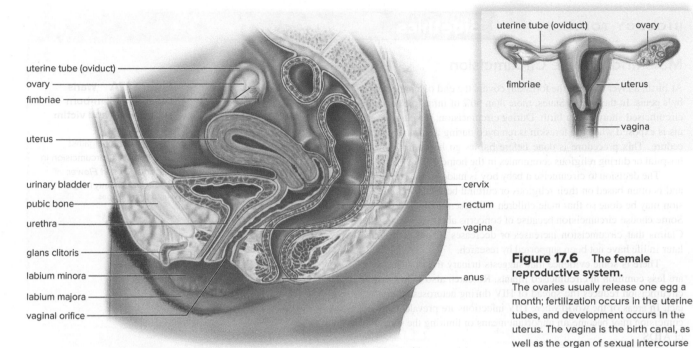

uterine tube (oviduct)
ovary
fimbriae
uterus

urinary bladder
pubic bone
urethra

glans clitoris

labium minora

labium majora

vaginal orifice

cervix

rectum

vagina

anus

Figure 17.6 **The female reproductive system.**
The ovaries usually release one egg a month; fertilization occurs in the uterine tubes, and development occurs in the uterus. The vagina is the birth canal, as well as the organ of sexual intercourse and the outlet for menstrual flow.

(radical hysterectomy). The vagina remains, so the woman can still engage in sexual intercourse.

Development of the embryo and fetus normally takes place in the uterus. This organ, sometimes called the womb, is approximately 5 cm wide in its usual state. It is capable of stretching to over 30 cm wide to accommodate a growing fetus. The lining of the uterus, called the **endometrium,** participates in the formation of the placenta (see Section 17.4). The endometrium supplies nutrients needed for embryonic and fetal development. The endometrium has two layers: a functional layer that is shed during each menstrual period and a basal layer of reproducing cells. In the nonpregnant female, the functional layer of the endometrium varies in thickness according to a monthly reproductive cycle called the uterine cycle.

A small opening in the cervix leads to the vaginal canal. The **vagina** is a tube that lies at a 45° angle to the small of the back. The mucosal lining of the vagina lies in folds and can extend. This is especially important when the vagina serves as the birth canal, and it facilitates sexual intercourse when the vagina receives the penis. The vagina also acts as an exit for menstrual flow. Several different types of bacteria normally reside in the vagina and create an acidic environment. While this environment is protective against the possible growth of pathogenic bacteria, sperm prefer the basic environment provided by seminal fluid.

External Genitals

The external genital organs of the female are known collectively as the **vulva** (Fig. 17.7). The vulva includes two large, hair-covered folds of skin called the labia majora. The labia majora extend backward from the mons pubis, a fatty prominence underlying the pubic hair. The labia minora are two small folds lying just inside the labia majora. They extend forward from the vaginal opening to encircle and form a foreskin for the glans clitoris. The glans clitoris is the organ of sexual arousal in females and, like the penis, contains a shaft of erectile tissue that becomes engorged with blood during sexual stimulation. As discussed in the Bioethics feature "Male and Female Circumcision," some cultures practice a form of circumcision that removes the external genitalia of the female.

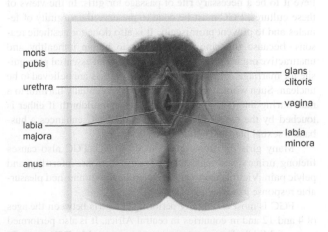

mons pubis

urethra

labia majora

anus

glans clitoris

vagina

labia minora

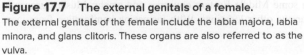

Figure 17.7 **The external genitals of a female.**
The external genitals of the female include the labia majora, labia minora, and glans clitoris. These organs are also referred to as the vulva.

BIOLOGY TODAY   **Bioethics**

Male and Female Circumcision

At birth, a layer of skin (the foreskin) covers the end of a male baby's penis. In the United States, more than 50% of infant males are circumcised shortly after birth. During circumcision, the glans penis is exposed when the foreskin is removed during a surgical procedure. This procedure is done before babies go home from the hospital or during religious ceremonies in the home.

The decision to circumcise a baby boy is made by the parents and is often based on their religious or cultural beliefs. Circumcision may be done so that male children will resemble their father. Some choose circumcision because of concerns about cleanliness. Claims that circumcision increases or decreases sexual pleasure later in life have not been supported by research.

There is some evidence that suggests urinary tract infections are less common in circumcised infants. Research also shows that circumcision reduces the spread of HIV during heterosexual contact. In areas of the world where HIV infections are prevalent, circumcision may become an important means of limiting the spread of AIDS.

As with any type of surgery, there are risks associated with circumcision. The most common complications are minor bleeding and localized infections that can be treated easily. One of the biggest concerns is the pain experienced by the baby during circumcision. The American Academy of Pediatrics (AAP) now recommends using a form of local anesthesia during the procedure. The AAP does not recommend or argue against circumcision of male babies.

However, the circumcision of females is a highly controversial topic. Female circumcision (also referred to as female genital cutting [FGC] or female genital mutilation) is done strictly for cultural or religious reasons, though no religion specifically calls for its practice. The procedure involves partially or totally cutting away the external genitalia of a female. Cultures that practice FGC believe it to be a necessary rite of passage for girls. In the views of these cultures, FGC must be done to preserve the virginity of females and to prevent promiscuity. It is also done for aesthetic reasons, because the clitoris is thought to be an unhealthy and unattractive organ. Moreover, FGC is seen as an essential prerequisite for marriage. Females with an intact clitoris are believed to be unclean. Such women are considered to be potentially harmful to a man during intercourse or to a baby during childbirth if either is touched by the clitoris. Many believe that FGC enhances a husband's sexual pleasure and a woman's fertility.

Many girls die from infection after FGC. FGC also causes lifelong urinary and reproductive tract infections, infertility, and pelvic pain. Victims report an absent or greatly diminished pleasurable response to sexual intercourse.

FGC is most commonly performed on girls between the ages of 4 and 12 and in countries in central Africa. It is also performed in some Middle Eastern countries and among Muslim groups in various other locations. With increasing immigration from these

Figure 17A   Waris Dirie, Somalian-born supermodel and victim of FGC.
Dirie advocates against female genital circumcision in her book *Desert Flower.*
© Sean Gallup/Getty Images News/Getty Images

countries, there are also greater numbers of women who have been subjected to FGC. Likewise, there are more girls in the United States who are at risk for FGC.

Thanks to the efforts of mutilation victim Waris Dirie (Fig. 17A) and others like her, the need to eliminate FGC is now discussed openly, and action is being taken in many countries to outlaw the practice. FGC is considered to be a violation of human rights by the United Nations, UNICEF, and the World Health Organization. It is illegal to perform FGC in many African and Middle Eastern countries, but the practice continues, because the laws are not enforced. In the United States, FGC is a criminal practice. In 1996, the United States granted asylum to a woman from Togo, who was trying to escape an arranged marriage and the FGC that would accompany it. Unfortunately, many immigrants to the United States continue the practice of FGC by sending their daughters abroad for the procedure or by importing someone to perform it. A number of educational approaches to eliminate FGC have been tried. These include community education that teaches about the harm done by FGC and the substitution of alternative rituals for the rite of passage to womanhood. Education may do even more to halt FGC, because more highly educated women are less likely to support having their daughters mutilated in this fashion.

Questions to Consider

1. In your view, is male circumcision unjustifiable? Why or why not?
2. Should families who accept the idea of FGC be allowed to immigrate?
3. How should the United States prosecute parents who have subjected their daughters to FGC?

The cleft between the labia minora contains the openings of the urethra and the vagina. The vagina may be partially closed by a ring of tissue called the hymen. The hymen is ordinarily ruptured by sexual intercourse or by other types of physical activities. If remnants of the hymen persist after sexual intercourse, they can be surgically removed.

The urinary and reproductive systems in the female are entirely separate. For example, the urethra carries only urine, and the vagina serves only as the birth canal and the organ for sexual intercourse.

Orgasm in Females

Upon sexual stimulation, the labia minora, the vaginal wall, and the clitoris become engorged with blood. The breasts also swell, and the nipples become erect. The labia majora enlarge, redden, and spread away from the vaginal opening.

The vagina expands and elongates. Blood vessels in the vaginal wall release small droplets of fluid that seep into the vagina and lubricate it. Mucus-secreting glands beneath the labia minora on either side of the vagina also provide lubrication for entry of the penis into the vagina. Although the vagina is the organ of sexual intercourse in females, the clitoris plays a significant role in the female sexual response. The extremely sensitive clitoris can swell to two or three times its usual size. The thrusting of the penis and the pressure of the pubic symphyses of the partners stimulate the clitoris.

Orgasm occurs at the height of the sexual response. Blood pressure and pulse rate rise, breathing quickens, and the walls of the uterus and uterine tubes contract rhythmically. A sensation of intense pleasure is followed by relaxation when organs return to their normal size. Females have no refractory period, and multiple orgasms can occur during a single sexual experience.

CHECK YOUR PROGRESS 17.3

1. Distinguish the structures of the female reproductive system that (a) produce the egg, (b) transport the egg, (c) house a developing embryo, and (d) serve as the birth canal.

2. Explain the purpose of the vagina and uterus in the female reproductive system.

3. Discuss why the urinary and reproductive systems are separate in a female.

CONNECTING THE CONCEPTS

For more information on the topics presented in this section, refer to the following discussions:

Section 18.1 outlines the steps in the fertilization of an egg by a sperm cell.

Section 18.2 examines the stages of fetal development in the uterus.

Sections 20.1 and **20.2** examine the characteristics of cancer cells and the causes of cancer.

17.4 The Ovarian Cycle

LEARNING OUTCOMES

Upon completion of this section, you should be able to

1. List the stages of the ovarian cycle and explain what is occurring in each stage.
2. Describe the process of oogenesis.
3. Summarize how estrogen and progesterone influence the ovarian cycle.

Hormone levels cycle in the female on a monthly basis, and the ovarian cycle drives the uterine cycle, as discussed in this section.

Ovarian Cycle: Nonpregnant

An ovary contains many **follicles,** and each one contains an immature egg called an oocyte. A female is born with as many as 2 million follicles, but the number has reduced to 300,000 to 400,000 by the time of puberty. Only a small number of follicles (about 400) ever mature, because a female usually produces only one egg per month during her reproductive years. As the follicle matures during the **ovarian cycle,** it changes from a primary to a secondary to a vesicular (Graafian) follicle (Fig. 17.8). Epithelial cells of a primary follicle surround a primary oocyte. Pools of follicular fluid bathe the oocyte in a secondary follicle. In a vesicular follicle, the fluid-filled cavity increases to the point that the follicle wall balloons out on the surface of the ovary.

Figure 17.9 traces the steps of **oogenesis.** A primary oocyte undergoes meiosis I, and the resulting cells are haploid with 23 chromosomes each. One of these cells is called a **polar body.** A polar body is a sort of cellular "trash can," because its function is simply to hold discarded chromosomes. The secondary oocyte undergoes meiosis II, but only if it is first fertilized by a sperm cell. If the secondary oocyte remains unfertilized, it never completes meiosis and will die shortly after being released from the ovary.

When appropriate, the vesicular follicle bursts, releasing the oocyte (often called an egg) surrounded by a clear membrane. This process is referred to as **ovulation.** Once a vesicular follicle has lost the oocyte, it develops into a **corpus luteum,** a glandlike structure. If the egg is not fertilized, the corpus luteum disintegrates.

As we discussed in Section 17.3, the ovaries produce eggs and the female sex hormones estrogen and progesterone. A primary follicle produces estrogen, and a secondary follicle produces estrogen and some progesterone. The corpus luteum produces progesterone and some estrogen.

Phases of the Ovarian Cycle

Similar to the testes, the hypothalamus has ultimate control of the ovaries' sexual function, because it secretes gonadotropin-releasing hormone, or GnRH. GnRH stimulates the anterior pituitary to produce FSH and LH, and these hormones control the ovarian cycle. The gonadotropic hormones are not present in constant amounts. Instead they are secreted at different rates during the cycle. For simplicity's sake, it is convenient to emphasize that during the first half,

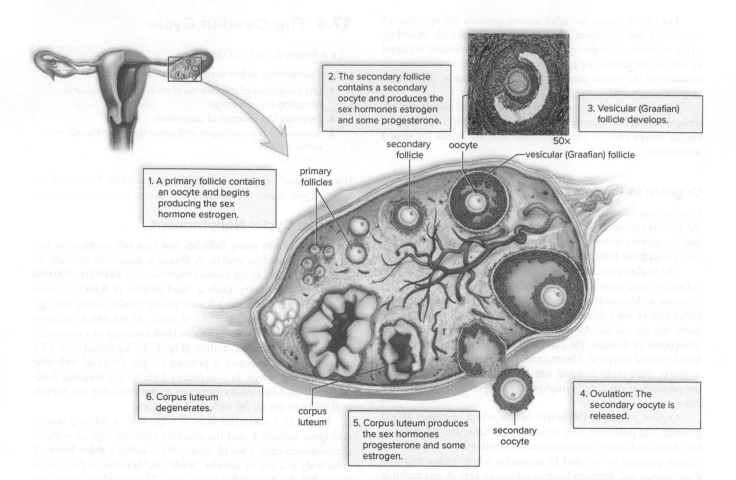

2. The secondary follicle contains a secondary oocyte and produces the sex hormones estrogen and some progesterone.

3. Vesicular (Graafian) follicle develops.

secondary follicle

oocyte

vesicular (Graafian) follicle

50x

primary follicles

1. A primary follicle contains an oocyte and begins producing the sex hormone estrogen.

6. Corpus luteum degenerates.

corpus luteum

5. Corpus luteum produces the sex hormones progesterone and some estrogen.

secondary oocyte

4. Ovulation: The secondary oocyte is released.

Figure 17.8 **The ovarian cycle.**
A single follicle goes through all stages (1–6) in one place in the ovary. As the follicle matures, layers of follicle cells surround a secondary oocyte. Eventually, the mature follicle ruptures, and the secondary oocyte is released. The follicle then becomes the corpus luteum, which eventually disintegrates.

© Ed Reschke

Figure 17.9 **Oogenesis produces egg cells.**
During oogenesis, the chromosome number is reduced from 46 to 23. Oogenesis produces a functional egg cell and nonfunctional polar bodies.

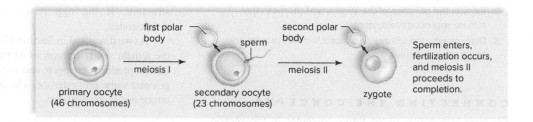

first polar body

second polar body

sperm

primary oocyte (46 chromosomes)

meiosis I

secondary oocyte (23 chromosomes)

meiosis II

zygote

Sperm enters, fertilization occurs, and meiosis II proceeds to completion.

or *follicular phase,* FSH promotes the development of follicles that primarily secrete estrogen (Fig. 17.10). As the estrogen level in the blood rises, it exerts negative feedback control over the anterior pituitary secretion of FSH. The follicular phase then comes to an end.

The estrogen spike at the end of the follicular phase has a positive feedback effect on the hypothalamus and pituitary gland. As a result, GnRH from the hypothalamus increases. A corresponding surge of LH is released from the anterior pituitary. The LH surge triggers ovulation at about day 14 of a 28-day cycle.

Next, the *luteal phase* begins. During the luteal phase of the ovarian cycle, LH promotes the development of the corpus luteum. The corpus luteum secretes high levels of progesterone and some estrogen. When pregnancy does not occur, the corpus luteum regresses and a new cycle begins with menstruation (Fig. 17.11).

Estrogen and Progesterone

Estrogen and **progesterone** affect not only the uterus but other parts of the body as well. Estrogen is largely responsible for the secondary sex characteristics in females, including body hair and fat distribution. In general, females have a more rounded appearance than males because of a greater accumulation of fat beneath the skin. Like males, females develop axillary and pubic hair during puberty. In females, the upper border of pubic hair is horizontal, but in males, it tapers toward the navel. Both estrogen and progesterone are also required for breast development. Other hormones are involved in milk production (prolactin) following pregnancy and milk letdown (oxytocin) when a baby begins to nurse.

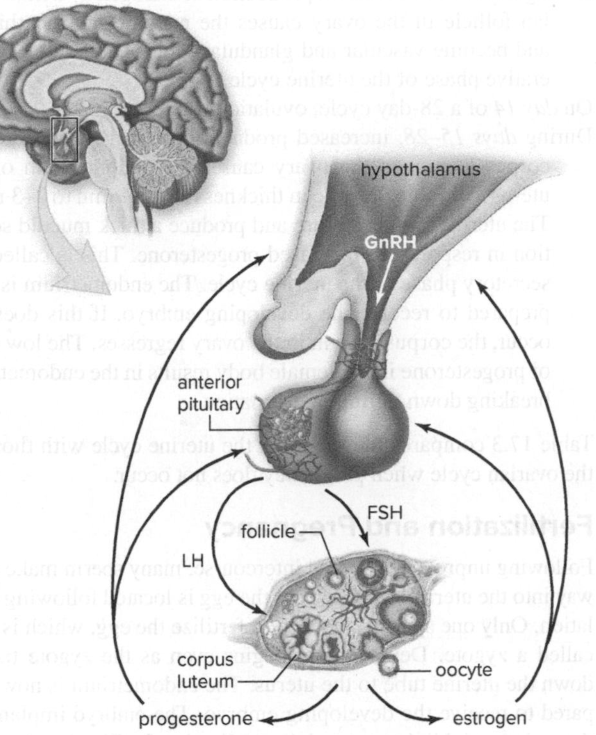

Figure 17.10   **The hormones that control the production of estrogen and progesterone by the ovaries.**
The hypothalamus produces gonadotropin-releasing hormone (GnRH). GnRH stimulates the anterior pituitary to produce follicle-stimulating hormone (FSH) and luteinizing hormone (LH). FSH stimulates the follicle to produce primarily estrogen, and LH stimulates the corpus luteum to produce primarily progesterone. Estrogen and progesterone maintain the sexual organs (e.g., uterus) and the secondary sex characteristics, and they exert feedback control over the hypothalamus and the anterior pituitary. Feedback control regulates the relative amounts of estrogen and progesterone in the blood.

Figure 17.11   **Female hormone levels during the ovarian and uterine cycles.**
During the follicular phase, FSH released by the anterior pituitary promotes the maturation of a follicle in the ovary. The ovarian follicle produces increasing levels of estrogen, which causes the endometrium to thicken during the proliferative phase of the uterine cycle. After ovulation and during the luteal phase of the ovarian cycle, LH promotes the development of the corpus luteum. Progesterone, in particular, causes the endometrial lining to become secretory. Menses, due to the breakdown of the endometrium, begins when progesterone production declines to a low level.

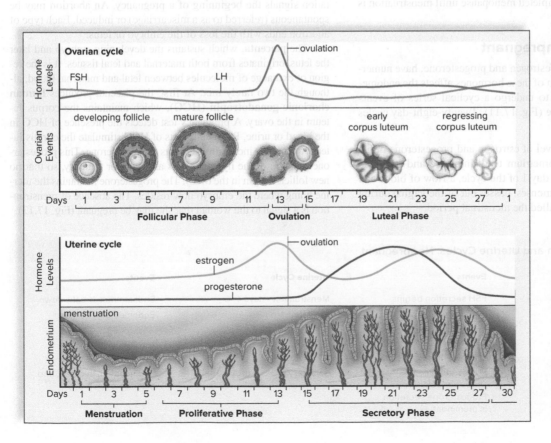

Do women make testosterone?

The adrenal glands and ovaries of women make small amounts of testosterone. Women's low testosterone levels may affect libido, or sex drive. The use of supplemental testosterone to restore a woman's libido has not been well researched.

By the way, men make estrogen, too. Some estrogen is produced by the adrenal glands. Androgens are also converted to estrogen by enzymes in the gonads and peripheral tissues. Estrogen may prevent osteoporosis in males.

The pelvic girdle is wider and deeper in females, so the pelvic cavity usually has a larger relative size compared with that of males. This means that females have wider hips than males and their thighs converge at a greater angle toward the knees. The female pelvis tilts forward, so females tend to have more of a lower back curve than males, an abdominal bulge, and protruding buttocks.

Menopause, the period in a woman's life during which the ovarian cycle ceases, is likely to occur between ages 45 and 55. The ovaries are no longer responsive to the gonadotropic hormones produced by the anterior pituitary, and the ovaries no longer secrete estrogen or progesterone. At the onset of menopause, menstruation becomes irregular, but as long as it occurs, it is still possible for a woman to conceive. Therefore, a woman is usually not considered to have completed menopause until menstruation is absent for a year.

Uterine Cycle: Nonpregnant

The female sex hormones, estrogen and progesterone, have numerous functions. One function of these hormones affects the endometrium, causing the uterus to undergo a cyclical series of events known as the **uterine cycle** (Fig. 17.11). Twenty-eight-day cycles are divided as follows:

During *days 1–5,* a low level of estrogen and progesterone in the body causes the endometrium to disintegrate and its blood vessels to rupture. On day 1 of the cycle, a flow of blood and tissues, known as the menses, passes out of the vagina during **menstruation,** also called the menstrual period.

During *days 6–13,* increased production of estrogen by a new ovarian follicle in the ovary causes the endometrium to thicken and become vascular and glandular. This is called the proliferative phase of the uterine cycle.

On *day 14* of a 28-day cycle, ovulation usually occurs.

During *days 15–28,* increased production of progesterone by the corpus luteum in the ovary causes the endometrium of the uterus to double or triple in thickness (from 1 mm to 2–3 mm). The uterine glands mature and produce a thick mucoid secretion in response to increased progesterone. This is called the secretory phase of the uterine cycle. The endometrium is now prepared to receive the developing embryo. If this does not occur, the corpus luteum in the ovary regresses. The low level of progesterone in the female body results in the endometrium breaking down during menstruation.

Table 17.3 compares the stages of the uterine cycle with those of the ovarian cycle when pregnancy does not occur.

Fertilization and Pregnancy

Following unprotected sexual intercourse, many sperm make their way into the uterine tubes, where the egg is located following ovulation. Only one sperm is needed to fertilize the egg, which is then called a zygote. Development begins even as the zygote travels down the uterine tube to the uterus. The endometrium is now prepared to receive the developing embryo. The embryo implants in the endometrial lining several days following fertilization. Implantation signals the beginning of a pregnancy. An abortion may be spontaneous (referred to as a miscarriage) or induced. Each type of abortion ends with the loss of the embryo or fetus.

The **placenta,** which sustains the developing embryo and later the fetus, originates from both maternal and fetal tissues. It is the region of exchange of molecules between fetal and maternal blood, although the two rarely mix. At first, the placenta produces **human chorionic gonadotropin (HCG),** which maintains the corpus luteum in the ovary. A pregnancy test detects the presence of HCG in the blood or urine. Rising amounts of HCG stimulate the corpus luteum to produce increasing amounts of progesterone. This progesterone shuts down the hypothalamus and anterior pituitary, so that no new follicles begin in the ovary. The progesterone maintains the uterine lining where the embryo now resides. The absence of menstruation is a signal to the woman that she may be pregnant (Fig. 17.12).

Table 17.3	Ovarian and Uterine Cycles: Nonpregnant		
Ovarian Cycle	**Events**	**Uterine Cycle**	**Events**
Follicular phase—days 1–13	FSH secretion begins.	Menstruation—days 1–5	Endometrium breaks down.
	Follicle maturation occurs.	Proliferative phase—days 6–13	Endometrium rebuilds.
	Estrogen secretion is prominent.		
Ovulation—day 14[1]	LH spike occurs.		
Luteal phase—days 15–28	LH secretion continues. Corpus luteum forms. Progesterone secretion is prominent.	Secretory phase—days 15–28	Endometrium thickens, and glands are secretory.

[1] assuming a 28-day cycle.

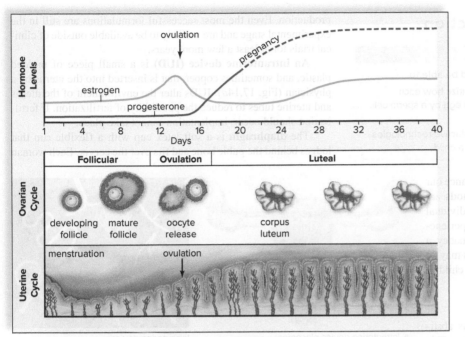

Figure 17.12 The effect of pregnancy on the corpus luteum and endometrium.

If pregnancy occurs, the corpus luteum does not regress. Instead, the corpus luteum is maintained and secretes increasing amounts of progesterone. Therefore, menstruation does not occur and the uterine lining, where the embryo resides, is maintained.

Eventually, the placenta produces progesterone and some estrogen. The corpus luteum is no longer needed and it regresses.

Many women use birth control pills to prevent pregnancy (see Section 17.5). The most commonly used pills include active pills, containing a synthetic estrogen and progesterone, taken for 21 days, followed by 7 days of taking inactive pills that do not contain these hormones (Fig. 17.13). The uterine lining builds up to some degree while the active pills are being taken. Progesterone decreases when the last of the active pills are taken, causing a minimenstruation to occur. Some women skip taking the inactive pills and start taking a new pack of active pills right away to skip menstruation (a period). Birth control pills are available that consist of 3 months of active pills. Women taking them have only four menstrual periods a year.

CHECK YOUR PROGRESS 17.4

1. Summarize the roles of estrogen and progesterone in the ovarian and uterine cycles.
2. Describe the changes that occur in the ovarian and uterine cycles during pregnancy.
3. Describe the changes that occur in the ovarian and uterine cycles when birth control pills are used.

CONNECTING THE CONCEPTS

For more information on the topics presented in this section, refer to the following discussions:

Section 16.6 provides additional information on the male sex hormones.

Section 18.1 outlines the steps in the fertilization of an egg by a sperm cell.

Section 19.4 examines how meiosis reduces the chromosome number during oogenesis.

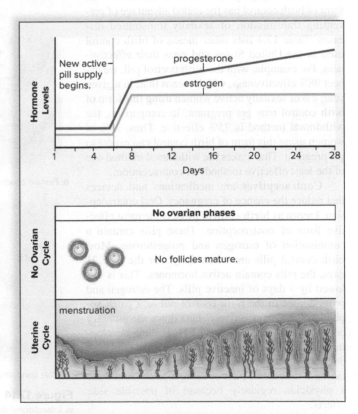

Figure 17.13 The effect of birth control pills on the ovarian cycle.

Active pills cause the uterine lining to build up, and this lining is shed when inactive pills are taken. Feedback inhibition of the hypothalamus and anterior pituitary means that the ovarian cycle does not occur.

17.5 Control of Reproduction

Several means are available to reduce or enhance our reproductive potential. **Birth control methods** are used to regulate the number of children an individual or a couple has. For individuals who are experiencing infertility, or an inability to achieve pregnancy, a number of assisted reproductive technologies may be used to increase the chances of conceiving a child.

Birth Control Methods

The most reliable method of birth control is abstinence—not engaging in sexual intercourse. This form of birth control has the added advantage of preventing transmission of sexually transmitted diseases. Table 17.4 lists other means of birth control used in the United States and rates their effectiveness. For example, with the birth control pill, we expect 98% effectiveness, which means that, in a given year, 2% of sexually active women using this form of birth control may get pregnant. In comparison, the withdrawal method is 75% effective. Thus, 25% of women using this form of birth control can expect to get pregnant. That makes the withdrawal method one of the least effective methods of contraception.

Contraceptives are medications and devices that reduce the chance of pregnancy. Oral contraception, known as **birth control pills,** is the most effective form of contraception. These pills contain a combination of estrogen and progesterone. Most birth control pills are taken daily. For the first 21 days, the pills contain active hormones. This is followed by 7 days of inactive pills. The estrogen and progesterone in the birth control pill or a patch applied to the skin effectively shuts down the pituitary production of both FSH and LH. Follicle development in the ovary is prevented. Because ovulation does not occur, pregnancy cannot take place. Women taking birth control pills or using a patch should see a physician regularly because of possible side effects.

A great deal of research is being devoted to developing safe and effective hormonal birth control for men. Implants, pills, patches, and injections are being explored as ways to deliver testosterone and/or progesterone at adequate levels to suppress sperm production. Even the most successful formulations are still in the experimental stage and are unlikely to be available outside of clinical trials for at least a few more years.

An **intrauterine device (IUD)** is a small piece of molded plastic, and sometimes copper, that is inserted into the uterus by a physician (Fig. 17.14a). IUDs alter the environment of the uterus and uterine tubes to reduce the possibility of fertilization. If fertilization should occur, implantation cannot take place.

The **diaphragm** is a soft latex cup with a flexible rim that lodges behind the pubic bone and fits over the cervix. Each woman

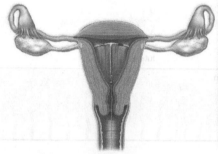

a. Intrauterine device placement

Intrauterine devices

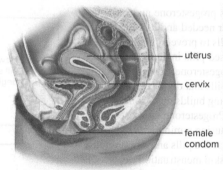

b. Female condom placement

uterus

cervix

female condom

Female condom

c. Male condom placement

Male condom

Figure 17.14   Placement of birth control devices.
a. Intrauterine devices mechanically prevent implantation and can contain progesterone to prevent ovulation, prevent implantation, and thicken cervical mucus. **b.** Female condom that is fitted inside the vagina prevents sperm entry and protects against STDs. **c.** Male condom that fits over the penis prevents sperm from entering the vagina and protects against STDs.

Table 17.4	Common Methods of Contraception			
Name	**Procedure**	**How Does It Work?**	**Effectiveness?**	**Health Risk**
Abstinence	Refrain from sexual intercourse	No sperm in vagina	100%	None; also protects against STDs
Natural family planning	Determine day of ovulation by keeping records	Intercourse avoided during the time that ovum is viable	80%	None
Withdrawal method	Penis withdrawn from vagina just before ejaculation	Ejaculation outside the woman's body; no sperm in vagina	75%	None
Douching	Vagina cleansed after intercourse	Washes sperm out of vagina	≥ 70%	May cause inflammation
Male condom	Sheath of latex, polyurethane, or natural material fitted over erect penis	Prevents entry of sperm into vagina; latex and polyurethane forms protect against STDs	89%	Latex allergy with latex forms; no protection against STDs with natural-material condoms
Female condom	Polyurethane liner fitted inside vagina	Prevents entry of sperm into vagina; some protection against STDs	79%	Possible allergy or irritation, urinary tract infection
Spermicide: jellies, foams, creams	Spermicidal products inserted into vagina before intercourse	Spermicide nonoxynol-9 kills large numbers of sperm cells.	50–80%	Irritation, allergic reaction, urinary tract infection
Contraceptive sponges	Sponge containing spermicide inserted into vagina and placed against cervix	Spermicide nonoxynol-9 kills large numbers of sperm cells.	72–86%	Irritation, allergic reaction, urinary tract infection, toxic shock syndrome
Combined hormone vaginal ring	Flexible plastic ring inserted into vagina; releases hormones absorbed into the bloodstream	Combined hormonal methods suppress ovulation by the combined actions of the hormones estrogen and progestin.	98%	Combined hormonal methods can cause dizziness; nausea; changes in menstruation, mood, and weight; rarely, cardiovascular disease, including high blood pressure, blood clots, heart attack, and strokes.
Combined hormone pill	Pills are swallowed daily; chewable form also available		98%	
Combined hormone 91-day regimen	Pills are swallowed daily; user has three or four menstrual periods a year		98%	
Combined hormone injection	Injection of long-acting hormone given once a month		99%	
Combined hormone patch	Patch is applied to skin and left in place for 1 week; new patch applied		98%	
Progestin-only minipill	Pills swallowed daily	Thickens cervical mucus, preventing sperm from contacting egg	98%	Irregular bleeding, weight gain, breast tenderness
Progesterone-only injection (Depo-Provera)	Injection of progestin once every 3 months	Inhibits ovulation; prevents sperm from reaching the egg; prevents implantation	99%	Irregular bleeding, weight gain, breast tenderness, osteoporosis possible
Emergency contraception	Should be taken shortly after unprotected intercourse	Suppresses ovulation by the combined actions of the hormones estrogen and progestin; prevents implantation	80%	Nausea, vomiting, abdominal pain, fatigue, headache
Diaphragm	Latex cup, placed into vagina to cover cervix before intercourse	Blocks entrance of sperm into uterus, spermicide kills sperm	90% with spermicide	Irritation, allergic reaction, urinary tract infection, toxic shock syndrome
Cervical cap	Latex cap held over cervix	Blocks entrance of sperm into uterus, spermicide kills sperm	90% with spermicide	Irritation, allergic reaction, toxic shock syndrome, abnormal Pap smear
Cervical shield	Latex cap in upper vagina, held in place by suction	Blocks entrance of sperm into uterus, spermicide kills sperm	90% with spermicide	Irritation, allergic reaction, urinary tract infection, toxic shock syndrome
Intrauterine device Copper T	Placed in uterus	Causes cervical mucus to thicken; fertilized embryo cannot implant	99%	Cramps, bleeding, infertility, perforation of uterus
Intrauterine device, progesterone-releasing type	Placed in uterus	Prevents ovulation; causes cervical mucus to thicken; fertilized embryo cannot implant	99%	Cramps, bleeding, infertility, perforation of uterus

must be properly fitted by a physician, and the diaphragm can be inserted into the vagina no more than 2 hours before sexual relations. Also, it must be used with spermicidal jelly or cream and should be left in place at least 6 hours after sexual relations. The cervical cap is a minidiaphragm.

The male and female **condoms** offer some protection against sexually transmitted diseases in addition to helping prevent pregnancy. Female condoms consist of a large polyurethane tube with a flexible ring that fits onto the cervix (Fig. 17.14*b*). The open end of the tube has a ring that covers the external genitals. A male condom is most often a latex sheath that fits over the erect penis (Fig. 17.14*c*). The ejaculate is trapped inside the sheath and thus does not enter the vagina. When used in conjunction with a spermicide, the protection is better than with the condom alone.

Contraceptive Injections and Vaccines

Contraceptive vaccines are in development. For example, a vaccine intended to immunize women against HCG, the hormone so necessary to maintaining the implantation of the embryo, was successful in a limited clinical trial. Because HCG is not normally present in the body, no autoimmune reaction is expected, but the immunization does wear off with time. Others believe that it would also be possible to develop a safe antisperm vaccine that could be used in women.

Contraceptive implants use a synthetic progesterone to prevent ovulation by disrupting the ovarian cycle. Most versions consist of a single capsule that remains effective for about 3 years. Contraceptive injections are available as progesterone only or a combination of estrogen and progesterone. The length of time between injections can vary from 1 to several months.

Emergency Contraception

Emergency contraception, or "morning-after pills," consists of medications that can prevent pregnancy after unprotected intercourse. The expression "morning-after" is a misnomer, in that some treatments can be started up to 5 days after unprotected intercourse.

The first FDA-approved medication produced for emergency contraception was a kit called Preven. Preven includes four synthetic progesterone pills; two are taken up to 72 hours after unprotected intercourse, and two more are taken 12 hours later. The hormone upsets the normal uterine cycle, making it difficult for an embryo to implant in the endometrium. One study estimated that Preven was 85% effective in preventing unintended pregnancies. The Preven kit also includes a pregnancy test; women are instructed to take the test first before using the hormone, because the medication is not effective on an established pregnancy.

In 2006 the FDA approved another drug, called Plan B One-Step, which is up to 89% effective in preventing pregnancy if taken within 72 hours after unprotected sex. It is available without a prescription to women age 17 and older. In August 2010,

ulipristal acetate (also known as ella) was also approved for emergency contraception. It can be taken up to 5 days after unprotected sex, and studies indicate it is somewhat more effective than Plan B One-Step. Unlike Plan B One-Step, however, a prescription is required.

Mifepristone, also known as RU-486 or the "abortion pill," can cause the loss of an implanted embryo by blocking the progesterone receptors of endometrial cells. This causes the endometrium to slough off, carrying the embryo with it. When taken in conjunction with a prostaglandin to induce uterine contractions, RU-486 is 95% effective at inducing an abortion up to the 49th day of gestation. Because of its mechanism of action, the use of RU-486 is more controversial compared to other medications, and while it is currently available in the United States for early medical abortion, it is not approved for emergency contraception.

Surgical Methods

Vasectomy and tubal ligation are two methods used to bring about sterility, the inability to reproduce (Fig. 17.15). **Vasectomy** consists of cutting and sealing the vas deferens from each testis so that the sperm are unable to reach the seminal fluid ejected at the time of orgasm. The sperm are then largely reabsorbed. Following this operation, which can be done in a doctor's office, the amount of ejaculate remains normal because sperm account for only about 1% of the volume of semen. Also, there is no effect on the secondary sex characteristics, because testosterone continues to be produced by the testes.

Tubal ligation consists of cutting and sealing the uterine tubes. Pregnancy rarely occurs, because the passage of the egg through the uterine tubes has been blocked. Using a method called laparoscopy, which requires only two small incisions, the surgeon inserts a small, lighted telescope to view the uterine tubes and a small surgical blade to sever them.

It is best to view a vasectomy or tubal ligation as permanent. Even following successful reconnection, fertility is usually reduced by about 50%.

SCIENCE IN YOUR LIFE

Are vasectomies 100% effective?

Vasectomies and tubal ligations are considered to be permanent forms of birth control. However, many men do not realize that it is still possible to father a child for several months following a vasectomy. This is because after the procedure some sperm remain in the vas deferens. Males who have had a vasectomy need to use alternate forms of birth control for 1 to 2 months or until their physician has performed a follow-up sperm count and verified that sperm are no longer present in the ejaculate. In very rare situations, the vas deferens may reconnect, allowing sperm to once again be ejaculated. While the only 100% effective form of contraception is abstinence, vasectomies are considered to be over 99.8% effective.

uterine tubes
(oviducts)

vas
deferens

testis

a.   b.

Figure 17.15   Vasectomies and tubal ligations.
a. Vasectomy involves making two small cuts in the skin of the scrotum. Each vas deferens is lifted out and cut. The cut ends are tied or sealed with an electrical current. The openings in the scrotum are closed with stitches. **b.** During tubal ligation, one or two small incisions are made in the abdomen. Using instruments inserted through the incisions, the uterine tubes are coagulated (burned), sealed shut with cautery, or cut and tied. The skin incision is then stitched closed.

Infertility

Infertility is the failure of a couple to achieve pregnancy after 1 year of regular, unprotected intercourse. Estimates of the prevalence of infertility vary, but most professional organizations predict that around 15% of all couples are infertile. The cause of infertility can be evenly attributed to the male and female partners.

Causes of Infertility

The most frequent cause of infertility in males is low sperm count and/or a large proportion of abnormal sperm, which can be due to environmental influences. It appears that a sedentary lifestyle coupled with smoking and alcohol consumption is most often the cause of male infertility. When males spend most of the day driving or sitting in front of a computer or TV, the testes' temperature remains too high for adequate sperm production.

Body weight appears to be the most significant factor in causing female infertility. In women of normal weight, fat cells produce a hormone called leptin, which stimulates the hypothalamus to release GnRH. FSH release and normal follicle development follow. In overweight women, leptin levels are higher, which impacts GnRH and FSH. The ovaries of many overweight women contain many small follicles that fail to ovulate. Other causes of infertility in females are blocked uterine tubes due to pelvic inflammatory disease (see Section 17.6) and endometriosis. **Endometriosis** is the presence of uterine tissue outside the uterus, particularly in the uterine tubes and on the abdominal organs. Backward flow of menstrual fluid allows living uterine cells to establish themselves in the abdominal cavity. The cells go through the usual uterine cycle, causing pain and structural abnormalities that make it more difficult for a woman to conceive.

Sometimes the causes of infertility can be corrected by medical intervention, so that couples can have children. If no obstruction is apparent and body weight is normal, it is possible to give females fertility drugs. These drugs are gonadotropic hormones that stimulate the ovaries and bring about ovulation. As discussed in the Bioethics feature "Should Infertility Be Treated?," these hormone treatments may cause multiple ovulations and multiple births.

Many couples who cannot reproduce in the usual manner adopt a child. Others sometimes try one of the assisted reproductive technologies discussed in the following paragraphs.

Assisted Reproductive Technologies

Assisted reproductive technologies consist of techniques used to increase the chances of pregnancy. Often, sperm and/or eggs are retrieved from the testes and ovaries, and fertilization takes place in a clinical or laboratory setting.

Artificial Insemination by Donor (AID)   During artificial insemination, sperm are placed in the vagina by a physician. Sometimes a woman is artificially inseminated by her partner's sperm. This is especially helpful if the partner has a low sperm count, because the sperm can be collected over time and concentrated, so that the sperm count is sufficient to result in fertilization. Often, however, a woman is inseminated by sperm acquired from a donor who is a complete stranger to her. At times, a combination of partner and donor sperm is used.

SCIENCE IN YOUR LIFE

How many babies are born annually in the United States using ART?

The very first IVF baby born in the United States was Elizabeth Carr on December 28, 1981. Since that time, assisted reproductive technologies (ART) have improved along with their success rates. In 2014 more than 70,000 babies were born in the United States as a result of ART. This represents almost 1% of the total conceptions in the United States.

BIOLOGY TODAY   **Bioethics**

Should Infertility Be Treated?

Every day, couples make plans to start or expand their families, yet for many, their dreams might not be realized because conception is difficult or impossible. Before seeking medical treatment for infertility, a couple might want to decide how far they are willing to go to have a child. Here are some of the possible risks.

Some of the Procedures Used

If a man has low sperm count or motility, artificial or intrauterine insemination of his partner with a large number of specially selected sperm may be done to stimulate pregnancy. Although there are dangers in all medical procedures, artificial insemination is generally safe.

   If a woman is infertile because of physical abnormalities in her reproductive system, she may be treated surgically. Whereas surgeries are now very sophisticated, they nonetheless have risks, including bleeding, infection, organ damage, and adverse reactions to anesthesia. Similar risks are associated with collecting eggs for in vitro fertilization (IVF). To ensure the collection of several eggs, a woman may be placed on hormone-based medications that stimulate egg production. Such medications may cause ovarian hyperstimulation syndrome—enlarged ovaries and abdominal fluid accumulation. In mild cases, the only symptom is discomfort; but in severe cases (though rare), a woman's life may be endangered. In any case, the fluid has to be drained.

   Usually IVF involves the creation of many embryos; the healthiest-looking ones are transferred into the woman's body. Others may be frozen for future attempts at establishing pregnancy, given to other infertile couples, donated for research, or destroyed. Of those that are transferred, none, one, or all might develop into fetuses. The significant increase in multifetal pregnancies in the United States in the last 15 years has been largely attributed to fertility treatment (Fig. 17B). Though the number of triplet and higher-number multiple pregnancies started to level off in 1999, twin pregnancies continue to climb.

   They may seem like a dream come true, but multifetal pregnancies are difficult. The mother is more likely to develop complications, such as gestational diabetes and high blood pressure, than are women carrying single babies. Positioning of the babies in the uterus may make vaginal delivery less likely, and there is likely a chance of preterm labor. Babies born prematurely face numerous hardships. Infant death and long-term disabilities are also more common with multiple births. This is true even of twins. Even if all babies are healthy, parenting "multiples" poses unique challenges.

What Happens to Frozen Embryos?

Despite potential trials, thousands of people undergo fertility treatment every year. Its popularity has brought a number of ethical issues to light. For example, the estimated high numbers of stored frozen embryos (a few hundred thousand in the United States) has

Figure 17B
Reproductive technologies may lead to mutliple births.
© Nancy R. Cohen/Getty RF

generated debate about their fate, complicated by the fact that the long-term viability of frozen embryos is not well understood. Scientists may worry that embryos donated to other couples are ones screened out from one implantation and not likely to survive. Some religious groups strongly oppose destruction of these embryos or their use in research. Patients for whom the embryos were created generally feel that they should have sole rights to make decisions about their fate. However, a fertility clinic may no longer be receiving monetary compensation for the storage of frozen embryos and may be unable to contact the couples for whom they were produced. The question then becomes whether the clinic now has the right to determine their fate.

Who Should Be Treated?

Additionally, because fertility treatment is voluntary, is it ever acceptable to turn some people away? What if the prospect of a satisfactory outcome is very slim or almost nonexistent? This may happen when one of the partners is ill or the woman is at an advanced age. Should a physician go ahead with treatment even if it might endanger a woman's (or baby's) health? Those in favor of limiting treatment argue that a physician has a responsibility to prevent potential harm to a patient. On the other hand, there is concern that if certain people are denied fertility for medical reasons, might they be denied for other reasons also, such as race, religion, sexuality, or income?

Questions to Consider

1. Should couples go to all lengths to have children even if it could endanger the life of one or both spouses?
2. Should couples with "multiples" due to infertility treatment receive assistance from private and public services?
3. To what lengths should society go to protect frozen embryos?
4. Do you think that anyone should be denied fertility treatment? If so, what factors do you think a doctor should take into consideration when deciding whether to provide someone fertility treatment?

A variation of AID is *intrauterine insemination* (*IUI*). In IUI, fertility drugs are given to stimulate the ovaries. Then the donor's sperm are placed in the uterus, rather than in the vagina.

If the prospective parents wish, sperm can be sorted into those believed to be X-bearing or Y-bearing to increase the chances of having a child of the desired sex. Fertilization of an egg with an X-bearing sperm results in a female child. Fertilization by a Y-bearing sperm yields a male child.

In Vitro Fertilization (IVF) During **in vitro fertilization (IVF)**, conception occurs in laboratory glassware. Ultrasound machines can now spot follicles in the ovaries that hold immature eggs; therefore, the latest method is to forgo the administration of fertility drugs and retrieve immature eggs by using a needle. The immature eggs are then brought to maturity in glassware, and then concentrated sperm are added. After about 2 to 4 days, the embryos are ready to be transferred to the uterus of the woman, who is now in the secretory phase of her uterine cycle. If desired, the embryos can be tested for a genetic disease, and only those found to be free of disease will be used. If implantation is successful, development is normal and continues to term.

Gamete Intrafallopian Transfer (GIFT) The term *gamete* refers to a sex cell, either a sperm or an egg. Gamete intrafallopian transfer (GIFT) was devised to overcome the low success rate (15–20%) of in vitro fertilization. The method is the same as in vitro fertilization, except the eggs and the sperm are placed in the uterine tubes immediately after they have been brought together. GIFT has the advantage of being a one-step procedure for the woman—the eggs are removed and reintroduced all at the same time. A variation on this procedure is to fertilize the eggs in the laboratory and then place the zygotes in the uterine tubes.

Surrogate Mothers Some women are contracted and paid to have babies. These women are called surrogate mothers. The sperm and even the egg can be contributed by the contracting parents.

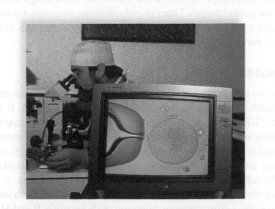

Figure 17.16   Intracytoplasmic sperm injection.
A microscope connected to a television screen is used to carry out intracytoplasmic sperm injection. A pipette holds the egg steady while a needle (not visible) introduces the sperm into the egg.
© CC Studio/SPL/Science Source

Intracytoplasmic Sperm Injection In this highly sophisticated procedure, a single sperm is injected into an egg (Fig. 17.16). It is used effectively when a man has severe infertility problems.

> **CHECK YOUR PROGRESS 17.5**
>
> 1. List the major forms of birth control in order of effectiveness.
> 2. Explain why vasectomies and tubal ligations are permanent forms of birth control.
> 3. Distinguish between an IVF and a GIFT procedure to compensate for infertility.

CONNECTING THE CONCEPTS

For more information on the hormones presented in this section, refer to the following discussions:

Section 16.2 explains the role of the gonadotropic hormones.

Section 16.6 describes the hormones produced by the female reproductive system.

17.6 Sexually Transmitted Diseases

> **LEARNING OUTCOMES**
>
> Upon completion of this section, you should be able to
>
> 1. Distinguish between sexually transmitted diseases (STDs) caused by viruses and those caused by bacteria.
> 2. Describe the causes and treatments of selected STDs.

Sexually transmitted diseases (STDs), sometimes referred to as sexually transmitted infections (STIs), are caused by viruses, bacteria, fungi, and parasites.

STDs Caused by Viruses

Among STDs caused by viruses, effective treatment is available for AIDS (acquired immunodeficiency syndrome) and genital herpes. However, treatment for HIV/AIDS and genital herpes cannot presently eliminate the virus from the person's body. Drugs used for treatment can merely slow replication of the viruses. Thus, neither viral disease is presently curable. Further, antiviral drugs have serious, debilitating side effects on the body.

HIV Infections

In Section 8.2 we explored the relationship between the HIV virus and AIDS, as well as some of the more common forms of treatment. At present there is no vaccine to prevent an HIV infection (although several are in trials), nor is there a cure for AIDS. The best course of action is to follow the guidelines for preventing transmission of STDs outlined in the Health feature "Preventing Transmission of STDs" later in this section.

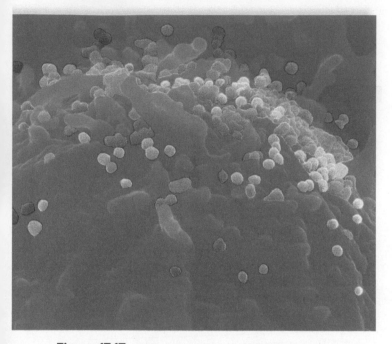

Figure 17.17   Cells infected by the HIV virus.
HIV viruses (yellow) can infect helper T cells (blue) as well as macrophages, which work with helper T cells to stem the infection.
© Dr. Olivier Schwartz/Institut Pasteur/Science Source

The primary host for HIV is a helper T lymphocyte, or helper T cell (Fig. 17.17), although macrophages are also infected by the virus. The helper T cells are the very cells that stimulate an immune response (see Section 17.3), so loss of these cells causes the immune system to become severely impaired in persons with AIDS. During the first stage of an HIV infection, symptoms are few, but the individual is highly contagious. Several months to several years after infection, the helper T-lymphocyte count falls. Following this decrease, infections, such as other sexually transmitted diseases, begin to appear. In the last stage of infection, called AIDS, the helper T-cell count falls way below normal. At least one opportunistic infection is present. Such diseases have the opportunity to occur only because the immune system is severely weakened. Persons with AIDS typically die from an opportunistic disease, such as *Pneumocystis* pneumonia.

There is no cure for AIDS. A treatment called highly active antiretroviral therapy (HAART) is usually able to stop HIV reproduction to the extent that the virus becomes undetectable in the blood. The medications must be continued indefinitely, because as soon as HAART is discontinued, the virus rebounds.

Genital Warts

Genital warts are caused by the human papillomaviruses (HPVs). Many times, carriers either do not have any sign of warts or merely have flat lesions. When present, the warts commonly are seen on the penis and foreskin of men and near the vaginal opening in women. A newborn can become infected while passing through the birth canal.

Individuals currently infected with visible warts may have those growths removed by surgery, freezing, or burning with lasers or acids. However, visible warts that are removed may recur. A vaccine has been released for the human papillomaviruses that most commonly cause genital warts. This development is an extremely important step in the prevention of cancer, as well as in the prevention of warts themselves. Genital warts, and specifically the HIV virus, are associated with cancer of the cervix (see chapter opener), as well as tumors of the vulva, vagina, anus, and penis. Researchers believe that these viruses may be involved in up to 90% of all cases of cancer of the cervix. HPV vaccinations, which are recommended for both women and men before the age of 26, might make such cancers a thing of the past.

Genital Herpes

Genital herpes is caused by herpes simplex virus. Type 1 usually causes cold sores and fever blisters, while type 2 more often causes genital herpes (Fig. 17.18).

Persons usually get infected with herpes simplex virus 2 when they are adults. Some people exhibit no symptoms. Others may experience a tingling or itching sensation before blisters appear on the genitals. Once the blisters rupture, they leave painful ulcers, which may take between 5 days and 3 weeks to heal. The blisters may be accompanied by fever; pain on urination; swollen lymph nodes in the groin; and in women, a copious discharge. At this time, the individual has an increased risk of acquiring an HIV infection.

After the ulcers heal, the disease is only latent, and blisters can recur, although usually at less frequent intervals and with milder symptoms. Fever, stress, sunlight, and menstruation are associated with recurrence of symptoms. Exposure to herpes in the birth canal can cause an infection in the newborn, which leads to neurological disorders and even death. Birth by cesarean section prevents this possibility. There are antiviral drugs available that reduce the number and length of outbreaks. However, these drugs are not a cure for genital herpes. Latex or polyurethane condoms are recommended by the FDA to prevent the transmission of the virus to sexual partners.

Hepatitis

Hepatitis infects the liver and can lead to liver failure, liver cancer, and death. Six known viruses cause hepatitis, designated A, B, C, D, E, and G. Hepatitis A is usually acquired from sewage-contaminated drinking water, but this infection can also be sexually transmitted through oral-anal contact. Hepatitis B is spread through sexual contact and by blood-borne transmission (accidental needlestick on the job, receiving a contaminated blood transfusion, a drug abuser sharing infected needles while injecting drugs, from mother to fetus, etc.). Simultaneous infection with hepatitis B and HIV is common, because both share the same routes of transmission. Fortunately, a combined vaccine is available for hepatitis A and B. It is recommended that all children receive the vaccine to prevent infection, and that adults receive vaccinations throughout their lives (see Section 7.4). Hepatitis C (also called *non-A, non-B hepatitis*) causes most cases of posttransfusion hepatitis. Hepatitis D and G are sexually transmitted, and hepatitis E is acquired from contaminated water. Screening of blood and blood products can prevent transmission of hepatitis viruses during a transfusion. Proper water-treatment techniques can prevent contamination of drinking water.

STDs Caused by Bacteria

Only STDs caused by bacteria are curable with antibiotics. Antibiotic resistance acquired by these bacteria may require treatment with extremely strong drugs for an extended period to achieve a cure.

Chlamydia

Chlamydia is named for the tiny bacterium that causes it, *Chlamydia trachomatis* (Fig. 17.19). The incidence of new chlamydia infections has steadily increased since 1984.

Chlamydial infections of the lower reproductive tract are usually mild or asymptomatic, especially in women. About 18 to 21 days after infection, men may experience a mild burning sensation on urination and a mucoid discharge. Women may have a vaginal discharge, along with the symptoms of a urinary tract infection. Chlamydia also causes cervical ulcerations, which increase the risk of acquiring HIV.

If the infection is misdiagnosed or if a woman does not seek medical help, there is a particular risk of the infection spreading from the cervix to the uterine tubes, so that pelvic inflammatory disease (PID) results. This very painful condition can result in

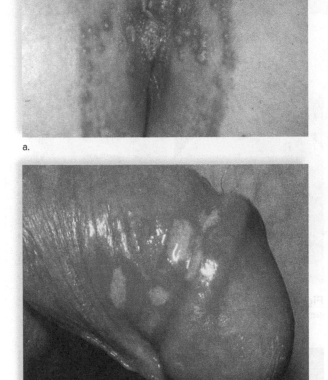

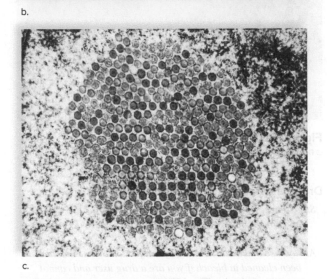

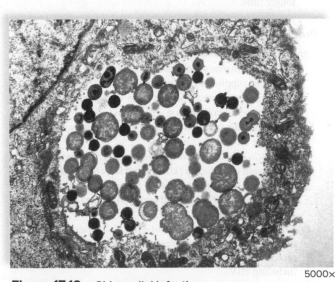

5000×

Figure 17.18 Herpes simplex virus 2 and genital herpes. Several types of viruses are associated with herpes. Genital herpes is usually caused by herpes simplex virus 2. Symptoms of genital herpes include an outbreak of blisters, which can be present on the labia of females (**a**) or on the penis of males (**b**). **c.** A photomicrograph of cells infected with the herpes simplex virus.

(a) © Bart's Medical Library/Phototake; (b) © Biophoto Associates/Science Source; (c) © David M. Phillips/Science Source

Figure 17.19 Chlamydial infection. The different stages of a *Chlamydia trachomatis* infection inside a cell are stained red, brown, and black.

© Biomedical Imaging Unit, Southampton General Hospital/ Science Source

380   **Unit 5**   Reproduction in Humans

 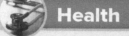
Preventing Transmission of STDs

Sexual Activities Transmit STDs

Abstain from sexual intercourse or develop a long-term monogamous (always the same partner) sexual relationship with a partner who is free of STDs (Fig. 17C).

Refrain from having multiple sex partners or having relations with someone who has multiple sex partners. If you have sex with two people and each of these has sex with two people, and so forth, the number of people who are relating is quite large.

Be aware that having relations with an intravenous drug user is risky, because the behavior of this group risks AIDS and hepatitis B. Be aware that anyone who already has another sexually transmitted disease is more susceptible to an HIV infection.

Avoid anal intercourse (in which the penis is inserted into the rectum), because this behavior increases the risk of an HIV infection. The lining of the rectum is thin, and infected CD4 T cells can easily enter the body there. Also, the rectum is supplied with many blood vessels, and insertion of the penis into the rectum is likely to cause tearing and bleeding that facilitate the entrance of HIV. The vaginal lining is thick and difficult to penetrate, but the lining of the uterus is only one cell thick at certain times of the month and does allow CD4 T cells to enter.

Uncircumcised males are more likely to become infected than circumcised males. This is because vaginal secretions, viruses, and bacteria may remain under the foreskin for a longer time.

Practice Safer Sex

Always use a latex condom during sexual intercourse if you are not in a monogamous relationship. Be sure to follow the directions supplied by the manufacturer for the use of a condom. At one time, condom users were advised to use nonoxynol-9 in conjunction with a condom, but testing shows that this spermicide has no effect on viruses, including HIV.

Avoid fellatio (kissing and insertion of the penis into a partner's mouth) and cunnilingus (kissing and insertion of the tongue into the vagina), because they may be a means of transmission. The mouth and gums often have cuts and sores that facilitate catching an STD.

Practice penile, vaginal, oral, and hand cleanliness. Be aware that hormonal contraceptives make the female genital tract receptive to the transmission of sexually transmitted diseases, including HIV.

Be cautious about using alcohol or any drug that may prevent you from being able to control your behavior.

Figure 17C   **Sexual activities transmit STDs.**
(left) © igormakarov/Shutterstock RF; (right) © David Raymer/Corbis

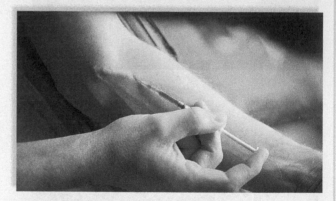

Figure 17D   **Sharing needles transmits STDs.**
© Don Mason/Getty RF

Drug Use Transmits HIV

Stop, if necessary, or do not start the habit of injecting drugs into your veins. Be aware that HIV and hepatitis B can be spread by blood-to-blood contact.

Always use a new sterile needle for injection or one that has been cleaned in bleach if you are a drug user and cannot stop your behavior (Fig. 17D).

Questions to Consider

1. Why might the use of female contraceptives actually increase the chances of contracting HIV?
2. What cells in the blood act as a host for HIV?

blockage of the uterine tubes, with the possibility of sterility and infertility. If a baby comes in contact with chlamydia during birth, inflammation of the eyes or pneumonia can result.

Gonorrhea

Gonorrhea is caused by the bacterium *Neisseria gonorrhoeae*. Diagnosis in the male is not difficult, because typical symptoms are pain upon urination and a thick, greenish-yellow urethral discharge. In females, a latent infection leads to pelvic inflammatory disease (PID), which may result in damage to the uterus, ovaries, and other reproductive structures. If a baby is exposed during birth, an eye infection leading to blindness can result. All newborns are given eyedrops to prevent this possibility.

Gonorrhea proctitis, an infection of the anus characterized by anal pain and blood or pus in the feces, also occurs in patients. Oral-genital contact can cause infection of the mouth, throat, and tonsils. Gonorrhea can spread to internal parts of the body, causing heart damage or arthritis. If, by chance, the person touches infected genitals and then touches his or her eyes, a severe eye infection can result. Up to now, gonorrhea was curable by antibiotic therapy. However, resistance to antibiotics is becoming more and more common, and *Neisseria gonorrhoeae* is now classified as a "superbug," meaning that it has developed resistance to a variety of antibiotics.

Syphilis

Syphilis is caused by a bacterium called *Treponema pallidum* (Fig. 17.20). As with many other bacterial diseases, penicillin is an effective antibiotic. Syphilis has three stages, often separated by latent periods, during which the bacteria are resting before multiplying again. During the primary stage, a hard chancre (ulcerated sore with hard edges) indicates the site of infection. The chancre usually heals spontaneously, leaving little scarring.

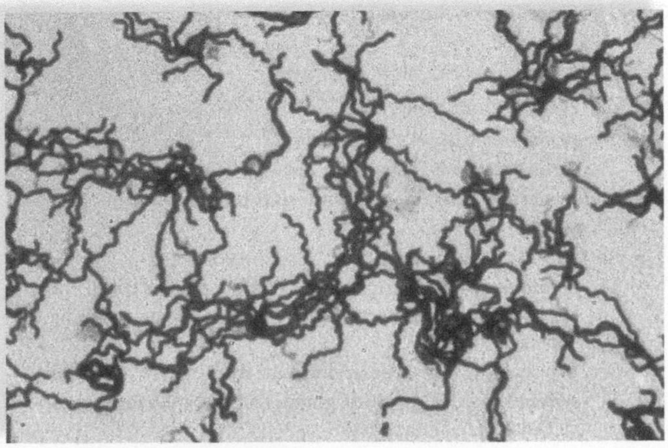

Figure 17.20 Syphilis.
Treponema pallidum, the cause of syphilis.
© Melba Photo Agency/Alamy RF

SCIENCE IN YOUR LIFE

Can you catch an STD from a toilet seat?
When HIV/AIDS was first identified in the mid-1980s, many people were concerned about being infected by the virus on toilet seats. Toilet seats are plastic and inert, so they're not very hospitable to disease-causing organisms. So if you're deciding whether to hover or sit, remember sitting on a toilet seat will not give you an STD.

During the secondary stage, the victim breaks out in a rash that does not itch and is seen even on the palms of the hands and the soles of the feet. Hair loss and infectious gray patches on the mucous membranes may also occur. These symptoms disappear of their own accord.

The tertiary stage lasts until the patient dies. During this stage, syphilis may affect the cardiovascular system by causing aneurysms, particularly in the aorta. In other instances, the disease may affect the nervous system, resulting in psychological disturbances. Also, gummas—large, destructive ulcers—may develop on the skin or within the internal organs.

Congenital syphilis is caused by syphilitic bacteria crossing the placenta. The child is born blind and/or with numerous anatomical malformations. Control of syphilis depends on prompt and adequate treatment of all new cases. Therefore, it is crucial for all sexual contacts to be traced, so that they can be treated. Diagnosis of syphilis can be made by blood tests or by microscopic examination of fluids from lesions.

Vaginal Infections

The term *vaginitis* is used to describe any vaginal infection or inflammation. It is the most commonly diagnosed gynecologic condition. Bacterial vaginosis (BV) is believed to cause 40–50% of the cases of vaginitis in the United States. Overgrowth of certain bacteria inhabiting the vagina causes vaginosis. A common culprit is the bacterium *Gardnerella vaginosis*. Overgrowth of this organism and subsequent symptoms can occur for nonsexual reasons. However, symptomless males can pass on the bacterium to women, who do experience symptoms.

The symptoms of BV are vaginal discharge that has a strong odor, a burning sensation during urination, and/or itching or pain in the vulva. Some women with BV have no signs of the infection. How women acquire these infections is not well understood. Having a new sex partner or multiple sex partners seems to increase the risk of getting BV, but females who are not sexually active get BV as well. Douching also appears to increase the incidence of BV. Women with BV are more susceptible to infection by other STDs, including HIV, herpes, chlamydia, and gonorrhea. Pregnant women with BV are at greater risk of premature delivery.

The yeast *Candida albicans*, and a protozoan, *Trichomonas vaginalis*, are two other causes of vaginitis. *Candida albicans* is

382   Unit 5 Reproduction in Humans

normally found living in the vagina. Under certain circumstances, its growth increases above normal, causing vaginitis. For example, women taking birth control pills or antibiotics may be prone to yeast infections. Both can alter the normal balance of vaginal organisms, causing a yeast infection. A yeast infection causes a thick, white, curdlike vaginal discharge and is accompanied by itching of the vulva and/or vagina. Antifungal medications inserted into the vagina are used to treat yeast infections. Trichomoniasis, caused by *Trichomonas vaginalis,* affects both males and females. The urethra is usually the site of infection in males. Infected males are often asymptomatic and pass the parasite to their partner during sexual intercourse. Symptoms of trichomoniasis in females are a foul-smelling, yellow-green, frothy discharge and itching of the vulva/vagina. Having trichomoniasis greatly increases the risk of infection by HIV. Prescription drugs are used to treat trichomoniasis, but if one partner remains infected, reinfection will occur. It is recommended that both partners in a sexual relationship be treated and abstain from having sex until the treatment is completed.

> ### CHECK YOUR PROGRESS 17.6
>
> 1. Explain what condition can occur due to a chlamydial or gonorrheal infection.
> 2. Identify a medical condition in women that is associated with genital warts.
> 3. Discuss the causes of most STDs.

CONNECTING THE CONCEPTS

For more information on the topics presented in this section, refer to the following discussions:

Section 8.1 explores the structure of both viruses and bacteria.

Section 8.2 provides a detailed examination of the HIV virus, its replication, and the disease AIDS.

Section 8.4 examines how antibiotic resistance occurs and its consequences in the treatment of disease.

CASE STUDY: CONCLUSION

The good news for Ann is that early detection of cervical cancer is critical to successful treatment of the disease. For individuals with cervical cancer, the survival rate for those who have early detection is almost 100%, versus a less than 5% survival rate for those in whom the cancer has begun to spread, or metastasize, to other organs. In Ann's case, her years of smoking cigarettes probably were a major factor in her development of cervical cancer. However, for many cases of cervical cancer, the cause is the human papillomavirus, or HPV. Over 15 forms of HPV have been linked to cervical cancers. In 2006 the Food and Drug Administration (FDA) approved an HPV vaccine for females. The vaccine is designed to be administered as three doses starting between the ages of 11 and 12 years. Recently the vaccine was also approved for males ages 9 to 26 to prevent genital warts and to reduce the chances that men will transmit HPV to their sexual partners. With the development of the HPV vaccine, it is hoped that the rates of cervical cancer in women will drop drastically over the next few decades.

STUDY TOOLS http://connect.mheducation.com

SMARTBOOK® Maximize your study time with McGraw-Hill SmartBook®, the first adaptive textbook.

SUMMARIZE

17.1 Human Life Cycle

The **reproductive system** is responsible for the production of **gametes** in both sexes. In females, the system also provides the location for fertilization. Following **zygote** formation, the female reproductive system protects and nourishes the developing fetus.

The life cycle of higher organisms requires two types of cell division:

- **Mitosis,** the growth and repair of tissues
- **Meiosis,** the production of gametes

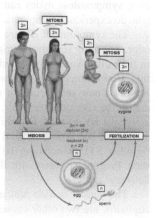

17.2 Male Reproductive System

The external genitals of males are

- The **penis** (organ of sexual intercourse)
- The **scrotum,** which contains the **testes**

Spermatogenesis, occurring in **seminiferous tubules** of the testes, produces **sperm.**

- **Sertoli cells** regulate the process of spermatogenesis.
- The **epididymis** stores mature sperm cells. A mature sperm consists of a head containing the **acrosome,** a middle section containing mitochondria, and a tail.
- Sperm pass from the **vas deferens** to the **urethra.**
- The **seminal vesicles, prostate gland,** and **bulbourethral glands** secrete fluids that aid the sperm.
- Sperm and secretions are called **semen** or seminal fluid.

Orgasm in males results in ejaculation of semen from the penis.

Circumcision is the surgical removal of the foreskin. **Erectile dysfunction (ED)** is a condition in which the male is unable to achieve or sustain an erection.

Hormonal Regulation in Males

- Hormonal regulation, involving secretions from the hypothalamus, the anterior pituitary, and the testes, maintains a fairly constant level of testosterone.
- **Follicle-stimulating hormone (FSH)** from the anterior pituitary promotes spermatogenesis.
- **Luteinizing hormone (LH)** from the anterior pituitary promotes **testosterone** production by **interstitial cells.**

17.3 Female Reproductive System

Oogenesis occurring within the **ovaries** typically produces one mature follicle each month.

- This follicle balloons out of the ovary and bursts, releasing an **egg** (ovum) that is moved by the **fimbriae** into the **uterine tubes.**
- The uterine tubes lead to the **uterus,** where **implantation** of the zygote and development occur. The **endometrium** is the lining of the uterus, which participates in the formation of the placenta.
- The **cervix** is the end of the uterus, which links to the vagina. A **Pap test** may be used to screen the cervix for cancer.
- The female external genital area is called the vulva. It includes the vaginal opening, the clitoris, the labia minora, and the labia majora.
- The **vagina** is the organ of sexual intercourse and the birth canal in females.

Orgasm in females culminates in contractions of the uterus and uterine tubes.

17.4 The Ovarian Cycle

Ovarian Cycle: Nonpregnant

- **Oogenesis** in females produces egg cells and **polar bodies.**
- The **ovarian cycle** is under the hormonal control of the hypothalamus and the anterior pituitary.
- During the cycle's first half, FSH from the anterior pituitary causes maturation of a **follicle** that secretes estrogen and some progesterone.
- After **ovulation** and during the cycle's second half, LH from the anterior pituitary converts the follicle into the **corpus luteum.**
- The corpus luteum secretes progesterone and some estrogen.
- **Menopause** represents that stage of a woman's life when the ovarian cycle ceases.

Uterine Cycle: Nonpregnant

Estrogen and progesterone regulate the **uterine cycle.**

- **Estrogen** causes the endometrium to rebuild.
- Ovulation usually occurs on day 14 of a 28-day cycle.
- **Progesterone** produced by the corpus luteum causes the endometrium to thicken and become secretory.
- A low level of hormones causes the endometrium to break down as **menstruation** occurs.

Fertilization and Pregnancy

If fertilization takes place, the embryo implants in the thickened endometrium.

- The corpus luteum is maintained because of **human chorionic gonadotropin (HCG)** production by the **placenta;** therefore, progesterone production does not cease.
- Menstruation usually does not occur during pregnancy.

17.5 Control of Reproduction

Contraceptives are **birth control methods** that reduce the chance of pregnancy.

- A few of these are the **birth control pill, intrauterine device (IUD), diaphragm,** and **condom.**
- Contraceptive vaccines, implants, and injections are becoming increasingly available.
- Surgical procedures, such as a **vasectomy** or **tubal ligation,** make the individual sterile.

Assisted reproductive technologies may help couples who are experiencing **infertility.** Infertility may be caused by a number of factors, including, **endometriosis** in females and alcohol consumption and smoking in males. Some examples of assisted reproductive technologies include:

- Artificial insemination by donor (AID)
- **In vitro fertilization (IVF)**
- Gamete intrafallopian transfer (GIFT)
- Intracytoplasmic sperm injection

17.6 Sexually Transmitted Diseases

STDs are caused by viruses, bacteria, fungi, and parasites.

STDs Caused by Viruses

- AIDS is caused by HIV (human immunodeficiency virus).
- Genital warts are caused by human papillomaviruses; these viruses cause warts or lesions on genitals and are associated with certain cancers.
- Genital herpes is caused by herpes simplex virus 2; it causes blisters on genitals.
- Hepatitis is caused by hepatitis viruses A, B, C, D, E, and G. Hepatitis A and E are usually acquired from contaminated water; B and C are from blood-borne transmission; and B, D, and G are sexually transmitted.

STDs Caused by Bacteria

- Chlamydia is caused by *Chlamydia trachomatis.*
- Gonorrhea is caused by *Neisseria gonorrhoeae.*
- Syphilis is caused by *Treponema pallidum.* It has three stages, with the third stage resulting in death.

Vaginal Infections

- Bacterial vaginosis commonly results from bacterial overgrowth. *Gardnerella vaginosis* often causes such infections.
- Infection with the yeast *Candida albicans* also occurs because of overgrowth, and antibiotics or hormonal contraceptives trigger this condition.
- The parasite *Trichomonas vaginalis* also causes vaginosis. This type affects both men and women, though men are often asymptomatic.

384   Unit 5   Reproduction in Humans

ASSESS

TESTING YOURSELF

Choose the best answer for each question.

17.1 Human Life Cycle

1. During the human life cycle, what process is responsible for reducing the number of chromosomes from 46 to the 23 found in the gametes?
   a. mitosis
   b. fertilization
   c. ovulation
   d. meiosis
   e. None of these are correct.

2. Which of the following are similar features of the reproductive systems of males and females?
   a. They are the site where meiosis occurs in the body.
   b. They produce sex hormones.
   c. They produce the gametes.
   d. All of these are correct.

17.2 Male Reproductive System

3. Label this diagram of the male reproductive system and nearby structures.

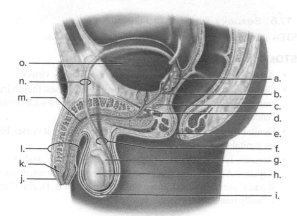

4. Testosterone is produced and secreted by
   a. spermatogonia.
   b. sustentacular cells.
   c. seminiferous tubules.
   d. interstitial cells.

5. Spermatogenesis occurs in this structure of the male reproductive system.
   a. prostate
   b. penis
   c. Sertoli cells
   d. seminiferous tubules
   e. None of these are correct.

17.3 Female Reproductive System

6. Label this diagram of the female reproductive system.

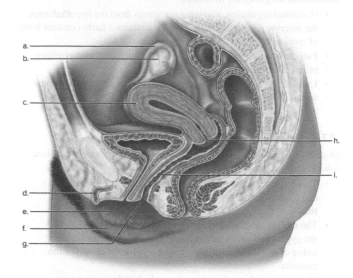

7. Implantation occurs in what structure of the female reproductive system?
   a. uterine tubes
   b. uterus
   c. vagina
   d. cervix
   e. None of these are correct.

8. This structure connects the ovary with the uterus.
   a. cervix
   b. vagina
   c. uterine tube
   d. endometrium

17.4 The Ovarian Cycle

9. The release of the oocyte from the follicle is caused by
   a. a decreasing level of estrogen.
   b. a surge in the level of follicle-stimulating hormone.
   c. a surge in the level of luteinizing hormone.
   d. progesterone released from the corpus luteum.

10. Which of the following is not an event of the ovarian cycle?
   a. FSH promotes the development of a follicle.
   b. The endometrium thickens.
   c. The corpus luteum secretes progesterone.
   d. Ovulation of an egg occurs.

11. During pregnancy,
   a. the ovarian and uterine cycles occur more quickly than before.
   b. GnRH is produced at a higher level than before.
   c. the ovarian and uterine cycles do not occur.
   d. the female secondary sex characteristics are not maintained.

17.5 Control of Reproduction

In questions 12–14, match each method of protection with a means of birth control in the key.

Key:

- **a.** vasectomy
- **b.** oral contraception
- **c.** intrauterine device (IUD)
- **d.** diaphragm
- **e.** male condom

12. Blocks entrance of sperm to uterus
13. Traps sperm and prevents STDs
14. Prevents implantation of an embryo

17.6 Sexually Transmitted Diseases

15. Which of the following can be treated using antibiotics?
    - **a.** genital herpes
    - **b.** hepatitis
    - **c.** chlamydia
    - **d.** HIV
    - **e.** None of these are correct.

16. The bacterium *Treponema pallidum* causes which of the following?
    - **a.** gonorrhea
    - **b.** syphilis
    - **c.** hepatitis
    - **d.** chlamydia

ENGAGE

THINKING CRITICALLY

1. Female athletes who train intensively often stop menstruating. The important factor appears to be the reduction of body fat below a certain level. Give a possible evolutionary explanation for a relationship between body fat in females and reproductive cycles.

2. The average sperm count in males is now lower than it was several decades ago. The reasons for this lower sperm count are not known. What data might be helpful in order to formulate a testable hypothesis?

3. Women who use birth control pills appear to have a lower risk of developing ovarian cancer, whereas the use of fertility-enhancing drugs (which increase the number of follicles that develop) may increase a woman's risk. Speculate about how these therapies might affect a woman's risk of developing ovarian cancer.

CHAPTER

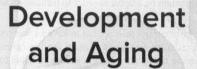

Development and Aging

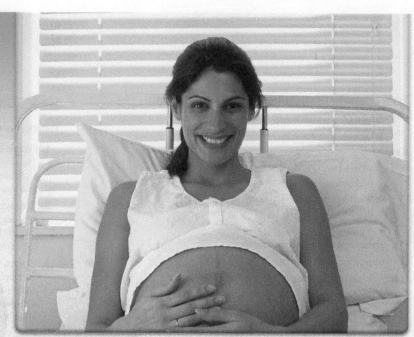

© John Slater/Getty RF

CHAPTER CONCEPTS

18.1 Fertilization
During fertilization, a sperm nucleus fuses with an egg nucleus. Once one sperm penetrates the plasma membrane, the egg undergoes changes that prevent any more sperm from entering.

18.2 Pre-embryonic and Embryonic Development
Pre-embryonic development occurs between fertilization and implantation in the uterine lining. By the end of embryonic development, all organ systems have been established and there is a mature and functioning placenta.

18.3 Fetal Development
During fetal development, the gender becomes obvious, the skeleton continues to ossify, fetal movement begins, and the fetus gains weight.

18.4 Pregnancy and Birth
During pregnancy, the mother gains weight as the uterus comes to occupy most of the abdominal cavity. A positive feedback mechanism that involves uterine contractions and oxytocin explains the onset and continuation of labor so that the child is born.

18.5 Aging
Development after birth consists of infancy, childhood, adolescence, and adulthood. Aging is influenced by both our genes and external factors.

BEFORE YOU BEGIN

Before beginning this chapter, take a few moments to review the following discussions:

Section 17.2 How does spermatogenesis produce sperm cells?

Section 17.4 How does oogenesis produce egg cells?

Section 17.4 What are the roles of estrogen and progesterone in the female reproductive system?

CASE STUDY: PREGNANCY TESTING

For several months, Amber and Kent had been trying to conceive a child. They had put off having children for several years while they pursued their careers. As they both approached the age of 40, they were beginning to feel the pressures of time. As a precautionary method, Amber had begun taking prenatal vitamins; additionally, she was much more aware of the content of her diet. Although neither of them was ever really into physical exercise, both began walking several times a week in preparation for what they hoped would be news that Amber was pregnant. Finally, after 2 months, Amber proudly announced that the home pregnancy test was positive! They immediately scheduled an appointment with their regular physician to prepare for the next stage of their lives.

Amber and Kent were both very satisfied with their choice of a doctor. At the first visit following the positive results of the home pregnancy test, their physician gave Amber a complete physical as well as a blood test to confirm pregnancy. The physician informed the new parents that a blood test was much more accurate in detecting levels of the pregnancy hormone, human chorionic gonadotropin (HCG), than over-the-counter (OTC) urine tests. The results of the blood test confirmed what Amber and Kent suspected, that in a period of just 40 weeks Amber and Kent would be parents.

Their physician promptly gave the parents-to-be a list of items to avoid. Amber was told to increase her level of exercise and watch her diet more closely. She needed to drink eight to ten glasses of water per day, as well as eat plenty of fruits and vegetables. The doctor informed them that it was crucial for Amber to inform her physician of any over-the-counter drugs she may want to take, especially in the first trimester. Her doctor told Amber that the first trimester was a period when critical organ systems developed in her baby and that alcohol and most OTC medications were now forbidden. Both Amber and Kent were up to the challenge and excited about the prospects of finally being parents.

As you read through the chapter, think about the following questions:

1. What is the role of the HCG hormone in pregnancy?
2. Why would the doctor ask Amber to check before taking over-the-counter drugs?
3. What physiological changes should Amber expect over the course of her pregnancy?

18.1 Fertilization

LEARNING OUTCOME

Upon completion of this section, you should be able to

1. Describe the steps in the fertilization of an egg cell by a sperm.

In Chapter 17 we examined the structure and function of the reproductive system in males and females. One of the functions of a reproductive system is to produce gametes (egg and sperm cells) for the production of a new individual. **Fertilization** is the union of a sperm and an egg to form a **zygote,** the first cell of that new individual (Fig. 18.1).

Steps of Fertilization

The tail of a sperm is a flagellum, which enables the sperm to swim toward the egg. The middle piece contains energy-producing mitochondria. The head contains a nucleus capped by a membrane-bound acrosome (see Fig 17.4d). The acrosome is an organelle containing digestive enzymes. Only the nucleus from the sperm head fuses with the egg nucleus. Therefore, the zygote receives cytoplasm and organelles only from the mother.

The plasma membrane of the egg is surrounded by an extracellular matrix termed the *zona pellucida.* In turn, the zona

SCIENCE IN YOUR LIFE

How many sperm compete to fertilize the egg?

Studies indicate that there are between 150 and 200 million sperm in a man's ejaculation. Of that number, only about 20 to 30 make it near the egg. Out of those, only a single sperm fertilizes the egg.

pellucida is surrounded by a few layers of adhering follicular cells, collectively called the *corona radiata.* These cells nourished the egg when it was in a follicle of the ovary.

During fertilization, several sperm penetrate the corona radiata. Several sperm attempt to penetrate the zona pellucida, but only one sperm enters the egg. The acrosome plays a role in allowing sperm to penetrate the zona pellucida. After a sperm head binds tightly to the zona pellucida, the acrosome releases digestive enzymes that forge a pathway for the sperm through the zona pellucida. When a sperm binds to the egg, the plasma membranes of egg and sperm fuse and the nucleus of the sperm enters the egg. Fusion of the sperm nucleus and the egg nucleus follows.

To ensure proper development, only one sperm should enter an egg. Prevention of polyspermy (entrance of more than one sperm) depends on changes in the egg's plasma membrane and in the zona pellucida. When a sperm comes in contact with the egg, a rapid release of Na$^+$ ions depolarizes the egg's plasma membrane,

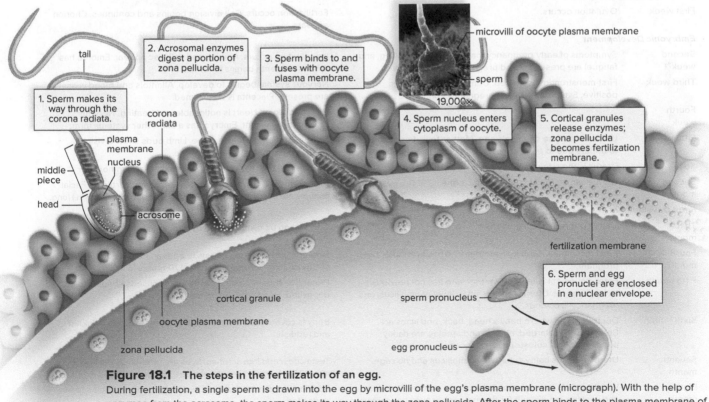

Figure 18.1   The steps in the fertilization of an egg.
During fertilization, a single sperm is drawn into the egg by microvilli of the egg's plasma membrane (micrograph). With the help of enzymes from the acrosome, the sperm makes its way through the zona pellucida. After the sperm binds to the plasma membrane of the egg, changes occur that prevent other sperm from entering the egg. Fertilization is complete when the sperm pronucleus and the egg pronucleus contribute their chromosomes to the zygote.
© David M. Phillips/Science Source

preventing the binding of any other sperm. In addition, vesicles called cortical granules release enzymes that cause the zona pellucida to become an impenetrable fertilization membrane. Now sperm cannot bind to the zona pellucida, either.

CHECK YOUR PROGRESS 18.1

1. Describe the steps in fertilization.
2. Distinguish between the functions of the corona radiata and the zona pellucida.
3. Explain what prevents multiple sperm from fertilizing the same egg.

CONNECTING THE CONCEPTS

For more information on egg and sperm cells, refer to the following discussions:

Section 17.2 explains how sperm are produced by spermatogenesis.

Section 17.4 explains how egg cells are produced by oogenesis.

18.2 Pre-embryonic and Embryonic Development

LEARNING OUTCOMES

Upon completion of this section, you should be able to

1. Recognize how cleavage, growth, morphogenesis, and differentiation all play a role in development.
2. Identify the extraembryonic membranes and provide a function for each.
3. Identify the organ systems that are formed from each of the primary germ layers.
4. Summarize the key events that occur at each stage of pre-embryonic and embryonic development.

Human development proceeds from pre-embryonic to embryonic development and then through fetal development. Table 18.1 outlines the major events during development.

Table 18.1	Human Development	
Time	**Events for Mother**	**Events for Baby**
Pre-embryonic Development		
First week	Ovulation occurs.	Fertilization occurs. Cell division begins and continues. Chorion appears.
Embryonic Development		
Second week	Symptoms of early pregnancy (nausea, breast swelling, and fatigue) are present. Blood pregnancy test is positive.	Implantation occurs. Amnion and yolk sac appear. Embryo has tissues. Placenta begins to form.
Third week	First menstruation is missed. Urine pregnancy test is positive. Symptoms of early pregnancy continue.	Nervous system begins to develop. Allantois and blood vessels are present. Placenta is well formed.
Fourth week		Limb buds form. Heart is noticeable and beating. Nervous system is prominent. Embryo has a tail. Other systems form.
Fifth week	Uterus is the size of a hen's egg. Mother feels frequent need to urinate due to pressure of growing uterus on her bladder.	Embryo is curved. Head is large. Limb buds show divisions. Nose, eyes, and ears are noticeable.
Sixth week	Uterus is the size of an orange.	Fingers and toes are present. Skeleton is cartilaginous.
Second month	Uterus can be felt above the pubic bone.	All systems are developing. Bone is replacing cartilage. Facial features are becoming refined. Embryo is about 38 mm (1.5 in.) long.
Fetal Development		
Third month	Uterus is the size of a grapefruit.	Gender can be distinguished by ultrasound. Fingernails appear.
Fourth month	Fetal movement is felt by a mother who has previously been pregnant.	Skeleton is visible. Hair begins to appear. Fetus is about 150 mm (6 in.) long and weighs about 170 grams (6 oz).
Fifth month	Fetal movement is felt by a mother who has not previously been pregnant. Uterus reaches up to level of umbilicus, and pregnancy is obvious.	Protective cheesy coating called vernix caseosa begins to be deposited. Heartbeat can be heard.
Sixth month	Doctor can tell where baby's head, back, and limbs are. Breasts have enlarged, nipples and areolae are darkly pigmented, and colostrum is produced.	Body is covered with fine hair called lanugo. Skin is wrinkled and reddish.
Seventh month	Uterus reaches halfway between umbilicus and rib cage.	Testes descend into scrotum. Eyes are open. Fetus is about 300 mm (12 in.) long and weighs about 1,350 grams (3 lb).
Eighth month	Weight gain is averaging about a pound a week. Standing and walking are difficult for the mother because her center of gravity is thrown forward.	Body hair begins to disappear. Subcutaneous fat begins to be deposited.
Ninth month	Uterus is up to rib cage, causing shortness of breath and heartburn. Sleeping becomes difficult.	Fetus is ready for birth. It is about 530 mm (20.5 in.) long and weighs about 3,400 grams (7.5 lb).

Processes of Development

As a human develops, these processes occur:

- **Cleavage.** Immediately after fertilization, the zygote begins to divide, so that there are first 2; then 4, 8, 16, and 32 cells; and so forth. Increase in size does not accompany these divisions (Fig. 18.2). Cell division during cleavage is mitotic, and each cell receives a full complement of chromosomes and genes.
- **Growth.** During embryonic development, cell division is accompanied by an increase in size of the daughter cells.
- **Morphogenesis.** Morphogenesis is the shaping of the embryo and is first evident when certain cells are seen to move, or migrate, in relation to other cells. By these movements, the embryo begins to assume various shapes.

- **Differentiation.** When cells take on a specific structure and function, differentiation occurs. The first system to become visibly differentiated is the nervous system.

Stages of Development

Pre-embryonic development encompasses the events of the first week; **embryonic development** begins with the second week and lasts until the end of the second month.

Pre-embryonic Development

The events of the first week of development are shown in Figure 18.2.

Immediately after fertilization, the zygote divides repeatedly as it passes down the uterine tube to the uterus. A **morula** is a compact ball of embryonic cells that becomes a **blastocyst.** The many cells of the blastocyst arrange themselves so that there is an **inner cell mass** surrounded by an outer layer of cells. The inner cell mass will become the **embryo,** and the layer of cells will become the chorion. The early appearance of the chorion emphasizes the complete dependence of the developing embryo on this extra-embryonic membrane.

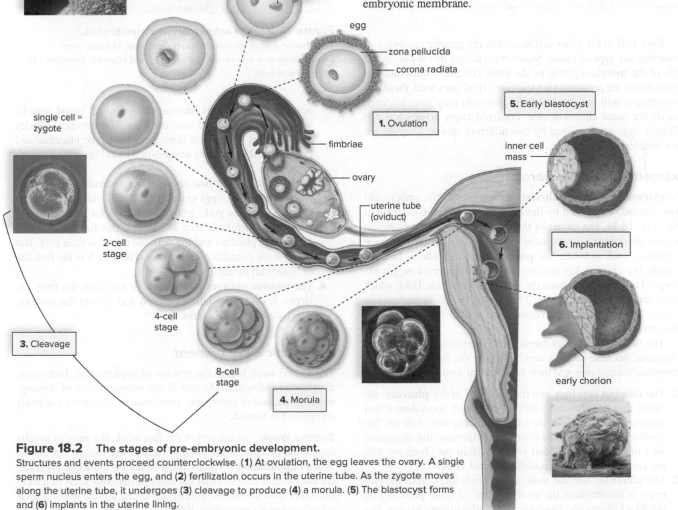

Figure 18.2   The stages of pre-embryonic development.
Structures and events proceed counterclockwise. (**1**) At ovulation, the egg leaves the ovary. A single sperm nucleus enters the egg, and (**2**) fertilization occurs in the uterine tube. As the zygote moves along the uterine tube, it undergoes (**3**) cleavage to produce (**4**) a morula. (**5**) The blastocyst forms and (**6**) implants in the uterine lining.

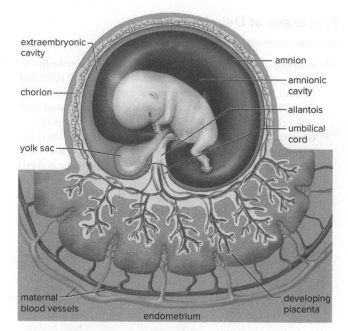

Figure 18.3   The extraembryonic membranes.
The chorion and amnion surround the embryo. The two other extraembryonic membranes, the yolk sac and allantois, contribute to the umbilical cord.

Each cell in the inner cell mass has the genetic capability of becoming any type of tissue. Sometimes, during development, the cells of the morula separate or the inner cell mass splits and two pre-embryos are present rather than one. If all goes well, these two pre-embryos will be identical twins, because they have inherited exactly the same chromosomes. Fraternal twins arise when two different eggs are fertilized by two different sperm. They do not have identical chromosomes.

Extraembryonic Membranes

The **extraembryonic membranes** are not part of the embryo and fetus. Instead, as implied by their name, they are outside the embryo (Fig. 18.3). The names of the extraembryonic membranes in humans are strange to us, because they are named for their function in animals, such as birds, that produce eggs with shells. In these animals, the chorion lies next to the shell and carries on gas exchange. The amnion contains the protective amniotic fluid, which bathes the developing embryo. The allantois collects nitrogenous wastes. The yolk sac surrounds the yolk, which provides nourishment.

The functions of the extraembryonic membranes are different in humans, because humans develop inside the uterus. The extraembryonic membranes and their functions in humans follow.

1. The **chorion** develops into the fetal half of the **placenta,** the organ that provides the embryo/fetus with nourishment and oxygen and takes away its waste. The chorionic villi are fingerlike projections of the chorion that increase the absorptive area of the chorion. Blood vessels within the chorionic villi are continuous with the umbilical blood vessels.
2. The **allantois,** like the yolk sac, extends away from the embryo. It accumulates the small amount of urine produced by the fetal kidneys and later gives rise to the urinary bladder. For

now, its blood vessels become the umbilical blood vessels, which take blood to and from the fetus. The umbilical arteries carry oxygen-poor blood from the fetus to the placenta, and the umbilical veins carry oxygen-rich blood from the placenta to the fetus.

3. The **yolk sac** is the first embryonic membrane to appear. In animals that have eggs encased by shells, such as birds, the yolk sac contains yolk, which is the food for the developing embryo. In mammals such as humans, this function is taken over by the placenta and the yolk sac contains little yolk. But the yolk sac contains plentiful blood vessels. It is the first site of blood cell formation.
4. The **amnion** enlarges as the embryo and then the fetus enlarges. It contains fluid to cushion and protect the embryo, which develops into a fetus.

Embryonic Development

The second week begins the process of implantation. Embryonic development lasts until the end of the second month of development. At the end of embryonic development, the embryo is easily recognized as human.

Second Week   At the end of the first week, the embryo usually begins the process of implanting itself in the wall of the uterus. When **implantation** is successful, a woman is clinically pregnant. On occasion, it happens that the embryo implants itself in a location other than the uterus, usually one of the uterine tubes. This is called an *ectopic pregnancy.* Because the uterine tubes are unable to expand to adjust for the growing embryo, this form of pregnancy is not successful and can pose health risks for the mother. During implantation, the chorion secretes enzymes to digest away some of the tissue and blood vessels of the endometrium of the uterus. The chorion also begins to secrete **human chorionic gonadotropin (HCG),** the hormone that is the basis for the pregnancy test. HCG acts as luteinizing hormone (LH) in that it maintains the corpus luteum past the time it normally disintegrates. It is being stimulated, so the corpus luteum secretes progesterone, which maintains the endometrial wall. The endometrium is maintained, so the expected menstruation does not occur.

The embryo is now about the size of the period at the end of this sentence. As the week progresses, the inner cell mass becomes the *embryonic disk,* and two more extraembryonic membranes form (Fig. 18.4*a, b*). The yolk sac is the first site of blood cell formation. The amniotic cavity surrounds the embryo (and then the fetus) as it develops. In humans, amniotic fluid acts as an insulator against cold and heat. It also absorbs shock, such as that caused by the mother exercising.

The major event, called **gastrulation,** turns the inner cell mass into the embryonic disk. Gastrulation is an example of morphogenesis, during which cells move or migrate. In this case, cells migrate to become tissue layers called **primary germ layers.** By the time gastrulation is complete, the embryonic disk has become an embryo with three primary germ layers: ectoderm, mesoderm, and endoderm. Figure 18.5 shows the significance of the primary germ layers. All the organs of an individual (Table 18.2) can be traced back to one of the primary germ layers.

Third Week Two important organ systems make their appearance during the third week. The nervous system is the first organ system to be visually evident. At first, a thickening appears along the entire posterior length of the embryo. Then, the center begins to fold inward, forming a pocket. The edges are called neural folds. When the neural folds meet at the midline, the pocket becomes a tube, called the neural tube. The neural tube later develops into the brain and the spinal cord.

Development of the heart begins in the third week and continues into the fourth week. At first, cells from both sides of the body

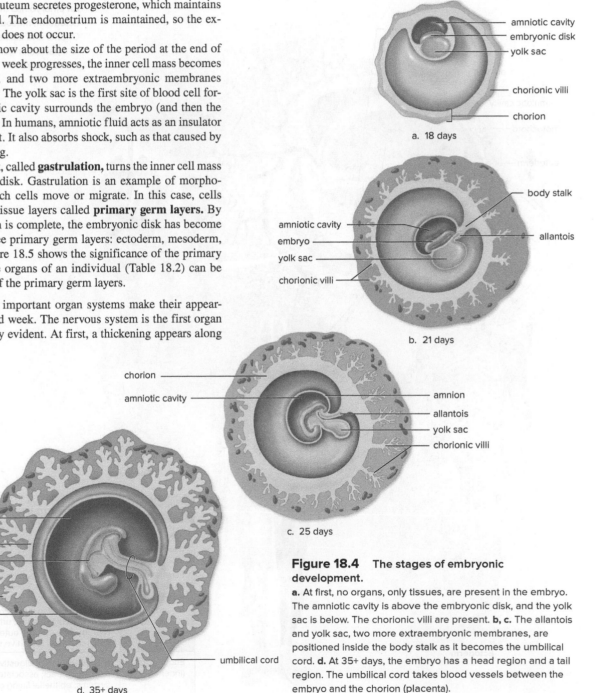

a. 18 days

b. 21 days

c. 25 days

d. 35+ days

Figure 18.4 The stages of embryonic development.

a. At first, no organs, only tissues, are present in the embryo. The amniotic cavity is above the embryonic disk, and the yolk sac is below. The chorionic villi are present. **b, c.** The allantois and yolk sac, two more extraembryonic membranes, are positioned inside the body stalk as it becomes the umbilical cord. **d.** At 35+ days, the embryo has a head region and a tail region. The umbilical cord takes blood vessels between the embryo and the chorion (placenta).

migrate to form the heart. When these fuse to form a continuous tube, the heart begins pumping blood, even though the chambers of the heart are not fully formed. The veins enter posteriorly, and the arteries exit anteriorly from this largely tubular heart. Later, the heart twists, so that all major blood vessels are located anteriorly.

Fourth and Fifth Weeks   At 4 weeks, the embryo is barely larger than the height of this print. A body stalk (future umbilical cord) connects the embryo to the chorion, which has treelike projections called **chorionic villi** (see Fig. 18.4c, d). The fourth extraembryonic membrane, the allantois, lies within the body stalk. Its blood vessels

Figure 18.5   The embryonic germ layers.
An embryo has three germ layers—ectoderm, mesoderm, and endoderm. Organs and tissues can be traced back to a particular germ layer, as indicated in this illustration.

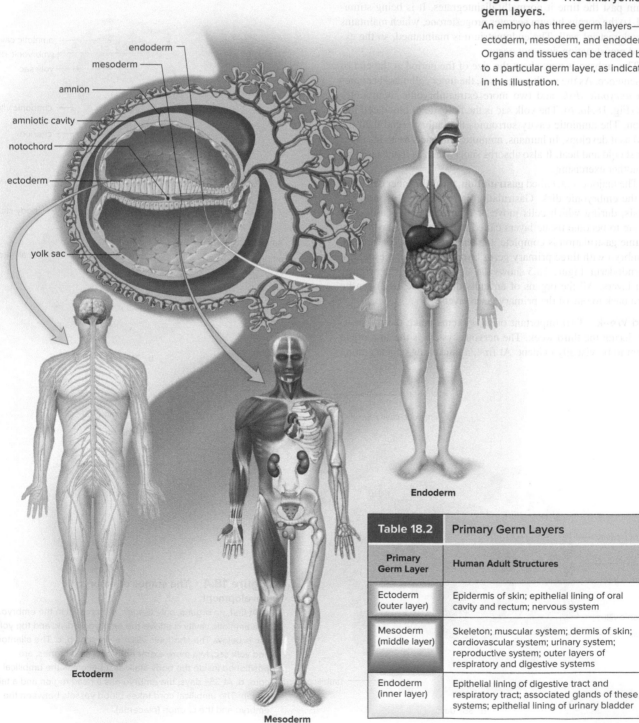

endoderm
mesoderm
amnion
amniotic cavity
notochord
ectoderm
yolk sac

Ectoderm

Mesoderm

Endoderm

Table 18.2	Primary Germ Layers
Primary Germ Layer	**Human Adult Structures**
Ectoderm (outer layer)	Epidermis of skin; epithelial lining of oral cavity and rectum; nervous system
Mesoderm (middle layer)	Skeleton; muscular system; dermis of skin; cardiovascular system; urinary system; reproductive system; outer layers of respiratory and digestive systems
Endoderm (inner layer)	Epithelial lining of digestive tract and respiratory tract; associated glands of these systems; epithelial lining of urinary bladder

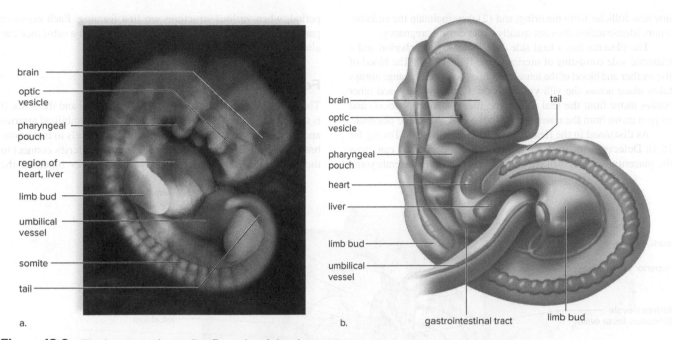

brain
optic vesicle
pharyngeal pouch
region of heart, liver
limb bud
umbilical vessel
somite
tail

a.

brain
optic vesicle
pharyngeal pouch
heart
liver
limb bud
umbilical vessel

tail

b.   gastrointestinal tract   limb bud

Figure 18.6   **The human embryo after 5 weeks of development.**
a. Scanning electron micrograph. **b.** The embryo is curled, so that the head touches the heart and liver, the two organs whose development is further along than the rest of the body. The organs of the gastrointestinal tract are forming, and the arms and the legs develop from the bulges called limb buds. The tail is an evolutionary remnant; its bones regress and become those of the coccyx (tailbone). The pharyngeal pouches become functioning gills in fishes and amphibian larvae; in humans, the first pair of pharyngeal pouches become the auditory tubes. The second pair become the tonsils, and the third and fourth become the thymus and the parathyroid glands.
(a) © Anatomical Travelogue/Science Source

become the umbilical blood vessels. The head and tail then lift up, and the body stalk moves anteriorly by constriction. Once this process is complete, the **umbilical cord** is fully formed (see Fig. 18.4*d*). The umbilical cord connects the developing embryo to the placenta.

Soon, limb buds appear (Fig. 18.6). Later, the arms and legs develop from the limb buds, and even the hands and feet become apparent. At the same time, during the fifth week, the head enlarges and the sense organs become more prominent. It is possible to make out the developing eyes and ears, and even the nose.

Sixth Through Eighth Weeks During the sixth through eighth weeks of development, the embryo changes to a form easily recognized as a human. Concurrent with brain development, the head achieves its normal relationship with the body as a neck region develops. The nervous system is developed well enough to permit reflex actions, such as a startle response to touch. At the end of this period, the embryo is about 38 mm (1.5 in.) long and weighs no more than an aspirin tablet, even though all organ systems have been established.

CHECK YOUR PROGRESS 18.2

1. Distinguish between the processes of morphogenesis and differentiation.
2. Describe the function of the extraembryonic membranes.
3. Summarize what occurs at each stage of pre-embryonic development and embryonic development.

CONNECTING THE CONCEPTS

For more information on the topics presented in this section, refer to the following discussions:

Section 4.7 summarizes the function of each of the organ systems in the body.

Section 17.4 examines the roles of HCG and progesterone in pregnancy.

18.3 Fetal Development

LEARNING OUTCOMES

Upon completion of this section, you should be able to

1. State the roles of progesterone and estrogen in fetal development.
2. Describe the flow of blood in a fetus and explain the role of the placenta.
3. Summarize the major events in the development of the fetus from 3 to 9 months.
4. Explain the process by which the male and female reproductive organs develop.

The **placenta** is the source of progesterone and estrogen during pregnancy. These hormones have two functions: (1) Because of negative feedback on the hypothalamus and anterior pituitary, they prevent any new follicles from maturing; and (2) they maintain the endometrium. Menstruation does not usually occur during pregnancy.

The placenta has a fetal side contributed by the chorion and a maternal side consisting of uterine tissue (Fig. 18.7*a*). The blood of the mother and blood of the fetus never mix, because exchange always takes place across the villi via diffusion. Carbon dioxide and other wastes move from the fetal side to the maternal side. Nutrients and oxygen move from the maternal side to the fetal side of the placenta.

As discussed in the Health feature "Preventing and Testing for Birth Defects" later in this section, harmful chemicals can cross the placenta, and this is of particular concern during the embryonic

period, when various structures are first forming. Each organ or part seems to have a sensitive period during which a substance can alter its normal function.

Fetal Circulation

The umbilical cord stretches between the placenta and the fetus. It is the lifeline of the fetus because it contains the umbilical arteries and vein (Fig. 18.7*b*). Blood in the fetal aorta travels to its various branches, including the iliac arteries. The iliac arteries connect to the *umbilical arteries* carrying oxygen (O_2)-poor blood to the

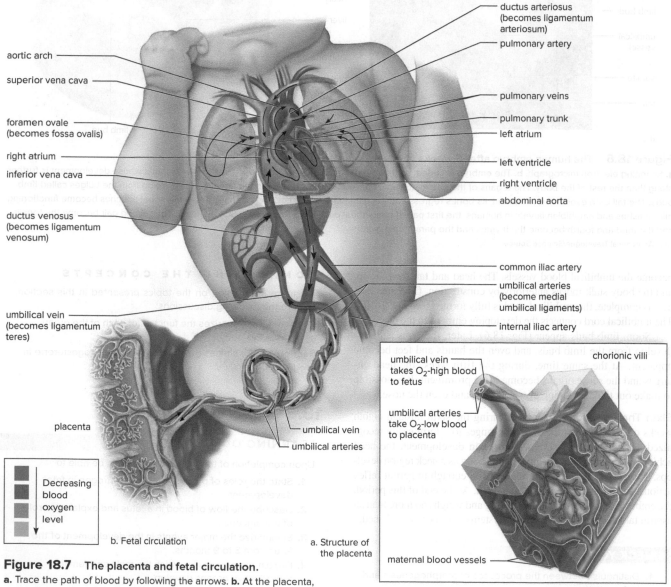

Figure 18.7   **The placenta and fetal circulation.**
a. Trace the path of blood by following the arrows. **b.** At the placenta, an exchange of molecules between fetal and maternal blood takes place across the walls of the chorionic villi. **a.** The flow of blood in the fetus differs from that in the adult (see Fig. 5.11) due to presence of the placenta. You can trace the path of blood by following the arrows.

Preventing and Testing for Birth Defects

Birth defects, or congenital disorders, are abnormal conditions that are present at birth. According to the Centers for Disease Control and Prevention (CDC), about 1 in 33 babies born in the United States has a birth defect. Genetic birth defects can sometimes be detected before birth by a variety of methods (Fig. 18A). However, these methods are not without risk.

Some birth defects are not serious, and not all can be prevented. But women can take steps to increase their chances of delivering a healthy baby.

Eat a Healthy Diet

Certain birth defects may occur because of nutritional deficiencies. For example, women of childbearing age are urged to make sure they consume adequate amounts of folic acid (a B vitamin) to prevent neural tube defects, such as spina bifida and anencephaly. In spina bifida, part of the vertebral column fails to develop properly and cannot adequately protect the spinal cord. With anencephaly, most of the fetal brain fails to develop. Anencephalic infants are stillborn or survive for only a few days after birth.

Fortunately, folic acid is plentiful in leafy green vegetables, nuts, and citrus fruits. The CDC recommends that all women of childbearing age get at least 400 micrograms (µg) of folic acid every day through supplements, in addition to eating a healthy diet rich in folic acid. Unfortunately, neural tube birth defects can occur just a few weeks after conception, when many women are still unaware that they are pregnant—especially if the pregnancy is unplanned.

Avoid Alcohol, Smoking, and Drug Abuse

Alcohol consumption during pregnancy is a leading cause of birth defects. In severe instances, the baby is born with fetal alcohol syndrome (FAS), estimated to occur in 0.2 to 1.5 of every 1,000 live births in the United States. Many children with FAS are underweight and have an abnormally small head, abnormal facial development, and intellectual disabilities. As they mature, children with FAS often exhibit a short attention span, impulsiveness, and poor judgment, as well as problems with learning and memory. Heavy alcohol use also reduces a woman's folic acid level, increasing the risk of neural tube defects.

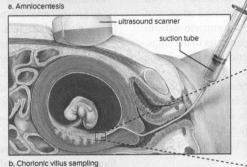
a. Amniocentesis

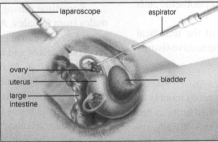
b. Chorionic villus sampling

c. Preimplantation genetic diagnosis

Figure 18A Methods for genetic defect testing before birth.
About 20% of all birth defects are due to genetic or chromosomal abnormalities, which may be detected before birth. **a.** Amniocentesis is usually performed from the fifteenth to the seventeenth week of pregnancy. **b.** Chorionic villus sampling is usually performed from the eighth to the twelfth week of pregnancy. **c.** Preimplantation genetic diagnosis can be performed prior to in vitro fertilization, either on oocytes that have been collected from the woman or on the early embryo.

Cigarette smoking causes many birth defects. Babies born to smoking mothers typically have low birth weight and are more likely to have defects of the face, heart, and brain than children of nonsmokers.

Illegal drugs should also be avoided. For example, cocaine causes blood pressure fluctuations that deprive the fetus of oxygen. Cocaine-exposed babies may have problems with vision and coordination and may be intellectually disabled.

Alert Medical Personnel If You Are or May Be Pregnant

Several medications that are safe for healthy adults may pose a risk to a developing fetus. Pregnant women who require immunizations should consult with their physicians.

Because the rapidly dividing cells of a developing embryo or fetus are very susceptible to damage from radiation, pregnant women should avoid unnecessary X-rays. If X-rays are unavoidable, the woman should notify the X-ray technician that she is pregnant, so that her fetus can be protected as much as possible.

Avoid Infections That Cause Birth Defects

Certain pathogens, such as rubella, toxoplasmosis, herpes simplex, cytomegalovirus, and Zika virus may cause birth defects.

Question to Consider

1. Besides tobacco, alcohol, and illegal drugs, what other potential risks should a pregnant woman avoid? Why?

placenta. The *umbilical vein* carries blood rich in nutrients and O_2 from the placenta to the fetus. The umbilical vein enters the liver and then joins the *ductus venosus* (venous duct). This merges with the inferior vena cava, a vessel that returns blood to the right atrium. This mixed blood enters the heart, and most of it is shunted to the left atrium through the *foramen ovale* (oval opening). The left ventricle pumps this blood into the aorta. Oxygen-poor blood that enters the right atrium is pumped into the pulmonary trunk. It then joins the aorta by way of the *ductus arteriosus* (arterial duct). Therefore, most blood entering the right atrium bypasses the lungs.

Various circulatory changes occur at birth due to the tying of the cord and the expansion of the lungs:

1. Inflation of the lungs. This reduces the resistance to blood flow through the lungs, resulting in an increased amount of blood flow from the right atrium to the right ventricle and into the pulmonary arteries. Now gas exchange occurs in the lungs, not at the placenta. Oxygen-rich blood returns to the left side of the heart through the pulmonary veins.
2. An increase in blood flow from the pulmonary veins to the left atrium. This increases the pressure in the left atrium, causing a flap to cover the foramen ovale. Even if this mechanism fails, passage of blood from the right atrium to the left atrium rarely occurs, because either the opening is small or it closes when the atria contract.
3. The ductus arteriosus closes at birth, because endothelial cells divide and block off the duct.
4. Remains of the ductus arteriosus and parts of the umbilical arteries and vein later are transformed into connective tissue.

Events of Fetal Development

Fetal development includes the third through the ninth months of development. At this time the fetus is recognizably human, but many refinements still need to be added. The fetus usually increases in size and gains the weight it needs to live as an independent individual.

Due to the rapid development of organs and tissues, the fetus is especially susceptible to environmental influences, such as chemicals and radiation. While procedures such as ultrasounds provide an indication of the overall rate of development and potential physical problems, there are also several methods of testing the fetus for genetic abnormalities. The Health feature "Preventing and Testing for Birth Defects" explores some of the more common options.

Third and Fourth Months

At the beginning of the third month, the fetal head is still very large relative to the rest of the body. The nose is flat, the eyes are far apart, and the ears are well formed. Head growth begins to slow down as the rest of the body increases in length. Fingernails, nipples, eyelashes, eyebrows, and hair on the head appear.

Cartilage begins to be replaced by bone as ossification centers appear in most of the bones. Cartilage remains at the ends of the long bones, and ossification is not complete until age 18 or 20 years. The skull has six large, membranous areas called **fontanels.** These permit a certain amount of flexibility as the head passes through the birth canal, and they allow rapid growth of the brain

SCIENCE IN YOUR LIFE

When can the heartbeat of a fetus first be detected?

A fetal heart will begin forming from tissues in the chest of the fetus first by forming a tube structure, which will later develop into the chambers of the heart. By the fifth week of fetal development, the heart has formed; it is too small to hear but it can be seen on an ultrasound. By week 10, the heart is fully developed and is beating at a rate of 150 to 195 beats per minute. The sounds of the heart at this point are often referred to as fetal heart tones (FHTs) and are very rapid due to the heart's small size; however, eventually they will settle into a rate of 120 to 160 beats per minute (usually after the twelfth week) and may even beat in synch with the mother's rate. The fetal heart can be heard through the end of the first trimester and into the beginning of the second using an amplification machine called a Doppler instrument, which bounces harmless sound waves off the heart. After that point, depending on the position of the fetus, a stethoscope can detect the heartbeat as the fetus and its heart get larger.

during infancy. Progressive fusion of the skull bones causes the fontanels to close, usually by 2 years of age.

Sometime during the third month, it is possible to distinguish males from females. As discussed later in this section, the presence of an *SRY* gene, usually on the Y chromosome, leads to the development of testes and male genitals. Otherwise, ovaries and female genitals develop. At this time, either testes or ovaries are located within the abdominal cavity. Later, in the last trimester of fetal development, the testes descend into the scrotal sacs (scrotum). Sometimes the testes fail to descend. In that case, an operation may be done later to place them in their proper location.

During the fourth month, the fetal heartbeat is loud enough to be heard when a physician applies a stethoscope to the mother's abdomen. At the end of this month, the fetus is about 152 mm (6 in.) in length and weighs about 171 g (6 oz).

Fifth Through Seventh Months

During the fifth through seventh months (Fig. 18.8), the mother begins to feel movement. At first there is only a fluttering sensation, but as the fetal legs grow and develop, kicks and jabs are felt. The fetus, though, is in the fetal position, with the head bent down and in contact with the flexed knees.

The wrinkled, translucent skin is covered by a fine down called **lanugo.** This, in turn, is coated with a white, greasy, cheeselike substance called **vernix caseosa,** which probably protects the delicate skin from the amniotic fluid. The eyelids are now fully open.

At the end of this period, the fetus's length has increased to about 300 mm (12 in.), and it weighs about 1,380 g (3 lb). It is possible that the baby will survive if born now.

Eighth Through Ninth Months

At the end of 9 months, the fetus is about 530 mm (20.5 in.) long and weighs about 3,400 g (7.5 lb). Weight gain is due largely to an

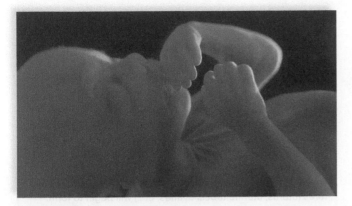

Figure 18.8   **A 5- to 7-month-old fetus.**
Wrinkled skin is covered by fine hair.
© James Stevenson/Science Source

accumulation of fat beneath the skin. Full-term babies have the best chance of survival. Premature babies are subject to various challenges, such as respiratory distress syndrome (because their lungs are underdeveloped), jaundice, and infections.

As the end of development approaches, the fetus usually rotates, so that the head is pointed toward the cervix. However, if the fetus does not turn, a breech birth (rump first) is likely. It is very difficult for the cervix to expand enough to accommodate this form of birth, and asphyxiation of the baby is more likely to occur. Thus, a *cesarean section* (incision through the abdominal and uterine walls) may be prescribed for delivery of the fetus.

Development of Male and Female Sex Organs

The sex of an individual is determined at the moment of fertilization. Males have a pair of chromosomes designated as X and Y, and females have two X chromosomes. On the Y chromosome, a gene called *SRY* (*s*ex-determining *r*egion of the *Y*) determines whether the gonadal tissue in the embryo will develop into the male or female sex organs. The protein encoded by the *SRY* gene

acts as a regulatory mechanism to control the expression, or function, of other developmental genes in the body (see Section 22.2).

Normal Development of the Sex Organs

Development of the internal and external sex organs depends on the presence or absence of the *SRY* gene.

Internal Sex Organs   During the first several weeks of development, it is impossible to tell by external inspection whether the unborn child is a boy or a girl. Gonads don't start developing until the seventh week. The tissue that gives rise to the gonads is called *indifferent,* because it can become testes or ovaries, depending on the action of hormones.

In Figure 18.9, notice that at 6 weeks, males and females have the same types of ducts. During this indifferent stage, an embryo has the potential to develop into a male or a female. If the *SRY* gene is present, a protein called *testis-determining factor* is produced that regulates the initial development of the testes. The **testosterone** produced by the testes (see Section 16.6) stimulates the Wolffian ducts to become male genital ducts. The Wolffian ducts enter the urethra, which belongs to both the urinary system and the reproductive system in males. An anti-Müllerian hormone causes the Müllerian ducts to regress. In the absence of an *SRY* gene, ovaries (rather than testes) develop from the same indifferent tissue. Now the Wolffian ducts regress, and because of an absence of testosterone, the Müllerian ducts develop into the uterus and uterine tubes. Estrogen has no effect on the Wolffian duct, which degenerates in females. A developing vagina also extends from the uterus. There is no connection between the urinary and genital systems in females.

At 14 weeks, the primitive testes or ovaries are located deep inside the abdominal cavity. An inspection of the interior of the

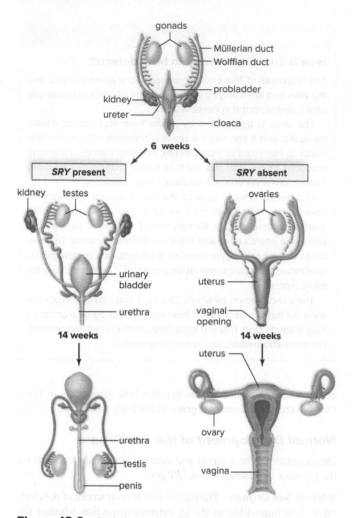

Figure 18.9   Development of the internal sex organs.
The formation of the internal male and female sex organs is largely determined by the presence or absence of the *SRY* gene on the Y chromosome.

ovaries would indicate that they already contain large numbers of tiny follicles, each having an ovum. Toward the end of development, in males the testes descend into the scrotal sac; in females the ovaries remain in the abdominal cavity.

External Sex Organs   Figure 18.10 shows the development of the external sex organs (genitals). These tissues are also indifferent at first—they can develop into either male or female sex organs. At 6 weeks, a small bud appears between the legs; this can develop into the male penis or the female clitoris. At 9 weeks, a urogenital groove bordered by two swellings appears. By 14 weeks, this groove has disappeared in males, and the scrotum has formed from the original swellings. In females, the groove persists and becomes the vaginal opening. Labia majora and labia minora are present instead of a scrotum. These changes are due to the presence or absence of the hormone dihydrotestosterone (DHT), which is manufactured in the adrenal glands and prostate glands from testosterone.

Why is the female gender sometimes referred to as the "default sex"?

The term *default sex* has to do with the presence or absence of the Y chromosome in the fetus. On the Y chromosome, the *SRY* (sex-determining region of the Y) gene produces a protein that will cause Sertoli cells in the testes to produce Müllerian-inhibiting substance (MIS). This causes Leydig cells in the testes to produce testosterone, which signals the development of the male sex organs (vasa deferentia, epididymides, penis, etc.). Without the *SRY* gene and this hormone cascade effect, female structures (uterus, uterine tubes, ovaries, etc.) will begin to form.

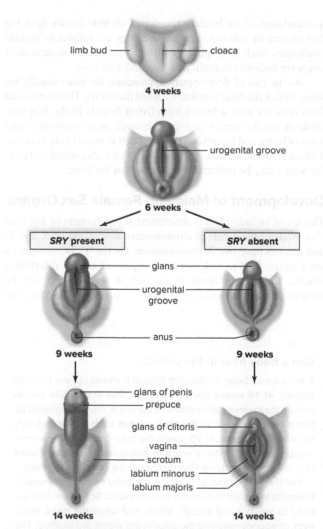

Figure 18.10   Development of the external sex organs.
The presence or absence of the *SRY* gene on the Y chromosome plays an important role in the development of the external sex organs (or genitals).

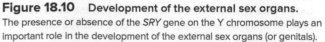

individual develops as a female because the receptors for testosterone are ineffective (Fig. 18.11). The external genitalia develop as female, and the Wolffian duct degenerates internally. The individual does not develop a scrotum, so the testes fail to descend and instead remain deep within the body. The individual develops the secondary sex characteristics of a female, and no abnormality is suspected until the individual fails to menstruate.

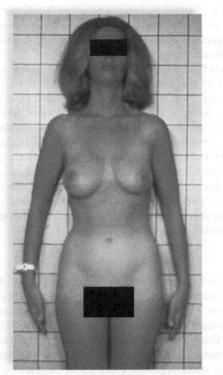

Figure 18.11   Androgen insensitivity affects sexual development.
This individual has a female appearance but the XY chromosomes of a male. She developed as a female because her receptors for testosterone are ineffective. Underdeveloped testes, instead of a uterus and ovaries, are in the abdominal cavity.
© Dr. Howard Jones, Eastern VA Medical School

Abnormal Development of the Sex Organs

It's not correct to say that all XY individuals develop into males. Some XY individuals become females (XY female syndrome). Similarly, some XX individuals develop into males (XX male syndrome). In individuals with XY female syndrome, a piece of the Y chromosome containing the *SRY* gene is missing (this is called a deletion). In individuals with XX male syndrome, the *SRY* gene has moved (this is called a translocation) to the X chromosome. The *SRY* gene causes testes to form, and then the testes secrete these hormones: (1) Testosterone stimulates development of the epididymides, vasa deferentia, seminal vesicles, and ejaculatory duct. (2) Anti-Müllerian hormone prevents further development of female structures and instead causes them to degenerate. (3) Dihydrotestosterone (DHT) directs the development of the urethra, prostate gland, penis, and scrotum.

Ambiguous Sex Determination   The absence of any one or more of these hormones results in ambiguous sex determination. The individual has the external appearance of a female, although the gonads of a female are absent.

In *androgen insensitivity syndrome,* these three types of hormones are produced by testes during development, but the

18.4 Pregnancy and Birth

Pregnancy

The major changes that take place in the mother's body during pregnancy (see Table 18.1) are due largely to the effects of the hormones progesterone and estrogen (Table 18.3).

Digestive System and Nutrition

When first pregnant, the mother may experience nausea and vomiting, loss of appetite, heartburn, constipation, and fatigue. These symptoms subside, and some mothers report increased energy levels and a general sense of well-being, despite an increase in weight. During pregnancy, the mother gains weight due to breast and uterine enlargement; the weight of the fetus; the amount of amniotic fluid; the size of the placenta; her own increase in total body fluid; and an increase in storage of proteins, fats, and minerals. The increased weight can lead to lordosis (swayback) and lower back pain.

Table 18.3	Effects of Placental Hormones on the Mother	
Hormone	**Chief Effects**
Progesterone	Relaxation of smooth muscle; reduced uterine motility; reduced maternal immune response to fetus
Estrogen	Increased uterine blood flow; increased renin-angiotensin-aldosterone activity; increased protein biosynthesis by the liver
Peptide hormones	Increased insulin resistance

A pregnant woman's metabolic rate may rise by up to 10–15% during pregnancy. While this may encourage overeating, the daily diet of a pregnant woman needs to increase by only about 300 kcal to meet the energy needs of the developing fetus. Of far greater importance is the quality of foods in the diet, because there is a greater demand on the woman's body for nutrients such as iron, calcium, and proteins.

The Circulatory System

Aside from an increase in weight, many of the physiological changes in the mother are due to the presence of the placental hormones that support fetal development. Progesterone decreases uterine motility by relaxing smooth muscle, including the smooth muscle in the walls of arteries. The arteries expand, and this leads to a low blood pressure that sets in motion the renin-angiotensin-aldosterone mechanism, promoted by estrogen. Aldosterone activity promotes sodium and water retention, and blood volume increases until it reaches its peak sometime during weeks 28 to 32 of pregnancy. Altogether, blood volume increases from 5 liters to 7 liters—a 40% rise. An increase in the number of red blood cells follows. With the rise in blood volume, cardiac output increases by 20–30%. Blood flow to the kidneys, placenta, skin, and breasts rises significantly. Smooth muscle relaxation also explains the common gastrointestinal effects of pregnancy. The heartburn experienced by many is due to relaxation of the esophageal sphincter and reflux of stomach contents into the esophagus. Constipation is caused by a decrease in intestinal tract motility.

The Respiratory System

Of interest is the increase in pulmonary values in a pregnant woman. The bronchial tubes relax, but this alone cannot explain the typical 40% increase in vital capacity and tidal volume. The increasing size of the uterus from a nonpregnant weight of 60–80 g to 900–1,200 g contributes to an improvement in respiratory functions. The uterus comes to occupy most of the abdominal cavity, reaching nearly to the xiphoid process of the sternum. This increase in size not only pushes the intestines, liver, stomach, and diaphragm superiorly but also widens the thoracic cavity. Compared with nonpregnant values, the maternal oxygen level changes little. Blood carbon dioxide levels fall by 20%, creating a concentration gradient favorable to the flow of carbon dioxide from fetal blood to maternal blood at the placenta.

Still Other Effects

The enlargement of the uterus may create problems. In the pelvic cavity, compression of the ureters and urinary bladder (Fig. 18.12)

can result in stress incontinence, or the involuntary leakage of urine from the urinary tract. Compression of the inferior vena cava, especially when lying down, decreases venous return, and the results are edema and varicose veins.

Aside from the steroid hormones progesterone and estrogen, the placenta also produces some peptide hormones. One of these makes cells resistant to insulin, and the result can be gestational diabetes. Some of the integumentary changes observed during pregnancy are also due to placental hormones. "Stretch marks" typically form over the abdomen and lower breasts in response to increased steroid hormone levels, rather than stretching of the skin. Melanocyte activity also increases during pregnancy. As a result, many women develop a dark line, the linea nigra, that extends from the pubic region to the umbilical region (belly button). In addition, darkening of certain areas of the skin, including the face, neck, and breast areolae, is common.

Birth

The uterus has contractions throughout pregnancy. At first these are light, lasting about 20 to 30 seconds and occurring every 15 to 20 minutes. Near the end of pregnancy, the contractions may become stronger and more frequent, so that a woman thinks she is in labor. "False labor" contractions are called **Braxton Hicks contractions.** The onset of true labor is marked by uterine contractions that occur regularly every 15 to 20 minutes and last for 40 seconds or longer.

A positive feedback mechanism can explain the onset and continuation of labor. Uterine contractions are induced by a stretching of the cervix, which also brings about the release of oxytocin from the posterior pituitary gland. Oxytocin stimulates the uterine muscles, both directly and through the action of prostaglandins. Uterine contractions push the fetus downward, and the cervix stretches even more. This cycle keeps repeating itself until birth occurs.

Prior to or at the first stage of **parturition,** the process of giving birth to an offspring, there can be a "bloody show" caused by expulsion of a mucous plug from the cervical canal. This plug prevented bacteria and sperm from entering the uterus during pregnancy.

Stage 1

During the first stage of labor, the uterine contractions occur in such a way that the cervical canal slowly disappears as the

---

SCIENCE IN YOUR LIFE

Does the length or width of the linea nigra indicate the sex of a baby?

The linea nigra occurs due to the secretions of melanocytes in a pregnant woman. The line may be darker in fair-skinned women, and the length and width of the line may vary even between pregnancies. However, there is no correlation between the existence of the linea nigra and the sex, or any other characteristics, of the developing fetus.

Figure 18.12   Changes to the internal anatomy of a pregnant woman.
The developing fetus compresses many of the organs in the body of the pregnant woman.

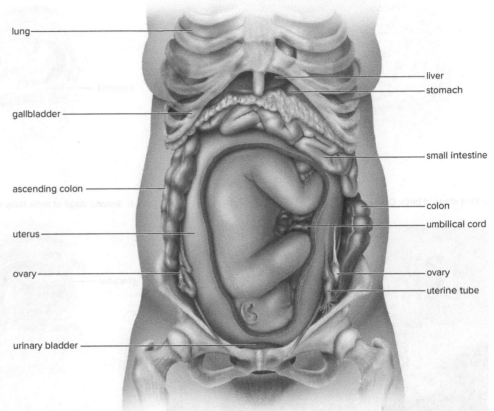

lung

liver

stomach

gallbladder

small intestine

ascending colon

colon

umbilical cord

uterus

ovary

ovary

uterine tube

urinary bladder

---

lower part of the uterus is pulled upward toward the baby's head. This process is called **effacement**, or "taking up the cervix." With further contractions, the baby's head acts as a wedge to assist with cervical dilation (Fig. 18.13*a*). If the amniotic membrane has not already ruptured, it is apt to do so during this stage, releasing the amniotic fluid, which leaks out of the vagina (an event sometimes referred to as "breaking water"). The first stage of parturition ends once the cervix is dilated completely.

Stage 2

During the second stage of parturition, the uterine contractions occur every 1 to 2 minutes and last about 1 minute each. They are accompanied by a desire to push, or bear down. As the baby's head gradually descends into the vagina, the mother's desire to push becomes greater. When the baby's head reaches the exterior, it turns, so that the back of the head is uppermost (Fig. 18.13*b*). To enlarge the vaginal orifice, an **episiotomy** is often performed. This incision, which enlarges the opening, is sewn together later. As soon as the head is delivered, the physician may hold the head and guide it downward while one shoulder and then the other emerges. The rest of the baby follows easily (Fig. 18.13*c*).

Once the baby is breathing normally, the umbilical cord is cut and tied, severing the child from the placenta. The stump of the cord shrivels and leaves a scar, the umbilicus (belly button).

Stage 3

The placenta, or **afterbirth**, is delivered during the third stage of parturition (Fig. 18.13*d*). About 15 minutes after delivery of the baby, uterine muscular contractions shrink the uterus and dislodge the placenta. The placenta then is expelled into the vagina. As soon as the placenta and its membranes are delivered, the third stage of parturition is complete.

CHECK YOUR PROGRESS 18.4

1. Identify the hormonal changes that occur during pregnancy.
2. Maternal blood carbon dioxide levels fall by 20% during pregnancy. How does this benefit the fetus?
3. Describe the three stages of labor.

CONNECTING THE CONCEPTS

For more information on the content of this section, refer to the following discussions:

Section 4.8 explains positive feedback mechanisms.

Section 11.4 examines how aldosterone regulates urine formation in the kidneys.

Section 17.4 examines the role of the female sex hormones estrogen and progesterone.

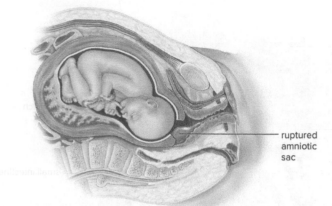

a. First stage of birth: Cervix dilates.

ruptured
amniotic
sac

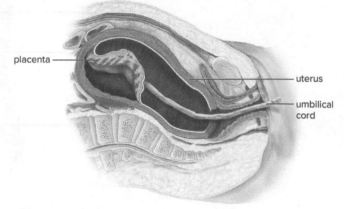

placenta

b. Second stage of birth: Baby emerges.

placenta

uterus

umbilical
cord

d. Third stage of birth: Afterbirth is expelled.

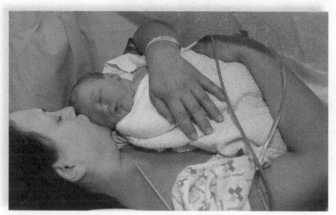

c. Baby has arrived.

Figure 18.13   The stages of birth.
Birth proceeds in three stages. The baby emerges in stage 2.
(c) © Rune Hellestad/Corbis

18.5 Aging

LEARNING OUTCOMES

Upon completion of this section, you should be able to

1. Summarize the hypotheses on why humans age.
2. Summarize the effects of aging on the organ systems of the body.

Development does not cease once birth has occurred but continues throughout the stages of life: infancy, childhood, adolescence, and adulthood. Infancy, the toddler years, and the preschool years are times of remarkable growth. During the birth to 5-year-old stage, humans acquire gross motor and fine motor skills. These include the ability to sit up and then to walk, as well as to hold a spoon and manipulate small objects. Language usage begins during this time and will become increasingly sophisticated throughout childhood. As infants and toddlers explore their environment, their senses—vision, taste, hearing, smell, and touch—mature dramatically. Socialization

is very important as a child forms emotional ties with its caregivers and learns to separate self from others. Babies do not all develop at the same rate, and there is a large variation in what is considered normal.

The preadolescent years, from 6 to 12 years of age, are a time of continued rapid growth and learning. Preadolescents form identities apart from parents, and peer approval becomes very important. Adolescence begins with the onset of puberty as the young person achieves sexual maturity. For girls, puberty begins between 10 and 14 years of age, whereas for boys it generally occurs between ages 12 and 16. During this time, the sex-specific hormones (see Section 16.6) cause the secondary sex characteristics to appear. Profound social and psychological changes are also associated with the transition from childhood to adulthood.

Aging encompasses the progressive changes from infancy until eventual death. Today, **gerontology,** the study of aging, is of great interest, because there are now more older individuals in our society than ever before. The number is expected to rise dramatically; in the next half-century, the number of people over age 65

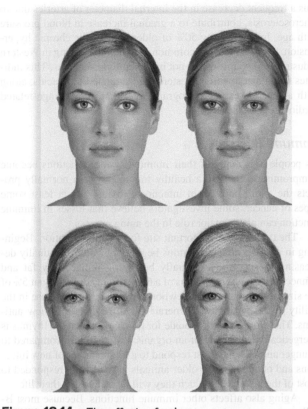

Figure 18.14   The effects of aging.
Aging is a slow process during which the body undergoes changes that eventually bring about death, even if no marked disease or disorder is present. Medical science is trying to extend the human life span and the health span, the length of time the body functions normally.
© Image Source/Getty RF

will increase 147%. The human life span is judged to be a maximum of 120 to 125 years. The present goal of gerontology is not necessarily to increase the life span but to increase the health span, the number of years that an individual enjoys the full functions of all body parts and processes (Fig. 18.14).

Cellular Aging

Aging is a complex process affected by multiple factors. Most scientists who study gerontology believe that aging is partly genetically preprogrammed. This idea is supported by the observation that longevity runs in families—that is, the children of long-lived parents tend to live longer than those of short-lived parents. As would also be expected, studies show that identical twins have a more similar life span than nonidentical twins.

Hormones

Many laboratory studies of aging have been performed in the nematode *Caenorhabditis elegans,* in which single-gene mutations have been shown to influence the life span. For example, mutations that

decrease the activity of a hormone receptor similar to the insulin receptor more than double the life span of the worms, which also behave and look like much younger worms throughout their prolonged lives. Interestingly, small-breed dogs, such as poodles and terriers, which may live 15 to 20 years, have lower levels of an analogous receptor compared to large-breed dogs that live 6 to 8 years.

Telomeres

Studies of the behavior of cells grown in the lab also suggest a genetic influence on aging. Most types of differentiated cells can divide only a limited number of times. One factor that may control the number of cell divisions is the length of the *telomeres,* sequences of DNA, at the ends of chromosomes. Telomeres protect the ends of chromosomes from deteriorating or fusing with other chromosomes. Each time a cell divides, the telomeres normally shorten, and cells with shorter telomeres tend to undergo fewer divisions (see Section 19.2). Some cells, such as stem cells, possess an enzyme called telomerase, which replenishes the length of the telomeres, effectively making stem cells immortal. Cancer cells, which behave in a similar manner to stem cells, frequently possess an active telomerase enzyme, which allows them to replicate continuously (see Section 20.1). Studies using stem cells and cancer cells have begun to close in on the genetic factors that cause cellular aging. For example, in 2012 researchers used *gene therapy* (see Section 22.4) to introduce an active telomerase enzyme into mice, thus slowing the aging process.

Mitochondria and Diet

The mitochondria are the powerhouses of the cell (see Section 3.6). As the mitochondria harvest the energy contained in carbohydrates, fats, and proteins, they generate free radicals. Free radicals are unstable molecules that carry an extra electron. To become stable, free radicals donate an electron to another molecule, such as DNA, proteins (e.g., enzymes), or lipids found in plasma membranes. Eventually these molecules become unable to function, and the cell loses internal functions. This may lead to cell death. Scientists have determined that high-calorie diets increase the levels of free radicals, thus accelerating cellular aging. Multiple studies on model organisms, including mice, have supported that a low-calorie diet can extend the life span. It is also possible to reduce the negative effects of free radicals by increasing one's consumption of natural antioxidants, such as those present in brightly colored and dark-green vegetables and fruits. Chemicals in nuts, fish, shellfish, and red wine have also been shown to reduce our exposure to free radicals and slow the aging process.

However, if aging were mainly a function of genes, we would expect to see much less variation in life span among individuals of a given species than is actually seen. For this reason, experts have estimated that in most cases genes account only for about 25% of what determines the length of life.

Damage Accumulation

Another set of hypotheses propose that aging involves the accumulation of damage over time. In 1900 the average human life expectancy was around 45 years. A baby born in the United States this year has a life expectancy of about 78 years. Because human genes have presumably not changed much in such a short time, most of this gain in life span is due to better medical care, along with the application of scientific knowledge about how to prolong our lives.

Two basic types of cellular damage can accumulate over time. The first type can be thought of as agents that are unavoidable—for example, the accumulation of harmful DNA mutations or the buildup of harmful metabolites. A second form involves the fact that proteins—such as the collagen fibers present in many support tissues—may become increasingly cross-linked as people age. This cross-linking may account for the inability of such organs as the blood vessels, heart, and lungs to function as they once did. Some researchers have now found that glucose has the tendency to attach to any type of protein, which is the first step in a cross-linking process. They are currently experimenting with drugs that can prevent cross-linking. However, other sources of cellular damage may be avoidable, such as a poor diet or exposure to the sun.

Effect of Age on Body Systems

In the preceding chapters we examined the structure and function of the major body systems. Aging reduces the ability of an organ system to perform these functions and in many cases impacts its ability to contribute to homeostasis. Therefore, it seems appropriate to first consider the effects of aging on the various body systems.

Integumentary System

As aging occurs, the skin becomes thinner and less elastic, because the number of elastic fibers decreases and the collagen fibers become increasingly cross-linked to each other, reducing their flexibility. There is also less adipose tissue in the subcutaneous layer; therefore, older people are more likely to feel cold. Together, these changes typically result in sagging and wrinkling of the skin.

As people age, the sweat glands also become less active, resulting in decreased tolerance to high temperatures. There are fewer hair follicles, so the hair on the scalp and the limbs thins out. Older people also experience a decrease in the number of melanocytes, making their hair gray and their skin pale. In contrast, some of the remaining pigment cells are larger, and pigmented blotches ("age spots") appear on the skin.

Cardiovascular System

Common problems with cardiovascular function are usually related to diseases, especially atherosclerosis. However, even with normal aging, the heart muscle weakens somewhat and may increase slightly in size as it compensates for its decreasing strength. The maximum heart rate decreases even among the most fit older athletes, and it takes longer for the heart rate and blood pressure to return to normal resting levels following stress. Some part of this decrease in heart function may also be due to blood leaking back through heart valves that have become less flexible.

Aging also affects the blood vessels. The middle layer of arteries contains elastic fibers, which, like collagen fibers in the skin, become more cross-linked and rigid with time. These changes, plus a frequent decrease in the internal diameter of arteries due to atherosclerosis, contribute to a gradual increase in blood pressure with age. Indeed, nearly 50% of older adults have chronic hypertension. Such changes are common in individuals living in Western industrialized countries but not in agricultural societies. This indicates that a diet low in cholesterol and saturated fatty acids, along with a sensible exercise program, may help prevent age-related cardiovascular disease.

Immune System

As people age, many of their immune system functions become compromised. Because a healthy immune system normally protects the entire body from infections, toxins, and at least some types of cancer, some investigators believe that losses in immune function can play a major role in the aging process.

The thymus is an important site for T-cell maturation. Beginning in adolescence, the thymus begins to involute, gradually decreasing in size and eventually becoming replaced by fat and connective tissue. The thymus of a 60-year-old adult is about 5% of the size of the thymus of a newborn, resulting in a decrease in the ability of older people to generate T-cell responses to new antigens. The evolutionary rationale for this may be that the thymus is energetically expensive for an organism to maintain; compared to younger animals that must respond to a high number of new infections and other antigens, older animals have already responded to most of the antigens to which they will be exposed in their life.

Aging also affects other immune functions. Because most B-cell responses are dependent on T cells, antibody responses also begin to decline. This, in turn, may explain why the elderly do not respond as well to vaccinations as young people do. This presents challenges in protecting older people against diseases such as influenza and pneumonia, which can otherwise be prevented by annual vaccination.

Not all immune functions decrease with age. The activity of natural killer cells, which are a part of the innate immune system, seems to change very little with age. Perhaps by investigating how these cells remain active throughout a normal human life span, researchers can learn to preserve other aspects of immunity in the elderly.

Digestive System

The digestive system is perhaps less affected by the aging process than other systems. Because secretion of saliva decreases, more bacteria tend to adhere to the teeth, causing more decay and periodontal disease. Blood flow to the liver is reduced, resulting in less efficient metabolism of drugs or toxins. This means that, as a person gets older, less medication is needed to maintain the same level in the bloodstream.

Respiratory System

Cardiovascular problems are often accompanied by respiratory disorders, and vice versa. Decreasing elasticity of lung tissues means that ventilation is reduced. Because we rarely use the entire vital capacity, these effects may not be noticed unless the demand for oxygen increases, such as during exercise.

Excretory System

Blood supply to the kidneys is also reduced. The kidneys become smaller and less efficient at filtering wastes. Salt and water balance are difficult to maintain, and the elderly dehydrate faster than young people. Urinary incontinence (lack of bladder control) increases with age, especially in women. In men, an enlarged prostate gland may reduce the diameter of the urethra, causing frequent or difficult urination.

Nervous System

Between the ages of 20 and 90, the brain loses about 20% of its weight and volume. Neurons are extremely sensitive to oxygen deficiency, and neuron death may be due not to aging itself but to reduced blood flow in narrowed blood vessels. However, contrary to previous scientific opinion, recent studies using advanced imaging techniques show that most age-related loss in brain function is not due to whatever loss of neurons is occurring. Instead, decreased function may occur due to alterations in complex chemical reactions or increased inflammation in the brain. For example, an age-associated decline in levels of dopamine can affect brain regions involved in complex thinking.

Perhaps more important than the molecular details, recent studies have confirmed that lifestyle factors can affect the aging brain. For example, animals on restricted-calorie diets developed fewer Alzheimer-like changes in their brains. For more on Alzheimer disease, see the Health feature "Alzheimer Disease" later in this section. Other positive factors that may help maintain a healthy brain include attending college (the "use it or lose it" idea), regular exercise, and sufficient sleep.

Sensory Systems

In general, with aging, more stimulation is needed for taste, smell, and hearing receptors to function as before. A majority of people over age 80 have a significant decline in their sense of smell, and about 15% suffer from anosmia, or a total inability to smell. The latter condition can be a serious health hazard, due to the inability to detect smoke, gas leaks, or spoiled food. After age 50, most people gradually begin to lose the ability to hear tones at higher frequencies, and this can make it difficult to identify individual voices and to understand conversation in a group.

Starting at about age 40, the lens of the eye does not accommodate as well, resulting in presbyopia, or difficulty focusing on near objects, which causes many people to require reading glasses as they reach middle age. Finally, cataracts and other eye disorders become much more common in the aged.

Musculoskeletal System

For the average person, muscle mass peaks between the ages of 16 and 19 for females and between 18 and 24 for males. Beginning in the twenties or thirties, but accelerating with increasing age, muscle mass generally decreases, due to decreases in both the size and number of muscle fibers. Most people who reach age 90 have 50% less muscle mass than when they were 20. Although some of this loss may be inevitable, regular exercise can slow this decline.

Like muscles, bones tend to shrink in size and density with age. Due to compression of the vertebrae, along with changes in posture, most of us lose height as we age. Those who reach age 80 will be about 2 in. shorter than they were in their twenties. Women lose bone mass more rapidly than men do, especially after menopause. Osteoporosis is a common disease in the elderly. Although some decline in bone mass is a normal result of aging, certain extrinsic factors are also important. A proper diet and a moderate exercise program have been found to slow the progressive loss of bone mass.

Endocrine System

As with the immune system, aging of the hormonal system can affect many organs of the body. These changes are complex, however, with some hormone levels tending to decrease with age, while others increase. The activity of the thyroid gland generally declines, resulting in a lower basal metabolic rate. The production of insulin by the pancreas may remain stable, but cells become less sensitive to its effects, resulting in a rise in fasting glucose levels of about 10 mg/dl each decade after age 50.

Human growth hormone (HGH) levels also decline with age, but it is very unlikely that taking HGH injections will "cure" aging, despite Internet claims. In fact, one study found that people with lower levels of HGH actually lived longer than those with higher levels.

Reproductive System

Testosterone levels are highest in men in their twenties. After age 30, testosterone levels decrease by about 1% per year. Extremely low testosterone levels have been linked to a decreased sex drive, excessive weight gain, loss of muscle mass, osteoporosis, general fatigue, and depression. However, the levels below which testosterone treatment should be initiated remain controversial. Testosterone replacement therapy, whether through injection, patches, or gels, is associated with side effects such as enlargement of the prostate, acne or other skin reactions, and the production of too many red blood cells.

SCIENCE IN YOUR LIFE

What genes may be associated with longevity?

In the past several years, researchers have begun to use new molecular techniques to unravel some of the mysteries as to why some individuals live past the age of 100—the centenarians. A variation of one gene, *FOXO3A*, has been found to be more prevalent in centenarians than in the general population. This gene regulates the insulin pathways of the body and appears to control the genetic mechanisms that protect cells against free radicals. Both insulin regulation and protection against free radicals have been known for some time to enhance longevity in a variety of organisms. Interestingly, *FOXO3A* is also believed to be involved in the process of apoptosis and may help protect the body against cancer. Although researchers do not think that *FOXO3A* is the sole gene for longevity, it is providing a starting point for larger studies on human aging.

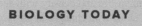
BIOLOGY TODAY **Health**

Alzheimer Disease

In 1900 the average life span in the United States was about 45 years of age. Today it is 78. Normal aging involves some changes in mental faculties, but many of the changes we associate with old age are related to disease, not aging. Two of the more common diseases are Alzheimer disease and Parkinson disease.

Alzheimer disease is characterized by the presence of abnormally structured neurons and a reduced amount of acetylcholine (ACh), primarily in an area of the brain called the hippocampus (see Fig. 14.12). A neuron that has been affected by Alzheimer disease has two characteristic features. Bundles of fibrous protein, called neurofibrillary tangles, extend from the axon to surround the nucleus of the neuron. Tangles form when the supporting protein, called tau, becomes malformed (Fig. 18B) and twists the neurofibrils, which are normally straight. In addition, protein-rich accumulations called amyloid plaques envelop branches of the axon. The plaques grow so dense that they trigger an inflammatory reaction that causes neuron death.

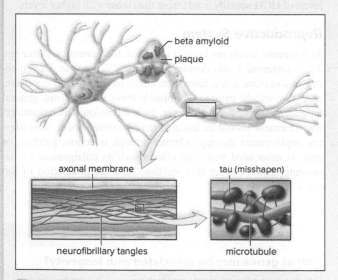

Figure 18B Tau protein and Alzheimer disease.
Some of the neurons of Alzheimer disease (AD) patients have beta amyloid plaques and neurofibrillary tangles. AD neurons are present throughout the brain but concentrated in the hippocampus and amygdala.

Treatment for Alzheimer Disease

Treatment involves using one of two categories of drugs. Cholinesterase inhibitors work at neuron synapses in the brain, slowing the activity of acetylcholinesterase, the enzyme that breaks down ACh. Allowing ACh to accumulate in synapses keeps memory pathways in the brain functional for a longer period. The second drug, memantine, blocks *excitotoxicity*, the tendency of diseased neurons to self-destruct. This recently approved medication is used only in moderately to severely affected patients. Using the drug allows neurons involved in memory pathways to survive longer in affected patients. Successes with these medications indicates that treatment for AD patients should begin as soon as possible after diagnosis and continue indefinitely. However, neither type of medication cures the disease; both merely slow the progress of symptoms, allowing the patient to function independently for a longer time. Additional research is currently under way to test the effectiveness of anticholesterol *statin* drugs, as well as anti-inflammatory medications, in slowing the progress of the disease.

Much of the current research on Alzheimer disease focuses on the prevention and cure of the disease. Scientists believe that a cure will require an early diagnosis, because it is thought that the disease may begin in the brain 15 to 20 years before symptoms develop. Currently, diagnosis can't be made with absolute certainty until the brain is examined at autopsy. A new test on the cerebrospinal fluid may allow early detection of amyloid proteins and a much earlier diagnosis. Researchers are also testing vaccines, which would target the patient's immune system to destroy amyloid plaques.

Early findings have shown that risk factors for cardiovascular disease also contribute to an increased incidence of Alzheimer disease. Risk factors for cardiovascular disease include elevated blood cholesterol and blood pressure, smoking, obesity, sedentary lifestyle, and diabetes mellitus. Thus, evidence suggests that a lifestyle tailored for good cardiovascular health may also prevent Alzheimer disease.

Questions to Consider

1. What is the role of the hippocampus, and how does this relate to the symptoms of Alzheimer disease?
2. How might anti-inflammatory drugs slow the progression of Alzheimer disease?

Menopause, the period in a woman's life during which the ovarian and uterine cycles cease, usually occurs between ages 45 and 55. The ovaries become unresponsive to the gonadotropic hormones produced by the anterior pituitary, and they no longer secrete estrogen or progesterone. At the onset of menopause, the uterine cycle becomes irregular, but as long as menstruation occurs, it is still possible for a woman to conceive.

Therefore, a woman is usually not considered to have completed menopause (and thus be infertile) until menstruation has been absent for a year.

The hormonal changes during menopause often produce physical symptoms such as "hot flashes" (caused by circulatory irregularities), dizziness, headaches, insomnia, sleepiness, and depression. To ease these symptoms, female hormone replacement therapy

(HRT) was routinely prescribed until 2002, when a large clinical study showed that in the long term, HRT caused more health problems than it prevented. For this reason, most doctors no longer recommend long-term HRT for the prevention of postmenopausal symptoms.

As a group, females live longer than males. It is likely that estrogen offers women some protection against cardiovascular disorders when they are younger. Males suffer a marked increase in heart disease in their forties, but an increase is not noted in females until after menopause, when women lead men in the incidence of stroke. Men remain more likely than women to have a heart attack at any age, however.

Conclusion

We have examined many adverse effects of aging; however, these effects are not inevitable (Fig. 18.15). Diet and exercise are factors that are under our personal control. Just as it is wise to make the proper preparations to remain financially independent when older, it is also wise to realize that, biologically, successful old age begins with the health habits developed when we are younger.

CHECK YOUR PROGRESS 18.5

1. Briefly describe the hypotheses of why we age.
2. Summarize the effects of aging on the various body systems.
3. Discuss the best way to keep healthy, even though aging occurs.

CONNECTING THE CONCEPTS

For more information on the organ systems presented in this section, refer to the following discussions:

Section 5.1 provides an overview of the cardiovascular system.

Section 11.1 provides an overview of the urinary system.

Section 14.1 provides an overview of the nervous system.

Figure 18.15   What steps can an individual take to increase health span?
Gerontology research has shown that regular physical exercise, as well as staying engaged both mentally and socially, can slow the progress of aging and lengthen the health span.
© Ronnie Kaufman/Corbis

CASE STUDY CONCLUSION

Over the course of the next few office visits, Amber's doctor performed a variety of tests. Because Amber was over 35 years old when she conceived her first child, the doctor recommended that a chorionic villus sampling test be done to test for birth defects, such as Down syndrome. The doctor also performed a glucose tolerance test to determine if Amber was experiencing gestational diabetes. An additional blood test, called an alpha-fetoprotein (AFP) test, screened for neural tube defects and additional evidence of Down syndrome. Much to the relief of Amber and Kent, all these tests came back normal.

Then, around week 20 of Amber's pregnancy, the doctor made an appointment for Amber to get an ultrasound exam, which is frequently used to confirm the due date of the baby but can also be used to look for birth defects such as cleft palate. Everything once again appeared normal. Finally, the technician asked the parents the question they had been waiting for: Were they interested in knowing the sex of their baby? Within a few minutes, Amber and Kent found out that in just a few months they would be the parents of a baby girl.

STUDY TOOLS   http://connect.mheducation.com

SMARTBOOK®   Maximize your study time with McGraw-Hill SmartBook®, the first adaptive textbook.

SUMMARIZE

18.1 Fertilization

Fertilization is the combination of an egg and sperm cell to produce a new individual, or **zygote.** During fertilization the acrosome of a sperm releases enzymes that digest a pathway for the sperm through the zona pellucida. The sperm nucleus then enters the egg and fuses with the egg nucleus.

18.2 Pre-embryonic and Embryonic Development

Cleavage, growth, morphogenesis, and **differentiation** are the processes of development. Development of the fetus may be divided into **pre-embryonic development** events (first week) and **embryonic development** events (second week and later).

Pre-embryonic Development

- Immediately after fertilization, the zygote begins to divide, first forming a **morula,** then a **blastocyst.** Within the blastocyst, the **inner cell mass** forms. This will become the **embryo.**
- The **extraembryonic membranes** (**chorion, allantois, yolk sac,** and **amnion**) begin to form.

Embryonic Development

- During the second week, **implantation** of the embryo occurs. Several hormones, including **human chorionic gonadotropin (HCG),** act on the uterus to adapt it for pregnancy. Within the embryo, **gastrulation** occurs, forming the **primary germ layers,** which will become the structures of the body.
- Starting in the third week, the development of organ systems begins, including the nervous system and circulatory system (heart).
- In the fourth week, the embryo connects to the chorion using **chorionic villi.** The formation of the **umbilical cord** establishes a connection to the placenta. The limb buds appear and by the fifth week the sense organs develop in the head.

18.3 Fetal Development

At the end of the embryonic period, all organ systems are established and there is a mature and functioning **placenta.** The umbilical arteries and umbilical vein take blood to and from the placenta, where exchanges take place. Fetal development occurs during the third to ninth months.

Fetal Circulation

- Fetal circulation supplies the fetus with oxygen and nutrients and rids the fetus of carbon dioxide and wastes.
- The venous duct joins the umbilical vein to the inferior vena cava. The oval duct and arterial duct allow the blood to pass through the heart without going to the lungs. **Fetal development** extends from the third through the ninth months.

Third and Fourth Months

- During the third and fourth months, the skeleton is becoming ossified. In the skull, the **fontanels** will allow the head to pass through the birth canal.

- The sex of the fetus becomes distinguishable. If an *SRY* gene is present, **testosterone** directs the development of the testes and male sex organs. Otherwise, ovaries and female sex organs develop.

Fifth to Ninth Months

- During the fifth through the ninth months, the fetus continues to grow and to gain weight. At this point, the skin is covered by a fine down (**lanugo**) and a protective layer (**vernix caseosa**).

18.4 Pregnancy and Birth

Pregnancy

Major changes take place in the mother's body during pregnancy.

- Weight gain occurs as the uterus occupies most of the abdominal cavity.
- Many complaints, such as constipation, incontinence, heartburn, darkening of certain skin areas, and pregnancy-induced diabetes, are due to the presence of placental hormones.

Birth

A positive feedback mechanism that involves uterine contractions (including **Braxton Hicks contractions**) and oxytocin explains the onset and continuation of labor.

- During stage 1 of **parturition** (birth), **effacement** assists in the dilation of the cervix.
- During stage 2, the child is born. An **episiotomy** may assist in the widening of the vaginal orifice.
- During stage 3, the **afterbirth** is expelled.

18.5 Aging

Development after birth consists of infancy, childhood, adolescence, and adulthood. The science of **gerontology** examines the progressive changes that occur during **aging.** As we age, these changes contribute to an increased risk of infirmity, disease, and death.

Cellular Aging

There are several factors that contribute to aging at the cellular level.

- Telomeres contribute to the life span of cells.
- Receptors for certain hormones may not work efficiently.
- Free radicals and other metabolites cause damage to cellular components.

Effect of Age on Body Systems

- Deterioration of organ systems can be prevented or reduced in part by using good health habits.

ASSESS

TESTING YOURSELF

Choose the best answer for each question.

18.1 Fertilization

1. Only one sperm enters an egg because
   a. sperm have an acrosome.
   b. the corona radiata gets larger.
   c. changes occur in the zona pellucida.
   d. the cytoplasm hardens.
   e. All of these are correct.

2. The fusion of a sperm and an egg cell initally produces which of the
following?
   a. blastocyst
   b. zygote
   c. morula
   d. gamete
   e. stem cell

18.2 Pre-embryonic and Embryonic Development

3. Label each of the indicated stages of pre-embryonic development.

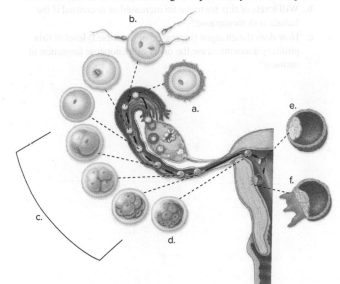

4. Which of these is mismatched?
   a. chorion—sense perception
   b. yolk sac—first site of blood cell formation
   c. allantois—umbilical blood vessels
   d. amnion—contains fluid that protects embryo

5. Which primary germ layer is not correctly matched to an organ
system or organ that develops from it?
   a. ectoderm—nervous system
   b. endoderm—lining of the digestive tract
   c. mesoderm—skeletal system
   d. endoderm—cardiovascular system

6. Which process involves the shaping of the embryo and cell
migration?
   a. cleavage
   b. differentiation
   c. growth
   d. morphogenesis

18.3 Fetal Development

7. Which association is not correct?
   a. third and fourth months—fetal heart has formed, but it does not beat
   b. fifth through seventh months—mother feels movement
   c. eighth through ninth months—usually head is now pointed
      toward the cervix
   d. All of these are correct.

8. Which of these structures is not a circulatory feature unique to the
fetus?
   a. arterial duct
   b. oval opening
   c. umbilical vein
   d. pulmonary trunk

9. Which of these statements is correct?
   a. Fetal circulation, like adult circulation, takes blood
      equally to a pulmonary circuit and a systemic circuit.
   b. Fetal circulation shunts blood away from the lungs
      but makes full use of the systemic circuit.
   c. Fetal circulation includes an exchange of substances
      between fetal blood and maternal blood at the placenta.
   d. Unlike adult circulation, fetal blood always carries
      oxygen-rich blood and therefore has no need for the
      pulmonary circuit.
   e. Both b and c are correct.

10. Which of the following does not occur if the *SRY* gene is present in
the fetus?
   a. The Wolffian duct becomes the male genital ducts.
   b. The Müllerian ducts disappear.
   c. The testes develop.
   d. The urethra and genital tracts remain separate.
   e. None of these are correct.

18.4 Pregnancy and Birth

11. Which of the following hormones is not matched correctly to its
effect on the mother?
   a. peptide hormones—increased resistance to insulin
   b. progesterone—reduced chances of the mother having
      an immune reaction to the fetus
   c. estrogen—increased uterine blood flow
   d. progesterone—relaxation of smooth muscle and decrease in
      blood pressure
   e. All of these are correct.

12. Which of the following is increased in the mother during
pregnancy?
   a. metabolic rate
   b. blood volume
   c. cardiac output
   d. All of these are correct.

18.5 Aging

13. After each cell division, these chromosomal structures shorten, thus
regulating the life span of a cell.
   a. mitochondria
   b. free radicals
   c. telomeres
   d. plasma membranes

14. Which of the following is associated with the aging process?
   a. reduction in the production of sex hormones, such as
      testosterone
   b. increased chances of dehydration
   c. decrease in bone density
   d. decrease in the ability of the senses to detect stimuli
   e. All of these are correct.

ENGAGE

THINKING CRITICALLY

Amber and Kent used a home pregnancy test to determine if she was pregnant. These tests detect the level of HCG (human chorionic gonadotropin) in the urine (see Section 18.2). This hormone is released following implantation of the embryo into the uterus, usually around 6 days after fertilization. Some tests claim that they are sensitive enough to detect HCG on the date that menstruation is expected to begin. However, doctors recommend waiting until menstruation is 1 week late. If pregnant, a woman's level of HCG rises with each passing day, and testing is more likely to be accurate. However, even with a negative test result, the woman may still be pregnant if HCG levels are too low to be detected at the time of the first test. The test should be repeated later if menstruation doesn't begin. The home pregnancy tests contain a positive control. This is a visual sign (usually a line or a +) that appears if the test is working correctly. If this line does not appear, the test is not valid and must be repeated.

1. At-home pregnancy tests check for the presence of HCG in a female's urine. Where does HCG come from? Why is HCG found in a pregnant woman's urine?

2. A blood test at a doctor's office can also check for the presence of HCG in a female's blood.
   a. Why would you expect to find HCG circulating in a pregnant female's blood?
   b. HCG is a protein, so how does HCG affect its target cells?

3. a. What pituitary hormone is checked with a blood test to diagnose menopause?
   b. Will levels of this hormone be increased or decreased if the female is in menopause?
   c. How does the changed (increased or decreased) level of this pituitary hormone cause the onset of menopause (cessation of menses)?

© MRP/Alamy

C H A P T E R

19

Patterns of Chromosome Inheritance

CASE STUDY: *BRCA1* AND THE CELL CYCLE

In 2013, actress Angelina Jolie announced to her shocked fans that she was going to undergo a double mastectomy (removal of breast tissue) to prevent breast cancer. Every year almost 233,000 American women are diagnosed with breast cancer. While Angelina did not have breast cancer, she has a history of this cancer in her family, and she had tested positive for a *BRCA1* (*breast cancer susceptibility gene 1*) gene mutation, linked to both breast and ovarian cancer. Cancer results from a failure to control the cell cycle, a series of steps that all cells go through prior to initiating cell division. *BRCA1,* and a similar gene, *BRCA2,* are important components of that control mechanism. Both of these genes are tumor suppressor genes. At specific checkpoints in the cell cycle, the proteins encoded by these genes check the DNA for damage. *BRCA1* acts as a gatekeeper, preventing cells from dividing continuously. Each cell normally has two copies of *BRCA1*, one inherited from each parent. In Angelina's case, the mutated version of *BRCA1* indicated that each of her cells only had a single functioning copy of the gene, and therefore she was at a higher risk of developing breast cancer in the future.

It is estimated that 1 in 833 people possess the *BRCA1* mutation associated with breast cancer. Although it is not the only genetic contribution to breast and ovarian cancer, it does play a major role. In this chapter we will examine not only how cells divide, but how the process of cell division is controlled.

As you read through the chapter, think about the following questions:

1. What are the roles of checkpoints in the cell cycle?
2. At what checkpoint in the cell cycle would you think that *BRCA1* would normally be active?
3. Why would a failure of the checkpoints in the cell cycle result in cancer?

CHAPTER CONCEPTS

19.1 Chromosomes
The genetic material in the cell is organized into chromosomes. A karyotype is a picture of chromosomes about to divide.

19.2 The Cell Cycle
The cell cycle consists of interphase and mitosis and is regulated by a series of checkpoints.

19.3 Mitosis
Mitosis is cell division in which the daughter cells have the same number and types of chromosomes as the mother cell.

19.4 Meiosis
Meiosis is cell division in which the daughter cells have half the number of chromosomes and different combinations of genes from the parent cell.

19.5 Comparison of Meiosis and Mitosis
Meiosis I uniquely pairs and separates the paired chromosomes, so that the daughter cells have half the number of chromosomes. Meiosis II is similar to mitosis, except the cells have half the number of chromosomes.

19.6 Chromosome Inheritance
Abnormalities in chromosome inheritance occur due to changes in chromosome number and changes in chromosome structure.

BEFORE YOU BEGIN

Before beginning this chapter, take a few moments to review the following discussions:

Section 2.7 What is the structure of a DNA molecule? How does this structure differ from that of RNA?

Section 3.4 What is chromatin?

Section 3.5 What are the functions of microtubules and actin filaments in a cell?

19.1 Chromosomes

LEARNING OUTCOMES

Upon completion of this section, you should be able to

1. Distinguish between a chromosome and chromatin.
2. Explain the purpose of a karyotype.
3. Describe the purpose of the centromere in relation to the sister chromatids.

Although the nucleus of a human cell is only about 5–8 μm long, it holds all the genetic material necessary to direct all the functions in the body. The genetic material is arranged into **chromosomes,** structures that assist in the transmission of genetic information from one generation to the next. The instructions in each chromosome are contained within genes, which in turn are composed of DNA (see Section 22.1).

Chromosomes also contain proteins that assist in the organizational structure of the chromosome. Collectively, the DNA and proteins are called **chromatin.** Humans have 46 chromosomes, which occur in 23 pairs. Twenty-two of these pairs are called *autosomes*. All these chromosomes are found in both males and females. One pair of chromosomes is called the *sex chromosomes,* because this pair contains the genes that control gender. Males have the sex chromosomes X and Y, and females have two X chromosomes. In Section 18.3 we explained that the Y chromosome contains the *SRY* gene that causes testes to develop.

A Karyotype

Physicians and prospective parents sometimes want to view an unborn child's chromosomes to determine whether a chromosomal abnormality exists. Any cell in the body except red blood cells, which lack a nucleus, can be a source of chromosomes for examination. In adults, it is easiest to obtain and use white blood cells separated from a blood sample for the purpose of looking at the chromosomes. For an examination of fetal chromosomes, a physician may recommend procedures such as chorionic villus sampling or amniocentesis. These processes are described more fully in the Health feature "Preventing and Testing for Birth Defects" in Section 18.3.

After a cell sample has been obtained, the cells are stimulated to divide in a culture medium. When a cell divides, chromatin condenses to form chromosomes. The nuclear envelope fragments, liberating the chromosomes. Next, a chemical is used to stop the division process when the chromosomes are most compacted and visible microscopically. Stains are applied to the slides, and the cells can be photographed with a camera attached to a microscope. Staining causes the chromosomes to have dark and light cross-bands of varying widths, and these can be used—in addition to size and shape—to help pair up the chromosomes. A computer is used to arrange the chromosomes in pairs (Fig. 19.1). The display is called a *karyotype.*

The karyotype in Figure 19.1 is that of a normal male. A normal karyotype tells us a lot about a body cell. First, we should notice that a normal body cell is diploid, meaning it has

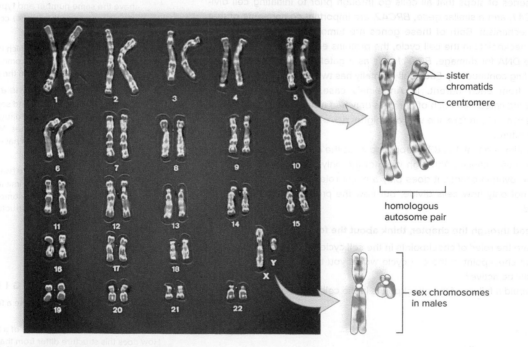

Figure 19.1   A karyotype of human chromosomes.
In body cells, the chromosomes occur in pairs. In a karyotype, the pairs have been numbered and arranged by size from largest to smallest. These chromosomes are duplicated, and each one is composed of two sister chromatids. This karyotype illustrates the 46 chromosomes of a male.
© CNRI/SPL/Science Source

the full complement of 46 chromosomes. How does it happen that almost all the cells in your body (red blood cells and liver cells are exceptions) have 46 chromosomes? A form of cell division called *mitosis* (see Section 19.3) begins when the fertilized egg starts dividing and ensures that every cell has 46 chromosomes.

The enlargement of a pair of chromosomes shows that in dividing cells each chromosome is composed of two identical parts, called **sister chromatids** (Fig. 19.1). These chromosomes are said to be *replicated* or *duplicated* chromosomes because the two sister chromatids contain the same genes. Genes are the units of heredity that control the cell. Replication of the chromosomes is possible only because each chromatid contains a DNA double helix.

The chromatids are held together at a region called the centromere. A **centromere** holds the chromatids together until a certain phase of mitosis, when the centromere splits. Once separated, each sister chromatid is a chromosome. In this way, a duplicated chromosome gives rise to two individual daughter chromosomes. When daughter chromosomes separate, the new cell gets one of each type and, therefore, a full complement of chromosomes.

SCIENCE IN YOUR LIFE

Does the number of chromosomes relate to the overall complexity of an organism?

In eukaryotes, like humans, the number of chromosomes varies considerably. A fruit fly has 8 chromosomes, and yeasts have 32. Humans have 46, and horses have 64. The largest number of chromosomes appears to be found in a particular type of fern. It has 1,252 chromosomes. The number of chromosomes doesn't seem to determine an organism's complexity.

CHECK YOUR PROGRESS 19.1

1. Explain the purpose of chromosomes in a cell.
2. Describe how a karyotype can be used to determine the number of chromosomes in a cell.
3. Explain why sister chromatids are genetically the same.

CONNECTING THE CONCEPTS

For more information on the topics in this section, refer to the following discussions:

Section 3.4 examines the role of the nucleus in a cell.

Section 3.4 explains the relationship of chromatin to the chromosomes.

Section 18.3 describes the stages of fetal development.

19.2 The Cell Cycle

LEARNING OUTCOMES

Upon completion of this section, you should be able to

1. List the stages of the cell cycle and state the purpose of each.
2. Describe the purpose of the checkpoints in the cell cycle.
3. Distinguish between mitosis and cytokinesis.

The **cell cycle** is an orderly process that has two parts: interphase and cell division. To understand the cell cycle, it is necessary to understand the structure of a cell (see Fig. 3.4). A human cell has a plasma membrane, which encloses the cytoplasm, the content of the cell outside the nucleus. In the cytoplasm are various organelles that carry on various functions necessary to the life of the cell. When a cell is not undergoing division, the chromatin (DNA and associated proteins) within a nucleus is a tangled mass of thin threads.

Interphase

As Figure 19.2 shows, most of the cell cycle is spent in **interphase.** This is the time when the organelles in the cell carry on their usual functions. As the cell continues through interphase, it gets ready to divide. The cell grows larger, the number of organelles doubles, and the amount of chromatin doubles as DNA replication occurs.

Interphase is divided into three main stages: the G_1 stage occurs before DNA synthesis; the S stage includes DNA replication; and the G_2 stage occurs after DNA replication. Originally *G* stood for "gaps"—times during interphase when DNA synthesis was not occurring. But now that we know growth happens during these

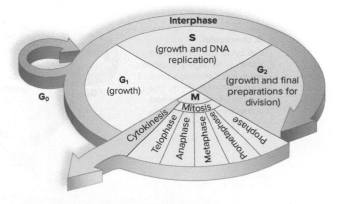

Figure 19.2   Stages of the cell cycle.
During interphase, which consists of stages G_1, S, and G_2, the cell gets ready to divide. During the mitotic stage, nuclear division and cytokinesis (cytoplasmic division) occur. The G_0 stage represents a holding stage outside the cell cycle.

stages, the *G* can be thought of as standing for "growth." Let us see what specifically happens during these stages.

G₁ stage. The cell returns to normal size and resumes its function in the body. A cell doubles its organelles (e.g., mitochondria and ribosomes), and it accumulates the materials needed for DNA synthesis.

S stage. A copy is made of all the DNA in the cell. DNA replication occurs, so each chromosome consists of two identical DNA double-helix molecules. These molecules occur in the strands called *sister chromatids*.

G₂ stage. The cell synthesizes the proteins needed for cell division, such as the protein found in microtubules. The role of microtubules in cell division is described in a later section.

The amount of time the cell takes for interphase varies widely. Some cells, such as nerve and muscle cells, typically do not complete the cell cycle and are permanently arrested in G_1. These cells are said to have entered a G_0 stage. Embryonic cells spend very little time in G_1 and complete the cell cycle in a few hours.

Mitosis and Cytokinesis

Following interphase, the cell enters the cell division part of the cell cycle. Cell division has two stages: M (for "mitotic") stage and cytokinesis. **Mitosis** is a type of nuclear division. Mitosis is also referred to as *duplication division,* because each new nucleus contains the same number and type of chromosomes as the former cell. **Cytokinesis** is division of the cytoplasm.

During mitosis, the sister chromatids of each chromosome separate, becoming chromosomes distributed to two daughter nuclei. When cytokinesis is complete, two daughter cells are now present. Mammalian cells usually require only about 4 hours to complete the mitotic stage.

The cell cycle, including interphase and cell division, occurs continuously in certain tissues. Right now your body is producing thousands of new red blood cells, skin cells, and cells that line your respiratory and digestive tracts. Mitosis is balanced by the process of **apoptosis,** or programmed cell death. Apoptosis occurs when cells are no longer needed or have become excessively damaged.

Cell Cycle Control

For a cell to reproduce successfully, the cell cycle must be controlled. The cell cycle is controlled by **checkpoints,** which can delay the cell cycle until certain conditions are met. The cell cycle has many checkpoints, but we will consider only three: G_1, G_2, and the mitotic checkpoint (Fig. 19.3). In addition, the cell cycle may be controlled by external factors, such as hormones and growth factors. Failure of the cell cycle control mechanisms may result in unrestricted cell growth, or cancer.

Checkpoints   The *G₁ checkpoint* is especially significant, because if the cell cycle passes this checkpoint, the cell is committed to divide. If the cell does not pass this checkpoint, it can enter a holding phase called G_0, during which it performs its normal functions but does not divide. The proper growth signals, such as certain growth factors, must be present for a cell to pass the G_1 checkpoint. Additionally, the integrity of the cell's DNA is also checked. If the DNA is damaged, proteins such as p53 can stop the cycle at this checkpoint and place the cell in G_0 phase. G_0 phase acts as a holding phase; if the DNA can be repaired, the cell may reenter the cell cycle. If not, then internal mechanisms cause the cell to undergo apoptosis. The cell cycle halts momentarily at the *G₂ checkpoint* until the cell verifies that DNA has replicated. This prevents the initiation of the M stage unless the chromosomes are duplicated. Also, if DNA is damaged, as from exposure to solar (UV) radiation or X-rays, arresting the cell cycle at this checkpoint

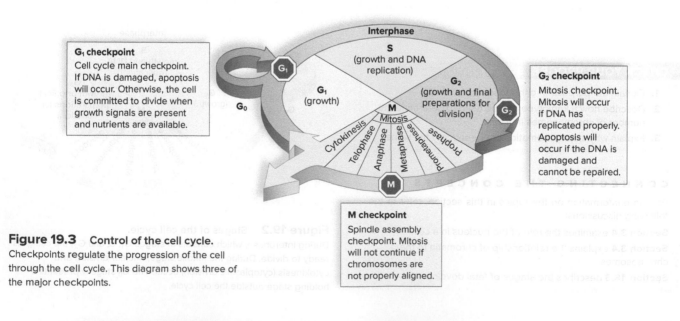

Figure 19.3   **Control of the cell cycle.**
Checkpoints regulate the progression of the cell through the cell cycle. This diagram shows three of the major checkpoints.

G₁ checkpoint
Cell cycle main checkpoint. If DNA is damaged, apoptosis will occur. Otherwise, the cell is committed to divide when growth signals are present and nutrients are available.

Interphase

S (growth and DNA replication)

G₁ (growth)

G₂ (growth and final preparations for division)

M

Cytokinesis · Telophase · Anaphase · Metaphase · Prometaphase · Prophase

Mitosis

G_0

G₂ checkpoint
Mitosis checkpoint. Mitosis will occur if DNA has replicated properly. Apoptosis will occur if the DNA is damaged and cannot be repaired.

M checkpoint
Spindle assembly checkpoint. Mitosis will not continue if chromosomes are not properly aligned.

allows time for the damage to be repaired so that it is not passed on to daughter cells.

Another cell cycle checkpoint occurs during the mitotic stage. The cycle hesitates between metaphase and anaphase to make sure the chromosomes are properly attached to the spindle and will be distributed accurately to the daughter cells. The cell cycle does not continue until every chromosome is ready for the nuclear division process.

External Control   The cell cycle control system extends from the plasma membrane to particular genes in the nucleus. Some external signals, such as hormones and growth factors, can stimulate a cell to go through the cell cycle. At a certain time in the menstrual cycle of females, the hormone progesterone stimulates cells lining the uterus to prepare the lining for implantation of a fertilized egg. Epidermal growth factor stimulates skin in the vicinity of an injury to finish the cell cycle, thereby repairing damage.

As shown in Figure 19.4, during reception an external signal delivers a message to a specific receptor embedded in the plasma membrane of a receiving cell. The signal is then relayed from the receptor to proteins inside the cell's cytoplasm. The proteins form a pathway called the signal transduction pathway because they pass the signal from one to the other. The last signal activates genes in the nucleus of the cell. The expression of these genes may either stimulate or inhibit the cell cycle. Genes called

proto-oncogenes stimulate the cell cycle, and genes called tumor suppressor genes inhibit the cell cycle. We will explore the action of these genes in more detail in Section 20.1.

CHECK YOUR PROGRESS 19.2

1. Describe the cell cycle, and list the locations of each phase and checkpoint.
2. Explain the purpose of the S phase in the cell cycle.
3. Explain how checkpoints help protect the cell against unregulated cell growth.
4. Summarize why external controls may be necessary to regulate the cell cycle.

CONNECTING THE CONCEPTS

For more information on the material presented in this section, refer to the following discussions:

Figure 16.5 illustrates how steroid hormones, such as progesterone, influence the internal activities of a cell.

Section 20.1 describes the differences between proto-oncogenes and tumor suppressor genes.

Section 20.2 explores how environmental factors, such as radiation, may cause cancer.

19.3 Mitosis

LEARNING OUTCOMES

Upon completion of this section, you should be able to

1. Explain the purpose of mitosis.
2. Explain the events that occur in each stage of mitosis.
3. State the purpose of cytokinesis.

The cell cycle, which includes mitosis, is very important to the well-being of humans. Mitosis is responsible for new cells in the developing embryo, fetus, and child. It is also responsible for replacement cells in an adult (Fig. 19.5). As we mentioned in

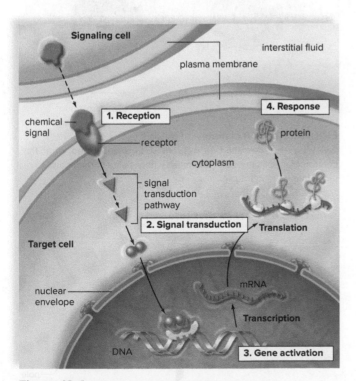

Figure 19.4   External controls of the cell cycle.
Growth factors stimulate a cell signaling pathway that stretches from the plasma membrane to the genes that regulate the occurrence of the cell cycle.

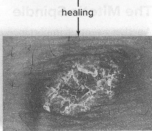

Figure 19.5   The importance of mitosis.
The cell cycle, including mitosis, occurs when humans grow and when tissues undergo repair.
(1): © Scott Camazine/Science Source;
(2): © Edward Kinsman/Science Source

Section 19.2, mitosis is often referred to as *duplication division,* because at the conclusion of mitosis the nuclei of the two new cells have the same number and types of chromosomes as the original cell. During mitosis, the cell that divides is called the **parent cell,** and the new cells are called **daughter cells.** Following mitosis, with the exception of rare mutations that may have occurred during DNA replication, the daughter cells are genetically identical to the parent cell.

Overview of Mitosis

During S phase of the cell cycle, replication of the DNA occurs (see Section 22.1), thus duplicating the chromosomes. Each chromosome now contains two identical parts, called *sister chromatids,* held together at a centromere. They are called sister chromatids because they contain the same genes.

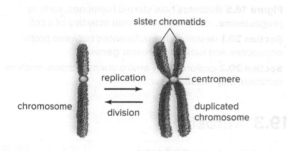

As mitosis begins, the proteins in the chromatin assist in causing the chromosomes to become highly condensed. Once this occurs, the chromosomes become visible under a light microscope. Figure 19.6 gives an overview of mitosis. For simplicity, only four chromosomes are depicted. Notice that there are two copies of each chromosome (one maternal and one paternal), so in this case the **diploid (2n)** number of chromosomes is four.

During mitosis, the centromeres divide and the sister chromatids separate. Following separation during mitosis, each chromatid is called a *chromosome.* Each daughter cell gets a complete set of chromosomes and is diploid (2n). Therefore, each daughter cell receives the same number and types of chromosomes as the parent cell. Each daughter cell is genetically identical to the other and to the parent cell.

The Mitotic Spindle

Another event of importance during mitosis is the duplication of the **centrosome,** the microtubule organizing center of the cell. After centrosomes duplicate, they separate and form the poles of the **mitotic spindle,** where they assemble the microtubules that make up the spindle fibers. The chromosomes are attached to the spindle fibers at their centromeres (Fig. 19.7). An array of microtubules called an *aster* (because it looks like a star) is also at the poles. Each centrosome contains a pair of **centrioles,** which consist of

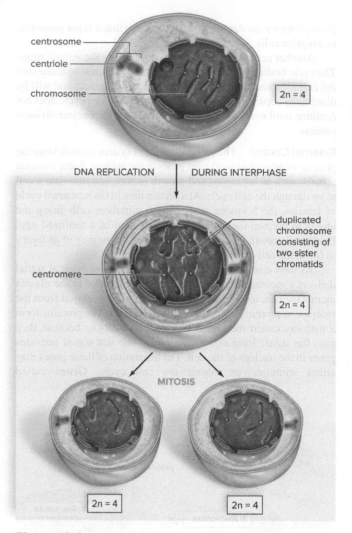

Figure 19.6 An overview of mitosis.
Following DNA replication, each chromosome is duplicated. When the centromeres split, the sister chromatids, now called chromosomes, move into daughter nuclei.

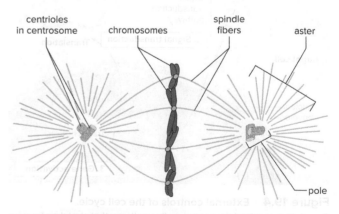

Figure 19.7 The mitotic spindle.
During mitosis, the centrioles separate, and the mitotic spindle, composed of microtubules, forms between them.

short cylinders of microtubules. The centrioles lie at right angles to one another. Centrioles are absent in plant cells, and their function in animals cells is not completely understood, although it is believed that they assist in the formation of the spindle that separates the chromatids during mitosis.

Phases of Mitosis

As an aid in describing the events of mitosis, the process is divided into phases: prophase, prometaphase, metaphase, anaphase, and telophase. Although the stages of mitosis are depicted as if they were separate, they are continuous. One stage flows from the other with no noticeable interruption.

Prophase

Several events occur during **prophase** that visibly indicate the cell is preparing to divide (Figure 19.8). The centrosomes outside the nucleus have duplicated, and they begin moving away from one another toward opposite ends of the nucleus. Spindle fibers appear between the separating centrosomes. The nuclear envelope begins to fragment. The nucleolus, a special region of DNA, disappears as the chromosomes coil and become condensed. The chromosomes are now clearly visible. Each is composed of two sister chromatids held together at a centromere.

Prometaphase

In **prometaphase** the spindle fibers attach to the centromeres as the chromosomes continue to shorten and thicken. During prometaphase, chromosomes are randomly placed in the nucleus (Fig. 19.8).

Metaphase

During **metaphase,** the spindle is fully formed. The *metaphase plate* is a plane perpendicular to the axis of the spindle and equidistant from the poles. The chromosomes, attached to spindle fibers at their centromeres, line up at the metaphase plate during metaphase. (Fig. 19.8).

Anaphase

At the start of **anaphase,** the centromeres uniting the sister chromatids divide. Then the sister chromatids separate, becoming chromosomes that move toward opposite poles of the spindle. Separation of the sister chromatids ensures that each cell receives a copy of each type of chromosome and thereby has a full complement of genes. Anaphase is characterized by the diploid (2n) number of chromosomes moving toward each pole. Remember that the number of centromeres indicates the number of chromosomes. Therefore, each pole receives four chromosomes: In Figure 19.8, two are shown in red and two are shown in blue.

Spindle Function in Anaphase The spindle brings about chromosomal movement. Two types of spindle fibers are involved in the movement of chromosomes during anaphase. One type extends from the poles to the equator of the spindle. There, they overlap. As mitosis proceeds, these fibers increase in length, which helps push the chromosomes apart. The chromosomes themselves are attached to other spindle fibers that extend from their centromeres to the poles. Because these fibers (composed of microtubules that can disassemble) become shorter as the chromosomes move toward the poles, they pull the chromosomes apart.

Spindle fibers, as stated earlier, are composed of microtubules. Microtubules can assemble and disassemble by the addition or subtraction of tubulin (protein) subunits. This is what enables spindle fibers to lengthen and shorten and what ultimately causes the movement of the chromosomes.

Telophase

Telophase begins when the chromosomes arrive at the poles. During telophase, the chromosomes become indistinct chromatin again. The spindle disappears as the nuclear envelope components reassemble in each cell. Each nucleus has a nucleolus, because each has a region of the DNA where ribosomal subunits are produced. Telophase is characterized by the presence of two daughter nuclei.

Cytokinesis

Cytokinesis is the division of the cytoplasm and organelles. In human cells, a slight indentation called a **cleavage furrow** passes around the circumference of the cell. Actin filaments form a contractile ring; as the ring becomes smaller, the cleavage furrow pinches the cell in half. As a result, each cell becomes enclosed by its own plasma membrane.

CHECK YOUR PROGRESS 19.3

1. Explain how the chromosome number of the daughter cell compares with the chromosome number of the parent cell following mitosis.
2. List the phases of mitosis, and explain what happens during each phase.
3. Describe how the cytoplasm is divided between the daughter cells following mitosis.

CONNECTING THE CONCEPTS

For more information on mitosis and cytokinesis, refer to the following discussions:

Section 3.4 examines the structure of the nucleus.

Section 3.5 describes the functions of both the microtubules and actin filaments in a nondividing cell.

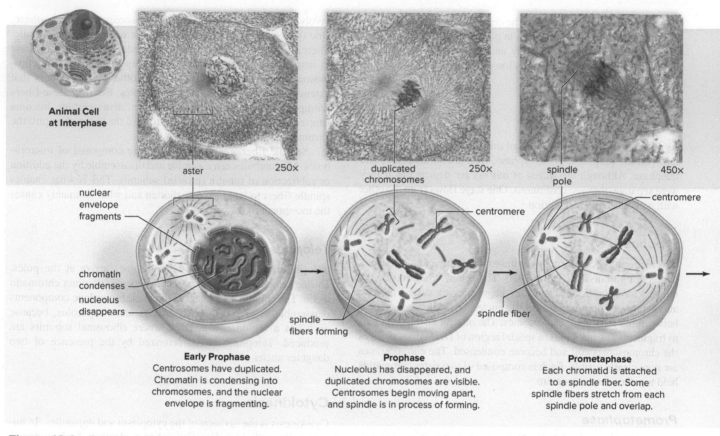

Animal Cell at Interphase

aster   250×

nuclear envelope fragments

chromatin condenses

nucleolus disappears

spindle fibers forming

Early Prophase
Centrosomes have duplicated.
Chromatin is condensing into chromosomes, and the nuclear envelope is fragmenting.

duplicated chromosomes   250×

centromere

spindle fiber

Prophase
Nucleolus has disappeared, and duplicated chromosomes are visible. Centrosomes begin moving apart, and spindle is in process of forming.

spindle pole   450×

centromere

Prometaphase
Each chromatid is attached to a spindle fiber. Some spindle fibers stretch from each spindle pole and overlap.

Figure 19.8   Stages of mitosis.
The stages of prophase, prometaphase, metaphase, anaphase, and telophase, all act to sort the chromosomes for the new daughter cells.
(1): © Ed Reschke; (2): © Ed Reschke; (3): © Michael Abbey/Science Source; (4-6): © Ed Reschke

19.4 Meiosis

LEARNING OUTCOMES

Upon completion of this section, you should be able to

1. List the stages of meiosis and describe what occurs in each stage.
2. Explain how meiosis increases genetic variation.
3. Differentiate between spermatogenesis and oogenesis with regard to occurrence and the number of functional gametes produced by each process.

Meiosis, or reduction division, reduces the chromosome number in the daughter cells. To do this, meiosis involves two consecutive cell divisions, without an intervening interphase. The end result is four daughter cells, each of which has one of each type of chromosome and, therefore, half as many chromosomes as the parent cell. The parent cell has the diploid (2n) number of chromosomes; the daughter cells have half this number, called the **haploid (n)** number of chromosomes. In addition, meiosis introduces genetic variation, which means that each of the resulting daughter cells is not a genetic replicate of the parent cell but, rather, possesses new

combinations of the genetic material. In animals, including humans, the daughter cells that result from meiosis may go on to become the gametes.

Overview of Meiosis

At the start of meiosis, the parent cell is diploid (2n), and the chromosomes occur in pairs. For simplicity's sake, Figure 19.9 has only two pairs of chromosomes. In this figure, the diploid (2n) number of chromosomes is four chromosomes. The short chromosomes are one pair, and the long chromosomes are another. The members of a pair are called **homologous chromosomes,** or *homologues,* because they look alike and carry genes for the same traits, such as type of hair or color of eyes. Notice that the parent cell (*top*) has the diploid (2n) number of chromosomes; the daughter cells (*bottom*) have the haploid (n) number of chromosomes, equal to two chromosomes.

Meiosis I

The two cell divisions of meiosis are called *meiosis I* and *meiosis II*. Prior to meiosis I, DNA replication has occurred and the chromosomes are duplicated. Each chromosome consists of two

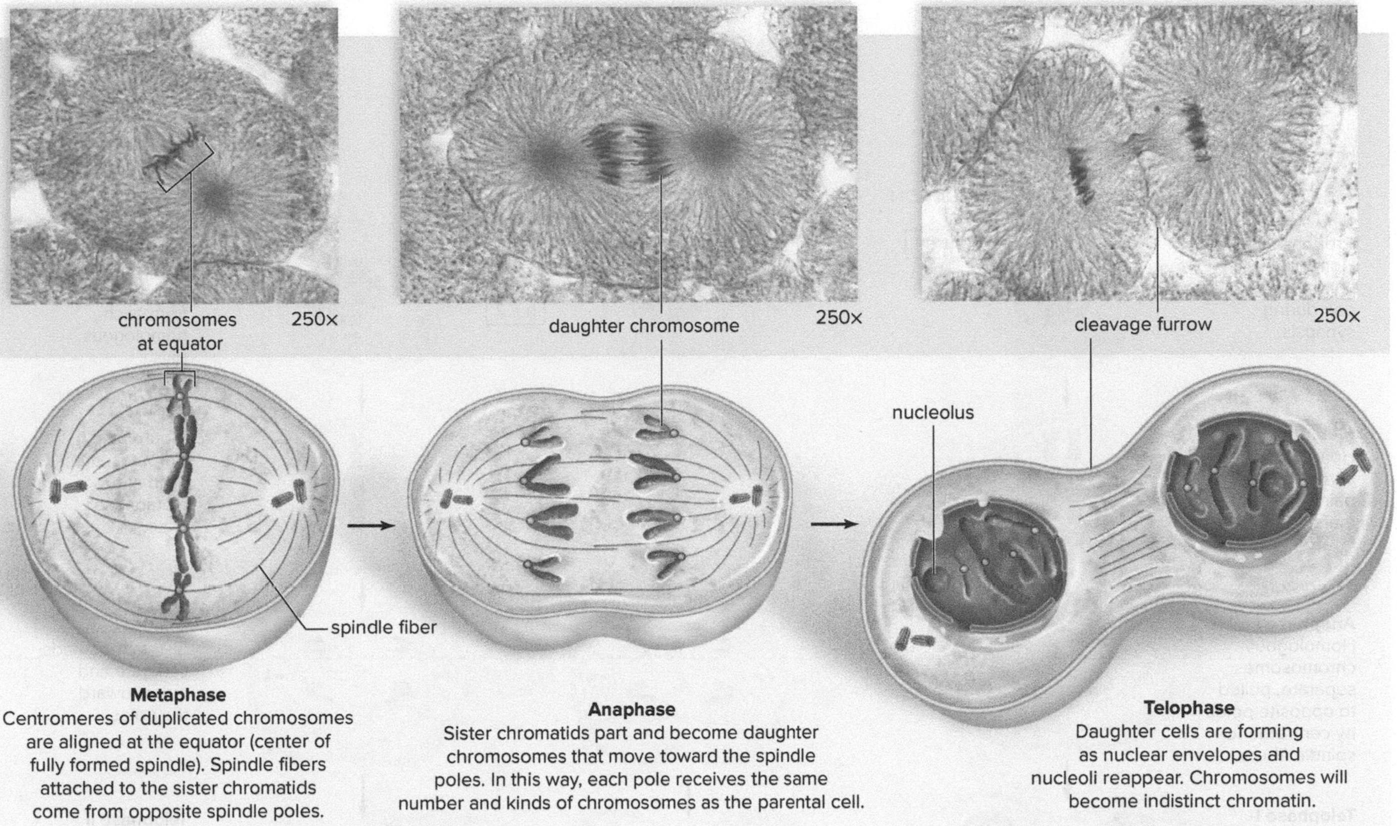

chromosomes at equator   250×

daughter chromosome   250×

cleavage furrow   250×

nucleolus

spindle fiber

Metaphase
Centromeres of duplicated chromosomes are aligned at the equator (center of fully formed spindle). Spindle fibers attached to the sister chromatids come from opposite spindle poles.

Anaphase
Sister chromatids part and become daughter chromosomes that move toward the spindle poles. In this way, each pole receives the same number and kinds of chromosomes as the parental cell.

Telophase
Daughter cells are forming as nuclear envelopes and nucleoli reappear. Chromosomes will become indistinct chromatin.

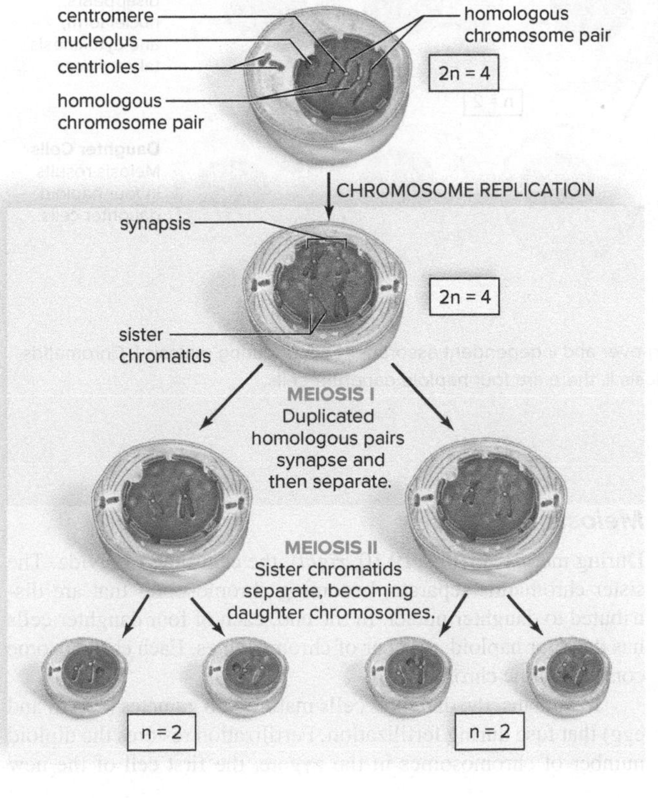

centromere
nucleolus
centrioles
homologous chromosome pair

homologous chromosome pair

2n = 4

CHROMOSOME REPLICATION

synapsis

2n = 4

sister chromatids

MEIOSIS I
Duplicated homologous pairs synapse and then separate.

MEIOSIS II
Sister chromatids separate, becoming daughter chromosomes.

n = 2

n = 2

chromatids held together at a centromere. During meiosis I (Figure 19.10, *top*), the homologous chromosomes come together and line up side by side. This is called **synapsis**, and it results in an association of four chromatids that stay in close proximity during the first two phases of meiosis I. Synapsis is significant, because its occurrence leads to a reduction of the chromosome number.

There are pairs of homologous chromosomes at the equator during meiosis I because of synapsis. Only during meiosis I is it possible to observe paired chromosomes at the equator. When the members of these pairs separate, each daughter nucleus receives one member of each pair. Therefore, each daughter cell now has the haploid (n) number of chromosomes, as you can verify by counting its centromeres. Each chromosome, however, is still duplicated. No replication of DNA occurs between meiosis I and meiosis II. The time between meiosis I and meiosis II is called **interkinesis.**

Figure 19.9   The results of meiosis.
DNA replication is followed by meiosis I when homologous chromosomes pair and then separate. During meiosis II, the sister chromatids become chromosomes that move into daughter nuclei.

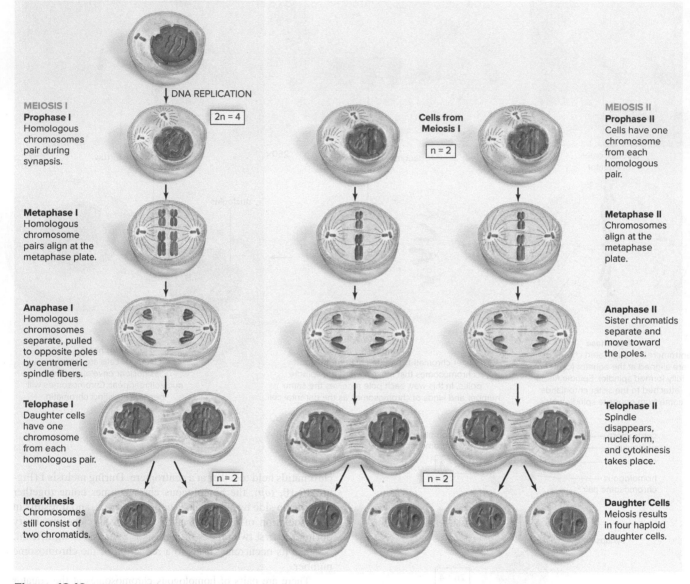

Figure 19.10   The phases of meiosis.
Homologous chromosomes pair and then separate during meiosis I. Crossing-over and independent assortment occur during meiosis I. Chromatids separate, becoming daughter chromosomes during meiosis II. Following meiosis II, there are four haploid daughter cells.

SCIENCE IN YOUR LIFE

How often do mistakes occur in meiosis?

It is estimated that 8% of all clinically recognized pregnancies have some form of chromosomal aberration. In a spontaneous abortion (typically referred to as a *miscarriage*), the frequency of chromosomal abnormalities rises to approximately 50%. Most of these are the result of errors during meiosis in parents with normal karyotypes.

Meiosis II

During meiosis II (Fig. 19.10, *right*), the centromeres divide. The sister chromatids separate, becoming chromosomes that are distributed to daughter nuclei. In the end, each of four daughter cells has the n, or haploid, number of chromosomes. Each chromosome consists of one chromatid.

In humans, the daughter cells mature into gametes (sperm and egg) that fuse during fertilization. Fertilization restores the diploid number of chromosomes in the zygote, the first cell of the new individual. If the gametes carried the diploid instead of the haploid number of chromosomes, the chromosome number would double with each fertilization. After several generations, the zygote would be nothing but chromosomes.

Meiosis and Genetic Variation

Meiosis is a part of sexual reproduction. The process of meiosis ensures that the next generation of individuals will have the diploid number of chromosomes and a combination of genetic characteristics different from that of either parent. Though both meiosis I and meiosis II have the same four stages of nuclear division as did mitosis (see Section 19.3), here we discuss only prophase I and metaphase I, because special events occur during these phases that introduce new genetic combinations into the daughter cells.

Prophase I

In prophase I, synapsis occurs, causing the homologous chromosomes to come together and line up side by side. Now, an exchange of genetic material may occur between the nonsister chromatids of the homologous pair (Fig. 19.11). This exchange is called **crossing-over.** Notice that in Figure 19.11 the crossing-over events (there may be more than one) have produced chromatids that are no longer identical. When the chromatids separate during meiosis II, the daughter cells receive chromosomes with recombined genetic material.

To appreciate the significance of crossing-over, it is necessary to realize that the members of a homologous pair can carry slightly different instructions for the same genetic trait. For example, one homologue may carry instructions for brown eyes and blond hair, and the corresponding homologue may carry instructions for blue eyes and red hair. Crossing-over causes the offspring to receive a different combination of instructions than the mother or the father received. Therefore, offspring can receive brown eyes and red hair or blue eyes and blond hair.

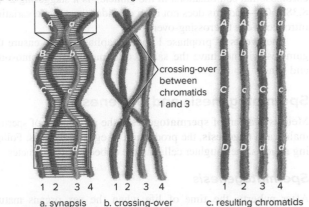

Figure 19.11 **Synapsis and crossing-over increase variability.** **a.** During meiosis I, duplicated homologous chromosomes undergo synapsis and line up with each other. **b.** During crossing-over, nonsister chromatids break and then rejoin in the manner shown. **c.** Two of the resulting chromosomes have a different combination of genes than they had before.

Metaphase I

During metaphase I, the homologous pairs align independently at the equator. This means that the maternal or paternal member may be oriented toward either pole. Figure 19.12 shows the eight possible orientations for a cell that contains only three pairs of chromosomes. The first four orientations will result in gametes that have different combinations of maternal and paternal chromosomes. The next four will result in the same types of gametes as the first four. For example, the first cell and the last cell will both produce gametes with either three red or three blue chromosomes.

Once all possible orientations are considered, the result will be 2^3, or 8, possible combinations of maternal and paternal chromosomes in the resulting gametes from this cell. In humans, in

Figure 19.12 **Independent alignment at metaphase I increases variability.**
When a parent cell has three pairs of homologous chromosomes, there are eight possible chromosome alignments at the equator due to independent assortment. Among the 16 daughter nuclei resulting from these alignments, there are eight different combinations of chromosomes.

whom there are 23 pairs of chromosomes, the number of possible chromosomal combinations in the gametes is a staggering 2^{23}, or 8,388,608—and this does not even consider the genetic variations introduced due to crossing-over.

The events of prophase I and metaphase I help ensure that gametes will not have the same combination of chromosomes and genes.

Spermatogenesis and Oogenesis

Meiosis is a part of **spermatogenesis,** the production of sperm in males, and **oogenesis,** the production of eggs in females. Following meiosis, the daughter cells mature to become the gametes.

Spermatogenesis

After puberty, the time of life when the sex organs mature, spermatogenesis is continual in the testes of human males. As many as 300,000 sperm are produced per minute, or over 400 million per day.

Spermatogenesis is shown in Figure 19.13, *top.* The *primary spermatocytes,* which are diploid (2n), divide during meiosis I to form two *secondary spermatocytes,* which are haploid (n). Secondary spermatocytes divide during meiosis II to produce four *spermatids,* which are also haploid (n). What's the difference between the chromosomes in haploid secondary spermatocytes and those in haploid spermatids? The chromosomes in secondary spermatocytes are duplicated and consist of two chromatids, whereas those in spermatids consist of only one. Spermatids mature into sperm (spermatozoa). In human males, sperm have 23 chromosomes, the haploid number. The process of meiosis in males always results in four cells that become sperm. In other words, all four daughter cells—the spermatids—become sperm.

Oogenesis

The ovary of a female contains many immature follicles (see Fig. 17.8). Each of these follicles contains a primary oocyte arrested in prophase I. As shown in Figure 19.13 (*bottom*), a primary oocyte, which is diploid (2n), divides during meiosis I into two cells, each of which is haploid. The chromosomes are duplicated. One of these cells, termed the *secondary oocyte,* receives almost all the cytoplasm. The other is the first polar body. A *polar body* acts as a trash can to hold discarded chromosomes. The first polar body contains duplicated chromosomes and occasionally completes meiosis II. The secondary oocyte begins meiosis II but stops at metaphase II and doesn't complete it unless a sperm enters during the fertilization process.

The secondary oocyte (for convenience, called the egg) leaves the ovary during ovulation and enters a uterine tube, where it may be fertilized by a sperm. If so, the oocyte is activated to complete the second meiotic division. Following meiosis II, there is one egg and two or possibly three polar bodies. The mature egg has 23 chromosomes. The polar bodies disintegrate, which is a way to discard unnecessary chromosomes while retaining much of the cytoplasm in the egg.

One egg can be the source of identical twins if, after one division of the fertilized egg during development, the cells separate and each one becomes a complete individual. On the other hand,

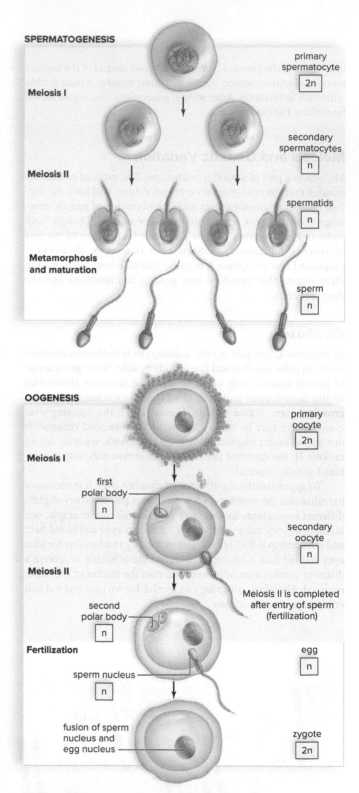

SPERMATOGENESIS

primary spermatocyte 2n

Meiosis I

secondary spermatocytes n

Meiosis II

spermatids n

Metamorphosis and maturation

sperm n

OOGENESIS

primary oocyte 2n

Meiosis I

first polar body n

secondary oocyte n

Meiosis II

second polar body n

Meiosis II is completed after entry of sperm (fertilization)

Fertilization

egg n

sperm nucleus n

fusion of sperm nucleus and egg nucleus

zygote 2n

Figure 19.13 A comparison of spermatogenesis and oogenesis in mammals.

Spermatogenesis produces four viable sperm, whereas oogenesis produces one egg and at least two polar bodies. In humans, both sperm and egg have 23 chromosomes each; therefore, following fertilization, the zygote has 46 chromosomes.

the occurrence of fraternal twins requires that two eggs be ovulated and then fertilized separately.

Significance of Meiosis

In animals, meiosis is a part of gametogenesis, production of the sperm and egg. One function of meiosis is to keep the chromosome number constant from generation to generation. The gametes are haploid, so the zygote has only the diploid number of chromosomes.

An easier way to keep the chromosome number constant is to reproduce asexually. Single-celled organisms such as bacteria, protozoans, and yeasts (a fungi) reproduce by binary fission.

Binary fission is a form of asexual reproduction, because one parent produces identical offspring. Binary fission is a quick and easy way to asexually reproduce many organisms within a short time. A bacterium can increase to over 1 million cells in about 7 hours, for example. Then, why do organisms expend the energy to reproduce sexually? It takes energy to find a mate, carry out a courtship, and produce eggs or sperm that may never be used for reproductive purposes. A human male produces over 400 million sperm per day, and very few of these will fertilize an egg.

Most likely, humans and other animals practice sexual reproduction that includes meiosis because it results in genetic recombination. Genetic recombination ensures that offspring will be genetically different from each other and their parents. Genetic recombination occurs because of crossing-over and independent alignment of chromosomes. Also, at the time of fertilization, parents contribute genetically different chromosomes to the offspring.

All environments are subject to a change in conditions. Those individuals able to survive in a new environment are able to pass on their genes. Environments are subject to change, so sexual reproduction is advantageous. It generates the diversity needed, so that at least a few will be suited to new and different environmental circumstances.

CHECK YOUR PROGRESS 19.4

1. Explain how, following meiosis, the chromosome number of the daughter cells compares to the chromosome number of the parent cell.
2. Explain how meiosis reduces the likelihood that gametes will have the same combination of chromosomes and genes.
3. Summarize the events during the two cell divisions of meiosis.
4. Compare and contrast the stages of oogenesis and spermatogenesis.

CONNECTING THE CONCEPTS

For more on the importance of meiosis, refer to the following discussions:

Figure 17.4 illustrates how meiosis relates to spermatogenesis.

Figure 17.9 demonstrates how meiosis produces eggs and polar bodies during oogenesis.

Figure 21.5 relates meiosis to the patterns of genetic inheritance.

19.5 Comparison of Meiosis and Mitosis

LEARNING OUTCOMES

Upon completion of this section, you should be able to

1. Distinguish between meiosis and mitosis with regard to the number of divisions and the number and chromosome content of the resulting cells.
2. Contrast the events of meiosis I and meiosis II with the events of mitosis.

Meiosis and mitosis are both nuclear divisions, but they differ in the number of cells produced and the genetic complement (haploid or diploid) of each of the daughter cells. Figure 19.14 provides a visual review of the similarities and differences between meiosis and mitosis.

General Comparison

DNA replication takes place only once prior to both meiosis and mitosis. Meiosis requires two nuclear divisions, but mitosis requires only one.

- Four daughter nuclei are produced by meiosis; following cytokinesis, there are four daughter cells. Mitosis followed by cytokinesis results in two daughter cells.
- The four daughter cells following meiosis are haploid (n) and have half the chromosome number of the parent cell (2n). The daughter cells following mitosis have the same chromosome number as the parent cell—the 2n, or diploid, number.
- The daughter cells from meiosis are not genetically identical to each other or to the parent cell. The daughter cells from mitosis are genetically identical to each other and to the parent cell.

The specific differences between these nuclear divisions can be categorized according to occurrence and process.

Occurrence

Meiosis occurs only at certain times in the life cycle of sexually reproducing organisms. In humans, meiosis occurs only in the reproductive organs and produces the gametes. Mitosis is more common, because it occurs in all tissues during growth and repair. Which type of cell division can lead to cancer? Mitosis can result in a proliferation of body cells. Abnormal mitosis can lead to cancer.

Process

Comparison of Meiosis I with Mitosis

These events distinguish meiosis I from mitosis (Table 19.1):

- Homologous chromosomes pair and undergo crossing-over during prophase I of meiosis but not during mitosis.
- Paired homologous chromosomes align at the equator during metaphase I in meiosis. These paired chromosomes have four chromatids altogether. Individual chromosomes align at the equator during metaphase in mitosis. They each have two chromatids.

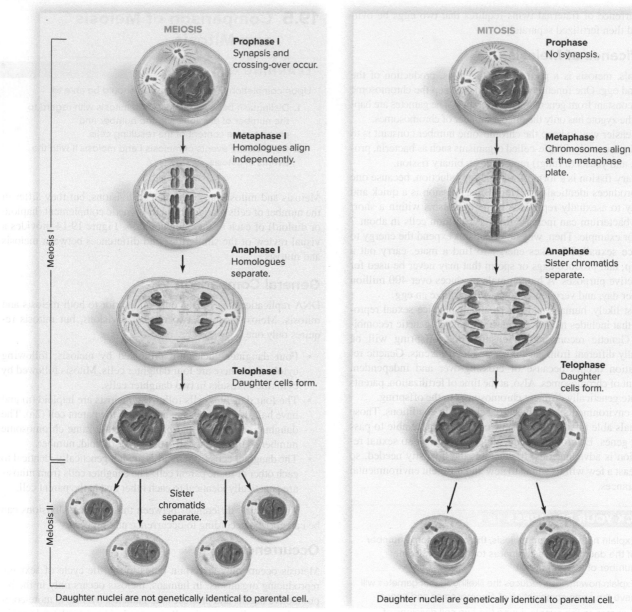

Figure 19.14   A comparison of meiosis and mitosis.
By comparing mitosis with meiosis, you can see why mitosis is referred to as duplication division and meiosis is called reduction division. Only in metaphase I are the homologous chromosomes paired at the equator. Members of homologous chromosome pairs separate during anaphase I; therefore, the daughter cells are haploid. The blue chromosomes were inherited from the paternal parent, and the red chromosomes were inherited from the maternal parent. The exchange of color between nonsister chromatids represents the crossing-over that occurs during meiosis I.

- This difference makes it easy to tell whether you are looking at mitosis, meiosis I, or meiosis II. For example, if a cell has 16 chromosomes, then 16 chromosomes are at the equator during mitosis but only 8 chromosomes during meiosis II. Only meiosis I has paired duplicated chromosomes at the equator.
- Homologous chromosomes (with centromeres intact) separate and move to opposite poles during anaphase I of meiosis. Centromeres split, and sister chromatids, now

called chromosomes, move to opposite poles during anaphase in mitosis.

Comparison of Meiosis II with Mitosis

The events of meiosis II are like those of mitosis (Table 19.2) except that, in meiosis II, the nuclei contain the haploid number of chromosomes. If the parent cell has 16 chromosomes, then the cells undergoing meiosis II have 8 chromosomes, and the daughter cells have 8 chromosomes, for example.

Table 19.1	Comparison of Meiosis I with Mitosis
Meiosis I	**Mitosis**
Prophase I	*Prophase*
Pairing of homologous chromosomes	No pairing of chromosomes
Metaphase I	*Metaphase*
Homologous duplicated chromosomes at equator	Duplicated chromosomes at equator
Anaphase I	*Anaphase*
Homologous chromosomes separate.	Sister chromatids separate, becoming daughter chromosomes, which move to the poles.
Telophase I	*Telophase*
Two haploid daughter cells	Two daughter cells, identical to the parent cell

Table 19.2	Comparison of Meiosis II with Mitosis
Meiosis II	**Mitosis**
Prophase II	*Prophase*
No pairing of chromosomes	No pairing of chromosomes
Metaphase II	*Metaphase*
Haploid number of duplicated chromosomes at equator	Duplicated chromosomes at equator
Anaphase II	*Anaphase*
Sister chromatids separate, becoming daughter chromosomes, which move to the poles.	Sister chromatids separate, becoming daughter chromosomes, which move to the poles.
Telophase II	*Telophase*
Four haploid daughter cells	Two daughter cells, identical to the parent cell

CHECK YOUR PROGRESS 19.5

1. List the similarities and differences between meiosis I and mitosis.
2. List the similarities and differences between meiosis II and mitosis.
3. Explain why a close examination of metaphase can indicate whether a cell is undergoing mitosis or meiosis.

CONNECTING THE CONCEPTS

For more on the roles of mitosis and meiosis, refer to the following discussions:

Section 17.2 examines the process of spermatogenesis and the male reproductive system.

Section 17.4 examines the process of oogenesis and the female reproductive system.

Section 20.1 explores how unrestricted mitosis causes cancer.

19.6 Chromosome Inheritance

LEARNING OUTCOMES

Upon completion of this section, you should be able to

1. Explain how nondisjunction produces monosomy and trisomy chromosome conditions.
2. Describe the causes and consequences of trisomy 21.
3. List the major syndromes associated with changes in the number of sex chromosomes.
4. Describe the effects of deletions, duplications, inversions, and translocations on chromosome structure.

Normally an individual receives 22 pairs of autosomes and two sex chromosomes. Each pair of autosomes carries alleles for particular traits. The alleles can be different, as when one contains instructions for freckles and one does not.

Changes in Chromosome Number

Some individuals are born with either too many or too few autosomes or sex chromosomes, most likely due to an error, called nondisjunction, during meiosis. **Nondisjunction** is the failure of the homologous chromosomes or daughter chromosomes to separate correctly during meiosis I and meiosis II, respectively. Nondisjunction may occur during meiosis I, when both members of a homologous pair go into the same daughter cell. It can also occur during meiosis II, when the sister chromatids fail to separate and both daughter chromosomes go into the same gamete. Figure 19.15 assumes that nondisjunction has occurred during oogenesis. Some abnormal eggs have 24 chromosomes, whereas others have only 22 chromosomes. If an egg with 24 chromosomes is fertilized with a normal sperm, the result is called a **trisomy,** because one type of chromosome is present in three copies (2n + 1). If an egg with 22 chromosomes is fertilized with a normal sperm, the result is called a **monosomy,** because one type of chromosome is present in a single copy (2n − 1).

Normal development depends on the presence of exactly two of each type of chromosome. An abnormal number of autosomes causes a developmental abnormality. Monosomy of all but the X chromosome is fatal. The affected infant rarely develops to full term. Trisomy is usually fatal, though there are some exceptions. Among autosomal trisomies, only trisomy 21 (Down syndrome) has a reasonable chance of survival after birth.

The chances of survival are greater when trisomy or monosomy involves the sex chromosomes. In normal XX females, one of the X chromosomes becomes a darkly-staining mass of chromatin called a **Barr body** (named after the person who discovered it). A Barr body is an inactive X chromosome. The Science feature "Barr Bodies and Dosage Compensation" provides additional information regarding Barr bodies.

We now know that the cells of females function with a single X chromosome just as those of males do. This is most likely the reason that a zygote with one X chromosome (Turner syndrome) can survive. Then, too, all extra X chromosomes beyond a single one become Barr bodies; this explains why poly-X females and XXY males are seen fairly frequently. An extra Y chromosome, called

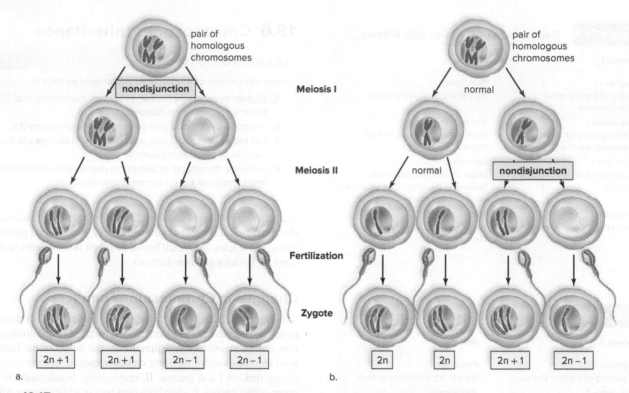

Figure 19.15   The consequences of nondisjunction of chromosomes during oogenesis.
a. Nondisjunction can occur during meiosis I and results in abnormal eggs that also have one more or one less than the normal number of chromosomes. Fertilization of these abnormal eggs with normal sperm results in a zygote with abnormal chromosome numbers. **b.** Nondisjunction can also occur during meiosis II if the sister chromatids separate but the resulting daughter chromosomes go into the same daughter cell. Then the egg will have one more or one less than the usual number of chromosomes. Fertilization of these abnormal eggs with normal sperm produces a zygote with abnormal chromosome numbers.

Jacobs syndrome, is tolerated in humans, most likely because the Y chromosome carries few genes. Jacobs syndrome (XYY) is due to nondisjunction during meiosis II of spermatogenesis. We know this because two Ys are present only during meiosis II in males.

Down Syndrome: An Autosomal Trisomy

The most common autosomal trisomy seen among humans is Down syndrome, also called trisomy 21. Persons with Down syndrome usually have three copies of chromosome 21, because the egg had two copies instead of one. However, about 20% of the time the sperm contributes the extra chromosome 21. The chances of a woman having a Down syndrome child increase rapidly with age, starting at about age 40. The reasons for this are still being investigated.

Although an older woman is more likely to have a Down syndrome child, most babies with Down syndrome are born to women younger than age 40, because this is the age group having the most babies. Karyotyping can detect a Down syndrome child. However, young women are not routinely encouraged to undergo the procedures necessary to get a sample of fetal cells (amniocentesis or chorionic villus sampling), because the risk of complications is greater than the risk of having a Down syndrome child. Fortunately, a test based on substances in maternal blood can help identify fetuses who may need to be karyotyped.

Are there trisomies of the other chromosomes besides chromosome 21?

There are other chromosomal trisomies. However, because most chromosomes are much larger than chromosome 21, the abnormalities associated with three copies of these other chromosomes are much more severe than those found in Down syndrome. The extra genetic material causes profound congenital defects, resulting in fatality. Trisomies of the X and Y chromosomes appear to be exceptions to this, as noted in the text.

Chromosome 8 trisomy occurs rarely. Affected fetuses generally do not survive to birth or die shortly after birth. There are also trisomies of chromosomes 13 (Patau syndrome) and 18 (Edwards syndrome). Again, these babies usually die within the first few days of life.

Down syndrome is easily recognized by these common characteristics: short stature; an eyelid fold; a flat face; stubby fingers; a wide gap between the first and second toes; a large, fissured tongue; a round head; and a palm crease, the so-called simian line. Unfortunately, intellectual disability, which can vary in intensity,

Barr Bodies and Dosage Compensation

Most people are familiar with calico cats, whose fur contains patches of orange, black, and white. These cats are genetic mosaics. A mosaic is formed by combining different pieces to form a whole (a stained glass window is one example). Likewise, in genetics, a mosaic is an individual whose cells have at least two—and sometimes more—different types of genetic expression. In the case of the calico cat, the fur colors are due to the expression of different genes. Some of the hair cells of these cats express the paternal copy of the gene. If an orange-haired father's copy of the gene is activated, a patch of orange hair develops. In other cells, the maternal gene is activated. A calico kitten with a black mother will grow black patches of hair scattered among the orange. Were you aware that human females are also mosaics?

The nucleus of human cells contains 46 chromosomes arranged into a set of 23 pairs. One chromosome from each pair is maternal, and the other is paternal. Each of the chromosomes in the first 22 pairs resembles its mate. Further, each member of a pair contains the same genes as the other member. Sex chromosomes that determine a person's gender are the last pair. Females have two X chromosomes, and males have one X and one Y chromosome. The Y chromosome is very small and contains far fewer genes than the X chromosome. Almost all the genes on the X chromosome lack a corresponding gene on the Y chromosome. Thus, females have two copies of X genes, whereas males have only one. The body compensates for this extra dose of genetic material by inactivating one of the X chromosomes in each cell of the female embryo. Inactivation occurs early in

development (at approximately the 100-cell stage). The inactivated X chromosome is called a Barr body, named after its discoverer. Barr bodies are highly condensed chromatin that appear as dark spots in the nucleus. Which X chromosome is inactivated in a given cell appears to be random. But every cell that develops from the original group of 100 cells will have the same inactivated X chromosome as its parent cell. Some of a woman's cells have inactivated the maternal X chromosome and other cells have inactivated the paternal X chromosome—she is a mosaic.

Problems with inactivation of the X chromosome in humans could be linked to the development of cancer. For example, women who have one defective copy of the breast cancer gene *BRCA1* have a greatly increased risk of developing breast and ovarian cancer. The BRCA1 protein produced from the gene is called a tumor suppressor. When the protein is functioning normally, it suppresses the development of cancer. The same protein is involved in X chromosome inactivation, although its exact role is uncertain. Presumably, increased cancer risk occurs because abnormal BRCA1 protein can neither inactivate the X chromosome nor function as a tumor suppressor.

Questions to Consider

1. Why would having an extra set of X chromosome genes be a problem for a female?
2. If X inactivation compensates for an extra X chromosome, why do Klinefelter males (XXY) have problems with development?

is also a characteristic. Chris Burke (Fig. 19.16*a*) was born with Down syndrome, and his parents were advised to put him in an institution. But Chris's parents didn't do that. They gave him the same loving care and attention they gave their other children, and it paid off. Chris is remarkably talented. He is a playwright, an actor, and a musician. He starred in *Life Goes On* (1989–1993), a TV series written just for him, and he is sometimes asked to be a guest star in other TV shows. His love of music and collaboration with other musicians have led to the release of several albums—like Chris, the songs are uplifting and inspirational. You can read more about this remarkable individual in his autobiography, *A Special Kind of Hero*.

The genes that cause Down syndrome are located on the bottom third of chromosome 21 (Fig. 19.16*b*). Extensive investigative work has been directed toward discovering the specific genes responsible for the characteristics of the syndrome. Thus far, investigators have discovered several genes that may account for various conditions seen in persons with Down syndrome. For example, they have located genes most likely responsible for the increased tendency toward leukemia, cataracts, accelerated rate of aging, and intellectual disabilities. The gene associated with the intellectual disabilities, called the

SCIENCE IN YOUR LIFE

Why is the age of a female a factor in Down syndrome?

One reason may be a difference in the timing of meiosis between males and females. Following puberty, males produce sperm continuously throughout their lives. In contrast, meiosis for females begins about 5 months after being conceived. However, the process is paused at prophase I of meiosis. Only after puberty are a selected few number of these cells allowed to continue meiosis as part of the female menstrual cycle. Because long periods of time may occur between the start and completion of meiosis, there is a greater chance that nondisjunction will occur; thus, as a female ages, there is a greater chance of producing a child with Down syndrome.

Gart gene, causes an increased level of purines in the blood, a finding associated with problems in intellectual development. One day it may be possible to control the expression of the *Gart* gene even before birth, so that at least this symptom of Down syndrome does not appear.

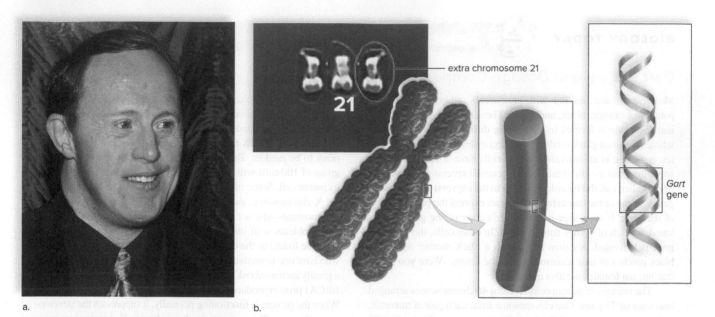

Figure 19.16   Down syndrome.
a. Chris Burke was born with Down syndrome. Common characteristics of the syndrome include a wide, rounded face and a fold on the upper eyelids. Intellectual disability, along with an enlarged tongue, makes it difficult for a person with Down syndrome to speak distinctly. **b.** Karotype of an individual with Down syndrome shows an extra chromosome 21. More sophisticated technologies allow investigators to pinpoint the location of specific genes associated with the syndrome, such as the *Gart* gene.
(a): © Scott Wintrow/Getty Images; (b): © CNRI/SPL/Science Source

Changes in Sex Chromosome Number

An abnormal sex chromosome number is the result of inheriting too many or too few X or Y chromosomes. Figure 19.15 can be used to illustrate nondisjunction of the sex chromosomes during oogenesis if you assume that the chromosomes shown represent X chromosomes. Nondisjunction during oogenesis or spermatogenesis can result in gametes that have too few or too many X or Y chromosomes.

A person with Turner syndrome (XO) is a female, and a person with Klinefelter syndrome (XXY) is a male. The term **syndrome** indicates that there are a group of symptoms that always occur together. This shows that in humans the presence of a Y chromosome, not the number of X chromosomes, determines maleness. The *SRY* gene, on the short arm of the Y chromosome, produces a hormone called *testis-determining factor*. This hormone plays a critical role in the development of male sex organs.

Turner Syndrome

From birth, an individual with Turner syndrome has only one sex chromosome, an X. As adults, Turner females are short, with a broad chest and folds of skin on the back of the neck. The ovaries, uterine tubes, and uterus are very small and underdeveloped. Turner females do not undergo puberty or menstruate, and their breasts do not develop. However, some have given birth following in vitro fertilization using donor eggs. They usually are of normal intelligence and can lead fairly normal lives if they receive hormone supplements.

Klinefelter Syndrome

One in 650 live males is born with two X chromosomes and one Y chromosome. The symptoms of this condition (referred to as "47, XXY") are often so subtle that only 25% are ever diagnosed, and those are usually not diagnosed until after age 15. Earlier diagnosis opens the possibility for educational accommodations and other interventions that can help mitigate common symptoms, which include speech and language delays. Those 47, XXY males who develop more severe symptoms as adults are referred to as having *Klinefelter syndrome*. All 47, XXY adults require assisted reproduction to father children. Affected individuals commonly receive testosterone supplementation beginning at puberty.

Poly-X Females

A poly-X female has more than two X chromosomes and extra Barr bodies in the nucleus. Females with three X chromosomes have no distinctive phenotype, aside from a tendency to be tall and thin. Although some have delayed motor and language development, most poly-X females do not have intellectual disabilities. Some may have menstrual difficulties, but many menstruate regularly and are fertile. Their children usually have a normal karyotype.

Females with more than three X chromosomes occur rarely. Unlike XXX females, XXXX females are more likely to possess problems with intellectual development. Various physical abnormalities are seen, but these females may menstruate normally.

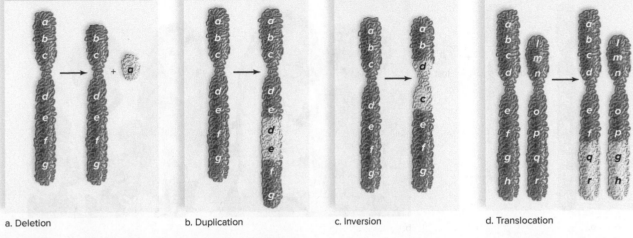

a. Deletion   b. Duplication   c. Inversion   d. Translocation

Figure 19.17   The various types of chromosomal mutations.
a. Deletion is the loss of a chromosome piece. **b.** Duplication occurs when the same piece is repeated within the chromosome. **c.** Inversion occurs when a piece of chromosome breaks loose and then rejoins in the reversed direction. **d.** Translocation is the exchange of chromosome pieces between nonhomologous pairs.

Jacobs Syndrome

XYY males with Jacobs syndrome can only result from nondisjunction during spermatogenesis. Affected males are usually taller than average, suffer from persistent acne, and tend to have speech and reading problems, but they are fertile and may have children. Despite the extra Y chromosome, there is no difference in behavior between XYY and XY males.

Changes in Chromosome Structure

Another type of chromosomal mutation is described as "changes in chromosome structure." Various agents in the environment, such as radiation, certain organic chemicals, or even viruses, can cause chromosomes to break. Ordinarily, when breaks occur in chromosomes, the two broken ends reunite to give the same sequence of genes. Sometimes, however, the broken ends of one or more chromosomes do not rejoin in the same pattern as before. The results are various types of chromosomal mutation.

Changes in chromosome structure include deletions, duplications, inversions, and translocations of chromosome segments. A **deletion** occurs when an end of a chromosome breaks off or when two simultaneous breaks lead to the loss of an internal segment (Fig. 19.17a). Even when only one member of a pair of chromosomes is affected, a deletion often causes abnormalities.

A **duplication** is the presence of a chromosomal segment more than once in the same chromosome (Fig. 19.17b). An **inversion** has occurred when a segment of a chromosome is turned around 180° (Fig. 19.17c). While most inversions do not present problems for the individuals, because all of the genes are present, the reversed sequence of genes can lead to problems during prophase of meiosis when crossing-over occurs. Often, inversions may lead to the formation of deletions and duplications (Fig. 19.18).

A **translocation** is the movement of a chromosome segment from one chromosome to another nonhomologous chromosome (see Fig. 19.17d). In 5% of cases, a translocation that occurred in a previous generation between chromosomes 21 and 14 is the cause of Down syndrome. In other words, because a portion of chromosome 21 is now attached to a portion of chromosome 14, the individual has three copies of the alleles that bring about Down syndrome when they are present in triplet copy. In these cases, Down syndrome is not related to the age of the mother but, instead, tends to run in the family of either the father or the mother.

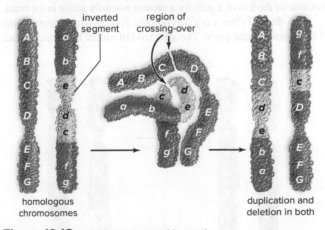

Figure 19.18   A chromosomal inversion.
Left: A segment of one homologue is inverted. In the shaded segment, *edc* occurs instead of *cde. Middle:* The two homologues can pair only when the inverted sequence forms an internal loop. After crossing-over, a duplication and a deletion can occur. *Right:* The homologue on the left has *AB* and *ab* sequences and neither *fg* nor *FG* genes. The homologue on the right has *gf* and *FG* sequences and neither *AB* nor *ab* genes.

Figure 19.19 A chromosomal deletion.
a. When chromosome 7 loses an end piece, the result is Williams syndrome. **b.** These children, although unrelated, have the same appearance, health, and behavioral problems.
(b): © The Williams Syndrome Association

Human Syndromes

Changes in chromosome structure occur in humans and lead to various syndromes, the genetics of which are just now being investigated.

Deletion Syndromes   Williams syndrome occurs when chromosome 7 loses a tiny end piece (Fig. 19.19). Children who have this syndrome look like pixies, with a turned-up nose, a wide mouth, a small chin, and large ears. Although their academic skills are poor, they exhibit excellent verbal and musical abilities. The gene that governs the production of the protein elastin is missing. This affects the health of the cardiovascular system and causes their skin to age prematurely. Such individuals are very friendly but need an ordered life, perhaps because of the loss of a gene for a protein normally active in the brain.

Cri du chat ("cat's cry") syndrome is seen when chromosome 5 is missing an end piece. The affected individual has a small head, is intellectually disabled, and has facial abnormalities. Abnormal development of the glottis and larynx results in the most characteristic symptom—the infant's cry resembles that of a cat.

Translocation Syndromes   A person who has both of the chromosomes involved in a translocation has the normal amount of genetic material and is healthy, unless the chromosome exchange broke an allele into two pieces. The person who inherits only one of the translocated chromosomes will no doubt have only one copy of certain alleles and three copies of certain other alleles. A genetics counselor begins to suspect a translocation has occurred when spontaneous abortions are commonplace and family members suffer from various syndromes.

Alagille syndrome occurs due to a translocation between chromosomes 2 and 20. People with this syndrome ordinarily have a deletion on chromosome 20. One consequence of this deletion is a

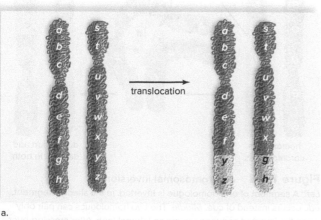

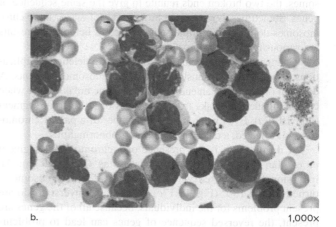

1,000×

Figure 19.20 A chromosomal translocation.
a. Translocations exchange material between nonhomologous chromosomes. **b.** One example occurs between chromosomes 22 and 9, resulting in chronic myeloid leukemia (CML). The pink cells in this micrograph are rapidly dividing white blood cells.
(b): © Jean Secchi/Dominique Lecaque/Roussel-Uclaf/CNRI/Science Source

combination of heart defects called *tetralogy of Fallot.* One of these defects is a hole between the chambers of the heart that allows oxygenated and deoxygenated blood to mix, a condition called *cyanosis. Clubbing,* or a widening of the tips of the fingers, may also occur. The symptoms of Alagille syndrome range from mild to severe, so some people may not be aware they have the syndrome.

Translocations can also be responsible for a variety of other disorders, including certain types of cancer. In the 1970s, new staining techniques revealed that a translocation from a portion of chromosome 22 to chromosome 9 is responsible for chronic myelogenous leukemia (Fig. 19.20). This translocated chromosome was called the Philadelphia chromosome. In Burkitt lymphoma, a cancer common in children in equatorial Africa, a large tumor develops from lymph glands in the region of the jaw. This disorder involves a translocation from a portion of chromosome 8 to chromosome 14.

CHECK YOUR PROGRESS 19.6

1. Explain what causes an individual to have an abnormal number of chromosomes.
2. Describe the specific chromosome abnormality of a person with Down syndrome.
3. Distinguish between a translocation and an inversion.
4. Describe the nondisjunction events that would cause Turner and Jacobs syndromes.

STUDY TOOLS http://connect.mheducation.com

SMARTBOOK® Maximize your study time with McGraw-Hill SmartBook®, the first adaptive textbook.

SUMMARIZE

19.1 Chromosomes

- The genetic material of the cell is organized as **chromosomes.** Chromosomes contain a combination of proteins and DNA called **chromatin.**
- Most human cells are diploid—therefore, chromosomes occur in pairs.
- Prior to mitosis, or duplication division, the chromosomes are replicated, forming **sister chromatids.** The sister chromatids are joined at the **centromere.**
- A karyotype is a visual display of an individual's chromosomes.

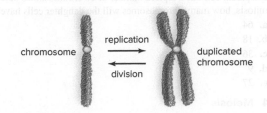

19.2 The Cell Cycle

The **cell cycle** occurs continuously and has several stages: G_1, S, G_2 (the **interphase** stages), and M (the mitotic stage), which includes **cytokinesis** and the stages of **mitosis.**

- In G_1, a cell doubles organelles and accumulates materials for DNA synthesis.

- In S, DNA replication occurs.
- In G_2, a cell synthesizes proteins needed for cell division.
- **Checkpoints** and external signals control the progression of the cell cycle. Cells that fail to pass checkpoints may enter G_0 phase and undergo **apoptosis.**

19.3 Mitosis

Mitosis is duplication division that ensures that the **daughter cells** have the **diploid (2n)** number and the same types of chromosomes as the **parent cell.** The **mitotic spindle** plays an important role in the separation of the sister chromatids during mitosis. The mitotic spindle is organized by the **centrosomes** of the cell. Centrosomes contain clusters of microtubules called **centrioles.**

The phases of mitosis are prophase, prometaphase, metaphase, anaphase, and telophase:

- **Prophase.** The nucleus dissolves and the chromosomes condense.
- **Prometaphase.** Chromosomes attach to spindle fibers.
- **Metaphase.** Chromosomes align at the equator.
- **Anaphase.** Chromatids separate, becoming chromosomes that move toward the poles.
- **Telophase.** Nuclear envelopes form around chromosomes; cytokinesis begins.

Cytokinesis is the division of cytoplasm and organelles following mitosis.

- Cytokinesis in animal cells involves the formation of a **cleavage furrow** to separate the cytoplasm.

CONNECTING THE CONCEPTS

For more information on the topics presented in this section, refer to the following discussions:

Section 18.3 explains how the *SRY* gene directs the formation of the male reproductive system.

Section 21.2 explores how chromosomes are involved in patterns of inheritance.

CASE STUDY   CONCLUSION

Approximately 10–15% of the women who are diagnosed with breast cancer have a hereditary form of the disease. This means that they inherited a genetic mutation that increases their risk of developing cancer. A genetic mutation does not guarantee that they will develop cancer, nor does it determine when or where they may develop cancer, if they do. Many of these mutations occur in proto-oncogenes or tumor suppressor genes. Angelina Jolie inherited a mutated *BRCA1* gene. The *BRCA1* gene is a tumor suppressor gene whose protein product is involved in DNA repair. Tumor suppressor genes act as gatekeepers for the cell cycle and thus control the rate at which cells divide.

19.4 Meiosis

Meiosis is reduction division that reduces the diploid (2n) chromosome number to a **haploid (n)** number. Meiosis involves two cell divisions—meiosis I and meiosis II.

Meiosis I

- **Homologous chromosomes** pair (**synapsis**) and then separate. **Interkinesis** follows meiosis I.

Meiosis II

- Sister chromatids separate, resulting in four cells with the haploid number of chromosomes that move into daughter nuclei.

Meiosis results in genetic recombination due to **crossing-over;** gametes have all possible combinations of chromosomes. Upon fertilization, the zygote is restored to a diploid number of chromosomes.

Spermatogenesis and Oogenesis

- **Spermatogenesis.** In males, spermatogenesis produces four viable sperm.
- **Oogenesis.** In females, oogenesis produces one egg and several polar bodies. Oogenesis goes to completion if the sperm fertilizes the developing egg.

19.5 Comparison of Meiosis and Mitosis

- In prophase I, homologous chromosomes pair; there is no pairing in mitosis.
- In metaphase I, homologous duplicated chromosomes align at equator.
- In anaphase I, homologous chromosomes separate.

19.6 Chromosome Inheritance

Meiosis is a part of gametogenesis (spermatogenesis in males and oogenesis in females) and contributes to genetic diversity.

Changes in Chromosome Number

- **Nondisjunction** changes the chromosome number in gametes, resulting in **trisomy (2n + 1)** or **monosomy (2n − 1)**.
- Autosomal syndromes include Down syndrome.

Changes in Sex Chromosome Number

- Nondisjunction during oogenesis or spermatogenesis can result in gametes that have too few or too many X or Y chromosomes.
- If more than one X chromosome is present in a cell, a **Barr body** may be formed.
- **Syndromes** include Turner, Klinefelter, poly-X, and Jacobs.

Changes in Chromosome Structure

- Chromosomal mutations can produce **deletions, duplications, inversions,** and **translocations.**
- These result in various syndromes, such as Williams, cri du chat (deletion), and Alagille, and certain cancers (translocation).

ASSESS

TESTING YOURSELF

Choose the best answer for each question.

19.1 Chromosomes

1. The point of attachment for two sister chromatids is the
   - **a.** centriole.
   - **b.** chromosome.
   - **c.** centromere.
   - **d.** karyotype.
   - **e.** chromatin.

2. Which of the following is/are produced by the process of DNA replication?
   - **a.** karyotype
   - **b.** spindle fibers
   - **c.** centromere
   - **d.** sister chromatids
   - **e.** chromatin

19.2 The Cell Cycle

3. Label the drawing of the cell cycle; then list the main events of the stages.

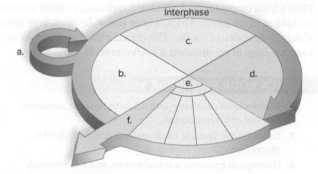

4. At which of the following checkpoints is the DNA checked for damage and, if damage is present, the cell is placed in G_0 phase?
   - **a.** M
   - **b.** G_1
   - **c.** G_2
   - **d.** None of these are correct.

19.3 Mitosis

In questions 5–9, match the statement to the phase of mitosis in the key.

Key:
   - **a.** metaphase
   - **b.** prometaphase
   - **c.** telophase
   - **d.** prophase
   - **e.** anaphase

5. Chromosomes line up at the equator.

6. Centromere splits and sister chromosomes move to opposite poles.

7. The nucleus dissolves and chromosomes condense.

8. The nucleus re-forms.

9. Spindle fibers attached to the sister chromatids.

10. If a parent cell has a diploid number of 18 chromosomes before mitosis, how many chromosomes will the daughter cells have?
    - **a.** 64
    - **b.** 18
    - **c.** 36
    - **d.** 9
    - **e.** 27

19.4 Meiosis

11. If a parent cell has 22 chromosomes, the daughter cells following meiosis II will have
    - **a.** 22 chromosomes.
    - **b.** 44 chromosomes.
    - **c.** 11 chromosomes.
    - **d.** All of these are correct.

12. Crossing-over occurs between
    a. sister chromatids of the same chromosome.
    b. chromatids of nonhomologous chromosomes.
    c. nonsister chromatids of a homologous pair.
    d. None of these are correct.

13. Which of these helps provide genetic diversity?
    a. independent alignment during metaphase I
    b. crossing-over during prophase I
    c. random fusion of sperm and egg nuclei during fertilization
    d. All of these are correct.

14. Polar bodies are produced during
    a. DNA replication.
    b. mitosis.
    c. spermatogenesis.
    d. oogenesis.
    e. None of these are correct.

19.5 Comparison of Meiosis and Mitosis

15. The pairing of homologous chromosomes occurs during which of the following?
    a. mitosis
    b. meiosis I
    c. meiosis II
    d. All of these are correct.

16. Sister chromatids separate during anaphase of which of the following?
    a. mitosis
    b. meiosis I
    c. meiosis II
    d. Both a and c are correct.

19.6 Chromosome Inheritance

17. Monosomy or trisomy occurs because of
    a. crossing-over.
    b. inversion.
    c. translocation.
    d. nondisjunction.

18. A person with Klinefelter syndrome is _____ and has _____ sex chromosomes.
    a. male; XYY
    b. male; XXY
    c. female; XXY
    d. female; XO

ENGAGE

BioNOW

Want to know how this science is relevant to your life? Check out the BioNow video below:

• Cell Division

What was the purpose of the rooting hormone in this experiment, and what part of the cell cycle do you think it was targeting?

Thinking Critically

1. Benign and cancerous tumors occur when the cell cycle control mechanisms no longer operate correctly. What types of genes may be involved in these cell cycle control mechanisms?

2. BPA is a chemical compound that has historically been used in the manufacture of plastic products. However, cells often mistake BPA compounds for hormones that accelerate the cell cycle. Because of this, BPA is associated with an increased risk of certain cancers.
    a. How might BPA interact with the cell cycle and its checkpoints?
    b. Why do you think that very small concentrations of BPA might have a large effect on the cell?

3. Explain how the separation of homologous chromosomes during meiosis affects the appearance of siblings (such that some resemble each other and others look very different from one another).

4. a. What would you conclude about the ability of nervous and muscular tissue to repair themselves if nerve and muscle cells are typically arrested in G_1 of interphase?
    b. What are the implications of this arrested state for someone who suffers a spinal cord injury or heart attack?

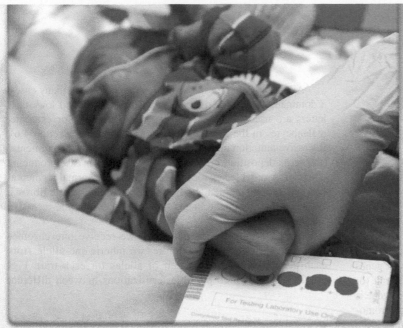

© Marmaduke St. John/Alamy

CHAPTER

21

Patterns of Genetic Inheritance

CASE STUDY: PHENYLKETONURIA

As part of the routine newborn screening performed on most children born in the United States and other developed countries, a high-performance liquid chromatography (HPLC) test was performed by taking a small amount of blood from a heel prick of 12-hour-old Patrick. The test came back positive for phenylketonuria (PKU). The doctor explained to Patrick's parents that PKU is a disorder in which the body has a deficiency in the hepatic enzyme phenylalanine hydroxylase (PAH).

PAH is an important enzyme the body needs to properly metabolize the amino acid phenylalanine into the amino acid tyrosine. When phenylalanine is not metabolized, it accumulates in the body and is converted into the compound phenylpyruvate. An accumulation of phenylpyruvate can lead to impaired brain development, intellectual disability, and seizure disorders. Patrick's parents wondered how he had developed this disorder. The doctor explained that it is a genetic disorder; the cause of the disorder was found in the DNA Patrick had acquired from both his parents. The fact that neither of Patrick's parents showed any signs of PKU indicated that this disease is inherited in an autosomal recessive manner, and that both of the parents are carriers for the disease.

As you read through the chapter, think about the following questions:

1. What is an autosomal recessive disorder?
2. How can people pass on conditions if they do not show any signs?
3. How does the environment influence the expression of a trait?

CHAPTER CONCEPTS

21.1 Genotype and Phenotype
A genotype consists of the genes for a particular trait. A phenotype consists of physical characteristics, such as blood type, eye color, or the operation of cellular pathways.

21.2 One- and Two-Trait Inheritance
In humans, each trait is controlled by two alleles. In most cases, dominant alleles mask recessive alleles. Many disorders, including those at the cellular level, are inherited in a dominant or recessive manner. It is possible to predict simple patterns of inheritance using Punnett squares and pedigrees.

21.3 Inheritance of Genetic Disorders
Inheritance of traits can be traced through generations of a family using a pedigree chart.

21.4 Beyond Simple Inheritance Patterns
There are other inheritance patterns beyond simple dominant or recessive ones. The environment and other alleles can both influence the phenotype.

21.5 Sex-Linked Inheritance
Not all traits on the sex chromosomes are associated with sex. Because males have only one X chromosome, the alleles on that chromosome are always expressed. Therefore, males are more apt to have an X-linked disorder than are females.

BEFORE YOU BEGIN

Before beginning this chapter, take a few moments to review the following discussions:

Section 2.7 What is the role of DNA in a cell?

Figures 17.4 and **17.9** How are sperm and egg cells produced?

Section 19.4 How does meiosis produce new combinations of alleles?

21.1 Genotype and Phenotype

LEARNING OUTCOMES

Upon completion of this section, you should be able to

1. Distinguish between a genotype and a phenotype.
2. Define *allele, gene, dominant,* and *recessive* as they relate to patterns of inheritance.
3. Given the genotype of an individual, identify the phenotype.

Genotype

Genotype refers to the genes of an individual. Recall that genes are segments of DNA on a chromosome that code for a trait (or characteristic). These genes are the units of heredity. Each gene is located in a specific position, or **locus** (pl., loci), on a chromosome. An **allele** is an alternate form of a gene. For example, if the trait the gene codes for is eye color, one allele contains the information for blue eyes while a different allele may produce brown eyes. Alleles are often classified as being either dominant or recessive. In general, **dominant alleles** mask (hide) the expression of **recessive alleles.** Therefore, if an allele is dominant, only one copy of that allele needs to be present for that trait to appear (or be expressed). If an allele is recessive, both of the chromosomes must possess the recessive allele for it to be expressed in the individual.

The terms *dominant* and *recessive* do not indicate the prevalence (or frequency) of a trait in the population but, instead, what is happening in the cell at the level of gene expression. A dominant allele may be very rare in a population, and the recessive alleles may be the most prevalent.

SCIENCE IN YOUR LIFE

Why are some alleles dominant to other alleles?

In a simple example, the dominant allele (*A*) codes for a particular protein. Let's assume this gene codes for an enzyme (protein) responsible for brown eye color. The recessive allele (*a*) is a mutated allele that no longer codes for the enzyme. At the molecular level, having the enzyme is dominant to lacking the enzyme. In other words, having brown in the eye is dominant over not having brown in the eye. Using this example, a homozygous dominant individual (*AA*) may have twice the amount of enzyme as a heterozygous individual (*Aa*). However, it may not be possible to detect a difference between homozygous and heterozygous, as long as there is enough enzyme to bring about the dominant phenotype. Half the amount of enzyme may still turn the eyes completely brown. Thus, a person with the genotype *Aa* would have eyes just as brown as a person with the genotype *AA*. A homozygous recessive individual (*aa*) makes no enzyme, so the brown phenotype is absent. Gene expression is discussed further in Section 22.2.

Alleles are often designated by abbreviations. In many cases, a dominant allele is assigned an uppercase letter, and lowercase letters are used for recessive alleles. In humans, for example, melanocytes in the skin produce pigmentation (see Section 4.6). Recessive mutation inhibits either the production of the pigmentation or its deposition into the skin cells, in either case producing albinism. A suitable key for these alleles is *A* for normal pigmentation and *a* for no pigmentation. Another example is cystic fibrosis, for which the dominant allele is designated *Cf* and the recessive allele *cf.*

For each pair of chromosomes, we receive one chromosome from each parent; therefore, we inherit one allele from each parent, resulting in a pair of alleles for each trait. Figure 21.1 shows three possible fertilizations between different

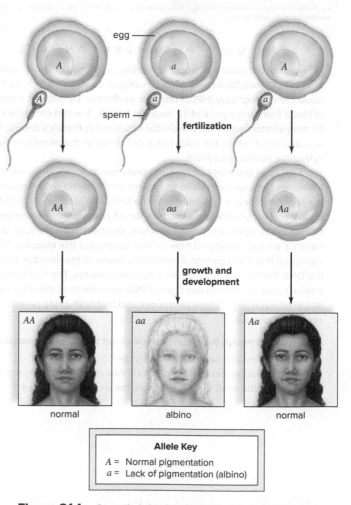

Figure 21.1   Genetic inheritance affects our characteristics.
For each trait, we inherit one allele from each parent. Therefore, we possess two alleles for every trait. The inheritance of a single dominant allele (resulting in either *AA* or *Aa*) causes an individual to have normal pigmentation; two recessive alleles (*aa*) cause an individual to have albinism.

alleles for the pigmentation trait and the resulting offspring of those fertilizations. In the first instance, the chromosomes of both the sperm and the egg carry the dominant trait, designated *A*, resulting in an individual with the alleles *AA*. This type of genotype is called **homozygous dominant.** In the second fertilization, the zygote has received two recessive alleles (*aa*), a genotype called **homozygous recessive.** In the third fertilization, the resulting individual has the alleles *Aa*, called a **heterozygous** genotype.

Phenotype

The physical appearance of a trait is called a **phenotype.** The phenotype is determined by the expression of the alleles in the genotype. Thus, we may generally state that the DNA determines the genotype and that proteins (gene products) determine the phenotype.

In Figure 21.1, the phenotypes are normal pigmentation (dominant phenotype) and no pigmentation (recessive phenotype). It is important to recognize that the genotype directs the phenotype of the individual. In most cases, the presence of a single dominant allele is all that is necessary to express the dominant phenotype (some exceptions are explained in Section 21.4). Notice that this is the case in the heterozygous individual (*Aa*) in Figure 21.1. A heterozygote shows the dominant phenotype, because the dominant allele needs only one copy to appear in the phenotype. Therefore, this individual has normal pigmentation. Homozygous recessive individuals (*aa*) have albinism, whereas homozygous dominant individuals (*AA*) have normal pigmentation.

From our example, you may get the impression that the phenotype has to be an easily observable trait. However, the phenotype can be any characteristic of the individual, including color blindness or a metabolic disorder, such as the lack of an enzyme to metabolize the amino acid phenylalanine.

CHECK YOUR PROGRESS 21.1

1. Define the following terms: *gene, allele, locus, chromosome, dominant,* and *recessive.*
2. Describe the difference between genotype and phenotype.
3. Summarize the three possible genotypes and their corresponding phenotypes.

CONNECTING THE CONCEPTS

The genotype of an individual is based on the information in the DNA of his or her cells. For more information on DNA, refer to the following discussions:

Sections 2.7 and **22.1** describe the basic structure of the DNA molecule.

Section 4.6 provides more information on the role of melanocytes in the skin.

Section 22.2 examines how the information in DNA is expressed as a protein.

21.2 One- and Two-Trait Inheritance

LEARNING OUTCOMES

Upon completion of this section, you should be able to

1. Understand how probability is involved in solving one- and two-trait crosses.
2. Calculate the probability of a specific genotype or phenotype in an offspring of a genetic cross.

A one-trait cross examines the patterns of inheritance of only a single set of alleles for a single characteristic. A two-trait cross explores the patterns of inheritance of the alleles for two different characteristics. For both types of crosses, it is first necessary to determine the gametes of both of the parents in the cross.

Forming the Gametes

During meiosis, the chromosome number of the cells that will form the gametes (egg and sperm) is divided in half (see Section 19.4). This is accomplished by the separation of homologous chromosomes. Each individual has 46 chromosomes, arranged as 23 homologous pairs. For each pair, one of the homologous chromosomes was originally from the mother, and the other was donated by the father. During meiosis, the homologous chromosomes, and the alleles they contain, are separated. Therefore, the sperm or egg has only 23 chromosomes. If reduction of the chromosome number did not occur, the new individual would have twice as many chromosomes after fertilization, which would not result in a viable embryo.

For example, let's say that the gene for pigmentation is on a particular chromosome. On the homologous chromosome originally from the mother, the allele is for normal pigmentation (*A*). On the father's paired chromosome, the allele is also an *A*. Therefore, *A* is the only option for alleles on either chromosome, so every gamete formed by this individual will carry an *A*. This occurs whether the gamete gets the mother's or the father's original chromosome. Similarly, if the homologous chromosome originally from the mother carries the recessive allele for pigmentation (*a*) and the father's chromosome also bears an *a*, then all gametes will have the *a* allele. However, if the individual is heterozygous, the the combination of alleles may be different. For example, the

SCIENCE IN YOUR LIFE

Aren't traits such as earlobe shape and dimples due to dominant and recessive alleles?

For a considerable amount of time geneticists thought that traits such as earlobe shape (attached or unattached), shape of the hairline (widow's peak), and the presence of dimples were examples of simple dominant and recessive inheritance. However, as we learn more about the 23,000 or so genes that make us human, we have discovered that these traits are actually under the control of multiple genes. These interactions complicate the expression of the phenotype, and thus they are not good examples of simple dominant and recessive allele combinations.

mother's homologous chromosome may have the *A* allele while the father's has an *a*. If this is the case, then half of the gametes formed will receive an *A* allele from the mother's homologue. The other half will get the father's homologue with the *a*.

Figure 21.2 shows the genotypes and phenotypes for a couple of observable traits in humans that have simple dominant and recessive relationships between the alles. Although many different alleles control finger length, a dominant allele (*S*) produces a condition called brachydactyly, or shortened fingers. There are also many factors that influence freckles, but a dominant allele (*F*) causes widespread freckling patterns on the body.

One-Trait Crosses

Parents often like to know the chances of having a child with a certain genotype and, therefore, a certain phenotype. To illustrate, consider a cross involving freckles. What happens when two parents without freckles have children? Will the children of this couple have freckles? In solving the problem, we will (1) use *F* to indicate the dominant allele for freckles and *f* to indicate the recessive allele of no freckles; (2) determine the possible gametes for each parent; (3) combine all possible gametes; and (4) finally, determine the genotypes and phenotypes of all the offspring. If both

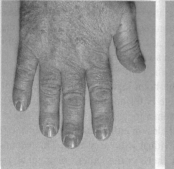

a. Short fingers: *SS* or *Ss*

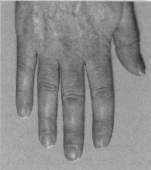

b. Long fingers: *ss*

c. Freckles: *FF* or *Ff*

d. No freckles: *ff*

Figure 21.2   **Examples of dominant and recessive traits.**
The allele for short fingers (brachydactyly) is dominant to long fingers.
The allele for freckles is dominant to no freckles.

(a and b): © McGraw-Hill Education/Bob Coyle, photographer; (c): © BananaStock/age fotostock RF; (d): © Creatas/PunchStock RF

parents do not have freckles, then their genotypes are both *ff*. The only gametes they can produce contain the *f* allele. All the children will therefore be *ff* and will not have freckles. In the following diagram, the letters indicate the genotypes of the parents. Each parent has only one type of gamete with regard to freckles; therefore, all the children have a similar genotype and phenotype.

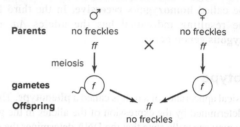

Let's also consider the results when a homozygous dominant man with freckles has children with a woman with no freckles. Will the children of this couple have freckles? The children are heterozygous (*Ff*) and have freckles. When writing a heterozygous genotype, always put the capital letter (for the dominant allele) first to avoid confusion.

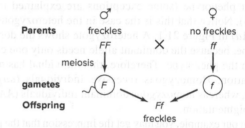

A one-trait cross is often referred to as a **monohybrid cross,** because it involves only a single trait. Notice that in this example the children are heterozygous with regard to one pair of alleles. If these individuals reproduce with someone else of the same genotype, will their children have freckles? In this problem (*Ff* × *Ff*), each parent has two possible types of gametes (*F* or *f*), and we must ensure that all types of sperm have an equal chance to fertilize all possible types of eggs. One way to do this is to use a **Punnett square** (Fig. 21.3), in which all possible alleles that may be found in the sperm are lined up vertically and all possible alleles for the

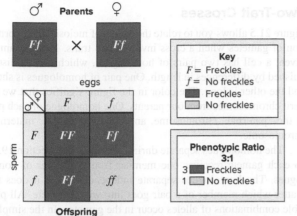

Figure 21.3   Expected results of a monohybrid cross.
A Punnett square diagrams the results of a cross. When the parents are heterozygous, each child has a 75% chance of having the dominant phenotype and a 25% chance of having the recessive phenotype.

eggs are lined up horizontally (or vice versa). Every possible combination of gametes occurs within the squares.

After we determine the genotypes and the phenotypes of the offspring, we can determine both the genotypic and phenotypic ratios. The genotypic ratio is 1 *FF*: 2 *Ff*: 1 *ff* or simply 1:2:1, but the phenotypic ratio is 3:1. Why? Three individuals will have freckles (the *FF* and the two *Ff*) and one will not have freckles (the *ff*).

This 3:1 phenotypic ratio is always expected for a monohybrid cross when one allele is completely dominant over the other. The exact ratio is more likely to be observed if a large number of matings take place and if a large number of offspring result. Only then do all possible types of sperm have an equal chance of fertilizing all possible types of eggs. Naturally, we do not routinely observe hundreds of offspring from a single type of cross in humans. The best interpretation of Figure 21.3 in humans is to say that each

child has three chances out of four to have freckles, or one chance out of four to not have freckles.

Every fertilization has exactly the same chance for allele combinations as the previous fertilization. For example, if two heterozygous parents already have three children with freckles and are expecting a fourth child, this child still has a 75% chance of having freckles and a 25% chance of not having freckles, just as each of its siblings did. The chance of achieving a new phenotype not previously shown does not increase with each fertilization; it stays exactly the same with every fertilization. Every new fertilization is not influenced by any previous fertilizations. Each one is considered an individual occurrence, each time subject to the probabilities of the gametes of the parents.

Determining If the Genotype Is Heterozygous or Homozygous Dominant

It is not possible to tell by inspection if a person expressing a dominant allele is homozygous dominant or heterozygous. However, it is sometimes possible to tell by the results of a cross. For example, Figure 21.4 shows two possible results when a man with freckles reproduces with a woman who does not have freckles. If the man is homozygous dominant, all his children will have freckles. If the man is heterozygous, each child has a 50% chance of having freckles. The birth of just one child without freckles indicates that the man is heterozygous.

The Punnett Square and Probability

Two laws of probability apply to genetics. The first is the product rule. According to this rule, the chance of two different events occurring simultaneously is equal to the multiplied probabilities of each event occurring separately. For example, what is the probability that a coin toss will be "heads"? There are only two options, so the probability of "heads" is 1 out of 2, or 50% (0.50). If we wanted to know what the probability was of a first coin toss being "heads"

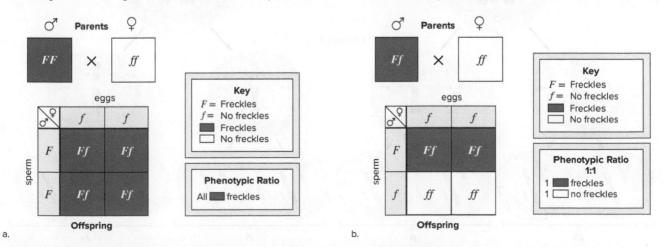

Figure 21.4   Determining if a dominant phenotype is homozygous or heterozygous.
The offspring of a monohybrid cross indicates if an individual with a dominant phenotype is homozygous or heterozygous. **a.** All offspring show the dominant characteristic, so the individual is most likely homozygous, as shown. **b.** The offspring show a 1:1 phenotypic ratio, so the individual is heterozygous, as shown.

and a second coin toss being "heads," we would use the product rule. *The product rule is often applied to cases in which the word "and" is used.* This would be ½ × ½ = ¼, or 25% (0.25). Probabilities range from 0.0 (0%, or an event that will not happen) to 1.0 (100%, or an event that will always happen). The Punnett square allows you to determine the probability that an offspring will have a particular genotype or phenotype. When you bring the alleles donated by the sperm and egg together into the same square, you are using the product rule. Both father and mother each give a chance of having a particular allele, so the probability for that allele in an offspring is the multiple of these two separate chances.

The second law of probability is the sum rule. Using this rule, individual probabilities can be added to determine total probability for an event. If we toss a coin and we want to know the probability that it will be either heads *or* tails, we use the sum rule. *The sum rule is often applied to cases in which the word "or" is used.* For example, if you want to determine the probability of having the dominant phenotype in a monohybrid cross, you need to add the probability of being either homozygous dominant, *or* heterozygous. When using the Punnett square, you use the sum rule when you add up the results of each square to determine the final phenotypic ratio.

Two-Trait Crosses

Figure 21.5 allows you to relate the events of meiosis to the formation of gametes when a cross involves two traits. In the example given, a cell has two pairs of homologues, which can be distinguished by differences in length. One pair of homologues is short, and the other is long. The color in the figure signifies that we inherit chromosomes from our parents. One homologue of each pair is the "paternal" chromosome, and the other is the "maternal" chromosome.

The homologues separate during meiosis I (see Section 19.4), so each gamete receives one member from each pair of homologues. The homologues separate independently, so it does not matter which member of a pair goes into which gamete. All possible combinations of alleles occur in the gametes. In the simplest of terms, a gamete in Figure 21.5 will *receive one short and one long chromosome of either color.* Therefore, all possible combinations of chromosomes and alleles are in the gametes.

Specifically, assume that the alleles for two genes are on these homologues. The alleles *S* and *s* are on one pair of homologues, and the alleles *F* and *f* are on the other pair of homologues. The

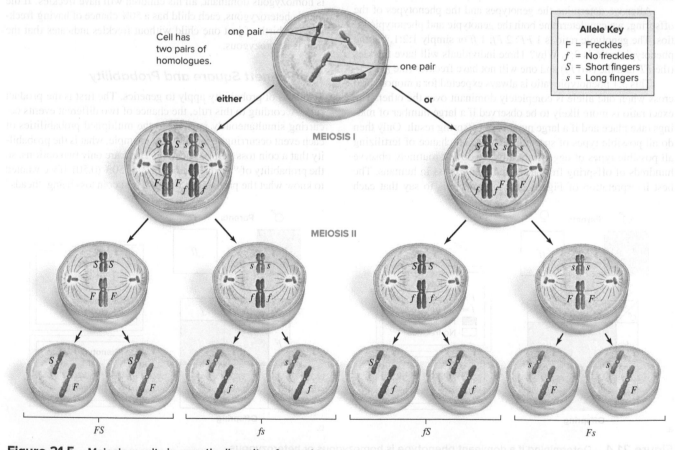

Allele Key
F = Freckles
f = No freckles
S = Short fingers
s = Long fingers

Figure 21.5   Meiosis results in genetic diversity of gametes.
A cell has two pairs of homologous chromosomes (homologues), recognized by length, not color. The long pair of homologues carries alleles for freckles and the short pair of homologues carries alleles for finger length. The homologues, and the alleles they carry, align independently during meiosis. Therefore, all possible combinations of chromosomes and alleles occur in the gametes, as shown in the last row of cells.

homologues separate, so a gamete will have either an *S* or an *s* and either an *F* or an *f*. They will never have two of the same letter. Also, because the homologues align independently at the equator, either the paternal or maternal chromosome of each pair can face either pole.

Therefore, there are no restrictions as to which homologue goes into which gamete. A gamete can receive either an *S* or an *s* and either an *F* or an *f* in any combination. In the end, the gametes will collectively have all possible combinations of alleles. You should be able to transfer this information to any cross that involves two traits. In other words, the process of meiosis explains why a person with the genotype *FfSs* would produce the gametes *FS*, *fs*, *Fs*, and *fS* in equal number.

The Dihybrid Cross

In the two-trait cross depicted in Figure 21.6, a person homozygous for freckles and short fingers (*FFSS*) reproduces with one who has no freckles and long fingers (*ffss*). Because this cross involves two traits, it is also referred to as a **dihybrid cross.** In this example, the gametes for the *FFSS* parent must be *FS* and the gametes for the *ffss* parent must be *fs*. Therefore, the offspring will all have the genotype *FfSs* and the same phenotype (freckles and short fingers). This genotype is called a dihybrid because the individual is heterozygous in two regards: presence of freckles and finger length.

When a dihybrid *FfSs* has children with another dihybrid who is *FfSs*, what gametes are possible? Each gamete can have only one letter of each type in all possible combinations. Therefore, these are the gametes for both dihybrids: *FS*, *Fs*, *fS*, and *fs*.

A Punnett square makes sure that all possible sperm fertilize all possible eggs. If so, these are the expected phenotypic results:

- 9 freckles and short fingers
- 3 freckles and long fingers
- 3 no freckles and short fingers
- 1 no freckles and long fingers.

This 9:3:3:1 phenotypic ratio is always expected for a dihybrid cross when simple dominance is present. We can use this expected ratio to predict the chances of each child receiving a certain phenotype. For example, the chance of getting the two dominant phenotypes together is 9 out of 16. The chance of getting the two recessive phenotypes together is 1 out of 16.

Two-Trait Crosses and Probability

It is also possible to use the rules of probability discussed earlier to predict the results of a dihybrid cross. For example, we know the probable results for two separate monohybrid crosses are as follows:

For freckles
- probability of freckles = ¾
- probability of no freckles = ¼

For finger length
- probability of short fingers = ¾
- probability of long fingers = ¼

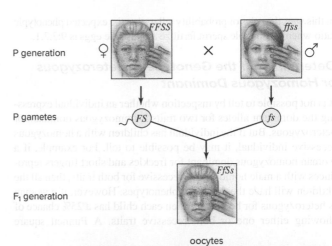

P generation ♀ FFSS × ffss ♂

P gametes FS × fs

F₁ generation FfSs

oocytes

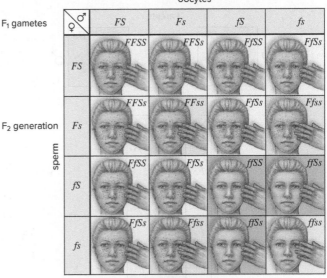

F₁ gametes

F₂ generation

sperm

♂ / ♀	FS	Fs	fS	fs
FS	FFSS	FFSs	FfSS	FfSs
Fs	FFSs	FFss	FfSs	Ffss
fS	FfSS	FfSs	ffSS	ffSs
fs	FfSs	Ffss	ffSs	ffss

Offspring

Allele Key
F = Freckles
f = No freckles
S = Short fingers
s = Long fingers

Phenotypic Ratio
9 ☐ Freckles, short fingers
3 ☐ Freckles, long fingers
3 ☐ No freckles, short fingers
1 ☐ No freckles, long fingers

Figure 21.6 Expected results of a dihybrid cross.
Each dihybrid can form four possible types of gametes, so four different phenotypes occur among the offspring in the proportions shown.

Using the product rule, we can calculate the probable outcome of a dihybrid cross as follows:

Probability of:
- freckles and short fingers: $\frac{3}{4} \times \frac{3}{4} = \frac{9}{16}$
- freckles and long fingers: $\frac{3}{4} \times \frac{1}{4} = \frac{3}{16}$
- no freckles and short fingers: $\frac{1}{4} \times \frac{3}{4} = \frac{3}{16}$
- no freckles and long fingers: $\frac{1}{4} \times \frac{1}{4} = \frac{1}{16}$

In this way, the rules of probability tell us that the expected phenotypic ratio when all possible sperm fertilize all possible eggs is 9:3:3:1.

Determining If the Genotype Is Heterozygous or Homozygous Dominant

It is not possible to tell by inspection whether an individual expressing the dominant alleles for two traits is homozygous dominant or heterozygous. But if the individual has children with a homozygous recessive individual, it may be possible to tell. For example, if a woman homozygous dominant for freckles and short fingers reproduces with a male homozygous recessive for both traits, then all the children will have the dominant phenotypes. However, if a woman is heterozygous for both traits, then each child has a 25% chance of showing either one or both recessive traits. A Punnett square

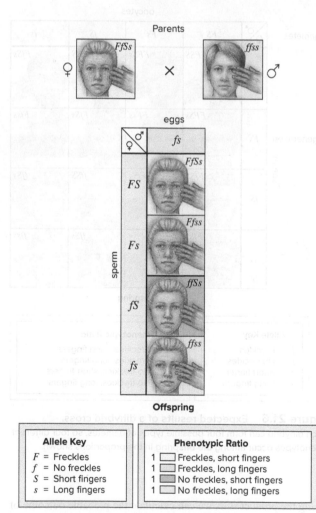

Parents

Allele Key	Phenotypic Ratio
F = Freckles	1 ☐ Freckles, short fingers
f = No freckles	1 ☐ Freckles, long fingers
S = Short fingers	1 ☐ No freckles, short fingers
s = Long fingers	1 ☐ No freckles, long fingers

Figure 21.7 Determining if an individual is homozygous dominant or heterozygous.
The results of this cross indicate that the individual with the dominant phenotypes is heterozygous for both traits, because some of the children are homozygous recessive for one or both traits. The chance of receiving any possible phenotype is 25%.

Table 21.1	Phenotypic Ratios of Common Crosses
Genotypes	**Phenotypes**
Monohybrid *Aa* × monohybrid *Aa*	3:1 (dominant to recessive)
Monohybrid *Aa* × recessive *aa*	1:1 (dominant to recessive)
Dihybrid *AaBb* × dihybrid *AaBb*	9:3:3:1 (9 both dominant: 3 dominant for one of the traits: 3 dominant for other trait: 1 both recessive)
Dihybrid *AaBb* × recessive *aabb*	1:1:1:1 (all possible combinations in equal number)

(Fig. 21.7) shows that the expected ratio is 1 freckles with short fingers: 1 freckles with long fingers: 1 no freckles with short fingers: 1 no freckles with long fingers, or 1:1:1:1.

For practical purposes, if a parent with the dominant phenotype in either trait has an offspring with the recessive phenotype, the parent has to be heterozygous for that trait. Also, it is possible to tell if a person is heterozygous by knowing the parentage. In Figure 21.7, no offspring showing a dominant phenotype is homozygous dominant for either trait. Why? The mother is homozygous recessive for that trait.

Table 21.1 gives the phenotypic results for certain crosses we have been studying. These crosses always give these phenotypic results. Therefore, it is not necessary to do a Punnett square to arrive at the results. To facilitate doing crosses, study Table 21.1, so that you can understand why these are the results expected for these crosses.

CHECK YOUR PROGRESS 21.2

1. Explain how the results of a dihybrid cross are related to the events of meiosis.

2. Predict what genotype the children will have if one parent is homozygous recessive for no freckles and homozygous dominant for short finger length (*ffSS*) and the other parent is homozygous dominant for freckles and homozygous recessive for long fingers (*FFss*).

3. Using a dihybrid cross as an example (see Fig. 21.6), explain how the gametes are formed by the process of meiosis.

CONNECTING THE CONCEPTS

For more information on the relationship between meiosis and patterns of inheritance, refer to the following discussions:

Section 17.2 explains gamete production in males.

Section 17.3 explores the process of gamete formation in females.

Section 19.4 describes how meiosis introduces genetic variation.

21.3 Inheritance of Genetic Disorders

LEARNING OUTCOMES

Upon completion of this section, you should be able to

1. Interpret a human pedigree to identify the pattern of inheritance for a trait.
2. Understand the genetic basis of select human autosomal dominant and autosomal recessive genetic disorders.

We inherit many different traits from our parents—not only our hair and eye color but also traits for diseases and disorders. Many of these diseases occur as a result of changes, or mutations, in our parents' genetic codes. The abnormal gene could be present in each of your parents' cells and thus passed down in the sperm or egg. Your parent may or may not have been affected by this genetic mutation. Alternatively, the genetic mutation might have occurred only in the sperm or egg that became a part of you. Some genetic diseases require two damaged alleles for the disease to manifest itself. Others need only one. When a genetic disorder is autosomal dominant, an individual with the alleles *AA* or *Aa* will have the disorder. When a genetic disorder is autosomal recessive, only individuals with the alleles *aa* will have the disorder. Genetic counselors often construct pedigrees to determine whether a condition that runs in the family is dominant or recessive. A pedigree shows the pattern of inheritance for a particular condition. Consider these two possible patterns of inheritance:

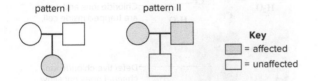

In both patterns, males are designated by squares and females by circles. Shaded circles and squares are affected individuals. A line between a square and a circle represents a mating. A vertical line going downward leads, in these patterns, to a single child. If there are more children, they are placed off a horizontal line. In the next sections we will explore which of these patterns represents an autosomal recessive pattern, and which represents an autosomal dominant pattern.

Autosomal Recessive Patterns of Inheritance

In pattern I, the child is affected but neither parent is. This can happen if the condition is recessive and the parents are *Aa*. The parents are **carriers,** because they carry the recessive trait in their DNA but their phenotype is dominant. Figure 21.8 shows a typical pedigree chart for a recessive genetic disorder. Other ways to recognize an autosomal recessive pattern of inheritance are also listed in the figure. If both parents are affected, all the children are affected. Why? The parents can pass on only recessive alleles for this condition. All children will be homozygous recessive, just like the parents.

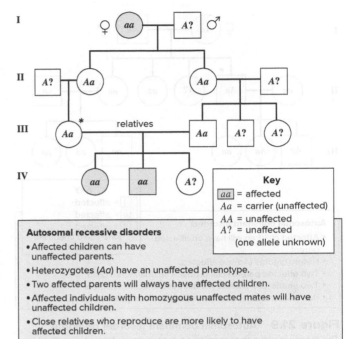

Autosomal recessive disorders
- Affected children can have unaffected parents.
- Heterozygotes (*Aa*) have an unaffected phenotype.
- Two affected parents will always have affected children.
- Affected individuals with homozygous unaffected mates will have unaffected children.
- Close relatives who reproduce are more likely to have affected children.
- Both males and females are affected with equal frequency.

Figure 21.8   Autosomal recessive disorder pedigree.
The list gives ways to recognize an autosomal recessive disorder. How would you know that the individual at the asterisk is heterozygous?[1]

Autosomal Dominant Pattern of Inheritance

In pattern II, the child is unaffected but the parents are affected. Of the two patterns, this one shows a dominant pattern of inheritance. The condition is dominant, so the parents can be *Aa* (heterozygous). The child inherited a recessive allele from each parent and, therefore, is unaffected. Figure 21.9 shows a typical pedigree for a dominant disorder. Other ways to recognize an autosomal dominant pattern of inheritance are also listed. When a disorder is dominant, an affected child must have at least one affected parent.

Genetic Disorders of Interest

Medical genetics has traditionally focused on disorders caused by single gene mutations; they are well understood due to their straightforward patterns of inheritance. It is estimated that there are over 4,000 identified disorders caused by single gene mutations in humans. Here, we will focus on only a few.

Autosomal Recessive Disorders

Inheritance of two recessive alleles is required for an autosomal recessive disorder to be the expressed phenotype.

Tay-Sachs Disease   Tay-Sachs disease is a well-known autosomal recessive disorder that occurs usually among Ashkenazic Jewish people (those from Central and Eastern Europe) and their

[1]Because she passed on the a allele to her first two children.

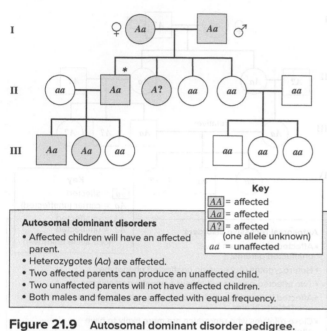

Key
$\boxed{AA}$ = affected
$\boxed{Aa}$ = affected
$\boxed{A?}$ = affected
        (one allele unknown)
aa = unaffected

Autosomal dominant disorders

- Affected children will have an affected parent.
- Heterozygotes (Aa) are affected.
- Two affected parents can produce an unaffected child.
- Two unaffected parents will not have affected children.
- Both males and females are affected with equal frequency.

Figure 21.9   Autosomal dominant disorder pedigree.
The list gives ways to recognize an autosomal dominant disorder. How would you know that the individual at the asterisk is heterozygous?[2]

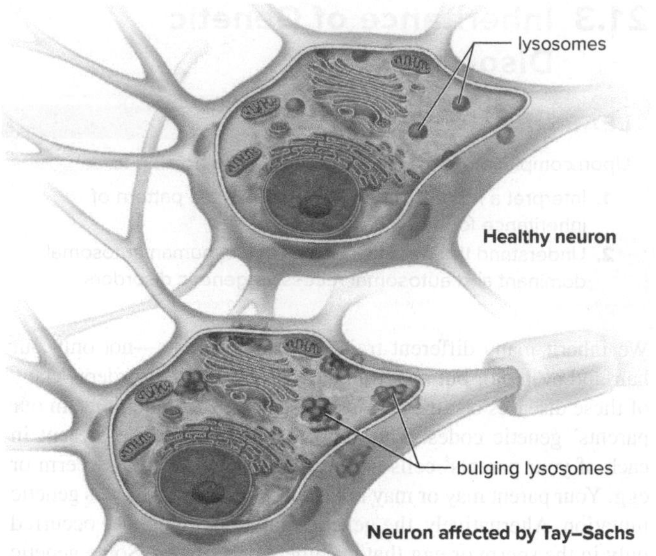

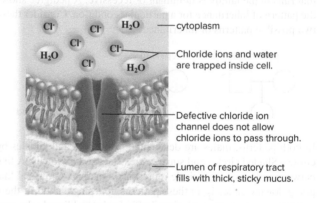

Figure 21.10   Neuron affected by Tay-Sachs disease.
In Tay-Sachs disease, a lysosomal enzyme is missing. This causes the substrate of that enzyme to accumulate within the lysosomes.

descendants. Tay-Sachs disease results from a lack of a lysosome enzyme, hex A, which clears out fatty acid proteins that build up in cells of the brain. Without this enzyme, the buildup will interfere with proper brain development and growth and cause malfunctions in vision, movement, hearing, and overall mental development. This impairment leads to blindness, seizures, and paralysis. Currently, there is no cure for Tay-Sachs disease; affected children normally die by the age of 5 (Fig. 21.10).

Cystic Fibrosis   Cystic fibrosis (CF) is an autosomal recessive disorder that occurs among all ethnic groups but is most prevalent in Caucasians. Cystic fibrosis is caused by a defective chloride ion channel that is encoded by the *cystic fibrosis conductance transmembrane regulator* (*CFTR*) allele on chromosome 7. It is estimated that 1 in 29 Caucasians in the United States carries this allele. Research has demonstrated that chloride ions (Cl^-) fail to pass through the defective version of the *CFTR* chloride ion channel (Fig. 21.11), which is located on the plasma membrane. Ordinarily, after chloride ions have passed through the channel to the other side of the membrane, sodium ions (Na^+) and water follow. It is believed that lack of water is the cause of the abnormally thick mucus in the bronchial tubes and pancreatic ducts.

By understanding the genetic basis of this disease, scientists have been able to develop treatments that have raised the average life expectancy for CF patients to as much as 35 years of age. Gene therapy (see Section 22.4) has also been successful in treating some forms of CF. Some scientists have suggested that the mutated

---

[2]Because he passed on the *a* allele to his third child.

Figure 21.11   Cystic fibrosis disease.
Cystic fibrosis is due to a faulty protein that is supposed to regulate the flow of chloride ions into and out of cells through a channel protein.

CFTR allele has persisted in the human population as a means of surviving potentially fatal diseases, such as cholera.

Sickle-Cell Disease   Sickle-cell disease is an autosomal recessive disorder in which the red blood cells are not biconcave disks like normal red blood cells. Many are sickle- or boomerang-shaped, and these red blood cells live for only about 2 weeks, unlike the average 4-month lifespan of a normal red blood cell. The defect is caused by an abnormal hemoglobin that differs from normal hemoglobin by one amino acid in the protein globin. The single amino acid change causes hemoglobin molecules to stack up and form insoluble rods. This causes the red blood cells to become sickle-shaped (see Section 6.2). This single gene defect can affect any race but is prevalent among African Americans; it is estimated that 1 in every 625 African Americans is affected by sickle-cell disease.

Sickle-shaped cells can't pass along narrow capillary passageways as disk-shaped cells can, so they clog the vessels, preventing adequate circulation. This results in anemia, tissue damage, jaundice, joint pain, and gallstones. Those affected by sickle-cell disease are also susceptible to many types of bacterial infections and have a higher incidence of stroke. Many treatment options, including blood transfusions and bone marrow transplants, are highly effective. The most common medicinal treatment, hydroxyurea, has been on the market for several decades and is considered one of the most effective daily treatments for the reduction in sickle-cell-related anemia, joint pain, and tissue damage.

Variations in the the sickle-cell gene enable heterozygous individuals to express variations of the recessive phenotype. Sickle-cell heterozygotes have sickle-cell traits in which the blood cells are normal unless they experience dehydration or mild oxygen deprivation. Intense exertion may cause sickling of some red blood cells for a short period of time. These patients can experience episodes and symptoms very similar to those of patients with the autosomal recessive genotype.

Autosomal Dominant Disorders

Inheritance of only one dominant allele is necessary for an autosomal dominant genetic disorder to be displayed. Here, we discuss just a few of the known autosomal dominant disorders.

Marfan Syndrome   The autosomal dominant disorder **Marfan syndrome** is caused by a defect in the production of an elastic connective tissue protein called fibrillin. This protein is normally abundant in the lens of the eye; the bones of limbs, fingers, and ribs; and the wall of the aorta and the blood vessels. This explains why the affected person often has a dislocated lens, long limbs and fingers, and a caved-in chest. The wall of the aorta is weak and can burst without warning. Marfan syndrome is considered a "rare" disorder, currently affecting less than 200,000 people in the United States, or less than 1 in every 2,000 individuals. Treatments for Marfan syndrome include beta blockers to control the cardiovascular symptoms, corrective lenses or eye surgery, and braces or orthopedic surgery for musculoskeletal symptoms.

Osteogenesis Imperfecta   **Osteogenesis imperfecta** is an autosomal dominant genetic disorder that results in weakened, brittle bones. Although at least nine types of the disorder are known, most are linked to mutations in two genes necessary to the synthesis of a type I collagen—one of the most abundant proteins in the human body. Collagen has many roles, including providing strength and rigidity to bone and forming the framework for most of the body's tissues. Because the mutant collagen can cause structural defects even when combined with normal collagen I, osteogenesis imperfecta is generally considered to be dominant.

Osteogenesis imperfecta, which has an incidence of approximately 1 in 5,000 live births, affects all racial groups similarly and has been documented since as long as 300 years ago. Some historians think that the Viking chieftain Ivar Ragnarsson, who was known as Ivar the Boneless and was often carried into battle on a shield, had this condition. In most cases, the diagnosis is made in young children who visit the emergency room frequently due to broken bones. Some children with the disorder have an unusual blue tint in the sclera, the white portion of the eye; reduced skin elasticity; weakened teeth; and heart valve abnormalities. The disorder is treatable with a number of drugs that help increase bone mass, but these drugs must be taken long-term.

Huntington Disease   An autosomal dominant neurological disorder that leads to progressive degeneration of brain cells (Fig. 21.12), **Huntington disease** is caused by a mutated copy of the gene for a protein called huntingtin. The defective gene contains segments of DNA in which the base sequence CAG repeats again and again. This type of structure, called a trinucleotide repeat, causes the huntingtin protein to have too many copies of the amino acid glutamine. The normal version of huntingtin has stretches of between 10 and 25 glutamic acids. If huntingtin has more than 36 glutamic acids, as is seen in the mutated Huntington gene, it changes shape and forms clumps inside neurons. These clumps attract other proteins to clump, rendering them inactive. One of these proteins that attaches itself to the clumps, called CBP, helps nerve cells survive.

The onset of symptoms for Huntington disease is normally not seen until later in life (average age of onset is late thirties to late forties), although it is not unusual for an affected person to develop symptoms as early as their late teens. Huntington disease has a range of symptoms but is normally characterized by uncontrolled movements, unsteady gait, dementia, and speech impairment. On average, patients live 15 to 20 years after onset of symptoms, as the disease progresses rapidly. Current effective treatments include medications that slow the progression of the disease. Additionally, dopamine blockers have been found to be very effective in reducing uncontrolled movements and improving eye-hand coordination and steadiness during walking.

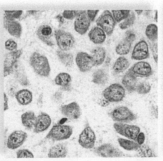
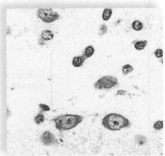

many neurons in normal brain   loss of neurons in Huntington brain

Figure 21.12   Huntington disease.
Huntington disease is caused by a loss of nerve cells.
© Dr. Hemachandra Reddy, The Neurological Science Institute, Oregon Health & Science University

BIOLOGY TODAY   **Bioethics**

Preimplantation Genetic Diagnosis

If prospective parents are heterozygous for one of the genetic disorders discussed in this section, they may want the assurance that their offspring will be free of the disorder. Determining the genotype of the embryo will provide this assurance. For example, if both parents are *Aa* for a recessive disorder, the embryo will develop normally if it has the genotype *AA* or *Aa*. On the other hand, if one of the parents is *Aa* for a dominant disorder, the embryo will develop normally only if it has the genotype *aa*.

Following in vitro fertilization (IVF), the zygote (fertilized egg) divides. When the embryo has eight cells (Fig. 21A*a*), removal of one of these cells for testing purposes has no effect on normal development. Only embryos that will not have the genetic disorders of interest are placed in the uterus to continue developing.

It is estimated that thousands of children have been born worldwide with normal genotypes following preimplantation embryo analysis for genetic disorders that run in their families. No American agency currently tracks these statistics, however. In the future, embryos that test positive for a disorder could be treated by gene therapy, so that they, too, would be allowed to continue to term.

Testing the egg is possible if the condition of concern is recessive. Recall that meiosis in females results in a single egg and at least two polar bodies (see Fig. 17.9). Polar bodies later disintegrate. They receive very little cytoplasm, but they do receive a haploid number of chromosomes. When a woman is heterozygous for a recessive genetic disorder, about half of the first polar bodies have received the mutated allele. In these instances, the egg received the normal allele. Therefore, if a polar body tests positive for a recessive mutated allele, the egg received the normal dominant allele. Only normal eggs are then used for IVF. Even if the sperm should happen to carry the mutation, the zygote will, at worst, be heterozygous. But the phenotype will appear normal.

Questions to Consider

1. Of the two diagnostic procedures described, does either seem more ethically responsible? Why?
2. Caring for an individual with a genetic condition can be very costly. Should society require preimplantation studies for the carriers of a genetic disease?

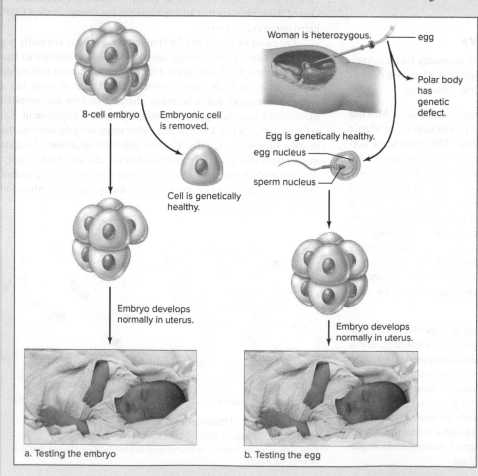

Figure 21A   The process of preimplantation genetic diagnosis.
a. Following IVF and cleavage, genetic analysis is performed on one cell removed from an eight-cell embryo. If it is found to be free of the genetic defect of concern, the seven-cell embryo is implanted in the uterus and develops into a newborn with a normal phenotype.
b. Chromosomal and genetic analysis is performed on a polar body attached to an egg. If the egg is free of a genetic defect, it is used for IVF and the embryo is implanted in the uterus for further development.
© Brand X/SuperStock RF

Woman is heterozygous.

egg

Polar body has genetic defect.

Egg is genetically healthy.

egg nucleus

sperm nucleus

8-cell embryo

Embryonic cell is removed.

Cell is genetically healthy.

Embryo develops normally in uterus.

Embryo develops normally in uterus.

a. Testing the embryo

b. Testing the egg

CHECK YOUR PROGRESS 21.3

1. Solve the following: In a pedigree, all the members of one family are affected. Based on this knowledge, list the genotypes of the parents (a) if the trait is recessive and (b) if the trait is dominant.
2. Predict the chances that homozygous normal parents for cystic fibrosis will have a child with cystic fibrosis.
3. Explain why some incidences of autosomal recessive disorders are higher in one race or culture.

CONNECTING THE CONCEPTS

Many of the diseases discussed in this section are associated with specific aspects of human physiology. For more information on these diseases (indicated in parentheses), refer to the following discussions:

Section 3.3 describes the function of proteins in the plasma membrane (cystic fibrosis).

Section 3.4 contains descriptions of the lysosomes (Tay-Sachs disease).

Section 4.2 reviews the role of connective tissue in the body (Marfan syndrome).

Section 6.2 overviews the role of the red blood cells (sickle-cell disease).

21.4 Beyond Simple Inheritance Patterns

LEARNING OUTCOMES

Upon completion of this section, you should be able to

1. Summarize how polygenic inheritance, pleiotropy, codominance, and incomplete dominance differ from simple one-trait crosses.
2. Explain how a combination of genetics and the environment can influence a phenotype.
3. Predict a person's blood type based on his or her genotype.

Certain traits, such as those studied in Section 21.2, are controlled by one set of alleles that follows a simple dominant or recessive inheritance. We now know of many other types of inheritance patterns.

Polygenic Inheritance

Polygenic traits, such as skin color and height, are governed by several sets of alleles. Each individual has a copy of all allelic pairs, possibly located on many different pairs of chromosomes. Each dominant allele codes for a product; therefore, the dominant alleles have a quantitative effect on the phenotype—that is, these effects are additive. The result is a *continuous variation* of phenotypes, resulting in a distribution of these phenotypes that resembles a bell-shaped curve. The more genes involved, the more continuous the variations and distribution of the phenotypes. Also,

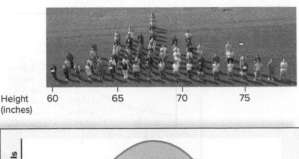

Height
(inches)   60   65   70   75

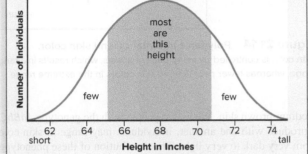

Figure 21.13   Height is a polygenic trait in humans.
When you record the heights of a large group of people chosen at random, the values follow a bell-shaped curve. Such a continuous distribution is because of control of a trait by several sets of alleles. Environmental effects are also involved.
© David Hyde and Wayne Falda/McGraw-Hill Education

environmental effects cause many intervening phenotypes. In the case of height, differences in nutrition bring about a bell-shaped curve (Fig. 21.13).

Skin Color

Skin color is the result of pigmentation produced by cells called melanocytes in the skin (see Section 4.6). We now know that there are over 100 different genes that influence skin color. For simplicity, skin color is an example of a polygenic trait that is likely controlled by many pairs of alleles.

Even so, we will use the simplest model and will assume that skin has only three pairs of alleles (*Aa* and *Bb* and *Cc*) and that each capital letter contributes pigment to the skin. When a very dark person reproduces with a very light person, the children have

SCIENCE IN YOUR LIFE

Is skin color a good indication of a person's race?

The simple answer to this question is no, an individual's skin color is not a true indicator of his or her genetic heritage. People of the same skin color are not necessarily genetically related. Because only a few genes control skin color, a person's skin color may not indicate his or her ancestors' origins. Scientists are actively investigating the genetic basis of race and have found some interesting relationships between a person's genetic heritage and medicine. This will be explored in greater detail in Section 23.5.

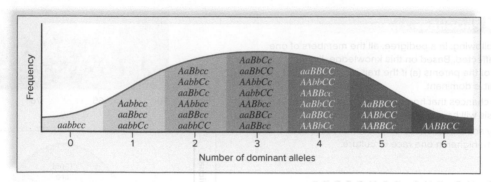

Figure 21.14   Polygenic inheritance and skin color.
Skin color is controlled by many pairs of alleles, which results in a range of phenotypes. The vast majority of people have skin colors in the middle range, whereas fewer people have skin colors in the extreme range.

medium-brown skin. When two people with the genotype *AaBbCc* reproduce with one another, individuals may range in skin color from very dark to very light. The distribution of these phenotypes typically follows a bell-shaped curve, meaning that few people have the extreme phenotypes and most people have the phenotype that lies in the middle. A bell-shaped curve is a common identifying characteristic of a polygenic trait (Fig. 21.14).

However, skin color is also influenced by the sunlight in the environment. Notice again that a range of phenotypes exists for each genotype. For example, individuals who are *AaBbCc* may vary in their skin color, even though they possess the same genotype, and several possible phenotypes fall between the two extremes. The interaction of the environment with polygenic traits is discussed below.

Multifactorial Traits

Many human disorders, such as cleft lip and/or palate, clubfoot, schizophrenia, diabetes, phenylketonuria (see chapter opener), and even allergies and cancers, are most likely controlled by polygenes subject to environmental influences. These are commonly called **multifactorial traits.** The coats of Siamese cats and Himalayan rabbits are darker in color at the ears, nose, paws, and tail (Fig. 21.15). Himalayan rabbits are homozygous for the allele *ch,* involved in the production of melanin. Experimental evidence suggests that the enzyme coded for by this gene is active only at a low temperature. Therefore, black fur occurs only at the extremities, where body heat is lost to the environment.

Recent studies have reported that all sorts of behavioral traits, such as alcoholism, phobias, and even suicide, can be associated with particular genes. However, in almost all cases the environment plays an important role in the severity of the phenotype. Therefore, they must be multifactorial traits. Current research focuses on determining what percentage of the trait is due to nature (inheritance) and what percentage is due to nurture (the environment). Some studies use identical and fraternal twins separated at birth and raised in different environments. The supposition is that if identical twins in different environments share the same trait, that trait is most likely inherited. Identical twins separated at birth are more similar in their intellectual talents, personality traits, and levels of lifelong happiness than are fraternal twins separated from

**Figure 21.15
Himalayan rabbit with
temperature-susceptible
coat color.**
It is believed that the ears, nose, and feet of this rabbit are dark because those are areas of lower body temperature.
© Neil Twigg/Alamy

birth. This substantiates the belief that behavioral traits are partly heritable. It also supports the belief that genes exert their effects by acting together in complex combinations susceptible to environmental influences.

Pleiotropy

Pleiotropy occurs when a single mutant gene affects two or more distinct and seemingly unrelated traits. For example, persons with

---

SCIENCE IN YOUR LIFE

Why do diet sodas carry the warning "Phenylketonurics: Contains Phenylalanine"?

The sweetener used in diet sodas is aspartame. Aspartame is formed by the combination of two amino acids: aspartic acid and phenylalanine. When aspartame is broken down by the body, phenylalanine is released. Phenylalanine can be toxic for those with PKU and must be avoided. Other foods high in phenylalanine include eggs, meat, milk, and bananas.

Figure 21.16   Marfan syndrome.

Marfan syndrome illustrates the multiple effects a single gene can have. Marfan syndrome is due to any number of connective tissue defects.
© Ed Reschke

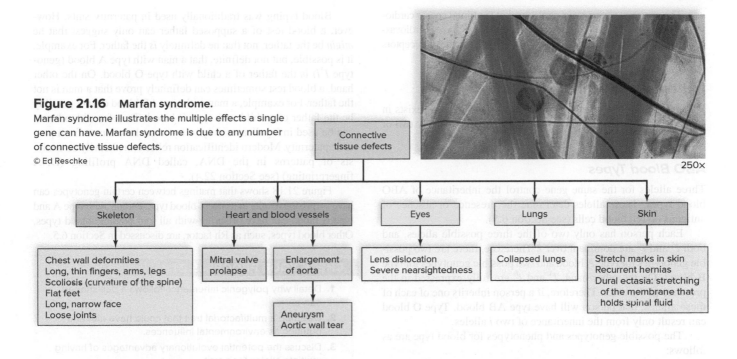

250×

Connective tissue defects

- **Skeleton**
  - Chest wall deformities
  - Long, thin fingers, arms, legs
  - Scoliosis (curvature of the spine)
  - Flat feet
  - Long, narrow face
  - Loose joints
- **Heart and blood vessels**
  - Mitral valve prolapse
  - Enlargement of aorta
    - Aneurysm
    - Aortic wall tear
- **Eyes**
  - Lens dislocation
  - Severe nearsightedness
- **Lungs**
  - Collapsed lungs
- **Skin**
  - Stretch marks in skin
  - Recurrent hernias
  - Dural ectasia: stretching of the membrane that holds spinal fluid

Marfan syndrome have disproportionately long arms, legs, hands, and feet; a weakened aorta; poor eyesight; and other characteristics (Fig. 21.16). All these characteristics are due to the production of abnormal connective tissue.

Marfan syndrome has been linked to a mutation in a gene (*FBN1*) on chromosome 15 that ordinarily specifies a functional protein called fibrillin. Fibrillin is essential for the formation of elastic fibers in connective tissue. Without the structural support of normal connective tissue, the aorta can burst, particularly if the person is engaged in a strenuous sport, such as volleyball or basketball. Flo Hyman may have been the best American woman volleyball player ever, but she fell to the floor and died at the age of only 31 because her aorta gave way during a game.

Incomplete Dominance and Codominance

Incomplete dominance occurs when the heterozygote is intermediate between the two homozygotes. For example, when a curly-haired individual has children with a straight-haired individual, their children have wavy hair. When two wavy-haired persons have children, the expected phenotypic ratio among the offspring is 1:2:1—one curly-haired child to two with wavy hair to one with straight hair. We can explain incomplete dominance by assuming that only one allele codes for a product and the single dose of the product gives the intermediate result.

Codominance occurs when alleles are equally expressed in a heterozygote. A familiar example is the human blood type AB, in which the red blood cells have the characteristics of both type A and type B blood. We can explain codominance by assuming that both genes code for a product, and we observe the results of both products being present. As we will see later in this section, blood type inheritance is also said to be an example of multiple alleles.

Incompletely Dominant Disorders

The prognosis in **familial hypercholesterolemia** parallels the number of LDL-cholesterol receptor proteins in the plasma membrane. A person with two mutated alleles lacks LDL-cholesterol receptors. A person with only one mutated allele has half the normal number of receptors, and a person with two normal alleles has the usual number of receptors. People with the full number of receptors do not have familial hypercholesterolemia. When receptors are completely absent, excessive cholesterol is deposited in various places in the body, including under the skin (Fig. 21.17).

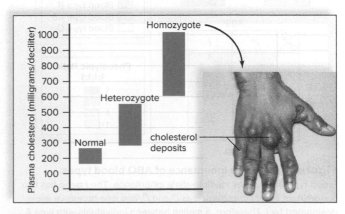

Plasma cholesterol (milligrams/deciliter)

Homozygote

Heterozygote

Normal

cholesterol deposits

Figure 21.17   The inheritance of familial hypercholesterolemia.

Familial hypercholesterolemia is incompletely dominant. Persons with one mutated allele have an abnormally high level of cholesterol in the blood, and those with two mutated alleles have a higher level still.
© Medical-On-Line/Alamy

The presence of excessive cholesterol in the blood causes cardio-vascular disease. Therefore, those with no receptors die of cardiovascular disease as children. Individuals with half the number of receptors may die when young or after they have reached middle age.

Multiple-Allele Inheritance

When a trait is controlled by **multiple alleles,** the gene exists in several allelic forms. However, each person can have only two of the possible alleles.

ABO Blood Types

Three alleles for the same gene control the inheritance of ABO blood types. These alleles determine the presence or absence of antigens on red blood cells (see Section 6.5).

Each person has only two of the three possible alleles, and both I^A and I^B are dominant over i. Therefore, there are two possible genotypes for type A blood and two possible genotypes for type B blood. On the other hand, I^A and I^B are fully expressed in the presence of the other. Therefore, if a person inherits one of each of these alleles, that person will have type AB blood. Type O blood can result only from the inheritance of two i alleles.

The possible genotypes and phenotypes for blood type are as follows:

Phenotype	Possible Genotypes
A	$I^A I^A$, $I^A i$
B	$I^B I^B$, $I^B i$
AB	$I^A I^B$
O	ii

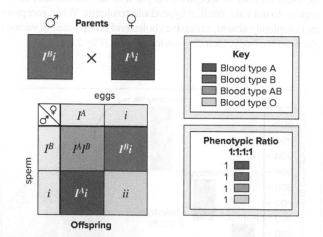

Figure 21.18 **The inheritance of ABO blood types.**
Blood type exemplifies multiple-allele inheritance. The *I* gene has two codominant alleles, designated as I^A and I^B, and one recessive allele, designated by i. Therefore, a mating between individuals with type A blood and type B blood can result in any one of the four blood types. Why? The parents are $I^A i$ and $I^B i$. If both parents were type AB blood, no child could have what blood type?[3]

[3]No child could have type O blood (ii genotype) from this cross.

Blood typing was traditionally used in paternity suits. However, a blood test of a supposed father can only suggest that he *might* be the father, not that he definitely *is* the father. For example, it is possible, but not definite, that a man with type A blood (geno-type $I^A i$) is the father of a child with type O blood. On the other hand, a blood test sometimes can definitely prove that a man is not the father. For example, a man with type AB blood cannot possibly be the father of a child with type O blood. Therefore, blood tests can be used in legal cases only to try to exclude a man from possible paternity. Modern identification relies more heavily on analysis of patterns in the DNA, called DNA profiling (DNA fingerprinting) (see Section 22.4).

Figure 21.18 shows that matings between certain genotypes can have surprising results in terms of blood type. Parents with type A and type B blood can have offspring with all four possible blood types. Other blood types, such as Rh factor, are discussed in Section 6.5.

CHECK YOUR PROGRESS 21.4

1. Detail why polygenic inheritance follows a bell-shaped curve.
2. Describe a multifactorial trait that could have diet and nutrition as environmental influences.
3. Discuss the potential evolutionary advantages of having multiple alleles for a trait.

CONNECTING THE CONCEPTS

For more information on the topics presented in this section, refer to the following discussions:

Section 4.6 provides more information on the melanocyte cells that control skin color.

Section 6.5 describes the basis of human blood types.

Section 23.5 explores the evolution of humans and human races.

21.5 Sex-Linked Inheritance

LEARNING OUTCOMES

Upon completion of this section, you should be able to

1. Understand the differences between autosomal and sex-linked patterns of inheritance.
2. Interpret a human pedigree to determine sex-linked inheritance of a trait.

Normally, both males and females have 23 pairs of chromosomes; 22 pairs are called **autosomes,** and 1 pair is the sex chromosomes. These are called **sex chromosomes** because they differ between the sexes. In humans, males have the sex chromosomes X and Y, and females have two X chromosomes. The Y chromosome contains the gene responsible for determining male gender.

Traits controlled by genes on the sex chromosomes are said to be **sex-linked.** An allele on an X chromosome is **X-linked,** and an allele on the Y chromosome is **Y-linked.** Most sex-linked genes are only on the X chromosomes. Very few Y-linked alleles associated with human disorders have been found on the much smaller Y chromosome.

Many of the genes on the X chromosomes, such as those that determine normal color vision as opposed to red-green color blindness, are unrelated to the gender of the individual. In other words, the X chromosome carries genes that affect both males and females. It would be logical to suppose that a sex-linked trait is passed from father to son or from mother to daughter, but this is not the case. A male always receives an X-linked allele from his mother, from whom he inherited an X chromosome. *The Y chromosome from the father does not carry an allele for the trait.* Usually, a sex-linked genetic disorder is recessive. Therefore, a female must receive two alleles, one from each parent, before she has the disorder.

X-Linked Alleles

When considering X-linked traits, the allele on the X chromosome is shown as a letter attached to the X chromosome. For example, this is the key for red-green color blindness, a well-known X-linked recessive disorder:

- X^B = normal color vision
- X^b = color blindness

The possible genotypes and phenotypes in both males and females follow.

Genotypes	Phenotypes
$X^B X^B$	Female who has normal color vision
$X^B X^b$	Carrier female who has normal color vision
$X^b X^b$	Female who is color-blind
$X^B Y$	Male who has normal color vision
$X^b Y$	Male who is color-blind

The second genotype is a carrier female. Although a female with this genotype appears normal, she is capable of passing on an allele for color blindness. Color-blind females are rare, because they must receive the allele from both parents. Color-blind males are more common, because they need only one recessive allele to be color-blind. The allele for color blindness must be inherited from their mother, because it is on the X chromosome. Males inherit the Y chromosome only from their father (Fig. 21.19).

Now let us consider a mating between a man with normal vision and a heterozygous woman (Fig. 21.19). What is the chance that this couple will have a color-blind daughter? A color-blind son? All daughters will have normal color vision, because they all receive an X^B from their father. The sons, however, have a 50% chance of being color-blind, depending on whether they receive an X^B or an X^b from their mother. The inheritance of a Y chromosome from their father cannot offset the inheritance of an X^b from their mother. The Y chromosome doesn't have an allele for the trait, so it can't prevent color blindness in a son. Notice in Figure 21.19 that the phenotypic results for sex-linked traits are given separately for males and females.

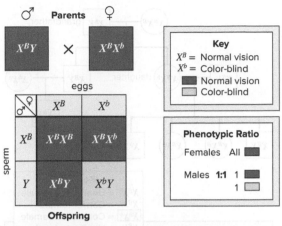

Figure 21.19   Results of an X-linked cross.
The male parent is normal, but the female parent is a carrier—an allele for color blindness is located on one of her X chromosomes. Therefore, each son has a 50% chance of being color-blind. The daughters will appear normal, but each one has a 50% chance of being a carrier.

Pedigree for X-Linked Disorders

Like color blindness, most sex-linked disorders are usually carried on the X chromosome. Figure 21.20 gives a pedigree for an *X-linked recessive disorder.* More males than females have the disorder, because recessive alleles on the X chromosome are always expressed in males. The Y chromosome lacks an allele for the disorder. X-linked recessive conditions often pass from grandfather to grandson, because the daughters of a male with the disorder are carriers. Figure 21.20 lists various ways to recognize a recessive X-linked disorder.

Only a few known traits are *X-linked dominant.* If a disorder is X-linked dominant, affected males pass the trait *only* to daughters, who have a 100% chance of having the condition. Females can pass an X-linked dominant allele to both sons and daughters. If a female is heterozygous and her partner is normal, each child has a 50% chance of escaping an X-linked dominant disorder. This depends on the maternal X chromosome that is inherited.

X-Linked Recessive Disorders of Interest

Color blindness is the inability to differentiate between certain color perceptions. Some forms of color blindness (red-green) are X-linked. There is no treatment for color blindness, but the disorder itself does not lead to a significant disability for the patient. Color blindness affects about 8–12% of Caucasian males and 0.5% of Caucasian females in the United States. Most people affected see brighter greens as tans, olive greens as browns, and reds as reddish-browns. A few cannot tell reds from greens at all. They see only yellows, blues, blacks, whites, and grays.

Duchenne muscular dystrophy is an X-linked recessive disorder characterized by a degeneration of the muscles. Symptoms, such as waddling gait, toe walking, frequent falls, and difficulty in rising, may appear as soon as the child starts to walk. Muscle weakness intensifies and respiratory and cardiovascular conditions

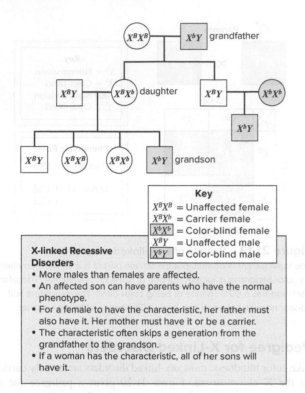

Key

$X^B X^B$	= Unaffected female
$X^B X^b$	= Carrier female
$X^b X^b$	= Color-blind female
$X^B Y$	= Unaffected male
$X^b Y$	= Color-blind male

X-linked Recessive Disorders

- More males than females are affected.
- An affected son can have parents who have the normal phenotype.
- For a female to have the characteristic, her father must also have it. Her mother must have it or be a carrier.
- The characteristic often skips a generation from the grandfather to the grandson.
- If a woman has the characteristic, all of her sons will have it.

Figure 21.20   X-linked recessive disorder pedigree.
This pedigree for color blindness exemplifies the inheritance pattern of an X-linked recessive disorder. The list gives various ways of recognizing the X-linked recessive pattern of inheritance.

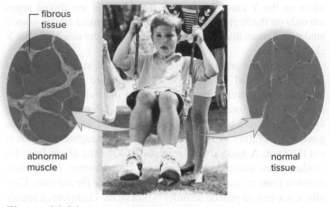

Figure 21.21   Muscular dystrophy.
In muscular dystrophy, an X-linked recessive disorder, calves enlarge because fibrous tissue develops as muscles waste away, due to lack of the protein dystrophin.

(left and right): © Dr. Rabi Tawil, Director, Neuromuscular Pathology Laboratory, University of Rochester Medical Center; (center): © Muscular Dystrophy Association

flapping, and distractibility. Females with the condition present with variable symptoms. Most of the same traits seen in males with fragile X syndrome have been reported in females as well, but often the symptoms are milder in females and present with lower frequency.

A person with fragile X syndrome does not make the fragile X mental retardation protein (FMRP). Lack of this protein in the brain results in the various manifestations of the disease. As the name implies, a gene defect is found on the X chromosome. The genetic basis of fragile X syndrome is similar to that seen in Huntington disease (see Section 21.3). In both cases, the gene in question has too many repeated copies of a DNA sequence containing three nucleotides (called a trinucleotide repeat). In fragile X syndrome, the DNA sequence is CGG. (Recall that in Huntington disease the repeated sequence is CAG.) Fewer than 59 copies of the repeated sequence is considered normal. Between 59 and 200 copies is considered "premutation." Generally, both males and females with the premutation genotype have normal intellect and appearance, although they can have subtle intellectual or behavioral symptoms. Persons whose DNA has over 200 copies of the repeat have "full mutation" and show the physical and behavioral traits of fragile X syndrome.

progress until the individual is confined to a wheelchair, normally by ages 7 to 10. Death usually occurs by ages 20 to 25. Therefore, affected males are rarely fathers. The recessive allele remains in the population by passage from carrier mother to carrier daughter.

The absence of a protein, now called dystrophin, is the cause of Duchenne muscular dystrophy. Much investigative work determined that dystrophin is involved in the release of calcium from the sarcoplasmic reticulum in muscle fibers. The lack of dystrophin causes calcium to leak into the cell, which promotes the action of an enzyme that dissolves muscle fibers. When the body attempts to repair the tissue, fibrous tissue forms (Fig. 21.21). This cuts off the blood supply, so that more and more cells die. Immature muscle cells can be injected into muscles, but it takes 100,000 cells for dystrophin production to increase 30–40%.

Fragile X syndrome is the most common cause of inherited mental impairment. These impairments can range from mild learning disabilities to more severe intellectual disabilities. It is also the most common known cause of *autism,* a class of social, behavioral, and communication disorders. Fragile X syndrome affects 1 out of every 4,000 males and 1 out of every 8,000 females, on average. Males with full symptoms of the condition have characteristic physical abnormalities—a long face, and prominent jaw, large ears, joint laxity (excessively flexible joints), and genital abnormalities. Other common characteristics include tactile defensiveness (dislike of being touched), poor eye contact, repetitive speech patterns, hand

SCIENCE IN YOUR LIFE

Why is this disease called "fragile" X syndrome?

The name of fragile X syndrome may make you think that the disease has something to do with a breakable X chromosome. Actually, the name refers to the appearance of the chromosome under a microscope. In extreme cases of fragile X syndrome, in which there are many copies of the trinucleotide repeat, a portion of the X chromosome appears to be hanging from a thread. However, the appearance of the chromosome is not a cause of the disease. Fragile X syndrome is a result of a malfunction in the fragile X mental retardation protein (FMRP).

The trinucleotide-repeat disorders, such as Huntington disease and fragile X syndrome, exhibit what is called *anticipation*. This means that the number of repeats in the gene can increase in each successive generation. For example, a female with 100 copies of the repeat is considered to have a premutation. When this female passes her X chromosome with the premutation to her offspring, the number of repeats may expand to over 200. This would result in a full mutation in her child. In a recent study, maternal premutations of between 90 and 200 repeats resulted in an expansion to full mutation in 80–100% of the offspring.

Hemophilia is an X-linked recessive disorder. There are two common types. Hemophilia A is due to the absence or minimal presence of a clotting factor known as factor VIII, and the less common hemophilia B is due to the absence of clotting factor IX. In the United States, 1 in every 5,000 males is affected with hemophilia. Of those, 80–85% specifically have the more common hemophilia A. Rarely are females affected by hemophilia, averaging 1 in every 50 million women in the United States. Hemophilia is called the bleeder's disease, because the affected person's blood either does not clot or clots very slowly. Although hemophiliacs bleed externally after an injury, they also bleed internally, particularly around joints. Hemorrhages can be stopped with transfusions of fresh blood (or plasma) or concentrates of the clotting protein. Also, factors VIII and IX are now available as biotechnology products.

CHECK YOUR PROGRESS 21.5

1. Solve the following: In a given family, a man and woman have two children, a boy and a girl, and both are color-blind. List the possible genotypes of the parents if both parents have normal vision.

2. Can a woman who is affected by an X-linked dominant disorder have a child who is not affected? Why or why not?

3. Discuss why X-linked disorders are more common than Y-linked disorders.

CONNECTING THE CONCEPTS

The sex-linked conditions described in this section are based on other systems of the human body. For more information, refer to the following discussions:

Section 6.4 provides more information on blood clotting and hemophilia.

Section 13.4 describes a variety of muscular disorders, including muscular dystrophy.

Section 18.3 outlines how genetics counselors obtain chromosomes to screen for diseases such as fragile X syndrome.

BIOLOGY TODAY **Science**

Hemophilia: The Royal Disease

The pedigree in Figure 21B shows why hemophilia is often referred to as "the Royal Disease." Queen Victoria of England, who reigned from 1837 to 1901, was the first of the royals to carry the gene. From her, the disease eventually spread to the Prussian, Spanish, and Russian royal families. In that era, monarchs arranged marriages between their children to consolidate political alliances. This practice allowed the gene for hemophilia to spread throughout the royal families. It is assumed that a spontaneous mutation arose either in Queen Victoria after her conception or in one of the gametes of her parents. However, in the book *Queen Victoria's Gene* by D. M. Potts, the author postulates that Edward Augustus, Duke of Kent, may not have been Queen Victoria's father. Potts suggests that Victoria may have instead been the illegitimate child of a hemophiliac male. Regardless of her parentage, had Victoria not been crowned, the fate of the various royal households may have been very different. The history of Europe also could have been dramatically different.

However, Victoria did become queen. Queen Victoria and her husband, Prince Albert, had nine children. Fortunately, only one son, Leopold, suffered from hemophilia. He experienced severe hemorrhages and died in 1884 at the age of 31 as a result of a minor

fall. He left behind a daughter, Alice, a carrier for the disease. Her son Rupert also suffered from hemophilia and in 1928 died of a brain hemorrhage as a result of a car accident. Queen Victoria's eldest son, Edward VII, the heir to the throne, did not have the disease; thus, the current British royal family is free of the disease.

Two of Queen Victoria's daughters, Alice and Beatrice, were carriers of the disease. Alice married Louis IV, the Grand Duke of Hesse. Of her six children, three were affected by hemophilia. Her son Frederick died of internal bleeding from a fall. Alice's daughter Irene married Prince Henry of Prussia, her first cousin. Two of their three sons suffered from hemophilia. One of these sons, Waldemar, died at age 56 due to the lack of blood-transfusion supplies during World War I. Henry, Alice's other son, bled to death at the age of 4.

Alice's daughter Alexandra married Nicholas II of Russia. Alexandra gave birth to four daughters before giving birth to Alexei, the heir to the Russian throne. It was obvious almost from birth that Alexei had hemophilia. Every fall caused bleeding into his joints, which led to crippling of his limbs and excruciating pain. The best medical doctors could not help Alexei. Desperate to

Continued

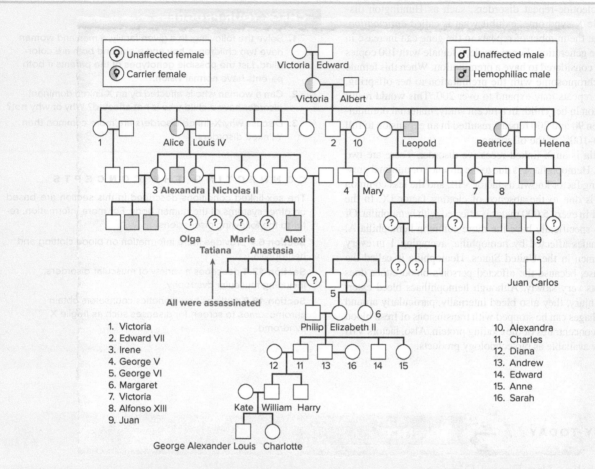

Figure 21B   **X-linked inheritance of hemophilia in royal families.**
Queen Victoria was a carrier, so each of her sons had a 50% chance of having the disorder, and each of her daughters had a 50% chance of being a carrier. This pedigree shows only the affected descendants. Many others are unaffected, including the members of the present British royal family.

relieve his suffering, his parents turned to the monk Rasputin. Rasputin was able to relieve some of Alexei's suffering by hypnotizing him and putting him to sleep. Alexandra and Nicholas, the czar and czarina, put unlimited trust in Rasputin. The illness of the only heir to the czar's throne, the strain Alexei's illness placed on the czar and czarina, and the power of Rasputin were all factors leading to the Russian Revolution of 1917. The czar and czarina, as well as their children, were all murdered during the revolution.

Queen Victoria's other carrier daughter, Beatrice, married Prince Henry of Battenberg. Her son Leopold was a hemophiliac, dying at 32 during a knee operation. Beatrice's daughter Victoria Eugenie married Alfonso XIII of Spain. Queen Ena, as Victoria Eugenie came to be known, was not popular with the Spanish people. Her firstborn son, Alfonso, the heir to the Spanish throne, did not stop bleeding on his circumcision. When it became obvious that she had given her son hemophilia, it is alleged that her husband

never forgave her. Like his cousin Rupert, Alfonso died in 1938 from internal bleeding after a car accident. Victoria's youngest son, Gonzalo, was also a hemophiliac whose life was claimed by a car accident in 1934.

Today, no members of any European royal family are known to have hemophilia. Individuals with the disease gene born in the late 1800s and early 1900s have all died, eliminating the gene from the current royal houses.

Questions to Consider

1. What was the probability that Alice's and Louis's sons would have hemophilia? What was the probability for their daughters? How does that relate to the actual occurrence in their children?
2. Assume that the mutation for hemophilia did not originate with Victoria. What does this tell you about the genotypes of her parents?

CASE STUDY: CONCLUSION

The physician referred Patrick's parents to the hospital's genetics counselor. Genetics counselors work in the medical field as a liaison between patients and members of all health-care disciplines. Their job descriptions include identifying couples at risk for passing on genetic disorders and working with patients affected by disorders and their families to better understand diagnoses, treatment options, and counseling.

The counselor explained that PKU is autosomal recessive in inheritance. She drew out a pedigree chart depicting both Patrick and his parents. Patrick was affected and neither of his parents was, which meant that both of his parents were carriers of the disorder. She explained how the diagnosis of PKU was made on

Patrick by use of the HPLC test and what the disorder might mean to his health and development. The characteristics of PKU— reduced brain development, seizures, and so on—can be avoided; because the problem is the buildup of phenylalanine levels, the main goal during developmental years is to eliminate or reduce the intake of phenylalanine. She explained that a diet restricting phenylalanine intake starting right away and continuing until Patrick finished puberty would result in little to no adverse effects. This diet, combined with prescribed protein supplements, would help Patrick avoid the buildup of phenylalanine in his neurons and would allow his brain to develop normally.

STUDY TOOLS http://connect.mheducation.com

SMARTBOOK® Maximize your study time with McGraw-Hill SmartBook®, the first adaptive textbook.

SUMMARIZE

21.1 Genotype and Phenotype

An allele is a variation of a gene. Each allele exists at a specific locus on a chromosome. *Genotype* refers to the alleles of the individual, and *phenotype* refers to the physical characteristics associated with these alleles. Dominant alleles mask the expression of recessive alleles.

- **Homozygous dominant** individuals have the dominant phenotype (e.g., *AA* = normal pigmentation).
- **Homozygous recessive** individuals have the recessive phenotype (e.g., *aa* = albino).
- **Heterozygous** individuals have the dominant phenotype (e.g., *Aa* = normal pigmentation).

21.2 One- and Two-Trait Inheritance

One-Trait Crosses

The first step in doing a problem with a one-trait cross, or **monohybrid cross,** is to determine the genotype and then the gametes.

- An individual has two alleles for every trait, but a gamete has one allele for every trait.

The next step is to combine all possible sperm with all possible eggs. If there are more than one possible sperm and/or egg, a **Punnett square** is helpful in determining the genotypic and phenotypic ratio among the offspring.

- For a monohybrid cross between two heterozygous individuals, a 3:1 ratio is expected among the offspring.
- For a monohybrid cross between a heterozygous and homozygous recessive individual, a 1:1 ratio is expected among the offspring.
- The expected ratio can be converted to the chance of a particular genotype or phenotype. For example, a 3:1 ratio = a 75% chance of the dominant phenotype and a 25% chance of the recessive phenotype.

Two-Trait Crosses

A problem consisting of two traits is often referred to as a **dihybrid cross.**

- If an individual is heterozygous for two traits, four gamete types are possible, as can be substantiated by knowledge of meiosis.
- For a cross between two heterozygous individuals (*AaBb* × *AaBb*), a 9:3:3:1 ratio is expected among the offspring.

- For a cross between a heterozygous and homozygous recessive individual (*AaBb* × *aabb*), a 1:1:1:1 ratio is expected among the offspring.

21.3 Inheritance of Genetic Disorders

A pedigree shows the pattern of inheritance for a trait from generation to generation of a family. This first pattern appears in a family pedigree for a recessive disorder—both parents are **carriers.** The second pattern appears in a family pedigree for a dominant disorder. Both parents are again heterozygous.

Trait is recessive.   Trait is dominant.

Genetic Disorders of Interest

- **Tay-Sachs disease, cystic fibrosis (CF),** and **sickle-cell disease** are autosomal recessive disorders.
- **Marfan syndrome, osteogenesis imperfecta,** and **Huntington disease** are autosomal dominant disorders.

21.4 Beyond Simple Inheritance Patterns

In some patterns of inheritance, the alleles are not just dominant or recessive.

Polygenic Inheritance

Polygenic traits, such as skin color and height, are controlled by more than one set of alleles. The alleles have an additive effect on the phenotype. **Multifactorial traits** are usually polygenic with an environmental influence.

Incomplete Dominance and Codominance

In **incomplete dominance** (e.g., **familial hypercholesterolemia**), the heterozygote is intermediate between the two homozygotes. In **codominance** (e.g., type AB blood), both dominant alleles are expressed equally.

Multiple-Allele Inheritance

In humans, an example of a trait involving **multiple alleles** is the ABO blood types. Every individual has two out of three possible alleles: I^A, I^B, or i. Both I^A and I^B are expressed. Therefore, this is also a case of codominance.

21.5 Sex-Linked Inheritance

X-Linked Alleles

Humans contain 22 pairs of **autosomes** and 1 pair of **sex chromosomes.** Traits on the sex chromosomes are said to be **sex-linked. X-linked** traits, such as those that determine normal vision as opposed to color blindness, are unrelated to the gender of the individual. Common X-linked genetic crosses are

- $X^B X^b \times X^B Y$: All daughters will be normal, even though they have a 50% chance of being carriers, but sons will have a 50% chance of being color-blind.
- $X^B X^B \times X^b Y$: All children will be normal (daughters will be carriers).

Pedigree for X-Linked Disorders

- A pedigree for an X-linked recessive disorder shows that the trait often passes from grandfather to grandson by way of a carrier daughter. Also, more males than females have the characteristic.
- Like most X-linked disorders, **color blindness, Duchenne muscular dystrophy, fragile X syndrome,** and **hemophilia** are recessive.

ASSESS

TESTING YOURSELF

Choose the best answer for each question.

21.1 Genotype and Phenotype

1. The _____ of an organism is determined by the information in the DNA, and the _____ is determined largely by proteins.
   a. phenotype; genotype
   b. locus; phenotype
   c. genotype; phenotype
   d. genotype; sex-linkage
   e. None of these are correct.

2. Which of the following terms refers to variations in a gene?
   a. locus
   b. carrier
   c. dominance
   d. alleles
   e. None of these are correct.

3. In which of the following can the phenotype be used to accurately predict the genotype?
   a. homozygous recessive
   b. homozygous dominant
   c. heterozygous
   d. None of these are correct.

21.2 One- and Two-Trait Inheritance

4. What possible gametes can be produced by *AaBb?*
   a. *Aa, Bb*
   b. *A, a, B, b*
   c. *AB, ab*
   d. *AB, Ab, aB, ab*

5. The genotype of an individual with the dominant phenotype can be determined best by reproduction with
   a. a homozygous recessive individual.
   b. a heterozygote.
   c. the dominant phenotype.
   d. None of these are correct.

6. In a dihybrid cross of *AaBb* × *AaBb,* what is the probability that offspring will have the dominant phenotype for trait A but the recessive phenotype for trait B?
   a. 1/16   d. 9/16
   b. 3/16   e. None of these are correct.
   c. 7/16

21.3 Inheritance of Genetic Disorders

7. Cystic fibrosis is a recessive trait. If two carriers have children, what is the probability that their child will have the disease?
   a. 0%   c. 50%   e. 100%
   b. 25%   d. 75%

8. Which of the following is correct regarding a dominant autosomal disorder?
   a. An allele in one of the parents may cause the disease in the offspring.
   b. Heterozygotes are affected by the disorder.
   c. Two unaffected parents do not produce offspring with the disorder.
   d. Two affected parents may produce offspring without the disorder.
   e. All of these are correct.

9. Which of the following disorders is caused by a loss of enzymes in the lysosomes of the cell?
   a. osteogenesis imperfecta
   b. cystic fibrosis
   c. Tay-Sachs disease
   d. Marfan syndrome
   e. Huntington disease

21.4 Beyond Simple Inheritance Patterns

10. Which of the following is not a feature of multifactorial inheritance?
    a. Effects of dominant alleles are additive.
    b. Genes affecting the trait may be on multiple chromosomes.
    c. Environment influences phenotype.
    d. Recessive alleles are harmful.

11. If a child has type O blood and the mother is type A, then which of the following might be the blood type of the child's father?
    a. A only
    b. B only
    c. O only
    d. A or O
    e. A, B, or O

12. A trait in which the heterozygotes have a phenotype that is intermediate between the dominant and recessive phenotypes is an indication of
    a. codominance.
    b. sex-linked trait.
    c. incomplete dominance.
    d. pleiotropy.
    e. None of these are correct.

13. Which of the following terms may be used to describe a disease that has multiple phenotypes?
    a. multifactorial
    b. codominance
    c. incomplete dominance
    d. sex-linked
    e. pleiotropy

21.5 Sex-Linked Inheritance

14. A couple wish to have children, but the father has an X-linked recessive trait. Assuming that the mother does not carry the trait, what percentage of their sons may inherit the trait?
    a. 0%   c. 50%   e. 100%
    b. 25%   d. 75%

15. A mother who is heterozygous for an X-linked recessive trait has children with a man who has the trait. What percentage of their daughters will exhibit the trait?
    a. 0%   c. 50%   e. 100%
    b. 25%   d. 75%

ENGAGE

BioNOW

Want to know how this science is relevant to your life? Check out the BioNow video below:

- Glowing Fish Genetics

How might an experiment be designed to test whether the pattern of inheritance in the glowfish is dominant or codominant?

THINKING CRITICALLY

In the case study, Patrick was affected with an autosomal recessive disorder, PKU. The chapter detailed many other autosomal recessive disorders, other types of genetic inheritance, and one- and two-trait inheritance patterns. Think about the basics learned from this chapter when answering the following questions:

1. In the pedigree for an autosomal recessive disorder in Section 21.3, the chart depicts a skip in the generations of affected individuals. Is this always the case for autosomal recessive disorders? Why or why not?

2. In two-trait crosses, does one trait being dominant have an effect on the inheritance of the second trait?

3. Would an X-linked disorder or an autosomal disorder appear more in a family pedigree? Explain your reasoning.

Unit 3 Movement and Support in Humans

CHAPTER

Skeletal System

© Southern Stock Corp/Corbis

CHAPTER CONCEPTS

12.1 Overview of the Skeletal System
Bones are the organs of the skeletal system. The primary tissues of the system are compact and spongy bone, various types of cartilage, and fibrous connective tissue in the ligaments.

12.2 Bones of the Axial Skeleton
The axial skeleton lies in the midline of the body and consists of the skull, the hyoid bone, the vertebral column, and the rib cage.

12.3 Bones of the Appendicular Skeleton
The appendicular skeleton consists of the bones of the pectoral girdle, upper limbs, pelvic girdle, and lower limbs.

12.4 Articulations
Joints are classified according to their degree of movement. Synovial joints are freely movable.

12.5 Bone Growth and Homeostasis
Bone is a living tissue that grows, remodels, and repairs itself. Bone homeostasis is performed by a variety of cells.

BEFORE YOU BEGIN

Before beginning this chapter, take a few moments to review the following discussions:

Section 4.1 What is the role of connective tissue in the body?

Section 4.8 How does the skeletal system contribute to homeostasis?

Section 9.6 What are the roles of calcium and vitamin D in the body?

CASE STUDY: KNEE REPLACEMENT

Jackie was an outstanding athlete in high school, and even now, in her early fifties, she tries to stay in shape. However, during her customary 3-mile jogs she has been having an increasingly hard time ignoring the pain in her left knee. She had torn some ligaments in her knee playing intramural and intermural volleyball in college, and it had never quite felt the same. In her forties, she was able to control the pain by taking over-the-counter medications, but 2 years ago she had had arthroscopic surgery to remove some torn cartilage and calcium deposits. Now that the pain was getting worse than before, she knew her best option might be a total knee replacement.

Although it sounds drastic, replacing old, arthritic joints with new, artificial ones is becoming increasingly routine. Almost 4 million Americans, and 1 in 20 individuals over the age of 50, have undergone either partial or total knee replacement surgery. During the procedure, a surgeon removes bone from the bottom of the femur and the top of the tibia and replaces each with caps made of metal or ceramic, held in place with bone cement. A plastic plate is installed to allow the femur and tibia to move smoothly against each other, and a smaller plate is attached to the kneecap (patella), so that it can function properly.

As you read through the chapter, think about the following questions:
1. What is the role of cartilage in the knee joint?
2. What specific portions of these long bones are being removed during knee replacement?
3. Why does Jackie's physical condition make her an ideal candidate for knee replacement?

12.1 Overview of the Skeletal System

LEARNING OUTCOMES

Upon completion of this section, you should be able to

1. State the functions of the skeletal system.
2. Describe the structure of a long bone and list the types of tissues it contains.
3. List the three types of cartilage found in the body and provide a function for each.

The **skeletal system** consists of two types of connective tissue: bone and the cartilage found at **joints.** In addition, **ligaments,** formed of fibrous connective tissue, join the bones.

Functions of the Skeleton

The skeleton does more than merely provide a frame for the body. In addition, it has the following functions:

Support. The bones of the legs support the entire body when we are standing, and bones of the pelvic girdle support the abdominal cavity.

Movement. The skeletal system works with the muscular system to provide movement.

Protection. The bones of the skull protect the brain; the rib cage protects the heart and lungs; and the vertebrae protect the spinal cord, which makes nervous connections to all the muscles of the limbs.

Production of blood cells. The skeleton plays an important role in the formation of blood. In the fetus, all bones in the fetus have red bone marrow to produce new blood cells. However, in adults, only certain bones produce blood cells.

Storage of minerals and fat. All bones have a matrix that contains calcium phosphate, a source of calcium ions and phosphate ions in the blood. Fat is stored in yellow bone marrow.

Anatomy of a Long Bone

The bones of the body vary greatly in size and shape. To better understand the anatomy of a bone, we will use a long bone (Fig. 12.1), a type of bone common in the arms and legs. The shaft, or main portion of the bone, is called the *diaphysis.* The diaphysis has a large **medullary cavity,** whose walls are composed of compact bone. The medullary cavity is lined with a thin, vascular membrane (the endosteum) and is filled with yellow bone marrow, which stores fat.

The expanded region at the end of a long bone is called an *epiphysis* (pl., epiphyses). The epiphyses are separated from the diaphyses by a small region of mature bone called the *metaphysis,* which contain the *epiphyseal plate,* a region of cartilage that allows for bone growth.

The epiphyses are composed largely of spongy bone that contains red bone marrow, where blood cells are made. The epiphyses are coated with a thin layer of hyaline cartilage, which is also called articular cartilage, because it occurs at a joint.

Except for the articular cartilage on the bone's ends, a long bone is completely covered by a layer of fibrous connective tissue called the **periosteum.** This covering contains blood vessels, lymphatic vessels, and nerves. Note in Figure 12.1 how a blood vessel penetrates the periosteum and enters the bone. Branches of the blood vessel are found throughout the medullary cavity. Other branches can be found in hollow cylinders called central canals within the bone tissue. The periosteum is continuous with ligaments and tendons connected to a bone.

Bone

Compact bone is highly organized and composed of tubular units called osteons. In a cross section of an osteon, bone cells called **osteocytes** lie in **lacunae** (sing., lacuna), tiny chambers arranged in concentric circles around a central canal (Fig. 12.1). Matrix fills the space between the rows of lacunae. Tiny canals called *canaliculi* (sing., canaliculus) run through the matrix. These canaliculi connect the lacunae with one another and with the central canal. The cells stay in contact by strands of cytoplasm that extend into the canaliculi. Osteocytes nearest the center of an osteon exchange nutrients and wastes with the blood vessels in the central canal. These cells then pass on nutrients and collect wastes from the other cells via gap junctions (see Fig. 3.17).

Compared with compact bone, **spongy bone** has an unorganized appearance (Fig. 12.1). It contains numerous thin plates, called *trabeculae,* separated by unequal spaces. Although this makes spongy bone lighter than compact bone, spongy bone is still designed for strength. Just as braces are used for support in buildings, the trabeculae follow lines of stress. The spaces of spongy bone are often filled with **red bone marrow,** a specialized tissue that produces all types of blood cells. The osteocytes of spongy bone are irregularly placed within the trabeculae. Canaliculi bring them nutrients from the red bone marrow.

Cartilage

Cartilage is not as strong as bone, but it is more flexible. Its matrix is gel-like and contains many collagenous and elastic fibers. The cells, called **chondrocytes,** lie within lacunae that are irregularly grouped. Cartilage has no nerves, making it well suited for padding joints where the stresses of movement are intense. Cartilage also has no blood vessels and relies on neighboring tissues for nutrient and waste exchange. This makes it slow to heal.

The three types of cartilage differ according to the type and arrangement of fibers in the matrix. *Hyaline cartilage* is firm and somewhat flexible. The matrix appears uniform and glassy, but actually it contains a generous supply of collagen fibers. Hyaline cartilage is found at the ends of long bones, in the nose, at the ends of the ribs, and in the larynx and trachea.

Fibrocartilage is stronger than hyaline cartilage, because the matrix contains wide rows of thick, collagenous fibers. Fibrocartilage is able to withstand both tension and pressure and is found where support is of prime importance—in the disks between the vertebrae and in the cartilage of the knee.

Elastic cartilage is more flexible than hyaline cartilage, because the matrix contains mostly elastin fibers. This type of cartilage is found in the ear flaps and the epiglottis.

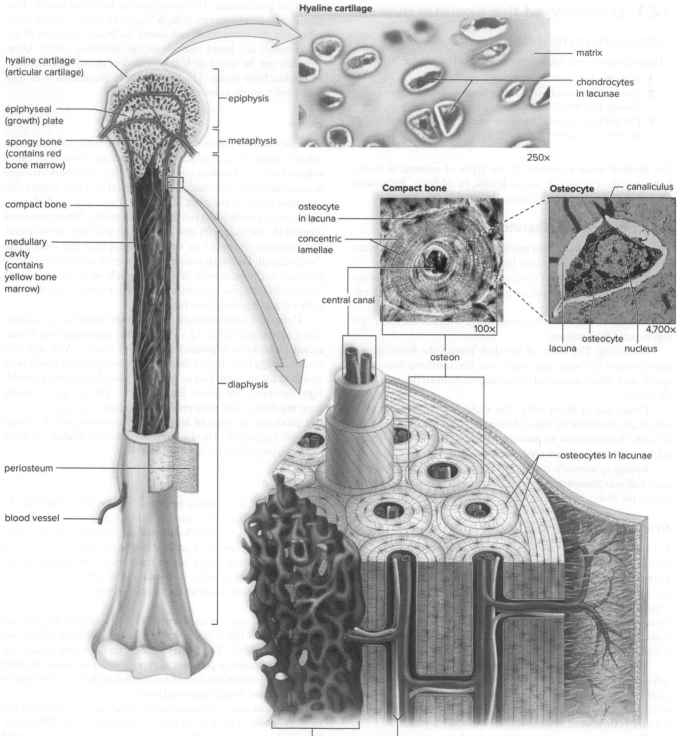

Figure 12.1   The anatomy of a long bone.

A long bone is formed of an outer layer of compact bone. Spongy bone, which lies beneath compact bone, may contain red bone marrow. The central shaft of a long bone contains yellow marrow, a form of stored fat. Periosteum, a fibrous membrane, encases the bone except at its ends. Hyaline cartilage covers the ends of bones.

(top) © Ed Reschke; (left) © Ed Reschke; (right) © Biophoto Associates/Science Source

Fibrous Connective Tissue

Fibrous connective tissue contains rows of cells called fibroblasts separated by bundles of collagenous fibers. This tissue makes up ligaments and tendons. Ligaments connect bone to bone. Tendons connect muscle to bone at a joint (also called an articulation).

CHECK YOUR PROGRESS 12.1

1. List the functions of the skeletal system.
2. Summarize the structure of a long bone by describing the differences in structure and function of compact and spongy bone.
3. Describe the three types of cartilage.

CONNECTING THE CONCEPTS

For a better understanding of the types of connective tissue presented in this section, refer to the following discussions:

Section 4.2 examines the general structure and function of the connective tissues of the body.

Section 6.1 provides an overview of the blood cells formed in the bone marrow.

Section 13.1 provides additional information on the function of tendons in the body.

12.2 Bones of the Axial Skeleton

LEARNING OUTCOMES

Upon completion of this section, you should be able to

1. Identify the bones of the skull, hyoid, vertebral column, and rib cage.
2. Identify the regions of the vertebral column.
3. Explain the function of the sinuses and intervertebral disks in relation to the axial skeleton.

The 206 bones of the skeleton are classified according to whether they occur in the axial skeleton or the appendicular skeleton (Fig. 12.2). The **axial skeleton** lies in the midline of the body and consists of the skull, hyoid bone, vertebral column, and the rib cage.

The Skull

The **skull** is formed by the cranium (braincase) and the facial bones. However, some cranial bones contribute to the structure of the face.

The Cranium

The cranium protects the brain. In adults, it is composed of eight bones fitted tightly together. In newborns, certain cranial bones are

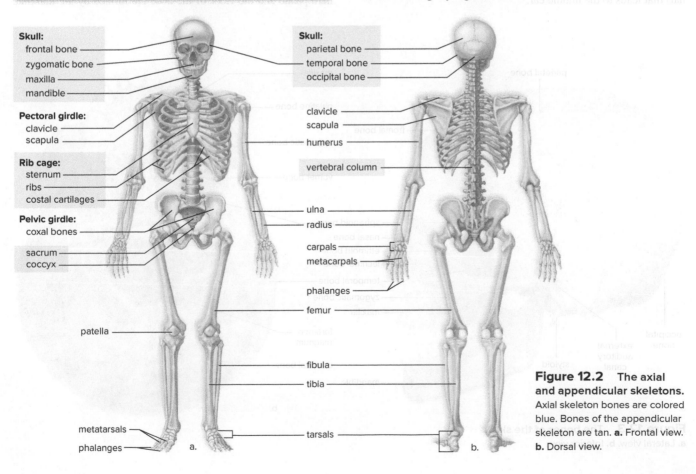

Figure 12.2   The axial and appendicular skeletons. Axial skeleton bones are colored blue. Bones of the appendicular skeleton are tan. **a.** Frontal view. **b.** Dorsal view.

Skull:
frontal bone
zygomatic bone
maxilla
mandible

Pectoral girdle:
clavicle
scapula

Rib cage:
sternum
ribs
costal cartilages

Pelvic girdle:
coxal bones

sacrum
coccyx

patella

metatarsals
phalanges

a.

Skull:
parietal bone
temporal bone
occipital bone

clavicle
scapula
humerus

vertebral column

ulna
radius

carpals
metacarpals

phalanges

femur

fibula
tibia

tarsals

b.

242   **Unit 3** Movement and Support in Humans

not completely formed. Instead, these bones are joined by membranous regions called **fontanels.** The fontanels usually close by the age of 16 months by the process of intramembranous ossification (see Section 12.5).

The major bones of the cranium have the same names as the lobes of the brain: frontal, parietal, occipital, and temporal. On the top of the cranium (Fig. 12.3a), the *frontal bone* forms the forehead, the *parietal bones* extend to the sides, and the *occipital bone* curves to form the base of the skull. Here there is a large opening, the **foramen magnum** (Fig. 12.3b), through which the spinal cord passes and becomes the brain stem. Below the much larger parietal bones, each *temporal bone* has an opening (external auditory canal) that leads to the middle ear.

The *sphenoid bone,* shaped like a bat with outstretched wings, extends across the floor of the cranium from one side to the other. The sphenoid is the keystone of the cranial bones, because all the other bones articulate with it. The sphenoid completes the sides of the skull and contributes to forming the orbits (eye sockets). The *ethmoid bone,* which lies in front of the sphenoid, also helps form the orbits and the nasal septum. The orbits are completed by various facial bones. The eye sockets are called orbits because we can rotate our eyes.

Some of the bones of the cranium contain the **sinuses,** air spaces lined by mucous membrane. The sinuses reduce the weight of the skull and give a resonant sound to the voice. Sinuses are named according to the bones in which they are located. The major sinuses are the frontal, sphenoid, ethmoid, and maxillary. A smaller set of sinuses, called the mastoid sinuses, drain into the middle ear. *Mastoiditis,* a condition that can lead to deafness, is an inflammation of these sinuses.

The Facial Bones

The most prominent of the facial bones are the mandible, the maxillae (sing., maxilla), the zygomatic bones, and the nasal bones.

The mandible, or lower jaw, is the only movable portion of the skull, and it forms the chin (Figs. 12.3 and 12.4). The maxillae form the upper jaw and a portion of the eye socket. Further, the hard palate and the floor of the nose are formed by the maxillae

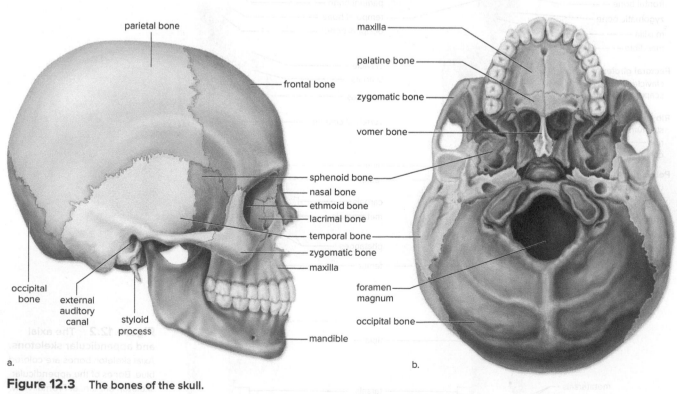

Figure 12.3 **The bones of the skull.**
a. Lateral view. **b.** Inferior view.

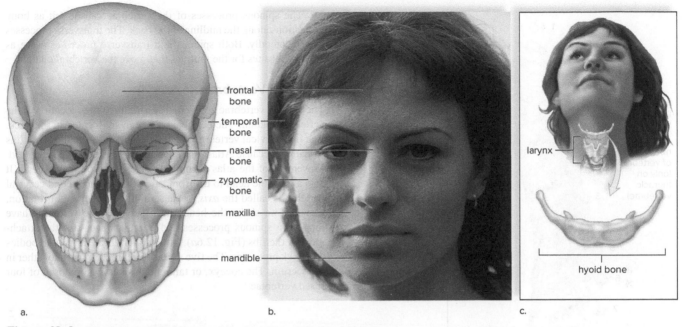

Figure 12.4   The bones of the face and the location of the hyoid bone.
a. The frontal bone forms the forehead and eyebrow ridges; the zygomatic bones form the cheekbones; and the maxillae have numerous functions. They assist in the formation of the eye sockets and the nasal cavity. They form the upper jaw and contain sockets for the upper teeth. The mandible is the lower jaw with sockets for the lower teeth. The mandible has a projection we call the chin. **b.** The maxillae, frontal, and nasal bones help form the external nose. **c.** The hyoid bone is located as shown.
(b) © Image100/Corbis RF

(anterior) joined to the palatine bones (posterior). Tooth sockets are located on the mandible and on the maxillae. The grinding action of the mandible and maxillae allows us to chew our food.

The lips and cheeks have a core of skeletal muscle. The *zygomatic bones* are the cheekbone prominences, and the *nasal bones* form the bridge of the nose. Other bones (e.g., ethmoid and vomer) are a part of the nasal septum, which divides the interior of the nose into two nasal cavities. The lacrimal bone (see Fig. 12.3*a*) contains the opening for the nasolacrimal canal, which drains tears from the eyes to the nose.

Certain cranial bones contribute to the face. The temporal bone and the wings of the sphenoid bone account for the flattened areas we call the temples. The frontal bone forms the forehead and has supraorbital ridges, where the eyebrows are located. Glasses sit where the frontal bone joins the nasal bones.

The exterior portions of ears are formed only by cartilage and not by bone. The nose is a mixture of bones, cartilages, and connective tissues. The cartilages complete the tip of the nose, and fibrous connective tissue forms the flared sides of the nose.

The Hyoid Bone

The *hyoid bone* is not part of the skull but is mentioned here because it is a part of the axial skeleton. It is the only bone in the body that does not articulate with another bone (Fig. 12.4*c*). It is attached to the temporal bones by muscles and ligaments and to the larynx by a membrane. The larynx is the voice box at the top of the

trachea in the neck region. The hyoid bone anchors the tongue and serves as the site for the attachment of muscles associated with swallowing. Due to its position, the hyoid bone does not fracture easily. In cases of suspicious death, however, a fractured hyoid is a strong indication of manual strangulation.

The Vertebral Column

The **vertebral column** consists of 33 vertebrae (Fig. 12.5). Normally the vertebral column has four curvatures that provide more resilience and strength for an upright posture than a straight column could provide. *Scoliosis* is an abnormal lateral (sideways) curvature of the spine. There are two other well-known abnormal curvatures. *Kyphosis* is an abnormal posterior curvature that often results in a "hunchback." An abnormal anterior curvature results in *lordosis,* or "swayback."

As the individual vertebrae are layered on top of one another, they form the vertebral column. The vertebral canal is in the center of the column, and the spinal cord passes through this canal. The intervertebral foramina (sing., foramen, "a hole or opening") are found on each side of the column. Spinal nerves branch from the spinal cord and travel through the intervertebral foramina to locations throughout the body. Spinal nerves control skeletal muscle contraction, among other functions. If a vertebra is compressed, or slips out of position, the spinal cord and/or spinal nerves might be injured. The result can be paralysis or even death.

The spinous processes of the vertebrae can be felt as bony projections along the midline of the back. The transverse processes extend laterally. Both spinous and transverse processes serve as attachment sites for the muscles that move the vertebral column.

Types of Vertebrae

The various vertebrae are named according to their location in the vertebral column. The cervical vertebrae are located in the neck. The first cervical vertebra, called the *atlas,* holds up the head. It is so named because Atlas, of Greek mythology, held up the world. Movement of the atlas permits the "yes" motion of the head. It also allows the head to tilt from side to side. The second cervical vertebra is called the *axis,* because it allows a degree of rotation, as when we shake the head "no." The thoracic vertebrae have long, thin spinous processes and articular facets for the attachment of the ribs (Fig. 12.6a). Lumbar vertebrae have large bodies and thick processes. The five sacral vertebrae are fused together in the sacrum. The coccyx, or tailbone, is usually composed of four fused vertebrae.

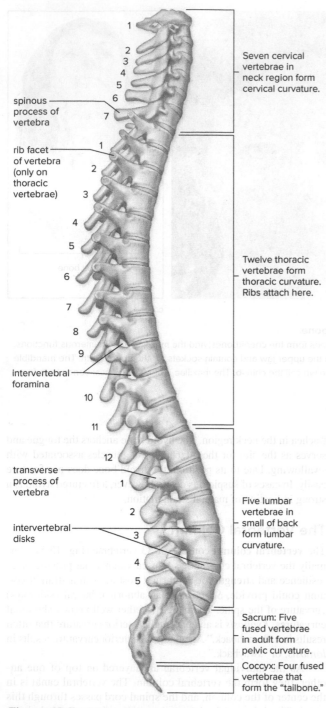

Figure 12.5   The vertebral column.
The vertebral column is made up of 33 vertebrae separated by intervertebral disks. The intervertebral disks make the column flexible. The vertebrae are named for their location in the vertebral column. For example, the thoracic vertebrae are located in the thorax. Humans have a coccyx, which is also called a tailbone.

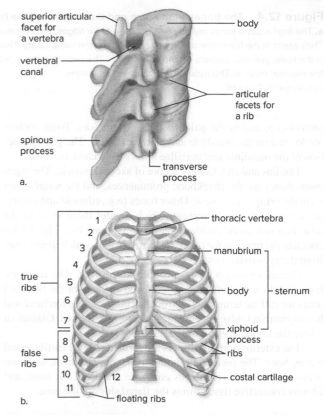

Figure 12.6   The thoracic vertebrae, ribs, and sternum.
a. The thoracic vertebrae articulate with one another and with the ribs at articular facets. A thoracic vertebra has two facets for articulation with a rib; one is on the body, and the other is on the transverse process. **b.** The rib cage consists of the 12 thoracic vertebrae, the 12 pairs of ribs, the costal cartilages, and the sternum. The rib cage protects the lungs and the heart.

Intervertebral Disks

Between the vertebrae are **intervertebral disks** composed of fibrocartilage that act as padding. The disks prevent the vertebrae from grinding against one another. They also absorb shock caused by movements such as running, jumping, and even walking. The presence of the disks allows the vertebrae to move as we bend forward, backward, and from side to side. Unfortunately, these disks become weakened with age and can herniate and rupture. Pain results if a disk presses against the spinal cord and/or spinal nerves. If that occurs, surgical removal of the disk may relieve the pain.

The Rib Cage

The rib cage, also called the thoracic cage, is composed of the thoracic vertebrae, the ribs and their associated cartilages, and the sternum (Fig. 12.6b). The rib cage is part of the axial skeleton.

The rib cage demonstrates how the skeleton is protective but also flexible. The rib cage protects the heart and lungs, yet it swings outward and upward upon inspiration and then downward and inward upon expiration.

The Ribs

A rib is a flattened bone that originates at the thoracic vertebrae and proceeds toward the anterior thoracic wall. There are 12 pairs of ribs. All 12 pairs connect directly to the thoracic vertebrae in the back. A rib articulates with the body and transverse process of its corresponding thoracic vertebra. Each rib curves outward and then forward and downward.

The upper seven pairs of ribs (ribs 1 through 7; Fig. 12.6b) connect directly to the sternum by means of a long strip of hyaline cartilage called costal cartilage. These are called "true ribs." Ribs 8 through 12 are called "false ribs" because their costal cartilage at the end of the ribs does not connect directly to the sternum. Ribs 11 and 12 are also called "floating ribs," because they have no connection with the sternum.

The Sternum

The *sternum* lies in the midline of the body. Along with the ribs, it helps protect the heart and lungs. The sternum, or breastbone, is a flat bone that has the shape of a knife.

The sternum is composed of three bones. These bones are the manubrium (the handle), the body (the blade), and the xiphoid process (the point of the blade). The manubrium articulates with the clavicles of the appendicular skeleton. Costal cartilages from the first pair of ribs also join to the manubrium. The manubrium joins with the body of the sternum at an angle. This is an important anatomical landmark, because it occurs at the level of the second rib and therefore allows the ribs to be counted. Counting the ribs is sometimes done to determine where the apex of the heart is located—usually between the fifth and sixth ribs.

The xiphoid process is the third part of the sternum. The variably shaped xiphoid process serves as an attachment site for the diaphragm, which separates the thoracic cavity from the abdominal cavity.

CHECK YOUR PROGRESS 12.2

1. List the bones of the axial skeleton.
2. Identify the bones of the cranium and face, and describe how they contribute to facial features.
3. Describe the various types of vertebrae, and state their function.

CONNECTING THE CONCEPTS

For more information on the interaction of the axial skeleton with other organ systems in the body, refer to the following discussions:

Section 10.4 examines how the rib cage is involved in respiration.
Section 14.2 details how the vertebral column and skull protect components of the central nervous system.

12.3 Bones of the Appendicular Skeleton

LEARNING OUTCOMES

Upon completion of this section, you should be able to

1. Identify the bones of the pelvic and pectoral girdles.
2. Identify the bones of the upper and lower limbs.

The **appendicular skeleton** consists of the bones within the pectoral and pelvic girdles and their attached limbs. A pectoral (shoulder) girdle and upper limb are specialized for flexibility. The pelvic (hip) girdle and lower limbs are specialized for strength.

SCIENCE IN YOUR LIFE

Why are human toes shorter than the fingers?

Though some scientists believe that toes are an example of a vestigial organ, there is growing evidence that short toes played an important role in our evolutionary history. According to some scientists, the shortness of our toes contributes to our ability to run long distances, a rare trait in the animal kingdom. Studies have shown that long toes require more energy to start and stop running. In most animals with toes, the fingers and toes are approximately the same length. As toe length shortens, the ability of the animal to run long distances increases. The shortness of our toes may have contributed to the success of our species in hunting large prey on the open plains of Africa.

The Pectoral Girdle and Upper Limb

The body has left and right **pectoral girdles.** Each consists of a scapula (shoulder blade) and a clavicle (collarbone) (Fig. 12.7). The *clavicle* extends across the top of the thorax. It articulates with (joins with) the sternum and the acromion process of the *scapula,*

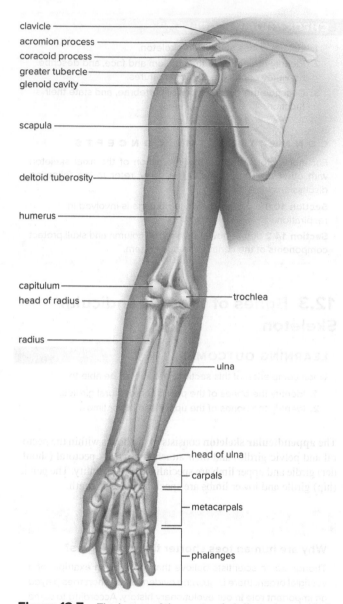

clavicle
acromion process
coracoid process
greater tubercle
glenoid cavity

scapula

deltoid tuberosity

humerus

capitulum
head of radius
trochlea

radius

ulna

head of ulna

carpals

metacarpals

phalanges

Figure 12.7 **The bones of the pectoral girdle and upper limb.**
The pectoral girdle consists of the clavicle (collarbone) and the scapula
(shoulder blade). The humerus is the single bone of the arm. The forearm
is formed by the radius and ulna. A hand contains carpals, metacarpals,
and phalanges.

a visible bone in the back. The muscles of the arm and chest attach
to the coracoid process of the scapula. The *glenoid cavity* of the
scapula articulates with and is much smaller than the head of the
humerus. This allows the arm to move in almost any direction but
reduces stability. This is the joint most apt to dislocate. Ligaments
and tendons stabilize this joint. Tendons that extend to the humerus
from four small muscles originating on the scapula form the *rotator
cuff.* Vigorous circular movements of the arm can lead to rotator
cuff injuries.

Pectoral girdle
- Scapula and clavicle

Upper limb
- Arm: humerus
- Forearm: radius and ulna
- Hand: carpals, metacarpals, and phalanges

The components of a pectoral girdle freely follow the movements
of the upper limb, which consists of the humerus in the arm and the
radius and ulna in the forearm. The *humerus,* the single long bone
in the arm, has a smoothly rounded head that fits into the glenoid
cavity of the scapula, as mentioned. The shaft of the humerus has
a tuberosity (protuberance) where the deltoid, a shoulder muscle,
attaches. You can determine, even after death, whether the person
did a lot of heavy lifting during his or her lifetime by the size of the
deltoid tuberosity.

The far end of the humerus has two protuberances, called
the capitulum and the trochlea, which articulate respectively with
the *radius* and the *ulna* at the elbow. The bump at the back of the
elbow is the olecranon process of the ulna.

When the upper limb is held so that the palm is turned forward, the radius and ulna are about parallel to each other. When the
upper limb is turned so that the palm is turned backward, the radius
crosses in front of the ulna, a feature that contributes to the easy
twisting motion of the forearm.

The hand has many bones, and this increases its flexibility.
The wrist has eight *carpal* bones, which look like small pebbles.
From these, five *metacarpal* bones fan out to form a framework for
the palm. The metacarpal bone that leads to the thumb is opposable to the other digits. An opposable thumb can touch each finger
separately or cross the palm to grasp an object. (*Digits* refers to
either fingers or toes.) The knuckles are the enlarged distal ends of
the metacarpals. Beyond the metacarpals are the *phalanges,* the
bones of the fingers and the thumb. The phalanges of the hand are
long, slender, and lightweight.

The Pelvic Girdle and Lower Limb

Figure 12.8 shows how the lower limb is attached to the pelvic
girdle. The **pelvic girdle** (hip girdle) consists of two heavy, large
coxal bones (hip bones). The **pelvis** is a basin composed of the
pelvic girdle, sacrum, and coccyx. The pelvis bears the weight of
the body, protects the organs within the pelvic cavity, and serves as
the place of attachment for the legs.

Pelvic girdle
- Coxal bones

Lower limb
- Thigh: femur
- Leg: tibia and fibula
- Foot: tarsals, metatarsals, and phalanges

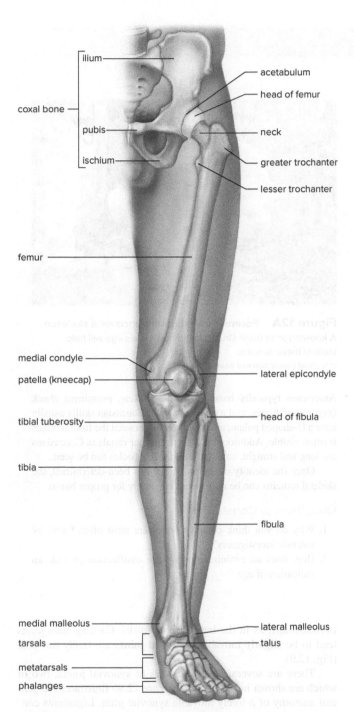

ilium

acetabulum

head of femur

coxal bone

pubis

neck

ischium

greater trochanter

lesser trochanter

femur

medial condyle

patella (kneecap)

lateral epicondyle

tibial tuberosity

head of fibula

tibia

fibula

medial malleolus

lateral malleolus

tarsals

talus

metatarsals

phalanges

Figure 12.8   The coxal bones and bones of the pelvis and lower limb.
The ilium, ischium, and pubis join at the acetabulum (hip socket) to form a coxal bone. The pelvis is completed by the addition of the sacrum and coccyx. The femur (thighbone) and tibia and fibula (shinbones) form the leg. Tarsals, metatarsals, and phalanges construct the foot.

Each *coxal bone* has three parts: the ilium, the ischium, and the pubis, which are fused in the adult (Fig. 12.8). The hip socket, called the acetabulum, occurs where these three bones meet. The ilium is the largest part of the coxal bones, and our hips form where it flares out. We sit on the ischium, which has a posterior spine, called the ischial spine, for muscle attachment. The *pubis,* from which the term *pubic hair* is derived, is the anterior part of a coxal bone. The two pubic bones are joined by a fibrocartilaginous joint called the pubic symphysis.

The male pelvis is different than the female pelvis. In the female, the iliac bones are more flared and the pelvic cavity is more shallow, but the outlet is wider. These adaptations facilitate the birthing process during vaginal delivery.

The *femur* (thighbone) is the longest and strongest bone in the body. The head of the femur articulates with the coxal bones at the acetabulum, and the short neck better positions the legs for walking. The femur has two large processes, the greater and lesser trochanters, which are places of attachment for thigh muscles, buttock muscles, and hip flexors. At its distal end, the femur has medial and lateral condyles that articulate with the *tibia* of the leg. This is the region of the knee and the *patella,* or kneecap. The patella is held in place by the quadriceps tendon, which continues as a ligament that attaches to the tibial tuberosity. At the distal end, the medial malleolus of the tibia causes the inner bulge of the ankle. The *fibula* is the more slender bone in the leg. The fibula has a head that articulates with the tibia and a distal lateral malleolus that forms the outer bulge of the ankle.

Each foot has an ankle, an instep, and five toes. The many bones of the foot give it considerable flexibility, especially on rough surfaces. The ankle contains seven *tarsal* bones, one of which (the talus) can move freely where it joins the tibia and fibula. The calcaneus, or heel bone, is also considered part of the ankle. The talus and calcaneus support the weight of the body.

The instep has five elongated *metatarsal* bones. The distal ends of the metatarsals form the ball of the foot. If the ligaments that bind the metatarsals together become weakened, flat feet are apt to result. The bones of the toes are called *phalanges,* just like those of the fingers. In the foot, the phalanges are stout and extremely sturdy.

CHECK YOUR PROGRESS 12.3

1. List the bones of the pectoral girdle and the upper limb.
2. List the bones of the pelvic girdle and the lower limb.
3. Describe how you can tell the difference in gender from looking at the bones of the pelvic girdle.

CONNECTING THE CONCEPTS

For more information on the limbs of the body, refer to the following discussions:

Figure 5.12 diagrams the major blood vessels of the arms and legs.

Figure 13.5 illustrates the major muscles of the arms and legs.

Section 14.2 details the areas of the brain that are responsible for the movement of the arms and legs.

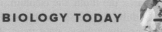 

Identifying Skeletal Remains

Regardless of how, when, and where human bones are found unexpectedly, many questions must be answered. How old was this person at the time of death? Are these the bones of a male or female? What was the ethnicity? Are there any signs that this person was murdered?

Clues about the identity and history of the deceased person are available throughout the skeleton (Fig. 12A). Age is approximated by *dentition,* or the structure of the teeth in the upper jaw (maxilla) and lower jaw (mandible). For example, infants between 0 and 4 months of age will have no teeth present; children approximately 6 to 10 years of age will have missing deciduous, or "baby," teeth; young adults acquire their last molars, or "wisdom teeth," around age 20. The age of older adults can be approximated by the number and location of missing or broken teeth. Studying areas of bone ossification also gives clues to the age of the deceased at the time of death. In older adults, signs of joint breakdown provide additional information about age. Hyaline cartilage becomes worn, yellowed, and brittle with age, and the hyaline cartilages covering bone ends wear down over time. The amount of yellowed, brittle, or missing cartilage helps scientists guess the person's age.

If skeletal remains include the individual's pelvic bones, these provide the best method for determining an adult's gender. The pelvis is shallower and wider in the female than in the male. The long bones, particularly the humerus and femur, give information about gender as well. Long bones are thicker and denser in males, and points of muscle attachment are bigger and more prominent. The skull of a male has a square chin and more prominent ridges above the eye sockets, or orbits.

Determining ethnic origin of skeletal remains can be difficult, because so many people have a mixed racial heritage. Forensic anatomists rely on observed racial characteristics of the skull. In general, individuals of African or African American descent have a greater distance between the eyes, eye sockets that are roughly rectangular, and a jaw that is large and prominent. Skulls of Native

Figure 12A   Forensic investigators uncover a skeleton.
A knowledge of bone structure and how bones age will help identify these remains.
© Michael Donne/Science Source

Americans typically have round eye sockets, prominent cheek (zygomatic) bones, and a rounded palate. Caucasian skulls usually have a U-shaped palate, and a suture line between the frontal bones is often visible. Additionally, the external ear canals in Caucasians are long and straight, so that the auditory ossicles can be seen.

Once the identity of the individual has been determined, the skeletal remains can be returned to the family for proper burial.

Questions to Consider

1. Why do you think compact bones are most often found by forensic investigators?
2. How does an examination of bone ossification provide an indication of age?

12.4 Articulations

LEARNING OUTCOMES

Upon completion of this section, you should be able to

1. List the three types of joints that connect bones.
2. Describe the structure and operation of a synovial joint.
3. Summarize the types of movement that are made possible by a synovial joint.

Bones are joined at the joints, classified as fibrous, cartilaginous, or synovial. Many fibrous joints, such as the **sutures** between the cranial bones, are immovable. Cartilaginous joints may be connected by hyaline cartilage, as in the costal cartilages that join the ribs to the sternum. Other cartilaginous joints are formed by fibrocartilage, as in the intervertebral disks. Cartilaginous joints tend to be slightly movable. **Synovial joints** are freely movable (Fig. 12.9).

There are several general classes of synovial joints, two of which are shown in Figure 12.9. Figure 12.9*b* illustrates the general anatomy of a freely movable synovial joint. Ligaments connect bone to bone and support or strengthen the joint. A fibrous joint capsule formed by ligaments surrounds the bones at the joint. This capsule is not shown in Figure 12.9 so that the inner structure of the joint may be revealed. The joint capsule is lined with synovial membrane, which secretes a small amount of synovial fluid to lubricate the joint. Fluid-filled sacs called bursae (sing., bursa) ease friction between bare areas of bone and overlapping muscles or between skin and tendons. The full joint contains menisci (sing., meniscus), which are C-shaped pieces of

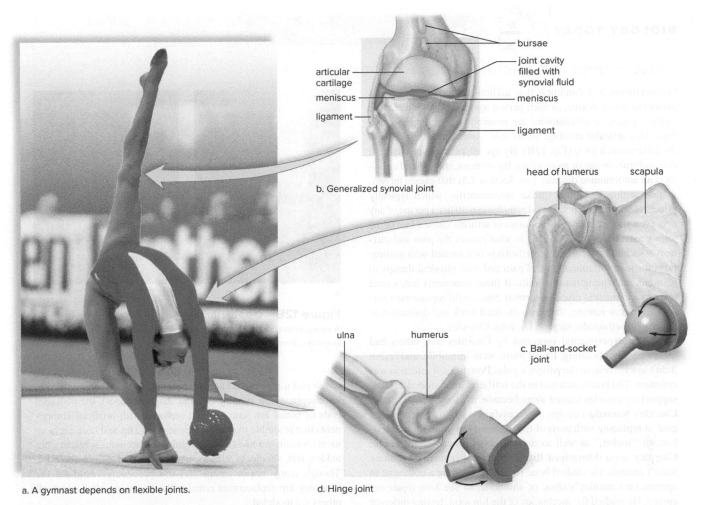

Figure 12.9   The structure of a synovial joint.
a. Synovial joints are movable and therefore flexible. **b.** The bones of joints are joined by ligaments that form a capsule. The capsule is lined with synovial membrane, which gives off synovial fluid as a lubricant. Bursae are fluid-filled sacs that reduce friction. Menisci (sing., meniscus), formed of cartilage, stabilize a joint, and articular cartilage caps the bones. **c.** Ball-and-socket joints form the hip and shoulder. **d.** Hinge joints construct the knee and elbow.
(a) © Gerard Vandystadt/Science Source

fibrocartilage cartilage between the bones. These give added stability and act as shock absorbers.

The ball-and-socket joints at the hips and shoulders allow movement in all planes, even rotational movement. The elbow and knee joints are synovial joints called hinge joints. Like a hinged door, they largely permit movement in one direction only. The Science feature "Osteoarthritis and Joint Replacement Surgery" examines the history of how joint replacement therapy was developed.

Movements Permitted by Synovial Joints

Intact skeletal muscles are attached to bones by tendons that span joints. When a muscle contracts, one bone moves in relation to another bone. The more common types of movements are described in Figure 12.10.

CHECK YOUR PROGRESS 12.4

1. List the three major types of joints.
2. Describe the basic movements of cartilaginous and fibrous joints, and give an example of each in the body.
3. Describe all the different movements of synovial joints, and give an example of each in the body.

CONNECTING THE CONCEPTS

For more information on ligaments and tendons, refer to the following discussion:

Section 4.2 describes the connective tissue found in the tendons and ligaments.

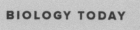 
BIOLOGY TODAY   **Science**

Osteoarthritis and Joint Replacement Surgery

Osteoarthritis is a condition that afflicts nearly everyone, to a greater or lesser degree, as each person ages. The bones that unite to form joints, or articulations, are covered with a slippery cartilage. This articular cartilage wears down over time, as friction in the joint wears it away (Fig. 12B). By age 80, people typically have osteoarthritis in one or more joints. By contrast, rheumatoid arthritis is an autoimmune disorder (see Section 7.5) that causes inflammation within the joint. Unlike osteoarthritis, which typically affects older people, rheumatoid arthritis can afflict a person of any age, even young children. Both forms of arthritis cause a loss of the joint's natural smoothness. This is what causes the pain and stiffness associated with arthritis. Arthritis is first treated with medications for joint inflammation and pain and with physical therapy to maintain and strengthen the joint. If these treatments fail, a total joint replacement is often performed. Successful replacement surgeries are now routine, thanks to the hard work and dedication of the British orthopedic surgeon Dr. John Charnley.

Early experimental surgeries by Charnley and others had been very disappointing. Fused joints were immobile, and fusion didn't always relieve the patient's pain. Postsurgical infection was common. The bones attached to the artificial joint eroded, and the supporting muscles wasted away because the joint wasn't useful. Charnley wanted to design a successful prosthetic hip, with the goal of replacing both parts of the diseased hip joint: the acetabulum, or "socket," as well as the ball-shaped head of the femur. Charnley soon determined that surgical experimentation alone wasn't enough. He studied bone repair, persuading a colleague to operate on Charnley's tibia, or shinbone, to see how repair occurred. He studied the mechanics of the hip joint, testing different types of synthetic materials. He achieved his first success using a hip socket lined with Teflon but soon discovered that the surrounding tissues became inflamed. After multiple attempts, his perfected hip consisted of a socket of durable polyethylene. Polyethylene is still used today as the joint's plastic component. The head of his prosthetic femur was a small, highly polished metal ball. Stainless steel, cobalt, and titanium, as well as chrome alloys, form the metal component today. Various techniques for cementing the polyethylene socket onto the pelvic bone had failed when bone pulled away from the cemented surface and refused to grow. Charnley's surgery used dental cement, slathered onto the bone surfaces. When the plastic components were attached, cement was squeezed into every pore of the bone, allowing the bone to regenerate and grow around the plastic. Finally, Charnley devised a specialized surgical tent and instrument tray to minimize infection.

Charnley's ideas were innovative and unorthodox, and he was reassigned to a former tuberculosis hospital, which he converted into a center for innovation in orthopedic surgery. His colleagues

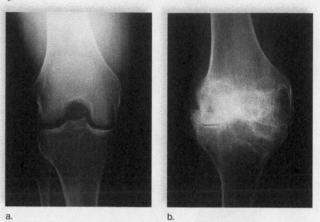

a.   b.

Figure 12B   Osteoarthritis.
A comparison of a normal knee (**a**) and a knee with osteoarthritis (**b**).
(a and b) © Scott Camazine/Science Source

developed a prosthetic knee joint similar to the Charnley hip. In knee replacement surgery (see the chapter opener), the damaged ends of bones are removed and replaced with artificial components that resemble the original bone ends. Hip and knee replacements remain the most common joint replacement surgeries, but ankles, feet, shoulders, elbows, and fingers can also be replaced. Though many improvements on the procedure continue, the Charnley hip replacement remains the technique after which all others are modeled.

When a joint replacement is complete, the patient's hard work is vital to ensure the success of the procedure. Exercise and activity are critical to the recovery process. After surgery, the patient is encouraged to use the new joint as soon as possible. The extent of improvement and range of motion of the joint depend on its stiffness before the surgery, as well as the amount of patient effort during therapy following surgery. A complete recovery varies in time from patient to patient but typically takes several months. Older patients can expect their replacements to last about 10 years. However, younger patients may need a second replacement if they wear out their first prosthesis. Still, individuals who have joint replacement surgery can expect an improved quality of life and a bright future with greater independence and healthier, pain-free activity.

Questions to Consider

1. Compare each component of Charnley's artificial joint with that of a real synovial joint.
2. What specifically in a joint does rheumatoid arthritis target?

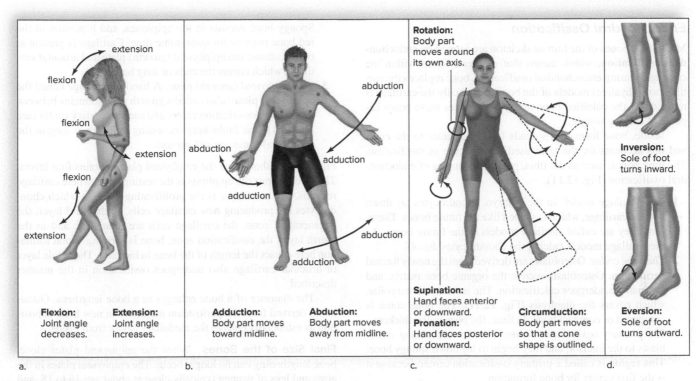

Figure 12.10 Synovial joints allow for a variety of movement.
a. Flexion and extension. **b.** Adduction and abduction. **c.** Rotation and circumduction. **d.** Inversion and eversion. Red dots indicate pivot points.

12.5 Bone Growth and Homeostasis

LEARNING OUTCOMES

Upon completion of this section, you should be able to

1. Summarize the process of ossification and list the types of cells involved.
2. Describe the process of bone remodeling.
3. Explain the steps in the repair of bone.

The importance of the skeleton to the human form is evident by its early appearance during development. The skeleton starts forming at about 6 weeks, when the embryo is only about 12 mm (0.5 in.) long. Most bones grow in length and width through adolescence, but some continue enlarging until about age 25. In a sense, bones can grow throughout a lifetime, because they are able to respond to stress by changing size, shape, and strength. This process is called remodeling. If a bone fractures, it can heal by bone repair.

Bones are living tissues, as shown by their ability to grow, remodel, and undergo repair. Several different types of cells are involved in bone growth, remodeling, and repair:

Osteoblasts are bone-forming cells. They secrete the organic matrix of bone and promote the deposition of calcium salts into the matrix.

Osteocytes are mature bone cells derived from osteoblasts. They maintain the structure of bone.

Osteoclasts are bone-absorbing cells. They break down bone and assist in returning calcium and phosphate to the blood.

Throughout life, osteoclasts are removing the matrix of bone and osteoblasts are building it up. When osteoblasts are surrounded by calcified matrix, they become the osteocytes within lacunae.

Bone Development and Growth

The term **ossification** refers to the formation of bone. The bones of the skeleton form during embryonic development in two distinctive ways: intramembranous ossification and endochondral ossification.

Intramembranous Ossification

Flat bones, such as the bones of the skull, are examples of intramembranous bones. In **intramembranous ossification,** bones develop between sheets of fibrous connective tissue. Here, cells derived from connective tissue cells become osteoblasts located in ossification centers. The osteoblasts secrete the organic matrix of bone. This matrix consists of mucopolysaccharides and collagen fibrils. Calcification occurs when calcium salts are added to the organic matrix. The osteoblasts promote calcification, or ossification, of the matrix. Ossification results in the formation of soft sheets, or trabeculae, of spongy bone. Spongy bone remains inside a flat bone. The spongy bone of flat bones, such as those of the skull and clavicles (collarbones), contains red bone marrow.

A periosteum forms outside the spongy bone. Osteoblasts derived from the periosteum carry out further ossification. Trabeculae form and fuse to become compact bone. The compact bone forms a bone collar that surrounds the spongy bone on the inside.

Endochondral Ossification

Most of the bones of the human skeleton are formed by **endochondral ossification,** which means that the bone forms within the cartilage. During endochondral ossification, bone replaces the cartilaginous (hyaline) models of the bones. Gradually the cartilage is replaced by the calcified bone matrix that makes these bones capable of bearing weight.

Inside, bone formation spreads from the center to the ends, and this accounts for the term used for this type of ossification. The long bones, such as the tibia, provide examples of endochondral ossification (Fig. 12.11).

1. *The cartilage model.* In the embryo, chondrocytes lay down hyaline cartilage, which is shaped like the future bones. Therefore, they are called cartilage models of the future bones. As the cartilage models calcify, the chondrocytes die off.
2. *The bone collar.* Osteoblasts are derived from the newly formed periosteum. Osteoblasts secrete the organic bone matrix, and the matrix undergoes calcification. The result is a bone collar, which covers the diaphysis (Fig. 12.11). The bone collar is composed of compact bone. In time, the bone collar thickens.
3. *The primary ossification center.* Blood vessels bring osteoblasts to the interior, and they begin to lay down spongy bone. This region is called a primary ossification center, because it is the first center for bone formation.
4. *The medullary cavity and secondary ossification sites.* The spongy bone of the diaphysis is absorbed by osteoclasts, and the cavity created becomes the medullary cavity. Shortly after birth, secondary ossification centers form in the epiphyses.

Spongy bone persists in the epiphyses, and it persists in the red bone marrow for quite some time. Cartilage is present at two locations: the epiphyseal (growth) plate and articular cartilage, which covers the ends of long bones.

5. *The epiphyseal (growth) plate.* A band of cartilage called the **epiphyseal plate** (also called a growth plate) remains between the primary ossification center and each secondary center (see Fig. 12.1). The limbs keep increasing in length as long as the epiphyseal plates are still present.

Figure 12.12 shows that the epiphyseal plate contains four layers. The layer nearest the epiphysis is the resting zone, where cartilage remains. The next layer is the proliferating zone, in which chondrocytes are producing new cartilage cells. In the third layer, the degenerating zone, the cartilage cells are dying off; and in the fourth layer, the ossification zone, bone is forming. Bone formation here causes the length of the bone to increase. The inside layer of articular cartilage also undergoes ossification in the manner described.

The diameter of a bone enlarges as a bone lengthens. Osteoblasts derived from the periosteum are active in new bone deposition as osteoclasts enlarge the medullary cavity from inside.

Final Size of the Bones   When the epiphyseal plates close, bone lengthening can no longer occur. The epiphyseal plates in the arms and legs of women typically close at about age 16 to 18, and they do not close in men until about age 20. Portions of other types of bones may continue to grow until age 25. **Hormones,** chemical messengers that are produced by one part of the body and act on a different part of the body, are secreted by the endocrine glands and

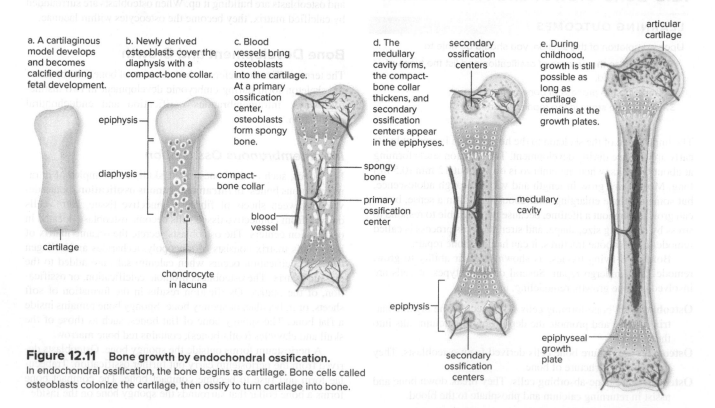

a. A cartilaginous model develops and becomes calcified during fetal development.

b. Newly derived osteoblasts cover the diaphysis with a compact-bone collar.

c. Blood vessels bring osteoblasts into the cartilage. At a primary ossification center, osteoblasts form spongy bone.

d. The medullary cavity forms, the compact-bone collar thickens, and secondary ossification centers appear in the epiphyses.

e. During childhood, growth is still possible as long as cartilage remains at the growth plates.

epiphysis

diaphysis

cartilage

chondrocyte in lacuna

compact-bone collar

blood vessel

spongy bone

primary ossification center

secondary ossification centers

medullary cavity

epiphysis

secondary ossification centers

epiphyseal growth plate

articular cartilage

Figure 12.11   Bone growth by endochondral ossification.
In endochondral ossification, the bone begins as cartilage. Bone cells called osteoblasts colonize the cartilage, then ossify to turn cartilage into bone.

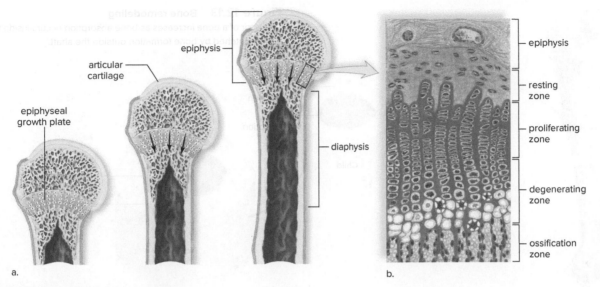

Figure 12.12   Increasing bone length.
a. Length of a bone increases when cartilage is replaced by bone at the growth plate. Arrows indicate the direction of ossification. **b.** Chondrocytes produce new cartilage in the proliferating zone, and cartilage becomes bone in the ossification zone closest to the diaphysis.

distributed about the body by the bloodstream. Hormones control the activity of the epiphyseal plate, as is discussed next.

Hormones Affect Bone Growth

Several hormones play an important role in bone growth.

Vitamin D is formed in the skin when it is exposed to sunlight, but it can also be consumed in the diet. Milk, in particular, is often fortified with vitamin D. In the kidneys, vitamin D is converted to a hormone that acts on the intestinal tract. The chief function of vitamin D is intestinal absorption of calcium. In the absence of vitamin D, children can develop rickets, a condition marked by bone deformities, including bowed long bones.

Growth hormone (GH) directly stimulates growth of the epiphyseal plate, as well as bone growth in general. However, growth hormone is somewhat ineffective if the metabolic activity of cells is not promoted. Thyroid hormone, in particular, promotes the metabolic activity of cells. Too little growth hormone in childhood results in dwarfism. Too much growth hormone during childhood (prior to epiphyseal fusion) can produce excessive growth and even gigantism (see Fig. 16.8). Acromegaly results from excess GH in adults following epiphyseal fusion. This condition produces excessive growth of bones in the hands and face (see Fig. 16.9).

Adolescents usually experience a dramatic increase in height, called the growth spurt, due to an increased level of sex hormones. These hormones apparently stimulate osteoblast activity. Rapid growth causes epiphyseal plates to become "paved over" by the faster-growing bone tissue within 1 or 2 years of the onset of puberty.

Bone Remodeling and Calcium Homeostasis

Bone is constantly being broken down by osteoclasts and re-formed by osteoblasts in the adult. As much as 18% of bone is recycled each year. This process of bone renewal, often called **bone remodeling,** normally keeps bones strong (Fig. 12.13). In Paget disease, new bone is generated at a faster-than-normal rate. This rapid remodeling produces bone that's softer and weaker than normal bone and can cause bone pain, deformities, and fractures.

Bone recycling allows the body to regulate the amount of calcium in the blood. To illustrate that the blood calcium level is critical, recall that calcium is required for blood to clot (see Section 6.4). Also, if the blood calcium concentration is too high, neurons and muscle cells no longer function. If calcium falls too low, nerve and muscle cells become so excited that convulsions occur. Calcium ions are also necessary for the regulation of cellular metabolism by acting in cellular messenger systems. Thus, the skeleton acts as a reservoir for storage of this important mineral—if the blood calcium rises above normal, at least some of the excess is deposited in the bones. If the blood calcium dips too low, calcium is removed from the bones to bring it back up to the normal level.

Two hormones in particular are involved in regulating the blood calcium level. Parathyroid hormone (PTH) stimulates osteoclasts to dissolve the calcium matrix of bone. In addition, parathyroid hormone promotes calcium reabsorption in the small intestine and kidney, increasing blood calcium levels. Vitamin D is needed for the absorption of Ca^{2+} from the digestive tract, which is why vitamin D deficiency can result in weak bones. It is easy to get enough of this vitamin, because your skin produces it when exposed to sunlight, and the milk you buy at the grocery store is fortified with vitamin D.

Calcitonin is a hormone that acts opposite to PTH. The female sex hormone estrogen can actually increase the number of osteoblasts; the reduction of estrogen in older women is often given as reason for the development of weak bones, called osteoporosis.

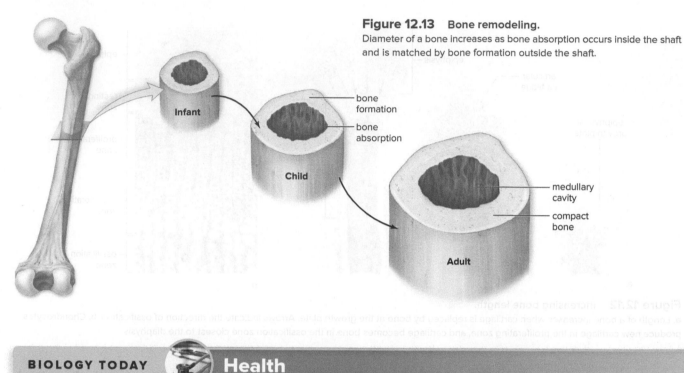

Figure 12.13   Bone remodeling.

Diameter of a bone increases as bone absorption occurs inside the shaft and is matched by bone formation outside the shaft.

You Can Avoid Osteoporosis

Osteoporosis is a condition in which the bones are weakened due to a decrease in the bone mass that makes up the skeleton. The skeletal mass continues to increase until ages 20 to 30. After that, there is an equal rate of formation and breakdown of bone mass until ages 40 to 50. Then, reabsorption begins to exceed formation, and the total bone mass slowly decreases (Fig. 12C).

Over time, men are apt to lose 25% and women 35% of their bone mass. But we have to consider that men—unless they have taken asthma medications that decrease bone formation—tend to have denser bones than women anyway. Whereas a man's testosterone (male sex hormone) level generally declines slowly after the age of 45, estrogen (female sex hormone) levels in women begin to decline significantly at about age 45. Sex hormones play an important role in maintaining bone strength, so this difference

means that women are more likely than men to suffer a higher incidence of fractures, involving especially the hip, vertebrae, long bones, and pelvis. Although osteoporosis may at times be the result of various disease processes, it is essentially a disease that occurs as we age.

How to Avoid Osteoporosis

Everyone can take measures to avoid having osteoporosis later in life. Adequate dietary calcium throughout life is an important

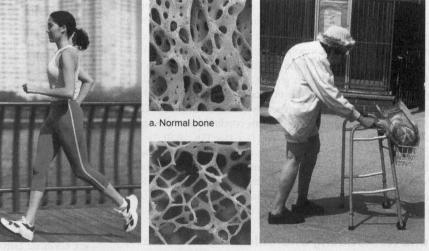

a. Normal bone

b. Osteoporosis

Figure 12C   Preventing osteoporosis.

Weight-bearing exercise, when we are young, can help prevent osteoporosis when we are older. **a.** Normal bone. **b.** Bone from a person with osteoporosis.

(left): © Corbis RF; (mid-top) © Susumu Nishinaga/ Science Source; (mid-bottom) © Ed Reschke/ Photolibrary/Getty Images; (right) © Bill Aaron/ PhotoEdit

Osteoporosis is discussed in the Health feature "You Can Avoid Osteoporosis." In the young adult, the activity of osteoclasts is matched by the activity of osteoblasts, and bone mass remains stable until about age 45 in women. After that age, bone mass starts to decrease.

Bone remodeling also accounts for why bones can respond to stress. If you engage in an activity that calls upon the use of a particular bone, the bone enlarges in diameter at the region most affected by the activity. During this process, osteoblasts in the periosteum form compact bone around the external bone surface and osteoclasts break down bone on the internal bone surface around the medullary cavity. Increasing the size of the medullary cavity prevents the bones from getting too heavy and thick. Today, exercises such as walking, jogging, and weight lifting are recommended. These exercises strengthen bone because they stimulate the work of osteoblasts instead of osteoclasts.

Bone Repair

Repair of a bone is required after it breaks or fractures. Fracture repair takes place over a span of several months in a series of four steps, shown in Figure 12.14:

1. *Hematoma.* After a fracture, blood escapes from ruptured blood vessels and forms a hematoma (mass of clotted blood) in the space between the broken bones. The hematoma forms within 6 to 8 hours.
2. *Fibrocartilaginous callus.* Tissue repair begins, and a fibro-cartilaginous callus fills the space between the ends of the broken bone for about 3 weeks.
3. *Bony callus.* Osteoblasts produce trabeculae of spongy bone and convert the fibrocartilage callus to a bony callus that joins the broken bones together. The bony callus lasts about 3 to 4 months.
4. *Remodeling.* Osteoblasts build new compact bone at the periphery. Osteoclasts absorb the spongy bone, creating a new medullary cavity.

In some ways, bone repair parallels the development of a bone except that the first step, hematoma, indicates that injury has occurred. Further, a fibrocartilaginous callus precedes the production of compact bone.

The naming of fractures tells you what type of break has occurred. A fracture is complete if the bone is broken clear through and incomplete if the bone is not separated into two parts. A

protection against osteoporosis. The National Osteoporosis Foundation (www.nof.org) recommends that adults under the age of 50 take in 1,000 mg of calcium per day. After the age of 50, the daily intake should exceed 1,200 mg per day.

A small daily amount of vitamin D is also necessary for the body to use calcium correctly. Exposure to sunlight is required to allow skin to synthesize a precursor to vitamin D. If you reside on or north of a "line" drawn from Boston to Milwaukee, to Minneapolis, to Boise, chances are you're not getting enough vitamin D during the winter months. Therefore, you should take advantage of the vitamin D present in fortified foods such as low-fat milk and cereal. If you are under age 50, you should be receiving 400–800 IU of vitamin D per day. After age 50, this amount should increase to 800–1,000 IU of vitamin D daily.

Very inactive people, such as those confined to bed, lose bone mass 25 times faster than people who are moderately active. On the other hand, moderate weight-bearing exercise, such as regular walking or jogging, is another good way to maintain bone strength (Fig. 12C).

Diagnosis and Treatment

Postmenopausal women with any of the following risk factors should have an evaluation of their bone density:

- White or Asian race
- Thin body type
- Family history of osteoporosis
- Early menopause (before age 45)
- Smoking
- A diet low in calcium or excessive alcohol consumption and caffeine intake
- Sedentary lifestyle

Bone density is measured by a method called dual-energy X-ray absorptiometry (DEXA). This test measures bone density based on the absorption of photons generated by an X-ray tube. Blood and urine tests are used to detect the biochemical markers of bone loss. Over the past several years, it has become easier for physicians to screen older women and at-risk men for osteoporosis.

If the bones are thin, it is worthwhile to take all possible measures to gain bone density, because even a slight increase can significantly reduce fracture risk. Although estrogen therapy does reduce the incidence of hip fractures, long-term estrogen therapy is rarely recommended for osteoporosis. Estrogen is known to increase the risk of breast cancer, heart disease, stroke, and blood clots. Other medications are available, however. Calcitonin, a thyroid hormone, has been shown to increase bone density and strength while decreasing the rate of bone fractures. Also, the bisphosphonates are a family of nonhormonal drugs used to prevent and treat osteoporosis. To achieve optimal results with calcitonin or one of the bisphosphonates, patients should also receive adequate amounts of dietary calcium and vitamin D.

Questions to Consider

1. How may long-term digestive system problems promote the chances of developing osteoporosis?
2. Why are individuals at risk for osteoporosis encouraged to increase their exercise regimes, including load-bearing exercises?

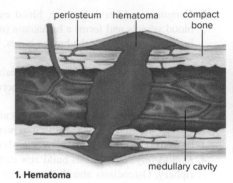

periosteum   hematoma   compact bone

1. Hematoma

medullary cavity

fibrocartilaginous callus

spongy bone

2. Fibrocartilaginous callus

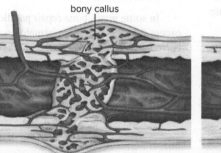

bony callus

3. Bony callus

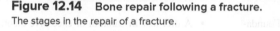

healed fracture

4. Remodeling

Figure 12.14   Bone repair following a fracture.
The stages in the repair of a fracture.

fracture is simple if it does not pierce the skin and compound if it does pierce the skin. Impacted means that the broken ends are wedged into each other. A spiral fracture occurs when the break is ragged due to twisting of a bone.

Blood Cells Are Produced in Bones

The bones of your skeleton contain two types of marrow: yellow and red. Fat is stored in yellow bone marrow, thus making it part of the body's energy reserves.

Red bone marrow is the site of blood cell production. The red blood cells are the carriers of oxygen in the blood. Oxygen is necessary for the production of ATP by aerobic cellular respiration. White blood cells also originate in the red bone marrow. The white cells are involved in defending your body against pathogens and cancerous cells; without them, you would soon succumb to disease and die.

CHECK YOUR PROGRESS 12.5

1. Describe how bone growth occurs during development.
2. Summarize the stages in the repair of bone.
3. Explain how the skeletal system is involved in calcium homeostasis.

CONNECTING THE CONCEPTS

For more on bone development and the hormones that influence bone growth, refer to the following discussions:

Section 9.6 provides additional information on inputs of vitamin D and calcium in the diet.

Section 16.2 examines the role of growth hormones in the body.

Section 16.3 describes the action of the hormones calcitonin and PTH.

CASE STUDY: CONCLUSION

For the first painful month or so after having her knee replaced, Jackie wondered if she had made the right decision. Just walking down the hall or up stairs was excruciating at first. Within 2 months, however, she was walking and swimming. Her physical therapist attributed her rapid return to her previous habits of staying in shape. But Jackie knows that without twenty-first-century medicine, she might have a difficult time walking by the time she is 60.

Still, she has been reminded by her doctor that all bones, even those of adults, are dynamic structures. Whereas her bone could be replaced by bone remodeling, the plastic and ceramic parts of her knees would eventually wear out. So there was a very good chance that she would have to undergo a repeat replacement of her knee in about 20 years. For Jackie, the ability to once again lead an active lifestyle was a worthwhile trade for a few months of discomfort.

SUMMARIZE

12.1 Overview of the Skeletal System

Functions of the **skeletal system:**

- It supports and protects the body.
- It produces blood cells.
- It stores mineral salts, particularly calcium phosphate. It also stores fat.
- Along with the muscles, it permits flexible body movement.

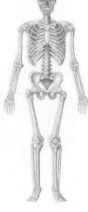

The bones of the skeleton are composed of bone tissues and cartilage. In a long bone,

- Cartilage covers the ends. **Periosteum** (fibrous connective tissue) covers the rest of the bone.
- **Spongy bone,** containing **red bone marrow,** is in the epiphyses.
- Yellow bone marrow is in the **medullary cavity** of the diaphysis.
- **Compact bone** makes up the wall of the diaphysis.
- Bone cells called **osteocytes** reside within the **lacunae** of compact bone.

Cartilage is a connective tissue that is more flexible than bone. Cartilage is formed by cells called **chondrocytes.**

Ligaments composed of **fibrous connective tissue** connect bones at **joints.**

12.2 Bones of the Axial Skeleton

The **axial skeleton** consists of the skull, the hyoid bone, the vertebral column, and the rib cage.

- The **skull** is formed by the cranium, which protects the brain, and the facial bones. Membranous regions called **fontanels** connect the bones at birth. **Sinuses** are air spaces that reduce the weight of the skull. The **foramen magnum** is the opening through which the spinal cord passes.
- The hyoid bone anchors the tongue and is the site of attachment of muscles involved with swallowing.
- The **vertebral column** is composed of vertebrae separated by shock-absorbing disks, which make the column flexible. **Intervertebral disks** separate and pad the vertebrae. The vertebral column supports the head and trunk, protects the spinal cord, and is a site for muscle attachment.
- The rib cage is composed of the thoracic vertebrae, ribs, costal cartilages, and sternum. It protects the heart and lungs.

12.3 Bones of the Appendicular Skeleton

The **appendicular skeleton** consists of the bones of the pectoral girdles, upper limbs, pelvic girdle, and lower limbs.

- The **pectoral girdles** and upper limbs are adapted for flexibility.
- The **pelvic girdle** and the lower limbs are adapted for supporting weight. The **pelvis** consists of the pelvic girdle, sacrum, and coccyx. The femur is the longest and strongest bone in the body.

12.4 Articulations

Bones are joined at joints, of which there are three types:

- Fibrous joints (such as the **sutures** of the cranium) are immovable.
- Cartilaginous joints (such as those between the ribs and sternum and the pubic symphysis) are slightly movable.
- **Synovial joints** (which have a synovial membrane) are freely movable.

12.5 Bone Growth and Homeostasis

Cells involved in growth, remodeling, and repair of bone are

- **Osteoblasts,** bone-forming cells
- **Osteocytes,** mature bone cells derived from osteoblasts
- **Osteoclasts,** which break down and absorb bone

Bone Development and Growth

- **Ossification** refers to the formation of bone.
- **Intramembranous ossification:** Bones develop between sheets of fibrous connective tissue. Examples are flat bones, such as bones of the skull.
- **Endochondral ossification:** Cartilaginous models of the bones are replaced by calcified bone matrix. Bone grows at a location called the **epiphyseal plate.**
- Bone growth is affected by vitamin D, growth hormone, and sex hormones.

Bone Remodeling and Its Role in Homeostasis

- **Bone remodeling** is the renewal of bone. Osteoclasts break down bone and osteoblasts re-form bone. Some bone is recycled each year.
- Bone recycling allows the body to regulate blood calcium.
- Two hormones, parathyroid hormone and calcitonin, direct bone remodeling and control blood calcium.

Bone Repair

Repair of a fracture requires the following four steps:

- Hematoma formation
- Fibrocartilaginous callus
- Bony callus
- Remodeling

ASSESS

TESTING YOURSELF

Choose the best answer for each question.

12.1 Overview of the Skeletal System

1. Spongy bone
   a. contains osteons.
   b. contains red bone marrow, where blood cells are formed.
   c. weakens bones.
   d. takes up most of a leg bone.
   e. All of these are correct.

2. Which of the following is not a function of the skeletal system?
   a. production of blood cells
   b. movement
   c. storage of minerals and fat
   d. production of body heat

3. These cells are responsible for the formation of cartilage.
   a. osteoclasts
   b. red blood cells
   c. chondrocytes
   d. osteoblasts

12.2   Bones of the Axial Skeleton

4. This bone is the only movable bone of the skull.
   a. sphenoid
   b. frontal
   c. mandible
   d. maxilla
   e. temporal

5. Which of the following is not involved in forming the shape of the face?
   a. nasal bones
   b. mandible
   c. zygomatic bones
   d. sternum

6. This area of the vertebral column is the location where the ribs attach.
   a. lumbar region
   b. cervical region
   c. thoracic region
   d. sacrum region

12.3   Bones of the Appendicular Skeleton

7. Which of the following is not a bone of the appendicular skeleton?
   a. the scapula
   b. a rib
   c. a metatarsal bone
   d. the patella

8. Label the following diagram of the human.

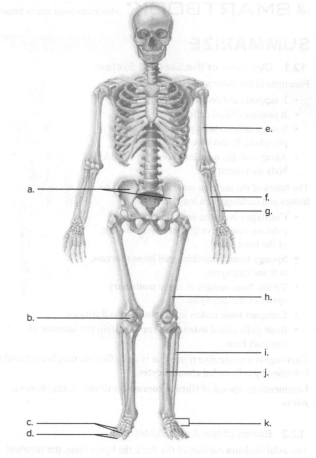

12.4   Articulations

9. This term is used to identify a joint in the body that is freely movable.
   a. fibrous
   b. cartilaginous
   c. synovial
   d. tendon

10. In which of the following types of movement does a synovial joint allow the appendage to increase its angle from the body?
    a. rotation
    b. extension
    c. flexion
    d. pronation

12.5 Bone Growth and Homeostasis

11. The bone cell responsible for breaking down bone tissue is the
    _____, whereas the bone cell that produces new bone tissue
    is the _____.
    a. osteoclast; osteoblast
    b. osteocyte; osteoclast
    c. osteoblast; osteocyte
    d. osteocyte; osteoblast
    e. osteoclast; osteocyte

12. In which of the following does bone form from cartilage?
    a. endochrondral ossification
    b. synovial ossification
    c. intramembrous ossification
    d. bone remodeling

ENGAGE

THINKING CRITICALLY

The ligaments that connect children's bones are flexible yet weak.
Dislocations of bones forming a synovial joint are common in children
and are usually not serious. Historically, this type of injury was termed
"nursemaid's elbow," indicating that the injury resulted from careless
handling of a child by a caregiver. Likewise, bone fractures are common
to children. The most common fracture in a child is called a "greenstick"
fracture, in which the bone splinters but does not break clean through. A
greenstick fracture is most common in the radius and ulna, from children

falling on their arms. Most strains, sprains, dislocations, and fractures
result from a child's active lifestyle. Injuries like these are treated
with pain management, maneuvers to return a bone/joint to normal,
immobilization in a cast or splint, and surgery if necessary. The vast
majority of these injuries heal quickly, with no lingering effects.
The child is encouraged to be as active as possible during the healing
process, because inactivity causes increased bone depletion. Balancing
safety with the need for children to exercise and play is critical for
normal growth.

1. What nutritional and personal habits would contribute to rapid
   bone repair?

2. Individuals who spend the majority of their day indoors (e.g.,
   residents in nursing homes) are more susceptible to fracture. Why?

3. Why do the broken bones of older people take much longer to
   mend than the broken bones of children and young adults?

4. Pediatricians are becoming increasingly concerned by the
   increased incidence of rickets in children eating a typical fast-food
   diet. What nutrients are missing from the diet?

5. Two athletes show up in the emergency room following a college
   football game. One has a fracture of the fibula. The second has a
   severe ankle sprain. Which player is most likely to return to play
   first? Why?

6. a. What stimulates the release of parathyroid hormone?
   b. What disease or diseases is (are) likely to result from
      hyperparathyroidism?

7. Why is the spinal cord almost always damaged when someone
   breaks one or more cervical vertebrae?

CHAPTER

7

The Lymphatic and Immune Systems

© ISM/Phototake

CHAPTER CONCEPTS

7.1 The Lymphatic System
The lymphatic vessels return excess interstitial fluid to cardiovascular veins. The lymphatic organs are important to immunity.

7.2 Innate Immune Defenses
Innate defenses are barriers that prevent pathogens from entering the body and mechanisms able to deal with minor invasions.

7.3 Adaptive Immune Defenses
Adaptive defenses specifically counteract an invasion in two ways: by production of antibodies and by outright killing of abnormal cells.

7.4 Acquired Immunity
The two main types of acquired immunity are immunization by vaccines and the administration of prepared antibodies.

7.5 Hypersensitivity Reactions
The immune system is associated with allergies, tissue reaction, and autoimmune disorders. Treatment is available for these, and research continues into finding new and better cures.

BEFORE YOU BEGIN

Before beginning this chapter, take a few moments to review the following discussions:

Section 2.6 How is a protein's structure related to its function?

Section 3.2 What are some differences between prokaryotic and eukaryotic cells?

Section 6.3 What is the role of white blood cells in defense against pathogens?

CASE STUDY: LUPUS

Abigail was a healthy and active teenager. She had a pretty unremarkable patient history that included nothing but the normal childhood diseases—croup when she was an infant, several ear infections, and a couple of bad bouts of the flu and bronchitis. She was up to date on all of her vaccinations. Over the last few months, however, she noticed that she was abnormally tired, her arms and legs ached, and her knees and elbows were bothering her. Initially she ignored these symptoms, but just a few weeks ago she developed a rash on her cheeks and across the bridge of her nose, which resembled a butterfly shape. Abigail thought that she might be sensitive to an ingredient in a new face soap she had recently switched to, so she quickly switched back to the old brand. The rash did not subside. Abigail suddenly began developing ulcers in her mouth, which interfered with eating and drinking. Within a few more weeks, Abigail also began experiencing some digestive issues—stomachaches after eating, periodic bouts of diarrhea, and a noticeable weight loss. Within another few weeks, Abigail began losing handfuls of hair. She decided that it was time to see the physician on campus.

The physician did a full exam on Abigail and ran a battery of tests over the next few days. The tests included a complete blood count (CBC), a urinalysis, various protein assays, and an ANA (antinuclear antibody) test, which is a test commonly used to aid in the diagnosis of many different autoimmune disorders. Once the results were in and a diagnosis was finally obtained, the doctor explained to Abigail that she had lupus, an autoimmune disease.

As you read through the chapter, think about the following questions:

1. What is an autoimmune disease?
2. Are the symptoms Abigail experienced common to autoimmune diseases?
3. How is an autoimmune disease acquired?

7.1 The Lymphatic System

The **lymphatic system** consists of lymphatic vessels and the lymphatic organs. This system, closely associated with the cardiovascular system, has four main functions that contribute to homeostasis: (1) Lymphatic capillaries absorb excess interstitial fluid and return it

to the bloodstream; (2) in the small intestines, lymphatic capillaries called lacteals absorb fats in the form of lipoproteins and transport them to the bloodstream; (3) the lymphatic system is responsible for the production, maintenance, and distribution of lymphocytes; and (4) the lymphatic system helps defend the body against pathogens.

Lymphatic Vessels

Lymphatic vessels form a one-way system of capillaries to vessels and, finally, to ducts. These vessels take lymph to cardiovascular veins in the shoulders (Fig. 7.1). As mentioned in Section 5.1, lymphatic capillaries take up excess interstitial fluid. Interstitial fluid is mostly water, but it also contains solutes (i.e., nutrients, electrolytes, and oxygen) derived from plasma. This fluid also contains cellular products (i.e., hormones, enzymes, and wastes) secreted by cells. The fluid inside lymphatic vessels is called **lymph.** Lymph is usually a colorless liquid, but after a meal it appears creamy because of its lipid content.

The lymphatic capillaries join to form lymphatic vessels that merge before entering either the thoracic duct or the right lymphatic duct. The larger thoracic duct returns lymph collected from

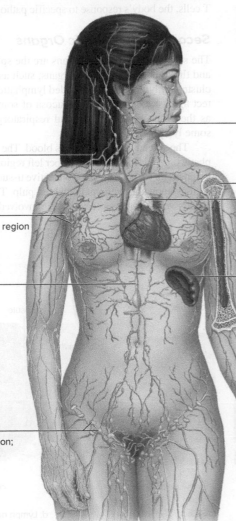

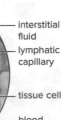

Right lymphatic duct: empties lymph into the right subclavian vein

Axillary lymph nodes: located in the underarm region

Thoracic duct: empties lymph into the left subclavian vein

Inguinal lymph nodes: located in the groin region; cleanse lymph and alert the immune system to pathogens

Tonsil: patches of lymphatic tissue; helps to prevent entrance of pathogens by way of the nose and mouth

Red bone marrow: site for the origin of all types of blood cells

Thymus: lymphatic tissue where T lymphocytes mature and learn to tell "self" from "nonself"

Spleen: cleanses the blood of cellular debris and bacteria, while resident lymphocytes respond to the presence of antigens

interstitial fluid

lymphatic capillary

tissue cell

blood capillary

Figure 7.1 Functions of the lymphatic system components.
Lymphatic vessels drain excess fluid from the tissues and return it to the cardiovascular system. The enlargement shows that lymphatic vessels, like cardiovascular veins, have valves to prevent backward flow. The lymph nodes, spleen, thymus, and red bone marrow are the main lymphatic organs that assist immunity.

the body below the thorax, the left arm, and left side of the head and neck into the left subclavian vein. The right lymphatic duct returns lymph from the right arm and right side of the head and neck into the right subclavian vein.

The construction of the larger lymphatic vessels is similar to that of cardiovascular veins, including the presence of valves. The movement of lymph within lymphatic capillaries is largely dependent on skeletal muscle contraction. Lymph forced through lymphatic vessels as a result of muscular compression is prevented from flowing backward by one-way valves.

Lymphatic Organs

The lymphatic organs are divided into two categories. The primary lymphatic organs include the red bone marrow and the thymus, whereas the lymph nodes and spleen represent the secondary lymphatic organs. Figure 7.2 shows tissue samples taken from the primary and secondary lymphatic organs.

The Primary Lymphatic Organs

Red bone marrow (Fig 7.2a) produces all types of blood cells. In a child, most bones have red bone marrow; in an adult, marrow is found only in the sternum, the vertebrae, the ribs, part of the pelvic girdle, and the upper ends of the humerus and femur. In addition to the red blood cells, bone marrow produces the various types of white blood cells: neutrophils, eosinophils, basophils, lymphocytes, and monocytes. Lymphocytes are either **B cells (B lymphocytes)** or **T cells (T lymphocytes)**. B cells mature in the bone marrow, but T cells mature in the thymus. Any B cell that reacts with cells of the body is removed in the bone marrow and does not

enter the circulation. This ensures that the B cells do not harm normal cells of the body.

The soft, bilobed **thymus** (Fig. 7.2b) is located in the thoracic cavity between the trachea and the sternum, superior to the heart. The thymus will begin shrinking in size before puberty and is noticeably smaller in an adult than in a child.

The thymus has two functions: (1) It produces thymic hormones, such as thymosin, thought to aid in the maturation of T lymphocytes. (2) Immature T lymphocytes migrate from the bone marrow through the bloodstream to the thymus, where they mature. Only about 5% of these cells ever leave the thymus. These T lymphocytes have survived a critical test: If any show the ability to react with the individual's cells, they die in the thymus. If they have potential to attack a pathogen, they can leave the thymus. The thymus is absolutely critical to immunity because without mature, properly functioning T cells, the body's response to specific pathogens is poor or absent.

Secondary Lymphatic Organs

The secondary lymphatic organs are the spleen, the lymph nodes, and the tonsils. Many other organs, such as the appendix, contain clusters of lymphatic tissue called lymphatic nodules that help protect against pathogens. The mucosa of some organ systems, such as the gastrointestinal tract and respiratory system, also contain some lymphatic tissue.

The **spleen** (Fig. 7.2c) filters blood. The spleen, the largest lymphatic organ, is located in the upper left region of the abdominal cavity posterior to the stomach. Connective tissue divides the spleen into regions known as white pulp and red pulp. The red pulp, which surrounds venous sinuses (cavities), is involved in filtering the blood.

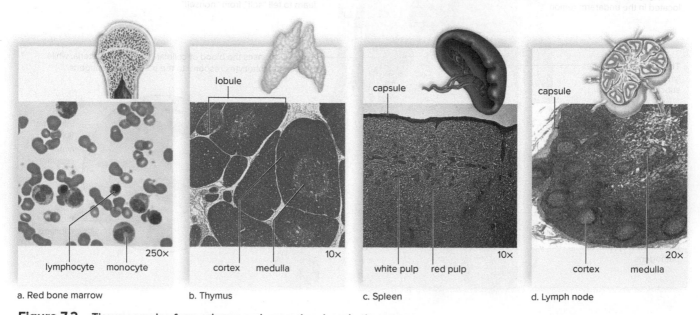

Figure 7.2   **Tissue samples from primary and secondary lymphatic organs.**
Red bone marrow (**a**) and the thymus (**b**) are the primary lymphatic organs. Blood cells, including lymphocytes, are produced in red bone marrow. B cells mature in the bone marrow, but T cells mature in the thymus. The spleen (**c**) and the lymph nodes (**d**) are secondary lymphatic organs. Lymph is cleansed in lymph nodes, and blood is cleansed in the spleen.

What does it mean when my lymph nodes are swollen?

Lymph nodes swell when they are fighting an infection. When the body is invaded by a bacterium or virus, individual nodes can swell from 1/2 to 2 inches in diameter. Cuts, burns, bites, rashes, and any break in the skin can cause an infection and thus the swelling of your lymph nodes. Swollen nodes near the groin mean infection on a leg or the lower abdomen; in your armpits, they mean infection on the arms or chest; and on the front of your neck, they mean an infection in the ears, nose, or throat. Some diseases, such as chickenpox, can cause all your nodes to swell.

Blood entering the spleen must pass through the sinuses before exiting. Here, macrophages that are like powerful vacuum cleaners engulf pathogens and debris, such as worn-out red blood cells.

The spleen's outer capsule is relatively thin, and an infection or a blow can cause the spleen to burst. Although the spleen's functions are replaced by other organs, a person without a spleen is often slightly more susceptible to infections and may have to receive antibiotic therapy indefinitely.

Lymph nodes (Fig. 7.2d), which occur along lymphatic vessels, filter lymph. Connective tissue forms a capsule and divides a lymph node into compartments. Each compartment contains a sinus that increases in size toward the center of the node. As lymph courses through the sinuses, it is exposed to macrophages, which engulf pathogens and debris. Lymphocytes, also present in sinuses, fight infections and attack cancer cells.

Lymph nodes are named for their location. For example, inguinal nodes are in the groin, and axillary nodes are in the armpits. Physicians often feel for the presence of swollen, tender lymph nodes in the neck as evidence that the body is fighting an infection. This is a noninvasive, preliminary way to help make such a diagnosis.

Lymphatic nodules are concentrations of lymphoid tissue not surrounded by a capsule. The *tonsils* are patches of lymphoid tissue located in a ring about the pharynx. The tonsils perform the same functions as lymph nodes; however, because of their location, they are the first to encounter pathogens and antigens that enter the body by way of the nose and mouth.

Peyer patches are located in the intestinal wall and in tissues within the appendix, a small extension of the large intestine, and encounter pathogens that enter the body by way of the intestinal tract.

CHECK YOUR PROGRESS 7.1

1. Describe how the lymphatic system contributes to fluid homeostasis in the body.
2. Detail the differences between a primary and a secondary lymphatic organ, and give an example of each.
3. Predict what could happen to the body if the lymphatic ducts did not allow lymph to drain.

CONNECTING THE CONCEPTS

As noted, the lymphatic system plays a role in the movement of fats and the return of excess fluid to the circulatory system. For more information on these functions, refer to the following discussions:

Section 5.1 examines how the lymphatic system interacts with the circulatory system.

Section 9.3 explores how the lymphatic system is involved in the processing of fat in the diet.

Figure 9.6 diagrams the location of the lymphatic vessels in the small intestine.

7.2 Innate Immune Defenses

LEARNING OUTCOMES

Upon completion of this section, you should be able to

1. List examples of the body's innate defenses.
2. Summarize the events in the inflammatory response.
3. Explain the role of the complement system.

We are constantly exposed to microbes such as viruses, bacteria, and fungi in our environment. Immunity is the capability of killing or removing foreign substances, pathogens, and cancer cells from the body. Mechanisms of innate, or nonspecific, immunity are fully functional without previous exposure to these invaders, whereas adaptive immunity (see Section 7.3) is initiated and amplified by exposure. As summarized in Figure 7.3, innate immune defenses include physical and chemical barriers; the inflammatory response (including the phagocytes and natural killer cells); and protective proteins, such as complement and interferons.

Innate defenses occur immediately or very shortly after infection occurs. With innate immunity, there is no recognition that an intruder has attacked before, and therefore no immunological "memory" of the attacker is present.

Physical and Chemical Barriers to Entry

The body has built-in barriers, both physical and chemical, that serve as the first line of defense against an infection by pathogens.

The intact skin is generally an effective physical barrier that prevents infection. The keratin of the skin prevents microbial growth, and the surface of the skin is constantly being lost to exfoliation (see Section 4.6). The skin also has the benefit of a chemical barrier in the form of secretions of sebaceous (oil) glands of the skin. This acidic mixture contains chemicals that weaken or kill certain bacteria on the skin.

Mucous membranes lining the respiratory, digestive, reproductive, and urinary tracts are also physical barriers to entry by pathogens. For example, the ciliated cells that line the upper respiratory tract sweep mucus and trapped particles up into the throat, where they can be coughed or spit out or swallowed.

Perspiration, saliva, and tears contain an antibacterial enzyme called **lysozyme.** Saliva also helps wash microbes off the teeth and

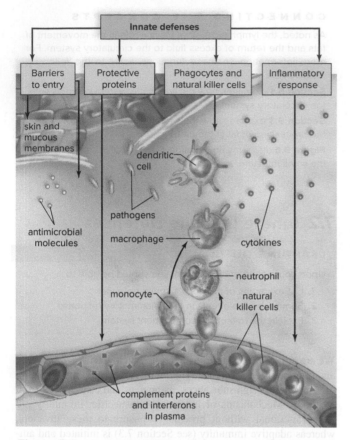

Figure 7.3   Overview of innate immune defenses.
Most innate defenses act rapidly to detect and respond to specific molecules expressed by pathogens.

tongue, and tears wash the eyes. Similarly, as urine is voided from the body, it flushes bacteria from the urinary tract.

The acid pH of the stomach inhibits growth or kills many types of bacteria. At one time it was thought that no bacterium could survive the acidity of the stomach. But now we know that ulcers are caused by the bacterium *Helicobacter pylori* (see Section 1.3). Similarly, the acidity of the vagina and its thick walls discourage the presence of pathogens.

Finally, a significant chemical barrier to infection is created by the normal flora, microbes that usually reside in the mouth, intestine, and other areas. By using available nutrients and releasing their own waste, these resident bacteria prevent potential pathogens from taking up residence. For this reason, chronic use of antibiotics can make a person susceptible to pathogenic infection by killing off the normal flora.

Inflammatory Response

The **inflammatory response** exemplifies the second line of defense against invasion by a pathogen. Inflammation employs mainly neutrophils and macrophages to surround and kill (engulf by phagocytosis) pathogens trying to get a foothold inside the body. Protective proteins are also involved. Inflammation is usually recognized by its four hallmark symptoms: redness, heat, swelling, and pain (Fig. 7.4).

The four signs of the inflammatory response are due to capillary changes in the damaged area, and all protect the body. Chemical mediators, such as **histamine,** released by damaged tissue cells and mast cells, cause the capillaries to dilate and become more permeable. Excess blood flow due to enlarged capillaries causes the skin to redden and become warm. Increased temperature in an inflamed area tends to inhibit growth of some pathogens. Increased blood flow brings white blood cells to the area. Increased

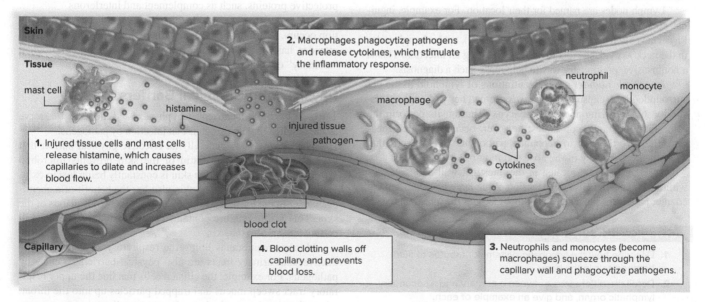

Figure 7.4   Steps of the inflammatory response.
1. Due to capillary changes in a damaged area and the release of chemical mediators, such as histamine by mast cells, an inflamed area exhibits redness, heat, swelling, and pain. **2.** Macrophages release cytokines, which stimulate the inflammatory and other immune responses. **3.** Monocytes and neutrophils squeeze through capillary walls from the blood and phagocytize pathogens. **4.** A blood clot can form a seal in a break in a blood vessel.

How do antihistamines work?

Once histamine is released from mast cells, it binds to receptors on other body cells. There, the histamine causes the symptoms associated with infections and allergies: sneezing, itching, runny nose, and watery eyes. Antihistamines work by blocking the receptors on the cells, so that histamine can no longer bind. For allergy relief, antihistamines are most effective when taken before exposure to the allergen.

permeability of capillaries allows fluids and proteins, including blood-clotting factors, to escape into the tissues. Clot formation in the injured area prevents blood loss. The excess fluid in the area presses on nerve endings, causing the pain associated with swelling. Together, these events summon white blood cells to the area.

As soon as the white blood cells arrive, they move out of the bloodstream into the surrounding tissue. The neutrophils are first and actively phagocytize debris, dead cells, and bacteria they encounter. The many neutrophils attracted to the area can usually localize any infection and keep it from spreading. If neutrophils die off in great quantities, they become a yellow-white substance called pus.

When an injury is not serious, the inflammatory response is short-lived and the healing process will quickly return the affected area to a normal state. Nearby cells secrete chemical factors to ensure the growth (and repair) of blood vessels and new cells to fill in the damaged area.

If, on the other hand, the neutrophils are overwhelmed, they call for reinforcements by secreting chemical mediators called **cytokines.** Cytokines attract more white blood cells, including monocytes, to the area. Monocytes are longer-lived cells, which become **macrophages,** even more powerful phagocytes than neutrophils. Macrophages can enlist the help of lymphocytes to carry out specific defense mechanisms.

Inflammation is the body's natural response to an irritation or injury and serves an important role. Once the healing process has begun, inflammation rapidly subsides. However, in some cases chronic inflammation lasts for weeks, months, or even years if an irritation or infection cannot be overcome. Inflammatory chemicals may cause collateral damage to the body, in addition to killing the invaders. Should an inflammation persist, anti-inflammatory

Why is aspirin used to alleviate so many symptoms?

The chemicals in aspirin decrease the body's ability to make prostaglandins. Prostaglandins, made by most of the body's tissues, are substances used as messengers in the perception and response to pain, fever, and muscle contractions. If the prostaglandin level is low, then the perception of pain, fever, and muscle contractions will be low. Aspirin also decreases the production of certain substances needed in the beginning stages of blood clotting, which is why it is prescribed to patients with certain cardiovascular clotting disorders.

medications, such as aspirin, ibuprofen, or cortisone, can minimize the effects of various chemical mediators.

Protective Proteins

The **complement system,** often simply called complement, is composed of a number of blood plasma proteins designated by the letter *C* and a number. These proteins "complement" certain immune responses, which accounts for their name. For example, they are involved in and amplify the inflammatory response—certain complement proteins can bind to mast cells and trigger histamine release. Others can attract phagocytes to the scene. Some complement proteins bind to the surface of pathogens already coated with antibodies, which ensures that the pathogens will be phagocytized by a neutrophil or macrophage.

Certain other complement proteins join to form a membrane attack complex that produces holes in the surface of bacteria. Fluids then enter the bacterial cells to the point that they burst (Fig. 7.5).

Interferons are proteins produced by virus-infected cells as a warning to noninfected cells in the area. Interferons bind to receptors of noninfected cells, causing them to prepare for possible attack by producing substances that interfere with viral replication. Interferons are used to treat certain viral infections, such as hepatitis C.

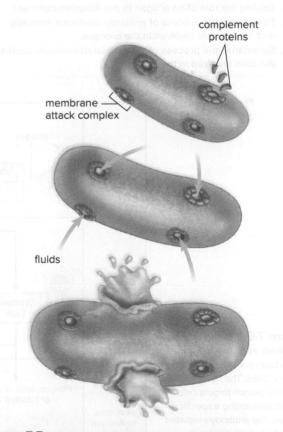

Figure 7.5 **Action of the complement system.**
When the immune response activates complement proteins in the blood plasma, they form a membrane attack complex that makes holes in bacterial cell walls and plasma membranes, allowing fluids to enter and causing the cell to burst.

CHECK YOUR PROGRESS 7.2

1. List some examples of the body's innate defenses.
2. Describe the blood cells associated with innate defenses, and detail how they function.
3. Discuss how the complement proteins got their name.

CONNECTING THE CONCEPTS

For more information on the topics presented in this section, refer to the following discussions:

Section 4.7 examines how the skin forms a physical barrier to the exterior environment.

Section 6.3 provides additional details on white blood cells.

Section 8.4 discusses the problems with the overuse of antibiotics.

7.3 Adaptive Immune Defenses

LEARNING OUTCOMES

Upon completion of this section, you should be able to

1. Explain the role of an antigen in the adaptive defenses.
2. Summarize the process of antibody-mediated immunity and list the cells involved in the process.
3. Summarize the process of cell-mediated immunity and list the cells involved in the process.

When innate (nonspecific) defenses have failed to prevent an infection, adaptive defenses come into play. Adaptive defenses overcome an infection by doing away with the particular disease-causing agent that has entered the body. Adaptive defenses also provide some protection against cancer.

How Adaptive Defenses Work

Adaptive defenses respond to large molecules, normally protein structures called **antigens** that the immune system recognizes as foreign to the body. Fragments of bacteria, viruses, molds, and parasitic worms can all be antigenic. Further, abnormal plasma membrane proteins produced by cancer cells may also be antigens. We do not ordinarily develop an immune response to the cells of our body, so it is said that the immune system is able to distinguish self (our cells) from nonself (pathogens).

Adaptive defenses primarily depend on the action of lymphocytes, which differentiate as either B cells (B lymphocytes) or T cells (T lymphocytes). B cells and T cells are capable of recognizing antigens because they have specific antigen receptors. These antigen receptors are plasma membrane proteins whose shape allows them to combine with particular antigens. Each lymphocyte has only one type of receptor. It is often said that the receptor and the antigen fit together like a lock and key. We encounter millions of different antigens during our lifetime, so we need a diversity of B cells and T cells to protect us against them. Remarkably, this diversification occurs during the maturation process. Millions of specific B cells and/or T cells are formed, increasing the likelihood that at least one will recognize any possible antigen. Both B cells and T cells then

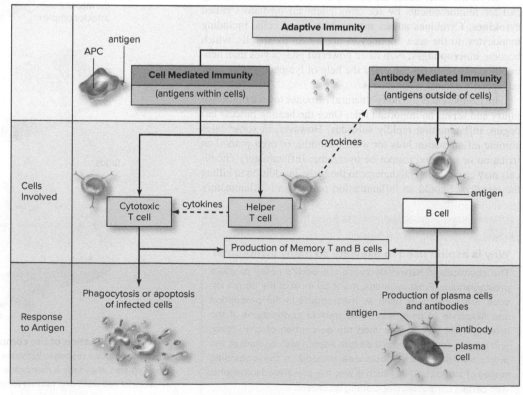

Figure 7.6   Overview of adaptive immune defenses.
The adaptive responses involve two branches. The cell-mediated immunity branch targets cells that are presenting a specific antigen. The antibody-mediated immunity branch produces antibodies that are located outside of the cells, such as the interstitial fluid.

have the ability to differentiate into a special form of lymphocyte that provides the immune system with a physiological memory.

There are two pathways that occur during adaptive immunity. In **cell-mediated immunity,** T cells target for destruction cells that are presenting a specific antigen. In **antibody-mediated immunity** (also called humoral immunity), B cells produce antibodies that target free antigens in the fluids of the body. The stages and interaction of these two pathways are shown in Figure 7.6.

B Cells and Antibody-Mediated Immunity

The receptor on a B cell is called a B-cell receptor (BCR). The clonal selection model (Fig. 7.7) states that an antigen selects, then binds to, the BCR of only one type of B cell. Then this B cell produces multiple copies of itself. The resulting group of identical cells is called a clone. Similarly, an antigen can bind to a T-cell receptor (TCR), and this T cell will clone.

Characteristics of B Cells

- Antibody-mediated immunity against pathogens
- Produced and mature in bone marrow
- Directly recognize antigen and then undergo clonal selection
- Clonal expansion produces antibody-secreting plasma cells as well as memory B cells.

B Cells Become Plasma Cells and Memory B Cells   Note in Figure 7.7 that each B cell has a specific BCR represented by shape. Only the B cell with a BCR that has a shape that fits the antigen (green circle) undergoes clonal expansion. During clonal expansion, cytokines secreted by helper T (T_H) cells (discussed later in this section) stimulate B cells to clone. Most of the cloned B cells become **plasma cells,** which circulate in the blood and lymph. Plasma cells are larger than regular B cells, because they have extensive rough endoplasmic reticulum. This is for the mass production and secretion of antibodies to a specific antigen. Antibodies identical to the BCR of the activated B cell are secreted from the plasma B cell. Some cloned B cells become memory cells, the means by which long-term immunity is possible. If the same antigen enters the system again, memory B cells quickly divide and transform into plasma cells. The correct type of antibody can be produced quickly by these plasma cells.

Once the threat of an infection has passed, the development of new plasma cells ceases, and those present undergo apoptosis. **Apoptosis** is the process of programmed cell death. It involves a cascade of specific cellular events leading to the death and destruction of the cell and removal of the cell remnants from the body as a waste product.

Defense by B cells is called humoral immunity, or antibody-mediated immunity, because activated B cells become plasma cells that produce antibodies. Collectively, plasma cells probably produce as many as 2 million different antibodies. A human doesn't have 2 million genes, so there cannot be a separate gene for each type of antibody. It has been found that scattered DNA segments can be shuffled and combined in various ways to produce the DNA sequence coding for the BCR unique to each type of B cell.

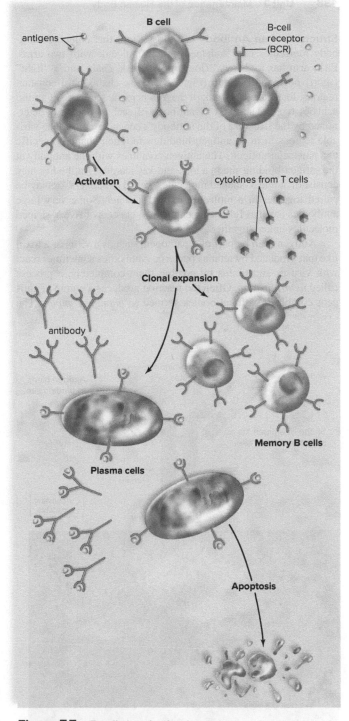

Figure 7.7   B cell clonal selection.

Each B cell has a B-cell receptor (BCR) designated by shape that will combine with a specific antigen. Activation of a B cell occurs when its BCR can combine with an antigen (colored green). In the presence of cytokines, the B cell undergoes clonal expansion, producing many plasma cells and memory B cells. These plasma cells secrete antibodies specific to the antigen, and memory B cells immediately recognize the antigen in the future. After the infection passes, plasma cells undergo apoptosis, also called programmed cell death.

138   Unit 2   Maintenance of the Human Body

Structure of an Antibody   The basic unit that composes antibody molecules is a Y-shaped protein molecule with two arms. Each arm has a "heavy" (long) polypeptide chain and a "light" (short) polypeptide chain (Fig. 7.8). These chains have constant regions, located at the trunk of the Y, where the sequence of amino acids is fixed. The class of antibody of each molecule is determined by the structure of the antibody's constant region. The variable regions form an antigen-binding site. Their shape is specific to a particular antigen. The antigen combines with the antibody at the antigen-binding site in a lock-and-key manner. Antibodies may consist of single Y-shaped molecules, called *monomers,* or may be paired together in a molecule termed a *dimer.* Some very large antibodies (such as IgM) are pentamers—clusters of five Y-shaped molecules linked together.

Antigens can be part of a pathogen, such as a virus or a toxin like that produced by tetanus bacteria. Antibodies sometimes react with viruses and toxins by coating them completely, a process called *neutralization.* Often the reaction produces a clump of antigens combined with antibodies, termed an *immune complex.* The

Table 7.1	Classes of Antibodies	
Class	**Presence**	**Function**
IgG	Main antibody type in circulation; crosses the placenta from mother to fetus	Binds to pathogens, activates complement, and enhances phagocytosis by white blood cells
IgM	Antibody type found in circulation; largest antibody; first antibody formed by a newborn; first antibody formed with any new infection	Activates complement and clumps cells
IgA	Main antibody type in secretions such as saliva and breast milk	Prevents pathogens from attaching to epithelial cells in digestive and respiratory tracts
IgD	Antibody type found on surface of immature B cells	Signifies readiness of B cell
IgE	Antibody type found as antigen receptors on mast cells in tissues	Responsible for immediate allergic response and protection against certain parasitic worms

antibodies in an immune complex are like a beacon that attracts white blood cells.

Classes of Antibodies   There are five classes of circulating antibodies, listed in Table 7.1. IgG antibodies are the major type in blood, and smaller amounts are found in lymph and interstitial fluid. IgG antibodies bind to pathogens and their toxins. IgG antibodies can cross the placenta from a mother to her fetus, so the newborn has temporary, partial immune protection. IgM antibodies are pentamers; they are the first antibodies produced by a newborn's body. IgM antibodies are the first to appear in blood soon after an infection begins and the first to disappear before the infection is over. They are good activators of the complement system. IgA antibodies are monomers or dimers containing two Y-shaped structures. They are the main type of antibody found in body secretions: saliva, tears, mucus, and breast milk. IgA molecules bind to pathogens and prevent them from reaching the bloodstream. The main function of IgD molecules seems to be to serve as antigen receptors on immature B cells. IgE antibodies are responsible for prevention of parasitic worm infections, but they can also cause immediate allergic responses.

Monoclonal Antibodies   Every plasma cell derived from the same B cell secretes antibodies against a specific antigen. These are **monoclonal antibodies,** because all of them are the same type and because they are produced by plasma cells derived from the same B cell. One method of producing monoclonal antibodies in vitro (outside the body) is depicted in Figure 7.9. B lymphocytes are removed from an animal, normally a lab mouse, and are

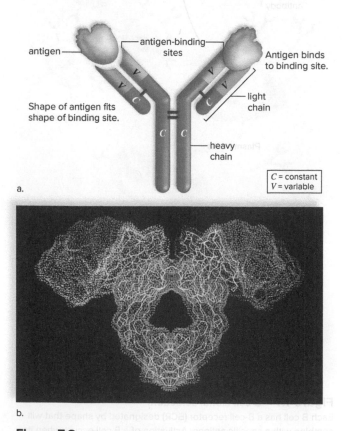

a.

b.

Figure 7.8   **The structure of an antibody.**
a. An antibody contains two heavy (long) polypeptide chains and two light (short) chains arranged so that there are two variable regions where a particular antigen is capable of binding with an antibody.
b. Computer model of an antibody molecule. The antigen combines with the two side branches.
(b) © Dr. Arthur J. Olson, Scripps Institute

infection common in young children. Because they can be used to distinguish between cancerous and normal tissue cells, they are also used to carry radioisotopes or toxic drugs to tumors, which can then be selectively destroyed. Trastuzumab (Herceptin) is a monoclonal antibody used in the treatment of breast cancer. It binds to a protein receptor on breast cancer cells and prevents the cancer cells from dividing as quickly. Antibodies that bind to cancer cells also can activate the complement system and can increase phagocytosis by macrophages and neutrophils.

T Cells and Cell-Mediated Immunity

Cell-mediated immunity is named for the action of T cells that directly attack diseased cells and cancer cells. Other T cells, however, release cytokines that stimulate both nonspecific and specific defenses.

How T Cells Recognize an Antigen   When a T cell leaves the thymus, it has a unique **T-cell receptor (TCR)**, just as B cells have. Unlike B cells, however, T cells are unable to recognize an antigen without help. The antigen must be displayed to them by an **antigen-presenting cell (APC)**, such as a macrophage. After phagocytizing a pathogen, such as a bacterium, APCs travel to a lymph node or the spleen, where T cells also congregate. In the meantime, the APC has broken the pathogen apart in a lysosome. A piece of the pathogen is then displayed in the groove of a **major histocompatibility complex (MHC)** protein on the cell's surface. The two classes of MHC proteins are called MHC I and MHC II.

Human MHC II proteins are called **human leukocyte antigens (HLAs).** These proteins are found on all of our body cells. There are three general groups of HLAs (HLA-A, HLA-B, and HLA-DR), each with a number of protein variations. Each person has a unique combination of HLAs. One exception is the HLAs of identical twins. Because identical twins arise from division of a single zygote, their HLA proteins are identical. MHC antigens are self proteins, because they mark the cell as belonging to a particular individual. The importance of self proteins in plasma membranes was first recognized when it was discovered that they contribute to the specificity of tissues and make it difficult to transplant tissue from one human to another. Comparison studies of the three classes of HLAs must always be carried out before a transplant is attempted. The greater the number of these proteins that match, the more likely the transplant will be successful.

When an antigen-presenting cell links a foreign antigen to the self protein on its plasma membrane, it carries out an important safeguard for the rest of the body. The T cell to be activated can compare the antigen and self protein side by side. The activated T cell, and all the daughter cells that it will form, can recognize foreign from self. These T cells go on to destroy cells carrying foreign antigens, while leaving normal body cells unharmed.

Clonal Expansion   In Figure 7.10, the T cells have specific TCRs, represented by their different shapes. A macrophage is presenting an antigen to a T cell that has the specific TCR that will combine with this particular antigen, represented by a green circle. The T cell is activated and undergoes clonal expansion. Many copies of the activated T cell are produced during clonal expansion.

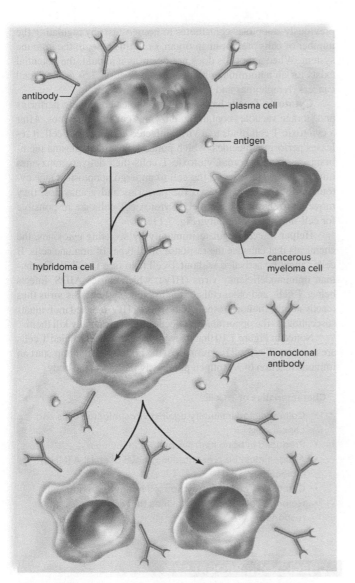

Figure 7.9   **The production of monoclonal antibodies.**
Plasma cells of the same type (derived from immunized mice) are fused with myeloma (cancerous) cells, producing hybridoma cells that are "immortal." Hybridoma cells divide and continue to produce the same type of antibody, called monoclonal antibodies.

exposed to a particular antigen. The resulting plasma cells are fused with myeloma cells (malignant plasma cells that live and divide indefinitely; they are immortal cells). The fused cells are called hybridomas—*hybrid-* because they result from the fusion of two different cells and *-oma* because one of the cells is a cancer cell.

At present, monoclonal antibodies are being used for quick and certain diagnosis of various conditions. For example, the hormone human chorionic gonadotropin (HCG) is present in the urine of a pregnant woman. A monoclonal antibody can be used to detect this hormone. Monoclonal antibodies are also used to identify infections such as H1N1 flu, HIV, and RSV, a respiratory virus

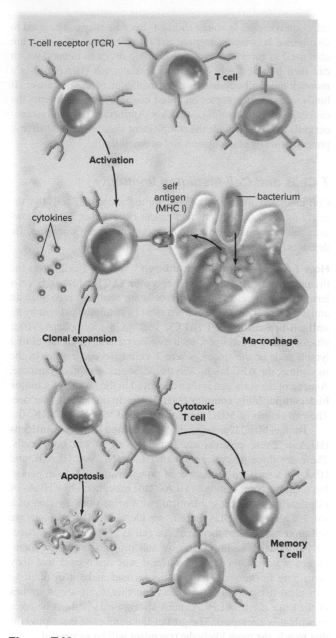

Figure 7.10 **The clonal selection model for T cells.**
Activation of a T cell occurs when its T-cell receptor (TCR) can combine with an antigen presented by a macrophage. In this example, cytotoxic T cells are produced. When the immune response is finished, they undergo apoptosis. A small number of memory T cells remain.

A subgroup of T cells recognizes APCs that display an antigen within the groove of an MHC I protein. These T cells will activate and become cytotoxic T cells. A subgroup of T cells recognizes APCs that display an antigen within the groove of an MHC II protein. These T cells will activate and become helper T cells. Helper T cells are necessary for regulating B cells.

As the illness disappears, the immune reaction wanes. Activated T cells become susceptible to apoptosis. As mentioned

previously, apoptosis contributes to homeostasis by regulating the number of cells present in an organ, or in this case, in the immune system. When apoptosis does not occur as it should, the potential exists for an autoimmune response (see Section 7.5) or for T-cell cancers (lymphomas and leukemias).

Cytotoxic T cells have storage vacuoles containing perforins and storage vacuoles containing enzymes called granzymes. After a cytotoxic T cell binds to a virus-infected cell or tumor cell, it releases perforin molecules, which punch holes in the plasma membrane, forming a pore. Cytotoxic T cells then deliver granzymes into the pore. These cause the cell to undergo apoptosis. Once cytotoxic T cells have released the perforins and granzymes, they move on to the next target cell. Cytotoxic T cells are responsible for cell-mediated immunity (Fig. 7.11).

Helper T cells regulate immunity by secreting cytokines, the chemicals that enhance the response of all types of immune cells. B cells cannot be activated without T-cell help (see Fig. 7.7). The human immunodeficiency virus (HIV), which causes AIDS, infects helper T cells and other cells of the immune system. The virus thus inactivates the immune response and makes HIV-infected individuals susceptible to the opportunistic infections that eventually kill them.

Notice in Figure 7.10 that a few of the clonally expanded T cells are **memory T cells.** They remain in the body and can jump-start an immune reaction to an antigen previously present in the body.

Characteristics of T Cells

- Cell-mediated immunity against virus-infected cells and cancer cells
- Produced in bone marrow, mature in thymus
- Antigen must be presented in groove of an HLA (MHC) molecule.
- Cytotoxic T cells destroy nonself antigen-bearing cells
- Helper T cells secrete cytokines that control the immune response.

CHECK YOUR PROGRESS 7.3

1. Detail how innate defense differs from adaptive defense.
2. Distinguish between the cells involved in targeting an antigen present within a cell of the body versus an antigen free in the interstitial fluid.
3. Explain how memory lymphocytes are formed and state their function.

CONNECTING THE CONCEPTS

For more information on the topics presented in this section, refer to the following discussions:

Section 6.3 summarizes the formation and specialization of lymphocytes.

Section 8.2 provides additional information on HIV and the AIDS epidemic.

Section 20.4 examines how immunotherapy using cytotoxic T cells can be used to treat cancer.

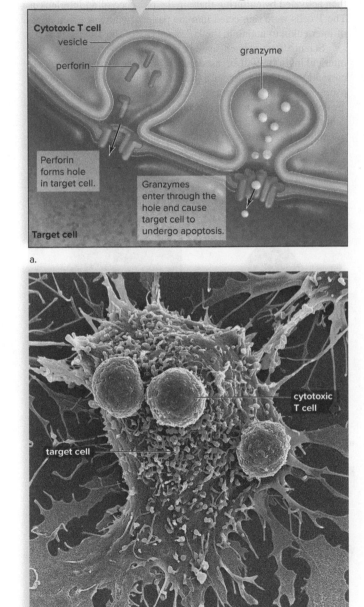

cytotoxic T cell

target cell
(virus-infected
or cancer cell)

Cytotoxic T cell

vesicle

perforin

granzyme

Perforin
forms hole
in target cell.

Granzymes
enter through the
hole and cause
target cell to
undergo apoptosis.

Target cell

a.

cytotoxic
T cell

target cell

b.   SEM 1,250x

Figure 7.11 **How cytotoxic T cells kill infected cells.**
a. Cytotoxic T cells bind to the target cell, punch holes in its membrane,
and inject chemicals that cause the cell to die. **b.** A micrograph of a
cytotoxic T cell in action.

(b) © Steve Gschmeissner/Science Source

7.4 Acquired Immunity

LEARNING OUTCOMES

Upon completion of this section, you should be able to
1. Distinguish between active and passive immunity.
2. Recognize the importance of cytokines in immunity.

Immunity occurs naturally through infection or is brought about artificially by medical intervention. The two types of acquired immunity are active and passive. In the process of **active immunity,** the individual alone produces antibodies against an antigen. In **passive immunity,** the individual is given prepared antibodies via an injection.

Active Immunity

Active immunity sometimes develops naturally after a person is infected with a pathogen. However, active immunity is often induced when a person is well to prevent future infection. Artificial exposure to an antigen through immunization can prevent future disease. The United States is committed to immunizing all children against the common types of childhood disease. A full list of recommended childhood vaccinations is available from the Centers for Disease Control and Prevention (CDC) website at www.cdc.gov/vaccines. Information on recommended adult vaccinations is provided in the Health feature "Adult Vaccinations."

Immunization involves the use of **vaccines,** substances that contain an antigen to which the immune system responds. Traditionally, vaccines are the pathogens themselves, or their products, that have been treated to be no longer virulent (no longer able to cause disease). Today it is possible to genetically engineer bacteria to mass-produce a protein from pathogens, and this protein can be used as a vaccine. This method is used to produce the vaccine for the viral-induced disease hepatitis B, and a vaccine for malaria made by the same method is currently going through FDA approval procedures.

After a vaccine is given, it is possible to follow an immune response by determining the amount of antibody present in a sample of plasma—this is called the *antibody titer.* After the first exposure to a vaccine, a primary response occurs. For the first several days no antibodies are present. Then the titer rises slowly, levels off, and gradually declines as the antibodies bind to the antigen or simply break down (Fig. 7.12). After a second exposure to the vaccine, a secondary response is expected. The titer rises rapidly to a level much greater than before. Then it slowly declines. The second exposure is called a "booster," because it boosts the antibody titer to a high level. The high antibody titer now is expected to help prevent disease symptoms, even if the individual is exposed to the disease-causing antigen.

Active immunity depends on the presence of memory B cells and memory T cells capable of responding to lower doses of antigen. Active immunity is usually long-lasting, although for certain vaccines a booster may be required after many years.

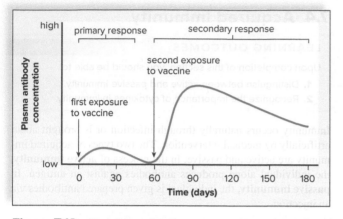

Figure 7.12   How immunizations cause active immunity.
During immunization, the primary response, after the first exposure to a vaccine, is minimal, but the secondary response, which may occur after the second exposure, shows a dramatic rise in the amount of antibody present in plasma.

Passive Immunity

Passive immunity occurs when an individual is given prepared antibodies or immune cells to combat a disease. These antibodies are not produced by the individual's plasma cells, so passive immunity is temporary. For example, newborn infants are passively immune to some diseases because IgG antibodies have crossed the placenta from the mother's blood (Fig. 7.13a). These antibodies soon disappear, and within a few months infants become more susceptible to infections. Breast-feeding prolongs the natural passive immunity an infant receives from the mother, because IgG and IgA antibodies are present in the mother's milk (Fig. 7.13b).

Even though passive immunity does not last, it is sometimes used to prevent illness in a patient who has been unexpectedly exposed to an infectious disease. Usually the patient receives a gamma globulin injection of serum that contains antibodies, in some cases taken from individuals who have recovered from the illness (Fig. 7.13c). For example, a health-care worker who suffers an accidental needlestick may come into contact with the blood from a patient infected with hepatitis virus. Immediate treatment with a gamma globulin injection (along with simultaneous vaccination against the virus) typically can prevent the virus from causing infection.

Cytokines and Immunity

Cytokines are signaling molecules produced by T lymphocytes, macrophages, and other cells. Cytokines regulate white blood cell formation and/or function, so they are being investigated as a possible adjunct therapy (treatments used in conjunction with the primary treatment) for cancer and AIDS. Both interferon, produced by virus-infected cells, and **interleukins,** produced by various white blood cells, have been used as immunotherapeutic drugs. These are used particularly to enhance the ability of the individual's T cells to fight cancer.

Most cancer cells carry an altered protein on their cell surface, so they should be attacked and destroyed by cytotoxic T cells. Whenever cancer develops, it is possible that cytotoxic T cells have not been activated. In that case, cytokines might awaken the immune system and lead to the destruction of the cancer. In one technique, researchers withdrew T cells from the patient and presented cancer cell antigens to the isolated T cells. The cells were then activated by culturing them in the presence of an interleukin. The T cells were reinjected into the patient, who was given doses of interleukin to maintain the killer activity of the T cells.

Scientists actively engaged in interleukin research believe that interleukins soon will be used as adjuncts for vaccines. They are currently used as treatment adjuncts for chronic diseases such as psoriasis, rheumatoid arthritis, and irritable bowel syndrome and are sometimes used to treat chronic infectious diseases and to treat cancer. Interleukin antagonists also may prove helpful in preventing skin and organ rejection, autoimmune diseases such as lupus and Crohn's disease, and allergies.

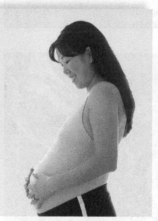

a. Antibodies (IgG) cross the placenta.

b. Antibodies (IgG, IgA) are secreted into breast milk.

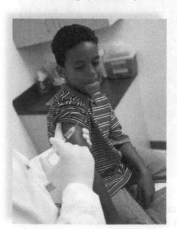

c. Antibodies can be injected by a physician.

Figure 7.13   Delivery mechanisms of passive immunity.
During passive immunity, antibodies are received (a) by crossing the placenta, (b) in breast milk, or (c) by injection. The body is not producing the antibodies, so passive immunity is short-lived.

(a) © John Lund/Drew Kelly/Blend Images/Corbis RF; (b) © Digital Vision/Getty RF; (c) © Photodisc Collection/Getty RF

BIOLOGY TODAY   Health

Adult Vaccinations

Many people mistakenly believe that you have received your full complement of vaccinations by the time you leave high school. In reality, being vaccinated is a lifelong activity. The Centers for Disease Control and Prevention (CDC) has identified a series of vaccinations that are recommended after the age of 18 (Table 7A). In many cases, vaccinations are recommended when an individual is determined to be at risk for a specific disease or condition. For example, while the vaccination for hepatitis B (HepB) may not be required, it is recommended for individuals who have had more than one sexual partner during a 6-month period, have been diagnosed with a sexually transmitted disease (STD; see Section 17.6), use injection drugs, or may have been exposed to blood or infected body fluid. In most cases, vaccinations are recommended as a protective measure even if you are not in an at-risk category.

As always, if you have questions regarding any of these diseases, or about your personal need for vaccinations, consult with your health-care provider. For more information on vaccination schedules from birth through adulthood, visit the CDC's website at www.cdc.gov/vaccines or the Immunization Action Coalition (www.immunize.org).

Questions to Consider

1. Why would some vaccines require multiple doses over an adult's lifetime?
2. Why would people over the age of 60 or 65 require different vaccinations?

Table 7A	Recommended Vaccination Schedule for Adults					
	Age group					
Vaccine	19–21 years	22–26 years	27–49 years	50–59 years	60–64 years	≥ 65 years
Influenza	← 1 dose annually →					
Tetanus, diphtheria, pertussis (Td/Tdap)	Substitute 1-time dose of Tdap for Td booster; then boost with Td every 10 years					
Varicella	← 2 doses →					
Human papillomavirus (HPV) female	← 3 doses →					
Human papillomavirus (HPV) male	← 3 doses →					
Shingles					← 1 dose →	
Measles, mumps, rubella (MMR)	← 1 or 2 doses →					
Pneumococcal 13-valent conjugate (PCV13)			← 1 dose →			← 1 dose →
Pneumococcal polysaccharide (PPSV23)		← 1 or 2 doses →				← 1 dose →
Meningococcal	← 1 or more doses →					
Hepatitis A	← 2 doses →					
Hepatitis B	← 3 doses →					
Haemophilus influenzae type b (Hib)	← 1 or 3 doses →					

■ For all persons in this category who meet the age requirements and who lack documentation of vaccination or have no evidence of previous infection; shingles vaccine recommended regardless of prior episode of shingles

■ Recommended if some other risk factor is present (e.g., on the basis of medical, occupational, lifestyle, or other indication)

□ No recommendation

CHECK YOUR PROGRESS 7.4

1. Define *acquired immunity,* and give some examples.
2. Describe how passive immunity is developed.
3. Compare the two types of immune therapies that can assist passive immunity.

CONNECTING THE CONCEPTS

For more information on the topics presented in this section, refer to the following discussion:

Section 20.4 examines how cytokines may be used to treat cancer.

7.5 Hypersensitivity Reactions

LEARNING OUTCOMES

Upon completion of this section, you should be able to

1. Explain what causes an allergic reaction.
2. Identify the causes of select autoimmune diseases.

Sometimes the immune system responds in a manner that harms the body, as when individuals develop allergies, receive an incompatible blood type (see Section 6.5), suffer tissue rejection, or have an autoimmune disease.

Allergies

Allergies are hypersensitivities to substances, such as pollen, food, or animal hair, that ordinarily would do no harm to the body. The responses to these antigens, called **allergens,** usually include some degree of tissue damage.

An **immediate allergic response** can occur within seconds of contact with the antigen. The response is caused by IgE antibodies (see Table 7.1). IgE antibodies are attached to receptors on the plasma membrane of mast cells in the tissues and to basophils in the blood. When an allergen attaches to the IgE antibodies on these cells, the cells release histamine and other substances that bring about the allergic symptoms. When pollen is an allergen, histamine stimulates the mucous membranes of the nose and eyes to release fluid. This causes the runny nose and watery eyes typical of hay fever. In a person who has asthma, the airways leading to the lungs constrict, resulting in difficult breathing accompanied by wheezing. When food contains an allergen, nausea, vomiting, and diarrhea often result.

Anaphylactic shock is an immediate allergic response that occurs because the allergen has entered the bloodstream. Bee stings and penicillin shots are known to cause this reaction, because both inject the allergen into the blood. Anaphylactic shock is characterized by a sudden and life-threatening drop in blood pressure due to increased permeability of the capillaries by histamine. Taking epinephrine can counteract this reaction until medical help is available.

People with allergies produce ten times more IgE than those without allergies. A new treatment using injections of monoclonal IgG antibodies for IgEs is being tested in individuals with severe food allergies. More routinely, injections of the allergen are given, so that the body will build up high quantities of IgG antibodies. The hope is that IgG antibodies will combine with allergens received from the environment before they have a chance to reach the IgE antibodies located in the membranes of mast cells and basophils.

A **delayed allergic response** is initiated by memory T cells at the site of allergen contact in the body. The allergic response is regulated by the cytokines secreted by both T cells and macrophages. A classic example of a delayed allergic response is the skin test for tuberculosis (TB). When the test result is positive, the tissue where the antigen was injected becomes red and hardened. This shows that there was prior exposure to the bacterium that causes TB. Contact dermatitis, which occurs when a person is allergic to poison ivy, jewelry, cosmetics, and many other substances that touch the skin, is also an example of a delayed allergic response.

Other Immune Problems

Certain organs, such as the skin, the heart, and the kidneys, could be transplanted easily from one person to another if the body did not attempt to reject them. Rejection of transplanted tissue results because the recipient's immune system recognizes that the transplanted tissue is not "self." Cytotoxic T cells respond by attacking the cells of the transplanted tissue.

Organ rejection can be controlled by carefully selecting the organ to be transplanted and administering **immunosuppressive** drugs. It is best if the transplanted organ has the same type of MHC antigens as those of the recipient, because cytotoxic T cells recognize foreign MHC antigens. Two well-known immunosuppressive drugs, cyclosporine and tacrolimus, act by inhibiting the production of certain T-cell cytokines.

Xenotransplantation is the use of animal organs instead of human organs in human transplant patients. Scientists have chosen to use the pig because animal husbandry has long included the raising of pigs as a meat source and pigs are prolific. Genetic engineering can make pig organs less antigenic. The ultimate goal is to make pig organs as widely accepted as type O blood.

An alternative to xenotransplantation exists because tissue engineering is making organs in the laboratory. Scientists have transplanted lab-grown urinary bladders into human patients. They hope that production of organs lacking HLA antigens will one day do away with the problem of rejection.

Immune system disorders occur when a patient has an immune deficiency or when the immune system attacks the body's own cells. When a person has an immune deficiency, the immune system is unable to protect the body against disease. Infrequently, a child may be born with an impaired immune system. For example, in **severe combined immunodeficiency disease** (SCID), both antibody- and cell-mediated immunity are lacking or inadequate. Without treatment, even common infections can be fatal. Bone marrow transplants and gene therapy have been successful in SCID patients. Acquired immune deficiencies can be caused by infections, chemical exposure, or radiation. Acquired immunodeficiency syndrome (AIDS) is a result of an infection with the human immunodeficiency virus (HIV). As a result of a weakened immune system, AIDS patients show a greater susceptibility to infections and have a higher risk of cancer (see Section 8.2).

When cytotoxic T cells or antibodies mistakenly attack the body's own cells, the person has an **autoimmune disease.** The exact cause of autoimmune diseases is not known, although it appears to involve both genetic and environmental factors. People with certain HLA antigens are more susceptible. Women are more likely than men to develop an autoimmune disease.

Sometimes the autoimmune disease follows an infection. For example, in **rheumatic fever,** antibodies induced by a streptococcal (bacterial) infection of the throat also react with heart muscle. This causes an inflammatory response, with damage to the heart muscle and valves. **Rheumatoid arthritis** (Fig. 7.14) is an autoimmune disease in which the joints are chronically inflamed. It is thought that antigen-antibody complexes, complement, neutrophils, activated T cells, and macrophages are all involved in the destruction of cartilage in the joints. A person with **systemic lupus erythematosus (SLE),** commonly just called *lupus,* has various symptoms, including a facial rash, fever, and joint pain. In these patients, damage to the central nervous system, heart, and kidneys can be fatal. SLE patients produce high levels of anti-DNA antibodies. All human cells (except red blood cells) contain DNA, so the symptoms of lupus interfere with tissues throughout the body. **Myasthenia gravis** develops when antibodies attach to and interfere with the function of neuromuscular junctions. The result is severe muscle weakness, eventually resulting in death from respiratory failure.

In **multiple sclerosis (MS),** T cells attack the myelin sheath covering nerve fibers, causing CNS dysfunction, double vision, and muscular weakness. Some now believe that MS is should be characterized as an immune-mediated disease, because a specific antigen has not been identified and the action of of the T cells may be in response to inflammation or failures of the immune system. Treatments for all of these diseases usually involve drugs designed to decrease the immune response.

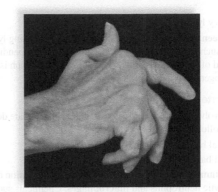

Figure 7.14   Rheumatoid arthritis.
Rheumatoid arthritis is due to recurring inflammation in skeletal joints. A variety of cells in the immune system, including T cells and B cells, participate in deterioration of the joints, which eventually become immobile.
© Southern Illinois University/Science Source

CHECK YOUR PROGRESS 7.5

1. Define the types of complications and disorders associated with the functioning of the immune system.
2. Detail how an antibody works during an allergic reaction.
3. Hypothesize why an autoimmune disorder sometimes develops after an infection.

CONNECTING THE CONCEPTS

For more information on the topics presented in this section, refer to the following discussions:

Section 8.2 examines how tuberculosis has become a worldwide epidemic.

Section 22.3 explores how gene therapy may be used to treat diseases such as SCID.

CASE STUDY: CONCLUSION

Lupus is an autoimmune disease. The immune system normally makes antibodies that attack foreign cells to keep the body healthy. In an autoimmune disease, the person's immune system makes antibodies that attack the healthy cells of the body, instead of invading pathogen cells. Abigail's immune system was attacking her, in addition to attacking any bacteria and viruses that got into her system. Lupus is also considered a rheumatic disease, or a disorder that affects the muscles, joints, and connective tissue. That explained the pain in her arms and legs.

The doctor went on to detail that she believed Abigail had a type of lupus called systemic lupus erythematosus (SLE). SLE is the most common form of lupus, affecting multiple organ systems. It is most commonly seen developing in people in their twenties and thirties, although it is not uncommon for symptoms to develop in people as young as 10 years old. The exact cause of lupus is unclear; it has been suggested that there is a genetic

predisposition to lupus that can be activated by infection, stress, and even increasing levels of estrogen. The doctor explained that 90% of the 1.5 million Americans living with lupus (an estimated 10,000 of them are children under 18) are female.

There is no cure for lupus and current treatments are aimed at managing the symptoms. The physician recommended that Abigail have a team of health-care professionals help her manage her lupus: a rheumatologist to manage her muscle and joint pain; a dermatologist to help with the periodic rashes; and a nephrologist, or kidney specialist, because lupus patients tend to develop kidney problems. Abigail is currently on a daily NSAID (nonsteroidal anti-inflammatory drug) to control muscle and joint pain. During a flare-up, she can also take corticosteroids to control inflammation. With proper care and caution, Abigail can keep her lupus in check, decrease the severity of flare-ups, and live a healthy and productive life.

STUDY TOOLS http://connect.mheducation.com

SMARTBOOK® Maximize your study time with McGraw-Hill SmartBook®, the first adaptive textbook.

SUMMARIZE

7.1   The Lymphatic System
The lymphatic system consists of lymphatic vessels that return lymph to cardiovascular veins.

The primary lymphatic organs are:

- The **red bone marrow,** where all blood cells are made and the **B cells (B lymphocytes)** mature.
- The **thymus,** where **T cells (T lymphocytes)** mature.

The secondary lymphatic organs are:

- The **spleen, lymph nodes,** and other organs containing lymphoid tissue, such as the tonsils, Peyer patches, and the appendix. Blood is cleansed of pathogens and debris in the spleen. Lymph is cleansed of pathogens and debris in the nodes.

7.2 Innate Immune Defenses

Immunity involves innate and adaptive defenses. The innate defenses include the following:

- Chemical barriers, such as **lysozyme** enzymes.
- Physical barriers to entry.
- The **inflammatory response,** which involves the action of phagocytic neutrophils and **macrophages.** Chemicals such as **histamine** and **cytokines** act as chemical signals.
- The **complement system** utilizes protective proteins and **interferons.**

7.3 Adaptive Immune Defenses

Adaptive defenses require B cells and T cells, also called B lymphocytes and T lymphocytes. The adaptive defenses respond to **antigens,** or foreign objects, in the body.

B Cells and Antibody-Mediated Immunity

- The clonal selection model explains how activated B cells undergo clonal selection with production of plasma cells and memory B cells, after their B-cell receptor (BCR) combines with a specific antigen.
- **Plasma cells** secrete antibodies and eventually undergo **apoptosis.** Plasma cells are responsible for **antibody-mediated immunity.**

- Most antibodies are Y-shaped molecules that have two binding sites for a specific antigen.
- Memory B cells remain in the body and produce antibodies if the same antigen enters the body at a later date.
- **Monoclonal antibodies,** produced by the same plasma cell, have various functions, from detecting infections to treating cancer.

T Cells and Cell-Mediated Immunity

- T cells possess a unique **T-cell receptor (TCR).** For a T cell to recognize an antigen, the antigen must be presented by an **antigen-presenting cell (APC),** such as a macrophage. Once digested within a lysosome, the antigen is presented on the **major histocompatibility complex (MHC)** of the cell. These MHC proteins belong to a class of molecules called **human leukocyte antigens (HLAs).**
- Activated T cells undergo clonal expansion until the illness has been stemmed. Then, most of the activated T cells undergo apoptosis. A few cells remain, however, as memory T cells.
- The two main types of T cells are cytotoxic T cells and helper T cells.
- **Cytotoxic T cells** kill on contact virus-infected cells or cancer cells, which bear nonself proteins. They are involved in the process of **cell-mediated immunity.**
- **Helper T cells** produce cytokines and stimulate other immune cells.
- Some activated T cells remain as **memory T cells** to combat future infections by the same pathogen.

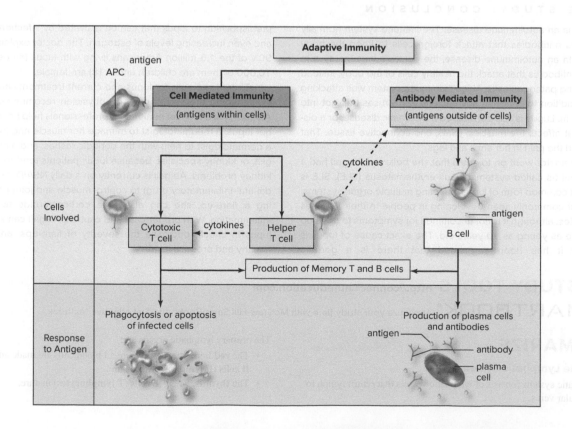

7.4 Acquired Immunity

- **Active immunity** can be induced by **immunization** using **vaccines** when a person is well and in no immediate danger of contracting an infectious disease. Active immunity depends on the presence of memory cells in the body.
- **Passive immunity** is needed when an individual is in immediate danger of succumbing to an infectious disease. Passive immunity is short-lived, because the antibodies are administered to—and not made by—the individual.
- Cytokines, including **interleukins,** are a form of passive immunity used to treat AIDS and to promote the body's ability to recover from cancer.

7.5 Hypersensitivity Reactions

Allergies occur when the immune system reacts vigorously to **allergens,** antigens that are not normally recognized as foreign.

- **Immediate allergic responses,** usually consisting of coldlike symptoms, are due to the activity of antibodies. One example is **anaphylactic shock.**
- **Delayed allergic responses,** such as contact dermatitis, are due to the activity of T cells.
- Tissue rejection occurs when the immune system recognizes a tissue as foreign. **Immunosuppressive** drugs may inhibit tissue rejection. Xenotransplantation is the use of animal tissue in place of human tissue.
- Immune deficiencies can be inherited or can be caused by infection, chemical exposure, or radiation. One example is **severe combined immunodeficiency disease (SCID),** in which adaptive responses are inoperative.
- **Autoimmune diseases** occur when the immune system reacts to tissues/organs of the individual as if they were foreign. Examples are **rheumatic fever, rheumatoid arthritis, systemic lupus erythematosus (SLE), myasthenia gravis,** and **multiple sclerosis (MS).**

ASSESS

TESTING YOURSELF

Choose the best answer for each question.

7.1 The Lymphatic System

1. Which of the following is a function of the spleen?
   a. produces T cells
   b. removes worn-out red blood cells
   c. produces immunoglobulins
   d. produces macrophages
   e. regulates the immune system

2. Which of the following is a function of the thymus?
   a. production of red blood cells
   b. secretion of antibodies
   c. production and maintenance of stem cells
   d. site for the maturation of T lymphocytes

3. Which of the following is a function of the secondary lymphatic organs?
   a. transport of lymph
   b. clonal selection of B cells
   c. location where lymphocytes encounter antigens
   d. All of these are correct.

7.2 Innate Immune Defenses

4. Which of the following is most directly responsible for the increase in capillary permeability during the inflammatory reaction?
   a. pain
   b. white blood cells
   c. histamine
   d. tissue damage

5. Which of the following is not a goal of the inflammatory reaction?
   a. bring more oxygen to damaged tissues
   b. decrease blood loss from a wound
   c. decrease the number of white blood cells in the damaged tissues
   d. prevent entry of pathogens into damaged tissues

6. Which of the following is not correct concerning interferon?
   a. Interferon is a protective protein.
   b. Virus-infected cells produce interferon.
   c. Interferon has no effect on viruses.
   d. Interferon can be used to treat certain viral infections.

7.3 Adaptive Immune Defenses

7. The adaptive immune defenses respond to which of the following?
   a. specific antigens
   b. general pathogens
   c. interferon
   d. histamine
   e. All of these are correct.

8. Which of the following does not pertain to B cells?
   a. have passed through the thymus
   b. have specific receptors
   c. are responsible for antibody-mediated immunity
   d. synthesize antibodies

9. Which of the following characteristics pertains to T cells?
   a. have specific receptors
   b. are of more than one type
   c. are responsible for cell-mediated immunity
   d. stimulate antibody production by B cells
   e. All of these are correct.

10. Human leukocyte antigens (HLAs) are involved in
    a. cell-mediated immunity.
    b. antibody-mediated immunity.
    c. the inflammatory response.
    d. complement.
    e. All of these are correct.

7.4 Acquired Immunity

11. Which of the following does not occur during a secondary immune response?
    a. Antibodies are made quickly and in great amounts.
    b. Antibody production lasts longer than in a primary response.
    c. Clonal selection occurs for B cells.
    d. All of these are correct.

12. Active immunity can be produced by
    a. having a disease.
    b. receiving a vaccine.
    c. receiving gamma globulin injections.
    d. Both a and b are correct.
    e. Both b and c are correct.

7.5 Hypersensitivity Reactions

13. A sudden drop in blood pressure in response to an antigen in the body is a characteristic of which of the following?
    a. inflammatory response
    b. passive immunity
    c. cell-mediated immunity
    d. anaphylactic shock
    e. None of these are correct.

14. Which of the following conditions occurs when antibodies attack the myelin sheath covering nerve fibers?
    a. lupus
    b. rheumatoid arthritis
    c. multiple sclerosis
    d. myasthenia gravis

ENGAGE

THINKING CRITICALLY

An allergic response is an overreaction of the immune system in response to an antigen. Such responses always require a prior exposure to the antigen. The reaction can be immediate (within seconds to minutes) or delayed (within hours). Insect venom reactions often involve the development of hives and itching. Asthmalike symptoms include shortness of breath and wheezing. Decreased blood pressure will eventually cause loss of consciousness. This immediate, severe allergic effect, called anaphylaxis, can be fatal if untreated. In addition to insect venom, food allergens such as those in milk, peanut butter, and shellfish may also elicit life-threatening symptoms. In these cases, IgE antibodies, histamine, and other inflammatory chemicals are the culprits involved in making the reaction so severe.

1. How are B cells involved in immediate allergic responses?

2. An allergist is a doctor who treats people with known allergies. What type of treatments do you think are used? Why?

3. Why do you think certain allergens affect some people more than others? Why are some people asymptomatic to a particular antigen, whereas others are affected?

4. Think of an analogy (something you're already familiar with) for the barrier defenses, such as your skin and mucous membranes.

5. Someone bitten by a poisonous snake should be given some antivenom (antibodies) to prevent death. If the person is bitten by the same type of snake 3 years after the initial bite, will he or she have immunity to the venom, or should the person get another shot of antivenom? Justify your response with an explanation of the type of immunity someone gains from a shot of antibodies.

CHAPTER 1

The Basics of Nutrition

Quiz Yourself

Take the following quiz to test your basic nutrition knowledge. The answers are on page 31.

1. There are four classes of nutrients: proteins, lipids, sugars, and vitamins.
   ___ T ___ F

2. Proteins are the most essential class of nutrients.
   ___ T ___ F

3. All nutrients must be supplied by the diet, because they cannot be made by the body.
   ___ T ___ F

4. Vitamins are a source of energy.
   ___ T ___ F

5. Milk, carrots, and bananas are examples of "perfect" foods that contain all nutrients.
   ___ T ___ F

connect
NUTRITION

www.mcgrawhillconnect.com

A wealth of proven resources are available on Connect® Nutrition including McGraw-Hill LearnSmart®, SmartBook®, NutritionCalc Plus, and many other dynamic learning tools. Ask your instructor about Connect.

CHAPTER **1**

The Basics of Nutrition

Quiz Yourself

Take the following quiz to test your basic nutrition knowledge; the answers are on page 31.

1. There are four classes of nutrients: proteins, lipids, sugars, and vitamins. _____ T _____ F

2. Proteins are the most essential class of nutrients. _____ T _____ F

3. All nutrients must be supplied by the diet, because they cannot be made by the body. _____ T _____ F

4. Vitamins are a source of energy. _____ T _____ F

5. Milk, carrots, and bananas are examples of "perfect" foods that contain all nutrients. _____ T _____ F

connect | NUTRITION   **www.mcgrawhillconnect.com**

A wealth of proven resources are available on Connect® Nutrition including McGraw-Hill LearnSmart®, SmartBook®, NutritionCalc Plus, and many other dynamic learning tools. Ask your instructor about Connect!

1.1 Nutrition: The Basics

Learning Outcomes

1 Explain why it is important to learn about foods and nutrition.

2 Identify factors that influence personal food choices.

3 Identify lifestyle factors that contribute to some of the leading causes of death in the United States.

4 List the six classes of nutrients, and identify a major role of each class of nutrient in the body.

5 Explain how to determine whether a substance is a phytochemical or an essential nutrient.

When you were an infant and a young child, your parents or other adult caregiv—ers were the "gatekeepers" of your food; they chose what you ate and prepared it, and you probably ate most of it. If you balked at eating steamed broccoli or baked salmon, they may have told you, "Eat your vegetables if you expect to get dessert," or "Finish that fish. People in Africa are starving!" As you grew older, your **diet,** your usual pattern of food choices, came increasingly under your control. Today, your diet is more likely to be composed of foods that you enjoy as well as can afford and probably those you can prepare easily or obtain quickly. Your family's ethnic and cultural background may also play a role in determining what you eat regularly. For example, do you eat tamales, tripe, goat, or kim chee because you ate these foods as a child? Numerous other factors influence your food choices, including friends and food advertising, as well as your beliefs and moods (Fig. 1.1).

Food is a basic human need for survival. You become hungry and search for something to eat when your body needs **nutrients,** the life—sustaining substances in food. Nutrients are necessary for the growth, maintenance, and repair of your body's cells. However, you have no instinctual drive that enables you to select the appro—priate mix of nutrients your body requires for proper functioning. To eat well, you need to learn about the nutritional value of foods and the effects that your diet can have on your health.

Simply having information about nutrients and foods and their effects on health may not be enough for people to change ingrained food—related behaviors; a person must be moti—vated to make such changes. Some people become motivated to improve their diets because they want to lose or gain weight. Others are so concerned about their health, they are motivated to change their eating habits in specific ways, such as by eating fewer salty or fatty foods. Many people, however, do not care if the food they eat is beneficial or harmful to their health.

diet usual pattern of food choices

nutrients chemicals necessary for proper body functioning

- Family
- Childhood experiences
- Peers • Ethnic background
- Education • Occupation • Income
- Rural vs. urban residence
- Food composition, convenience, and availability • Food flavor, texture, and appearance • Religious beliefs
- Nutritional beliefs • Health beliefs
- Current health status • Habits
- Advertising and media
- Moods

Figure 1.1 What influences your eating practices? Numerous factors influence food choices, including food advertising, peers, income, moods, and personal beliefs.

Why Learn about Nutrition

Why should you care about your diet? In the United States, poor eating habits contribute to several leading causes of death, including heart disease, some types of cancer, stroke, and type 2

4   Chapter 1 The Basics of Nutrition

diabetes (Fig. 1.2). Results of a national study that followed over 350,000 older adult Americans for 10 years indicated the likelihood of dying was 20 to 25% lower for subjects who followed nationally recommended dietary guidelines.[1] According to the *2015–2020 Dietary Guidelines for Americans,* people can reduce their chances of developing serious diseases that contribute to premature deaths by consuming more fruits, vegetables, unsalted nuts, fat–free or low–fat dairy products, and whole–grain cereals, as well as exercising regularly.[2]

Are you concerned about the nutritional quality of your diet? The fact that you are taking this course indicates you have a strong interest in nutrition and a desire to learn more about the topic. A major objective of this textbook is to provide you with the basic information you need to better understand how your diet can influence your health. Managing your diet is your responsibility. We will not tell you what to eat to guarantee optimal health: No one can make that promise. After read–ing this textbook and learning about foods and the nutrients they contain, you can use the information to make informed decisions concerning the foods you eat. Fur–thermore, you will be able to evaluate your diet and decide if it needs to be changed.

Each chapter of this textbook begins with "Quiz Yourself," a brief true–or–false quiz to test your knowledge of the material covered in the chapter. Each major section of a chapter ends with "Concept Checkpoints," a series of multiple–choice questions that can help you determine whether you understood the major concepts in the section. Answers to the "Concept Checkpoints" are given in Appendix G. At the end of each chapter, you will find the answers to the opener quiz, as well as a group of multiple–choice questions that test your understanding of the material in the chapter. The answers to those questions are also provided in Appendix G. References for information cited in chapters are in Appendix H.

Introduction to Nutrition

nutrition scientific study of nutrients and how the body uses these substances

chemistry study of the composition and characteristics of matter and changes that can occur to it

Nutrition is the scientific study of nutrients, chemicals necessary for proper body functioning, and how the body uses them. Understanding nutrition requires learning about chemistry. **Chemistry** is the study of the composition and char–acteristics of matter, and changes that can occur to it. Matter is anything that takes up space and has mass or weight (on Earth). The air you breathe, this textbook, and even your body consist of chemicals and are forms of matter.

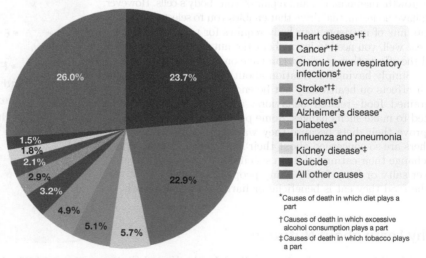

Source: Hoyert DL, Jiaquan X: Deaths: Preliminary data for 2011. *National Vital Statistics Reports* 61[6], 2012.

Figure 1.2 Ten leading causes of U.S. deaths (preliminary data, 2011). Lifestyle factors contribute to many of the 10 leading causes of death in the United States.

"There are chemicals in our food!" This statement may sound frightening, but it is true. Food is mat—ter; therefore, it contains chemicals, some of which are nutrients.

There are six classes of nutrients: carbohydrates, fats and other lipids, proteins, vitamins, minerals, and water. Your body is comprised of these nutrients (Fig. 1.3). Although an average healthy young man and woman have similar amounts of vitamins, minerals, and carbohydrates in their bodies, the young woman has less water and protein, and considerably more fat.

Table 1.1 presents major roles of nutrients in your body. In general, your body uses certain nutrients for energy, growth and development, and regulation of processes, including the repair and maintenance of cells. A **cell** is the smallest living functional unit in an organism, such as a human being. There are hun—dreds of different types of cells in your body. Cells do not need food to survive, but they need the nutri—ents in food to carry out their metabolic activities. **Metabolism** is the total of all chemical processes that occur in living cells, including chemical reactions (changes) involved in generating energy, making pro—teins, and eliminating waste products.

Understanding nutrition also involves learning about human *physiology*, the study of how the body functions. Chapter 4 (Body Basics) prepares you for

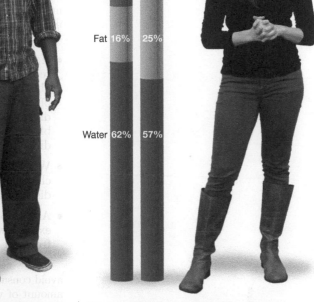

Figure 1.3 **Comparing composition.** These illustrations present the approximate percentages of nutrients that comprise the bodies of a healthy young man and woman. Note that the amount of vitamins in the human body is so small, it is not shown.

TABLE 1.1   Major Functions of Nutrients in the Body

Nutrient	Major Functions
Carbohydrates	Energy (most forms)
Lipids	Energy (fat)
	Cellular development, physical growth and development
	Regulation of body processes (certain chemical messengers, for example)
	Absorption of certain vitamins
Proteins	Production of structural components, such as cell membranes, and functional components, such as enzymes
	Cellular development, growth, and maintenance
	Regulation of body processes (certain chemical messengers, for example)
	Immune function and fluid balance
	Energy
Vitamins	Regulation of body processes, including cell metabolism
	Maintenance of immune function, production and maintenance of tissues, and protection against agents that can damage cellular components
Minerals	Regulation of body processes, including fluid balance and metabolism; formation of certain chemical messengers; structural and functional components of various substances and tissues; physical growth, maintenance, and development
Water	Maintenance of fluid balance, regulation of body temperature, elimination of wastes, and transportation of substances
	Participant in many chemical reactions

cell smallest living functional unit in an organism

metabolism total of all chemical processes that take place in living cells

essential nutrient nutrient that must be supplied by food

deficiency disease state of health that occurs when a nutrient is missing from the diet

phytochemicals compounds made by plants that are not nutrients

the study of nutrition by presenting basic information about chemistry and human physiology. Chapters 5 (Carbohydrates), 6 (Fats and Other Lipids), 7 (Proteins), 8 (Vitamins), and 9 (Water and Minerals) provide information about the functions of nutrients in the body.

What Is an Essential Nutrient?

The body can synthesize (make) many nutrients, such as the lipids cholesterol and fat, but about 50 nutrients are dietary essentials. An **essential nutrient** must be supplied by food, because the body does not synthesize the nutrient or make enough to meet its needs. Water is the most essential nutrient.

There are three key features that help identify an essential nutrient:

- If the nutrient is missing from the diet, a **deficiency disease** occurs as a result. The deficiency disease is a state of health characterized by certain abnormal physiological changes. (*Physiological* refers to the functioning of the body.) Visible or measurable changes are referred to as *signs* of disease. Disease signs include rashes, failure to grow properly, and elevated blood pressure. *Symptoms* are subjective complaints of ill health that are difficult to observe and measure, such as dizziness, fatigue, and headache.

- When the missing nutrient is added to the diet, the abnormal physiological changes are corrected. As a result, signs and symptoms of the deficiency disorder resolve as normal functioning is restored and the condition is cured.

- After scientists identify the nutrient's specific roles in the body, they can explain why the abnormalities occurred when the substance was missing from the diet.

If you wanted to test your body's need for vitamin C, for example, you could avoid consuming foods or vitamin supplements that contain the vitamin. When the amount of vitamin C in your cells became too low for them to function normally, you would develop physical signs of *scurvy*, the vitamin C deficiency disease. Early in the course of the deficiency, tiny red spots that are actually signs of bleeding under the skin (tiny bruises) would appear where the elastic bands of your clothing applied pressure. When you brushed your teeth, your gums would bleed from the pressure of the toothbrush. If you cut yourself, the wound would heal slowly or not at all. If you started consuming vitamin C–containing foods again, the deficiency signs and symptoms would disappear within a few days as your body recovered. By reading about vitamin C in Chapter 8, you will learn that one of the physiological roles of vitamin C is maintaining a substance in your body that literally holds cells together. This substance is also needed to produce scar tissue for wound healing. Thus, vitamin C meets all the required features of an essential nutrient.

Table 1.2 lists nutrients that are generally considered to be essential. Fortunately, the human body is designed to obtain these substances from a wide variety of foods. Chapter 3 provides information about ways to plan nutritious diets.

What Are Nonnutrients?   Some foods contain nonnutrients—substances that are not nutrients, yet they may have healthful benefits. Plants make hundreds of nonnutrients called **phytochemicals** (*phyto* = plant). Caffeine, for example, is a phytochemical naturally made by coffee plants that has a stimulating effect on the body. Many phytochemicals are antioxidants that may reduce risks of heart disease and certain cancers. An **antioxidant** protects cells and their components from being damaged or destroyed by exposure to certain harmful environmental and internal factors. Not all phytochemicals, however, have beneficial effects on the body; some are *toxic* (poisonous) or can interfere with the absorption of nutrients. Scientific research that explores the effects of phytochemicals on the body is ongoing. Table 1.3 lists several phytochemicals that are currently under scientific investigation, identifies rich food sources of these compounds, and indicates their biological effects on the body, including possible health benefits.

Dietary Supplements

Many Americans purchase dietary supplements such as vitamin pills and herbal extracts to improve their health. The Dietary Supplement and Health Education Act of 1994 (DSHEA) allows manufacturers to classify nutrient supplements and certain herbal products as foods.[3] The DSHEA defines a **dietary supplement** as a product (excluding tobacco) that contains a vitamin, a mineral, an herb or other plant product, an amino acid, or a dietary substance that supplements the diet by increasing total intake. According to scientific evidence, some dietary supplements, such as vitamins and certain herbs, can have beneficial effects on health. However, results of scientific testing also indicate that many popular dietary supplements are not helpful and may even be harmful. The "Nutrition Matters" feature in Chapter 2 ("What Are Dietary Supplements?") discusses dietary supplements. Information about specific dietary supplements is also woven into chapters where it is appropriate.

TABLE 1.2   Essential Nutrients for Humans

Water	Glucose[†]	Fats that contain linoleic and alpha-linolenic acids
Vitamins:	**Minerals:**	
A	Calcium	
B vitamins	Chloride	
Thiamin	Chromium	**The following amino acids are generally recognized as essential:**
Riboflavin	Copper	
Niacin	Iodine	
Pantothenic acid	Iron	
Biotin	Magnesium	Histidine
Folic acid (folate)	Manganese	Leucine
B-6	Molybdenum	Isoleucine
B-12	Phosphorus	Lysine
Choline*	Potassium	Methionine
C	Selenium	Phenylalanine
D**	Sodium	Threonine
E	Sulfur	Tryptophan
K	Zinc	Valine

*The body makes choline but may not make enough to meet needs. Often classified as a *vitamin-like* compound.

**The body makes vitamin D after exposure to sunlight, but a dietary source of the nutrient is often necessary.

[†]A source of glucose is needed to supply the nervous system with energy and spare protein from being used for energy.

antioxidant substance that protects other compounds from being damaged or destroyed by certain factors

dietary supplements nutrient preparations, certain hormones, and herbal products

---

Concept **Checkpoint 1.1**

  1. Identify at least two of the 10 leading causes of death that are diet related.
  2. Identify at least four factors that influence your eating habits.
  3. List the six major classes of nutrients.
  4. What is the smallest living functional unit in the body?
  5. What are three key factors that determine whether a substance is an essential nutrient?
  6. What is a phytochemical?
  7. Define "dietary supplement."

8   Chapter 1   The Basics of Nutrition

TABLE 1.3   Phytochemicals of Scientific Interest

Classification and Examples	Rich Food Sources	Biological Effects/Possible Health Benefits
Carotenoids		May reduce risk of certain cancers, may reduce risk of macular degeneration (a major cause of blindness)
Alpha-carotene, beta-carotene, lutein, lycopene, zeaxanthin	Orange, red, yellow fruits and vegetables; egg yolks	
Phenolics		Antioxidant activity; may inhibit cancer growth, may reduce risk of heart disease
Quercetin	Apples, tea, red wine, onions, olives, raspberries, cocoa	
Catechins	Green and black tea, chocolate, plums, apples, berries, pecans	
Naringenin, hesperitin	Citrus fruits	
Anthocyanins	Red, blue, or purple fruits and vegetables	
Resveratrol	Red wine, purple grapes and grape juice, dark chocolate, cocoa	
Isoflavonoids	Soybeans and other legumes	
Lignans	Flaxseed, berries, whole grains, bran, nuts	
Tannins	Tea, coffee, chocolate, blueberries, grapes, persimmons	
Ellagic acid	Raspberries, strawberries, cranberries, walnuts, pecans, pomegranates	
Monterpenes	Oranges, lemons, grapefruit, cherries	
Organosulfides		Antioxidant effects; may improve immune system functioning and reduce the risk of heart disease
Isothiocyanates, indoles, allylic sulfur compounds	Garlic, onions, leeks, cruciferous vegetables (broccoli, cauliflower, cabbage, kale, bok choy, collard and mustard greens)	
Alkaloids		Stimulant effects
Caffeine	Coffee, tea, kola nuts, cocoa	
Glycosides		May kill certain microbes, inhibit certain cancers, and reduce risk of heart disease
Saponins	Chickpeas, beans, oats, grapes, olives, spinach, garlic, quinoa	
Capsaicinoids		May provide some pain relief
Capsaicin	Chili peppers	
Fructooligosaccharides		May stimulate the growth of beneficial bacteria in the human intestinal tract
	Onions, bananas, asparagus, wheat	

1.2 Factors That Influence Americans' Health

Learning Outcomes

1 Explain why people should be concerned about their lifestyle and risk factors for chronic diseases.

2 Compare Americans' current typical eating habits to the population's typical eating habits in 1970.

3 Describe the general goals of *Healthy People 2020*.

As mentioned in the opener of this chapter, poor eating habits contribute to several of the leading causes of death in the United States. Note in Figure 1.2 that heart disease is the leading cause of death for all Americans, and cancer is the second leading cause of death. In 2011, these two diseases accounted for almost 50% of all deaths.[4]

Conditions such as heart disease and cancer are *chronic* diseases. Chronic diseases usually take many years to develop and have complex causes. A **risk factor** is a personal characteristic that increases your chances of developing a chronic disease. For example, genetic background or family history is an important risk factor for heart disease. If your father's father had a heart attack before he was 55 years old and your mother is being treated for having a high blood cholesterol level (a risk factor for heart disease), your family history indicates you have a higher−than−average risk of having a heart attack. For many people, however, having a family history of a chronic disease does not mean that they definitely will develop the condition. Other risk factors that contribute to health are age, environmental conditions, psychological factors, access to health care, and lifestyle practices.

Lifestyle is a person's usual way of living that includes dietary practices, physical activity habits, use of drugs such as tobacco and alcohol, and other typical patterns of behavior. Your lifestyle may increase or reduce your chances of developing a chronic disease or delay its occurrence for years, even decades. Poor diet, cigarette smoking, and excess alcohol consumption, for example, are risk factors that increase the likelihood of heart disease, stroke, and many forms of cancer. Cigarette smoking is the primary cause of preventable cancer deaths, but dietary habits and physical activity patterns also contribute to the devel−opment of certain cancers.[5,6] Additionally, poor diet and lack of physical activ−ity can result in obesity, a condition characterized by the accumulation of too much body fat. Obesity is a risk factor for numerous health problems, including heart disease, certain cancers, type 2 diabetes, and *hypertension* (chronic high blood pressure).

Chapter 5 discusses diabetes, and Chapter 6 explains the role of diet and other lifestyle factors in the development of heart disease and hypertension. The Chapter 8 "Nutrition Matters" feature takes a closer look at the diet and cancer connection. Chapter 10 (Energy Balance and Weight Control) provides informa−tion about obesity.

Our Changing Eating Habits

Americans' diets have changed significantly over the past 40 years.[7] According to U.S. Department of Agriculture (USDA) estimates, we eat less red meat, eggs, and milk, and more fish, poultry, and cheese than in 1970. Our diet also supplies more food energy from flour and cereal products than in 1970, but *refined* grain foods, such as white bread and pasta, make up the majority of these products. In general, the more refined a food is, the more processing it has undergone before it reaches your plate, and as a result, the food has lost vitamins, minerals, and

Did You Know?

Your genetic makeup influences the effects of diet on your health as well as disease susceptibility. *Nutritional genomics* or *nutrigenomics* is a relatively new area of nutrition research that explores complex interactions among gene functioning, diet and other lifestyle choices, and the environment.

risk factor personal characteristic that increases a person's chances of developing a disease

lifestyle usual way of living, including dietary practices and physical activity habits

Smoking is the leading cause of preventable death in the United States.

10   Chapter 1 The Basics of Nutrition

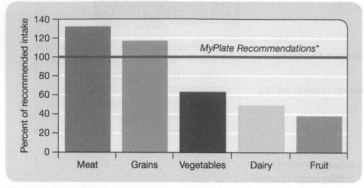

*Data based on a 2000-calorie diet.

Source: Calculated by ERS/USDA based on data from various sources (see Loss-Adjusted Food Availability Documentation). U.S. Department of Agriculture, Agricultural Research Service: *Food availability (per capita) data system.* Data as of February 2013.

Figure 1.4 Americans' diets generally do not meet dietary recommendations.

Did You Know?

Overall, the health status of minorities lags behind that of the rest of the U.S. population. Efforts to improve the health of minorities is a major focus of *Healthy People 2020* nutrition-related programs.

other beneficial naturally occurring substances. Compared to past years, Americans are eating more fruits and veg-etables, but many people do not consume enough to meet recommended amounts (Fig. 1.4).

In 2010, the typical American diet provided more added fat, added sugar, and total food energy than in 1970 (Table 1.4).[7] If a person's energy intake is more than needed, especially for physical activity, his or her body fat increases. Nationwide surveys indicate that Americans are fatter than in previous decades. Dietary practices, how-ever, should not receive all the blame for this unhealthy finding; during the same period, we have become increas-ingly dependent on various labor–saving gadgets and machines that make our lives easier but also reduce the amount of energy we need to expend. Chapter 10 examines weight management in detail.

Healthy People

Since the late 1970s, health promotion and disease preven-tion have been the focus of public health efforts in the United States. A primary focus of such efforts is developing educational programs that can help people prevent chronic and infectious diseases, birth defects, and other serious health problems. In many instances, it is more practical and less expensive to prevent a serious health condition than to treat it.

Healthy People 2010, a report issued in 2000 by the U.S. Department of Health and Human Services (DHHS), included 467 specific national health promo-tion and disease prevention objectives that were to be met by 2010. The main goals of *Healthy People 2010* were to promote healthful lifestyles and reduce prevent–able death and disability among Americans.

In early 2011, DHHS issued *Healthy People 2020*, a report that includes national health promotion and disease prevention objectives to be met by 2020. The "vision" of *Healthy People 2020* is "A society in which all people live long, healthy lives."[8] *Healthy People 2020* goals encourage Americans to:

- attain higher–quality, longer lives that are free of preventable disease, disability, injury, and premature death;

- achieve health equity by eliminating disparities to improve the health of all groups;

- create social and physical environments that promote good health for all;

- promote quality of life, healthy development, and healthy behaviors across all life stages.

TABLE 1.4 Changing Dietary Patterns: Energy Intakes and Added Fats and Sugars (per Person)

Dietary Component (per day)	1970	2010
Food energy	2064 Calories	2538 Calories
Added fats	1.6 oz	2.8 oz
Added sugars (equivalent to teaspoons of sugar)	20.8 teaspoons	23.0 teaspoons

Source: USDA, Economic Research Service: *Food availability (per capita) data system.*
http://www.ers.usda.gov/data-products/food-availability-%28per-capita%29-data-system/.aspx#.Ue8s-G0qmSo
Accessed: February 21, 2014

TABLE 1.5   Some *Healthy People 2020* Objectives: Nutrition and Weight Status (NWS)

Goal: Promote health and reduce chronic disease associated with diet and weight.

Goal Number	Objective's Short Title
NWS 8	Healthy weight in adults
NWS 9	Obesity in adults
NWS 10	Obesity in children and adolescents
NWS 14	Fruit intake
NWS 15	Vegetable intake
NWS 16	Whole grain intake
NWS 17	Solid fat and added sugar intake
NWS 18	Saturated fat intake
NWS 19	Sodium intake
NWS 20	Calcium intake
NWS 21	Iron deficiency in young children and in females of childbearing age

Healthy People 2020 has several major nutrition—related objectives, some of which are listed in Table 1.5. You can access more information about these objectives at the government's website (http://www.healthypeople.gov/2020/topicsobjectives2020/default.aspx).

Concept Checkpoint 1.2

8. What is a risk factor?
9. Explain how your lifestyle can affect your health.
10. Discuss how Americans' eating habits have changed since 1970.
11. Identify at least one main diet-related objective of *Healthy People 2020*.

1.3 Metrics for Nutrition

Learning Outcomes

1. Identify basic units of the metric system often used in nutrition.
2. Use the caloric values of macronutrients and alcohol to estimate the amount of energy (kcal) in a food.

Scientists classify specific nutrients according to their chemical composition and major functions in the body. Nutrients can also be classified based on how much of them are in food. Americans usually refer to length in terms of inches and feet, weight in pounds, and amounts of food in familiar household measures (e.g., teaspoons, tablespoons, cups). Scientists, however, generally use metric values to report length (*meter*), weight (*gram*), and volume (*liter*). The following section provides a basic review of the metric system. Appendix A provides common English—to—metric and metric—to—household unit conversions.

12   Chapter 1 The Basics of Nutrition

TABLE 1.6 Common Metric Prefixes in Nutrition

kilo- (k) = one thousand
deci- (d) = one-tenth (0.1)
centi- (c) = one-hundredth (0.01)
milli- (m) = one-thousandth (0.001)
micro- (mc or µ) = one-millionth

kilocalorie or **Calorie** heat energy needed to raise the temperature of 1 liter of water 1° Celsius; measure of food energy

macronutrients nutrients needed in gram amounts daily and that provide energy; carbohydrates, proteins, and fats

micronutrients vitamins and minerals

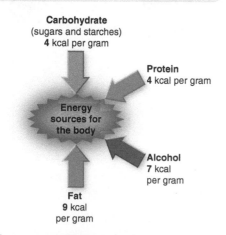

Carbohydrate
(sugars and starches)
4 kcal per gram

Protein
4 kcal per gram

Energy sources for the body

Alcohol
7 kcal per gram

Fat
9 kcal per gram

Figure 1.5 Energy sources for the body. Most forms of carbohydrate supply 4 kcal/g; protein also provides 4 kcal/g. Fat supplies 9 kcal/g, and alcohol (a nonnutrient) provides 7 kcal/g.

Metric Basics

The metric prefixes *micro–, milli–, centi–, deci–,* and *kilo–* indicate whether a measurement is a fraction or a multiple of a meter (m), gram (g), or liter (l or L) (Table 1.6).

There are approximately 2.54 centimeters (cm) per inch. To obtain your approximate height in centimeters, multiply your height in inches by 2.54. For example, a person who is 5′5″ in height (65″) measures about 165 cm (65 × 2.54) in length. There are approximately 28 g in an ounce and 454 g in a pound. A kilogram (*kilo* = 1000) equals 1000 g or about 2.2 pounds. To determine your weight in kilograms (kg), divide your weight in pounds by 2.2. A person who weighs 130 pounds, for example, weighs about 59 kg.

Assume that a small raisin weighs 1 gram. If you cut this raisin into 1000 equal pieces, then each piece weighs 1 milligram (*milli* = 1000). Thus, 1000 milligrams (mg) equal 1 gram (g). Imagine cutting a small raisin into 1 million equal pieces. Each piece of raisin would weigh 1–millionth of a gram, or a microgram (mcg or µg). Amounts of nutrients in blood are often reported as the number of milligrams or micrograms of the substance per deciliter of blood. For example, a normal blood glucose level for a healthy fasting person is 90 milligrams/deciliter (90 mg/dl).

What's a Calorie?   Running, sitting, studying—your body uses energy even while sleeping. Every cell in your body needs energy to carry out its various activities. As long as you are alive, you are constantly using energy. You are probably familiar with the term ***calorie,*** the unit that describes the energy content of food. A calorie is the heat energy necessary to raise the temperature of 1 g (1 ml) of water 1° Celsius (C). A calorie is such a small unit of measurement, the amount of energy in food is reported in 1000–calorie units called kilocalories or Calories. Thus, a **kilocalorie** (kcal) or **Calorie** is the heat energy needed to raise the temperature of 1000 g (a liter) of water 1° Celsius (C). A small apple, for example, supplies 40,000 calories or 40 kcal or 40 Calories. If no number of kilocalories is specified, it is appropriate to use "calories." In this textbook, the term *kilocalories* (kcal) is interchangeable with *food energy* or simply *energy*.

A gram of carbohydrate and a gram of protein each supply about 4 kcal; a gram of fat provides about 9 kcal (Fig. 1.5). Although alcohol is not a nutrient, it does provide energy; a gram of pure alcohol furnishes 7 kcal. If you know how many grams of carbohydrate, protein, fat, and/or alcohol are in a food, you can estimate the number of kilocalories it provides. For example, if a serving of food contains 10 g of carbohydrate and 5 g of fat, multiply 10 by 4 (the number of kcal each gram of carbohydrate supplies). Then multiply 5 by 9 (the number of kcal each gram of fat supplies). By adding the two values (40 kcal from carbohydrate and 45 kcal from fat), you will determine that this food provides 85 kcal/serving.

Macronutrients and Micronutrients

Carbohydrates, fats, and proteins are referred to as **macronutrients** because the body needs relatively large amounts (grams) of these nutrients daily. Vitamins and minerals are **micronutrients,** because the body needs very small amounts (milligrams or micrograms) of them to function properly. In general, a serving of food supplies grams of carbohydrate, fat, and protein, and milligram or micro–gram quantities of vitamins and minerals. It is important to understand that macronutrients supply energy for cells, whereas micronutrients do not. Although the body requires large amounts of water, this nutrient provides no energy and is not usually classified as a macronutrient.

Amounts of nutrients present in different foods vary widely, and even the same food from the same source can contain different amounts of nutrients. Therefore, food composition tables and nutrient analysis software generally indicate average amounts of nutrients in foods. By using these tools, however, you can obtain approximate values for each nutrient measured and estimate your nutrient intake.

Concept **Checkpoint 1.3**

12. Scientists generally use which metric values to report volume, weight, and length?
13. A person weighs 154 pounds. How many kilograms does this person weigh?
14. A slice of whole-wheat bread supplies approximately 13 g of carbohydrate, 1 g of fat, 3 g of protein, and 11 g of water. Based on this information, estimate the number of kilocalories this food provides.
15. Which nutrients are classified as macronutrients? Which are classified as micronutrients?

1.4 Key Nutrition Concepts

Learning Outcomes

1. Give examples of empty-calorie, energy-dense, and nutrient-dense foods.
2. Discuss key basic nutrition concepts, such as the importance of eating a variety of foods and why food is the best source of nutrients.

Before learning about the nutrients and their roles in health, it is important to grasp some key basic nutrition concepts (Table 1.7). The content in the chapters that follow will build upon these key concepts and can help you make more informed choices concerning your dietary practices.

Concept 1: Most Naturally Occurring Foods Are Mixtures of Nutrients

Which foods do you think of when you hear the words *protein* or *carbohydrate?* You probably identify meat, milk, and eggs as sources of protein; and potatoes, bread, and candy as sources of carbohydrate. Most naturally occurring foods, however, are mixtures of nutrients. In many instances, water is the major nutrient in foods. For example, an 8–fluid–ounce serving of fat–free milk is about 91% water by weight, but it is an excellent source of protein and supplies carbohydrate, very little fat, and several vitamins and minerals. A 6–ounce plain white potato baked in its skin is 75% water and only about 23% carbohydrate by weight. The baked potato also supplies iron and potassium (minerals) and vitamins C and niacin.

Many sweet snacks are sources of nutrients other than sugar, a carbohydrate. Although sugar comprises about 44% of the weight of a chocolate with almonds candy bar, over one–third of the sweet snack's energy is from fat. The candy bar also contains small amounts of protein, iron, calcium, vitamin A, and the B–vitamin riboflavin. Figure 1.6 compares the energy, water, protein, carbohydrate, fat, and calcium contents of a 6–ounce baked potato, a slice of whole–wheat bread, 8 ounces of fat–free milk, and a chocolate–glazed doughnut (4–inch diameter) You can find information about the energy and nutrient contents of foods by using "What's in the Foods You Eat *Search Tool*" at the U.S. Department of Agriculture's website: www.ars.usda.gov/Services/docs.htm?docid=17032.

TABLE 1.7   Key Basic Nutrition Concepts

- Most naturally occurring foods are mixtures of nutrients.
- Variety can help ensure the nutritional adequacy of a diet.
- There are no "good" or "bad" foods.
- Enjoy eating all foods in moderation.
- For each nutrient, there is a range of safe intake.
- Food is the best source of nutrients and phytochemicals.
- There is no "one size fits all" approach to planning a nutritionally adequate diet.
- Foods and the nutrients they contain are not cure-alls.
- Malnutrition includes *under*nutrition as well as *over*nutrition.
- Nutrition is a dynamic science.

14   Chapter 1 The Basics of Nutrition

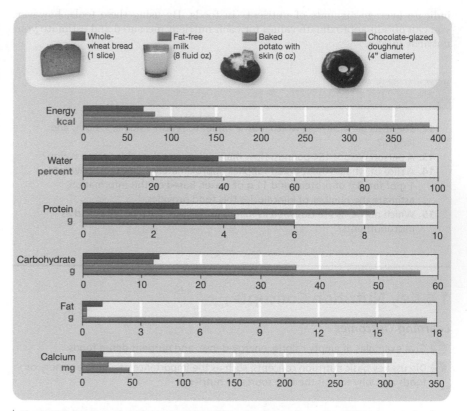

Figure 1.6 Energy and nutrient comparison. These foods contribute very different amounts of energy, water, protein, carbohydrate, fat, and calcium to diets.

| Figure 1.7 **MyPlate.**

Pumpkin pie is a good source of beta-carotene, a substance the body can convert to vitamin A. Because the pie is made with eggs and milk, this holiday favorite is also a good source of protein.

Concept 2: Variety Can Help Ensure the Nutritional Adequacy of a Diet

No natural food is "perfect" in that it contains all nutrients in amounts that are needed by the body. To help ensure the nutritional adequacy of your diet, choose a diet that contains a variety of foods from each food group that is shown in Figure 1.7, including fruits, low−fat or fat−free dairy products, and whole grains. To make menu planning more interesting and dishes more appealing, try unfa− miliar foods and new recipes for preparing your usual fare. Chapter 3 (Planning Nutritious Diets) provides information about the food groups and practical menu planning tools, such as the MyPlate plan. MyPlate is a personalized approach to menu planning that can help you incorporate a variety of foods from all food groups into your daily diet.

Concept 3: There Are No "Good" or "Bad" Foods

Are some foods "good" and others "bad" for your body? If you think there are such foods, which ones are good and which are bad? Do you sometimes feel guilty about eating "junk foods"? What is a junk food? Should pizza, chips, candy, doughnuts, ice cream, and sugar−sweetened soft drinks be classified as junk food?

No food deserves the label of "bad" or "junk," because all foods have nutritional value. For example, many people think pumpkin pie is a junk food. Pumpkin pie, however, is a good source of protein, the mineral iron, and the phytochemical beta−carotene that the body can convert to vitamin A. Even sugar—sweetened soft drinks provide water and the carbohydrate sugar, a source of energy. Although pies, doughnuts, and ice cream contain a lot of fat and sugar, these foods also supply small amounts of protein, vitamins, and minerals to diets. Healthy diets, however, generally contain limited amounts of such foods.

Empty-Calorie Foods

Some foods and beverages, such as bacon, candy, pastries, snack chips, and alco—holic or sugar—sweetened drinks, are described as sources of "empty calories." An **empty—calorie** food contributes a large portion of its energy from unhealthy solid fat, added sugar, and/or alcohol.[9] Therefore, people should limit their intake of empty—calorie foods. Consuming too much food energy in relation to one's needs can result in depositing excess body fat. Furthermore, eating too many empty—calorie foods may displace more nutritious foods from the diet. Chapter 3 provides more information about empty—calorie foods.

Nutrient Density

Certain foods are more nutritious than others. A **nutrient—dense** food contains more vitamins and minerals in relation to its unhealthy fat, added sugar, and/or alcohol contents. Broccoli, leafy greens, fat—free milk, orange juice, lean meats, and whole—grain cereals are examples of nutrient—dense foods. Figure 1.8 com—pares the nutritional values of 8—fluid—ounce servings of a sugar—sweetened soft drink and fat—free milk. Note that milk supplies water, protein, and certain vitamins and minerals, whereas the soft drink supplies water and carbohydrate but is a poor source of protein and micronutrients. A nutritious diet contains a variety of nutrient—dense foods.

Energy Density

Energy density describes the energy value of a food in relation to the food's weight. For example, a chocolate, cake—type frosted doughnut that weighs about 2 ounces provides 242 kcal; 5 medium strawberries also weigh about 2 ounces, but they provide only 19 kcal. You would have to eat nearly 64 of the strawber—ries to obtain the same amount of food energy that is in the chocolate doughnut. Therefore, the doughnut is an energy—dense food in comparison to the berries. In general, high—fat foods such as doughnuts are energy dense because they are concentrated sources of energy. Most fruits are not energy dense, because they contain far more water than fat.

Figure 1.9 compares a group of foods that each weigh about the same but differ in their energy densities. Not all energy—dense foods are empty—calorie foods. Nuts, for example, are high in fat and, therefore, energy dense. However, nuts are also nutrient dense because they contribute protein, vitamins, miner—als, and fiber to diets. Most forms of fiber are classified as carbohydrates.

A food *is* bad for you if it contains toxic substances or is contaminated with bacteria, viruses, or microscopic animals that cause food—borne illness. Chapter 12 (Food Safety Concerns) focuses on food safety concerns, including major types of food—borne illnesses and how to prevent them.

Concept 4: Enjoy Eating All Foods in Moderation

Dietary **moderation** involves obtaining enough nutrients from food to meet one's needs while avoiding excessive amounts and balancing calorie intake with calorie expenditure, primarily by physical activity. This can be accomplished by choosing nutrient—dense foods, limiting serving sizes, and incorporating moderate— to

83 kcal	91 kcal
8.26 g protein	0.17 g protein
299 mg calcium	5 mg calcium
247 mg phosphorus	25 mg phosphorus
0.446 mg riboflavin	0 mg riboflavin
149 µg vitamin A	0 µg vitamin A

8 fluid ounces   8 fluid ounces

Figure 1.8 Comparing nutrient densities. Although the milk and soft drink have similar caloric contents, milk is a much better source of proteins and micronutrients.

empty calorie describes food or beverage that supplies excessive amounts of unhealthy solid fat, added sugars, and/or alcohol

nutrient-dense describes food or beverage that has more vitamins and minerals in relation to its unhealthy fat, added sugar, and/or alcohol contents

energy density energy value of a food in relation to the food's weight

moderation obtaining adequate amounts of nutrients while balancing calorie intake with calorie expenditure

16   Chapter 1 The Basics of Nutrition

vigorous—intensity physical activities into your daily routine. Although mod—eration requires planning meals and setting aside time for physical activity daily, it can help you achieve your health and fitness goals. If, for example, you overeat during a meal or snack, you can regain dietary moderation and balance by eating less food and exercising more intensely during the next 24 hours.

Eliminating all empty—calorie foods from your diet is not generally recommended or necessary. If your core diet is comprised primarily of nutrient—dense foods and meets your nutritional needs, including some empty—calorie items adds enjoyment to living when they are consumed in moderation. Physically active individuals, such as athletes in training programs, often find it difficult to consume enough energy from foods to sustain healthy body weights, unless they include some empty—calorie items in their diets.

When a diet meets nutritional needs, including some empty-calorie items such as these brownies adds enjoyment when such foods are consumed in moderation.

physiological dose amount of a nutrient that is within the range of safe intake and enables the body to function optimally

megadose generally defined as 10 times the recommended amount of a vitamin or mineral

Concept 5: For Each Nutrient, There Is a Range of Safe Intake

By eating a variety of nutrient—dense foods, you are likely to obtain adequate and safe amounts of each nutrient. The **physiological dose** of a nutrient is the amount that is within the range of safe intake and enables the body to func—tion optimally. Consuming less than the physiological dose can result in mar—ginal nutritional status. In other words, the person's body has just enough of the nutrient to function adequately, but that amount is not sufficient to overcome the added stress of infection or injury. If a person's nutrient intake falls below the marginal level, the individual is at risk of developing the nutrient's deficiency disease. For example, the recommended amounts of the B—vitamin niacin are 16 mg for men and 14 mg for women. People whose diets contain little or no nia—cin are at risk of developing *pellagra*, the vitamin's deficiency disease.

Most people require physiological amounts of micronutrients. A **megadose** is generally defined as an amount of a vitamin or mineral that is at least 10 times the recommended amount of the nutrient.[10] When taken in high amounts, many vitamins behave like drugs and can produce unpleasant and even toxic side effects. For example, physicians sometimes use megadoses of the B—vitamin niacin to treat high blood cholesterol levels, but such amounts may cause painful facial flushing and liver damage. Minerals have very narrow ranges of safe intakes.

Many consumers take megadoses of vitamin and/or mineral supplements without consulting physicians, because they think the micronutrients will prevent or treat ailments such as the common cold or heart disease. For most people, consuming amounts of nutrients that exceed what is necessary for good health is economically wasteful and could be harmful to the body. "More is not always better," when it relates to optimal nutrition.

Figure 1.9 **Energy density.** Although each of these portions of food weigh about the same, they differ in their energy densities. For example, you would need to eat over 4 cups of whole strawberries to consume the same amount of energy in a 3-ounce, broiled hamburger patty (10% fat).

In their natural states, most commonly eaten foods do not contain toxic levels of vitamins and minerals. You probably do not need to worry about consuming toxic levels of micronutrients, unless you are taking megadoses of vitamin/mineral supplements or eating large amounts of foods that are fortified with these nutrients regularly. The diagram shown in Figure 1.10 illustrates the general concept of deficient, safe, and toxic intake ranges for nutrients such as vitamins and minerals. Chapters 8 and 9 provide more information about micronutrients, including deficiencies and toxicities.

Concept 6: Food Is the Best Source of Nutrients and Phytochemicals

The most natural, reliable, and economical way to obtain nutrients and beneficial phytochemicals is to base your diet on a variety of "whole" and minimally processed foods. Plant foods naturally contain a variety of nutrients and phytochemicals, but processing the foods often removes some of the most healthful parts. For example, a wheat kernel is stripped of its germ and outer hull (bran) during refinement into white flour (Fig. 1.11). Wheat germ is a rich source of vitamin E and beneficial lipids. Wheat bran contains fiber and certain phytochemicals, and it is a concentrated source of micronutrients. The endosperm that remains is primarily starch (a form of carbohydrate) with some protein and very small amounts of micronutrients and fiber. By replacing refined grain products, such as white bread, with whole–grain products, you can increase the likelihood of obtaining a wide variety of nutrients and phytochemicals.

In addition to eating food, many people take nutrient supplements in the form of pills, powders, bars, wafers, or beverages. The human body, however, is designed to obtain nutrients from foods, not supplements. In some instances, nutrients from food are more available, that is, more easily digested and absorbed, than those in supplements.

It is important to understand that nutrient supplements do not contain everything one needs for optimal nutrition. For example, they do not contain the wide variety of phytochemicals found in plant foods. Although supplements that contain phytochemicals are available, they may not provide the same healthful benefits as consuming the plants that contain these compounds. Why? Nutrients and phytochemicals may need to be consumed together to provide the desirable effects in the body. Food naturally contains combinations of these chemicals in very small amounts and certain proportions. There is nothing "natural" about gulping down handfuls of supplements.

Some individuals have increased needs for certain nutrients, particularly micronutrients. People who have chronic illnesses, digestive disorders that interfere with nutrient absorption, and certain inherited disorders may require supplemental nutrients. Additionally, many older adults may need higher amounts of vitamins and other nutrients than those found in food. Because it is often difficult

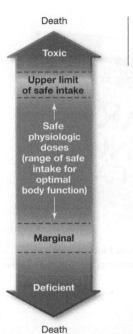

Figure 1.10 Intake continuum. For each nutrient, there is a range of safe intake.

Death

Toxic

Upper limit of safe intake

Safe physiologic doses (range of safe intake for optimal body function)

Marginal

Deficient

Death

Dietary supplements should not be considered substitutes for nutrient-dense food.

This product is a functional food because it was manufactured with ingredients that may reduce the body's cholesterol level.

to plan and eat nutritious menus each day, taking a supplement that contains a variety of vitamins may be advisable, even for healthy adults.[11] In general, there appears to be little danger in taking a dietary supplement that provides 100% of recommended amounts of the micronutrients daily.[12] However, healthy adults should consider taking such supplements as an "insurance policy" and not a substitute for eating a variety of nutrient–dense foods.

Concept 7: There Is No "One Size Fits All" Approach to Planning a Nutritionally Adequate Diet

By using food guides presented in Chapter 3, you can individualize your diet so that it is nutritionally adequate and suits your food likes and dislikes, budget, and lifestyle. Individualizing a diet does not mean only eating foods that "match" your blood type, hair color, personality, or shoe size. If someone promotes a diet based on such personal traits, steer clear of the diet and the promoter. Consider this: Human beings would not have survived as a species for thousands of years if their diets had to be matched to physical characteristics or personalities.

Physicians often prescribe special diets, sometimes referred to as *medical nutrition therapies*, for people with chronic health conditions such as diabetes. Even the nutritional needs of healthy people vary during different stages of their lives. Chapter 13 (Nutrition for a Lifetime) provides information about the importance of diet during pregnancy, childhood, and other stages of the life cycle.

Concept 8: Foods and the Nutrients They Contain Are Not Cure-Alls

Although specific nutrient deficiency diseases, such as scurvy, can be cured by eating foods that contain the nutrient that is missing or in short supply, nutrients do not "cure" other ailments. Diet is only one aspect of a person that influences his or her health. By making certain dietary changes, however, a person may be able to prevent or forestall the development of certain diseases, or possibly lessen their severity if they occur.

Although there is no legal definition for "functional foods," such products have health–related purposes.[13] Functional foods are often manufactured to boost nutrient intakes or help manage specific health problems. For example, consumers who want to increase their calcium intake can purchase orange juice

Figure 1.11 What is white flour? During refinement, a wheat kernel is stripped of its nutrient-rich germ and bran. The endosperm (white flour) that remains is mostly starch.

Bran

Endosperm

Germ

that has the mineral added to it. Certain margarine substitutes contain phyto—chemicals that interfere with the body's ability to absorb cholesterol from food and, as a result, may lower the risk of heart disease. Although some functional foods can help Americans improve their health, more research is needed to determine their benefits as well as possible harmful effects.

Concept 9: Malnutrition Includes *Under*nutrition as Well as *Over*nutrition

Malnutrition is a state of health that occurs when the body is improperly nour—ished. Everyone must consume food and water to stay alive, yet despite the abundance and variety of nutritious foods, many Americans consume nutrition—ally poor diets and suffer from malnutrition as a result. Some people select nutri—tionally inadequate diets because they lack knowledge about nutritious foods or the importance of nutrition to health. Low—income people, however, are at risk for malnutrition because they have limited financial resources for making wise food purchases. Other people who are at risk of malnutrition include those who have severe eating disorders, are addicted to drugs such as alcohol, or have cer—tain serious medical problems. This chapter's "Nutrition Matters" feature dis—cusses the international problem of *under*nutrition.

Although many people associate malnutrition with undernutrition and starvation, *over*nutrition, the long—term excess of energy or nutrient intake, is also a form of malnutrition. Overnutrition is often characterized by obesity. You may be surprised to learn that overnutrition is more common in the United States than undernutrition (Fig. 1.12). Obesity is widespread in countries where most people have the financial means to buy food, have an ample food supply, and obtain little exercise. Chapter 10 provides information about obesity.

Concept 10: Nutrition Is a Dynamic Science

As researchers continue to explore the complex relationships between diets and health, nutrition information constantly evolves. As a result, dietary practices and recommendations undergo revision as new scientific evidence becomes avail—able and is reviewed and accepted by nutrition experts. Unfortunately such changes can be confusing to the general public, who expect medical researchers to provide definite answers to their nutrition—related questions and rigid advice concerning optimal dietary practices.

Even nutrition educators find it difficult to keep up with the vast num—ber of research articles published in scientific journals. Chapter 2 explains how nutrition research is conducted using scientific methods. Furthermore, Chapter 2 provides information to help you become a better consumer of nutrition and health information that appears in popular sources such as magazines, infomercials, and the Internet.

Figure 1.12 Obesity. Obesity is a prevalent nutrition-related health problem in many nations.

malnutrition state of health that occurs when the body is improperly nourished

MY DIVERSE PLATE

Locusts

In parts of Africa, Cambodia, and the Philippines, many people eat locusts, especially when the insects are plentiful. Popular ways to cook locusts include removing the wings and legs before frying with seasonings or placing locusts on skewers and roasting them over hot embers. The legs and wings are removed from the grilled insects before they are cooked or eaten. Over 60% of the dry weight of a locust is protein, so the insect is an excellent source of the macronutrient.

Source: Food and Agricultural Organization, http://www.fao.org/ag/locusts/en/info/info/faq/

Concept **Checkpoint 1.4**

16. Identify at least five of the key nutrition-related concepts presented in this section.
17. What is the difference between an empty-calorie and a nutrient-dense food?
18. What is the difference between a physiological dose and a megadose of a nutrient?

1.5 Nutrition Matters: Undernutrition—A Worldwide Concern

Learning Outcomes

① Discuss factors that contribute to undernutrition in the world.

② Describe how undernutrition during pregnancy and childhood can affect a child's physical and intellectual development.

③ Identify major federal food assistance programs and the populations served by each program.

④ Discuss how sustainable agriculture can improve the environment.

Over 6.5 billion people inhabit the Earth. In 2009, an estimated 1 billion of these persons were chronically undernourished and on the brink of starvation.[14] Chronic undernutrition is a condition that occurs when a person's long−term energy and nutrient intakes are insufficient to meet his or her needs.

Many factors contribute to undernutrition (Fig. 1.13). Poverty and lack of access to nutritious food are serious problems, particularly in sub−Saharan Africa and certain regions of Asia, where decades of civil unrest, wars, and the AIDS epidemic have left millions of people impover−ished and living in uncertainty. Furthermore, unfavorable weather conditions and crop failures can cause regional food shortages. In many developing countries, impoverished people lack supplies of clean cooking and drinking water. Throughout the world, lack of access to clean water causes the majority of all diseases and more than one−third of all deaths (Fig. 1.14).

Undernutrition During Periods of Growth

When undernutrition occurs during periods of rapid growth, such as pregnancy, infancy, and childhood, the long−term effects can be devastating. Each year, maternal and child undernutrition contributes to 3.5 million deaths; nutrition−related factors such as under−nutrition and vitamin A deficiency are responsible for 35% of deaths in children under 5 years of age.[15] The vast majority of childhood deaths associated with under−nutrition occur among poor populations in developing countries, particularly in Africa and Southeast Asia.[16]

Figure 1.14 Unsafe water source. In developing countries, lack of clean cooking and drinking water contribute to the spread of infectious diseases.

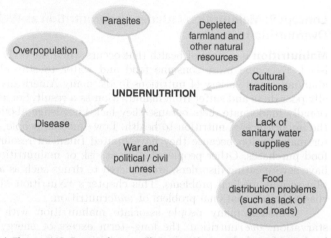

Figure 1.13 Factors that contribute to undernutrition. Many factors, including war, disease, and overpopulation, contribute to undernutrition in developing countries.

Diagram labels: Parasites; Depleted farmland and other natural resources; Overpopulation; Cultural traditions; UNDERNUTRITION; Disease; Lack of sanitary water supplies; War and political / civil unrest; Food distribution problems (such as lack of good roads)

Undernutrition During Pregnancy. Women who are undernourished during pregnancy are more likely to die while giving birth than pregnant women who are adequately nourished. Furthermore, malnourished pregnant women have a high risk of giving birth to infants that are born too soon. These babies often suffer from breathing problems and have low birth weights—conditions that increase their risk of dying during their first year of life. Each year, an estimated 18 million low−birth−weight infants are born in the world.[17] The vast majority of low−birth−weight infants are born in developing countries. Chapter 13 provides more information about the importance of adequate nutrition during pregnancy.

Undernutrition During Infancy. As explained in Chapter 13, breast milk is the best food for young infants because it is sanitary, is nutritionally adequate, and provides babies with immu−nity to some infectious diseases. In developing countries, many new mothers do not exclusively breastfeed their babies for more than a few weeks.[15] Although infant formulas are nutritious substitutes for breast milk, they do not provide immunity to diseases, and they are generally more expensive.

To increase the volume of infant formula that they can afford to give their children, poor parents in developing countries often add excessive amounts of water. This practice dilutes the nutritional value of the formula and increases the likelihood of contaminating it with disease–causing microbes. Infants who drink formula that has been mixed with unsanitary water can develop diarrhea that causes loss of body water (*dehydration*) and death.

Ideally, babies should be exclusively breast fed for their first six months and then consume breast milk in addition to solid foods well into their second year.

Undernutrition During the Preschool Years. In undernourished children, nutrient deficiencies are responsible for stunted physical growth, delayed physical development, blindness, impaired intellectual development, and premature death (Fig. 1.15). In the United States and other developed countries, children are usually well nourished and vaccinated against common childhood diseases such as measles. In poorer nations, however, many children are malnourished and not protected against infectious agents, such as the virus that causes measles. Measles can be a life–threatening illness in undernourished children, because their immune systems do not function normally.

Undernutrition in the United States Undernutrition also occurs in wealthy, developed nations such as the United States. In some instances, undernutrition is not due to poverty in these countries. For example, many people suffering from anorexia nervosa and chronic alcoholism are undernourished despite having enough money to purchase food. Nevertheless, Americans with low incomes have a higher risk of malnutrition than members of the population who are in higher income categories. Between 2008–2012, 14.9% of the population were living at or below the U.S. Department of Health and Human Services *poverty guideline*.[18] In 2011, the poverty guideline was $22,350 for a family of four.[19] In 2014, this guideline was $23,850 for a family of four. Most American households are *food secure*, which means the people in those households have access to and can purchase sufficient food to lead healthy, active lives. In 2011, **food insecurity** was reported in almost 15% of all households in the United States.[20] Food insecurity describes individuals or families who are concerned about running out of food or not having enough money to buy more food. People who are unemployed, work in low–paying jobs, or have excessive medical and housing expenses often experience food insecurity. Food insecurity may also affect elderly Americans who live on fixed incomes, especially if they are forced to choose between purchasing nutritious food and buying life–extending medications.

Charities and churches in many cities operate food pantries and "soup kitchens" to feed food–insecure people (Fig. 1.16). In addition to the help provided by the private sector, low–income individuals can obtain food aid from federal food assistance programs. Table 1.8 summarizes information about major federally subsidized food programs in the United States. Although not every eligible food–insecure person has access to or takes advantage of the aid, federal food assistance programs protect most American children from hunger and undernutrition. For more information

food insecurity situation in which individuals or families are concerned about running out of food or not having enough money to buy more food

Figure 1.15 Chronic undernutrition. This photograph shows a group of undernourished children outside a Nigerian orphanage during the late 1960s.

Figure 1.16 Feeding the hungry. In many cities, charities and churches operate food pantries and "soup kitchens" to feed food-insecure people.

TABLE 1.8   Major Federally Subsidized Food Programs in the United States

Program	General Eligibility Requirements	Description
Supplemental Nutrition Assistance Program (SNAP)	Low-income individuals and families	Participants use an electronic benefit transfer (debit) card to purchase allowable food items.
Commodity Distribution Program	Certain low-income groups, including pregnant women, preschool-age children, and the elderly	In some states, state agencies distribute USDA surplus foods to eligible people.
Women, Infants, and Children (WIC)	Low-income pregnant or breastfeeding women, infants, and children under 5 years of age who are at nutritional risk	Participants receive checks or vouchers to purchase milk, cheese, fruit juice, certain cereals, infant formula, and other specific food items at grocery stores. Nutrition education is also provided.
School Lunch and School Breakfast Programs	Low-income children of school age	Certain schools receive subsidies from the government to provide free or reduced-price nutritionally balanced lunches and breakfasts.
Elderly Nutrition Program	Age 60 or older (no income guidelines)	Provides grants for sites to provide nutritious congregate and home-delivered meals
Child and Adult Care Food Program	Children enrolled in organized childcare programs and seniors in adult care programs	Site receives reimbursement for nutritious meals and snacks supplied to participants.
Food Distribution Program on Indian Reservations	Low-income American Indian or non-Indian households on reservations; members of federally recognized Native American tribes	Distribution of monthly food packages. This program is an alternative to SNAP and includes a nutrition education component.

about the federal government's nutrition assistance programs, visit www.nutrition.gov/food–assistance–programs.

World Food Crisis: Finding Solutions   Reducing hunger through food aid programs is a major goal of the United Nations. The World Food Program and United Nations Children's Fund (UNICEF) are agencies within the United Nations that provide high–quality food for undernourished populations. UNICEF also supports the development and distribution of ready–to–use therapeutic food (RUTF) to treat severe undernutrition among young children in developing countries. *Plumpy'Nut*, for example, is

an energy– and nutrient–dense paste made from a mixture of peanuts, powdered milk, oil, sugar, vitamins, and minerals. During processing, the paste is placed in foil packets to keep the food clean and make it easy to transport to remote places without refrigeration. In 2013, UNICEF supplied over 37,000 tons of RUTFs to feed starving children in developing nations.[21]

The Promise of Biotechnology.   **Biotechnology** involves the use of living things—plants, animals, microbes—to manufacture new products. Biotechnology in agriculture has led to the development of crops that supply higher yields, resist pests, or are tolerant of drought conditions. By increasing food production or modifying the nutritional content of foods, biotechnology offers another way of alleviating the world food crisis.

Genetic modification methods, such as *genetic engineering*, involve scientific methods that alter an animal or plant's hereditary material (**genes** or DNA). For example, genes that produce a desirable trait are transferred from

Any child who attends a school that participates in the School Lunch Program can purchase a nutritious lunch. After selecting from the menu, the child enters his or her personal identification number (PIN) into the device shown in the photo. The device records the purchase and debits the child's school lunch account. By using this system, the program protects the identity of children who receive free or reduced-price lunches.

biotechnology using living things to manufacture new products

genetic modification techniques that alter an organism's DNA

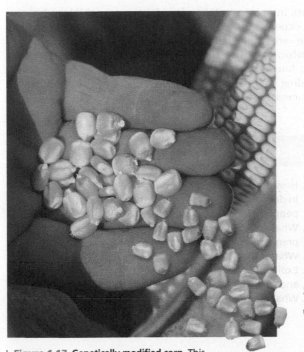

Figure 1.17 Genetically modified corn. This seed corn is the result of genetic engineering.

one organism into the DNA of a second organism, altering its genes. Most of the cotton, corn, and soybeans grown in the United States are the result of genetic engineering (Fig. 1.17).[22] These crops have been genetically altered to resist pests and tolerate chemicals that farmers use to kill pests (pesticides). In the future, genetic engineering of food crops will provide the opportunity to enhance the plants' nutritional qualities.

According to Dr. J. Craig Venter, geneticist and founder of the Institute for Genomic Research, the safety of genetically engineered crops destined for human consumption has been tested extensively.[23] Some scientists, however, have raised concerns that *genetically modified organisms (GMOs)* introduce new proteins into the food chain, creating the potential for environmental harm. The U.S. Food and Drug Administration (FDA) regulates the safety of genetically engineered foods. Nevertheless, researchers continue to examine the long-term safety of GMOs.

Feeding the World, Protecting Natural Resources. Our current system of food production relies primarily on conventional agricultural methods. In general, conventional farming requires considerable amounts of water and pesticides that can harm the environment. Irrigation systems often remove fresh water from rivers and other natural sources at a faster rate than it is restored. This activity reduces water flow to many communities. The water that runs off conventional farms can carry with it precious topsoil and pesticides that pollute waterways. Such farming methods also release greenhouse gases, especially carbon dioxide and methane, which contribute to global warming. Furthermore, the need for new farmland often requires cutting down trees so that forests can be converted to croplands. The loss of forests eliminates native animal and plant habitats. About 40% of the Earth's land (excluding Greenland and Antarctica) is used for food production; very little suitable land remains to be farmed.[24] What can be done to feed the world's population without destroying the Earth's natural resources?

What's Sustainable Agriculture?   **Sustainable agriculture** involves farming methods that meet the demand for more food without depleting natural resources and harming the environment. The challenge is finding ways for farmers and ranchers to make the conversion from primarily conventional farming techniques to sustainable agriculture. Farming needs to be profitable for farmers and ranchers, so any switch from conventional to sustainable agricultural methods must not reduce their profit margins.

To solve the problems created by conventional agricultural methods, an international team developed the following points for establishing a universal policy:[24]

- Stop expanding agricultural activity, especially into tropical forests and grasslands.
- Find ways to improve crop yields on existing farms. Biotechnology in agriculture has led to the development of crops that supply higher yields, resist pests, or are tolerant of drought conditions. By increasing food production or modifying the nutritional content of foods, biotechnology offers a way of reducing the world food crisis.
- Find ways to use natural resources and pesticides more efficiently. Use irrigation systems that apply water directly to a plant's base instead of spraying it into the air, where much of the water evaporates.
- Rely more on nonchemical methods of pest management (see Chapter 12).
- Eat less meat. Sixty percent of the world's crops (primarily grains) are grown for human consumption. Most of the remaining crops are used to feed cattle and other farm animals. It takes about 30 pounds of grains to produce 1 pound of hamburger. By reducing the consumption of meat, especially beef, more grains could be produced to feed people. Grass-fed beef also spares grains for human consumption, because grass is not eaten by people.

sustainable agriculture farming methods that do not deplete natural resources or harm the environment while meeting the demand for food

- Reduce food waste—about 30% of food is wasted. In many instances, the food spoils before it is eaten or it is thrown out as garbage. Smaller portion sizes and bet—ter menu planning can reduce the amount of food that people waste each day.

Taking Action. Poverty and hunger have always plagued humankind; the causes of poverty and hunger are complex and, therefore, difficult to eliminate. Nevertheless, certain social, political, economic, and agricultural changes can reduce the number of people who are chronically hungry. In the short run, wealthy countries can provide food aid to keep impoverished people from starving to death. Families and small farmers in underdeveloped nations need to learn new and more efficient methods of growing, processing, preserving, and distributing nutritious regional food prod—ucts. Additionally, governments can support programs that encourage breastfeeding and fortify locally grown or com—monly consumed foods with vitamins and minerals that are often deficient in local diets.

In the long run, population control is critical for preserv—ing the Earth's resources for future generations. Impoverished parents in poor countries often have many children because they expect only a few to survive to adulthood. When people are financially secure, adequately nourished, and well educated, they tend to have fewer, healthier children. Thus, long—term ways to slow population growth include providing well—paying jobs, improving public education, and increasing access to health care services.

Concept **Checkpoint 1.5**

19. How do unfavorable environmental and political factors in developing countries affect the health status of people living in those nations?
20. What effects can undernutrition have on the health of pregnant women and young children?
21. What is the "WIC program"?
22. Explain the difference between conventional and sustainable agricultural methods.
23. What is a genetically modified organism?

Chapter References

See Appendix H.

Summary

1.1 Nutrition: The Basics

- Lifestyle choices, including poor eating habits and lack of physical activity, contribute to the development of many of the leading causes of premature deaths for American adults, including heart disease, cancer, stroke, and diabetes. However, you may be able to extend your life span and improve your quality of life by applying what you learn about nutrition and the role of diet and health.

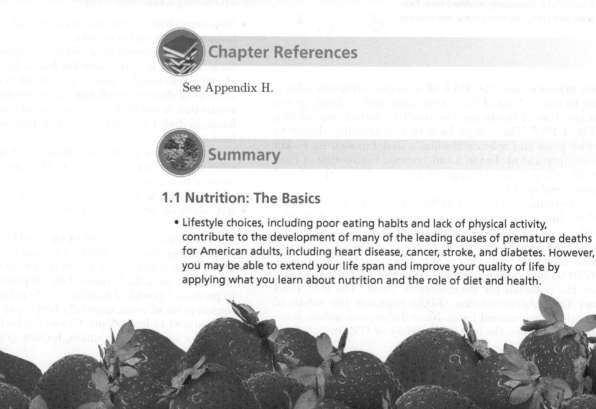

- There are six classes of nutrients: carbohydrates, lipids, proteins, vitamins, minerals, and water. The body needs certain nutrients for energy, growth and development, and regulation of processes, including the repair and maintenance of cells. The human body can synthesize many nutrients, but about 50 nutrients are dietary essentials that must be supplied by food.

- Nonnutrients, which include phytochemicals, are substances in food that may have healthful benefits. Many phytochemicals are antioxidants that protect cells from being damaged or destroyed by exposure to certain environmental factors. However, some phytochemicals are toxic. The Dietary Supplement Health and Education Act of 1994 (DSHEA) allows manufacturers to classify herbal products and nutrient supplements as dietary supplements.

1.2 Factors That Influence Americans' Health

- Heart disease is the leading cause of death for all Americans. Chronic diseases, such as heart disease, are complex conditions that have multiple risk factors. A risk factor is a personal characteristic that increases a person's chances of developing diseases. In many instances, people can live longer and healthier by modifying their diets, increasing their physical activity, and altering other aspects of their lifestyles. Objectives to improve the status of Americans' health, including nutrition-related programs, are an important focus of *Healthy People 2020.*

1.3 Metrics for Nutrition

- Scientists generally use metric values when measuring volume, weight, and length. The metric prefixes *micro-, milli-, deci-, centi-,* and *kilo-* indicate whether a measurement is a fraction or a multiple of a meter, gram, or liter. Approximately 28 g are in an ounce and 454 g are in a pound; a kilogram equals 1000 grams or about 2.2 pounds. Each gram equals 1000 milligrams or 1 million micrograms.

- Every cell needs energy. A Calorie is the heat energy needed to raise the temperature of 1 liter of water 1° Celsius (C). Calories or kilocalories (kcal) are used to indicate the energy value in food. If no number of kilocalories is specified, it is appropriate to use "calories." A gram of carbohydrate and a gram of protein each supply about 4 kcal; a gram of fat provides about 9 kcal. Although alcohol is not a nutrient, a gram of pure alcohol furnishes 7 kcal.

- Carbohydrates, fats, and proteins are referred to as macronutrients because the body needs relatively large amounts of these nutrients daily. Vitamins and minerals are micronutrients, because the body needs very small amounts. Although the body requires large amounts of water, this nutrient provides no energy and is not usually classified as a macronutrient.

1.4 Key Nutrition Concepts

- There are several key points to understanding nutrition. Most naturally occurring foods are mixtures of nutrients, but no food contains all the nutrients needed for optimal health. Thus, nutritionally adequate diets include a variety of foods from all food groups. Instead of classifying foods as "good" or "bad," people can focus on eating all foods in moderation and limiting empty-calorie foods. For each nutrient, there is a range of safe intake. Healthy people should rely on eating a variety of foods to meet their nutrient needs instead of taking dietary supplements. Foods and the nutrients they contain are not cure-alls. There is no "one size fits all" approach to planning a nutritionally adequate diet. Malnutrition includes overnutrition as well as undernutrition. Finally, nutrition is a dynamic science; new scientific information about nutrients and their roles in health is constantly emerging. Therefore, ways the science of nutrition is applied, such as dietary recommendations, also change.

1.5 Nutrition Matters: Undernutrition—A Worldwide Concern

- Poverty and undernutrition are commonplace in many developing countries. Impoverished people must often cope with infectious diseases and polluted water supplies. In developing countries, poor sanitation practices and lack of clean cooking and drinking water contribute to diseases and deaths. In undernourished children, nutrient deficiencies are responsible for stunted physical growth, delayed physical development, blindness, impaired intellectual development, and premature death. Chronic undernutrition depresses the body's immune functioning, increasing the risk of death from infectious diseases, such as measles, especially in childhood. The vast majority of childhood deaths associated with undernutrition occur among poor populations in developing countries, particularly in sub-Saharan Africa and Southeast Asia. When undernutrition occurs during the first 5 years of life, the effects can be devastating to the child's brain and result in permanent learning disabilities. Additionally, chronically undernourished children do not grow normally and tend to be shorter if they survive to adulthood.

- Reducing hunger through food aid programs is a major goal of the United Nations. Biotechnological advances in agriculture have led to the development of crops that supply higher yields, resist pests, or are tolerant of drought conditions. Conventional farming methods can cause soil loss and add pesticides to water supplies. Sustainable agriculture refers to farming methods that do not deplete natural resources or harm the environment while meeting the demand for food.

Recipe for 🗃 Healthy Living

Food Preparation Basics (Yes, You *Can* Cook!)

By learning how to prepare dishes, experiment with recipe ingredients, and use a variety of spices and herbs as seasonings, you can make home-cooked meals that are more tasty, more appealing, and lower in fat, sugar, salt, and calories than the usual choices at fast-food restaurants. Additionally, you can save money by making your meals and snacks instead of purchasing them from restaurants and vending machines.

At the end of each chapter, you will find the "Recipe for Healthy Living," a nutritious, easy-to-prepare recipe. Each recipe includes a list of ingredients, instructions, and some information concerning the energy and selected nutrient contents in a serving of the product. The "MyPlate" icon indicates which of the USDA's food groups are primarily represented in the recipe (see Fig.1.7). The circle graph shows approximate percentages of total calories for each macronutrient in the food. The bar graph indicates approximate percentages of Daily Values (DVs) for energy and some key nutrients. Daily Values are a set of nutrient standards used for food labeling purposes (see Chapter 3).

Even if you've had little or no cooking experience, you can learn the basics of preparing foods. Some cooks don't measure ingredients; they know from experience how to estimate amounts of foods and seasonings to add when preparing dishes. Until you feel confident with your food preparation skills, it is best to follow recipes and measure ingredients carefully.

You'll need some basic food preparation equipment to get started. You don't have to spend a lot of money, but buy well-made stainless steel (rustproof) cooking utensils and mixing bowls that will last for decades. Baking pans should also be stainless steel. A square or rectangular tempered-glass baking dish can be used for a variety of cooking needs, including heating foods in a toaster oven or microwave oven.

Understanding how to use household measurements is a good place to begin when learning how to cook. Purchase a set of metal measuring spoons that includes ⅛ teaspoon (tsp), ¼ tsp, ½ tsp, 1 tsp, and 1 tablespoon (Tbsp) measures. You'll also need a set of plastic or metal measuring cups that includes the following measures: ¼ cup, ⅓ cup, ½ cup, and 1 cup. These cups are used to measure dry ingredients such as flour or sugar. Finally, purchase a 2-cup glass or clear plastic measuring pitcher that is marked to indicate fluid ounces. This pitcher is used for measuring liquid ingredients such as water, milk, and oil.

To measure dry ingredients, fill the appropriate measuring cup or spoon to the top, and skim off the excess with the straight edge of a knife. To measure liquid ingredients, use a liquid measuring pitcher. Fill the pitcher to the desired amount, and place it on a level surface. Crouch down so you are at eye level with the fluid's level, and then carefully add more or remove some fluid as needed.

HOUSEHOLD UNITS

Common household units often used for measuring food ingredients and their commonly used abbreviations are listed below. Ounces (oz) are a measure of weight; *fluid* ounces are a measure of volume. Appendix A provides information about English-to-metric and metric-to-household unit conversions.

COMMON HOUSEHOLD UNITS FOR MEASURING FOOD INGREDIENTS

3 tsp = 1 Tbsp	1 cup = 8 fluid ounces (oz)
4 Tbsp = ¼ cup	1 cup = ½ pint
5 Tbsp + 1 tsp = ⅓ cup	2 cups = 1 pint
8 Tbsp = ½ cup	4 cups or 2 pints = 1 quart
16 Tbsp = 1 cup	4 quarts = 1 gallon

28   **Chapter 1** The Basics of Nutrition

Low-Fat Applesauce Oatmeal Muffins

The following muffin recipe is simple and will give you an opportunity to practice measuring dry and liquid ingredients. This recipe makes 12 small muffins, so you'll need a muffin tin with 12 muffin cups. Each muffin supplies about 168 kcal, 4.6 g fat, 27.0 g digestible carbohydrate, 4.5 g protein, 1.5 g fiber, and 5.7 mg iron.

INGREDIENTS:

1 ½ cups quick oats, enriched, uncooked
1 ¼ cups all-purpose enriched flour
1 tsp baking powder
¾ tsp baking soda
1 tsp ground cinnamon
¼ tsp ground nutmeg
1 cup unsweetened applesauce
½ cup fat-free milk
½ cup brown sugar
3 Tbsp vegetable oil
1 medium egg
vegetable oil cooking spray

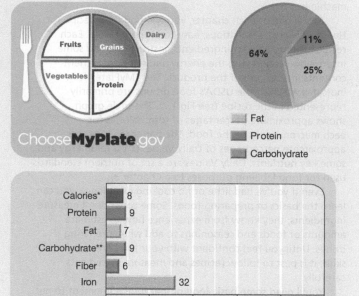

*2000 daily total kcal
**Digestible forms

PREPARATION STEPS:

1. Preheat oven to 400° F. Spray vegetable oil spray lightly on the bottom of each cup of the muffin tin.

2. Combine oats, flour, baking powder, baking soda, and spices in a large bowl. Stir until well mixed. By using a large spoon, form a depressed area (a "well") in the center of the dry ingredients.

3. In another bowl, break the egg and use a fork to beat the egg to blend the white and yolk into a yellow mixture.

4. Add applesauce, milk, brown sugar, and oil to the beaten egg, and stir with a large spoon until ingredients are well mixed.

5. Pour the applesauce-containing mixture into the "well" of dry ingredients in the first bowl. Stir gently and just until the dry ingredients have been moistened by the applesauce mixture. Do not be concerned if small lumps of dry ingredients are in the batter. Do not beat or overmix the ingredients; otherwise, the muffins will form air tunnels and have peaked rather than rounded tops.

6. Spoon batter into muffin cups until the cup is half full of batter.

7. Bake 20 minutes or until muffins are golden brown. Use pot holders to protect your hands when taking the muffin tin out of the oven. Cool muffins for about 5 minutes before removing them from the tin. Muffins can be stored in a closed container in the refrigerator for up to a week. Before eating, warm each muffin in a microwave oven for about 15 seconds.

Tip: For easier cleanup, soak the bowl that contained the batter in cold, soapy water.

connect | NUTRITION   Further analyze this and other recipes through activities on Connect at www.mcgrawhillconnect.com.

Personal Dietary Analysis

1. For 1 week, keep grocery and convenience store receipts.

   a. How much money did you spend on foods purchased at these markets?

   b. Which foods were the most expensive items purchased?

   c. How much money did you spend on empty-calorie foods and beverages such as salty snacks, cookies, soft drinks, and candy? _____

   d. What percentage of your food dollars were spent on empty-calorie foods? _____ (Divide the amount of money spent on empty-calorie foods by the total cost of food for the week. Move the decimal point over 2 places to the right and place a percent sign after the number.)

   e. How much money did you spend on nutrient-dense foods such as whole-grain products, fruits, and vegetables? _____

   f. What percentage of your food dollars were spent on nutrient-dense foods? _____ (Divide the amount of money spent on nutrient-dense foods by the total cost of food for the week. Move the decimal point over 2 places to the right and place a percent sign after the number.)

2. For 1 week, keep a detailed log of your usual vending machine purchases, including the item(s) purchased and amount of money spent for each purchase.

   a. What types of foods and beverages did you buy from the machines?

   b. How many soft drinks did you consume each day? _____

   c. How much money did you spend on vending machine foods and beverages? _____

   d. Based on this week's vending machine expenditures, estimate how much money you spend on such purchases in a year. _____

3. For 1 week, keep a detailed log of your usual fast-food consumption practices, including fast-food purchases at convenience stores. List the types of food and beverages you purchased and amount of money you spent.

   a. According to your weekly record, how often do you buy food from fast-food places and convenience stores? _____

   b. What types of foods did you usually buy?

   c. How much money did you spend on fast foods? _____

   d. Based on this week's expenditures, estimate how much money you spend on fast-food purchases in a year. _____

connect |NUTRITION

Complete this Personal Dietary Analysis activity online at www.mcgrawhillconnect.com.

30   **Chapter 1** The Basics of Nutrition

Critical Thinking

1. Identify at least six factors that influence your food and beverage selections. Which of these factors is the most important? Explain why.

2. Consider your current eating habits. Explain why you think your diet is or is not nutritionally adequate.

3. "Everything in moderation." Explain what this state-ment means in terms of your diet.

4. If you were at risk of developing a chronic health con-dition that could be prevented by changing your diet,

would you make the necessary changes? Explain why or why not.

5. Have you ever used certain foods or dietary supplements, such as vitamins, to treat or prevent illnesses? If you have, describe the situations and discuss which foods or supplements were used.

6. What actions have you taken or can you take to help hun-gry or food—insecure people obtain adequate nutrition?

Practice Test

Select the best answer.

1. Diet is a

   a. practice of restricting energy intake.
   b. pattern of food choices.
   c. method of reducing portion sizes.
   d. technique to reduce carbohydrate intake.

2. Which of the following conditions is not one of the 10 leading causes of death in the United States?

   a. tuberculosis
   b. cancer
   c. heart disease
   d. stroke

3. The nutrients that provide energy are

   a. carbohydrates, vitamins, and lipids.
   b. lipids, proteins, and minerals.
   c. vitamins, minerals, and proteins.
   d. proteins, fats, and carbohydrates.

4. _____ refers to all chemical processes that occur in living cells.

   a. Physiology   b. Catabolism
   c. Anatomy   d. Metabolism

5. Phytochemicals

   a. are essential nutrients.
   b. may have healthful benefits.
   c. should be avoided.
   d. are in animal sources of food.

6. Which of the following foods is energy and nutrient dense?

   a. peanut butter
   b. sugar—sweetened soft drink
   c. fat—free milk
   d. iceberg lettuce

7. Which of the following foods is a rich source of phytochemicals?

   a. hamburger
   b. fish
   c. peaches
   d. chicken

8. An antioxidant is a(an)

   a. essential nutrient found only in animal foods.
   b. dietary supplement that is available without prescription.
   c. substance that protects cell components from being damaged or destroyed.
   d. nonnutrient produced by plants that provides health benefits.

9. In the United States, the primary cause of preventable cancer deaths is

   a. physical inactivity.
   b. tobacco use.
   c. high—fat diet.
   d. excessive alcohol intake.

10. Lena weighs 165 pounds. What is her weight in kilograms?

    a. 75 kg
    b. 7.5 kg
    c. 82 kg
    d. 8.2 kg

11. A serving of food contains 10 g carbohydrate, 2 g pro-tein, and 4 g fat. Based on this information, a serving of this food supplies _____ kcal.

    a. 64
    b. 74
    c. 84
    d. 94

12. A serving of food supplies 20 g carbohydrate, 4 g protein, 10 g fat, and 50 g water. Which of the following statements is true about a serving of the food?

    a. Fat provides the most food energy.
    b. Carbohydrate provides the most food energy.
    c. Water provides the most food energy.
    d. Fat provides about 25% of total calories.

13. Which of the following foods is the most nutrient dense?

    a. potato chips
    b. broccoli
    c. butter
    d. chocolate chip cookie

14. Which of the following statements is false?

    a. A megadose is 10 times the recommended amount of a nutrient.
    b. Megadoses of nutrients may behave like drugs in the body.
    c. In general, megadoses of nutrients are safe to consume.
    d. A physiological dose of a vitamin is less than a megadose of the vitamin.

15. The _____ Program enables eligible low-income participants to use a special debit card to purchase food at authorized stores.

    a. Nutritious Food Purchase
    b. Supplemental Nutrition Assistance
    c. Healthy Diets for All
    d. Eat Better for Less

LEARNSMART ADVANTAGE

Get the most out of your study of nutrition with McGraw-Hill's innovative suite of adaptive learning products including McGraw-Hill LearnSmart®, SmartBook®, LearnSmart Achieve®, and LearnSmart Prep®. Visit www.learnsmartadvantage.com.

Answers to Quiz Yourself

1. There are four classes of nutrients: proteins, lipids, sugars, and vitamins. **False** (p. 5)

2. Proteins are the most essential class of nutrients. **False** (p. 6)

3. All nutrients must be supplied by the diet, because they cannot be made by the body. **False** (p. 6)

4. Vitamins are a source of energy. **False** (p. 12)

5. Milk, carrots, and bananas are examples of "perfect" foods that contain all nutrients. **False** (p. 14)

CHAPTER **2**

Evaluating Nutrition Information

Quiz Yourself

Before reading Chapter 2, test your knowledge of scientific methods and reliable sources of nutrition information by taking the following quiz. The answers are on page 59.

1. Scientists use anecdotes as scientific evidence to support their findings. _____ T _____ F

2. Popular health-related magazines typically publish articles that have been peer reviewed. _____ T _____ F

3. By conducting a prospective epidemiological study, medical researchers can determine risk factors that may influence health. _____ T _____ F

4. Dietary supplements include vitamin pills as well as products that contain echinacea, ginseng, and garlic. _____ T _____ F

5. In general, registered dietitians are reliable sources of food and nutrition information. _____ T _____ F

2.1 Nutrition: Science for Consumers

Learning Outcomes

1. Explain the basic steps of the scientific method.
2. Explain the importance of having controls when performing experiments.
3. Design a nutrition-related study that involves human subjects.
4. Explain why nutrition information derived from anecdotes is not evidence based.
5. Discuss why similar scientific studies often have different results.

We consume food, and we consume nutrition information. There seems to be no way to avoid nutrition information: If you browse shelves of books and magazine at a bookstore, watch television, listen to the radio, or shop for groceries, you will encounter information about the subject. Even family members and friends contribute to the flood of nutrition information. Much of the information from such popular sources is not **evidence based,** that is, it is not supported by scientific evidence. The challenge for you and other consumers is to understand how scientists collect evidence about nutrition and health, and how to analyze this information to determine whether it is factual and based on solid evidence (reliable) or misinformation that is unsupported by the facts.

How do nutrition scientists determine facts about foods, nutrients, and diets? Why do nutrition scientists seem to contradict themselves so much? How can you evaluate the reliability of nutrition information? Where can you obtain up–to–date, accurate nutrition information? This chapter will provide answers to these questions and help you become a more critical and careful consumer.

evidence based information that is based on results of scientific studies

anecdotes reports of personal experiences

Understanding the Scientific Method

In the past, nutrition facts and dietary practices were often based on intuition, common sense, "conventional wisdom" (tradition), or **anecdotes** (reports of personal experiences). Today, *registered dietitians* and other nutrition experts discard conventional beliefs, explanations, and practices when the results of current scientific research no longer support them.

Scientists ask questions about the natural world, such as: "How do cells make proteins?" and "What causes stomach ulcers?" To obtain answers for their questions, researchers design studies that follow generally accepted methods. Figure 2.1 presents the general steps nutrition researchers take when conducting scientific investigations. The following sections take a closer look at some common methods that scientists use to collect nutrition information and establish nutrition facts.

Laboratory Experiments

An experiment is a systematic way of testing a hypothesis (question). Because of safety and ethical concerns, nutrition scientists often conduct experiments on small mammals before performing similar research on humans. Certain kinds of mice and rats are raised for experimentation purposes (Fig. 2.2). These rodents are inexpensive to house in laboratories, and their food and other living conditions can be carefully controlled. An experiment that uses whole living organisms,

34   Chapter 2 Evaluating Nutrition Information

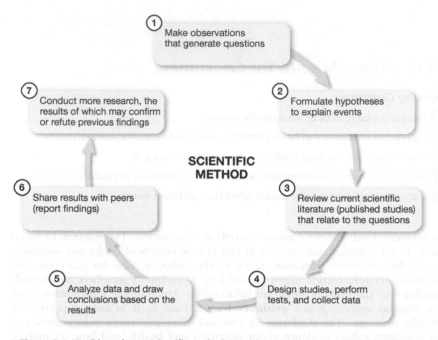

Figure 2.1 Nutrition science: Scientific method. Nutrition scientists generally follow these steps when conducting research.

treatment group group being studied that receives a treatment

control group group being studied that does not receive a treatment

variable personal characteristic or other factor that changes and can influence an outcome

Figure 2.2 Rodents for research. Nutrition scientists often conduct *in vivo* experiments on small rodents that are raised for experimentation purposes.

such as mice, is called an *in vivo* experiment. Nutrition researchers also perform controlled laboratory experiments on cells or other components derived from living organisms. These studies are *in vitro* or "test tube" experiments.

Experiments generally involve the basic steps shown in Figure 2.1. A team of nutrition scientists, for example, makes observations and generates questions that result in the development of a hypothesis. According to their hypothesis, consuming "chemical X" in charcoal−grilled meat is harmful. To test this hypothesis, the scientists divide 100 genetically similar 3−week old mice into two groups of 50 mice. One group **(treatment group)** is fed a certain amount of chemical X daily for 52 weeks; the second group **(control group)** does not receive the treatment during the period (Fig. 2.3).

Why is a control group necessary? Having a control group enables scientists to compare results between the two study groups to determine whether the treatment had any effect. A **variable** is a characteristic or other factor that can change and influence an outcome. Many variables can influence the outcome of an experimental study. Therefore, scientists who want to determine the effect or effects of a single variable, such as chemical X intake, need to control the influence of other variables. Therefore, all other conditions, including timing of feedings and amount of handling by caregivers must be the same for both groups of mice. If researchers design an experiment in which they fail to control variables that are not being tested, their findings are likely to be unclear or inaccurate.

For the duration of this study, the scientists examine the mice regularly for signs of health problems and record their results (data). If the mice in the treatment group are as healthy as the mice in the control group at the end of this experiment, the researchers may conclude that mice can safely consume the amount of chemical X used in the study on a daily basis for a year.

Researchers are cautious when drawing conclusions from results of *in vitro* experiments, because components removed from a living thing may not function the same way they do when they are in the entire life form.

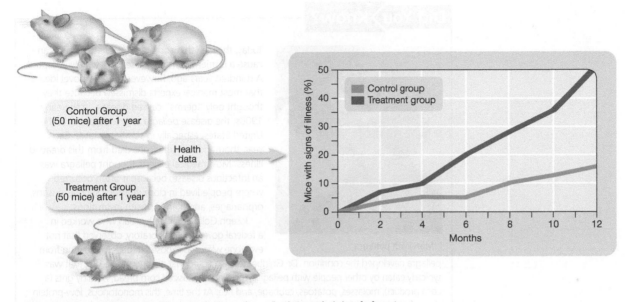

Figure 2.3 An experiment. Based on the findings shown in the graph, is it safe for mice to consume chemical X daily for a year?

Medical researchers must also be careful when applying the results of *in vivo* animal studies to people, because of the physiological differences between humans and other animals. Nevertheless, scientists are often able to determine the safety and effectiveness of treatments by conducting research on laboratory animals before engaging in similar testing on humans. Two types of research that involve human subjects are *experimental* (intervention) studies and *observational* studies. Such investigations can provide clues about the causes, progression, and prevention of diet—related diseases.

Human Research: Experimental (Intervention) Studies

Nutrition scientists often conduct experimental studies to obtain information about health conditions (*outcomes*) that may result from specific dietary practices. When conducting an experimental study involving human subjects, researchers usually randomly divide a large group of people into treatment and control groups.

For example, every other person who enrolls in a study is placed in the treatment group. The remaining subjects become control group members. Random assignment helps ensure that the members of the treatment and control groups have similar variables, such as age and other characteristics. All subjects will be instructed to maintain their usual lifestyle during the duration of the study, except for the activities required by their participation in the research.

Then the scientists provide all study participants with the same instructions and a form of intervention, such as a dietary supplement or experimental food. However, only members of the treatment group actually receive the treatment. Subjects in the control group are given a **placebo.** Placebos are not simply "sugar pills"; they are a fake treatment, such as a sham pill, injection, or medical procedure. The placebo mimics the treatment. For example, a placebo dietary supplement pill looks, tastes, and smells like the supplement pill with an active ingredient that is given subjects in the treatment group. The placebo pill,

placebo fake treatment, such as a sham pill, injection, or medical procedure

Did You ⟩ Know?

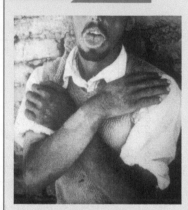

| Man with pellagra

Today, the idea that something missing in diets can cause a nutrient deficiency disease is widely accepted. A hundred years ago, however, it was a novel idea that most medical experts dismissed because they thought only "germs" caused disease. In the early 1900s, the disease *pellagra* was widespread in the United States, especially in southern states. Each year, thousands of Americans died from this dreaded illness. Most medical experts thought pellagra was an infectious disease, because it often occurred where people lived in close quarters, such as prisons, orphanages, and mental health institutions.

Joseph Goldberger, a physician who worked in a federal government laboratory, observed that not everyone who was exposed to people suffering from pellagra developed the condition. Dr. Goldberger also noted that prisoners ate a diet that was typically eaten by other people with pellagra. The diet emphasized corn bread, hominy grits (a corn product), molasses, potatoes, cabbage, and rice. At the time, this monotonous, low-protein diet was associated with poverty throughout the southern United States. He also observed that people who did not develop pellagra had higher incomes and ate more meat, milk, and fresh vegetables. Based on his observations, Goldberger rejected the medical establishment's notion that pellagra was an infectious disease. He proposed the idea that pellagra resulted from the lack of something in poor people's diet and the missing dietary factor was in meat, milk, and other foods eaten regularly by people with high incomes. To test his dietary hypothesis, Goldberger gave these foods to children in two Mississippi orphanages and patients in a Georgia mental institution who were suffering from pellagra, and they were cured of the disease. Many members of the medical establishment, however, rejected his finding that a poor diet was the cause of pellagra.

To satisfy his critics, Goldberger enrolled a group of healthy Mississippi prison inmates in an experiment that involved consuming the corn- and molasses-based diet commonly eaten in the southern states at the time. After a few months, more than half of the inmates developed pellagra. Once again, however, many of Goldberger's critics rejected his finding that poor diet was the cause of pellagra.

In 1916, Dr. Goldberger experimented on himself and some volunteers during what they called a "filth party." The group applied secretions taken from inside the nose and throat of a patient with pellagra into their noses and throats; they also swallowed pills made with flakes of skin scraped from the rashes of people with the disease. Additionally, Goldberger and one of his colleagues gave each other an injection of blood from a person who had pellagra. If

| *Dr. Joseph Goldberger*

pellagra were infectious, filth-party participants should have contracted the disease—but none of them did. Despite the results of Dr. Goldberger's extraordinary experiment, a few physicians still resisted the idea that pellagra was associated with diet.[1]

Dr. Goldberger died in 1929—8 years before Dr. Conrad Elvehjem and his team of scientists at the University of Wisconsin isolated a form of the vitamin niacin from liver extracts. Elvehjem and his colleagues discovered niacin cured "black tongue," a condition affecting dogs that was similar to pellagra.[2] Soon after Elvehjem's discovery, other scientists determined that niacin was effective in treating pellagra, and the medical establishment finally accepted the fact that the disease was the result of a dietary deficiency.

however, has *inert* ingredients; that is, the pill contains substances that do not produce any measurable physical changes. Providing placebos to members of the control group enables scientists to compare the extent of the treatment's response with that of the placebo.

What Is the Placebo Effect? People may report positive or negative reactions to a treatment even though they received the placebo. If a patient believes a medical treatment will improve his or her health, the patient is more likely to report positive results for the therapy. Such wishful thinking is called the **placebo effect.**

People who take certain herbal products or use other unconventional medical therapies to prevent or treat diseases are often convinced the products and treatments are effective, despite the general lack of scientific evidence to support their beliefs. Such personal findings may be examples of the placebo effect. However, placebos can produce beneficial physiological and psychological changes, particularly in conditions that involve pain.[3] Because subjects in the control group believe they are receiving a real treatment, their faith in the "treatment" can stimulate the release of chemicals in the brain that alter pain perception, reducing their discomfort. Therefore, when people report that a treatment was beneficial, they may not have been imagining the positive response, even when they were taking a placebo.

Double-Blind Studies

Human experimental studies are usually **double–blind studies;** that is, neither the investigators nor the subjects are aware of the subjects' group assignments. Codes are used to identify a subject's group membership, and this information is not revealed until the end of the study. Maintaining such secrecy is important during the course of a human study involving placebos, because researchers and subjects may try to predict group assignments based on their expectations. If the investigators who interview the participants are aware of their individual group assignments during the study (a single–blind study), they may unwittingly convey clues to each subject, perhaps in the form of body language, that could influence the subject's belief about being in the experimental or control group. Subjects who suspect they are in the control group and taking a placebo may report no changes in their condition, because they expect a placebo should have no effect on them. On the other hand, subjects who think they are in the treatment group could insist that they feel better or have more energy as a result of the treatment, even though the treatment may not have produced any measurable changes in their bodies. Ideally, subjects should not be able to figure out their group assignment while researchers are collecting information from them.

Human Research: Epidemiological Studies

For decades, medical researchers have noted differences in rates of chronic diseases and causes of death among various populations. The most common type of diabetes, for example, occurs more frequently among Native American, Hispanic, and non–Hispanic African–American adults than among non–Hispanic, white American adults.[4] To understand why this difference exists, medical researchers rely on the findings of epidemiological studies.

Epidemiology (*ehp–e–dee–me–all'–uh–jee*) is the study of the occurrence, distribution, and causes of health problems in populations. Epidemiologists often use physical examinations of people to obtain health data, such as height and weight. Additionally, they may collect other kinds of information by conducting surveys. Such surveys question people about their personal and family medical histories, environmental exposures, health practices, and attitudes. Since 1999, National Nutrition and Health Examination Survey (NHANES)

placebo effect response to a placebo

double-blind study experimental design in which neither the participants nor the researchers are aware of each participant's group assignment

epidemiology study of the occurrence, distribution, and causes of health problems in populations researchers have used interviews and physical examinations to assess the health and nutritional status of a nationally representative sample of Americans. Data collected from NHANES help epidemiologists determine the prevalence of major diseases, risk factors for such diseases, and national standards for measurements that are associated with health status, including height, weight, and blood pressure.

In cases involving chronic diseases such as heart disease and cancer, it is often difficult to determine a single variable that is responsible for the development of the condition. Multiple factors, including a person's *genetic susceptibility* (inherited proneness), exposure to certain environmental conditions, and diet as well as other lifestyle practices can influence his or her likelihood of developing a disease.

By conducting studies that explore differences in dietary practices and disease occurrences among populations, nutrition epidemiologists may learn much about the influence of diet on health. If one group of people is more likely to develop a certain health disorder than another group and the two populations consume very different diets, scientists can speculate about the role diet plays in this difference.

Observational Epidemiological Studies   Most epidemiological research is observational and involves either case–control study or cohort study designs (Fig. 2.4). In a **case–control study,** individuals with a health condition (cases) such as heart disease or breast cancer are matched to persons with similar characteristics who do not have the condition (controls). Information such as personal and family medical histories, eating habits, and other lifestyle behaviors are collected from each participant in the study. By analyzing the results of case–control studies, researchers identify factors that may have been responsible for the illness. Scientists, for example, may be able to identify dietary practices that differ between the two groups, such as long–term fruit and vegetable intakes.

In a **cohort study,** epidemiologists collect and analyze various kinds of information about a large group of people over time. The scientists are generally interested in making associations between exposure to a specific factor and the subsequent development of health conditions. Cohort studies can be *retrospective* or *prospective*. Retrospective means "to look back" and prospective means "to look forward" in time. (See Figure 2.4.) In a retrospective cohort study, researchers collect information about a group's past exposures and identify current health outcomes. For example, nutritional epidemiologists might examine whether a group of people who have stomach cancer consumed more charcoal–broiled meat (the exposure) in the past than a group of people with similar characteristics who do not have stomach cancer. In a prospective cohort study, a group of healthy people are followed over a time period and any diseases that eventually develop are recorded. Scientists then try to identify links between exposures and diseases that occurred between the beginning and end of the study period.

The Framingham Heart Study that began in 1949 in Framingham, Massachusetts, is one of the most well–known prospective studies. At the beginning of the study, the over 5200 healthy participants (men and women) underwent extensive physical examinations and questioning about their family and personal medical histories as well as their lifestyle practices. Over the following years, a group of medical researchers periodically collected data concerning each participant's health and, if the person died, cause of death. The scientists analyzed this information and found relationships between a variety of personal characteristics and health outcomes. Findings from the Framingham Heart Study identified numerous risk factors for heart disease, including elevated

case-control study study in which individuals who have a health condition are compared with individuals with similar characteristics who do not have the condition

cohort study study that measures variables of a group of people over time

EPIDEMIOLOGICAL STUDIES

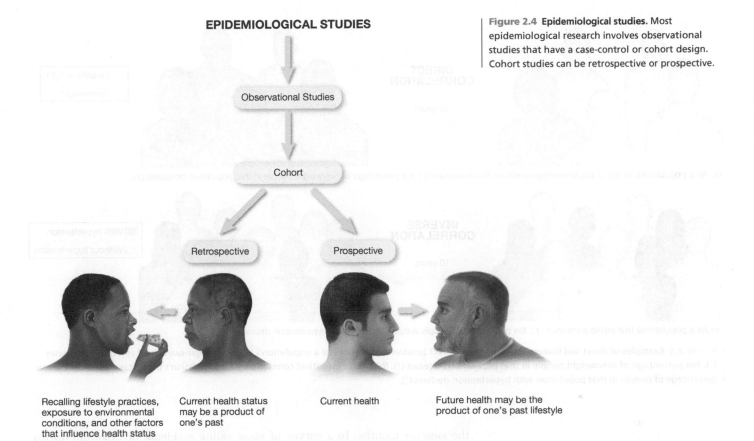

Figure 2.4 **Epidemiological studies.** Most epidemiological research involves observational studies that have a case-control or cohort design. Cohort studies can be retrospective or prospective.

Recalling lifestyle practices, exposure to environmental conditions, and other factors that influence health status

Current health status may be a product of one's past

Current health

Future health may be the product of one's past lifestyle

blood cholesterol levels, cigarette smoking, and hypertension. Today, medical researchers are still collecting information from the original Framingham Heart Study participants as well as their descendants.

Limitations of Epidemiological Studies Epidemiological studies cannot establish *causation*, that is, whether a practice is responsible for an effect. When two different natural events occur simultaneously within a population, it does not necessarily mean they are correlated. A **correlation** is a relationship between variables. A correlation occurs when two variables change over the same period; for example, when a population's intake of sugar—sweetened soft drinks increases, the percentage of overweight people in the population also increases (Fig. 2.5a). In this case, the correlation is *direct* or *positive* because the two variables—body weight and regular soft drink consumption—are changing in the same direction; they are both increasing. An *inverse* or *negative* correlation occurs when one variable increases and the other one decreases (the variables change in opposite directions). An example of an inverse correlation is the relationship between fruit intake and hypertension; as a population's fruit consumption increases, the per-centage of people with hypertension in that population decreases (Fig. 2.5b).

What appears to be a correlation between a behavior and an outcome could be a coincidence, that is, a chance happening, and not an indication of a *cause—and—effect* relationship between the two variables. For example, in a survey of lemonade consumption in Colorado over a 10—year period, we might observe that fewer people drank lemonade during the winter than during

correlation relationship between two variables

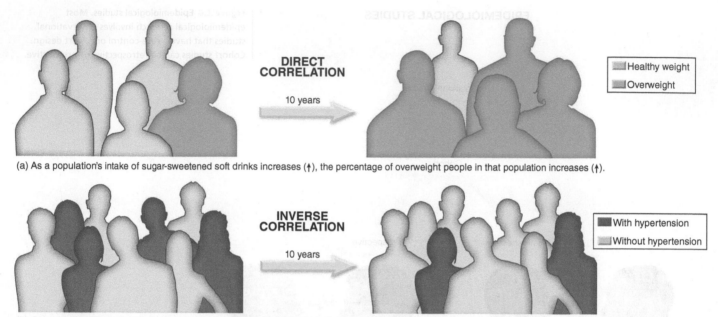

(a) As a population's intake of sugar-sweetened soft drinks increases (↑), the percentage of overweight people in that population increases (↑).

(b) As a population's fruit intake increases (↑), the percentage of people in that population with hypertension decreases (↓).

Figure 2.5 Examples of direct and inverse correlations. (*a*) Direct (positive) correlation: As a population's intake of sugar-sweetened soft drinks increases (↑), the percentage of overweight people in that population increases (↑). (*b*) Inverse (negative) correlation: As a population's fruit intake increases (↑), the percentage of people in that population with hypertension declines (↓).

the summer months. In a survey of snow skiing accidents in Colorado during the same 10–year period, we might also find that snow skiing accidents were more likely to occur during the winter than in the summer. Thus, as lemonade consumption declined, snow skiing accidents increased. Does this mean lem–onade consumption is inversely correlated to skiing accidents and people who do not drink lemonade have a greater risk of having a skiing accident at this time of year? It is more likely that the relationship between snow skiing and lemonade drinking is coincidental, because both activities are associated with seasonal weather conditions. Although this example is obviously far–fetched, it illustrates the problems scientists can have when analyzing results of epide–miological studies.

Analyzing Data, Drawing Conclusions, and Reporting Findings

Nutrition researchers use a variety of statistical methods to analyze data collected from observations and experiments. These methods may enable the researchers to find relationships between the variables and health outcomes that were studied. As a result, scientists can determine whether their hypotheses are supported by the data.

When an experiment or study is completed and the results analyzed, researchers summarize the findings and seek to publish articles with informa–tion about their investigation in scientific journals. Before articles are accepted for publication, they undergo **peer review,** a critical analysis conducted by a group of "peers." Peers are investigators who were not part of the study but are experts involved in related research. If peers agree that a study was well conducted, its results are fairly represented, and the research is of interest to

peer review expert critical analysis of a research article before it is published

the journal's readers, these scientists are likely to recommend that the journal's editors publish the article. Examples of peer—reviewed medical and nutrition journals include the *The New England Journal of Medicine, Journal of the American Medical Association,* and the *Journal of the American College of Nutrition.*

Research Bias   Scientists expect other researchers to avoid relying on their personal attitudes and biases ("points of view") when collecting and analyzing data, and to evaluate and report their results objectively and honestly. This process is important because much of the scientific research that is conducted in the United States is supported financially by the federal government, nonprofit foundations, and drug companies and other private industries. Some funding sources can have certain expectations or biases about research outcomes, and as a result, they are likely to finance studies of scientists whose research efforts support their interests. The beef industry, for example, might not fund scientific investigations to find connections between high intakes of beef and the risk of certain cancers. On the other hand, the beef industry might be interested in supporting a team of scientists whose research indicates that a high protein diet that contains plenty of beef is useful for people who are trying to lose weight.

Peer—reviewed journals usually require authors of articles to disclose their affiliations and sources of financial support. Such disclosures may appear on the first page or at the end of the article. By having this information, readers can decide on the reliability of the findings. Although peer review helps ensure that the scientists are as ethical and objective as possible, it is impossible to eliminate all research bias.

Spreading the News   After the results of a study are published in a nutrition—related journal or reported to health professionals attending a meeting of a nutrition or medical society, the media (e.g., newspapers, magazines, Internet news sources) may receive notice of the findings. If the information is simplistic and sensational, such as a finding that drinking green tea can result in weight loss, it is more likely to be reported in the popular press. In many instances, you learn about the study's results when they are reported in a television or radio news broadcast as a 15— or 30—second "sound bite." Such sources generally provide very little information concerning the way the study was conducted or how the data were collected and analyzed.

Popular sources of nutrition information, such as magazines and the Internet, generally do not subject articles or blogs to peer review or other scientific scrutiny, and as a result, they may feature faulty, biased information. For example, a health news column in a popular magazine may report findings from a few nutrition journal articles that support the use of garlic supplements for reducing blood cholesterol levels. However, you may conclude that the column is biased if it excludes results of other studies that do not indicate such benefits. You can often distinguish a peer—reviewed scientific journal from a popular magazine simply by looking at their covers and skimming their pages. Compared to scientific journals, magazines typically have more colorful, attractive covers and photographs, and their articles are shorter and easier for the average person to read (Fig. 2.6).

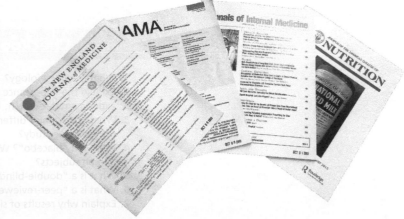

| Examples of peer-reviewed medical and nutrition journals.

Figure 2.6 Judging by the cover. Consumers can be trained to look for features, such as "busy," brightly colored covers, that distinguish peer-reviewed scientific journals from popular magazines. Also, popular sources of nutrition information, such as these magazines, are readily available at supermarkets and convenience stores.

It is important to keep in mind that sensational media coverage of a medical "breakthrough" is not necessarily an indication of the value or quality of research that resulted in the news story or magazine article. The results of one study are rarely enough to gain widespread acceptance for new or unusual findings or to provide a basis for nutritional recommendations. Thus, the findings obtained by one research team must be supported by those generated in other studies. If the results of several scientific investigations conducted under similar conditions confirm the original researchers' conclusions, then these findings are more likely to be accepted by other nutrition scientists.

Confusion and Conflict

One day, the news highlights dramatic health benefits from eating garlic, dark chocolate, brown rice, or cherries. A few weeks later, the news includes reports of more recent scientific investigations that do not support the earlier findings. When consumers become aware of conflicting results generated by nutrition studies, they often become confused and disappointed. As a result, some people may mistrust the scientific community and think nutrition scientists do not know what they are doing.

Consumers need to recognize that conflicting findings often result from differences in the ways various studies are designed. Even when investigating the same question, different groups of scientists often conduct their studies and analyze the results differently. For example, the numbers, ages, and physical conditions of subjects; the type and length of the study; the amount of the treatment provided; and the statistical tests used to analyze results typically vary among studies. Additionally, individual genetic differences often contribute to a person's response to a treatment. Not only are people genetically different, they also have different lifestyles, and they typically recall dietary information and follow instructions concerning health care practices differently. These and other factors can influence the results of nutrition research involving human subjects.

The science of nutrition is constantly evolving; old beliefs and practices are discarded when they are not supported by more recent scientific evidence, and new principles and practices emerge from the new findings. By now you should understand that science involves asking questions, developing and testing hypotheses, gathering and analyzing data, drawing conclusions from data, and, sometimes, accepting change.

Concept **Checkpoint 2.1**

1. What is epidemiology?
2. Explain the importance of having a control group when conducting experimental research.
3. What is the major difference between a prospective study and a retrospective study?
4. What is a "placebo"? Why are placebos often used in studies involving human subjects?
5. What is a "double-blind study"?
6. What is a "peer-reviewed" article?
7. Explain why results of similar studies may provide different findings.

2.2 Nutrition Information: Fact or Fiction

Learning Outcomes

1 Explain why there is so much nutrition misinformation.

2 Discuss how people can become more critical and careful consumers of nutrition information.

3 Identify common "red flags" that are signs of nutrition misinformation.

While "channel surfing" one afternoon, you stop and watch the host of a televised home shopping program promote FatMegaMelter, his company's brand of a dietary supplement for losing weight. According to the host, the supplement contains a chemical derived from a plant that grows naturally in South Africa. This amazing chemical reduces the appetite for fattening foods, enabling an overweight person taking FatMegaMelter to lose up to 30 pounds in 30 days, without the need to exercise more or eat less. The host interviews an attractive young actress who claims to have lost a lot of weight after she started taking FatMegaMelter pills. A few days later, a friend mentions that she has lost 3 pounds since she began taking this product a week ago. You would like to lose a few pounds without resorting to restricting your food intake or exercising. Should you take FatMegaMelter? The supplement helped the actress and your friend; will it help you?

Although the actress's health history appears to be compelling evidence that the weight–loss supplement is effective, her information is a **testimonial,** a personal endorsement of a product. People are usually paid to provide their testimonials for advertisements; therefore, their remarks may be biased in favor of the product. Your friend's experience with taking the same weight–loss product is intriguing, but it is an anecdote and not *proof* that FatMegaMelter promotes weight loss. When your source of nutrition information is a testimonial, anecdote, or advertisement, you cannot be sure that the information is based on scientific facts and, therefore, reliable.

testimonial personal endorsement of a product

Become a Critical Consumer of Nutrition Information

People may think they have learned facts about nutrition by reading popular magazine articles or best–selling books; visiting Internet websites; or watching television news, infomercials, or home shopping programs. In many instances, however, they have been misinformed. To be a careful consumer, do not assume that all nutrition information presented in the popular media is reliable. The First Amendment to the U.S. Constitution guarantees freedom of the press and freedom of speech, so people can provide nutrition information that is not true. Thus, the First Amendment does not protect consumers with freedom from nutrition misinformation or false nutrition claims.

The U.S. Food and Drug Administration (FDA) can regulate nutrition– and health–related claims on product labels, but the agency cannot prevent the spread of health and nutrition misinformation published in books or pamphlets or presented in television or radio programs. As a consumer, you are responsible for questioning and

Be wary of ads for nutrition-related products that rely on testimonials and anecdotes.

44   **Chapter 2**   Evaluating Nutrition Information

researching the accuracy of nutrition information as well as the credentials of the people making nutrition–related claims.

Promoters of worthless nutrition products and services often use sophisticated marketing methods to lure consumers. For example, some promoters of dietary supplements claim their products are "scientifically tested," or they include citations to what appear to be scientific journal articles in their ads or articles. Consumers, however, cannot be certain the information is true. Few dietary supplements have been thoroughly evaluated by reputable scientists. In some instances, these products have been scientifically tested, but the bulk of the research has shown that most dietary supplements, other than vitamins and minerals, provide little or no measurable health benefits. Nevertheless, promoters of nonnutrient dietary supplements usually ignore the scientific evidence and continue to sell their goods to an unsuspecting, trusting public. The "Nutrition Matters" feature at the end of this chapter focuses on dietary supplements.

Consumers also need to be alert for promoters' use of **pseudoscience,** the presentation of information masquerading as factual and obtained by scientific methods. In many instances, pseudoscientific nutrition or physiology information is presented with complex scientific–sounding terms, such as "enzymatic therapy" or "colloidal extract." Such terms are designed to convince people without science backgrounds that the nutrition–related information is true. Often, promoters of nutrition misinformation try to confuse people by weaving false information with facts into their claims, making the untrue material seem credible too.

Although people's lives have improved as a result of scientific advancements in medicine, the general public tends to mistrust scientists, medical professionals, and the pharmaceutical industry. Promoters of nutrition misinformation exploit this mistrust to sell their products and services. For example, they may tell consumers that physicians rely on costly diagnostic methods and treatments for serious diseases because they are more interested in making money than doing what is best for their patients, such as recommending a dietary supplement. Are physicians driven by the desire to make money from their patients' illnesses, and do they hide information about natural cures from them?

Over the past 100 years, people's lives have been greatly improved by contributions of medical researchers. As a group, physicians are dedicated to improving their patients' health and saving lives. Physicians have nothing to gain from concealing a cure from the public. They strive to diagnose and treat diseases using scientifically tested and approved techniques. Moreover, a physician may face a malpractice lawsuit if he or she fails to diagnose and treat a condition effectively. Additionally, physicians have much to gain from treating their patients kindly and effectively. Consider this: If you follow a physician's advice and have positive results, are you likely to be that doctor's patient for a long time and recommend the practitioner to others?

If your car is not functioning properly, you probably would want people who have the best training, tools, and equipment to determine the problem and repair it. If you think something is wrong with your body, it is prudent to seek information and opinions from medical professionals who have the best training and experience to diagnose and treat health disorders.

pseudoscience presentation of information masquerading as factual and obtained by scientific methods

Ask Questions

If you are like most people, you do not want to waste your money on things you do not need or that are useless or potentially harmful. How can you become a more careful, critical consumer of nutrition—related information or products? The following questions should help you evaluate various sources of nutrition information:

- *What motivates the authors, promoters, or sponsors to provide the information? Do you think they are more interested in your health and well—being or in selling their products?* Salespeople often have favorable biases toward the things they sell, and therefore, they may not be reliable sources of information about these products. A clerk in a dietary supplements outlet store, for example, may wear a white lab coat to look as though he or she has a science or medical educational background, but you should keep in mind that the clerk was hired to sell dietary supplements and may have little or no scientific training. Furthermore, salespeople who work in such outlets may be unwilling to inform customers about the potential health hazards of taking certain products, particularly when they earn a commission from each sale.

- *Is the source scientific, such as an article from a peer—reviewed nutrition journal?* In general, popular sources of nutrition information, such as best—selling books and articles in magazines, are not peer—reviewed by scientists. Additionally, radio or TV programs that promote nutrition information may actually be sophisticated advertisements for nutrition—related products.

- *If a study is cited, how was the research conducted? Did the study involve humans or animals? If people participated in the study, how many subjects were involved in the research? Who sponsored the study?* As mentioned earlier in this chapter, epidemiological studies are not useful for finding cause—and—effect relationships. Additionally, the results of studies involving large numbers of human subjects are more reliable than studies of animals. Sponsors may influence the outcomes of the studies they fund.

- *To provide scientific support for claims, does the source cite respected nutrition or medical journals or mention reliable experts?* Be careful if you see citations in popular nutrition or health books and magazines. Promoters of nutrition misinformation may refer to scientific—appearing citations from phony medical journals to convince people that their information is reliable. Furthermore, be wary of nutrition experts introduced or identified as "Doctor" because they may not be physicians or scientists. Furthermore, a so—called nutrition expert who is referred to as "Doctor" may not have a doctorate degree (Ph.D.) in human nutrition from an accredited university. Such experts may have obtained their degrees simply by purchasing them on the Internet or through a mail—order outlet, without having taken appropriate coursework or graduated from an accredited university or college.

Did You > Know?

In 2010, a federal district court ruled in favor of the Federal Trade Commission in a case involving companies that used unproven claims to promote "Chinese Diet Tea" and "Bio-Slim Patch." The court fined the companies nearly $2 million for claiming that the products would enable people to lose weight without diet and exercise.[5]

If this person appeared on a television show or in a magazine advertisement, would you consider him to be a reliable source of nutrition information? Explain why you would or would not trust his nutrition-related advice.

Practicing medicine without the proper training and licensing is illegal. How—ever, providing nutrition information and advice without the proper training and licensing is legal. **Quackery** involves promoting useless medical treatments, such as copper bracelets to treat arthritis.

To obtain information about a nutrition expert's credentials, enter the person's name at an Internet search engine and evaluate the results. For example, is the person associated with an accredited school of higher education or a government agency such as the U.S. Department of Agriculture? You can also visit www.quackwatch.org and submit an "Ask a Question" e—mail requesting information about a person's credentials from the site's sponsors.

quackery promotion of useless medical treatments

Look for Red Flags

To become a critical consumer of nutrition information, you need to be aware of "red flags," clues that indicate a source of information is unreliable. Common red flags include the following:

1. **Promises of quick and easy remedies for complex health—related problems:** "Our product helps you lose weight *without* exercising or dieting," or "Garlic cures heart disease."

2. **Claims that sound too good to be true:** "Our all—natural product blocks fat and calories from being absorbed, so you can eat everything you like and still lose weight." Such claims are rarely true. Remember, if the claim sounds too good to be true, it probably is not true.

3. **Scare tactics that include sensational, frightening, false, or misleading statements about a food, dietary practice, or health condition:** "Dairy products cause cancer," or "Eating sugar causes hyperactivity."

4. **Personal attacks on the motives and ethical standards of registered dietitians or conventional scientists:** "Dietitians and medical researchers don't want you to know the facts about natural cures for cancer, diabetes, and heart disease because it will dry up their funding." Such statements indicate unsubstantiated biases against bona fide nutrition experts and the scientific community.

5. **Statements about the superiority of certain dietary supplements or unconventional medical practices:** "Russian scientists have discovered the countless health benefits of taking Siberian ginseng," or "Colon cleansing with herbs is the only cure for intestinal cancer."

6. **Testimonials and anecdotes as evidence of effectiveness:** "I lost 50 pounds in 30 days using this product," or "I rubbed this vitamin E—containing lotion on my scar and it disappeared in days." As mentioned earlier, these sources of information are unreliable. Reliable nutrition information is based on scientific evidence.

7. **Information that promotes a product's benefits while overlooking its risks:** "Our all—natural supplement boosts your metabolism naturally so it won't harm your system." Anything you consume, even water, can be toxic in high doses. Beware of any source of information that fails to mention the possible side effects of using a dietary supplement or nutrition—related treatment.

8. **Vague, meaningless, or scientific—sounding terms to impress or confuse consumers:** "Our *all—natural, clinically tested, patented, chelated* dietary supplement works best."

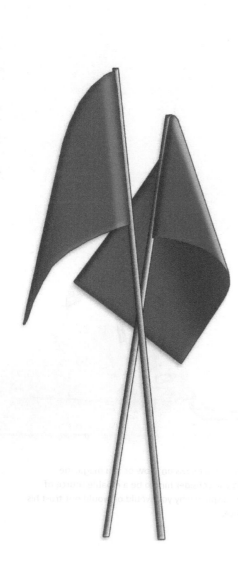

9. **Sensational statements with incomplete references of sources:** "Clinical research performed at a major university and published in a distinguished medical journal indicates food manufacturers have added ingredients to products that make you hungry and fat," or "Millions of Americans suffer from various nutritional deficiencies." Which "major university" and "distinguished medical journal"? What study reported that "millions of Americans" are deficient in nutrients?

10. **Recommendations based on a single study:** "Research conducted at our private health facility proves coffee enemas can cure cancer."

11. **Information concerning nutrients or human physiology that is not supported by reliable scientific evidence:** "This book explains how to combine certain foods based on your blood type," or "Most diseases are caused by undigested food that gets stuck in your guts," or "People with alkaline bodies don't develop cancer."

12. **Results disclaimers, usually in small or difficult–to–read print:** "Results may vary," or "Results not typical" (Fig. 2.7). Disclaimers are clues that the product may not live up to your expectations or the manufacturer's claims.

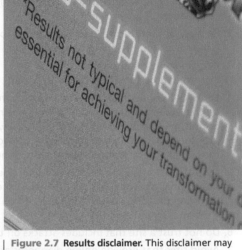

Figure 2.7 Results disclaimer. This disclaimer may be a red flag indicating the product has limited effectiveness, despite its promoter's claims.

Using the Internet Wisely

You can find abundant sources of information about nutrition and the benefits of dietary supplements on the Internet. However, you must be careful and consider the sources. Who or what organization sponsors the site? Is the information intended to promote sales? Be wary if the site discusses benefits of dietary supplements and enables you to purchase these products online. Furthermore, a site is likely to be unreliable if it includes comprehensive disclaimers such as "The manufacturer is not responsible or obligated to verify statements," or "The FDA has not evaluated this website. This product is not intended to diagnose, cure, or prevent any disease." Also avoid sites that publish disclaimers such as "The nutrition and health information at this site is provided for educational purposes only and not

Food & Nutrition tips

If you are looking for a recipe for guacamole, cranberry chutney, or sweet and sour cabbage, simply use the Internet—it is like having a cookbook at your fingertips. Recipes for nearly every food and from various countries and ethnic groups are available on the Internet, and you can also find menu planning and cooking tips from this vast resource.

When searching the Web for recipes, you need to recognize that many food manufacturers use the sites to promote their products in recipes. If the brand name of a product is mentioned in the recipe, you can usually substitute another company's product. Additionally, recipes do not always provide accurate information about the nutrients and calories in a serving of food, and you cannot be certain that the recipes have been tested for quality. Therefore, it is a good idea to check more than one site for a recipe and compare the information.

TABLE 2.1 Tips for Searching Nutrition Information on the Internet

To be a Careful Consumer of Internet Sources of Information:

1. Use multiple sites, especially government sites such as the Centers for Disease Control and Prevention (www.cdc.gov) and the Food and Drug Administration (www.fda.gov), as well as the sites of nationally recognized nutrition- or health-related associations such as the Academy of Nutrition and Dietetics (www.eatright.org) and the American Heart Association (www.americanheart.org).

2. Be wary of sites that have surveys for you to complete, advertisements for diet-related products, and promotions in pop-up windows.

3. Rely primarily on sites that are managed or reviewed by a group of qualified health professionals. Blogs might be fun and interesting to read, but they are not necessarily reliable.

4. Look for the Health on the Net symbol at the bottom of the main page of the website. The Health on the Net Foundation is a nonprofit, international organization that promotes the HONcode, a set of principles for standardizing the reliability of health information on the Internet. Currently, website sponsors are not required to follow HONcode standards. For more information about HONcode, you can visit the organization's website (www.hon.ch/).

5. Do not trust information at a site that does not indicate valid sources, such as well-respected peer-reviewed scientific journals or nationally recognized universities or medical centers. Contributing authors and their credentials should be identified; when they are, perform an online search of the scientific journals, as well as the authors' names and credentials to determine their validity.

6. Do not trust a site that includes attacks on the trustworthiness of the medical or scientific establishment.

7. Avoid sites that provide online diagnoses and treatments.

8. Be wary of commercial sites (*.com) with links to government sites or the sites of well-known medical, nutrition, or scientific associations. An unreliable *.com site can be linked to reliable sites without having received their endorsements.

9. Avoid providing your personal information at the site because its confidentiality may not be protected.

For more tips, visit: http://ods.od.nih.gov/Health_Information/How_To_Evaluate_Health_Information_on_the_Internet_Questions_and_Answers.aspx.

Be wary of nutrition information provided at websites that sell diet-related products.

as a substitute for the advice of a physician or dietitian. The author and owner of this site are not liable for personal actions taken as a result of the site's contents."

Be wary of websites that are authored or sponsored by one person, or sites that promote or sell products for profit (*.com), because such sources of information may be biased. In general, websites sponsored by nationally recognized health associations such as the Academy of Nutrition and Dietetics, (www.eatright.org) and nonprofit organizations such as the National Osteoporosis Foundation (www.nof.org) are reliable sources of nutrition information. Government agencies (*.gov) and nationally accredited colleges and universities (*.edu) are also excellent sources of credible nutrition information. Table 2.1 presents some tips for using the Internet to obtain reliable nutrition information.

The Federal Trade Commission (FTC) enforces consumer protection laws and investigates complaints about false or misleading health claims that appear on the Internet. For information to help you evaluate nutrition and health–related claims, visit the agency's website (www.ftc.gov/bcp/edu/pubs/consumer/health/hea07.shtm). To complain about a product, you can complete and submit the FTC's complaint form at the website or call the agency's toll–free line (1–877–382–4357).

Concept **Checkpoint 2.2**

8. What is the difference between a testimonial and an anecdote?

9. List at least three "red flags" that may indicate a questionable source of nutrition information.

10. List at least three tips for using the Internet as a reliable source of nutrition information.

2.3 Reliable Nutrition Experts

Learning Outcome

1 Explain how to identify reliable nutrition experts.

registered dietitian (RD), registered dietitian nutritionist (RDN), or licensed dietitian nutritionist (LDN) college-trained health care professional who has extensive knowledge of foods, nutrition, and dietetics

If you have questions about food or nutrition, where do you find factual answers? Although many states regulate and license people who call themselves nutritionists, you cannot always rely on someone who refers to him— or herself as a "nutritionist" or "nutritionalist" for reliable nutrition information, because there are no standard legal definitions for these descriptors. Should you ask a physician for nutrition advice? Physicians are not necessarily the best sources of nutrition information, because most doctors do not have extensive college coursework in the subject.

If your university or college has a nutrition or dietetics department, you are likely to find nutrition experts, including professors, registered dietitians, and reg— istered dietitian nutritionists, who are faculty members. A **registered dietitian (RD), registered dietitian nutritionist (RDN), or licensed dietitian nutritionist (LDN)** is a college—trained health care professional who has extensive knowledge of foods, nutrition, and *dietetics*, the application of nutrition and food information to treat many health—related conditions. The titles "registered dietitian (RD)" and "registered dietitian nutritionist (RDN)" are legally protected.

You can also locate registered dietitians by consulting the phone directories, contacting your local dietetic association or dietary department of a local hospital, or visiting the Academy of Nutrition and Dietetics website (www.eatright.org) or the Dietitians of Canada's website (www.dietitians.ca).

Becoming a Registered Dietitian Nutritionist

There are three major professional divisions for RDs, RDNs, and LDNs: clinical dietetics, community nutrition, and food service systems management. Clinical dietitians can work as members of medical teams in hospitals or clinics. Clinical dietitians can also work as community nutritionists in public health settings or as dietary counselors in private practice or with wellness programs. Food service sys— tems management dietitians direct food systems in hospitals, schools, or other set— tings. Although most registered dietitians work in health care settings, some are educators or researchers.

An RD/RDN/LDN has completed a baccalaureate degree program approved by the Accreditation Council for Education in Nutrition and Dietetics of the Academy of Nutrition and Dietetics, the largest organization of dietitians in the United States. As undergraduate students, dietetics majors are required to take a wide variety of college—level courses, including food and nutrition sciences,

organic chemistry, biochemistry, biology, physiology, microbiology, food service systems management, business, and communications classes. If you are attending a major university, you can check the course or program catalog at your school to determine whether an accredited dietetics program is offered.

In addition to taking the required college coursework, the student dietitian must complete a *supervised practice program* (*SPP*) that provides professional training in a health care facility such as a hospital, a food service company, or a community health care agency such as a state or local health department. Finally, this individual has to pass the national registration examination to become certified as an RD. After becoming certified, RDs are also required to fulfill continuing education requirements to maintain their certification. The Academy of Nutrition and Dietetics provides information about becoming an RD and roles these professionals play in health care settings.

Concept **Checkpoint 2.3**

11. What is the difference between a nutritionist and a registered dietitian nutritionist?
12. List three ways of locating reliable nutrition experts.

2.4 Nutrition Matters: What Are Dietary Supplements?

Learning Outcomes

1 Explain the difference between conventional medicine and complementary and alternative medicine (CAM).

2 Explain how the FDA regulates medicines differently than dietary supplements.

3 Discuss the risks and benefits of taking dietary supplements.

Do you take a daily vitamin or mineral pill because you are concerned about the nutritional quality of your diet? Do you use herbal pills or extracts to strengthen your immune system, boost your memory, or treat illnesses such as the common cold? If you follow any of these practices, you are not alone. According to results of national surveys, almost 50% of the American population takes one or more dietary supplements regularly.[6]

According to the Dietary Supplement and Health Education Act of 1994 (DSHEA), a dietary supplement is a product (other than tobacco) that

- adds to a person's dietary intake and contains one or more dietary ingredients, including nutrients or *botanicals* (herbs or other plant material)

- is taken by mouth
- is not promoted as a conventional food or the only item of a meal or diet[7]

Dietary supplements include nutrient pills, protein powders, and herbal extracts, as well as energy bars and drinks. Many dietary supplements are often referred to as "nutraceuticals," but there is no legal definition for this term.

In the United States, the most commonly used dietary supplements are **multivitamin/mineral (MV/M)** products.[8] There is no standard definition for the contents of a MV/M supplement, but such products may contain several vitamins and minerals.[6] Among American adults, the most popular nonvitamin, nonmineral dietary supplements are fish oil or "omega 3," glucosamine, echinacea, and flaxseed oil and pills. Some people use dietary supplements, particularly those containing nutrients, because the products are recommended by their physicians or dietitians. Physicians, for example, may prescribe a prenatal MV/M supplement for their pregnant patients. Most dietary supplements are available without the need for prescriptions, so people can take them without their doctors' knowledge and approval. When researchers asked a group of people why they used dietary supplements, subjects gave a variety of reasons, including to boost their nutrient intakes, to prevent certain diseases, to obtain more energy, to enhance good health, and to treat existing ailments.[9]

Table 2.2 provides information about some non-micronutrient dietary supplements that are popular among adult Americans. Benefits and risks of supplementing diets with micronutrients are discussed in Chapters 8 and 9.

What Is Complementary and Alternative Medicine?

The use of herbal products and other dietary supplements to treat disease or promote good health is an aspect of **complementary and alternative medicine (CAM).** CAM includes a variety of health care practices and products that are not accepted by the majority of physicians and other conventional health care providers. In 2007, approximately 38% of American adults and 12% of American children used CAM therapies, including chiropractic manipulations, homeopathy, naturopathy, and massage therapy.[10] Among American adults, taking nonvitamin, nonmineral natural products was the most popular form of CAM therapy. However, there is little scientific evidence that supports the usefulness as well as the safety of taking most nonnutrient dietary supplements, including botanicals.[10]

A few types of CAM are gaining acceptance among conventional medical practitioners, primarily because there is sufficient scientific support for the practices. For example, species of "unfriendly" bacteria can overpopulate the large intestine when a person takes an antibiotic for infection. The overgrowth of these bacteria can cause cramping and diarrhea. Some physicians recommend probiotics in yogurt or tablet form for patients who are taking antibiotics. Research has shown that certain probiotics can help prevent or limit diarrhea that results from antibiotic use.[11]

The practice of using CAM with conventional medicine is called *integrative medicine*. The National Center for Complementary and Integrative Health (NCCIH), an agency within the National Institutes of Health, funds research intended to increase scientific evidence about the usefulness and safety of CAM practices.

How Are Dietary Supplements Regulated?

The U.S. Food and Drug Administration (FDA) is the federal agency that is responsible for ensuring the safety and effectiveness of medications and other health-related products. The FDA strictly regulates the development, production, and marketing of new medications (drugs). A drug is a substance, natural or human-made, that alters body functions. As a result, drugs can produce beneficial as well as harmful effects on the body. Before marketing a new drug, the manufacturer must submit evidence to the FDA indicating that the product has been tested extensively and is safe and effective. If FDA experts have serious concerns about a medication's side effects or question its usefulness, the agency may reject the manufacturer's petition to sell the product.

When consumed, many dietary supplements act as drugs in the body. However, the FDA regulates dietary supplements as foods, not medications.[12] As a result, dietary supplement manufacturers can bypass most of the strict regulations that the FDA applies to the introduction of new medications into the marketplace. Supplement manufacturers, for example, generally do not need FDA approval before manufacturing or marketing their products. Additionally, the manufacturers are not required to provide the FDA with scientific evidence indicating their products provide measurable health benefits. Manufacturers, however, must notify the FDA and provide the agency with information about the safety of any supplement that contains dietary ingredients that were not marketed in dietary supplements prior to 1994, unless the substance had been used in foods.

The FDA regulates the labeling of dietary supplements, including the kinds of claims that are permitted on labels. The "Food and Dietary Supplement Labels" section of Chapter 3 provides information about supplement labeling.

The FDA's role in regulating dietary supplements generally begins after products enter the marketplace.[13] Supplement manufacturers are required to keep records concerning reports they receive about serious adverse (negative) health effects that may have been caused by their products. Furthermore, the manufacturers must also inform the FDA about such reports. Consumers and health care professionals can also report health problems that are possibly associated with supplement use directly to the FDA.

When the FDA determines that a particular supplement presents a significant or unreasonable risk of harm, the agency alerts consumers about the risk and seeks to recall the product, that is, initiates efforts to have it removed

---

multivitamin/mineral (MV/M) describes a dietary supplement that contains vitamins and minerals

complementary and alternative medicine (CAM) variety of health care practices that are not accepted by the majority of conventional medical practitioners

TABLE 2.2 Some Popular Dietary Supplements

Dietary Supplement	Major Claims	Known Health Effects	
		Benefits	Risks
Alfalfa	Treats kidney problems and improves urine flow Relieves arthritis symptoms	May be effective in lowering total cholesterol and "bad" cholesterol levels, but little scientific evidence that it has other benefits	Although alfalfa leaves may be safe to ingest, consuming alfalfa seeds may be hazardous to health; may lower blood sugar levels, which could be dangerous for people with diabetes
Bitter orange	Useful for causing weight loss and treating heartburn, upset stomach, and constipation	None	May increase heart rate and blood pressure, which could result in stroke
Chondroitin	Relieves joint damage associated with arthritis	Some scientific evidence supports health benefit claims, but more research is needed. Often combined with glucosamine	Some products may contain poisonous levels of the mineral manganese.
Coenzyme Q-10	Increases exercise tolerance, prevents heart disease and cancer, and reverses signs of aging	Antioxidant made by the body and involved in energy metabolism Insufficient scientific evidence to support most claims	May improve heart function Low toxicity but may interfere with certain blood thinners
Echinacea	Boosts immune system Prevents the common cold and reduces cold symptoms	May reduce cold symptoms if taken in the early stage of the infection process May reduce recurrence of vaginal yeast infections Not effective for treating recurrent genital herpes outbreaks	Generally safe for short-term use but may provoke allergic response or intestinal upset; some products may be contaminated with arsenic and lead
Evening primrose oil	Treats eczema (a common skin condition) Relieves arthritis and postmenopausal symptoms	Little scientific evidence to support health benefit claims	Long-term safety has not been established.
Fish oil	Prevents heart disease and stroke Cures rheumatoid arthritis Reduces depression and risk of Alzheimer's disease	Lowers elevated blood triglyceride (fat) levels, but consuming fatty fish may be more helpful in reducing heart disease risk than taking fish oil supplements Can slightly lower blood pressure May reduce pain and stiffness associated with rheumatoid arthritis More research is need to determine other health benefits.	Taking more than 3 g/day may interfere with blood clotting, increasing the risk of hemorrhagic stroke. Can reduce blood vitamin E concentration
Flaxseed and flaxseed oil	Acts as a laxative (flaxseed) Reduces blood cholesterol levels	Nonanimal source of omega-3 fatty acids Seeds have laxative effects. May benefit people with heart disease, but more research is needed	Generally safe but may cause diarrhea
Garlic	Lowers blood cholesterol levels	May slow the development of atherosclerosis that can result in heart attack and stroke May reduce the risk of stomach and colon cancers May reduce elevated blood pressure	Can cause allergic reaction, cause unpleasant body odor, and interfere with prescription blood thinners
Ginger	Treats "morning sickness" and other forms of nausea Relieves stomach upsets Relieves joint and muscle pain	Can safely treat morning sickness and may reduce other forms of nausea Lack of scientific evidence to support other health benefit claims	In general, few side effects when taken in small amounts; powdered ginger may cause intestinal upset

Sources: National Institutes of Health, National Center for Complementary and Alternative Medicine: Health topics A-Z http://nccam.nih.gov/health/atoz.htm
Accessed: July 31, 2014

TABLE 2.2 Some Popular Dietary Supplements *(Continued)*

Dietary Supplement	Major Claims	Known Health Effects	
		Benefits	Risks
Ginkgo biloba	Improves memory Reduces the risk of Alzheimer's disease and other forms of dementia	Taking ginkgo leaf extracts by mouth may produce mild improvements in cognitive (thinking) processes and reduce dizziness. Lack of scientific evidence to support many other health benefit claims	Reacts with several prescription medications May increase the risk of bleeding and cause allergic reactions, headaches, intestinal upsets, and nausea Ginkgo seeds are toxic.
Ginseng (Asian)	Boosts overall health Treats erectile dysfunction (male impotence)	May lower elevated blood glucose levels and benefit immune system Lack of scientific evidence to support other health benefit claims	May cause headaches, sleep disturbances, allergic responses, and gastrointestinal upsets Long-term use may increase risk of toxicity.
Glucosamine sulfate	Relieves joint damage associated with arthritis	Some scientific evidence supports health benefit claims, but more research is needed (frequently used with chondroitin).	Appears to be safe but may cause mild gastrointestinal side effects, including nausea and heartburn
Green tea	Prevents or treats cancer Promotes weight loss Reduces blood cholesterol levels	Results of some laboratory studies indicate green tea protects against cancer or reduces cancer cell growth, but results of human studies are not conclusive. Lack of reliable evidence to support other health benefit claims, including promoting weight loss	Green tea extracts may damage the liver. Caffeine content may cause sleep disturbances, irritability, and digestive upset.
Kava	Reduces stress	Potential harm of using kava outweighs any benefit.	Toxic—can damage the liver May cause abnormal muscle movements, yellowed skin, and sleepiness
L-arginine	Treats heart disease Improves male sexual functioning Improves mental functioning of older adults Lowers blood pressure Increases male fertility	Amino acid (component of proteins) Does not prevent heart attacks May reduce recovery time after surgery and improve erectile function More research is needed to support other health benefits.	Probably safe when taken for short term but may cause side effects, including abdominal pain, diarrhea, gout, breathing problems, and low blood pressure May worsen recurrent herpes outbreaks Should not be taken by people who are recovering from a heart attack, because the supplement may cause another heart attack
Melatonin	Treats some sleep disorders Prevents jet lag Treats cancer, headaches, and irritable bowel syndrome Delays the aging process	May be effective for treating certain sleep disorders and preventing jet lag May help relieve withdrawal symptoms in smokers who quit tobacco use Lack of evidence that the supplement is useful for other conditions	Probably safe for short-term use, but people should not drive or operate heavy machinery for 4–5 hours after taking the supplement Interacts with several prescription medications and other herbs that produce sedation (calming effects) May interfere with female fertility and worsen depression in people with the condition
St. John's wort	Reduces depression	At this time, most studies do not support using the supplement to treat depression.	May interact with other herbal products and many medications, including prescription antidepressants and oral contraceptives

from the market.[14] In most instances, the manufacturer voluntarily recalls the product after determining there is a problem with it or being notified by the FDA about the problem. In some cases, however, the FDA requests a recall. If the FDA determines that the manufacturer's response to the recall is inadequate, the agency can take enforcement steps, such as initiating legal action against the company to seize products or stop producing the items.

Using Dietary Supplements Wisely

When used properly, many dietary supplements, particularly micronutrient products, are generally safe. Herbal supplements, however, are made from plants that may have toxic parts. Comfrey, pennyroyal, sassafras, kava, lobelia, and ma huang are among the plants known to be highly toxic or cancer—causing. Products containing material from these plants should be avoided. The use of botanical products can also evoke allergic or inflammatory responses that often result in signs and symptoms of skin, sinus, or respiratory illnesses. Herbal teas may contain pollens and other parts of plants that can cause allergies, particularly in people who are sensitive to the herbs or their related species. Echinacea (purple cone flower) is related to ragweed, a plant that is often associated with seasonal respiratory allergies. When people who are allergic to ragweed pollen take supplements that contain echinacea, they may develop allergic responses that mimic symptoms of the common cold (watery eyes, runny nose, and sneezing). In some instances, inflammatory responses, such as asthma attacks, can occur after exposure to echinacea or other plants. Asthma can be a life—threatening condition. Therefore, people who have asthma or allergies should be very careful when using botanical supplements.

Consumers also need to be aware that medicinal herbs may contain substances that interact with prescription or over—the—counter medications as well as other herbs. Such responses can produce unwanted and even dangerous side effects (see Table 2.2). Ginkgo biloba, for example, can interact with aspirin, increasing the risk of bleeding. Garlic, ginseng, and vitamin E supplements can also increase bleeding. Kava and valerian act as sedatives (calming agents) and can amplify the effects of anesthetics and other medications used during surgery. Therefore, consult a physician or pharmacist before using any dietary supplement or giving such products to your children. Additionally, treat dietary supplements as drugs: store them away from children and provide your physicians and other health care professionals with a list of the ones you are taking.

If you use or are thinking about using one or more dietary supplements:

- Determine whether the supplement is necessary. Some people have medical reasons for taking dietary supplements that contain one or more micronutrients, such as folic acid, calcium, or vitamin D. Discuss your need for the supplement with your physician or a registered dietitian before you purchase or use the product. This action is particularly important if you are pregnant, are breastfeeding a baby, or have a chronic medical condition such as diabetes or heart disease.
- Consult a physician as soon as you develop signs and symptoms of a serious illness. Using supplements to treat serious diseases instead of seeking conventional medical care that has proven effectiveness is a risky practice. In these instances, delaying or forgoing useful medical treatment may result in the worsening of the condition or even be life threatening.
- Be wary of claims made about a supplement's benefits and investigate the claims used to promote the product. The following government websites provide reliable information about dietary supplements:

U.S. National Library of Medicine http://www.nlm .nih.gov/medlineplus/herbalmedicine.html

Food and Drug Adminstration www.fda.gov/Food /DietarySupplements/default.htm

National Institutes of Health, National Center for Complementary and Integrative Health https:// nccih.nih.gov/health/integrative—health

Office of Dietary Supplements http://ods.od.nih.gov/

- Determine hazards associated with taking the supplement. Information about the risks and benefits of various dietary supplements can be found at the **Office of Dietary Supplements'** website: http://ods.od.nih .gov/factsheets/dietarysupplements/.
- Avoid using dietary supplements as substitutes for nutritious foods. Plant foods provide a wide array of phytochemicals, many of which may have health benefits when taken in their natural forms—foods. When these substances are isolated from plants and manufactured into supplements, they may lose their beneficial properties.

If you experience negative side effects after using a particular dietary supplement, it is a good idea to be examined by a physician immediately. Furthermore, you as well as your physician should report the problem to the FDA's MedWatch program by calling (800) FDA—1088 or visiting the agency's website: http://www.fda.gov/Safety /MedWatch/HowToReport/default.htm.

It is important to recognize that the manufacturing of dietary supplements is a profitable industry in the

United States. In 2011, Americans spent $30 billion on such products.[15] In many instances, however, people do not need dietary supplements, and they are wasting their money by purchasing them—money that could be better spent on natural sources of nutrients and phyto—chemicals, particularly fruits, vegetables, and whole—grain cereals.[16]

13. List at least three examples of complementary and alternative medical practices.

14. Explain why a prescription medication that is used to treat the common cold is not a dietary supplement.

15. List at least two examples of dietary supplements.

Chapter References

See Appendix H.

Summary

2.1 Nutrition: Science for Consumers

- Scientists ask questions about the natural world and follow generally accepted methods to obtain answers to these questions. Nutrition research relies on scientific methods that may involve making observations, asking questions and developing possible explanations, performing tests, collecting and analyzing data, drawing conclusions from data, and reporting on the findings. Other scientists can test the findings to confirm or reject them.

- Epidemiology is the study of the occurrence, distribution, and causes of health problems in populations. By studying differences in dietary practices and disease occurrences among populations, epidemiologists can suggest nutrition-related hypotheses for the prevalence of certain diseases. Epidemiological studies cannot indicate whether two variables are correlated, because the relationship could be a coincidence.

- Researchers summarize the findings and seek to publish articles with information about their investigations in scientific journals. Before articles are accepted for publication, they undergo peer review. Scientists generally do not accept a hypothesis or the results of a study until they are supported by considerable research evidence. Media coverage of a medical breakthrough is not necessarily an indication of the value or quality of research that resulted in the news story. More research is often necessary for scientists to determine whether the results are valid and can be generalized.

- Consumers may think scientists do not know what they are doing when conflicting research findings are reported in the media. Conflicting findings often result because different teams of researchers use different study designs when investigating the same hypothesis. Furthermore, each team of scientists may analyze the results differently. Other factors, such as genetic and lifestyle differences, can also influence the results of nutrition research involving human subjects. The science of nutrition is constantly evolving.

2.2 Nutrition Information: Fact or Fiction

- Although testimonials and anecdotes are often used to promote nutrition-related products and services, consumers cannot be sure that this information is reliable or based on scientific facts. Personal observations are not evidence of a cause-and-effect relationship because many factors, such as lifestyle and environment, can influence outcomes.

- Popular magazine articles, best-selling trade books, Internet websites, television news reports, and other forms of media are often unreliable sources of nutrition information. Consumers need to be careful and question the reliability of such sources, because the First Amendment to the U.S. Constitution guarantees freedom of the press and freedom of speech.

- Consumers need to ask questions to determine the author's reasons for promoting the information. Consumers should also look for red flags, such as scare tactics and claims that sound too good to be true.

- Much of the nutrition information that is on the Internet is unreliable and intended to promote sales. Websites sponsored by nonprofit organizations, nationally recognized health associations, government agencies, and nationally accredited colleges and universities are generally reliable sources of information.

2.3 Reliable Nutrition Experts

- Although some states regulate and license nutritionists, there is no standard legal definition for "nutritionist" in the United States. For reliable food, nutrition, and dietary information, consumers can consult persons with degrees in human nutrition from accredited institutions of higher learning, such as nutrition instructors and registered dietitians, registered dietitian nutritionists, or licensed dietitian nutritionists.

2.4 Nutrition Matters: What Are Dietary Supplements?

- A dietary supplement is a product (other than tobacco) that adds to a person's dietary intake, contains one or more dietary ingredients, is taken by mouth in tablet or other forms, and is not promoted as a conventional food or the only item of a meal or diet.

- Dietary supplements include nutrient pills, protein powders, and herbal extracts, as well as energy bars and drinks. In many instances, people do not need dietary supplements. Healthy people should focus on obtaining nutrients and phytochemicals from foods, particularly fruits, vegetables, and whole-grain cereals. Before taking a dietary supplement, discuss the matter with your physician.

Recipe for Healthy Living

Grandma's Chicken Soup

Long before the advent of over-the-counter antihistamines and cough syrups, there was chicken soup. Sometimes referred to as "Jewish penicillin," chicken soup has been used as a cold remedy for over 1000 years. Chicken soup is not a cure for the common cold. However, results of a laboratory study indicated chicken soup contains substances that can subdue the body's inflammatory response to upper respiratory tract infections. This inflammatory response typically results in common cold symptoms such as cough and excess nasal discharge. Although the soup's specific actions on cold-causing microbes still need to be determined, consuming a soothing, warm bowl of chicken soup contributes to the sick person's fluid and other nutrient intake at a time when he or she may not feel like eating anything else. Even if you don't have a cold, the following chicken soup recipe is delicious and easy to make. You can freeze the soup in small, covered plastic containers for future meals.

Source: Rennard BO and others: Chicken soup inhibits neutrophil chemotaxis in vitro. *Chest* 118(4):1, 2000.

This recipe makes approximately 6 cups of soup. A 1-cup serving of the soup supplies approximately 135 kcal, 19 g of protein, 3 g fat, 323 mg sodium, 431 mg potassium, and 6.4 mg niacin.

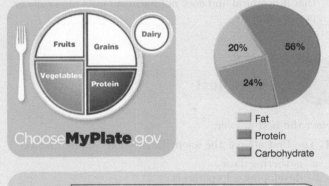

INGREDIENTS:

- 1 package of raw chicken wings, approx. 3 to 4 lbs
- 1 large onion, cut in wedges
- 4 large carrots, cleaned and cut into 3-inch lengths
- ⅛ tsp black pepper
- 1 chicken bouillon cube
- 3 large celery stalks, cleaned and cut into 3-inch lengths
- ⅛ tsp paprika
- ⅛ tsp thyme
- ⅛ tsp curry seasoning
- few parsley sprigs (optional)

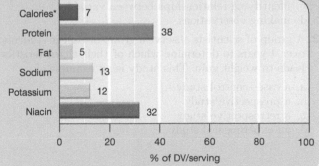

PREPARATION STEPS:

1. Place the raw chicken in a large cooking pot and add enough cold water to cover chicken, approximately 2 quarts of water.

2. Add onion, carrots, celery, pepper, bouillon cube, and spices to chicken and water; turn burner on high. When mixture comes to a boil, reduce heat to medium and cover the pot with a lid. Soup should boil for at least an hour.

3. Turn off the heat, remove chicken wings from the soup, and place them in a bowl. Cover and refrigerate.

4. Cover soup and refrigerate for 12 hours.

5. Skim chicken fat from top of soup. Remove skin from the wings and discard skin. Separate the meat from the bones, discard bones, and add the meat to the soup. Reheat soup before eating; sprinkle with parsley sprigs, if desired.

6. Cover and store leftover soup in refrigerator for up to 3 days, or freeze.

Note: When you reheat the soup, you can also add your favorite soup ingredients, such as frozen vegetables, broccoli florets, kale, whole-wheat noodles, or cooked brown rice.

connect | NUTRITION   Further analyze this and other recipes through activities on Connect at www.mcgrawhillconnect.com.

58   **Chapter 2** Evaluating Nutrition Information

Critical Thinking

1. A news broadcaster reports the results of a study in which people who took fish oil and vitamin E supplements daily did not reduce their risk of heart attack. Moreover, the researchers stopped the study when they determined the supplements increased the subjects' risk of stroke! Explain how you would determine whether this information is reliable.

2. Explain how you can verify the reliability of advice about dietary supplements provided at an Internet website.

3. Design a study that involves observing a nutrition-related practice of college students, such as vending machine choices or fast-food preferences, and share your idea with the class. Your study should be designed so that it is ethical and does not harm subjects physically or psychologically.

4. A group of scientists conduct a study to determine risk factors for breast cancer. According to their results, women who consume soy foods have a lower risk of breast cancer than women who do not eat soy foods. Think of two questions this finding is likely to generate that could be answered by further scientific investigation.

5. Browse through popular health-related magazines to find an article or advertisement that relates to nutrition, and make a copy of the article or advertisement. Analyze each sentence or line of the article or advertisement for signs of unreliability. Is the article or advertisement a reliable source of information? Explain why it is or why it is not.

Practice Test

Select the best answer.

1. The first step of the scientific method usually involves
   a. gathering data.
   b. developing a hypothesis.
   c. identifying relationships between variables.
   d. making observations.

2. A group of scientists observe a group of college students over 4 years to determine which of their characteristics leads to weight gain. This study is an example of
   a. a case-control study.
   b. a prospective study.
   c. a retrospective study.
   d. an experimental study.

3. An aspect of _____ involves studying causes of health problems in a population.
   a. epidemiology
   b. technobiology
   c. diseasiology
   d. censusology

4. Comparing individuals with iron-deficiency anemia to individuals who have very similar characteristics but are healthy would be an example of
   a. a prospective study.
   b. an anecdotal study.
   c. a retrospective study.
   d. a case-control study.

5. Generally, epidemiological studies
   a. establish causation.
   b. prove correlations.
   c. cannot determine cause-and-effect relationships.
   d. are experimental-based research efforts that examine two variables.

6. Which of the following journals does not have peer-reviewed articles?
   a. *Journal of the American Medical Association*
   b. *The New England Journal of Medicine*
   c. *Journal of the American College of Nutrition*
   d. *Men's Journal*

7. The government agency that enforces consumer protection laws by investigating false or misleading health–related claims is the

   a. Federal Trade Commission (FTC).
   b. Environmental Protection Agency (EPA).
   c. Agricultural Research Service (ARS).
   d. Centers for Disease Control and Prevention (CDC).

8. A testimonial is

   a. an unbiased report about a product's value.
   b. a scientifically valid claim.
   c. a personal endorsement of a product.
   d. a form of scientific evidence.

9. Which of the following websites is most likely to provide biased and unreliable nutrition information?

   a. the site of a nationally recognized health association (*.org)
   b. a site that promotes or sells dietary supplements (*.com)
   c. the site of a U.S. government agency (*.gov)
   d. an accredited college or university's site (*.edu)

10. A fake treatment is a(an)

   a. anecdote.
   b. double–blind study.
   c. pseudoscience experiment.
   d. placebo.

11. Which of the following substances would be classified as a dietary supplement according to the Dietary Supplement and Health Education Act of 1994?

   a. tobacco   c. ginseng
   b. aspirin   d. ibuprofen

12. The _____ is the federal agency that tries to ensure the safety and effectiveness of health–related products.

   a. FDA   c. EPA
   b. FTC   d. USGS

Answers to Quiz Yourself

1. Scientists use anecdotes as scientific evidence to support their findings. **False.** (p. 33)

2. Popular health-related magazines typically publish articles that have been peer-reviewed. **False.** (p. 45)

3. By conducting a prospective epidemiological study, medical researchers can determine risk factors that may influence health. **True.** (p. 38)

4. Dietary supplements include vitamin pills as well as products that contain echinacea, ginseng, and garlic. **True.** (p. 50)

5. In general, registered dietitians are reliable sources of food and nutrition information. **True.** (p. 49)

≡LEARNSMART
ADVANTAGE

Get the most out of your study of nutrition with McGraw-Hill's innovative suite of adaptive learning products including McGraw-Hill LearnSmart®, SmartBook®, LearnSmart Achieve®, and LearnSmart Prep®. Visit www.learnsmartadvantage.com.

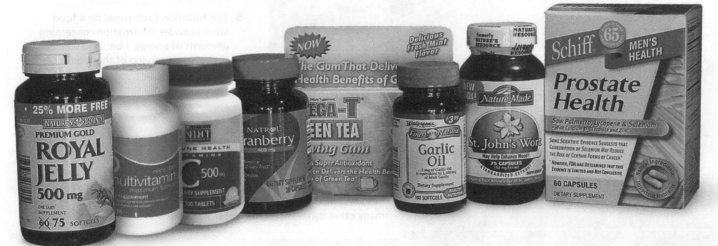

CHAPTER 3

Planning Nutritious Diets

Quiz Yourself

Before reading the rest of Chapter 3, test your knowledge of dietary standards, recommendations, and guides, as well as nutrient labels, by taking the following quiz. The answers are found on page 97.

1. According to the latest U.S. Department of Agriculture food guide, fruits and vegetables are combined into one food group. _____ T _____ F

2. According to the recommendations of the *2015–2020 Dietary Guidelines for Americans,* it is acceptable for certain adults to consume alcoholic beverages in moderation. _____ T _____ F

3. Last week, Colin didn't consume the recommended amount of vitamin C for a couple of days. Nevertheless, he is unlikely to develop scurvy, the vitamin C deficiency disease. _____ T _____ F

4. The Food and Drug Administration develops Dietary Guidelines for Americans. _____ T _____ F

5. The Nutrition Facts panel on a food label provides information concerning amounts of energy, fiber, and sodium that are in a serving of the food. _____ T _____ F

Mc Graw Hill Education **connect**
|NUTRITION   **www.mcgrawhillconnect.com**

A wealth of proven resources are available on Connect® Nutrition including McGraw-Hill LearnSmart®, SmartBook®, NutritionCalc Plus, and many other dynamic learning tools. Ask your instructor about Connect!

3.1 From Requirements to Standards

Learning Outcomes

1 Explain the difference between a dietary requirement and a dietary allowance.

2 Identify the various dietary standards and explain how they can be used.

When you shop for groceries, do you sometimes feel overwhelmed by the vast array of foods that are available? If your answer is "yes," your response is not surprising, considering the average supermarket offered nearly 44,000 items in 2013.[1] Every time you enter a supermarket, you are likely to find food items that were not on the shelves during your last visit to the store. In 2010, for example, over 21,500 new food and beverage products were introduced into the marketplace.[2]

Chapter 1 introduced some key nutrition concepts, including the need for dietary adequacy, moderation, balance, and a variety of foods. Chapter 2 described how you can become a more careful consumer of nutrition information. However, you are also a consumer of food. With so many grocery items from which to choose, what are the primary factors that influence your food purchases? Do you select foods simply because they taste good, are reasonably priced, or are easy to prepare? Do you ever consider the effects certain foods may have on your health before you purchase them?

Your lifestyle reflects your health—related behaviors, including your dietary practices and physical activity habits. Americans of all ages may reduce their risk of chronic disease by adopting nutritious diets and engaging in regular physical activity. However, consumers need practical advice to help them make decisions that can promote more healthy lifestyles.

Chapter 3 discusses dietary standards, including how the standards are established and used. The information in this chapter also presents practical ways to plan a nutritionally adequate, well—balanced diet using tools such as the Dietary Guidelines and MyPlate. Furthermore, Section 3.5 explains how to interpret and use nutrition—related information that appears on food and dietary supplement labels.

What Is a Nutrient Requirement?

By using research methods discussed in Chapter 2, scientists have been able to estimate the amount of many nutrients required by the body. A **requirement** can be defined as the smallest amount of a nutrient that maintains a defined level of nutritional health.[3] In general, this amount, when consumed daily, prevents the nutrient's deficiency disease. The requirement for a particular nutrient varies to some degree from person to person. A person's age, sex, general health status, physical activity level, and use of medications and drugs are among the factors that influence his or her nutrient requirements.

Many nutrients are stored in the body, including vitamin D and most minerals. Major storage sites include the liver, body fat, and bones. Other nutrients, such as vitamin C and most B vitamins, are not stored by the body. For optimal nutrition, you need to consume enough of those nutrients to maintain storage levels. Your body uses its nutrient stores much like you can

requirement smallest amount of a nutrient that maintains a defined level of nutritional health

use a savings account to help manage your money. When you have some extra cash, it is wise to place the money in a savings account, so you can withdraw some of the reserves to meet future needs without going into debt. When your consumption of certain nutrients is more than enough to meet your needs, the body stores the excess. When your intake of a stored nutrient is low or needs for this nutrient become increased, such as during recovery from illness, your body withdraws some from storage. As a result of having optimal levels of stored nutrients, you may recover more quickly and avoid or delay developing deficiencies of those nutrients.

Dietary Reference Intakes

Dietary Reference Intakes (DRIs) encompass a variety of daily energy and nutrient intake standards that nutrition experts in the United States use as references when making dietary recommendations. DRIs are intended to help people reduce their risk of nutrient deficiencies and excesses, prevent disease, and achieve optimal health.[4] The standards (Fig. 3.1) are the Estimated Average Requirement (EAR), which includes Estimated Energy Requirement (EER); Recommended Dietary Allowance (RDA), Adequate Intake (AI), and Tolerable Upper Intake Level (UL).

A group of nutrition scientists, the **Food and Nutrition Board (FNB)** of the Institute of Medicine, develop DRIs. Periodically, members of the board adjust DRIs as new information concerning human nutritional needs and dietary adequacy becomes available. You can find tables for the latest DRIs on the last pages of this book. The following sections provide basic information about the various DRI standards. It is important to become familiar with these terms, because we refer to them in this and other chapters.

Estimated Average Requirement

An **Estimated Average Requirement (EAR)** is the daily amount of the nutrient that meets the needs of 50% of healthy people who are in a particular *life stage/sex group*. Life stage/sex groups classify people according to age, sex, and whether females are pregnant or breastfeeding. A typical 20–year–old female college student, for example, would be classified as a female, between 19 and 30 years old, and not pregnant or breastfeeding.

To establish an EAR for a nutrient, the Food and Nutrition Board identifies a physiological marker, a substance in the body that reflects proper functioning and can be measured. This marker indicates whether the level of a nutrient in the body is adequate. A marker for vitamin C, for example, is the amount of the vitamin in certain blood cells. When these cells contain nearly all the vitamin C they can hold, the body has an optimal supply of the vitamin. Thus, a physician can diagnose whether a patient is vitamin C deficient by taking a blood sample from the person and measuring the vitamin C content of certain blood cells.

Estimated Energy Requirement   The **Estimated Energy Requirement (EER)** is the average daily energy intake that meets the needs of a healthy person who is maintaining his or her weight. Dietitians can use EERs to evaluate an individual's energy intake. The EER takes into account the person's physical

Dietary Reference Intakes (DRIs) various energy and nutrient intake standards for Americans

Food and Nutrition Board (FNB) group of nutrition scientists who develop DRIs

Estimated Average Requirement (EAR) amount of a nutrient that meets the needs of 50% of healthy people in a life stage/sex group

Estimated Energy Requirement (EER) average daily energy intake that meets the needs of a healthy person maintaining his or her weight

DIETARY REFERENCE INTAKES (DRIs)

Estimated Average Requirement (EAR)

Recommended Dietary Allowance (RDA)

Estimated Energy Requirement (EER)

Tolerable Upper Intake Level (UL)

Adequate Intake (AI)

Figure 3.1 Dietary Reference Intakes. The Dietary Reference Intakes (DRIs) encompass a variety of terms that represent standards for energy and nutrient recommendations.

activity level, height, and weight, as well as sex and life stage. Because the EER is an average figure, some people have energy needs that are higher or lower. Chapter 10 provides formulas for calculating your EER.

Recommended Dietary Allowances

The **Recommended Dietary Allowances (RDAs)** are standards for recommending daily intakes of several nutrients. RDAs meet the nutrient needs of nearly all healthy individuals (97 to 98%) in a particular life stage/sex group. To establish an RDA for a nutrient, nutrition scientists first determine its EAR. Then scientists add a "margin of safety" amount to the EAR that allows for individual variations in nutrient needs and helps maintain tissue stores (Fig. 3.2). For example, the adult EAR for vitamin C is 60 mg for women who are not pregnant or breastfeeding and 75 mg for men.[3] However, the adult RDA for vitamin C is 15 mg higher than the EAR: 75 mg for women who are not pregnant or breastfeeding and 90 mg for men. Thus, the margin of safety for vitamin C is 15 mg. Because smoking cigarettes increases the need for vitamin C, smokers should add 35 mg to their RDA for the nutrient.

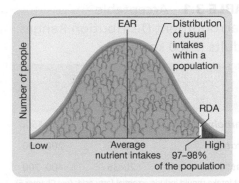

Figure 3.2 Establishing RDAs. A nutrient's RDA is high enough to meet or exceed the requirements of 97 to 98% of the population for the nutrient. In other words, about 98% of the population will have their needs for the nutrient met by just consuming the RDA amount.

Adequate Intakes

In some instances, nutrition scientists are unable to develop RDAs for nutrients because there is not enough information to determine human requirements. Until such information becomes available, scientists set **Adequate Intakes (AIs)** for these nutrients. To establish an AI, scientists record eating patterns of a group of healthy people and estimate the group's average daily intake of the nutrient. If the population under observation shows no evidence of the nutrient's deficiency disorder, the researchers conclude that the average level of intake must be adequate and use that value as the AI (Fig. 3.3). Vitamin K and the mineral potassium are among the nutrients that have AIs instead of RDAs.

Tolerable Upper Intake Level

Nutrition scientists also establish a **Tolerable Upper Intake Level (Upper Level or UL)** for many vitamins and minerals. The UL is the highest average amount of a nutrient that is unlikely to harm most people when the amount is consumed daily (see Fig. 3.3).[4] The risk of a toxicity disorder increases when a person regularly consumes amounts of a nutrient that exceed its UL. The UL for vitamin C, for example, is 2000 mg/day for adults.

Recommended Dietary Allowances (RDAs) standards for recommending daily intakes of several nutrients

Adequate Intakes (AIs) dietary recommendations that assume a population's average daily nutrient intakes are adequate because no deficiency diseases are present

Tolerable Upper Intake Level (Upper Level or UL) standard representing the highest average amount of a nutrient that is unlikely to be harmful when consumed daily

Acceptable Macronutrient Distribution Ranges (AMDRs) macronutrient intake ranges that are nutritionally adequate and may reduce the risk of diet-related chronic diseases

Acceptable Macronutrient Distribution Ranges

The results of scientific research suggest that food energy sources (macronutrients) are associated with risk of developing certain diet—related chronic diseases, such as heart disease. **Acceptable Macronutrient Distribution Ranges (AMDRs)** indicate ranges of carbohydrate, fat, and protein intakes that provide adequate amounts of vitamins and minerals and may reduce the risk of diet—related chronic diseases.[4] The AMDR for carbohydrates, for example, is 45 to 65% of total energy intake. If a person's total energy intake is 2300 kcal/day, then his or her recommended carbohydrate intake is 1035 to 1495 kcal/day. To obtain the range of energy from carbohydrate, multiply total kcal/day (in this case, 2300 kcal) by 0.45 (45%) and then

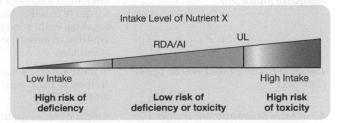

Figure 3.3 Adequate Intakes and Upper Limits. Consuming too much or not enough of a nutrient can cause health problems.

TABLE 3.1 Acceptable Macronutrient Distribution Ranges: Adults (2000 kcal/day)

Macronutrient	AMDR (% of total energy intake)	Calories
Carbohydrate	45–65	900–1300
Protein	10–35	200–700
*Fat**	20–35	400–700

* Fat intake should include essential fatty acids (see Chapter 6).

multiply 2300 kcal by 0.65 (65%). Table 3.1 lists adult AMDRs for a person who consumes 2000 kcal/day.

Applying Nutrient Standards

Table 3.2 summarizes information about the DRIs. Dietitians refer to DRIs as standards for planning nutritious diets for groups of people and evaluating the nutritional adequacy of a population's diet. Nevertheless, RDAs and AIs are often used to evaluate an individual's dietary practices.[4] Your diet is likely to be nutritionally adequate if your average daily intake for each nutrient meets the nutrient's RDA or AI value. If your diet consistently supplies less than the EAR for a nutrient, you may be at risk of eventually developing the nutrient's deficiency disorder (see Fig. 3.3). On the other hand, if your intake of a nutrient is consistently above its UL, you are at risk of developing that nutrient's toxicity disorder. Nutrient toxicity disorders are more likely to occur when people take high doses of individual nutrient supplements, particularly vitamins and minerals. If you do not take large doses of nutrient supplements and you eat reasonable amounts of food, your risk of developing a nutrient toxicity disorder is low.

Nutritional standards have a variety of commercial applications. Pharma—ceutical companies refer to DRIs when developing formulas that replace breast milk for infants and special formulas for people who cannot consume regular foods. As a result, babies can be nourished by consuming commercially prepared formulas, and adults who are unable to swallow can survive for years on formula feedings administered through tubes inserted into their bodies.

For nutrition labeling purposes, the Food and Drug Administration (FDA) uses RDAs to develop a set of standards called *Daily Values (DVs)*. Consumers may find DVs useful for comparing the nutritional contents of similar foods. The "Food and Dietary Supplement Labels" section of this chapter provides more information about nutritional labeling, including DVs.

TABLE 3.2 Summary of Dietary Reference Intakes

Standard	Definition	Example
Estimated Average Requirement (EAR)	Amount of a nutrient that meets the needs of 50% of healthy people who are in a particular life stage/sex group	**Vitamin C** 75 mg/day for males and 60 mg/day for females ages 19 through 50 years
Recommended Dietary Allowance (RDA)	Amount of a nutrient that meets the needs of nearly all healthy individuals (97.5%) in a particular life stage/sex group	**Vitamin C** 90 mg/day for males (nonsmokers) and 75 mg/day for females ages 19 through 50 years (nonsmokers)
Adequate Intake (AI)	Amount of a nutrient that is considered to be adequate based on the population's typical intakes, but there is not enough scientific information available to determine an RDA for the nutrient at this time	**Vitamin C** 40 mg/day for infants from birth through 6 months of age
Tolerable Upper Intake Level or Upper Limit (UL)	Highest average amount of a nutrient that is unlikely to harm most people when the amount is consumed daily	**Vitamin C** 2000 mg/day for adults
Acceptable Macronutrient Distribution Range (AMDR)	Ranges of carbohydrate, fat, and protein intakes that provide adequate amounts of micronutrients and may reduce the risk of developing certain diet-related chronic diseases	See Table 3.1

Concept **Checkpoint 3.1**

1. What is the difference between an RDA and an AI?
2. Describe how scientists establish the RDA for a nutrient.
3. Explain how an EER differs from an RDA or AI.
4. Discuss how dietitians, pharmaceutical companies, and the FDA use nutrient standards.

3.2 Major Food Groups

Learning Outcome

1 List major food groups, and identify foods that are typically classified in each group.

The DRIs are not practical for planning menus, so nutrition experts develop more consumer—friendly food (dietary) guides. In general, such guides classify foods into major food groups according to their natural origins and key nutrients. Major food groups are usually grains, dairy products, fruits, vegetables, and protein—rich foods. In most instances, dietary guides also provide recommendations concern—ing amounts of foods from each group that should be eaten daily. The following points identify major food groups and summarize key features of each group.

Grains include products made from wheat, rice, corn, barley, and oats.

- **Grains** include products made from wheat, rice, and oats. Pasta, noodles, and flour tortillas are members of this group because wheat flour is their main ingredient. In general, 1 ounce of a grain food is equivalent to 1 slice of bread, 1 cup of ready—to—eat cereal, or ½ cup of cooked rice, pasta, or cereal such as oatmeal. Although corn is a type of grain, it is often used as a vegetable in meals. Cornmeal and popcorn, however, are usually grouped with grain products.

  Carbohydrate (starch) and protein are the primary macronutrients in grains. In the United States, refined grain products can also be good sources of several vitamins and minerals when they have undergone enrichment or fortification. **Enrichment** is the addition of specific amounts of iron and certain B vitamins to cereal grain products such as flour and rice. In general, enrichment replaces some of the nutrients that were lost during processing. **Fortification** is the addition of any nutrient to food, such as adding calcium to orange juice, vitamins A and D to milk, and numerous vitamins and minerals to ready—to—eat breakfast cereals.

  Dietary guides generally recommend choosing foods made with whole grains instead of refined grains. According to the FDA, whole grains are the intact, ground, cracked, or flaked seeds of cereal grains, such as wheat, buckwheat, oats, corn, rice, wild rice, rye, and barley.[5] Compared to refined grain products, foods made from whole grains naturally contain more fiber as well as micronutrients that are not replaced during enrichment.

- **Dairy foods** include milk and products made from milk that retain their calcium content after processing, such as yogurt and hard cheeses. Dairy foods are also excellent sources of protein, phosphorus (a mineral), and riboflavin (a B vitamin). Additionally, most of the milk sold in the United States is fortified with vitamins A and D.

  Foods and beverages made from soy beans (soy "milk" and soy "cheese") can substitute for cow's milk if they are fortified with calcium and other

enrichment addition of specific amounts of iron and certain B vitamins to cereal grain products

fortification addition of any of nutrient to food

Dairy products, especially yogurt and hard cheeses, are excellent sources of calcium, protein, phosphorus, and riboflavin. Additionally, milk is often fortified with vitamins A and D.

micronutrients. Ice cream, pudding, and frozen yogurt are often grouped with dairy foods, even though they often have high sugar and fat contents. Although cream cheese, cream, and butter are made from cow's milk they are not included in this group, because they have little or no calcium and are high in fat.

Most dietary guides recommend choosing dairy products that have most of the fat removed, such as fat–free or low–fat milk. (Fat–free milk may also be referred to as nonfat or skim milk.) Compared to whole milk, which is about 3.25% fat by weight, low–fat milk contains only 1% fat by weight and is often called "1% milk."

In general, 1 cup of fat–free milk has the calcium content of ⅔ cup of plain, low–fat yogurt or frozen yogurt; 2 cups of low–fat cottage cheese; 1½ ounces of natural cheese such as Swiss or cheddar; or 2.3 ounces of processed cheese. To obtain about the same amount of calcium as in 1 cup of fat–free milk, you would have to eat almost 1⅔ cups of regular vanilla ice cream. This amount of ice cream provides 490 kcal and about 26 g of fat, whereas 1⅔ cups of fat–free milk supplies about 135 kcal and less than 1 g of fat.

- ***Protein–rich foods*** include beef, pork, lamb, fish, shellfish, liver, and poultry. Beans, eggs, nuts, and seeds are included with this group because these protein–rich foods can substitute for meats. One ounce of food from this group generally equals 1 ounce of meat, poultry, or fish; ¼ cup cooked dry beans or dry peas; 1 egg; 1 tablespoon of peanut butter; or ½ ounce of nuts or seeds. One–fourth cup of tofu, a food made from soybeans, can substitute for 1 ounce of meat, fish, or poultry.

  Foods in the protein group are rich sources of micronutrients, especially iron, zinc, and B vitamins. In general, the body absorbs minerals, such as iron and zinc, more easily from animal foods than from plants.

  Some dietary guides use fat content to categorize meats and other protein–rich foods. According to these guides, low–fat cottage cheese and the white meat of turkey are very lean meats; ground beef that is not more than 15% fat by weight and tuna are lean meats. Pork sausage, bacon, regular cheeses, and hot dogs are examples of high–fat meats.

- ***Fruits*** include fresh, dried, frozen, sauced, and canned fruit, as well as 100% fruit juice. In general, 1 cup of food from this group equals 1 cup of fruit or fruit juice, or ½ cup of dried fruit, such as raisins or apricots.[6] Most fruits are low in fat and good sources of phytochemicals and micronutrients, especially the mineral potassium and vitamins C and folate. Additionally, whole or cut–up fruit is a good source of fiber. Although 100% juice is a source of phytochemicals and can count toward one's fruit intake, the majority of choices from this group should be whole or cut–up fruits.[7] Whole or cutup fruits are healthier options than juices because they contain more dietary fiber.

- ***Vegetables*** include fresh, cooked, canned, frozen, and dried/dehydrated vegetables, and 100% vegetable juice. Vegetables may be further grouped into dark green, orange, and starchy categories. Some guides include dried beans and peas in the vegetable group as well as in the meat and meat substitutes group. In general, 1 cup of food from this group equals 1 cup of raw or cooked vegetables, 1 cup vegetable juice, or 2 cups of uncooked leafy greens, such as salad greens. Many vegetables are good sources of micronutrients, fiber, and phytochemicals. Furthermore, many vegetables are naturally low in fat and energy.

Other Foods

Food guides may include an oils group and a group for empty–calorie foods or beverages. Oils include canola, corn, and olive oils, as well as other fats that are liquid at room temperature. Certain spreadable foods made from vegetable oils,

Dry beans, peas, eggs, nuts, and seeds are protein-rich foods that can substitute for meat.

MY DIVERSE PLATE

MyPlate

Tomatillos

For centuries, the people of Central America have grown and eaten tomatillos ("husk-tomatoes"). After the papery husk is removed, the fruit can be roasted, chopped, and mixed with ground chili peppers to form sauces, such as salsa verde (green sauce). Three medium tomatillos provide about 33 kcal, 2 g fiber, and 12 mg vitamin C.

such as mayonnaise, soft or "tub" margarine, and salad dressing, are also classi‑fied as oils. Nuts, olives, avocados, and some types of fish have high fat contents but these kinds of fat are "healthy" fats that do not contribute to heart disease (see Chapter 6). Some food guides group these foods with oils. Oils are often good sources of fat soluble vitamins.

Solid fats, such as beef fat, butter, stick margarine, and shortening, are fairly hard at room temperature. Solid fat is a source of "unhealthy" *saturated* fats that are associated with an increased risk of cardiovascular disease (CVD). Although cream and coconut oil are liquid or soft at room temperature, these foods are classified as solid fats. Chapter 6 discusses how dietary fats can affect health.

Empty‑calorie foods generally contain a lot of added sugar, alcohol, and/or solid fat. Sugary foods ("sweets") include candy, regular soft drinks, jelly, and other foods that contain high amounts of sugar added during processing or preparation. Sugary foods and alcoholic beverages typically supply energy but few or no micronutrients.

It is important to note that the nutritional content of foods within each group often varies widely. For example, 3.5 ounces of fresh sliced apples and 3.5 ounces of fresh orange slices each supply about 50 kcal. However, the apples contribute about 4 mg of vitamin C, whereas oranges supply about 46 mg of the vitamin to diets (Fig. 3.4). Therefore, dietary guides generally recommend that people choose a variety of foods from each food group when planning daily meals and snacks.

solid fats fats that are fairly hard at room temperature

Concept **Checkpoint 3.2**

5. List at least three foods that are generally classified as grain products.
6. What is the difference between nutrient fortification and nutrient enrichment?
7. List at least four foods that are generally classified as dairy products.
8. Why are dry beans often classified with meat?
9. According to the information in this section of Chapter 3, how many cups of dried apricots are nutritionally equivalent to 2 cups of fresh apricots?
10. Most dietary guides classify eggs and nuts with meat. Why?
11. Identify at least two foods that are classified as solid fat.

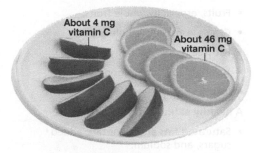

About 4 mg vitamin C

About 46 mg vitamin C

Figure 3.4 Comparing apples to oranges. The nutritional content of foods within each group often varies widely.

Did You Know?

The Dietary Guidelines form the basis of the federal government's nutrition policy, which serves as a framework for national, state, and local health promotion as well as food and nutrition programs. Dietary Guidelines are also used for menu planning by individuals and health care professionals.[8] Furthermore, food and beverage manufacturers can apply the guidelines to develop healthier products that appeal to consumers.

To revise the 2010 version of the dietary guidelines, officials with the U.S. Department of Health and Human Services (USDHHS) and the U.S. Depart‑ment of Agriculture (USDA) appointed a Dietary Guidelines Advisory Committee (DGAC) comprised of nationally recognized medical and nutrition experts. DGAC members reviewed the scientific evidence concerning the role of foods in health, before preparing the *Scientific Report of the 2015 Dietary Guidelines Advisory Committee*.[8] This publication contained recommendations for the development of the *2015–2020 Dietary Guidelines for Americans*. In February 2015, the overseeing government agencies made the DGAC report available for the public to read and provide input.

According to the DGAC report, a healthy diet contains more fruits, vegetables, whole grains, low- or nonfat dairy products, seafood, legumes and nuts than the typical diet of the general American population.[8] Additionally, a healthy diet contains fewer refined grains, red and processed meats, sodium, and sugar-sweetened foods and beverages than the typical American eating pattern. Such eating patterns should be flexible so food choices can be varied and individualized to meet a person's preferences, medical needs, and economic situation. The federal government incorporated some but not all of the DGAC's recommendations into the *2015–2020 Dietary Guidelines for Americans*.[9]

68   Chapter 3 Planning Nutritious Diets

TABLE 3.3 *2015–2020 Dietary Guidelines for Americans*: Overarching Guidelines

- Follow a healthy eating pattern across the lifespan.
- Focus on variety, nutrient density, and amount of food.
- Limit calories from added sugars and saturated fats and reduce sodium intake.
- Shift to healthier food and beverage choices.
- Support healthy eating patterns for all.

TABLE 3.4 A Healthy Eating Pattern

Includes:
• A variety of vegetables;
• Fruits, especially whole fruits;
• Grains, especially whole grains;
• Fat-free or low-fat dairy products;
• A variety of protein foods; and
• Oils.
A healthy eating pattern limits:
• Saturated fats and trans fats, added sugars, and sodium.

3.3 Dietary Guidelines

Learning Outcome

1 List at least four overarching guidelines of the *2015–2020 Dietary Guidelines for Americans* and provide recommendations of each one.

Heart disease, cancer, hypertension (chronically elevated blood pressure), and diabetes mellitus (commonly referred to as *diabetes*) are among the leading causes of disability and death among Americans. According to a considerable amount of scientific evidence, risk of these diseases is strongly linked with certain lifestyles, particularly poor dietary choices and lack of regular physical activity. As required by law, the USDHHS and the USDA publish the *Dietary Guidelines for Americans* (Dietary Guidelines), a set of general nutrition–related lifestyle recommendations that are intended for healthy people over 2 years of age.[8] The Dietary Guidelines are designed to promote adequate nutritional status and good health, and to reduce the risk of major nutrition–related chronic health conditions, such as obesity and cardiovascular disease. These guidelines are updated every 5 years.

Table 3.3 indicates the overarching guidelines of the *2015–2020 Dietary Guidelines*, which focus on encouraging healthy eating patterns. Table 3.4 lists key components of a healthy eating pattern, according to the Dietary Guidelines. The following information includes recommendations about each overarching guideline.[8] You can learn more about the Dietary Guidelines by visiting: http://health.gov/dietaryguidelines/2015/guidelines/ .

Follow a Healthy Eating Pattern Across the Lifespan

- All food and beverage choices matter.
- People should choose a healthy eating pattern that has an appropriate number of calories to achieve and maintain a healthy body weight, is nutritionally adequate, and reduces the risk of diet–related chronic diseases.

Focus on Variety, Nutrient Density, and Amount of Food

To meet nutrient needs within calorie limits, choose a variety of nutrient–dense foods from all food groups and consume recommended amounts.

- Consume a variety of vegetables from all subgroups, including dark green, red, and orange, legumes (beans and peas), starchy, and other vegetables.
- Consume a variety of fruits, especially whole fruits.
- Consume grains, at least half of which are whole grains.
- Consume fat–free or low–fat dairy foods, including milk, yogurt, cheese, and/or fortified soy products.
- Eat a variety of protein foods, including seafood, lean meats and poultry, eggs, legumes, nuts, seeds, and soy products.
- Consume oils or cook with oils.

Limit Calories from Added Sugars and Saturated Fats and Reduce Sodium Intake

- Consume less than 10% of daily calories from added sugars. Added sugars contribute calories to foods and beverages, but they lack essential nutrients. For people consuming 2000 kcal per day, the upper limit of 10% of total calories is 200 kcal, the amount of energy in about 12 teaspoons of sugar.
- Consume less than 10% of daily calories from saturated fats.
- Consume less than 2300 mg of sodium per day. Increased sodium intake is associated with increased risk of hypertension and cardiovascular disease. Salt is the major source of sodium in diets.

Shift to Healthier Food and Beverage Choices

- Choose nutrient–dense foods and beverages from all food groups to replace less healthy products.
- Consider cultural and personal preferences when shifting foods and beverages to healthier choices.

Recommendations for Specific Population Groups

Women who are capable of becoming pregnant, are pregnant, or are breastfeeding:

- Consume 8 to 12 ounces of seafood per week from a variety of seafood types. Certain seafood contain fats that may improve an infant's health. Seafood that are rich in these particular fats include salmon, herring, sardines, and trout.
- Do not eat tilefish, shark, swordfish, and king mackerel because they may contain high amounts of the toxic chemical methylmercury.
- Consume iron–rich foods or take an iron supplement, if recommended by a physician or other qualified health care provider. Iron is a "nutrient of public health concern" for pregnant females.
- Do not consume alcohol.

    To reduce the risk of birth defects, women who are capable of becoming pregnant should obtain 400 mcg of folic acid each day by consuming fortified foods and/or taking supplements that contain the vitamin.

Support Healthy Eating Patterns for All

- Everyone has a role in creating and supporting healthy eating patterns in multiple settings throughout the country.
- Health professionals and policymakers should use multiple strategies to promote healthy eating and physical activity behaviors across all segments of society. Such strategies can include developing educational resources that inspire individuals to take appropriate actions with regard to their food and beverage choices.

Applying the Dietary Guidelines

The Dietary Guidelines include several food and nutrition–related messages for consumers, such as "Consume more nutrient–dense vegetables" (Table 3.5). Table 3.6 suggests practical ways people can apply the Dietary Guidelines' recommendations to their usual food choices. However, making recommended dietary and other lifestyle changes does not always reduce risk factors for disease.

TABLE 3.5 Selected Messages from *2015-2020 Dietary Guidelines for Americans*

- Increase the variety of protein foods consumed and incorporate about 8 ounces per week of various seafood into meals. Young children should eat less seafood than older children and adults.
- Consume more nutrient-dense vegetables.
- Choose more nutrient-dense fruits for snacks, desserts, or in side dishes.
- Choose enriched grain products and make at least half your grains whole grains.
- Choose lower fat versions of milk, yogurt, and cheese.
- Compare sodium in foods and choose the foods with the lowest sodium content.
- Drink water instead of sugary drinks.
- Choose foods that provide potassium, dietary fiber, calcium, and vitamin D, which are "nutrients of public health concern," because Americans tend to consume them in limited amounts.
- Achieve or maintain a healthy body weight.
- Consuming three to five 8-oz cups of coffee per day (up to 400 mg/day of caffeine) is acceptable within a healthy eating pattern.
- Consume as little cholesterol as possible while following a healthy diet.
- If one consumes alcohol, the beverage should be consumed in moderation and only by adults of legal drinking age. "Moderation" is up to one drink per day for women and up to two drinks per day for men. People should not begin to drink alcohol or drink more for any reason. Furthermore, certain individuals should not consume alcohol, especially pregnant women.

| *2015–2020 Dietary Guidelines for Americans*

For example, a man who has hypertension may find that his blood pressure remains dangerously elevated after several months of exercising, limiting his salt intake, and maintaining a healthy weight for his height. In this case, genetic factors may be influencing the man's health more than his lifestyle, and medica—tion may be necessary to reduce his blood pressure.

TABLE 3.6 Applying the Dietary Guidelines to One's Usual Food Choices

If One Usually Eats:	Consider Replacing with:
White bread and rolls	Whole-wheat bread and rolls
Sugary breakfast cereals	Low-sugar, high-fiber cereal sweetened with berries, bananas, peaches, or other fruit
Cheeseburger, French fries, and a regular (sugar-sweetened) soft drink	Roasted chicken or turkey sandwich, baked beans, fat-free or low-fat milk, or soy milk
Potato salad or cole slaw	Leafy greens or three-bean salad
Doughnuts, chips, or salty snack foods	Small bran muffin or whole-wheat bagel topped with peanut butter or soy nut butter, unsalted nuts, or dried fruit
Regular soft drinks	Water, fat-free or low-fat milk, or 100% fruit juice
Boiled vegetables	Raw or steamed vegetables (often retain more nutrients than boiled)
Breaded and fried meat, fish, or poultry	Broiled or roasted meat, fish, or poultry
Fatty meats such as barbecued ribs, sausage, and hot dogs	Chicken, turkey, or fish; lean meats such as ground round
Whole or 2% milk, cottage cheese with 4% fat, or yogurt made from whole milk	1% or fat-free milk, low-fat cottage cheese (1% fat), or low-fat yogurt
Ice cream	Frozen yogurt
Cream cheese on a bagel	Low-fat cottage cheese (mashed) or reduced-fat cream cheese or pea-nut butter (if appropriate)
Creamy salad dressings or dips made with mayonnaise or sour cream	Oil and vinegar dressing, reduced-fat salad dressings, or dips made from low-fat sour cream or plain yogurt
Chocolate chip or cream-filled cookies	Fruit-filled bars, oatmeal cookies, or fresh fruit
Salt added to season foods	Herbs, spices, or lemon juice

Concept **Checkpoint 3.3**

Respond to the following points according to recommendations of the Dietary Guidelines (2015–2020 version).

12. What are two overarching guidelines of the Dietary Guidelines?
13. A healthy person who is 23 years of age should limit his sodium intake to less than _____ per day.
14. List at least three of the key recommendations of the Dietary Guidelines.
15. Replace solid fats with _____.
16. Consume less than _____% of total calories from saturated fat.
17. Consume less than _____ % of total calories from added sugars.
18. What percentage of your intake of grains foods should be whole grains?
19. An adult woman who drinks alcohol and is not pregnant should limit her alcohol intake to no more than _____ drinks per day.
20. Adult men who drink alcohol should limit their alcohol consumption to no more than _____ drinks per day.
21. Which nutrients are "of public health concern" in the American diet?

3.4 Food Guides

Learning Outcomes

1 Use MyPlate to develop nutritionally adequate daily menus.

2 Compare MyPlate with the Exchange System.

For over 100 years, the USDA has issued specific dietary recommendations for Americans. In 1943, the USDA issued the first food guide based on RDAs for the general public to use. By the mid–1950s, the USDA simplified the original food guide to include only four food groups: milk, meat, fruit and vegetable, and bread and cereal. The recommendations of the "Basic Four" provided the foun– dation for an adequate diet while supplying about 1200 to 1400 kcal/day. Extra servings of food could be added to the basic diet plan for people who had higher energy needs.

In 1992, the USDA introduced the Food Guide Pyramid (Fig. 3.5). Unlike earlier dietary guides, the Food Guide Pyramid incorporated knowledge about the health benefits and risks associated with certain foods and ranked food groups according to their emphasis in menu planning. The Food Guide Pyramid displayed the groups in a layered format with grain products at the base to establish the foundation for a healthy diet. Fruit and vegetable groups occupied the next layer of the Food Guide Pyramid, followed by a layer shared by the milk and milk products, and meat and meat substitutes groups. Fatty and sugary foods formed the small peak of the Pyramid, a visual reminder that people should limit their intake of these foods.

Although the Food Guide Pyramid became a familiar feature on many pack– aged foods, the USDA released the *MyPyramid Plan* in 2005 (Fig. 3.6). The MyPyramid Plan was a *food guidance system*, which was based on *Dietary Guidelines for Americans, 2005*. In addition to providing foods and nutrition information, the MyPyramid.gov website emphasized the importance of physical activity and enabled consumers to monitor their activity levels. In 2011, the USDA replaced the MyPyramid Plan with *MyPlate*, another interactive dietary and menu planning guide accessible at a website.

MyPlate

MyPlate (www.choosemyplate.gov) includes a variety of food, nutrition, and physical activity resources for consumers that are based on the recommenda– tions of the Dietary Guidelines. MyPlate differs from the two previous USDA food guides in that it no longer has six food groups depicted by boxes or stripes within a pyramid (Fig. 3.7). MyPlate focuses on five different food groups: fruits, vegetables, protein foods, grains, and dairy.[10] According to the USDA, "oils" is not a food group.[11] The government agency, however, notes the need for some fat in the diet.

To learn more about MyPlate's five food groups, visit www.choosemyplate.gov and click on "MyPlate" in the menu bar to obtain a list of food groups. Click on each food group to find practical information about foods in the group, including how much food should be eaten, scientifically supported health benefits of foods, and helpful food–related tips. The site also has information and tips concerning weight management and calories, as well as physical activity.

Choosemyplate.gov has a wide variety of helpful interactive tools, including "SuperTracker," an excellent tool for developing nutritionally adequate daily food plans, and recording and monitoring dietary intake and physical activity habits.

| Figure 3.5 **Food Guide Pyramid.**

| Figure 3.6 **MyPyramid Plan.**

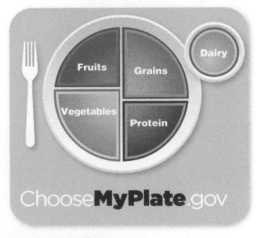

| Figure 3.7 **MyPlate.**

MyPlate USDA's interactive Internet dietary and menu planning guide

The "Food Tracker" feature of SuperTracker enables people to determine the energy and nutrient contents of their favorite recipes.

Major Sources of Empty Calories

Empty calories include energy from alcoholic beverages and foods that contain high amounts of added sugars and/or solid fats. Many commonly eaten foods include various amounts of empty calories. According to the USDA, the foods and beverages that supply the most empty calories in Americans' diets are:

- Cakes, cookies, pastries, and doughnuts
- Sugar–sweetened soft drinks, sports drinks, and fruit drinks
- Cheese (source of solid fat)
- Pizza (source of solid fat)
- Ice cream[10]

Tips for "Building a Better Plate"   The "Ten Tips" page of the MyPlate web–site includes some helpful information and tips to help consumers make healthier food selections:

- Make half of your grains whole grains.
- Add more vegetables to your day.
- Focus on fruits.
- Enjoy your food but eat less.
- Vary your protein routine.

Using MyPlate for Menu Planning

MyPlate has 12 different nutritionally adequate daily food patterns that sup–ply from 1000 to 3200 kcal/day (http://www.choosemyplate.gov/MyPlate–Daily–Checklist). Each pattern can be individualized to meet various personal characteristics, including age, sex, physical activity level, and food likes and dislikes.

MyPlate dietary patterns include foods and beverages that contain little or no empty calories. After a person consumes recommended amounts of nutritious foods from each food group (and oils), a small number of calories remain. The 2000 kcal dietary pattern, for example, has only 260 kilocalories remaining, which is less than the energy in two 12–ounce sugar–sweetened soft drinks. People can use up these remaining calories by choosing foods that contain a lot of solid fat and/or added sugars (empty–calorie foods), or healthy foods such as fresh fruits and vegetables.

To use MyPlate as a personalized menu planning guide, visit http://www.choosemyplate.gov and click on "SuperTracker" and then "Create Your Pro–file." Fill in boxes that request information, including your age, sex, weight, height, and estimated level of physical activity. After you provide this infor–mation, MyPlate estimates your daily energy needs and indicates how much food you should eat from each of the food groups daily to meet your recom–mended energy level. Table 3.7 indicates MyPlate's food intake recommenda–tions for average healthy young adults who consume 1800 to 3200 kilocalories per day.

TABLE 3.7 MyPlate: Recommendations for Average, Healthy 20-Year-Old Adults

MyPlate Guidelines (Daily)	Women	Men
Kilocalories	1800–2400	2600–3200
Fruit	2 cups	2–2.5 cups
Vegetables	2.5–3 cups	3.5–4.0 cups
Grains	6–8 oz	9–10 oz
Protein foods	5.0–6.5 oz	6.5–7 oz
Dairy	3 cups	3 cups
Oils	5–7 tsp	8–11 tsp

Overall, MyPlate can be helpful for planning menus because it promotes food variety, nutritional adequacy, and moderation. You can also use MyPlate to evaluate the nutritional quality of your daily diet by recording your food and beverage choices, classifying your choices into food groups, and estimating your intake of servings from each food group.

A computer and Internet access are necessary to use the program. Many people, particularly older adults, are unfamiliar with personal computers and may find the interactive www.choosemyplate.gov website challenging and frustrating to use. You may encounter some difficulties when using MyPlate to evaluate your diet's adequacy. How do you classify menu items that combine small amounts of foods from more than one group, such as pizza, sandwiches, and casseroles? A slice of pizza, for example, has thin crust made with wheat flour (grains), tomato sauce (vegetable), and cheese (dairy). The first step is to determine the ingredients and classify each into an appropriate food group. Estimate the number of cups or ounces of each ingredient and record the amounts contributed from a particular food group. The slice of pizza may provide ¼ cup of a vegetable, 2 ounces of grains, and ¼ cup of dairy. Another problem you may have when using MyPlate is judging portion sizes without keeping handy a battery of measuring cups and a scale for weighing foods. Figure 3.8 provides convenient ways to estimate typical portions using familiar objects, including a tennis ball and bar of soap.

The USDA has also developed MyPlate menu planning tools for children and pregnant or breastfeeding women. These guides can also be accessed at www.choosemyplate.gov. For information about MyPlate guides for various life stages, see Chapter 13.

MyPlate for Losing Weight

The "My Weight Manager" page at https://www.supertracker.usda.gov/ provides information about planning nutritionally adequate diets for persons who are trying to lose weight. If you would like to lose weight, start by obtaining your personalized daily food plan at https://www.supertracker.usda.gov/ . Click on "Create Your Profile." In the box for "Weight," fill in your present weight; in the box for height, fill in your height. If you are too heavy for your height, the program will let you know and provide a food plan that will help you reach a healthy weight for your height (see Chapter 10). One way to reduce your calorie intake without sacrificing the nutritional adequacy of your diet is

Dairy group   Vegetable group   Grain group

Classifying foods that combine ingredients from different food groups is challenging. This slice of pizza, for example, has crust (grains), tomato sauce and tomatoes (vegetable), and cheese (dairy).

to eat smaller amounts of empty–calorie foods or eliminate them altogether. Additionally, you can increase the amount of time that you are physically active each day.

MyPlate: Physical Activity   Although you may be busy while performing daily activities, you may not be moving your body enough to strengthen your mus–cles and prevent unwanted weight gain. To obtain important health benefits, you should engage in moderate or vigorous physical activity every day.[12] Choosemyplate.gov includes some information about physical activity, including examples of activities that are moderate or vigorous (http://www.choosemyplate.gov/physical–activity). Chapter 11 provides more information about physical activity and the importance of a physically active lifestyle.

Other Food Guides

The USDA's original Food Guide Pyramid inspired the development of other food pyramids for people who follow cultural and ethnic food traditions that differ from the mainstream American ("Western") diet. The "Nutrition Matters" feature at the end of Chapter 3 discusses various cultural, ethnic, and religious influences on American dietary practices. The "Nutrition Matters" feature also includes illustrations of the traditional Latin American Diet (see Fig. 3.16) Mediterranean Diet (see Fig. 3.17), and the Asian Diet Pyramids (see Fig. 3.18). Health Canada, the federal agency responsible for helping Canadians achieve better health, also has a food guide, "Eating Well with Canada's Food Guide". Go to this website: http://hc–sc.gc.ca/fn–an/food–guide–aliment/index–eng.php , to access this interactive guide.

Do Americans Follow Dietary Recommendations?

Analysis of government food consumption data indicates that most Americans do not follow the Dietary Guidelines.[13] In 2003–2004, the typical diet of Americans who were 2 years of age and older did not provide recommended amounts of fruit, vegetables, whole grains, and fat–free or low–fat milk.[13] Furthermore,

Figure 3.8 Estimating portion sizes. You can use familiar items such as these to estimate portion sizes.

4 dice = 1 oz cheese

Computer mouse = 1/2 to 2/3 cup
(baked potato, ground or chopped food)

Tennis ball = 1/2 to 2/3 cup
(medium or small fruit)

the diet generally contained too much added sugar, solid fats, and sodium. It is apparent that the public needs to learn more about the importance of choosing a variety of foods and applying MyPlate to everyday menu planning.

What Is the Exchange System?

Many chronic diseases require special diets to prevent or delay complications. Diabetes, for example, is easier to control when the person's diet has about the same macronutrient composition from day to day. The **Exchange System** is a valuable tool for estimating the energy, protein, carbohydrate, and fat content of foods. The system was originally developed by a committee of the Academy of Nutrition and Dietetics and the American Diabetes Association for planning diets of people with diabetes, a condition characterized by abnormal carbohydrate metabolism. Because the Exchange System makes it relatively easy to plan nutritious calorie–reduced meals and snacks, it is also useful for people who are trying to lose weight.

The Exchange System categorizes foods into three broad groups: carbohydrates, meat and meat substitutes, and fats.[14] The foods within each group have similar macronutrient composition, regardless of whether the food is from a plant or animal. For example, the carbohydrate group includes fruits, vegetables, and grains, as well as milk products. Nuts and seeds are grouped with fats. Meats and meat substitutes are grouped according to their fat content. Cheeses are in the meat and meat substitutes group because of their high protein and fat content. Thus, the Exchange System classifies foods differently than MyPlate does.

Within each of the three major food groups, the Exchange System provides *exchange lists* of specific types of foods. The specified amount of a food listed in an exchange list provides about the same amount of macronutrients and calories as each of the other specified amounts of foods in that list. According to the fruit list, for example, an orange is equivalent to a small apple, a kiwifruit, one–half of a fresh pear, or one–half of a large grapefruit. This equality allows people to plan a wide variety of nutritious menus by exchanging one food for another within each list. For more information about the Exchange System, you can visit

Exchange System method of classifying foods into lists based on macronutrient composition

Did You Know?

Many kinds of fresh fruit make quick and easy snacks that can be carried in backpacks, purses, and briefcases. Fresh fruit such as apples, oranges, tangerines, kiwifruit, and grapes can be kept for a few days at room temperature in a fruit bowl. You can store fresh fruits for longer periods by placing them in the refrigerator. Banana peels, however, turn dark brown when the fruit is refrigerated, so it is best to store bananas at room temperature, but refrigerated bananas are still good to eat.

Baseball or human fist = 1 cup (large apple or orange, or 1 cup serving of ready-to-eat cereal)

Bar of soap or deck of cards = 3 oz meat

Small yo-yo = 1 standard bagel or English muffin

the Academy of Nutrition and Dietetics' website (www.eatright.org) to order easy—to—read publications such as *Eating Healthy with Diabetes* or the *ADA Guide to Eating Right When You Have Diabetes*.

Carbohydrate counting ("counting carbs") is another meal planning technique that people with diabetes can use to control their blood sugar lev—els. The American Diabetes Association offers information about counting carbohydrates (http://www.diabetes.org/food—and—fitness/food/what—can—i—eat/understanding—carbohydrates/carbohydrate—counting.html). You will learn more about diabetes in the section of Chapter 5 that discusses this serious disease in detail.

Concept **Checkpoint 3.4**

22. List four tips for "building a better plate," according to MyPlate.
23. Explain how to use MyPlate to evaluate the nutritional adequacy of an individual's daily food choices.
24. According to the USDA, which foods supply most of the empty calories in Americans' diets?
25. Describe how the Exchange System differs from MyPlate.

3.5 Food and Dietary Supplement Labels

Learning Outcomes

1 Use the Nutrition Facts panel to make more nutritious food choices.

2 Identify nutrition-related claims the FDA allows on food and dietary supplement labels.

Consumers can use information on food labels to determine ingredients and to compare energy and nutrient contents of packaged foods and beverages. In the United States, the FDA regulates and monitors information that can be placed on food labels, including claims about the health benefits of ingredients. Today, nearly all foods and beverages sold in grocery stores must have labels that provide the product's name, manufacturer's name and address, and amount of product in the package (Fig. 3.9a). Producers and sellers of fresh and frozen fruits and vegetables; fresh poultry, fish, and shellfish; and a few other food items must declare the product's *country of origin* either on the packaging or where the product is located in stores. Furthermore, products that have more than one ingredient must display a list of the ingredients in descending order according to weight.

Nutrition Facts Panel

Consumers can find specific nutrition—related information about many packaged foods simply by reading the products' labels. The FDA requires food manufactur—ers to use a special format, the **Nutrition Facts panel,** to display information about the energy and nutrient contents of products (Fig. 3.9b). The Nutrition Facts panel indicates the amount of a serving size, in household units as well as grams, and the number of servings in the entire container.

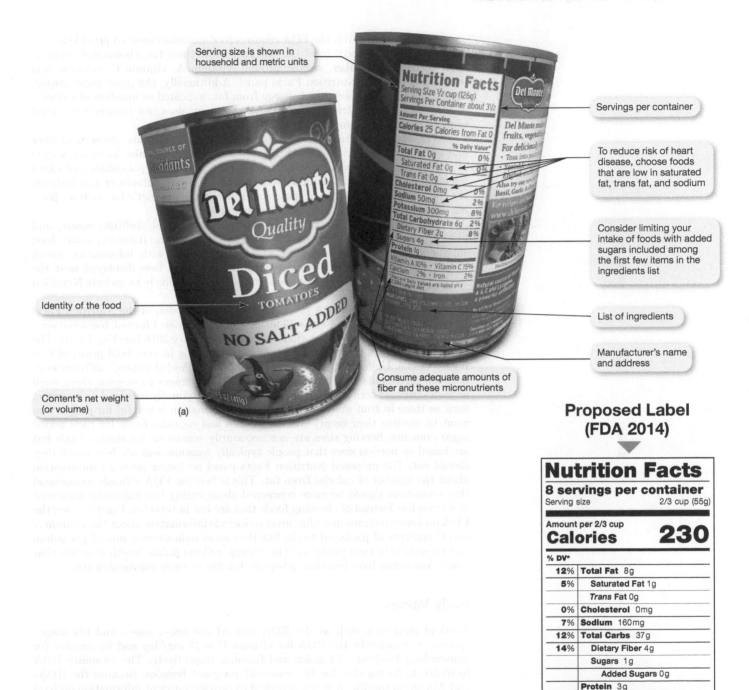

Serving size is shown in household and metric units

Servings per container

To reduce risk of heart disease, choose foods that are low in saturated fat, trans fat, and sodium

Consider limiting your intake of foods with added sugars included among the first few items in the ingredients list

List of ingredients

Manufacturer's name and address

Identity of the food

Content's net weight (or volume)

Consume adequate amounts of fiber and these micronutrients

(a)

Nutrition Facts
Serving Size ½ cup (126g)
Servings Per Container about 3½

Amount Per Serving		
Calories 25 Calories from Fat 0		
		% Daily Value*
Total Fat 0g		0%
Saturated Fat 0g		0%
Trans Fat 0g		
Cholesterol 0mg		0%
Sodium 50mg		2%
Potassium 300mg		8%
Total Carbohydrate 6g		2%
Dietary Fiber 2g		8%
Sugars 4g		
Protein 1g		
Vitamin A 10% • Vitamin C 15%		
Calcium 2% • Iron 2%		

*Percent Daily Values are based on a 2,000 calorie diet.

Proposed Label (FDA 2014)
▼

	Nutrition Facts	
	8 servings per container	
	Serving size	2/3 cup (55g)
	Amount per 2/3 cup	
	Calories	**230**
% DV*		
12%	**Total Fat** 8g	
5%	Saturated Fat 1g	
	Trans Fat 0g	
0%	**Cholesterol** 0mg	
7%	**Sodium** 160mg	
12%	**Total Carbs** 37g	
14%	Dietary Fiber 4g	
	Sugars 1g	
	Added Sugars 0g	
	Protein 3g	
10%	**Vitamin D** 2mcg	
20%	**Calcium** 260mg	
45%	**Iron** 8mg	
5%	**Potassium** 235mg	

* Footnote on Daily Values (DV) and calories reference to be inserted here.

(b)

Figure 3.9 What's in a food? (a) Nearly all packaged foods and beverages sold in grocery stores must have labels that provide specific information, including the manufacturer's name and address. (b) The Nutrition Facts panel displays information about energy and nutrient contents of food products.

As of January 2016, the FDA requires food manufacturers to provide infor-mation about the food's total fat, saturated fat, trans fat, cholesterol, sodium, total carbohydrate, fiber, sugars, protein, vitamin A, vitamin C, calcium, and iron contents in the Nutrition Facts panel. Additionally, the panel must display the total amount of energy and energy from fat, indicated as numbers of calories, in a serving. The Nutrition Facts panel, however, does not translate the total number of calories from fat into a percentage.

The panel uses grams (g) and milligrams (mg) to indicate amounts of fiber and nutrients in a serving of food. Food manufacturers can also include amounts of polyunsaturated and monounsaturated fats, as well as potassium and other micronutrients, in the Nutrition Facts panel. If the manufacturer has fortified the food with the nutrients or made claims about the product's fat content, list-ing these particular food components is required.

Foods such as fresh fruits and vegetables, fish and shellfish, meats, and poultry are not required to have Nutrition Facts labels. However, many food suppliers and supermarket chains provide consumers with information about their products' nutritional content on posters or shelf tags displayed near the foods. In the future, fresh foods such as raw meats are likely to include Nutrition Facts panels on their labels.

Early in 2014, the FDA proposed an updated version of the Nutrition Facts panel, which is shown in Figure 13.9b. The proposed panel format has some sig-nificant changes to the format that was used in January 2016 (see Fig. 13.9a). The new panel displays the number of calories per serving in very bold print, so it is highly visible. Under "Sugars," a new component, "Added sugars," differentiates between ingredients that are added to foods or beverages to sweeten them, such as high-fructose corn syrup, from sugars that are naturally in a food or beverage, such as those in fruit and cow's milk. Such information is helpful for people who want to monitor their empty-calorie intakes and compare foods for their added sugar contents. Serving sizes are not necessarily consistent for similar foods but are based on portion sizes that people typically consume and not how much they should eat. The proposed Nutrition Facts panel no longer provides information about the number of calories from fat. This is because FDA officials recommend that consumers should be more concerned about eating less unhealthy saturated and trans fats instead of choosing foods that are low in total fat. Furthermore, the FDA no longer requires manufacturers to include information about the vitamin A and C contents of packaged foods, but they must indicate amounts of potassium and vitamin D in their products. This change reflects public health concerns that many Americans have less than adequate intakes of these micronutrients.

Daily Values

Nutrient standards such as the RDA and AI are sex-, age-, and life stage-specific. For example, the RDA for vitamin C is 75 mg/day and 65 mg/day for nonsmoking 18-year-old males and females, respectively. The vitamin's RDA increases to 80 mg/day for 18-year-old pregnant females. Because the RDAs and AIs are so specific, it is not practical to provide nutrient information on food labels that refers to these complex standards. To help consumers evaluate the nutritional content of food products, FDA developed the **Daily Values (DVs)** for labeling purposes. Compared to the RDAs, the DVs are a more simplified and practical set of nutrient standards. The adult DV for a nutrient is based on a standard diet that supplies 2000 kcal/day. Not all nutrients have DVs, but they have been established for total fat, total carbohydrate, fiber, and several vitamins and minerals. As of early 2016, there are no DVs for added sugars or trans fat.

Appendix B lists current (as of January 2016) and proposed DVs. A set of DVs that applies to people over 4 years of age is used for foods and beverages

Daily Values (DVs) set of nutrient intake standards developed for labeling purposes

that adults consume. Three other sets of DVs are used on labels of foods intended for infants, children between 1 and 4 years of age, and pregnant or breastfeeding women.

Although the DVs are often the highest RDA or AI for a particular nutrient, in many instances, they are based on recom— mendations of public health experts. For example, the RDA for carbohydrate is 130 g/day for people over 1 year of age. The DV for carbohydrate, however, is 300 g/day (2015 value). This amount reflects the general dietary recommendations that carbohydrate can contribute 60% of a person's total energy intake, or 1200 kcal (300 g × 4 kcal/g of carbohydrate) of a 2000 kcal/day diet. For people older than 1 year of age, no RDA or AI has been set for daily fat intake. However, DV for fat is 65 g/day. This amount meets the general recommendation that fat intake can be about 30% of a person's total energy intake for a 2000 kcal/day diet.

When evaluating or planning nutritious menus, your goal is to obtain at least 100% of the DVs for fiber, vita— mins, and minerals each day. On the other hand, you may need to limit your intake of foods that have high %DVs of total fat, saturated fat, and sodium (Fig. 3.10). High intakes of these nutrients may have negative effects on your health. Thus, your goal is to consume less than 100% of the DV for total fat, sat— urated fat, and sodium each day. The general rule of thumb: A food that supplies 5%DV or less of a nutrient is a low source of the nutrient; a food that provides 20%DV or more is a high source of the nutrient.[15]

Percents of DVs are designed to help consumers compare nutrient contents of packaged foods to make more healthful choices. However, most people do not eat just packaged foods. Fresh fruits and vegetables, as well as most restaurant meals, do not have labels or menus with information about %DVs per serving. Therefore, many consumers will underestimate their nutrient intakes, if they do not consider the contribution that unlabeled foods make to their diets.

It is important to note the description of a serving size and the number of servings per container when using nutritional labeling information to estimate your intakes of energy, fiber, and nutrients in the food. A common mistake people make when using a Nutrition Facts panel is assuming the information applies to the entire package. For example, the Nutrition Facts panel on a pack— age of food indicates there are four servings in the container. If you eat all the container's contents, you must multiply the information concerning calories, fat, and other food components by four. Why? Because you ate four servings and the nutritional information on the Nutrition Facts panel applies to only *one* serving.

Make Your Calories Count, an interactive program developed by the FDA, helps consumers use Nutrition Facts on food labels to plan nutritionally adequate diets while managing calorie intake. You can access the program by visiting the website http://www.fda.gov/food/ingredientspackaginglabeling/labelingnutrition/ucm275438.htm and downloading "Make Your Calories Count," an interactive training module. The FDA also provides "The Food Label and You," a video that you can watch at http://www.fda.gov/food/ingredientspackaginglabeling/labelingnutrition/ucm275409.htm.

What About Restaurant and Vending Machine Foods?

A section of the *Patient Protection and Affordable Care Act* of 2010 requires restaurants and similar retail food establishments with 20 or more locations to list calorie content information for standard menu items on restaurant menus and menu boards.[16] Information about total calories, fat, saturated fat, cholesterol, sodium, total carbohydrates, sugars, fiber, and total protein contents of menu items must be available in writing when the customer requests it. According

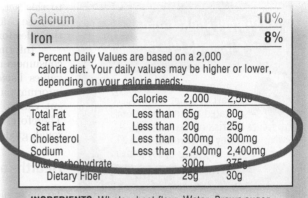

Calcium		10%
Iron		8%

* Percent Daily Values are based on a 2,000 calorie diet. Your daily values may be higher or lower, depending on your calorie needs:

	Calories	2,000	2,500
Total Fat	Less than	65g	80g
Sat Fat	Less than	20g	25g
Cholesterol	Less than	300mg	300mg
Sodium	Less than	2,400mg	2,400mg
Total Carbohydrate		300g	375g
Dietary Fiber		25g	30g

INGREDIENTS: Whole wheat flour, Water, Brown sugar, Wheat gluten, Cracked wheat , Wheat bran, Yeast, Salt, Molasses, Soybean oil, Calcium propionate (preservative)

Figure 3.10 Nutrients to limit. High intakes of saturated fat and sodium can have negative effects on your health. The appearance of this panel is likely to change when new DVs are published.

80   Chapter 3 Planning Nutritious Diets

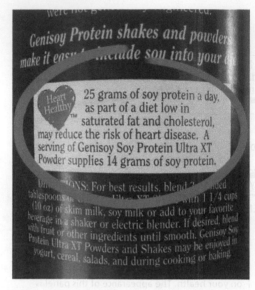

Figure 3.11 Label claims. The FDA permits food manufacturers to include certain health claims on food labels.

to this act, companies that maintain 20 or more food vending machines must disclose calorie contents of certain items. The FDA is responsible for developing the rules for providing the nutrition information.

Information about the calorie contents of restaurant foods can help consumers make healthier menu selections. However, the accuracy of the caloric values listed by restaurants can vary.[17] The displayed or published nutrition information may give a close estimate of the food's actual energy and nutrient values, but portions are not exactly the same every time a food is served. Therefore, calorie levels posted at restaurants should be used by consumers as a rough guide for making healthier food choices.

Health- and Nutrition-Related Claims

To make their foods more appealing to consumers, manufacturers often promote products as having certain health benefits or high amounts of nutrients. A health claim describes the relationship between a food, food ingredient, or dietary supplement and the reduced risk of a nutrition–related condition. The FDA permits food manufacturers to include certain health claims on food labels (Fig. 3.11). For example, an allowable health claim may state, "Diets low in saturated fat may reduce the risk of heart disease."

For the FDA to allow a health claim on a product label, the claim should:

- indicate that the product has health benefits only when it is part of a daily diet;
- be complete, easy to understand, honest, and not misleading;
- refer to a product that contains 10% or more of the DV for vitamins A and C, calcium, iron, fiber, or protein, *before* being fortified with nutrients. (This condition does not apply to dietary supplements.);
- be for a product intended for people who are 2 years of age or older;
- use *may* or *might* to describe the relationship between the product and disease. For example, "Diets containing foods that are good sources of potassium and that are low in sodium may reduce the risk of high blood pressure and stroke" is an allowable claim. However, the claim "Reduces the risk of stroke" would not be permitted on a label;
- not quantify any degree of risk reduction. For example, a claim that states, "Reduces risk of cancer by 41%" would not be allowed because it specifies the degree of risk reduction;
- indicate that many factors influence disease.

The FDA requires specific wording for certain health claims that are allowed on labels. Table 3.8 lists some permissible health claims that can be used for labeling purposes. For more information, visit FDA's website at www.fda.gov and search for "qualified health claims."

As of 2015, the FDA will not approve health claims for foods that contain more than 13 g of fat, 4 g of saturated fat, 60 mg of cholesterol, or 480 mg of sodium per serving. For example, calcium is a mineral that strengthens bones and protects them from *osteoporosis*, a condition in which bones become brittle and break easily. Whole milk is a rich source of calcium. Nevertheless, the label on a carton of whole milk cannot include a health claim about calcium and osteo–porosis, because the milk contains more than 4 g of saturated fat per serving. In addition, the product must meet specific conditions that relate to the health claim. For example, a claim regarding the benefits of eating a low–fat diet is allowed only if the product contains 3 g or less of fat per serving, which is the FDA's standard definition of a low–fat food.

TABLE 3.8 Examples of Permissible Health Claims for Food Labels (2015)

Dietary Factor/Health Condition	Example of Permissible Health Claim
Certain lipids and heart disease	"While many factors affect heart disease, diets low in saturated fat and cholesterol may reduce the risk of this disease."
Diet and heart disease	"Diets low in saturated fat and cholesterol and rich in fruits, vegetables, and grain products that contain some types of dietary fiber, particularly soluble fiber, may reduce the risk of heart disease, a disease associated with many factors."
Calcium, exercise, and osteoporosis (a disease that weakens bones)	"Regular exercise and a healthy diet with enough calcium help teen and young adult white and Asian women maintain good bone health and may reduce their high risk of osteoporosis."
Sodium (a mineral) and high blood pressure	"Diets low in sodium may reduce the risk of high blood pressure, a disease associated with many factors."
Folate (a B vitamin) and neural tube defects (conditions in which the skull and spine do not form properly before birth)	"Healthful diets with adequate folate may reduce a woman's risk of having a child with a brain or spinal cord defect."
Fruits and vegetables and risk of cancer	"Foods that are low in fat and contain dietary fiber, vitamin A, or vitamin C may reduce the risk of some types of cancer, a disease associated with many factors. Broccoli is high in vitamins A and C, and it is a good source of dietary fiber."

Source: U.S. Food and Drug Administration, Center for Food Safety and Applied Nutrition. *A food labeling guide.* 2013. http://www.fda.gov/food/guidanceregulation/guidancedocumentsregulatoryinformation/labelingnutrition/ucm2006828.htm Accessed: June 9, 2014

Structure/Function Claims

A structure/function claim describes the role a nutrient or dietary supplement plays in maintaining a structure, such as bone, or promoting a normal function, such as digestion. The FDA allows structure/function claims such as "cal-cium builds strong bones" or "fiber maintains bowel regularity" (Fig. 3.12). Structure/function statements cannot claim that a nutrient, food, or dietary supplement can be used to prevent or treat a serious health condition. For example, the FDA would not permit a claim that a product "promotes low blood pressure," because that claim implies the product has druglike effects and can treat high blood pressure.

Nutrient Content Claims

The FDA permits labels to include claims about levels of nutrients in packaged foods. Nutrient content claims can use terms such as *free*, *high*, or *low* to describe how much of a nutrient is in the product. Additionally, nutrient content claims can use terms such as *more* or *reduced* to compare amounts of nutrients in a product to those in a similar product. This claim is often used for an item that substitutes for a *reference food*, a similar and more familiar food. For example, a "reduced–fat" salad dressing has considerably less fat than its reference food, regular salad dressing.

Table 3.9 lists some legal definitions for common nutrient content claims that were allowed on labels in 2015. Note that a product may con-tain a small amount of a nutrient such as fat or sugar, yet the Nutrition Facts panel can indicate the amount as "0 g." For example, the Nutrition Facts panel may indicate that a serving of food supplies "0" grams of trans fat, even though the food actually supplies less than 0.5 g of trans fat. As a result, it is possible to consume some trans fats from processed foods even though labels indicate a serving of each food does not contain this type of fat. When the FDA introduces

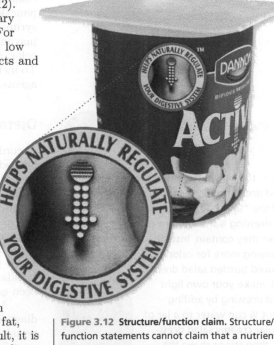

Figure 3.12 Structure/function claim. Structure/function statements cannot claim that a nutrient, food, or dietary supplement can be used to prevent or treat a serious health condition.

TABLE 3.9 Legal Definitions for Common Nutrient Content Claims (2015)

Sugar	• **Sugar free:** The product provides less than 0.5 g of sugar per serving. • **Reduced sugar:** The food contains at least 25% less sugar per serving than the reference food.
Calories	• **Calorie free:** The food provides fewer than 5 kcal per serving. • **Low calorie:** The food supplies 40 kcal or less per serving. • **Reduced or fewer calories:** The food contains at least 25% fewer kcal per serving than the reference food.
Fat	• **Fat free:** The food provides less than 0.5 g of fat per serving. • **Low fat:** The food contains 3 g or less fat per serving. Two-percent milk is not "low fat," because it has more than 3 g of fat per serving. The term *reduced fat* can be used to describe 2% milk. • **Reduced or less fat:** The food supplies at least 25% less fat per serving than the reference food.
Cholesterol	• **Cholesterol free:** The food contains less than 2 mg of cholesterol and 2 g or less of saturated fat per serving.
Fiber	• **High fiber:** The food contains 5g or more fiber per serving. Foods that include high-fiber claims on the label must also meet the definition for low fat. • **Good source of fiber:** The food supplies 2.5 to 4.9 g of fiber per serving.
Meat and poultry products regulated by USDA	• **Extra lean:** The food provides less than 5 g of fat, 2 g of saturated fat, and 95 mg of cholesterol per serving. • **Lean:** The food contains less than 10 g of fat, 4.5 g of saturated fat, and 95 mg of cholesterol per serving.

the new labeling format, specific amounts of such ingredients, such as trans fat, may need to be shown. To learn more about the FDA's regulations concerning nutrient claims, visit the agency's website (http://www.fda.gov/Food/Ingredients PackagingLabeling/LabelingNutrition/ucm2006873.htm).

Other Descriptive Labeling Terms

According to the FDA, a *light* or *lite* food has at least one–third fewer kilo–calories or half the fat of the reference food. For example, a tablespoon of lite pancake syrup has one–third fewer kcal than a tablespoon of regular pancake syrup, and a tablespoon of light mayonnaise has less than half the fat of regular mayonnaise. The term *light* may also describe such properties as texture and color, as long as the label explains the intent: for example, "light brown sugar." To include the term *natural* on the label, the food must not contain food coloring agents, synthetic flavors, or other unnatural substances (as of February 2016).

Dietary Supplement Labels

According to federal law, every dietary supplement container must be properly labeled (Fig. 3.13). The label must include the term "dietary supplement" or a similar term that describes the product's particular ingredient, such as "herbal supplement" or "vitamin C supplement." Dietary supplement labels are also required to display the list of ingredients, manufacturer's address, and suggested dosage. Furthermore, the label must include facts about the product's contents in a special format—the "Supplement Facts" panel (see Fig. 3.13). The panel pro-vides information about the serving size; amount per serving; and percent Daily Value (%DV) for ingredients, if one has been established. Daily Values (DVs) are standard desirable or maximum intakes for several nutrients, but DVs have not been established for nonnutrient products.

According to the FDA, dietary supplements are not intended to treat, diagnose, cure, or alleviate the effects of diseases. Therefore, the agency does not permit manufacturers to market a dietary supplement product as a treatment or cure for a disease, or to relieve signs or symptoms of a disease. Although such products generally cannot prevent diseases, some can improve health or reduce the risk of certain diseases or conditions. Thus, the FDA allows supplement

Food & Nutrition tip

Often, the only difference between a creamy salad dressing, such as ranch or blue cheese, and the "light" version of the dressing is the amount of water they contain. Instead of paying more for calorie-reduced bottled salad dress-ings, make your own light salad dressing by adding about ¼ cup water to a jar of regular creamy salad dress-ing, then stir or shake the mixture.

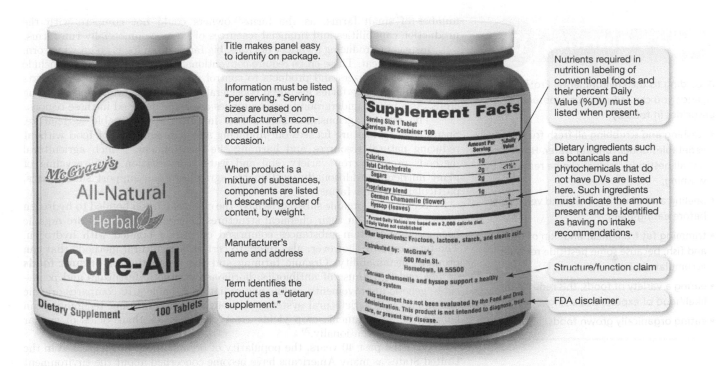

Figure 3.13 Supplement Facts label. A nutrient supplement label must list the product's ingredient(s), serving size, amount(s) per serving, suggested use, manufacturer and the company's address, and %DV, if one has been established. If a health claim appears on the supplement's label, the claim must be followed by the FDA disclaimer.

manufacturers to display structure/function claims on labels. Manufacturers of iron supplements, for example, may have a claim on the label that states: "Iron is necessary for healthy red blood cell formation." If the FDA has not reviewed a claim, the label must include the FDA's disclaimer indicating that the claim has not been evaluated by the agency (Fig. 3.14).

The FDA does not require dietary supplement manufacturers or sellers to provide evidence that labeling claims are accurate or truthful before they appear on product containers. However, manufacturers that include structure/function claims on labels must notify the FDA about the claims within 30 days after intro— ducing the products into the marketplace. If FDA officials question the safety of a dietary supplement or the truthfulness of claims that appear on supplement labels, manufacturers are responsible for providing the agency with evidence that their products are safe and the claims on labels are honest and not misleading.

The FDA requires dietary supplement manufacturers to evaluate the purity, quality, strength, and composition of their products before marketing them. The regulations are designed to result in the production of supplements that contain the ingredients listed on the label, are wholesome, contain standard amounts of ingredients per dose, and are properly packaged and accurately labeled.

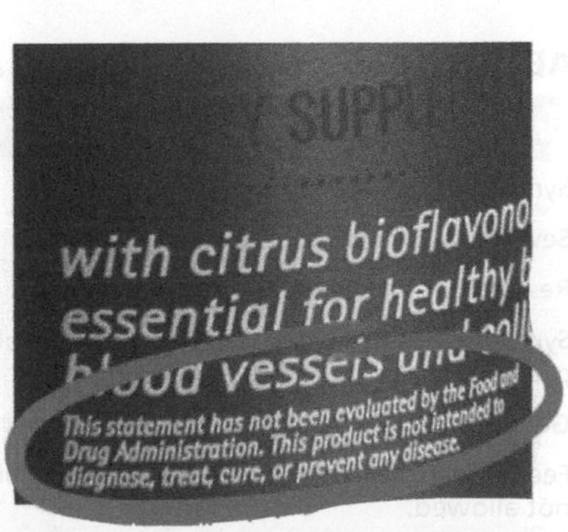

Organic Food

By the late twentieth century, emphasis on increasing agricultural production resulted in an inexpensive and abundant food supply in the United States. How— ever, the rise of agribusiness also resulted in social, economic, and environmental costs. Rural agricultural communities experienced a dramatic decline in the

Figure 3.14 Label disclaimer. The FDA permits dietary supplement manufacturers to include certain health-related claims on their product labels. However, the label of products bearing such claims also must display this disclaimer.

84   Chapter 3 Planning Nutritious Diets

According to the Environmental Protection Agency, you can reduce your exposure to pesticides in food by:

- washing and scrubbing all fresh fruits and vegetables under running water. However, not all pesticide residues can be removed by washing;

- peeling and trimming fruits and vegetables before eating them;

- trimming fat from meat and skin of poultry and fish, because some pesticide residues accumulate in fat;

- eating a variety of foods; this reduces the likelihood of exposure to a single pesticide;

- eating organically grown foods.

organic foods foods produced without the use of antibiotics, hormones, synthetic fertilizers and pesticides, genetic improvements, or spoilage-killing radiation

number of small farms, as the farms' owners could not compete with the production capabilities and financial resources of large, commercially run farms.

Instead of producing a variety of crops, big farms often focus on growing corn, soybeans, or wheat. These crops require conventional farming methods that include heavy use of fertilizers and products to control pests (*pesticides*). In some parts of the country, large farms also need considerable amounts of water for irrigating crops. As a result, underground water supplies are being depleted in these regions.

The rise in agribusiness helped fuel interest in sustainable agriculture. Sustainable agriculture focuses on producing adequate amounts of food without reducing natural resources and harming the environment.[18] Such agricultural methods promote crop variety, soil and water conservation, and recycling of plant nutrients. Additionally, sustainable agriculture can support small farms, particularly organic farms.

Technically, organic substances have the element carbon bonded to hydrogen (another element) in their chemical structures. Therefore, all foods are organic because they contain substances comprised of carbon bonded with hydrogen. The term *organic*, however, also refers to certain agricultural methods that can promote sustainability. Organic farming and the production of **organic foods** do not rely on the use of antibiotics, hormones, synthetic fertilizers and pesticides, genetic improvements, or ionizing radiation.[19] Table 3.10 compares organic and nonorganic agricultural systems. Although organic farming techniques can benefit the environment, crop yields are typically lower than yields of similar crops grown conventionally.[20]

Over the past 40 years, the popularity of organic foods has increased in the United States as many Americans have become concerned about the environment and the safety and nutritional value of the food supply. Sales of organic foods have increased steadily since the 1990s, even though these products are usually more expensive than the same foods produced by conventional farming methods.[21] According to the Food Marketing Institute, Americans spent an estimated 31.5 billion on organic foods and beverages in 2011.[22]

People who purchase organically grown foods often think the products are better for their health and more nutritious than conventionally produced foods. Few well-designed studies have compared nutrient and phytochemical contents of organically grown foods to their conventionally grown counterparts. Nevertheless, some general trends have been determined. In general, organic food crops are not more nutritious than conventionally grown food crops.[23] Organic

TABLE 3.10 Comparing Organic and Nonorganic Farming Systems

Organic	Nonorganic
Synthetic fertilizers are not allowed.	Limited restrictions on fertilizers
Sewage sludge products are not allowed.	Sludge products may be used on some fields.
Restrictions on use of raw manure on fields used for food crops	Few restrictions on raw manure use for edible crop fields
Synthetic pesticides are not allowed; natural pest management practices are encouraged.	Any government-approved pesticide may be used according to label instructions. Natural pest management practices may also be used.
Genetically modified organisms (GMOs) are not allowed.	Government-approved GMOs are permitted.
Feeding livestock mammal and poultry by-products and manure is not allowed.	Certain mammal and poultry by-products are allowed in livestock feed.
Use of growth hormones and antibiotics in livestock production is not allowed.	Government-approved hormone and antibiotic treatments are permitted.
Food irradiation (a food safety method) is not allowed.	Food irradiation may be used.
Detailed record keeping and site inspections by regulators are required.	Some records are required, but no on-site checks by regulators are necessary.

TABLE 3.11   Organic Labeling Categories

"100% Organic" (may use USDA seal)	100% organic ingredients, including processing aids Must identify organic ingredients
"Organic" (may use USDA seal)	Contains at least 95% organic ingredients Remaining 5% of ingredients are on USDA's allowable list of allowed ingredients Must identify organic ingredients
"Made with organic ingredients" (may not use USDA organic seal)	Contains 70 to 95% certified organic ingredients Must identify organic ingredients

Source: U.S. Department of Agriculture: *Labeling organic products.* (ND). http://www.ams.usda.gov/AMSv1.0/
Accessed: August 4, 2013

Figure 3.15 Organic food logo. Foods that have been certified "organic" may use the USDA's symbol.

crops, however, may contain fewer pesticides than conventionally grown crops.[24] Nevertheless, more research is needed to determine whether there are health advantages to eating organic foods.

Labeling Organic Foods

To protect consumers, the USDA developed and implemented rules for the organic food industry. A food product cannot be labeled "organic" unless its production meets strict national standards. For labeling purposes, organic food manufacturers can use the circular "USDA Organic" symbol on the package (Fig. 3.15). This symbol indicates the products meet USDA's standards for organic food. According to the USDA, there are three organic labeling categories (Table 3.11). Note that certain foods can have the organic symbol on the package, yet they may contain small amounts of nonorganic ingredients. For more information about the gov—ernment's organic food standards, visit the USDA's National Organic Program's website (http://www.ams.usda.gov/AMSv1.0/nop).

Concept **Checkpoint 3.5**

26. Identify at least one limitation of using %DVs to determine your nutrient intakes.
27. Explain how you can use nutritional information provided on food and dietary supplement labels to become a more careful consumer.
28. What is the difference between a health claim and a structure/function claim? What is a nutrient content claim? Give an example of each type of claim.
29. Discuss the role of the FDA in protecting consumers from false nutrition and health claims on food and dietary supplement labels.

3.6 Using Dietary Analysis Software

Learning Outcomes

1 Explain why different dietary analysis software programs may provide different values for energy and nutrient contents for the same food item.

2 Use the U.S. Department of Agriculture's websites to estimate the nutritional value of various foods.

How much selenium, magnesium, and niacin are in an ounce of Swiss cheese? Have you ever wanted information about nutrients in a food that are not listed on the Nutrition Facts panel? In the past, people relied on food composition

Valencia oranges and other produce may vary in nutrient content depending on numerous factors, including growing conditions.

tables, lists of commonly eaten foods that provide amounts of energy, fiber, macronutrients, and several micronutrients. Today, people can determine the energy and nutrient contents of their food choices by using a dietary analy-sis software program. Furthermore, people with Internet access can obtain the information from certain websites.

Dietary analysis software and websites can be quick and easy tools for determining nutrient and energy contents of a specific food. However, the val-ues provided by these resources are not necessarily exact amounts. The same type of plant food may vary in nutrient content depending on hereditary fac-tors, age, growing conditions, and production methods. Therefore, scientists generally analyze several samples of a particular food to determine their nutri-ent contents, and then the researchers average the results. For example, if the amount of energy in three Valencia oranges that each weigh about 4 ounces (120 g) were 55, 60, and 62 kcal, respectively, the value listed in the food com-position table for a Valencia orange weighing 4 ounces would be 59 kcal, the average of the three. In many instances, values for certain nutrients are miss-ing. This occurs when accurate data concerning the complete nutrient analysis of the food are unavailable.

The following section discusses some government–sponsored websites that provide practical tools for evaluating food intakes and physical activity habits. The Personal Dietary Analysis feature at the end of this chapter provides an opportunity for you to practice using dietary analysis software.

Government-Sponsored Dietary Analysis Websites

In addition to www.choosemyplate.gov, the USDA sponsors other websites to help you assess the energy and nutrient contents of your food intake. The "What's in the Food You Eat *Search Tool*" (www.ars.usda.gov/Services/docs.htm?docid=17032) is one such site. Another USDA–sponsored site that provides extensive information regarding the energy and nutrient content of food is the National Nutrient Database for Standard Reference. You can access this nutrient database by visiting www.nal.usda.gov/fnic/foodcomp/search. To keep current, USDA–sponsored websites are updated regularly to provide information about new products and serving sizes.

Concept **Checkpoint 3.6**

30. Identify at least two reliable sources of information about the energy and nutrient contents of foods and beverages.

3.7 Nutrition Matters: The Melting Pot

Learning Outcomes

1 Discuss how various ethnic and religious groups influence Americans' dietary patterns.

2 Identify religion-based dietary restrictions.

Wherever you live or travel in the United States, you're likely to find restaurants that serve a wide variety of ethnic fare, such as Italian, Thai, Vietnamese, or Middle Eastern dishes. Although your primary food selection and cooking habits probably reflect your cultural/ethnic heritage, you likely enjoy foods from other cultures and ethnic groups.

This section examines the influences that the dietary practices of certain cultures and ethnic groups have had on the American diet and the possible effects of these practices on health. Traditional ethnic diets are often based on dishes containing small amounts of animal foods and larger amounts of locally grown fruits, vegetables, and unrefined grains. However, these foods are typically the first to be abandoned as immigrants *assimilate*, that is, blend into the general population over time. After an immigrant population has assimilated fully, the prevalence of chronic diseases such as cardiovascular disease, type 2 diabetes, and high blood pressure often increases among them, partly as a result of adopting less healthy eating practices.

Northwestern European Influences

Immigrants from northwestern European regions or countries such as the United Kingdom, Scandinavia, and Germany established the familiar "meat−and−potatoes" diet that features a large portion of beef or pork served with a smaller portion of potatoes. In the past, the potatoes were either boiled or mashed; today, they are usually fried. This mainstream American diet, often referred to as a "Western" diet, provides large amounts of animal protein and fat, and lacks fruits, whole grains, and a variety of green vegetables. Such diets are associated with high rates of serious chronic diseases, particularly CVD and type 2 diabetes, which are discussed in later chapters of this textbook.

Hispanic Influences

The Hispanic (people with Spanish ancestry) population is now the largest minority group in the United States. Many Hispanic−Americans migrated to the United States from Mexico. The traditional Mexican diet included corn, beans, chili peppers, avocados, papayas, and pineapples. Many supermarkets in the United States sell other plant foods that are often incorporated into Mexican meals, such as fresh chayote, cherimoya, jicama, plantains, and cactus leaves and fruit. Such fruits and vegetables add fiber and a variety of nutrients, phytochemicals, vivid colors, and interesting flavors to Mexican dishes (Figure 3.16).

Authentic Mexican meals are based primarily on rice, tortillas, and beans, depending on the region. However, many non−Hispanic Americans do not like to eat meals limited to these inexpensive yet nutritious plant foods.

OLDWAYS
HEALTH THROUGH HERITAGE

Latin American Diet Pyramid
La Pirámide de la Dieta Latinoamericana

Carne y Dulces
Con menos frecuencia

Meats and Sweets
Less often

Beba Agua
Drink Water

Pollo, Huevos, Quesos, y Yogur
En raciones moderadas, diariamente a semanalmente

Poultry, Eggs, Cheese, and Yogurt
Moderate portions, daily to weekly

Cerveza y Vino
En moderatión
Beer and Wine
In moderation

Pescado y Mariscos
Frecuentemente, por lo menos dos veces a la semana

Fish and Seafood
Often, at least two times per week

Frutas, Vegetales, Granos (principalmente enteros), Frijoles, Nueces, Leguminosas, y Semillas, Hierbas, y Especias
Base cada alimentación en estas comidas

Fruits, Vegetables, Grains (mostly whole), Beans, Nuts, Legumes and Seeds, Herbs, and Spices
Base every meal on these foods

Este Físicamente Activo; Disfrute su Comida con Otros.

Be Physically Active; Enjoy Meals with Others.

Illustration by George Middleton

© 2009 Oldways Preservation and Exchange Trust   www.oldwayspt.org

Figure 3.16 Latin American Diet Pyramid.
Source: www.oldwayspt.org

To appeal to people with more Western food preferences, "Mexican" fast—food restaurants in the United States often serve dishes that contain large portions of high—fat beef topped with sour cream and cheese. Diets that contain high amounts of these and other solid fats are associated with excess body fat, CVD, and type 2 diabetes.

Italian and Other Mediterranean Influences

The traditional Italian diet of pasta and other grain products, olive oil, fish, nuts, fruits, and vegetables is healthier than the Western diet. Pasta, a product made from wheat flour and water, is the core of the traditional Italian diet. To many Americans *pasta* is spaghetti topped with tomato sauce, meatballs, and grated Parmesan cheese. However, Italians eat a variety of different forms of pasta, such as penne, linguini, acini de pepe, and rotini, along with sauces that are often meatless. Pizza, a dish from southern Italy, is one of the most frequently consumed foods in the United States. Unlike traditional Italian pizza that has a thin crust and is lightly covered with tomatoes, basil (a leafy herb), and mozzarella cheese, many Americans choose thick—crust pizza topped with tomato sauce, plenty of shredded mozzarella cheese, and dotted with fatty pork sausage or pepperoni.

Dietary pyramids or plans developed by governmental agencies or private organizations have plant foods as the core of a healthy diet. The Mediterranean Diet Pyramid shown in Figure 3.17 is based on traditional dietary practices of Greece, southern Italy, and the island of Crete. Grains, fruits, and vegetables, particularly beans and potatoes, form the foundation of this diet. Red meat is rarely eaten. Main dishes often include seafood and poultry, and wine may be included with meals. Although the Mediterranean Diet Pyramid allows as much as 35% of total calories as fat in the diet, much of the fat is from olive oil. Olive oil is a rich source of a type of fat that reduces rather than increases the risk of CVD. Chapter 6 provides more information about oils and fats and their roles in health.

African Heritage Diets

Over the past several decades, the diets of African Americans changed significantly so they now incorporate regional food preferences. In some parts of the United States, for example, the traditional African—American diet includes sweet potato pie, fried chicken, pork, black—eyed peas, and "greens," the nutritious leafy parts of plants such as kale, collards, mustard, turnip, and dandelion. To add flavor, greens may be cooked with small pieces of smoked pork.

Although sweet potatoes, dried peas, and leafy vegetables provide fiber and a variety of vitamins and minerals, fried foods and salt—cured pork products contribute undesirable levels of fat and sodium to the diet. High—fat diets are associated with obesity, and high—sodium diets raise the risk of hypertension. You will learn more about the role of diet in the development of hypertension in Chapters 6 and 9. For more information about African heritage diets and foods, visit http://oldwayspt.org/programs/african—heritage—health .

Asian Influences

Traditional Asian foods, such as Chinese, Japanese, Vietnamese, Thai, and Korean cuisines, are similar and generally feature large amounts of vegetables, rice, or noodles combined with small amounts of meat, fish, or shellfish. The variety of vegetables used in Asian dishes adds color,

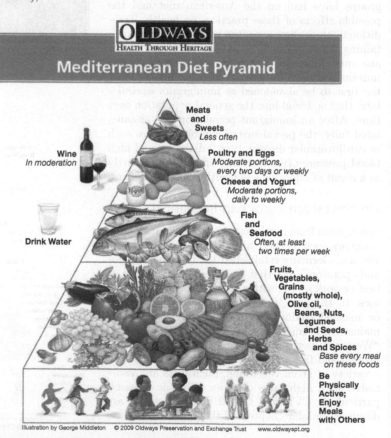

Figure 3.17 Mediterranean Diet Pyramid. The Mediterranean Diet Pyramid is based on traditional dietary practices of Greece, southern Italy, and the island of Crete. Source: www.oldwayspt.org.

flavor, texture, phytochemicals, and nutrients to meals. Additionally, Asian dishes often include flavorful sauces and seasonings made from plants, such as soy sauce, rice wine, gingerroot, garlic, scallions, peppers, and sesame seeds. The Asian Diet Pyramid, shown in Figure 3.18, illustrates the traditional Asian dietary pattern, which generally provides inadequate amounts of calcium from milk and milk products. However, using calcium–rich or calcium–fortified foods can add the mineral to diets.

Chinese foods are popular among Americans. Many Americans, however, do not favor dishes that feature seafood and contain large portions of vegetables and grains, because they believe meat should form the basis of a meal. Thus, North American Chinese restaurants that specialize in Cantonese, Szechwan, or Mandarin cuisines typically offer menu items that contain much larger portions of animal foods such as beef and chicken than authentic dishes. Furthermore, American–Chinese foods are often prepared with far greater amounts of fat than are used in true Chinese cooking.

Traditional Chinese food preparation methods, particularly steaming and stir–frying, tend to preserve the vitamins and minerals in fresh vegetables. Stir–frying involves cooking foods in a lightly oiled, very hot pan for a short period of time. Unlike Western methods of deep-fat frying or boiling vegetables, stir–frying vegetables keeps them crisp and colorful.

Rice is the staple food in the traditional Japanese diet. Additionally, fish, poultry, pork, and foods made from soybeans provide protein in this diet. The Japanese people eat sushi, small pieces of raw fish or shellfish that are usually served rolled in or pressed into rice and served with vegetables and seaweed. American–Japanese restaurants often feature sushi, and many non–Japanese Americans like to order the exotic dish.

Some of the longest–lived people in the world reside on Okinawa, a tiny island south of the main Japanese islands. The traditional diet of fresh vegetables, minimal amounts of salt and animal protein (mainly from pork and fish), and moderate amounts of fat may protect the island's population from premature heart disease and stroke. Younger Okinawans have adopted more western dietary practices, such as eating "fast food," and as a result, their life expectancy is not as long as their grandparents.[25]

Not all Japanese are as healthy as the older generations of Okinawans. The people living on the Japanese island of Honshu consume high amounts of salt, which is the principal dietary source of the mineral sodium. High sodium intakes increase the risk of hypertension, and this disease is very common among the Honshu population.

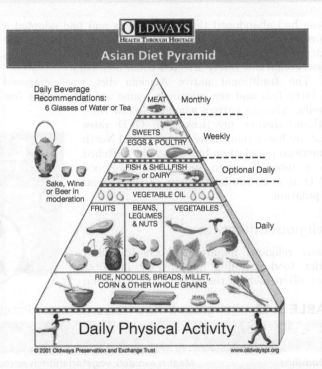

Figure 3.18 Asian Diet Pyramid. The Asian Diet Pyramid dietary pattern generally provides inadequate amounts of calcium from milk and milk products.
Source: www.oldwayspt.org

Native American Influences

In the past, some Native Americans were hunter–gatherers, depending on wild vegetation, fish, and game for food. Other Native Americans learned to grow vegetable crops, including tomatoes, corn, and squash. In general, the traditional Native American diet was low in sodium and fat and high in fiber. During the last half of the twentieth century, many Native Americans abandoned their traditional diets and adopted the typical Western diet. The negative health effects of this lifestyle change have been significant. Before the 1930s, for example, members of the Pima tribe in the southwestern United States primarily ate native foods that included low–fat game animals and high–fiber desert vegetation. By the end of the century, most American

Pima had abandoned their native diets and had adopted a more Western diet. Today, obesity and type 2 diabetes are extremely prevalent among the Pima, whereas in the past, these conditions rarely affected tribal members.

The traditional native Alaskan diet was composed of fatty fish and sea mammals, game animals, and a few plants. Alaskan natives who still follow traditional dietary practices have CVD rates that are lower than those in the general North American population, but those who switched to a more Western diet have developed CVD at rates similar to those of the general population.

Religious Influences

Many religions require members to follow strict food handling and dietary practices that often include the prohibition of certain foods and beverages (see Table 3.12). According to Jewish dietary laws, for example, meat and poultry products must be kept separate from milk products. Milk products are not used to prepare foods that contain meat or poultry, nor are they served with them. A cheeseburger, for example, is not *kosher.* "Kosher" refers to a specific procedure concerning killing, butchering, and preparation activities that makes food acceptable for the religion's followers to eat. Fruits, grains, and vegetables are "neutral" foods that can be eaten with meals that contain either meat or dairy products. However, vegetables cooked with meat become a "meat" food and cannot be served with milk; peaches served with cottage cheese become a "milk" food and cannot be eaten with meat or poultry. Today many American Jews do not follow their religion's complex dietary laws as closely as their ancestors did.

TABLE 3.12 Religious Influences on Dietary Practices

Religion	Dietary practices*
Buddhist	Meat is avoided; vegetarianism is encouraged.
Eastern Orthodox	Meat and fish restrictions; fasting and specific food abstinence during certain holidays
Hindu	Beef is forbidden, but dairy products are "pure" for consumption. Pork may be restricted. Alcohol is avoided. Fasting is often encouraged.
Islam	Pork; birds of prey; reptiles; insects, except locusts; most gelatins; and alcohol are prohibited (*ha-raam*). Ritual killing of animals that are permitted as food (*ha-lal*) Stimulant beverages (i.e., coffee and tea) are avoided. Fasting from all food and drink (daytime) during month of Ramadan and certain other religious holidays
Jewish	Only kosher foods are acceptable. "Tref" (*trayf*) refers to prohibited foods. Pork and shellfish are prohibited. Eating meat with dairy is prohibited. Consuming blood is forbidden. Raw meat is soaked in cold water to remove blood, salted for 1 hour, and then rinsed. Eggs, fruits, and vegetables can be eaten with either meat or dairy foods. Eggs, however, are inspected to make sure they do not contain blood specks. Only fish with fins and scales can be eaten. Only land animals that have split hooves and chew their cud can be eaten, and only the front half of the cud-chewing animal is used. Ritual killing of certain animals is required. Fasting and specific food restrictions for certain holidays
Mormon	Do not drink alcohol, coffee, and tea Fasting is practiced regularly.
Roman Catholic	Fasting before communion; fasting and specific food abstinence during certain holidays
Seventh Day Adventist	Animal product consumption generally limited to milk, milk products, and eggs (lacto-ovo vegetarianism) Alcohol and beverages containing stimulants are prohibited.

* Some religions have extensive rules governing food-related practices, but many people do not follow their religion's dietary guidelines fully or at all.

Bagels with smoked salmon (*lox*), pickled herring, cream cheese, dill pickles, corned beef, and pastrami are popu—lar among the Ashkenazi, the predominant group of Jews in America. Although many non—Jews enjoy eating these traditional Ashkenazic foods, such items may be too high in sodium and animal fat to be healthy.

Chapter References

See Appendix H.

Summary

3.1 From Requirements to Standards

- A requirement is the smallest amount of a nutrient that maintains a defined level of health. Numerous factors influence nutrient requirements. Scientists use information about nutrient requirements and storage capabilities to establish specific dietary recommendations. The Dietary Reference Intakes (DRIs) are various energy and nutrient intake standards for Americans. An Estimated Average Requirement (EAR) is the amount of the nutrient that meets the needs of 50% of healthy people in a particular life stage/sex group. The Estimated Energy Requirement (EER) is used to evaluate a person's energy intake. The Recommended Dietary Allowances (RDAs) meet the needs of nearly all healthy individuals (97 to 98%) in a particular life stage/sex group. When nutrition scientists are unable to determine an RDA for a nutrient, they establish an Adequate Intake (AI) value. The Tolerable Upper Intake Level (UL) is the highest average amount of a nutrient that is unlikely to harm most people when the amount is consumed daily.

- DRIs can be used for planning nutritious diets for groups of people and evaluating the nutritional adequacy of a population's diet. RDAs and AIs are often used to evaluate an individual's dietary practices. For nutrition labeling purposes, FDA uses RDAs to develop Daily Values (DVs).

3.2 Major Food Groups

- Food guides generally classify foods into groups according to their natural origins and key nutrients. Such guides usually feature major food groups. Some food guides also include groups for oils and empty-calorie foods or beverages.

3.3 Dietary Guidelines

- The Dietary Guidelines is a set of general nutrition-related lifestyle recommendations designed to promote adequate nutritional status and good health, and to reduce the risk of major chronic nutrition-related health conditions.

3.4 Food Guides

- Choosemyplate.gov is an online, interactive food intake and physical activity guide that is based on Dietary Guidelines. Most Americans do not follow the government's dietary recommendations.

- The Exchange System, a tool for estimating the calorie and macronutrient contents of foods, categorizes foods into three broad groups. The foods within each group have similar macronutrient composition. A specified amount of food in an exchange list provides about the same amount of macronutrients and calories as each of the other specified amounts of foods in that list. Carbohydrate counting is a method that people can use for planning menus.

3.5 Food and Dietary Supplement Labels

- Consumers can use information on food labels to determine ingredients and compare nutrient contents of packaged foods and beverages. The FDA regulates and monitors information that can be placed on food labels, including claims about the product's health benefits. Nearly all foods and beverages sold in supermarkets must be labeled with the product's name, manufacturer's name and address, amount of product in the package, and ingredients listed in descending order by weight. Furthermore, food labels must use a special format for listing specific information on the Nutrition Facts panel.

- The Daily Values (DVs) are a practical set of nutrient standards for labeling purposes. The nutrient content in a serving of food is listed on the label as a percentage of the DV (%DV). Not all nutrients have DVs. A dietary goal is to obtain at least 100% of the DVs for fiber, vitamins, and minerals (except sodium) each day.

- The FDA permits food manufacturers to include certain health claims on food labels. However, the agency requires that health claims meet certain guidelines and, in some instances, use specific wording. A structure/function claim describes the role a nutrient plays in the body. Structure/function statements cannot claim that a nutrient or food can be used to prevent or treat a serious health condition.

- Organic foods are produced without the use of antibiotics, hormones, synthetic fertilizers and pesticides, genetic improvements, or food irradiation. In general, organic food crops are not more nutritious than similar conventionally grown foods. More research is needed to determine whether there are health advantages to eating organic foods. A food product cannot be labeled "organic" unless its production meets strict national standards.

3.6 Using Dietary Analysis Software

- Dietary analysis software and websites can be quick and easy tools for determining nutrient and energy contents of a specific food.

3.7 Nutrition Matters: The Melting Pot

- Traditional ethnic diets are often based on dishes containing small amounts of animal foods and larger amounts of locally grown fruits, vegetables, and unrefined grains. However, these foods are typically abandoned as people migrate to other countries and assimilate into the general population. After an immigrant population has assimilated fully, the prevalence of chronic diseases such as cardiovascular disease, type 2 diabetes, and high blood pressure often increases among them, partly as a result of adopting unhealthy eating practices. Many religions require members to follow strict food handling and dietary practices that often include the prohibition of certain foods and beverages.

Recipe for Healthy Living

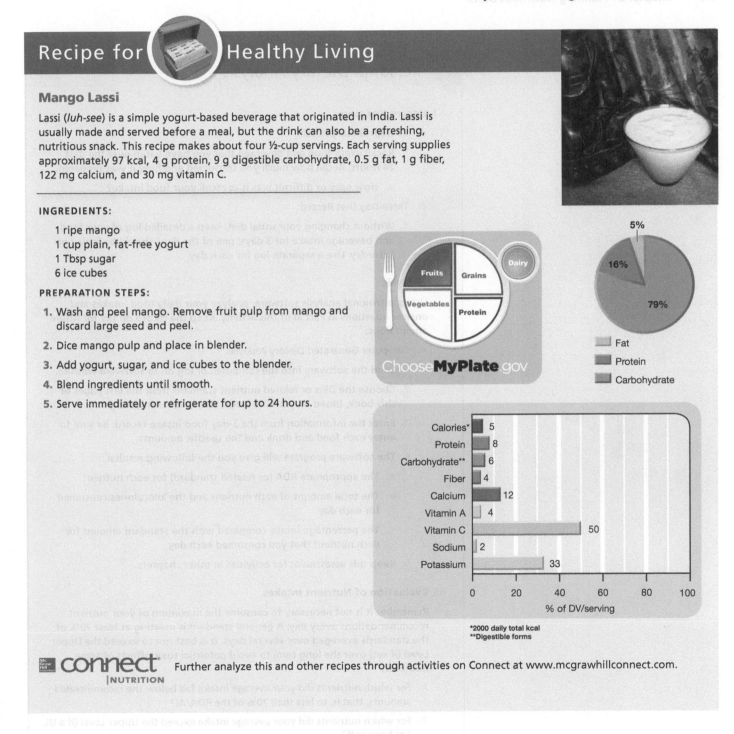

Mango Lassi

Lassi (*luh-see*) is a simple yogurt-based beverage that originated in India. Lassi is usually made and served before a meal, but the drink can also be a refreshing, nutritious snack. This recipe makes about four ½-cup servings. Each serving supplies approximately 97 kcal, 4 g protein, 9 g digestible carbohydrate, 0.5 g fat, 1 g fiber, 122 mg calcium, and 30 mg vitamin C.

INGREDIENTS:

1 ripe mango
1 cup plain, fat-free yogurt
1 Tbsp sugar
6 ice cubes

PREPARATION STEPS:

1. Wash and peel mango. Remove fruit pulp from mango and discard large seed and peel.

2. Dice mango pulp and place in blender.

3. Add yogurt, sugar, and ice cubes to the blender.

4. Blend ingredients until smooth.

5. Serve immediately or refrigerate for up to 24 hours.

Fruits | Grains
Vegetables | Protein
Dairy

ChooseMyPlate.gov

5%
16%
79%

☐ Fat
☐ Protein
☐ Carbohydrate

	% of DV/serving
Calories*	5
Protein	8
Carbohydrate**	6
Fiber	4
Calcium	12
Vitamin A	4
Vitamin C	50
Sodium	2
Potassium	33

0   20   40   60   80   100
% of DV/serving

*2000 daily total kcal
**Digestible forms

Further analyze this and other recipes through activities on Connect at www.mcgrawhillconnect.com.

Personal Dietary Analysis

I. Record Keeping

A. 24-Hour Dietary Recall

1. Recall every food and beverage that you have eaten over the past 24 hours. Recall how much you consumed and how it was prepared.

   a. How easy or difficult was it to recall your food intake?

B. Three-Day Diet Record

1. Without changing your usual diet, keep a detailed log of your food and beverage intake for 3 days; one of the days should be Friday or Saturday. Use a separate log for each day.

II. Analysis

Using nutritional analysis software, analyze your daily food intakes and answer questions in Part III of this activity. Keep the record on file for future applications.

A. Computer-Generated Dietary Analysis

1. Load the software into the computer, or log on to software website.

2. Choose the DRIs or related nutrient standard from the last pages of this book, based on your life stage, sex, height, and weight.

3. Enter the information from the 3-day food intake record. Be sure to enter each food and drink and the specific amounts.

4. The software program will give you the following results:

   a. The appropriate RDA (or related standard) for each nutrient

   b. The total amount of each nutrient and the kilocalories consumed for each day

   c. The percentage intake compared with the standard amount for each nutrient that you consumed each day

5. Keep this assessment for activities in other chapters.

III. Evaluation of Nutrient Intakes

Remember it is not necessary to consume the maximum of your nutrient recommendations every day. A general standard is meeting at least 70% of the standards averaged over several days. It is best not to exceed the Upper Level (if set) over the long term to avoid potential toxic effects of some nutrients.

A. For which nutrients did your average intake fall below the recommended amounts, that is, to less than 70% of the RDA/AI?

B. For which nutrients did your average intake exceed the Upper Level (if a UL has been set)?

IV. MyPlate

This activity determines how your diet stacks up when compared to the amounts of foods from each food group that are recommended by MyPlate.

A. Refer to your 3-day diet record. Classify each food item in the appropriate food group of MyPlate. For each food group, indicate whether you ate the recommended amount daily for your sex, age, height, weight, and physical activity level. Note that some of your food choices—pizza, for example—may contribute to more than one food group. Enter a minus sign (–) if your total falls below the MyPlate recommendation or a plus sign (+) if it equals or exceeds the daily recommendation for each food group.

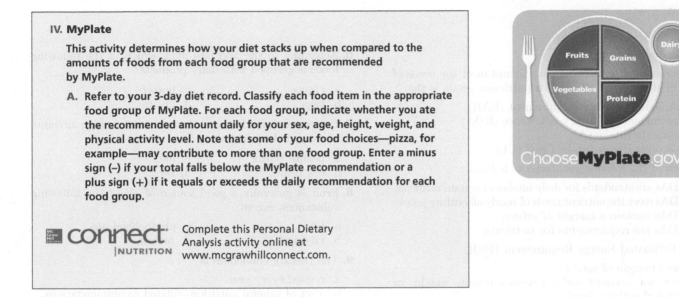

Complete this Personal Dietary Analysis activity online at www.mcgrawhillconnect.com.

Critical Thinking

1. Your friend takes several dietary supplements daily, and as a result, his vitamin B–6 intake is 50 times higher than the RDA for the vitamin. You would like to con-vince him to stop taking the supplements. To support your advice, which nutrient standards would you show him? Explain why.

2. Why should consumers use MyPlate to plan menus instead of the DRIs?

3. How do your added sugars, sodium, and saturated fat intakes compare to the recommendations of the latest Dietary Guidelines?

4. Examine Table 3.6. Which foods in the left–hand col-umn do you eat regularly? Why are those foods listed in that column?

5. The ingredient list on a package of crackers includes veg-etable oil. What can you do to learn which type of veg-etable oil is in the product?

6. Visit the USDA's website (www.ars.usda.gov/Services/docs. htm?docid=17032) to access "What's in the Foods You Eat *Search Tool,*" a database for searching the nutritional content of foods. To practice using this search tool, find the number of kilocalories and the amounts of fiber, vitamin C, iron, and caffeine in 1 cup of raw jicama, 1 cup of 2% milk with added vitamin A, and ¼ cup of dry roasted, salt–added sunflower seed kernels (no hulls).

7. According to a newspaper article, an 8–oz serving of fat–free milk contains 15 mcg of folate (a B vitamin). Another source of nutrition information indicates that an 8–oz serving of fat–free milk contains 12 mcg of folate. Explain why both sources of information can be correct.

Practice Test

Select the best answer.

1. The amount of a nutrient that should meet the needs of half of the healthy people in a particular group is the

   a. Estimated Average Requirement (EAR).
   b. Recommended Dietary Allowance (RDA).
   c. Adequate Intake (AI).
   d. Tolerable Upper Intake Level (UL).

2. Which of the following statements is false?

   a. RDAs are standards for daily intakes of certain nutrients.
   b. RDAs meet the nutrient needs of nearly all healthy people.
   c. RDAs contain a margin of safety.
   d. RDAs are requirements for nutrients.

3. The Estimated Energy Requirement (EER)

   a. has a margin of safety.
   b. does not account for a person's height, weight, or physical activity level.
   c. is based on the average daily energy needs of a healthy person.
   d. reflects a person's actual daily energy needs.

4. A diet is likely to be safe and nutritionally adequate if

   a. average daily intakes for nutrients meet RDA or AI values.
   b. intakes of various nutrients are consistently less than EAR amounts.
   c. nutrient intakes are consistently above ULs.
   d. vitamin supplements are included.

5. Nutritional standards, such as the RDAs, are not

   a. used to develop formula food products.
   b. the basis for establishing DVs.
   c. used to evaluate the nutritional adequacy of diets.
   d. the basis for developing AIs.

6. According to the MyPlate plan, which of the following foods is grouped with dairy products?

   a. cheese   c. butter
   b. eggs   d. cream

7. Protein−rich food sources that also contain high amounts of saturated fat include

   a. peanut butter.   c. nuts.
   b. dry beans.   d. beef.

8. Fruit is generally a good source of all of the following substances, except

   a. fiber.   c. phytochemicals.
   b. vitamin C.   d. protein.

9. The Dietary Guidelines is

   a. revised every year.
   b. a set of general nutrition−related recommendations.
   c. published by the Centers for Disease Control and Prevention.
   d. used to develop DVs.

10. Which of the following foods would be classified as "empty calories" by MyPlate?

    a. chocolate syrup   c. white bread
    b. fat−free milk   d. corn oil

11. Which of the following statements is true?

    a. According to MyPlate, vegetable oils are grouped into the "Fats and Oils" food group.
    b. The MyPlate menu planning guide cannot be individualized to meet a person's food preferences.
    c. A person can use MyPlate to evaluate his or her diet's nutritional adequacy.
    d. MyPlate was the first food guide developed for Americans.

12. The Exchange System

    a. classifies foods in the same groups as MyPlate.
    b. has exchange lists based on macronutrient contents.
    c. is useful only for people who have diabetes.
    d. incorporates high−protein foods with high−carbohydrate foods.

13. Which of the following information was not provided by the Nutrition Facts panel in 2015?

    a. percentage of calories from fat
    b. amount of carbohydrate per serving
    c. serving size
    d. amount of trans fat per serving

14. Daily Values are

a. for people who consume 1200 to 1500 kilocalorie diets.
b. based on the lowest RDA or AI for each nutrient.
c. dietary standards developed for food—labeling purposes.
d. used to evaluate the nutritional adequacy of a popu—lation's diet.

15. People who follow Islamic dietary rules will not consume

a. pork.
b. rice.
c. beef.
d. milk.

Answers to Quiz Yourself

1. According to the latest U.S. Department of Agriculture food guide, fruits and vegetables are combined into one food group. **False.** (p. 71)

2. According to the recommendations of the *2015–2020 Dietary Guidelines for Americans,* it is acceptable for certain adults to consume alcoholic beverages in moderation. **True.** (p. 69)

3. Last week, Colin didn't consume the recommended amount of vitamin C for a couple of days. Nevertheless, he is unlikely to develop scurvy, the vitamin C deficiency disease. **True.** (p. 64)

4. The Food and Drug Administration develops Dietary Guidelines for Americans. **False.** (p. 68)

5. The Nutrition Facts panel on a food label provides information concerning amounts of energy, fiber, and sodium that are in a serving of the food. **True.** (p. 77)

LEARNSMART
ADVANTAGE

Get the most out of your study of nutrition with McGraw-Hill's innovative suite of adaptive learning products including McGraw-Hill LearnSmart®, SmartBook®, LearnSmart Achieve®, and LearnSmart Prep®. Visit www.learnsmartadvantage.com.

CHAPTER 13

Nutrition for a Lifetime

Quiz Yourself

What steps can young women take to prepare for pregnancy? Compared to breast milk, do infant formulas provide the same health benefits for infants? When is the best time to begin feeding solid foods to infants? Which nutrients are most likely to be deficient in diets of older adults? While reading this chapter, you will learn answers to these questions. Test your knowledge of nutrition during various life stages by taking the following quiz. The answers are found on page 535.

1. During pregnancy, a mother-to-be should double her food intake because she's "eating for two." _____ T _____ F

2. The natural size of a woman's breasts is not a factor in determining her ability to breastfeed her baby. _____ T _____ F

3. Caregivers should add solid foods to an infant's diet within the first month after the baby is born. _____ T _____ F

4. Over the past few decades, the prevalence of obesity has increased among American children. _____ T _____ F

5. Compared to younger persons, older adults have lower risks of nutritional deficiencies. _____ T _____ F

13.1 Introduction to Nutrition for a Lifetime

Learning Outcomes:

1 Identify the life stages.

2 Explain why it is important to learn about nutrition concerns for pregnancy, lactation, childhood, and the older adult years.

The chapter opening portrait features a young woman during her eighth month of pregnancy, looking forward to a bright future. Thanks to technological and medical advances that occurred during the twentieth century, her baby has an excellent chance of enjoying a long, healthy life.

If you are a woman, are you pregnant? Do you already have children? If you have children, were they breastfed or formula−fed? Do you live with and help care for an elderly parent or grandparent? These may seem to be personal ques−tions, but many undergraduate college students do not fit the stereotype of being 18 to 22 years of age, having no children, and residing away from home.

Most of the nutrition recommendations presented in this textbook apply to people who are "adults"—loosely defined as the period when a person is 19 to 70 years of age.[1] This chapter focuses on the differing nutrition needs and health concerns of people who are in specific *life stages*. These particular life stages are the **prenatal period** or pregnancy, the time between conception and birth; **lactation** (milk production for breastfeeding); infancy; childhood; adolescence; and the older adult period that generally spans from 70 years of age until death.

Why is it necessary to learn some basic information about nutrition−related concerns during various life stages? If you do not have children, you may become a parent in the future. If your parents and grandparents are relatively young and vigorous now, you can expect them to experience declining physical functioning as they grow older. Finally, you need to recognize that most of these changes are normal and will affect you as well.

Today in the United States, many of the leading causes of death are chronic diseases, such as heart disease and cancer. Long−term health−related practices, including dietary and physical activity habits, often contribute to the develop−ment of these diseases. Whether you enjoy overall good health or suffer from one or more disabling physical ailments as you grow older depends not only on your life−style choices but also on several other factors, including your heredity, relationships, environment, income, education level, and access to health care. Achieving and maintaining a healthy body weight is critical to enjoying good health throughout life. This chapter also includes information about obesity during childhood and adolescence.

prenatal period time between conception and birth; pregnancy

lactation milk production

Concept **Checkpoint 13.1**

1. John is 79 years of age. According to the general definition of *adult,* is he an adult or an "older adult"?
2. For women, which life stage involves milk production for breastfeeding?

494   Chapter 13 Nutrition for a Lifetime

conception moment when a sperm enters an egg (fertilization)

uterus female reproductive organ that protects the developing organism during pregnancy

embryo human organism from 14 days to 8 weeks after conception

fetus human organism from 8 weeks after conception until birth

13.2 Pregnancy

Learning Outcomes

1 Discuss the roles of the placenta and uterus during pregnancy.

2 Explain why an infant's birth weight is an important aspect of the baby's health during its first year of life.

3 List major physiological changes that occur during pregnancy, and identify typical nutrition-related discomforts associated with this stage of life.

4 Discuss the importance of appropriate weight gain during pregnancy, and identify recommended ranges of weight that pregnant women should gain.

5 Explain why prenatal care and a nutritious diet are important for the health of the pregnant woman and her unborn offspring.

"It's positive!" Each day, the results of pregnancy testing are a source of excite-ment, relief, or concern for thousands of women. About 50% of pregnancies are unplanned in the United States.[2] Therefore, all sexually active women of child-bearing age should be aware of their likelihood of becoming pregnant. Regardless of whether a pregnancy is planned or not, dietary practices before and during pregnancy play a major role in the course of the pregnancy and the primary outcome—a healthy infant.

The prenatal period (*gestation*) encompasses the time from **conception,** the moment a male sperm cell enters a female egg cell, until the birth of a *full-term* infant, about 38 to 42 weeks later. During the first 2 weeks after conception, the fertilized egg (*ovum*) divides repeatedly, forming a mass of cells that enters the woman's **uterus,** the female reproductive organ that protects the developing organism. The mass of cells buries itself into the nutrient-rich lining of the uterus (implantation) and continues to develop. For the next 6 weeks, the rapidly dividing mass of cells, called an **embryo,** increases in size and forms organs. Eight weeks after conception, the developing human being is referred to as a **fetus** (Fig. 13.1).

Figure 13.1 Prenatal development: Conception to fetus. During the first 2 weeks after conception, the fertilized egg divides repeatedly, forming a mass of cells that eventually enters the uterus and buries itself into the organ's nutrient-rich lining. From 14 days through 8 weeks after conception, the rapidly dividing mass of cells is called an embryo. Eight weeks after conception and until its birth, the developing human being is referred to as a fetus.

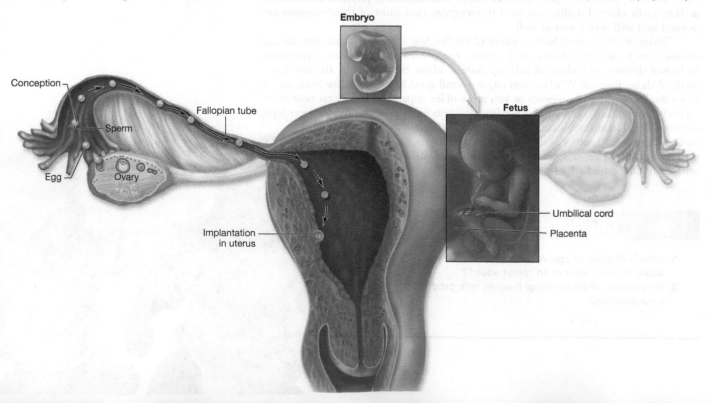

Embryo

Conception

Sperm

Fallopian tube

Egg

Ovary

Implantation in uterus

Fetus

Umbilical cord

Placenta

The prenatal period is often divided into three stages or *trimesters*. During the first trimester, the embryo/fetus develops most of its organs, and by the end of this period, the fetus can move. The first trimester is a critical stage in human development because nutrient deficiencies or excesses and exposure to toxic compounds, such as alcohol, are most likely to have devastating effects on the embryo/fetus. However, many women who are in their first trimester do not realize they are pregnant.

As the second trimester begins, the fetus is still very tiny, about 2½ to 3 inches in length, and weighs only about an ounce. However, the fetus is beginning to look more like a human infant: It has fully formed arms, hands, fingers, legs, feet, and toes. The fetus's organs continue to grow and mature in their ability to function. As the fetus moves around, its mother becomes increasingly aware of its presence within her body.

By the beginning of the third trimester, the fetus is approximately 10 inches long (from crown to rump) and weighs about 2 pounds. During this trimester, the fetus will nearly double in length and multiply its weight by three to four times. Thus, a healthy fetus usually weighs about 6 to 8 pounds and is 19 to 21 inches long by the time it is full–term and ready to be born.

Throughout the prenatal period, the embryo/fetus depends entirely on its mother for survival. During most of the pregnancy, the expectant mother nourishes her embryo/fetus through the **placenta,** the organ of pregnancy that connects the uterus to the embryo/fetus via the *umbilical cord* (see Fig. 13.1). The role of the placenta is to transfer nutrients and oxygen from the mother's bloodstream to the embryo/fetus. Additionally, the placenta transfers wastes from the embryo/fetus to the mother's bloodstream, so her body can eliminate them. Unfortunately, the placenta does not filter many microbes and toxic substances, such as alcohol and nicotine, from the mother's blood. Thus, agents of infection and harmful chemicals can pass through the placenta, enter the embryo/fetus, and cause disease, birth defects, or embryonic/fetal death.

A fetus generally needs to spend at least 37 weeks developing within the uterus to be physiologically mature enough to survive after birth without the need for special care. A fetus's weight depends on the supply of nutrients that it receives through the placenta.[3] If the placenta fails to grow properly, the developing fetus is likely to be born too soon and be lighter than average at birth.

Low-Birth-Weight and Preterm Newborns

Birth weight is a major factor that determines whether a baby is healthy and survives his or her first year of life. A **high–birth–weight (HBW)** baby weighs more than approximately 8.8 pounds at birth. A large baby is difficult to deliver vaginally and in many cases requires birth by *caesarian section* (C–section). A C–section involves surgical removal of the fetus from the mother's uterus.

Low–birth–weight (LBW) infants generally weigh less than 5½ pounds at birth. LBW is the leading cause of death among American infants who are less than 28 days of age.[4] In 2012, 8% of infants born in the United States were low birth weight.[5] Pregnant females who are under 15 years of age or 45 to 54 years of age are more likely to give birth to LBW infants than women in other age groups.[4] Additionally, women who smoke during pregnancy are at risk to have LBW babies.[6] Low birth weight is often associated with premature or preterm births. In 2012, 11.5% of births in the United States were preterm; that is, they occurred before the thirty–seventh week of pregnancy.[5]

Early preterm infants are born before 34 weeks of gestation.[7] In 2010, 3.5% of babies born in the United States were early preterm infants. Such infants are more likely to have serious health problems or die soon after birth than babies delivered after 34 weeks of pregnancy.[8] An early preterm infant who is born

placenta organ of pregnancy that connects the uterus to the embryo/fetus via the umbilical cord

high-birth-weight (HBW) describes baby who weighs more than 8.8 pounds at birth

low-birth-weight (LBW) describes baby generally weighing less than 5½ pounds at birth

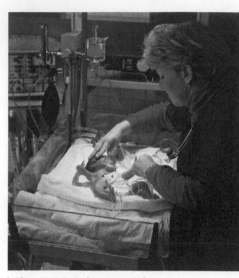

| Figure 13.2 **Early preterm infant.**

prolactin hormone that stimulates milk production after delivery

morning sickness nausea and vomiting associated with pregnancy

Did You Know?

In 2012, Kate Middleton, wife of Great Britian's Prince William, was hospitalized for 3 days because of excessive vomiting during early pregnancy. She recovered and gave birth to a healthy baby boy on July 22, 2013. In 2014, she experienced severe morning sickness with her second pregnancy.

after about 26 weeks of pregnancy may survive if cared for in a hospital nursery for high–risk newborns (Fig. 13.2). However, the tiny infant's body will not have stores of fat and certain minerals that normally accumulate during the last month of pregnancy. Additionally, early preterm babies are likely to have conditions that complicate their medical care and food intake, such as breathing difficulties and weak sucking and swallowing abilities.

Nutrition-Related Signs of Pregnancy

During pregnancy, a woman's body undergoes major physiological changes, such as increased blood volume, breast size, and levels of several hormones. These adaptations enable her body to nourish and maintain the developing embryo/fetus, as well as produce milk for her infant after its birth. However, some of the physical changes cause discomfort for the pregnant woman.

In the first trimester, most women experience physical signs that they are pregnant, such as enlarged breasts and "morning sickness." Other common nutrition–related signs as well as complaints of pregnancy include extreme tiredness, swollen feet, constipation, and heartburn. In most cases, such discomforts do not create serious complications, and they resolve within a few months.

Breast Changes

During pregnancy, hormones signal the breasts to increase in size in preparation for lactation. The mother's pituitary gland in the brain produces **prolactin,** a hormone that stimulates the development of milk–producing tissue in the breasts. However, a pregnant woman's breasts do not form milk, because high levels of progesterone, a hormone that helps maintain pregnancy, inhibit milk production.[9] After birth, the level of progesterone drops rapidly, essentially removing the "brakes" from the breasts' ability to produce milk.

Morning Sickness

A common sign of pregnancy is **morning sickness,** nausea that is sometimes accompanied by vomiting. The name "morning sickness" is misleading because the queasy feeling can occur at any time of the day. The cause of this unpleasant condition is unclear, but it may be the result of the pregnant woman's body adapting to higher levels of female hormones. Additionally, emotional stress and certain foods can contribute to nausea. The condition generally begins early in the first trimester, and most women are no longer affected by the sixteenth week of pregnancy.[10] However, some women experience nausea and vomiting occasionally throughout their pregnancies.

To help control mild morning sickness, pregnant women can avoid odors and foods, such as fried or greasy foods, that trigger nausea. Some women find that eating crackers and drinking some water helps reduce the likelihood of feeling nauseated, especially before they get out of bed in the morning. Furthermore, eating smaller but more frequent meals and nutritious snacks can be helpful.

If the nausea and vomiting contribute to weight loss of more than 2 pounds, the pregnant woman should contact her physician for treatment. Morning sickness that persists beyond the fourth month of pregnancy should also be brought to the attention of a physician. During pregnancy, excessive vomiting is harmful because it can lead to dehydration and nutritional deficiencies.

Fatigue in Pregnancy

Early in pregnancy, the mother's blood volume expands to approximately 150% of normal. The number of red blood cells, however, increases by only 20 to 30%, and this change occurs more gradually. As a result, the pregnant woman develops *physiological anemia*, a condition characterized by a lower concentration of red blood cells in the bloodstream. This form of anemia is a normal response to pregnancy, rather than the result of inadequate nutrient intake. Nevertheless, physiological anemia may be responsible for the extreme tiredness experienced by pregnant women during their first trimester. As their red blood cell numbers increase, expectant mothers report having more energy, especially during the second trimester. By the third trimester, however, most pregnant women are easily fatigued again, possibly because carrying a rapidly growing fetus is physically demanding.

What Is Edema?

High levels of certain hormones can cause various tissues to retain fluid during pregnancy. Although the extra fluid causes some minor swelling (edema), especially in the hands and feet, the condition is normal. In most cases, mild edema does not require treatment such as restricting salt intake or taking diuretics. Edema, however, can be a sign of trouble if hypertension and the appearance of extra protein in the urine accompany the swelling. The "Importance of Prenatal Care" section of this chapter discusses hypertension during pregnancy.

Digestive Tract Discomforts

During pregnancy, certain hormones produced by the placenta relax muscles of the digestive tract. As a result, intestinal movements slow down and digested material takes longer to pass through the tract, increasing the likelihood of constipation (see the "Fiber and Health" section of Chapter 5). To help prevent constipation, pregnant women should consume adequate amounts of fiber and fluids. During pregnancy, the Adequate Intake (AI) for fiber is 28 g/day, and the AI for total water is 3 L/day.[1] If constipation still persists after making these dietary changes, the pregnant woman should discuss this concern with her physician.

Heartburn is another common complaint of pregnant women. As the fetus grows, the uterus pushes upward in the mother's abdominal cavity and applies pressure on her stomach. When this occurs, stomach acid can enter the esophagus, causing heartburn (see the Chapter 4 "Nutrition Matters"). To help avoid heartburn, the pregnant woman can consume smaller meals, avoid lying down after eating, eat less fatty foods, and learn to identify and avoid foods that seem to contribute to heartburn. If heartburn continues to be bothersome, the woman should consult her physician and discuss other ways to treat the condition.

Pregnancy: General Dietary Recommendations

Ideally, women of childbearing age should take steps to ensure good health before becoming pregnant. For example, women can analyze the nutritional adequacy of their diets and choose to eat foods that correct any marginal or deficient intakes. Prior to pregnancy, sedentary women can begin an exercise regimen; overweight or obese women can lose some excess weight; and women who smoke can join smoking cessation programs. The time to remedy faulty lifestyle practices and increase chances of having a healthy pregnancy and baby is long before pregnancy occurs.

During pregnancy, the mother-to-be should follow a diet that meets her own nutritional needs as well as those of her developing offspring. Depending on the trimester, an expectant woman's requirements for energy (calories), protein, and many other nutrients are greater than her needs prior to pregnancy. Nevertheless, a pregnant woman does not need to double her usual food intake just because she is "eating for two." Table 13.1 compares Recommended Dietary Allowances (RDAs) for energy and selected nutrients that apply to healthy 25-year-old nonpregnant and pregnant women.

TABLE 13.1 Comparing Selected DRIs: 25-Year-Old Nonpregnant and Pregnant Women

Energy/ Nutrient*	Nonpregnant	Pregnant
Kilocalories	Estimated Energy Requirement (EER)	First Trimester = EER + 0
		Second Trimester = EER + 340
		Third Trimester = EER + 452
Protein	46 g/day	71 g/day
Vitamin C	75 mg/day	85 mg/day
Thiamin	1.1 mg/day	1.4 mg/day
Niacin	14 mg/day	18 mg/day
Folate	400 mcg/day	600 mcg/day
Vitamin D	15 mcg/day	15 mcg/day
Calcium	1000 mg/day	1000 mg/day
Iron	18 mg/day	27 mg/day
Iodine	150 mcg/day	220 mcg/day

* RDA

Source: Data from Institute of Medicine: *Dietary Reference Intakes.*

TABLE 13.2 Sample Menu for a 25-Year-Old Pregnant Woman (Second Trimester)

Breakfast
¾ cup cooked oatmeal, made with ½ cup fat-free milk and sprinkled with ¼ cup raisins
½ cup calcium-fortified orange juice
Mid-morning snack
½ cup calcium-fortified orange juice
1 rectangular graham cracker
2 Tbsp peanut butter
Lunch
Cheese sandwich
2 slices whole-grain bread
1 slice American cheese
2 slices tomato
¼ cup leaf lettuce
2 tsp mayonnaise-type low-calorie salad dressing
1 cup apple slices
1 cup fat-free milk
½ cup orange sherbet
Mid-afternoon snack
1 whole-grain English muffin, toasted
1 Tbsp soft margarine
2 tsp jelly
½ cup fat-free milk
Dinner
Broiled salmon filet, 5 oz
1¼ cups mixed salad greens
1 Tbsp low-calorie Italian dressing
½ cup enriched white rice
1 cup steamed broccoli
2 small dinner rolls
1 Tbsp soft margarine
Evening snack
1 cup frozen yogurt

Energy Needs

In the first trimester, a pregnant woman's daily energy requirement (*Estimated Energy Requirement* or *EER*) is essentially the same as a nonpregnant woman's, because the embryo/fetus is quite small (see Table 13.1). However, the fetus grows rapidly during the second and third trimesters, and the pregnant woman requires more energy and nutrients to support its growth as well as her own body's needs. During the second trimester, the expectant mother should consume approximately 340 more kilocalories per day than her prepregnancy EER. Throughout the third trimester, she should add about 450 kcal per day to her prepregnancy EER (see Table 13.1). If a woman is physically active during her pregnancy, she may need to increase her kilocalorie intake by even more than these levels. Why? As the pregnant woman gains weight, her muscles require more energy to move her body. The average expectant mother, however, reduces her physical activity level during the third trimester, conserving energy.

Folate and Iron Needs

A pregnant woman's requirements for folate and iron are 50% higher than those of a nonpregnant woman. It is important for women to enter pregnancy with adequate folate status, because embryos need the vitamin to support rapid cell division. As discussed in Chapter 8, pregnant women who are folate deficient have high risk of giving birth to infants with neural tube defects, such as spina bifida (see Fig. 8.25). To obtain adequate folate, women of childbearing age as well as pregnant women should include rich food sources of folate in their diets, such as green leafy vegetables, and take a vitamin/mineral supplement that supplies at least 400 mcg of *folic acid*, a form of folate.

As the pregnant woman's blood volume expands, her need for iron increases because her body must make more hemoglobin for the extra red blood cells. Additionally, the woman's body transfers iron to the fetus to build its stores of the mineral. If women fail to meet their iron needs during pregnancy, their iron stores can be severely depleted, and they can develop iron deficiency anemia. Pregnant women who are iron deficient have high risk of giving birth prematurely and having low-birth-weight infants.[11]

Even when their diets include good sources of iron such as red meats and enriched cereals, pregnant women often need a supplemental source of iron. Thus, most physicians recommend special prenatal multiple vitamin/mineral supplements that contain iron for their pregnant patients.

Menu Planning for Pregnant Women

Rather than view pregnancy as a time to splurge by eating energy-dense empty-calorie foods, the mother-to-be should obtain the extra calories from nutrient-dense foods. For example, drinking an additional cup of fat-free milk, eating a bowl of an enriched whole-grain cereal, and taking a prenatal supplement each day can supply extra kilocalories as well as protein, fiber, and micronutrients. Table 13.2 presents a day's meals and snacks for a sedentary 25-year-old woman who is in her second trimester of pregnancy. Her prepregnancy EER was 2000 kcal, so her sample menu is based on MyPlate recommendations for 2400 kcal, enough to cover her increased EER during this trimester.

Is Fish Safe to Eat During Pregnancy? Fish and shellfish (e.g., clams, shrimp, and crabs) are excellent sources of many minerals, omega-3 fatty acids, and high-quality protein. However, most fish and shellfish contain very small amounts of methylmercury, a compound that contains the toxic mineral mercury.[12] Certain kinds of fish and shellfish, however, contain higher levels of methylmercury than others. When a pregnant woman eats these foods, the methylmercury in them can eventually reach the developing fetus and damage its nervous system. Chapter 3 provides recommendations for safe levels of fish consumption by pregnant women.

What About Cravings?

The stereotype of a pregnant woman who craves pickles and ice cream is not simply a myth. Cravings are common during this stage of life. However, ask pregnant women to identify the foods they crave, and you are likely to get a variety of responses. The causes of cravings are unknown, but they may be responses to the hormonal changes associated with pregnancy or to the emotional state of the mother-to-be. In other instances, specific food cravings may simply reflect the pregnant woman's family traditions. Unless food cravings contribute to excess weight gain, they are generally harmless.

Some women develop **pica,** the practice of eating nonfood items such as laundry starch, chalk, cigarette ashes, and soil. Some studies have linked pica with iron and zinc deficiency, but it is not clear if pica is the result or the cause of such deficiencies. Pregnant women should refrain from practicing pica, especially eating clay or soil. Soil may contain substances that interfere with the absorption of minerals in the intestinal tract. Furthermore, eating soil can be harmful because the dirt may be contaminated with toxic substances, such as lead and pesticides, and pathogenic microbes.

pica practice of eating nonfood items

Weight Gain During Pregnancy

Nearly all pregnant women experience weight gain. In fact, gaining an appropriate amount of weight is crucial during pregnancy. How much weight a woman should gain depends on her prepregnancy weight. Women who were underweight prior to pregnancy should gain 28 to 40 pounds; women whose prepregnancy weights were within the healthy range can expect to gain 25 to 35 pounds.[13] Women who were overweight before they became pregnant should gain 15 to 25 pounds, and obese women should gain 11 to 20 pounds during pregnancy. The recommendations are higher for women who are pregnant with more than one fetus. For example, a healthy woman who is carrying twins may gain as much as 54 pounds during pregnancy.[14]

In 2011, 48% of women in the United States gained more than the recommended amount of weight during pregnancy.[13] Women who gain excess weight during pregnancy are likely to retain the extra pounds long after their babies are born. Furthermore, expectant mothers who gain excessive amounts of weight are more likely to give birth to high-birth-weight (HBW) babies. When compared to newborns with healthy weights, HBW infants have higher risk of being injured during the birth process and of having birth defects. Furthermore, HBW infants are more likely to develop obesity, diabetes, and hypertension at some point in their lives.[15] In 2011, about 7% of babies born in the United States were HBW.[13]

Underweight women who do not gain enough weight during pregnancy are at risk of having preterm or low-birth-weight (LBW) infants. Underweight pregnant women should try to reach healthy weights by the end of the first trimester and then meet the recommended weight-gain goals. Obese women have a greater risk of developing hypertension as well as type 2 diabetes during pregnancy. Obese pregnant women are also at risk of giving birth to HBW babies.[15] However, women should not try to lose weight while they are pregnant because calorie restriction may harm the fetus.

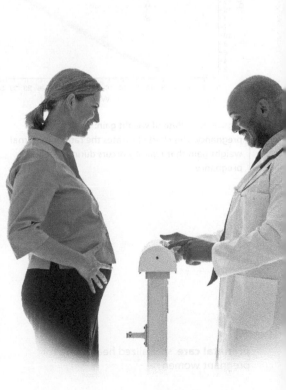

500   Chapter 13   Nutrition for a Lifetime

TABLE 13.3   Distribution of Weight Gain During Pregnancy

Tissue	Approximate Pounds
Maternal	
Blood	3
Breasts	2
Uterus	2
Fat, protein, and retained fluid	11
Fetus	7.5
Placenta	1.5
Amniotic fluid*	2.0

* Protective fluid that surrounds fetus.

Source: March of Dimes, *Your pregnant body.* 2009. http://www.marchofdimes.org/pregnancy/your-pregnant-body.aspx Accessed September 12, 2014

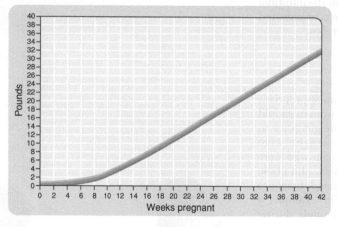

Figure 13.3 Rate of weight gain: Healthy pregnancy. This chart illustrates the rate of maternal weight gain that typically occurs during a healthy pregnancy.

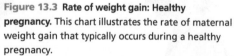

prenatal care specialized health care for pregnant women

Accounting for the Weight Gain

It is important to understand that much of the weight a woman gains during a healthy pregnancy is not body fat. By the end of a full–term pregnancy, the average fetus weighs about 7½ pounds, and the placenta and *amniotic fluid* that surrounds the fetus account for about 3½ pounds. The remaining weight is comprised of tissues and fluids the mother's body gains during pregnancy (*maternal weight* gain). Table 13.3 indicates the typical distribution of weight that is gained during this life stage.

Rate of Weight Gain

For an expectant mother, the rate of weight gain is important, as well as the amount of weight gained. Most pregnant women add up to 4 pounds of weight during the first trimester. Throughout the rest of their pregnancies, healthy women typically gain at a faster rate, 3 to 4 pounds *each* month. Figure 13.3 charts the course of weight gain in a healthy pregnancy. Note how the rate reaches a steady pace of about 1 pound/week during the second and third tri-mesters. During the second and third trimesters, recommended weight gains are higher for underweight women and lower for overweight or obese women.

The Importance of Prenatal Care

Ideally, women of childbearing age should plan for pregnancy and receive dietary advice before becoming pregnant. If this is not possible, *prenatal care* should begin early in pregnancy, because many medical problems that may occur during this life stage can be diagnosed and treated before the health of the mother or her fetus are threatened. **Prenatal care** is specialized to meet the health care needs of pregnant women. Routine prenatal health care includes measuring and monitoring the pregnant woman's weight, blood pressure, blood glucose level, and uterine growth. The prenatal health care provider may also discuss various con-cerns with the expectant mother, such as morning sickness, safe types of physical activity, what to expect during the birth process, and basic infant care skills. Additionally, the health care pro-vider can advise the pregnant woman to make appropriate lifestyle choices, such as avoiding the use of tobacco, alcohol, and illegal substances. Women who receive adequate prenatal care are more likely to have good pregnancy outcomes, including babies who have healthy birth weights, than women who do not receive such care.[16]

During pregnancy, it is important for a woman to decide whether she will breastfeed her baby. Pregnant women who decide to breastfeed their babies should inform their physicians and learn as much as they can about breastfeeding early in their pregnancy.

Gestational Diabetes

According to estimates, 2 to 10% of pregnant women in the United States develop type 2 diabetes during pregnancy (*gestational diabetes*).[17] When a woman has gestational diabetes, her fetus receives too much glucose and converts the excess into fat. Thus, women with this form of diabetes often give birth to HBW babies. After birth, these infants often have difficulty controlling their own blood glu-cose levels and are at risk of becoming overweight as children.

Gestational diabetes can be detected during routine prenatal care. For more information about diabetes during pregnancy, see Chapter 5.

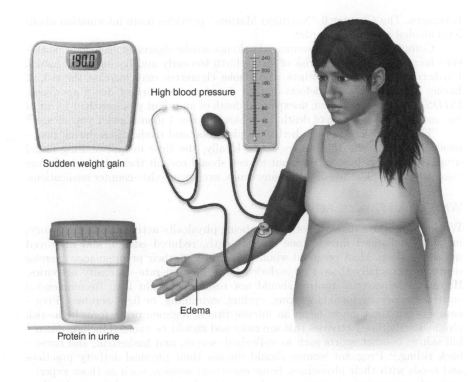

Major signs of preeclampsia include sudden weight gain, elevated blood pressure, edema, and protein in urine.

High blood pressure

Sudden weight gain

Edema

Protein in urine

Gestational Hypertension

Hypertension is a common complication of pregnancy. In the United States, 3 to 5% of pregnant women develop high blood pressure.[18] Rapid weight gain, especially after the fifth month of pregnancy, could be a sign **gestational hypertension** (formerly called "pregnancy–induced" hypertension). Approximately 15 to 25% of women with gestational hypertension develop a more severe form of the condition, called *preeclampsia (pre–e–klamp'–see–a)*.[18] Preeclampsia is characterized by sudden, dramatic increase in weight that is due to edema, particularly of the hands, calves, and face; hypertension; and protein in urine.

Pregnant women who have high risk of preeclampsia are those who are under 20 or over 35 years of age, are obese, have a history of diabetes or hypertension, are African American, and are carrying more than one fetus.[18] If a woman suffering from preeclampsia develops convulsions, her condition is called *eclampsia (e–klamp'–see–a)*. In the United States, eclampsia is the second leading cause of death among pregnant women.[19]

At present, the only effective treatment for preeclampsia and eclampsia is delivering the fetus, but infants born before the twenty–fourth week of pregnancy are unlikely to survive. If the fetus is older than 24 weeks, its mother may be hospitalized for treatment. This practice helps physicians monitor the mother's condition and enables the fetus to mature until it has a better chance of surviving after a premature birth.

Drug Use

Exposure to alcohol and tobacco is harmful to the embryo/fetus. Women who drink alcohol during pregnancy are at risk of having a child with a fetal alcohol spectrum disorder such as FAS (see Fig. 6.27). Scientists do not know if there is a "safe" amount of alcohol that pregnant women can consume; therefore, women of childbearing age who are sexually active or pregnant should avoid alcoholic

gestational hypertension type of hypertension that can develop during pregnancy

beverages. The Chapter 6 "Nutrition Matters" provides more information about fetal alcohol spectrum disorder.

Compared to pregnant women who do not smoke cigarettes, expectant moth—ers who smoke have higher risk of giving birth too early and having LBW babies. Furthermore, expectant mothers who smoke cigarettes may increase the risk of having babies with birth defects or that die of *sudden infant death syndrome* (*SIDS*). SIDS is the sudden, unexplained death of an infant younger than 1 year of age and the leading cause of death for babies between 1 month and 1 year of age.[20]

The use of illegal drugs, herbal supplements, and medications during preg—nancy can also harm the embryo/fetus. Ideally, the time to quit abusing illegal drugs is before pregnancy. Pregnant women should consult their physicians before using herbal supplements or taking any drugs, even over—the—counter medications.

What About Physical Activity?

Women can derive many benefits from being physically active during pregnancy, including enhanced muscle tone and strength, reduced edema, and improved mood and sleep. Most pregnant women can continue their prepregnancy exercise regimens, especially those that included low— or moderate—intensity activities. However, the exercise routine should not result in weight loss. Recommended activities generally include walking, cycling, swimming, or light aerobics. Preg—nancy is not the time to begin an intense fitness regimen or perform high—risk physical activities. Activities that are risky and should be avoided include down—hill skiing; contact sports such as volleyball, soccer, and basketball; and horse—back riding.[21] Pregnant women should discuss their physical activity practices and needs with their physicians. Some expectant women, such as those experi—encing hypertension or premature labor contractions, may need to restrict their physical activity.

Most pregnant women can continue their prepregnancy exercise regimens, especially those that included low- or moderate-intensity activities.

Concept **Checkpoint 13.2**

3. When is an embryo referred to as a fetus?

4. What is the role of the placenta?

5. What is a major factor that determines whether a newborn baby is healthy and survives its first year of life?

6. Why is gestational hypertension dangerous?

7. Identify at least three different nutrition-related signs of pregnancy.

8. How much weight should a woman at a healthy weight gain during pregnancy; how much weight should she gain if she was underweight before becoming pregnant? How much weight should she gain if she was overweight or obese before pregnancy?

9. Why is having adequate folate and iron status important for pregnant women?

10. Discuss the harmful effects that a pregnant woman's alcohol consumption and cigarette smoking can have on her embryo/fetus.

13.3 Infant Nutrition

Learning Outcomes

1. Discuss the physiological processes of lactation and breastfeeding.
2. Discuss the nutrient and energy needs of a lactating woman.
3. Describe benefits that women derive from breastfeeding and infants derive from consuming their mother's milk.
4. Compare the energy and nutrient contents of human milk, cow's milk, and infant formulas.
5. Describe signs that an infant is ready to eat solid foods, and identify appropriate foods for infants.
6. Discuss a healthy infant's rate of growth.

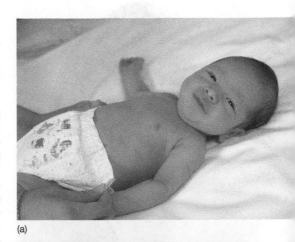

(a)

Rapid physical growth characterizes infancy, the life stage that extends from birth to about 2 years of age. During the first 4 to 6 months of life, a healthy baby doubles its birth weight, and by 1 year of age, an infant's birth weight has tripled. Additionally, an infant's length increases by 50% during its first year of life. Thus, if a baby girl weighs 7 pounds and is 20 inches long at birth, you would expect her to weigh 21 pounds and be 30 inches long by her first birthday (Fig. 13.4).

Compared to older children, an infant needs more energy and nutrients per pound of body weight to support its rapid growth.[1] If an infant's diet lacks adequate energy and nutrients, the baby's growth may slow or even stop. The following sections take a closer look at infant nutrition, including breastfeeding and other infant feeding practices.

Breast Milk Is Best Milk

Two hundred years ago, if a new mother was unable to breastfeed her baby, the child faced certain death—unless a woman who was producing breast milk could be located to suckle (*nurse*) the infant. Today, a new mother can choose to nurse her baby or feed the child an **infant formula,** a synthetic food that simulates human milk. Although both foods provide adequate nutrition for young babies, breast—feeding provides benefits beyond nutrition for the new mother as well as her infant.

Human milk is uniquely formulated to meet the nutrient needs of a newborn baby. During the first couple of days after giving birth, the new mother's breasts produce **colostrum** (*co—loss'—trum*), a yellowish fluid that does not look like milk. (Some women report that colostrum leaked from their breasts late in the pregnancy.)[22] By the end of the first week of lactation, colostrum has undergone a transition to *mature milk*. If you compare the appearance of mature human milk to cow's milk, you will notice that breast milk is more watery than cow's milk and may have a slightly bluish color.

If they are unaware that colostrum is secreted by breasts soon after birth, women may think something is wrong with their ability to produce milk. However, colostrum is a very important first food for babies, because the fluid contains antibodies and immune system cells that can be absorbed by the infant's immature digestive tract. Colostrum also contains a substance that encourages the growth of a type of bacteria, *Lactobacillus bifidus* (*L. bifidus*), in the infant's GI tract. Such biologically active substances help an infant's body fight infections and hasten the maturation of the baby's immune system. Thus, breastfed infants, especially those who are exclusively breastfed, have lower risks of allergies and gastrointestinal, respiratory, and ear infections than formula—fed infants.[23] Furthermore, breastfed babies are less likely to develop childhood asthma, leukemia, obesity, sudden infant death syndrome, and type 1 diabetes than infants who are not breastfed.

(b)

Figure 13.4 Growth rates during infancy. A healthy newborn baby (*a*) grows rapidly during its first year. During the first 4 to 6 months of life, a baby doubles its birth weight, and by 1 year of age, an infant's birth weight has tripled (*b*). Additionally, an infant's length increases by 50% during its first year of life.

---

infant formula synthetic food that simulates human milk

colostrum initial form of breast milk that contains anti-infective properties

504   Chapter 13 Nutrition for a Lifetime

American infants who are breastfed have a lower infant mortality rate than American babies who are not.

Human milk is a rich source of lipids, including cholesterol, and fatty acids such as linoleic acid, *arachidonic acid* (*AA*), and *docosahexaenoic acid* (*DHA*). An infant's nervous system, especially the brain and eyes, depends on AA and DHA for proper development. Furthermore, the fat in breast milk helps supply the energy needed to maintain the infant's overall growth.

The practice of breastfeeding also provides some important advantages for parents, particularly the new mother. Breastfeeding is more convenient and economical than using infant formula. Human milk is readily available; there is no need to purchase cans of infant formula and have them on hand. As milk leaves the breast, it is always fresh, free of bacteria, and ready to feed without mixing, bottling, or warming. Because human milk production requires a considerable amount of energy, lactating women can lose the extra body fat gained during pregnancy faster than mothers who use infant formula. Additionally, women who breastfeed their babies have lower risks of breast cancer (before menopause) and ovarian cancer than women who do not breastfeed. Some of these benefits depend on whether a woman breastfeeds exclusively, that is, provides no other foods, and the number of months the mother nurses her infant. Table 13.4 lists these and several other advantages of breastfeeding.

The Milk Production Process: Lactation

When an infant suckles, nerves in the mother's nipple signal her brain to release prolactin and **oxytocin** (*ox–e–tose'–in*) into her bloodstream. Prolactin stimulates specialized cells in breasts to form milk. These cells carry out the lactation process by synthesizing some nutrients and removing others from the mother's bloodstream and adding them to her milk. Oxytocin plays a different role in establishing successful lactation. This hormone signals breast tissue to "let down" milk. The *let–down reflex* enables milk to travel in several tubes (ducts) to the nipple area. A reflex is a physical response that is automatic and not under conscious control. When let–down occurs, the infant removes the milk by continued sucking (Fig. 13.5). Shortly before the flow of milk begins, the lactating woman often feels a tingling sensation in her nipples, a signal that let–down is occurring.

TABLE 13.4   Advantages of Breastfeeding

Advantages for Infants
Human milk
• Is free of bacteria as it leaves the breast.
• Supplies antibodies and immune cells.
• Is easily digested.
• Reduces risk of food allergies, especially to proteins in infant formulas and cow's milk.
• Changes in composition over time to meet the changing needs of a growing infant.
• Contains zinc, iron, and other minerals in highly absorbable forms.
• Decreases risks of ear, intestinal, and respiratory infections.
• May reduce the risk of asthma, obesity, and type 1 diabetes in childhood.

Advantages for New Mothers
Breastfeeding
• Reduces uterine bleeding after delivery.
• Promotes shrinkage of the uterus to its prepregnancy size.
• Decreases the risk of breast cancer (before menopause) and ovarian cancer.
• May promote maternal weight loss.
• May enhance bonding with the infant.
• Is less expensive and more convenient than feeding infant formula.

oxytocin hormone that elicits the "let-down" response and causes the uterus to contract

Did You Know?

When a new mother breastfeeds her newborn immediately after delivery, oxytocin signals her uterus to contract, reducing the risk of excessive uterine bleeding.

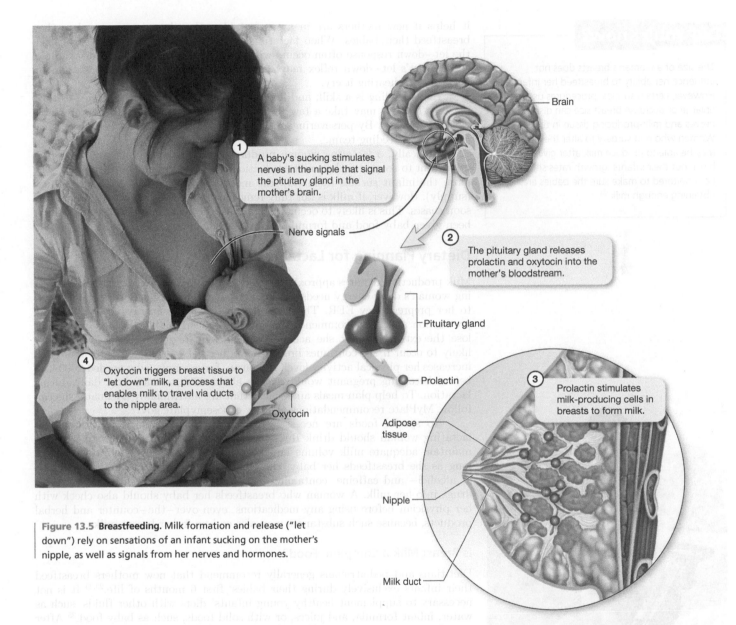

① A baby's sucking stimulates nerves in the nipple that signal the pituitary gland in the mother's brain.

Brain

Nerve signals

② The pituitary gland releases prolactin and oxytocin into the mother's bloodstream.

Pituitary gland

④ Oxytocin triggers breast tissue to "let down" milk, a process that enables milk to travel via ducts to the nipple area.

Oxytocin

Prolactin

③ Prolactin stimulates milk-producing cells in breasts to form milk.

Adipose tissue

Nipple

Milk duct

Figure 13.5 Breastfeeding. Milk formation and release ("let down") rely on sensations of an infant sucking on the mother's nipple, as well as signals from her nerves and hormones.

Embarrassment, emotional stress and tension, pain, and fatigue can easily block the let–down reflex. For example, if a lactating mother is tense or upset, let–down does not occur, and her infant will not be able to obtain milk when it suckles. When this happens, the hungry infant becomes frustrated and angry, and the mother may respond by becoming even more tense and upset, setting up a vicious cycle. At this point, new mothers often give up breastfeeding, reporting that they tried to suckle their babies but were unable to "produce" milk.

Lactating women need to be aware of the connection between their emotional state and failure to let down. To smooth the path to successful lactation, it helps if new mothers are in a comfortable, relaxed environment when they breastfeed their babies. When lactation and breastfeeding are well established, the let—down response often occurs without the need for suckling. For example, the mother's let—down reflex may be triggered just by thinking about nursing her infant or hearing it cry.

Breastfeeding is a skill, and like other skills, it takes some practice to fully master. Thus, it may take a few weeks for the new mother to feel comfortable with the process. By persevering, she and her baby are likely to become a suc—cessful breastfeeding team.

Typically, a lactating woman produces over 3 cups of milk per day.[9] It is important to recognize that milk production relies on "supply and demand." The more the infant suckles (demand), the more milk its mother's breasts produce (supply). However, if milk is not fully removed from the breasts, milk production soon ceases. This is likely to occur when infants are not hungry because they have been given baby food and formula to supplement breast milk feedings.

Dietary Planning for Lactating Women

Milk production requires approximately 800 kcal every day. However, the lactat—ing woman's daily energy needs can be met by adding only about 300 to 400 kcal to her prepregnancy EER. The difference between the energy needed for milk production and the recommended energy intake can enable the new mother to lose the extra body fat she accumulated during pregnancy. This loss is more likely to occur if she continues breastfeeding her baby for 6 months or more and increases her physical activity level. A woman, for example, who needed 2000 kcal before becoming pregnant would require about 2300 to 2400 kcal daily during lactation. To help plan meals and snacks that are nutritionally adequate, she can follow MyPlate recommendations at www.choosemyplate.gov.

No special foods are necessary to sustain milk production. However, a lactating woman should drink fluids every time her infant suckles to help her maintain adequate milk volume and keep her body properly hydrated. For as long as she breastfeeds her baby, the lactating mother should limit her intake of alcohol— and caffeine—containing beverages because her body secretes these drugs into her milk. A woman who breastfeeds her baby should also check with her physician before using any medications, even over—the—counter and herbal products, because such substances may also end up in her breast milk.

Is Breast Milk a Complete Food?

Dietitians and pediatricians generally recommend that new mothers breastfeed their infants exclusively during their babies' first 6 months of life.[23,25] It is not necessary to supplement healthy young infants' diets with other fluids, such as water, infant formula, and juices, or with solid foods, such as baby food.[25] After an infant reaches 6 months of age, breastfeeding should continue, but the infant can also be offered some appropriate solid foods. Breastfeeding may be combined with infant foods until the child's first birthday. However, there is no reason why children cannot be breastfed for longer periods. Throughout the world, many mothers continue to nurse their babies well past the babies' first birthdays, but in the United States, this practice is uncommon.

Although breast milk is highly nutritious, it is not a complete food for all infants. Human milk may contain inadequate amounts of vitamins D and B—12, and the minerals iron and fluoride. The American Academy of Pediatrics (AAP) recommends all breastfed infants be given a supplement that supplies 400 IU of vitamin D per day until they are consuming that amount of the vita—min from food or infant formula. Exposing the infant to some sun can also help meet part of the child's vitamin D needs (Fig. 13.6). If a lactating woman is a

Figure 13.6 Vitamin D and infants. Exposing an infant's skin to some direct sunlight enables the baby's body to form vitamin D.

total vegetarian and she does not consume a source of vitamin B–12, she should consult her physician concerning the need for vitamin B–12 supplementation. When breastfed infants are about 6 months old, they should also be consuming some iron–containing solid foods, because the amount of iron in their mother's milk may no longer meet their needs. Furthermore, a fluoride supplement may be necessary for breastfed babies. Before giving any dietary supplements to their baby, parents or caregivers should discuss their infant's nutritional needs with the child's physician.

Quitting Too Soon

Nearly all healthy women are physically capable of breastfeeding their infants. In 2011, 79.2% of American women started breastfeeding their babies soon after birth.[26] Within 2 days of birth, 19.4% of the breastfed babies were also consum— ing formula. By the time the infants were 6 months old, 49.4% continued to be breastfed. By their first birthday, only about 27% of the babies were still being nourished with their mother's milk.

Women who breastfeed their newborns often stop the practice within 6 months. There are many reasons why women discontinue nursing their infants too soon. New mothers often quit because they lack information about and support for breastfeeding their babies. Some women discontinue breastfeeding because of uncertainty over how much milk their babies are consuming. Baby bottles are marked to indicate ounces, so a mother who bottle–feeds her infant can easily measure the amount of formula consumed. A lactating mother, how— ever, has to observe her baby for cues indicating the child is full. When a breast— feeding baby is no longer interested in nursing and stops, its mother has to assume the infant is satisfied with the feeding. A well–nourished breastfed infant will gain weight normally and generally have six or more wet diapers as well as one or two soft bowel movements per day. Parents or caregivers who are con— cerned about their infants' food intake or nutritional status should consult their physician immediately.

Many new mothers discontinue breastfeeding before their babies are 6 months old because they need to return to work and have caregivers feed their babies. Although lactating women can learn to express milk from their breasts and preserve it for later feedings, many workplaces do not have comfortable, private facilities for women to express milk and then store it safely.

To enhance the likelihood that a nursing mother continues to breastfeed, it is helpful to enlist the support of a female relative or friend who has successfully breastfed her children. Furthermore, the woman's partner needs to understand and appreciate the function of the human breast as a source of nearly perfect nourishment for infants. New mothers are unlikely to begin and continue nursing their babies without their partners' support. La Leche League is an international organization dedicated to providing education and support for breastfeeding women (1–877–4–LALECHE or www.llli.org). Also, hospitals may employ lac— tation consultants or specialists. Lactation consultants are often nurses who are trained to provide information and advice about breastfeeding. For more infor— mation about breastfeeding, visit http://www.cdc.gov/breastfeeding/.

This mother is using an electric device to express milk in a private room at her workplace. She will chill the milk and give it to her baby's caregiver for bottle-feeding.

Infant Formula Feeding

Not every woman wants or is able to breastfeed her baby. Infant formulas are a safe and nutritionally adequate source of nutrients for babies who are not breastfed (Fig. 13.7). To produce artificial milk for babies, infant formula manu— facturers alter cow's milk to improve its digestibility and nutrient content. Infant

508   Chapter 13   Nutrition for a Lifetime

Figure 13.7 Infant formulas. Infant formulas provide a safe and nutritionally adequate source of nutrients for babies who are not breastfed.

casein major protein in cow's milk

formulas generally contain heat—treated proteins from cow's milk, lactose and/or sucrose, and vegetable oil. Infant formulas generally lack cholesterol, but some of these products have the fatty acids DHA and AA added to them. Vitamins and minerals are added to the product, and in some instances, infant formula contains higher levels of micronutrients than human milk. Although infant formulas mimic the water, macronutrient, and micronutrient content of human milk, their compositions are not identical to human milk (Table 13.5). Formula manufacturers have been unable to duplicate human antibodies and other unique immune system factors that are in breast milk.

An interesting feature of human milk is that its fat content changes during each feeding, which usually lasts about 20 minutes. In the beginning of the session, the mother's milk is low in fat, but as her infant continues to suckle, the fat content of her milk gradually increases.[27] The higher fat content of the "hind milk" may make the baby feel satisfied and, as a result, discontinue feeding. Infant formulas, however, have uniform composition; that is, they do not change their fat content during a feeding session. Thus, the mother or infant caregiver is more likely to control the amount of formula the baby consumes, possibly leading to overfeeding. Nevertheless, the overall energy content of human milk is about the same as that of infant formulas (about 20 kcal per ounce).

Experts with the AAP recommend that caregivers provide an iron—fortified infant formula for babies who are not breastfed. Not all infant formulas contain iron, so it is important to read the product's label before purchasing it. Formula—fed babies may also need a source of fluoride, but caregivers should check with their infants' physicians before providing a supplement containing the mineral. For babies who are allergic to infant formulas made from cow's milk proteins, similar products made with soy or other proteins are available.

What About Cow's Milk?

Why not feed fresh fluid cow's milk to an infant? Cow's milk is too high in minerals and protein and does not contain enough carbohydrate to meet an infant's nutrient needs (see Table 13.5). In addition, infants have more difficulty digesting **casein** (*kay'—seen*), the major protein in cow's milk, than the major proteins in human

TABLE 13.5 Comparing Approximate Compositions of Human Milk, Cow's Milk, and Iron-Fortified Infant Formulas (per Ounce)

Milk or Iron-Fortified Formula	Energy (kcal/oz)	Protein (g/oz)	Carbo-hydrate (g/oz)	Fat (g/oz)	Choles-terol (mg/oz)	Iron (mg/oz)	Calcium (mg/oz)
Human milk	22.0	0.32	2.12	1.35	4.00	0.01	10.0
Cow's milk, whole	19.0	0.96	1.46	0.99	3.00	0.01	34.0
Cow's milk, fat-free	10.0	1.03	1.52	0.02	1.00	0.01	37.0
Cow's milk protein-based formulas							
Similac with iron	20.0	0.41	2.10	1.08	1.00	0.36	16.0
Enfamil with iron	19.0	0.42	2.19	1.07	0.00	0.36	16.0
Soy protein-based formulas							
ProSobee with iron	19.0	0.50	1.86	1.07	0.00	0.36	21.0
Similac Isomil with iron	20.0	0.49	2.04	1.09	0.00	0.36	21.0

Source: Data from U.S. Department of Agriculture, Agricultural Research Service. What's in the foods you eat *search tool, 5.0.* http://www.ars.usda.gov/services/docs.htm?docid=17032 Accessed February 20, 2014

milk. Cow's milk can also contribute to intestinal bleeding and iron deficiency.[28] Thus, whole cow's milk should not be fed to infants until they are 1 year of age.[29]

Whole milk is major source of saturated fat in young children's diets. According to the AAP, reduced—fat forms of milk can be given to children who are between 1 and 2 years of age, but only as part of a diet that supplies 30% of total calories from fat.[29] To reduce the risk of developing cardiovascular disease later in life, children over age 2 years should consume low—fat or fat—free dairy products.[29]

Allergies   Allergies are immune system responses to the presence of foreign proteins in the body. Allergies to proteins in foods, especially cow's milk proteins, often begin in infancy and may persist through childhood. Signs and symptoms of food allergies typically include the following:

- Vomiting, diarrhea, intestinal gas and pain, bloating, or constipation

- Itchy, swollen, or reddened skin

- Runny nose and breathing difficulties, such as asthma

Compared to breastfed infants, formula—fed babies have a greater risk of food allergies. When a woman has a personal or family history of food allergies, she may be able to prevent her children from developing such allergies if she breastfeeds her babies exclusively for 6 months. Infants rarely develop allergic reactions to food proteins that enter breast milk from the mother's bloodstream.

Introducing Solid Foods

Before 6 months of age, babies' nutritional needs can generally be met with human milk and/or infant formula. Solid ("complementary" or "baby") foods should not be introduced to infants until they are about 6 months of age.[30] At this age, many infants need the additional calories supplied by solid foods. Breastfed babies may also need a dietary source of iron, because their stores of the mineral are usually exhausted about 6 months after birth. Nevertheless, caregivers should continue to provide human milk or iron—fortified infant formula as the foundation of the baby's diet for the first year.

Many new parents are anxious to start feeding their young infants solid food. However, babies are not physically mature enough to consume solids before they are 4 to 6 months of age. For example, a baby's kidney functions are quite limited until the child is about 4 to 6 weeks of age. Additionally, an infant's digestive tract cannot readily digest starch before the child is about 3 months old.

Infants are born with the **extrusion reflex,** an involuntary response that occurs when a solid or semisolid object is placed in an infant's mouth. As a result of this reflex, a young baby thrusts its tongue forward, pushing the object out of its mouth. Thus, trying to feed the infant solid foods is a messy, frustrating process, as the child automatically pushes the food out of its mouth. Liquid foods, such as breast milk or infant formula, do not elicit the extrusion reflex, so the baby swallows fluids.

As the infant reaches 4 to 6 months of age, the extrusion reflex disappears, and the child has developed the physiological abilities to digest, metabolize, and excrete a wider range of foods. Moreover, a 6—month—old infant can usually sit up with back support and coordinate muscular control over his or her mouth and neck movements. These signs indicate the baby is ready physically to eat solid foods, is less likely to choke on such foods, and can turn his or her head away from food when full.

Weaning is the gradual process of shifting an infant from breastfeeding or bottle—feeding to drinking from a cup and eating solid foods. Pediatricians often

Food & Nutrition tip

Do not heat infant formula or human milk in a microwave oven. The heat can destroy immune factors in human milk and create hot spots that can scald an infant's tongue.

extrusion reflex involuntary response in which a young infant thrusts its tongue forward when a solid or semisolid object is placed in its mouth

weaning gradual process of shifting from breastfeeding or bottle-feeding to drinking from a cup and eating solid foods

Did You Know?

Many parents think adding solid foods to infants' diets helps babies sleep through the night. Actually, this developmental milestone generally occurs around 3 to 4 months of age, regardless of what infants are eating.

| Figure 13.8 **Learning to drink from a 'sippy' cup.**

recommend introducing an iron—fortified infant cereal made from rice as the first solid food. However, pureed meat or chicken are better sources of iron for babies. After feeding the infant a solid food for the first time, caregivers should offer the food to the baby for at least 5 days and observe the infant for signs and symp—toms of food allergy. If the infant appears to tolerate the food, caregivers can add a new food to the baby's diet, such as another type of meat or a cooked, strained vegetable. As each new food is introduced, caregivers should wait 3 to 5 days before adding a different food to the child's diet.[30] If the infant develops diarrhea, vomiting, or a rash during this period, he or she may be allergic to the new food.

It is a good idea to avoid giving mixed foods such as casseroles or commercially prepared baby food "dinners" to infants. If the baby has an aller—gic response after eating a food mixture, it will be difficult to determine which ingredient was responsible. Serving mixed foods is acceptable when the child has eaten each ingredient individually without having an allergic response.

Infants who have a high risk of food allergy have a parent or sibling who has a history of allergies, including food allergy. Foods that are associated with allergic responses in infants include egg whites, chocolate, nuts, and cow's milk. Therefore, caregivers should not offer these foods to high—risk babies under 6 months of age. Many babies outgrow food allergies during childhood, but some children remain allergic to the foods through adulthood.

Many varieties of strained baby food are available at the supermarket. Single—food items, such as carrots or peas, are more nutrient—dense choices for feeding infants than mixed dinners and desserts. Most brands have no added salt, but some fruit desserts contain a lot of added sugar. As an alternative, caregiv—ers can prepare their own baby food by taking plain, unseasoned cooked foods and pureeing them in a blender. If a large amount of the item is blended, the pureed food can be poured into an ice cube tray, covered with a plastic bag, and frozen. When it is feeding time, an ice cube portion of the baby food can be popped out of the tray and warmed.

At about 6 to 8 months of age, the baby's first set of teeth, the "primary teeth," begin to appear. These teeth are important for proper nutrition because they help the child bite and chew food. By 8 to 12 months of age, most infants can use their fingers to pick up and chew "finger foods" such as crackers, toast, and cooked string beans. Babies can also hold a bottle and practice drinking from a special cup ("sippy cup") that has a lid with a spout (Fig. 13.8). Babies need to practice self—feeding skills, even if it means playing with food and creating messes. By about 10 months of age, many infants are mastering self—feeding and making the transition from baby foods to menu items that the rest of the family enjoys.

What Not to Feed an Infant

By the end of the first year, an infant should be consuming many different foods—grain products, meats, fruits, and vegetables—along with breast milk or infant formula. Introducing a baby to various foods helps the child learn about different tastes, odors, and textures. However, certain foods and beverages are not appropriate for infants. Avoid feeding an infant these things:

- **Honey.** This product may contain spores of *Clostridium botulinum* that can produce a potentially fatal toxin in children who are under 1 year old (see Chapter 12).

- **Excessive infant formula or human milk.** Depending on their age, most infants need less than 30 ounces of human milk or infant formula daily. A

| Babies need to practice self-feeding skills, even if it means playing with food and creating messes.

Food & Nutrition tips

When feeding solid foods to an infant:

- Use a baby-sized spoon—a small spoon with a broad handle.
- Hold the infant comfortably on your lap, as for breastfeeding or bottle-feeding, but in a more upright position to ease swallowing.
- Add some breast milk or infant formula to the cereal, and place a small dab of the semisolid food on the spoon's tip. Gently place the spoon on the infant's tongue and tilt it so the food slides onto the tongue. If the infant spits it out, do not continue with the feeding.
- Expect the infant to take only two or three bites during these early feeding sessions.

child who drinks too much milk may not eat enough solid foods that contain nutrients lacking in milk.

- **Semisolid baby cereal in a baby bottle that has the nipple opening enlarged.** This practice contributes to overfeeding and does not help the child learn self−feeding skills.

- **Candy, flavored gelatin water, or soft drinks.** These items provide few micronutrients.

- **Small pieces of hard or coarse foods.** Foods such as hot dogs (unless finely cut into sticks, not coin shapes), whole nuts, grapes, chunks of cooked meat, raw carrots, popcorn, and peanut butter can cause choking. Caregivers should supervise meals to keep young children from stuffing too much food in their mouths.

- **Excessive amounts of apple or pear juice.** The fructose and *sorbitol*, a sugar alcohol, contained in these juices can lead to diarrhea. Also, if the infant drinks fruit juice or fruit drinks rather than breast milk or infant formula, the child may not be receiving adequate amounts of calcium and other essential minerals.

- **Unpasteurized (raw) milk.** Raw milk may be contaminated with bacteria or viruses.

- **Goat's milk.** Goat's milk is low in iron, folate, and vitamins C and D.

Baby Bottle Caries

At bedtime, many caregivers place infants in their cribs with a baby bottle contain− ing formula, juice, or a sugar−sweetened drink. This practice is not recommended, because the sleepy infant sucks slowly, allowing the carbohydrate−containing fluid to bathe the child's teeth and provide a source of nutrients for bacteria that stick to teeth. These bacteria produce acids that dissolve tooth enamel, causing cavities to form in the teeth (*dental caries*). Dentists often refer to this condition as "baby bottle caries." To reduce the risk of baby bottle caries, infants should be given only water in their bedtime bottles.

Concept Checkpoint 13.3

11. What is the "let-down reflex"?
12. How does lactation affect a new mother's energy needs?
13. What is colostrum, and why is it a valuable first food for breastfed babies?
14. Dietitians and other health experts recommend that infants be breastfed exclusively during their first _____ months of life.
15. List at least five benefits that infants derive from breastfeeding.
16. Identify at least three benefits that women derive from breastfeeding their babies.
17. Compare the energy, macronutrient, and calcium contents of an ounce of human milk with those of an ounce of cow's milk.
18. Identify at least three physiological indications that an infant is ready to eat solid foods.
19. How much should a healthy infant's weight increase during its first year of life?

13.4 The Preschool Years

Learning Outcomes

1 Identify some major nutrition-related health concerns facing American preschool children.

2 Summarize practical suggestions for encouraging healthy eating habits among preschool children.

3 Describe steps caregivers can take to improve the nutritional status of preschool children.

Figure 13.9 Age-appropriate portion sizes. Healthy young children should not be expected to eat adult-size portions of food. Each of these children is eating half a sandwich, a reasonable amount for their age.

Childhood can be divided into the preschool period (2 to 5 years of age), the school—age period (6 to 11 years of age), and adolescence (12 to 19 years of age). In this section, we focus on some major nutrition concerns of preschool children. The rapid growth rate that characterizes the first 12 months of life tapers off quickly during the preschool years and proceeds at a slow but steady rate until the end of childhood. If an average infant's growth rate did not slow down, he or she might weigh about 190 pounds and be about 5 feet, 7 inches tall by 3 years of age! However, the average 3—year—old weighs about 32 pounds and is about 3 feet in height.

The preferred growth standard for children who are 2 to 20 years of age is the *body mass index (BMI)—for—age*. The BMI—for—age is a number calculated from the child's height and weight. BMI charts for children are both sex— and age—specific (see Appendix F). An *overweight* child has a BMI—for—age that is at or above the 85th percentile and lower than the 95th percentile for children of the same age and sex.[31] An *obese* child has a BMI—for—age that is at or above the 95th percentile for children of the same age and sex.

TABLE 13.6   Preschool Children: Daily Food Plan Based on MyPlate Recommendations

Energy/Food Group	2 Years	3 to 5 Years
Kilocalories*	1000	1400
Grains	3 oz	5 oz
Vegetables	1 cup	1½ cups
Fruits	1 cup	1½ cups
Dairy	2 cups	2½ cups
Protein foods	2 oz	4 oz

* Kilocalorie estimates are based on age and 30 to 60 minutes of physical activity.

Source: U.S. Department of Agriculture: *MyPlate*. www.choosemyplate.gov/myplate/index.aspx. Accessed July 26, 2014

As the growth rate slows after infancy, preschoolers' appetites decrease because they do not need as much food. Parents and other caregivers must recognize that a 3—year—old child should not be expected to eat as eagerly as he or she did as an infant. Furthermore, children do not have the stomach capacity to eat adult—size portions of foods (Fig. 13.9). When planning meals and snacks for children, caregivers should emphasize nutrient—dense foods, such as lean meats, low—fat dairy products, whole—grain cereals, fruits, nuts, and vegetables. Although many ready—to—eat cereals are sweetened with sugar, it is not necessary to eliminate such foods. Caregivers, however, should read product labels and choose varieties with less added sugar. Additionally, it is important to monitor children's intake of sweets, because sugary items can crowd out more nutritious foods from their diets. Table 13.6 presents a day's food group selections, based on MyPlate recommendations, that are appropriate for children who are 2 to 5 years of age.

Snacks

Snacking is not necessarily a bad habit, especially if snacks are nutrient dense and fit into the child's overall diet. Nutritious snacks can be offered at midmorning or midafternoon, when the child is likely to become hungry between meals. A healthy 4— or 5—year—old child can safely eat raw vegetables without fear of choking. Nutritious dips, such as the yogurt dip in this chapter's "Recipe for Healthy Living," may make raw vegetables more appealing to children. Table 13.7 lists some nutritious snacks that children tend to like.

Fostering Positive Eating Behaviors

Parents often refer to their preschool children as "picky eaters" because the youngsters do not eat everything offered to them. Furthermore, it is not unusual for children to have "food jags," periods in which they refuse to eat a food that they liked in the past or want to eat only a particular food, such as peanut butter and jelly sandwiches or cereal and milk. Picky eating and food jags may be expressions of a child's growing need for independence. Caregivers should avoid nagging, forcing, and bribing children to eat. Instead, caregivers can offer the children a variety of healthy foods each day and allow the youngsters to choose which items and how much to eat.

Many children, especially preschool children, resist eating new foods. The temperature, appearance, texture, and taste of a food influence whether children will sample it. For example, young children often reject lumpy or hot—temperature

TABLE 13.7   Nutritious Snacks

- Peanut butter spread on graham crackers
- Fruit smoothies (see Chapter 9 "Recipe for Healthy Living")
- Fruit salad (or cut-up fruit)
- Mini-pizzas (half an English muffin, topped with tomato sauce and mozzarella cheese, and heated in toaster oven or microwave oven)
- Plain, low-fat yogurt topped with granola or fresh fruit
- Peanuts, cashews, or sunflower seeds
- Cheese melted on whole-wheat crackers
- Dried fruit
- Trail mix
- Ready-to-eat cereal
- Vegetable sticks dipped in hummus

Eating vegetables may become more appealing when children help grow, select, or prepare fresh produce.

Food & Nutrition tips

- Foods with bright colors, crisp textures, and sweet or mild flavors usually appeal to children. When planning meals, consider including foods with these attractive characteristics.

- As a parent, you may want to consider having the "one bite policy." According to this policy, your child should try at least one bite of each new food provided at mealtimes.

- To stimulate your child's appetite, try serving food on a small colorful plate that is designed to appeal to young children.

- Keep in mind that you are your children's role model for food choices and physical activity habits. If you eat a variety of nutrient-dense foods and are physically active, your children are likely to eat such foods and be active as well.

foods. Sometimes children object to having foods mixed together such as in stews and casseroles, even though they like the ingredients when served separately. It is not unusual for young children to dislike vegetables that have strong flavors or odors, such as broccoli, onions, and asparagus. The idea of eating vegetables may become more appealing when children help grow, select, or prepare fresh produce. Nevertheless, it is important to recognize that everyone, including a child, is entitled to dislike certain foods.

The social atmosphere can make mealtimes enjoyable or unbearable, which in turn influences a child's desire to eat. Mealtimes should be happy, social occasions to enjoy healthful foods with parents or other caregivers. The kitchen table should not become a battleground in which adults use threats or bribes to force children to eat unfamiliar foods. For example, avoid telling a child, "You'll just sit there until you clean your plate" or "You can have a cupcake if you eat your peas." When a child refuses to eat, have the youngster remain at the table for a while. If the child continues to be disinterested in eating, remove the food and wait until the next scheduled meal or snack.

Healthy children are not in danger of starving if they skip a meal. A child who is not hungry at mealtimes may have eaten a snack before the meal at a friend's home. If a child's lack of appetite persists, caretakers should consult the child's physician to rule out illness.

Common Food-Related Concerns

Nutrition–related problems that often affect preschool children are iron deficiency, dental caries, food allergies, and obesity. Food allergies are discussed in Chapter 7. Section 13.7 focuses on obesity during childhood and adolescence.

Iron Deficiency

Iron deficiency can lead to decreased physical stamina and learning ability, and resistance to infection. The best way to prevent iron deficiency in children is to provide foods that are good sources of iron, such as lean meat and enriched breads and cereals. Milk and other dairy products are poor sources of iron, so caregivers may need to limit daily servings of foods from this food group. Preschool children should consume 2 to 2.5 cups/day of fat–free or low–fat milk or equivalent dairy products.[32] Chapter 9 provides more information about iron deficiency.

Dental Caries

Many preschool children have had one or more dental caries by the time they enter school. If dental caries are not treated, jaw pain, gum infection, and tooth loss can occur. The following tips can help reduce the risk of dental caries in children:

- Brush teeth with a pea–sized amount of fluoride–containing toothpaste twice daily.

- Provide routine pediatric dental care and fluoridated drinking water.

- Any carbohydrate can contribute to dental caries, so reduce the number of snacks the child eats. Also, provide the child with more nutrient–dense snacks, such as raw fruits and vegetables or pieces of cheese.[33]

- If preschoolers want to chew gum, have them chew sugarless gum to reduce the risk of dental caries.[34]

Concept **Checkpoint 13.4**

20. What is a "food jag"?
21. Discuss effects that iron deficiency can have on children.
22. List at least three steps caregivers can take to reduce the risk of dental caries in children.

13.5 School-Age Children

Learning Outcomes

1 Compare the typical eating patterns of school-age children with those of preschool children.

2 Identify some major nutrition-related health concerns facing American school-age children.

3 Summarize practical suggestions for encouraging healthy eating habits among school-age children.

Many school—age children adopt diets that are nutritionally inadequate.[35] Compared to preschoolers, older children often skip breakfast. Furthermore, school—age children typically consume more foods away from home and more fried items and sweetened beverages than younger children. Diets of school—age children tend to provide excessive amounts of solid fat, added sugars, and sodium.[35,36] Excessive intakes of fat and sugar contribute to the development of obesity, and high intake of sodium may contribute to hypertension among children.

School—age children often do not eat recommended amounts of fruits and vegetables, and the youngsters typically consume less than recommended amounts of dietary fiber. Low fiber intake contributes to constipation; as many as 10% of American children suffer from chronic constipation.[37]

Table 13.8 presents a day's food recommendations for healthy school—age children, based on MyPlate. The www.choosemyplate.gov website has a special

TABLE 13.8 Six- to 11-Year-Old Children: Daily Food Plan Based on MyPlate Recommendations

Energy/Food Group	Age/Sex 6 Years		Age 7–8 Years	Age/Sex 9 Years		Age 10–11 Years	
	Girls	Boys	Both	Girls	Boys	Girls	Boys
Kilocalories*	1400	1600	1600	1600	1800	1800	2000
Grains	5 oz	5 oz	5 oz	5 oz	6 oz	6 oz	6 oz
Vegetables	1.5 cups	2 cups	2 cups	2 cups	2.5 cups	2.5 cups	2.5 cups
Fruits	1.5 cups	1.5 cups	1.5 cups	1.5 cups	1.5 cups	1.5 cups	2 cups
Dairy	2.5 cups	2.5 cups	3 cups	3 cups	3 cups	3 cups	3 cups
Protein foods	4 oz	5 oz	5 oz	5 oz	5 oz	5 oz	5.5 oz

* Kilocalorie estimates are based on age, sex, and 30 to 60 minutes of physical activity.

Source: U.S. Department of Agriculture: ChooseMyPlate.gov: Supertracker & other tools: Daily food plans & worksheets. http://www.choosemyplate.gov/supertracker-tools/daily-food-plans.html Accessed February 23, 2014

series of web pages for children who are 6 to 11 years of age. Children can visit the "MyPlate Kids' Place" website and play the interactive "Blast Off Game." To test the game, visit http://www.choosemyplate.gov/kids/index.html.

Caregivers can help improve children's diets by encouraging youngsters to eat breakfast regularly. Children who routinely eat breakfast are more likely to have better diets and healthier body weights than children who skip this meal.[38] Breakfast menus do not need to feature traditional fare such as bacon, eggs, waffles, or pancakes. For example, leftovers from the previous night's dinner can be eaten for breakfast. Convenient "fast breakfasts" that school–age children can prepare quickly include ready–to–eat cereal with milk and fruit, cottage cheese and fruit, a peanut butter and jelly sandwich, or yogurt topped with trail mix or pieces of fresh fruit.

Parents and other caregivers need to be concerned about foods that are available at school and obtain answers to the following questions: What kinds of foods are offered for school breakfasts and lunches? Does the school have vend–ing machines accessible to youngsters? If so, what kinds of foods and beverages are sold from these machines? Do vending machines offer competitively priced, nutrient–dense foods? What can be done to ensure that the machines and the school's cafeteria provide nutritious foods that children will eat? Furthermore, what efforts are being made to teach children about proper nutrition while they are in school?

Food & Nutrition tips

The following tips can help you improve your child's diet:

- Guide your family's food choices instead of dictating what they eat.
- Eat meals together as a family as often as possible.
- If necessary, reduce the amount of fat, especially saturated and trans fat, in your family's diet.
- Do not place your child on a restrictive diet, unless the diet is recommended by the child's physician.
- Avoid using food as a reward or punishment.
- Encourage the child to drink water instead of sugar-sweetened beverages.
- Keep healthy snacks (such as fat-free or low-fat milk, fresh fruit, and vegetables) on hand.
- Serve at least 5 servings of fruits and vegetables each day.
- Discourage eating meals or snacks while watching TV.
- Encourage the child to eat a nutrient-dense breakfast daily.

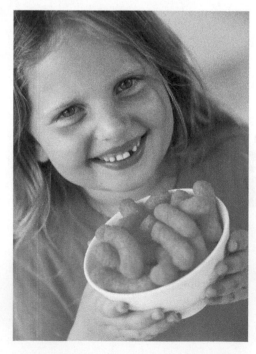

Parents and other caregivers need to be concerned about their children's food choices.

Concept **Checkpoint 13.5**

23. Discuss how young children's eating patterns often change when they enter school.

24. List at least three tips for improving diets of school-age children.

13.6 Adolescence

Learning Outcomes

1 Discuss puberty and how it affects an adolescent's energy and nutrient needs.

2 Identify some major nutrition-related health concerns facing American adolescents.

Adolescence is the life stage in which a child matures physically into an adult. During adolescence, the reproductive organs increase in size and begin functioning properly. Furthermore, individuals typically attain their full height by the end of adolescence.[39] During this life stage, youth also develop emotionally, intellectually, and socially as they prepare for their adult roles.

Healthy adolescents learn to function independently of their adult caregivers. Thus, youths face a variety of lifestyle choices, including decisions regarding eating and physical activity habits. Such decisions often set the stage for the quality of their health in adulthood. For many teens, however, pressure to conform to fads and be influenced by other adolescents ("peer pressure") negatively affects their diets and overall health.

Puberty signals the end of childhood. Most boys begin puberty when they are between 10 and 12 years of age; most girls begin puberty between 8 and 10 years of age.[39] Puberty is a period characterized by dramatic physical changes, including increases in height and weight, known as the adolescent "growth spurt."

Most girls begin their growth spurt between 10 and 13 years of age. Boys begin their growth spurt later than girls—generally when they are between 12 and 15 years of age. Girls usually begin menstruating during their growth spurt. A girl's skeletal growth is almost complete about 2 years after her first menstrual period, whereas boys typically continue to gain stature until they are in their early twenties. The timing of puberty and growth spurts can vary widely, primarily due to genetic, environmental, and nutritional factors. Figure 13.10 shows a group of adolescents who are about the same age but are at different stages of physical maturity.

When their growth spurts begin, adolescents eat more to support their higher energy needs. If maturing boys and girls choose to eat nutritious foods and maintain a high level of physical activity, they can take advantage of their increased hunger and gain lean body mass without gaining excess body fat.

Nutrition-Related Concerns of Adolescents

People generally establish their future eating habits and physical activity practices when they are teenagers. According to results of a nationwide survey, many youth are not following healthy diets. In 2013, 19% of the students had not consumed milk and 13% had skipped breakfast during the same period of time.[41] According

adolescence life stage in which a child matures physically into an adult

Did You Know?

Many teenagers are plagued by *acne*—pimples, blackheads, and reddening of the skin—that often occurs on the face, upper back, and chest. Many people think acne is caused by eating certain foods, especially greasy foods and chocolate. However, there is a lack of scientific evidence that links specific foods with acne. According to physicians who treat skin disorders (*dermatologists*), hormonal changes normally associated with puberty cause acne.[40]

Figure 13.10 Different rates of physical maturity. Although these adolescents are about the same age, they are in different stages of physical maturity.

to findings of this survey, only about 47% of the high school students met recom—mended levels of physical activity during the 7 days before the survey.

Adolescents whose diets rely heavily on energy—dense foods purchased at fast—food restaurants or vending machines may be setting the stage for the development of obesity, type 2 diabetes, heart disease, and other serious chronic diseases. Obesity, eating disorders, and low iron and calcium intakes are major nutrition—related concerns of adolescents. Youth, especially teenage girls, are at risk of developing disordered eating practices and eating disorders. You can learn more about eating disorders by reading the Chapter 10 "Nutrition Matters." In this chapter, Section 13.7 discusses adolescent obesity.

Iron and Calcium Intakes

Adolescent boys may become iron deficient during their growth spurt because their iron intakes do not keep up with their bodies' needs for the mineral. Ado—lescent girls are also at risk of iron deficiency, especially if their diets lack iron—rich foods and they have heavy menstrual blood losses. Iron deficiency leads to increased fatigue and decreased ability to concentrate and learn. Teenagers need to understand why iron is important for good health and incorporate reliable food sources of the mineral in their diets (see Chapter 9). Over the last 20 years, many adolescents have switched from drinking milk to drinking soft drinks. Dietitians and other nutrition experts are concerned that many adolescents have inadequate calcium intakes because of this practice. Inadequate calcium intake during ado—lescence is associated with decreased bone mass and increased likelihood of bone fractures later in life. To encourage youth to consume adequate amounts of cal—cium, parents or other caregivers should explain the importance of the mineral to bone health and provide calcium—rich foods and beverages during meals and snacks. Adolescents should consume 3 cups/day of fat—free or low—fat milk or equivalent dairy products. Furthermore, teenagers need to be aware that physi—cal activity can strengthen bones, whereas smoking cigarettes is a risk factor for *osteoporosis*, a condition characterized by loss of bone density. To learn more about this condition, see the "Major Minerals" section of Chapter 9.

Vegetarianism

Some teenagers adopt vegetarian diets as a way of defining their identity and asserting independence from their caregivers. Although vegetarian diets can be healthy alternatives to the typical American diet, some youth use vegetarianism to mask disordered eating behaviors (see Chapter 10's "Nutrition Matters").[42] When planning their diets, teenage vegans need to include foods that supply adequate amounts of calcium, iron, and zinc, and vitamins D and B—12. For information to help plan well—balanced, nutritionally adequate diets, teens can use the recommendations of the MyPlate food guide that are appropriate for their age, sex, and physical activity level. Chapter 7 discusses vegetarianism in more detail.

Adolescents should consume 3 cups/day of fat-free or low-fat milk or equivalent dairy products.

Concept **Checkpoint 13.6**

25. At what age does the adolescent growth spurt usually occur in boys? At what age does the growth spurt generally occur in girls?

26. Why are intakes of iron and calcium important during adolescence?

13.7 Childhood Obesity

Learning Outcomes

1 Provide definitions for *overweight, obesity,* and *extreme obesity* in childhood and adolescence.

2 Identify health consequences of childhood obesity.

3 Discuss the prevalence of and factors that contribute to childhood obesity.

4 Discuss strategies for preventing and treating childhood obesity.

Over the past few decades, U.S. public health officials became concerned about the increasing prevalence of obesity among children and adolescents ("child–hood obesity"). Approximately 17% of American children who are between the ages of 2 and 19 years are obese.[43] Between 1980 and 2008, the prevalence of obesity among American children who are between 6 and 19 has almost tripled (Fig. 13.11).[44] There is some good news: Obesity rates among low–income preschoolers are declining.[45] Nevertheless, more obese American children are classi–fied as having extreme obesity than in the past.[46]

Defining Obesity in Children

Health care professionals use BMI–for–age charts that are available from the Centers of Disease Control and Prevention to determine children's and ado–lescents' weight status. The BMI for children is calculated in the same way as for adults, but BMIs for children are plotted on sex–specific growth charts (see Appendix F). Children and adolescents whose BMI–for–age is greater than or equal to (≥) the 85th percentile and less than (<) the 95th percentile are overweight, and youngsters who are at or above the 95th percentile are obese (Table 13.9). Although there is no generally accepted definition for extreme obe–sity that applies to children, BMI–for–age at or above the 97th percentile is typically used to identify children who have extreme obesity.[44]

Health Problems Associated with Childhood Obesity

Compared to children who have healthy body weights, obese children and ado–lescents are more likely to have elevated blood pressure, cholesterol, and glu–cose levels.[45] These chronic conditions are risk factors for cardiovascular disease (CVD). According to results of one study, 70% of obese children had at least one risk factor for CVD, and 39% of obese children had two or more risk factors.[31] Table 13.10 lists chronic health problems that obese children are more likely to have than children who have healthy body weights.

Many obese children and adolescents do not "grow out" of their excess body. Overweight or obese preschool–age children are five times as likely as pre–school children who have healthy weights to be overweight or obese as adults.[45] Furthermore, overweight or obese children are more likely to be *extremely* obese when they are adults.[31]

Childhood Obesity: Contributing Factors

There is no single cause of excess body fat in children, but researchers have iden–tified multiple factors that are associated with the development of the condi–tion.[47] As in cases of adult obesity, the development of childhood obesity results

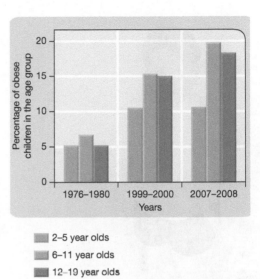

Figure 13.11 Prevalence of obesity among American children aged 2 to 19 years, for selected years 1980 through 2008.

TABLE 13.9 Weight Status Classifications: Children and Adolescents (Ages 2 to 19)

Age	BMI-for-Age Percentile
Desirable weight	> 5th to < 85th
Overweight	≥ 85th to < 95th
Obese	≥ 95th
Extreme obesity*	≥ 97th

* No official definition

TABLE 13.10   Chronic Health Problems Associated with Childhood Obesity

- Impaired glucose tolerance, insulin resistance, and type 2 diabetes
- Breathing problems, including sleep apnea and asthma
- Musculoskeletal problems, including joint discomfort
- Fatty liver disease, gallstones, and gastroesophageal reflux (heartburn)
- Social and psychological problems, such as discrimination and poor self-esteem

Source of information: Centers for Disease Control and Prevention: Overweight and obesity: *Basics about childhood obesity.* Updated April 2012. http://www.cdc.gov/obesity/childhood/basics.html Accessed January 23, 2014

from complex interactions among multiple factors (see Chapter 10). The following sections examine the roles of genetic, biological, and environmental factors that contribute to childhood obesity.

Genetic and Other Biological Factors

Scientific evidence supports the role of inherited (genetic) and other biological factors in the development of childhood obesity, especially in cases of obesity that begin early in life.[48] Some of the biological factors that contribute to obesity include:[48]

- **Having overfat parents.** Children of overfat parents have a greater risk of obesity than children whose parents have healthy weights. If both parents are obese, the child has 10 times the risk of obesity as a child who has only one obese parent.

- **Having a mother who was overfat during pregnancy.** A mother's weight during pregnancy is a more important predictor of childhood obesity than the father's body weight. When compared to children whose mothers have a healthy body weight during pregnancy, babies born to overweight mothers are nearly three times as likely to be overweight. Furthermore, obese women are more likely than women who have healthy body weights to have large babies, and such infants have a high risk of childhood obesity.

- **Having a mother who gained too much weight and/or had diabetes during pregnancy.** Women who gain too much weight during pregnancy or have diabetes are more likely to give birth to high-birth-weight (HBW) babies. Such children are also at risk of developing excess body fat in childhood.

- **Having a mother who smoked during pregnancy.** Although the reasons are unclear, women who smoke during pregnancy set the stage for the future development of overweight and obesity in their babies.

- **Being undernourished during prenatal development.** Poor nutrition (undernutrition) during pregnancy contributes to delivery of a low-birth-weight (LBW) infant. Such infants are more likely to develop hypertension, CVD, and type 2 diabetes later in life, which are chronic diseases associated with obesity. At this point, scientists have been unable to explain why prenatal undernutrition contributes to hypertension, CVD, and type 2 in adulthood.

Biological factors, however, are not entirely responsible for the current obesity epidemic. In many cases, it is difficult to determine whether genes play a more important role than environmental factors in the development of childhood obesity. Is a child obese because the youngster inherited genes from his or her parents that "program" for obesity? Or is a child obese because his or her caregivers provide an excess of empty-calorie, energy-dense foods and do not encourage the child to be physically active?

Impact of the Child's Environment

In the United States, many children are exposed to an environment that encour—ages overeating and consumption of empty—calorie foods. Additionally, the environment often does not provide children with opportunities to participate in enough physical activity. Table 13.11 lists these and other environmental factors that contribute to childhood obesity. Public health measures to prevent obesity among children generally focus on modifying the environment.

Preventing Childhood Obesity

In 2010, the White House Task Force on Childhood Obesity published the report *Solving the Problem of Childhood Obesity Within a Generation*.[49] The task force report included recommendations to reduce the percentage of American children who are obese to 5% within the next 20 years. To download the entire report of the White House Task Force on Childhood Obesity, visit www.letsmove.gov/about .

Fostering Healthy Lifestyles

The Institute of Medicine developed a set of policy recommendations that may reduce the likelihood of obesity among preschool—age children.[51] Some of the institute's major recommendations focused on specific physical activity and dietary behaviors:

- New mothers should breastfeed their babies exclusively for the first 6 months of life and continue breastfeeding along with introducing appropriate foods after 6 months.

- Communities and child care providers should provide opportunities for children to be physically active throughout the day.

- Limit children's exposure to TV and forms of digital media ("screen time") to less than 2 hours per day.

  Specific steps that caregivers can take to help children achieve and maintain a body weight are listed in the "Food & Nutrition Tips" box on page 516.

Treating Childhood Obesity

The treatment goal for managing overweight and obese young children and ado—lescents is to slow the rate of weight gain without interfering with normal growth and physical development. This goal can be accomplished by balancing the calo—ries children consume with the calories they use for physical activity and need for

Did You Know?

Let's Move! America's Move to Raise a Healthier Generation of Kids is a comprehensive national program that focuses on ways to prevent childhood obesity in the United States. Major components of the program include making healthier foods available in schools and increasing opportunities for children to be physically active.[50] To learn more about *Let's Move!*, visit http://www.letsmove.gov/.

TABLE 13.11   Environmental Factors That Contribute to Childhood Obesity

- Easy access to empty-calorie foods and drinks at or near schools
- Limited access to healthy and affordable foods, particularly in areas that have many convenience stores and fast-food restaurants
- Advertising of empty-calorie foods that targets youth
- Lack of set periods for daily physical activity in schools and safe places to be active in many communities
- Large portion sizes of foods sold from vending machines and in restaurants and grocery stores
- Excess exposure to television and other media
  - TV viewing and use of other digital media contribute to childhood obesity because the sedentary activities can reduce the time children spend being physically active.

Source: Centers for Disease Control and Prevention: *Overweight and obesity: A growing problem: What causes childhood obesity?* Last updated April 2013. http://www.cdc.gov/obesity/childhood/problem.html Accessed February 25, 2014

growth. Encouraging more physical activity, especially for sedentary children, is also recommended.

Caregivers should not place a child or youth on a weight reduction diet without consulting the child's physician.[52] For severely obese adolescents, treat—ment approaches that go beyond dietary changes and increased physical activity are often necessary. Such interventions may include prescription medication and weight loss surgery (see Chapter 10).

Bariatric Surgery for Youth

Bariatric (weight loss) surgery can improve the health of adolescents with extreme obesity.[53] According to a review of bariatric surgery outcomes in the United States, the surgeries are safe for adolescents. At this time, however, the adjust—able gastric banding procedure has not been approved for use with patients who are under 18 years of age.

To qualify for bariatric surgery, an adolescent should have:

- extreme obesity (BMI>40);

- failed to lose weight after 6 months of trying to reduce his or her weight;

- attained his or her adult height (skeletal maturity), which is generally at 13 years of age for girls and 15 years of age for boys; and

- developed serious chronic conditions that are associated with obesity, such as type 2 diabetes or sleep apnea, which may improve after surgery.[53]

Regardless of one's age, bariatric surgery is a drastic measure to lose excess body weight and involves some risks. Thus, caregivers and health care providers should carefully determine whether an extremely obese adolescent is a suitable candidate for bariatric surgery. For example, is the adolescent emotionally ready to handle the surgery and make the necessary lifestyle changes to achieve good health and well—being after the procedure?

Concept Checkpoint 13.7

27. Define *overweight, obese,* and *extremely obese* for children as defined by the Centers for Disease Control and Prevention.
28. List at least three health consequences of childhood obesity.
29. List at least three factors that contribute to the development of childhood obesity.
30. What information is used to determine whether an obese adolescent qualifies for bariatric surgery?

13.8 Nutrition for Older Adults

Learning Outcomes

1 Explain the difference between life expectancy and life span.

2 Identify physiological changes that are associated with the normal aging process.

3 Discuss nutrient needs for older adults.

4 Identify nutrients that are often lacking in diets of older adults.

5 Discuss steps caregivers can take to improve nutrient intakes of older persons.

In 1900, the life expectancy of a baby born in the United States was only 47 years. **Life expectancy** is the length of time a person born in a specific year, such as 1900, can expect to live. One hundred years ago, the top three leading causes of death for Americans were pneumonia, influenza, and other infectious diseases. By 2011, life expectancy in the United States rose to almost 79 years.[54] Major factors that contributed to increased life expectancy during the past century include improved diets, housing conditions, and public sanitation, as well as advances in medicine.

According to the U.S. Census Bureau, 13.7% of the U.S. population were 65 years of age or older in 2012.[55] By 2060, government experts estimate that a little over 20% of Americans will be in this age group. Americans who are the "oldest old"—85 years of age or older—comprise one of the fastest–growing segments of the U.S. population. In 2000, 1.5% of Americans were in that age group. By 2010, 1.8% of the population were 85 years of age or older. By 2060, about 4.3% of Americans will be 85 years of age or older.[56]

Although more Americans are living longer than their ancestors, they are not necessarily living well. Chronic diseases are among the leading causes of death in the United States (see Figure 1.2). These diseases are associated with lifestyles that include smoking, eating a poor diet, and being physically inactive.[57]

George John Blum of St. Louis, Missouri, circa 1900. In 1900, the life expectancy of a baby born in the United States was only 47 years.

The Aging Process

The aging process begins at conception and is characterized by numerous predictable physical changes. By the time you are 65 years of age, you will have reached the final life stage, *older adulthood*. What causes people to age is unclear. Scientists who study the aging process have learned that cell structure and function inevitably decline with time, leading to many of the physiological changes shown in Table 13.12. Eventually, most cells lose the ability to regenerate their internal parts, and they die. As more and more cells in an organ die, the organ

life expectancy length of time an average person born in a specific year can expect to live

TABLE 13.12 Aging: Normal Physiological Changes

Body System	Changes
Digestive	Reduced saliva, gastric acid, and intrinsic factor secretion; increased heartburn and constipation
Skin, hair, and nails (integument)	Graying hair; drier skin and hair; skin loses elasticity and forms wrinkles; skin bruises easily
Musculoskeletal	Bone-forming cells become less active, resulting in bone loss that can lead to tooth loss and bones that fracture easily; fractures heal more slowly; joints become stiff and painful; muscle mass declines, resulting in loss of strength and stamina
Nervous	Decreased brain weight, reduced production of neurotransmitters, delayed transmission of nervous impulses, loss of short-term memory, and reduced sensory abilities (e.g., vision, hearing, smell, and taste)
Lymphatic (immune)	Reduced functioning resulting in increased vulnerability to cancer and infections
Circulatory	Hardening of the arteries, reduced cardiac output, increased risk of blood clots
Endocrine	Decreased production of reproductive, growth, and thyroid hormones
Respiratory	Reduced lung capacity, increased vulnerability to respiratory infections
Urinary	Increased loss of functional kidney cells, resulting in decreased blood filtration rate; loss of bladder control
Reproductive	Men: Decreased male hormone production and sperm count Women: Declining female hormone production, cessation of menstrual cycles, and loss of fertility

senescence declining organ functioning and increased vulnerability

life span maximum number of years an organism can live

loses its functional capacity, and as a result, other organs fail and body systems are adversely affected. When this happens, the person soon dies. **Senescence** (*se—ness'—enz*) refers to declining organ functioning and increased vulnerability to disease that occur after a person reaches physical maturity.

Extending the Human Life Span

Life span refers to the maximum number of years an organism such as a human can live. To date, a Frenchwoman, Jeanne Calment, had the longest documented human life span—122 years. Some scientists think the human life span can be lengthened considerably just by making certain dietary changes. This chapter's "Nutrition Matters" takes a closer look at the role of diet and longevity.

Growing old is a normal and natural process. Your body ages, regardless of dietary and other health—related practices you follow. Nevertheless, scientists have found a strong genetic component to human longevity. If you have ances-tors who are very old or lived to be 90 years of age or more, you may have inher-ited "longevity genes." If your ancestors were not so fortunate, to some extent, you can control the rate at which you age. How? By making responsible healthy lifestyle decisions while you are still young, such as selecting a nutritious diet, exercising regularly, and avoiding tobacco. Your focus should not be simply on living longer but on living longer *and* healthier.

Common Nutrition-Related Concerns

Compared to younger persons, older adults have greater risk of nutritional defi-ciencies because of physiological changes associated with the normal aging pro-cess. Other factors that can influence an older person's nutritional status include illnesses, medications, low income, and lack of social support.

Diets of older Americans, particularly older women, often provide inad-equate amounts of vitamins A, D, and B—12 and minerals, particularly calcium and potassium.[36] In the United States, fewer than half (41.8%) of older adults consume 2 or more servings of fruit each day, and less than a third (29.6%) of this population eats 3 or more servings of vegetables each day.[58] Furthermore, over 80% of people who are 71 years of age and older consume more empty calories than recommended.[59] Table 13.13 shows recommended amounts from

TABLE 13.13   What Americans 71 Years of Age and Older Eat Compared to USDA Recommendations

	Food Group				
	Fruit (cups)	Vegetables (cups)	Grains (oz. equivalents)	Dairy (cups)	Protein (oz. equivalents)
*MyPlate Recommendations**					
Men (51 years of age and older)	2	2.5	6	3	5.5
Women (51 years of age and older)	1.5	2	5	3	5
Percentage of people who consumed recommended amount (estimated)					
Men	23	12	55	7	46
Women	34.5	13	53	3.6	40

* Amounts are for people who obtain fewer than 30 minutes/day of moderate physical activity, beyond their normal daily activities.

Adapted from Krebs-Smith SM and others: Americans do not meet federal dietary recommendations. *Journal of Nutrition* 140 (10): 1832, 2010.

U.S. Department of Agriculture (USDA) MyPlate food groups and percentages of men and women ages 71 years and older who meet the recommendations. The following sections discuss some of the major health concerns that often affect the nutritional status of older adults. Some of these conditions have been discussed in previous chapters.

Changes in Body Weight

As the human body ages, its need for energy decreases.[1] In senescence, muscle mass declines as some muscle cells shrink or die. The loss of muscle mass leads to a decrease in muscular strength and basal metabolism. The aging body typically loses lean tissue and gains fat tissue. Increased body fat results from overeating and lack of physical activity, but even athletic men and lean women usually gain some central body fat after they are 50 years of age. Being overfat may increase the bone density of older adults and result in stronger bones,[60] but having too much body fat increases the risk of type 2 diabetes, hypertension, cardiovascular disease, and osteoarthritis. For more information about overweight and obesity, see Chapter 10.

Compared to healthy younger adults, people who are over 70 years of age have a higher risk of nutrient deficiencies, because their food intake tends to decrease as their metabolic rates and physical activity levels decline. Despite having lower energy needs, however, older adults need the same or even higher amounts of vitamins and minerals. Meeting micronutrient needs while eating less food can be difficult for older persons to accomplish.

After reaching 70 years of age, it is not unusual for people to lose some weight. Several factors can contribute to weight loss among older adults (Table 13.14). Older adults may eat less because they have lost the ability to taste and smell food. Loss of teeth and difficulty swallowing can also result in decreased food consumption. Declines in normal *cognitive* functioning (thought processes) resulting from conditions such as Alzheimer's disease or reduced blood flow to the brain can contribute to poor nutritional status. People who lack normal cognitive functioning may be unable to make decisions regarding planning nutritious meals, as well as to shop for and prepare food. Conditions that interfere with mobility and flexibility, such as arthritis and osteoporosis, can also interfere with food shopping and preparation activities. Social and economic factors often play a role in reduced food intake. Many older people live alone and on fixed incomes, circumstances that are associated with depression and inability to afford adequate amounts of nutritious food. In many instances, very old people refuse to eat and, as a result, lose considerable amounts of weight, a situation that hastens their death.

For older adults who find that food no longer tastes "good," adding more spices may improve the taste of food and, as a result, stimulate weak appetites. Efforts to make mealtimes social events, such as inviting friends to share potluck meals together, can enhance older adults' mental outlooks and spark their interest in eating. Older adults can increase or maintain their weight by consuming energy—dense snacks between meals, such as cheese, milkshakes, nuts, or oatmeal cookies. If weight loss becomes significant, a physician should be consulted to determine the cause.

Physical Inactivity

Many of the undesirable physical changes we associate with growing old are the result of a lifetime of physical inactivity. Regardless of a person's age, a physically active lifestyle increases muscle strength and mobility, improves balance, slows bone loss, and boosts emotional well—being. Most older adults can benefit from performing aerobic and strength—training activities

TABLE 13.14   Reduced Food Intake Among Older Adults: Contributing Factors

- Reduced ability to taste and smell food
- Difficulty swallowing
- Loss of teeth
- Loss of normal cognitive function
- Lack of income
- Depression
- Reduced mobility and flexibility

Did You Know?

You are never too old to gain some benefits from exercise. Any form of physical activity, from swimming to performing household chores, can help extend an older person's longevity.[61]

Many older adults do not like to wear dentures because they can be uncomfortable.

regularly. Before embarking on a program to increase physical fitness, however, sedentary older adults should consult their physicians concerning appropriate activities.

Tooth Loss

In the 1950s, surveys of Americans indicated that the majority of older adults had lost all their natural teeth. Since then, the percentage of older adults who retain all or most of their teeth has increased in the United States. Adults should have 28 natural teeth. In 2010–2012, about 8% of Americans who were 18 years of age or older had lost all of their teeth.[62] Moreover, approximately 23% of Americans who were 65 years or older had lost all their natural teeth. Tooth loss is related to long–term poor dental hygiene, cigarette smoking, and poor dietary practices. By following recommended dental hygiene practices, obtaining regular dental care, and avoiding tobacco use, you can greatly increase your chances of keeping most of your teeth as you age.

Excessive tooth loss can lead to faulty eating habits. People who lack teeth often avoid crisp or chewy foods, such as fresh fruits, vegetables, whole–grain cereals, and meat. According to results of a study involving over 300 older adults, subjects who had 10 or fewer teeth consumed considerably less than the recommended amounts of fruits, vegetables, meat and beans, and oils when compared to older adults who had more than 10 teeth.[63] Although dentures that replace natural teeth can enable some people to chew normally, many older adults do not like to wear them because they can be uncomfortable. When a person has difficulty chewing food, serving soft foods such as ground meats, cooked vegetables, pureed fruits, and puddings can stimulate the individual's appetite.

Intestinal Tract Problems

Constipation is a major complaint of older adults. By increasing their intakes of fiber–rich foods, such as whole–grain products and vegetables, older adults may be able to have more regular bowel movements (see the "Fiber" section of Chapter 5). Dehydration contributes to constipation, so older persons should make sure their fluid intake is adequate.

As a person ages, his or her stomach secretes less hydrochloric acid (HCl) and intrinsic factor. These changes can contribute to poor absorption of vitamin B–12 and the development of vitamin B–12 deficiency and pernicious anemia. Older adults may be able to meet their vitamin B–12 needs by eating foods fortified with the micronutrient or taking vitamin B–12 supplements. Some older adults, however, must take injections of the B vitamin to prevent pernicious anemia (see Chapter 8). Older persons are also at risk of iron deficiency because reduced stomach acid production may hinder iron absorption. Furthermore, many older adults take aspirin regularly, and this practice can cause intestinal bleeding that can lead to iron deficiency anemia. Intestinal ulcers and cancer can also cause blood loss from the digestive tract. The discovery of blood in bowel movements needs to be reported to a physician—regardless of one's age.

Many older adults take one or more prescription drugs daily. Although such medications can improve health and quality of life of older adults, some drugs interfere with the body's absorption and/or use of certain nutrients. Additionally, older adults often take one or more dietary supplements regularly. According to results of a national survey conducted in 2003–2006, 70% of adults ages 71 and older took at least 1 dietary supplement regularly.[64] Nutrient supplements, such as multivitamin/multimineral supplements, were the most widely used type of dietary supplement. Certain dietary supplements, including herbal products, can reduce or amplify the effects of prescribed medications. Therefore, older adults should notify their physicians about their use of all dietary supplements. A few foods also interfere with prescribed drugs. Grapefruit juice, for example, can alter the potency of certain medications that are used to lower blood pressure or cholesterol.

Depression in Older Adults

In 2008, 16% of women and 11% of men age 65 and over reported having symp−toms of depression.[65] Situations that contribute to depression among the older adult population include coping with chronic illness or loss of mobility, and isolation and loneliness as family members and friends move away or die. If the depressed person loses interest in cooking and eating, weight loss and nutri−ent deficiencies are likely to occur. In many instances, depression can be man−aged with medication, but social support and psychological counseling may be necessary as well. Without proper treatment, depressed persons, especially males, are at risk of alcoholism and suicide. In 2009, non−Hispanic white men who were 85 years of age and older were more likely to commit suicide than other Americans.[65]

Dietary Planning in Older Adulthood

MyPlate can provide the basis for planning nutritionally adequate meals and snacks for healthy older adults. However, amounts of foods recommended in these diet plans may not provide enough vitamin D and vitamin B−12 for older adults. By regularly consuming fortified and/or enriched foods, older

![Food & Nutrition tips]

The following suggestions can help caregivers improve nutrient intakes of older adults:

- Emphasize nutrient-dense foods when planning daily menus.

- Try new foods, seasonings, and ways of preparing foods.

- Have easy-to-prepare, nutrient-dense foods on hand for times when the older person is too tired to cook large meals.

- Serve meals in well-lit or sunny areas, and plan appealing meals by using foods with different flavors, colors, shapes, textures, and smells.

- Plan occasions for the older adult to share cooking responsibilities and eat meals with friends or relatives.

- Encourage the older person to eat at a senior center whenever possible. Investigate community resources for helping the older adult obtain groceries, cook, or manage other daily care needs.

- Encourage the older adult to be physically active.

- If biting and chewing are difficult for an older adult, chop, grind, or blend tough or crisp foods.

- Prepare extra amounts of soup, stew, or casserole, so leftovers can be frozen for future meals.

People enjoying the social benefits of dining together at a community center for independent older adults.

Many communities in the United States offer the Meals on Wheels program in which volunteers deliver nutritious meals prepared at a senior center to qualified, homebound older adults.

adults can increase their intakes of these micronutrients. In many instances, older adults can also benefit from taking a daily multiple vitamin/mineral supplement.

Friends, relatives, and health care personnel should be alert for indications of poor nutrient intakes among older people, especially those who are at risk and live in nursing homes or other long–term care facilities. For example, family members can make sure the older adult's nutrient needs are met by visiting the person's residence during mealtimes, observing the foods that are offered, and, if necessary, helping the older adult eat. Additionally, monitoring the older person's weight can indicate whether long–term food intake has been adequate. Older adults who live at home may need help planning nutritionally adequate diets. In these instances, registered dietitians can be consulted to provide personalized dietary advice.

Community Nutrition Services for Older Adults

The Chapter 1 "Nutrition Matters" provides information about popular community–based nutrition services for American older adults. You can obtain information regarding locally available nutrition services for older people from medical clinics, private practitioners, hospitals, and health maintenance organizations in your area. To learn more about nutrition–related programs for older adults, visit the following websites: National Institute on Aging, www.nia.nih.gov/; American Geriatrics Society, www.americangeriatrics.org/; and Administration on Aging, www.aoa.gov/.

Concept **Checkpoint 13.8**

31. What is the difference between *life expectancy* and *life span*?

32. Identify at least five physiological changes that are associated with the normal aging process.

33. Explain why nutrient needs for older adults are often higher than those for younger persons.

34. List at least four nutrients that are often lacking in diets of older adults.

35. Suggest at least three ways caregivers can improve nutrient intakes of older persons.

13.9 Nutrition Matters: In Search of the Fountain

Learning Outcomes

1. Discuss at least two aging theories.
2. Explain the effects of calorie restriction on the aging process.
3. Identify steps people can take to extend their life expectancy.

In 1513, Spanish explorer Juan Ponce de León sailed to the southeastern coastal region of North America and discovered an area he named "Land of Flowers" (Florida). Ponce de León was on a mission to find gold, but he was also eager to locate a natural spring that supposedly had magical powers. According to Native Americans in the area, elderly people who drank the spring's water regained their youthful looks and vigor. Unfortunately, Ponce de León never found gold or the mythical "fountain of youth" in Florida. Nevertheless, many older adults still seek ways to combat aging, especially by taking certain hormones and dietary supplements promoted as having age–defying properties. Older Americans spend considerable amounts of money on such products, some of which may be harmful in the long run. Promoters of antiaging formulas or therapies claim their treatments can stop, and even reverse, the process of aging. Is there any reliable scientific evidence to support claims that you can take something to stay young longer?

Claims that a nutritional fountain of youth exists are simply not true. Currently, scientific evidence does not support the use of antiaging therapies that include taking antioxidants and hormones.[66] Scientists have determined that consuming a nutritious diet and obtaining adequate amounts of physical activity can promote good health as one ages.[66] Nevertheless, researchers are conducting experiments to better understand the process of aging and the keys to longevity.

Biogerontologists are scientists who study the biology of aging. Biogerontologists have proposed several theories to explain why aging occurs and why some people live longer than others. According to one of these theories, longevity results from the body's ability to maintain and repair the damage done by a lifetime of exposure to the environment and the effects of everyday "wear and tear." Some multicellular organisms are able to live longer when they can improve their abilities to repair damage to their DNA, reduce the toxicity of free radicals, and replace nonfunctioning cells. Antioxidants reduce the toxic effects of free radicals (see Chapter 8), and organisms produce a variety of antioxidants to control free radical production.

| Ponce de León.

Scientific studies, however, provide little evidence that increasing one's intake of antioxidants slows the aging process.[66]

One area of biogerontological research that shows some promise is the use of *calorie restriction (CR)* to extend longevity. Although CR provides fewer calories than an organism's usual diet, the dietary pattern supplies all essential nutrients. Since the 1930s, scientists have studied the effects of CR on the health and life spans of various species of multicellular organisms. According to some research findings, CR can increase life spans of various organisms, including some kinds of rodents, fruit, flies, and yeast.[66] Results of other studies, however, were not so promising, because the animals either had the same or shorter life spans when compared to controls.

Even if scientists provide evidence that any form of CR adds some years to the human life span, would you be interested in reducing your food intake considerably to extend your life? How enjoyable would your life be if you ate only 900 kcal daily? What is important to you: how long you can live, or how *well* you live?

The science of biogerontology is still in its beginning stages; researchers have much to learn about the aging process before they can develop safe ways to enhance longevity. We already know that you can reduce your risk of dying prematurely from chronic diseases such as heart disease, hypertension, type 2 diabetes, and many forms of cancer by adopting healthy lifestyles. Rather than wait until the fountain of youth becomes a reality, you can take charge of your health now by consuming a nutritionally adequate diet, obtaining regular moderate— to vigorous—intensity physical activity, maintaining a healthy weight, avoiding tobacco products, limiting your alcohol consumption, and having regular physical checkups.

Concept **Checkpoint 13.9**

36. According to scientific evidence, which dietary modification may extend the life expectancies of organisms that include fruit flies and rodents?

37. List three steps you can take that may extend your life expectancy.

Chapter References

See Appendix H.

Summary

13.1 Introduction to Nutrition for a Lifetime

- The leading causes of death for Americans are chronic diseases: heart disease, cancer, and stroke. Lifestyles, especially dietary practices and physical activity patterns, contribute to the development of these chronic conditions. Other factors that influence a person's overall health include heredity, relationships, environment, income, education level, and access to health care.

13.2 Pregnancy

- Embryonic/fetal life is characterized by rapid rates of cell division, resulting in a dramatic increase in cell numbers. The first trimester of pregnancy is a critical stage in human development because inadequate or excessive nutrient intakes as well as exposure to toxic compounds can have devastating effects on the embryo/fetus during this period. The placenta is the organ of pregnancy that transfers nutrients and oxygen from the mother's bloodstream to her embryo/fetus. The placenta also transfers wastes from the embryo/fetus to the mother's bloodstream so her body can eliminate them.

- Women of childbearing age should take steps to ensure they are in good health prior to becoming pregnant. During pregnancy, the woman's body undergoes various physiological changes. These changes enable her body to nourish and maintain the developing fetus, as well as to produce milk for her infant after its birth. A pregnant woman should follow a diet that meets her own nutritional needs as well as those of her developing offspring. The mother-to-be can use MyPlate to develop nutritionally adequate daily menus, but she may also need to take a prenatal vitamin/mineral supplement.

- Women whose prepregnancy weights were within the healthy range can expect to gain 25 to 35 pounds during pregnancy. Women who gain excess weight during pregnancy may retain the extra weight long after delivery.

- Monitoring weight gain is an important aspect of prenatal care. Rapid weight gain, especially after the fifth month of pregnancy, could be a sign of gestational hypertension. Underweight women who do not gain enough weight during pregnancy are at risk of having preterm or low-birth-weight infants. Obese women have a greater risk of developing hypertension and type 2 diabetes during pregnancy.

13.3 Infant Nutrition

- Breast milk is the best first food for infants. Compared to babies who are not breastfed, breastfed infants have lower risks of allergies and of gastrointestinal, respiratory tract, and ear infections. Women who breastfeed their babies can also derive some important benefits from the practice, such as losing extra fat gained during pregnancy.

- When an infant suckles, nerves in the nipple signal the mother's brain to release prolactin and oxytocin into her bloodstream. Oxytocin is necessary for the let-down reflex and causes the uterus to contract. Milk production relies on "supply and demand." If the breasts are not emptied fully, milk production soon ceases. To support milk production, the lactating mother needs about 400 to 500 extra kilocalories daily.

- Growth is very rapid during infancy. Health care practitioners can assess growth in infants and children by measuring body weight, height (or length), and head circumference over time. For the first 6 months, the infant's nutrient needs can be met by human milk or iron-fortified infant formula. Breastfed babies need vitamin D and possibly iron and fluoride supplements.

- Most infants do not need solid foods before 6 months of age. The first solid food offered to babies should be an iron-containing food such as an iron-fortified infant cereal, meat, or poultry. New foods should be added one at a time, and the child should be observed for allergy signs and symptoms. Whole cow's milk should not be fed to babies until they are 1 year of age.

13.4 The Preschool Years

- It is normal for a preschooler's appetite to decline as the child's growth rate tapers off. Additionally, it is not unusual for preschool children to be "picky eaters" or embark on "food jags." Caregivers should avoid nagging, forcing, and bribing children to eat, but instead offer a variety of healthy food choices and allow the child to choose what and how much to eat. Nutrition-related problems that often affect preschool children are iron deficiency, dental caries, obesity, and food allergies.

532   Chapter 13 Nutrition for a Lifetime

13.5 School-Age Children

- School-age children often skip breakfast, and they tend to consume more foods away from home, larger portions of food, and more fried foods and sweetened beverages. Children who eat breakfast are more likely to have better diets and healthier body weights than children who skip this meal. Diets of many school-age children fail to supply recommended amounts of calcium and potassium while providing too much sodium.

13.6 Adolescence

- A child matures physically into an adult during adolescence. For many teens, pressure to conform to fads and be influenced by other adolescents negatively affects their diets and overall health. Obesity, eating disorders, and low iron and calcium intakes are major nutrition-related concerns of adolescents.

13.7 Childhood Obesity

- Public health experts are very concerned about the increasing prevalence of obesity among children in the United States. Overfat children have higher risks of elevated blood pressure, cholesterol, and glucose levels than children whose weights are within the healthy range. Overfat children may also have higher risk of hypertension, heart disease, and type 2 diabetes later in life. Such children are also more likely to have low self-esteem and become obese as adults.

13.8 Nutrition for Older Adults

- The aging process is characterized by numerous predictable physical changes. Senescence refers to declining organ functioning and increased vulnerability to disease that occurs after a person reaches physical maturity. Although genetics play a role in determining longevity, lifestyle practices and environmental conditions influence a person's rate of aging. People may be able to live longer and healthier by making responsible healthy lifestyle decisions while they are still young.

- Factors that can influence an older person's nutritional status include illnesses, tooth loss, medications, low income, depression, and lack of social support. Diets of older adults, particularly older women, often provide inadequate amounts of vitamins D, A, and B-12 and minerals such as calcium and potassium. Friends, relatives, and health care personnel should be alert for indications of poor nutrient intakes among older people, especially those who live in nursing homes or other long-term care facilities.

13.9 Nutrition Matters: In Search of the Fountain

- According to biogerontologists, longevity results from the body's ability to maintain and repair the damage done by a lifetime of exposure to the environment and the effects of everyday "wear and tear." Little credible scientific evidence exists to support the use of antiaging therapies that include taking hormones or megadoses of vitamins and antioxidants. Researchers are conducting experiments to better understand the process of aging and the keys to longevity.

Recipe for 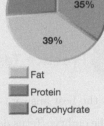 Healthy Living

Vegetable Dip

You can make low-fat versions of fruit or vegetable dips by replacing sour cream or mayonnaise in recipes with plain, low-fat yogurt. This vegetable dip recipe makes approximately five ¼-cup servings of dip. Each serving provides approximately 46 kcal, 3 g protein, 2 g fat, 90 mg calcium, 160 mg sodium, and 120 mg potassium

INGREDIENTS:

1 cup plain, low-fat yogurt
3 Tbsp calorie-reduced ranch dressing
¼ tsp curry powder (optional)

PREPARATION STEPS:

1. In a small bowl, combine yogurt with the dressing and stir until well blended.

2. Refrigerate until ready to serve.

3. Serve chilled in a bowl that is surrounded with fresh pieces of raw vegetables.

4. Discard any remaining dip.

Further analyze this and other recipes through activities on Connect at www.mcgrawhillconnect.com.

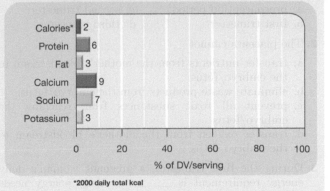

Critical Thinking

1. One of your friends just found out that she is pregnant. Although her BMI is within the healthy range, she is concerned about gaining too much weight during pregnancy. What advice would you provide concerning the need to gain some weight during this life stage? If your friend's prepregnancy weight was 125 pounds, how much weight would be appropriate for her to gain during pregnancy?

2. Your pregnant friend wants your advice concerning whether she should breastfeed or formula-feed her baby. After reading Chapter 13, what information would you provide to help your friend decide to breastfeed?

3. Olivia is a healthy 2-month-old baby. Olivia's mother, Kara, wants to replace Olivia's iron-fortified infant formula with the same fresh fluid 2% milk that she drinks. What advice would you give to Kara concerning the appropriateness of making such a decision?

4. Marcus is 8 years old, and his weight is in the overweight range. His caregivers are also overweight, but they seem to be concerned about Marcus's excess body weight. What advice would you provide his caregivers to help Marcus achieve a healthy body weight?

5. Are your parents, grandparents, and great-grandparents still alive? If any of your ancestors died before they were 60 years of age, can you identify their causes of death and factors that contributed to their deaths? What lifestyle changes can you make now that can help you achieve a longer, healthier lifetime?

Practice Test

Select the best answer.

1. The embryo/fetus develops most of its organs during the
   a. preconception period.   c. second trimester.
   b. first trimester.   d. third trimester.

2. The placenta cannot
   a. transfer nutrients from the mother's bloodstream to the embryo/fetus.
   b. eliminate waste products from the embryo/fetus.
   c. prevent all toxic substances from reaching the embryo/fetus.
   d. transfer oxygen from the mother's bloodstream to the embryo/fetus.

3. During the first trimester, a pregnant woman's daily energy requirement is _____ her daily energy needs before she became pregnant.
   a. 300 kcal lower than
   b. about the same as
   c. 300 kcal higher than
   d. 500 kcal higher than

4. Women with prepregnancy weights within the healthy range should gain _____ pounds during pregnancy.
   a. 10−20   c. 25−35
   b. 20−25   d. 35−50

5. Preeclampsia is a form of _____ that can develop during pregnancy.
   a. hypertension   c. cancer
   b. diabetes   d. anemia

6. Which of the following statements is true?
   a. A woman's energy needs are higher during the first trimester than at any other time in pregnancy.
   b. Using infant formula to bottle-feed a baby is more convenient and less expensive than breastfeeding a baby.
   c. Oxytocin is necessary for the "let-down" reflex to occur.
   d. The American Pediatric Association recommends feeding fresh whole milk to infants when they are 6 months of age.

7. A healthy infant who weighs 6.5 pounds at birth can be expected to weigh _____ pounds by her first birthday.
   a. 13.0   c. 19.5
   b. 16.5   d. 23.5

8. Breastfed infants are _____ than babies who are fed infant formula.
   a. more likely to have diarrhea
   b. less likely to have cystic fibrosis
   c. more likely to have respiratory infections
   d. less likely to have ear infections

9. Which of the following factors is associated with increased risk of obesity during childhood?

   a. having a family history of obesity
   b. eating 3 to 5 servings of fresh fruit daily
   c. being a full–term infant
   d. taking dietary supplements that contain zinc and vitamin C

10. Which of the following practices has been scientifically shown to extend the life spans of certain flies and rodents?

   a. taking antioxidant supplements
   b. eating a high–protein diet
   c. performing vigorous physical exercise
   d. consuming a calorie–restricted diet

▦▎LEARNSMART·
ADVANTAGE

Get the most out of your study of nutrition with McGraw-Hill's innovative suite of adaptive learning products including McGraw-Hill LearnSmart®, SmartBook®, LearnSmart Achieve®, and LearnSmart Prep®. Visit www.learnsmartadvantage.com.

Answers to Quiz Yourself

1. During pregnancy, a mother-to-be should double her food intake because she's "eating for two." **False.** (p. 497)

2. The natural size of a woman's breasts is not a factor in determining her ability to breastfeed her baby. **True.** (p. 506)

3. Caregivers should add solid foods to an infant's diet within the first month after the baby is born. **False.** (p. 509)

4. Over the past few decades, the prevalence of obesity has increased among American children. **True.** (p. 519)

5. Compared to younger persons, older adults have lower risks of nutritional deficiencies. **False.** (p. 525)

Online Supplements

connect®

Connect Online Access for Human Biology, 15th Edition

McGraw-Hill Connect is a digital teaching and learning environment that improves performance over a variety of critical outcomes. With Connect, instructors can deliver assignments, quizzes and tests easily online. Students can practice important skills at their own pace and on their own schedule.

HOW TO REGISTER

Using a <u>Print Book</u>?
To register and activate your Connect account, simply follow these easy steps:
1. **Go to the Connect course web address provided by your instructor or visit the Connect link set up on your instructor's course within your campus learning management system.**
2. **Click on the link to register.**
3. **When prompted, enter the Connect code found on the inside back cover of your book and click Submit. Complete the brief registration form that follows to begin using Connect.**

Using an <u>eBook</u>?
To register and activate your Connect account, simply follow these easy steps:
1. **Upon purchase of your eBook, you will be granted automatic access to Connect.**
2. **Go to the Connect course web address provided by your instructor or visit the Connect link set up on your instructor's course within your campus learning management system.**
3. **Sign in using the same email address and password you used to register on the eBookstore. Complete your registration and begin using Connect.**

Note: Access Code is for one use only. If you did not purchase this book new, the access code included in this book is no longer valid.

Need help? Visit mhhe.com/support